GREAT AMERICAN BRAND NAME RECIPES COOKBOOK

Publications International, Ltd.

ISBN 0-88176-836-7

Library of Congress Catalog Card Number: 89-60929

MINUTE® is a registered trademark of General Foods Corporation.

Pictured on the front cover: Top row, left to right—Northwest Cheesecake Supreme *(page 306)*, Rainbow Fruit Salad *(page 75)*, Cheese-Stuffed Beef Rolls *(page 194)*. Middle row, left to right—Ginger Pineapple Mold *(page 73)*, Marinated Kabobs *(page 134)*, Marinated Shrimp & Vegetables *(page 90)*. Bottom row, left to right—Marinated Beef Salad *(page 85)*, Choco-Coconut Cake Roll *(page 345)*, Broccoli and Pasta *(page 218)*.

Pictured on the back cover: Top row, left to right—Fresh Vegetable Salad *(page 64)*, New Orleans Crumb Cake *(page 350)*, Garden Chicken Salad *(page 84)*. Middle row, left to right—Ham Pasta Primavera *(page 204)*, Cool and Creamy Cucumber Spread *(page 11)*, Caribbean Fudge Pie *(page 325)*. Bottom row, left to right—Fluffy Grasshopper Pie *(page 327)* Golden Gate Grill *(page 243)*, Shantung Chicken *(page 149)*.

CONTENTS

Your Guide to Great Cooking 5

Appetizers 6

Beverages 32

Soups 42

Salads 62

Meats 94

Poultry 138

Fish & Shellfish 170

Main-Dish Casseroles 190

Pasta 204

Side Dishes 214

Pizza & Sandwiches 236

Eggs, Cheese & Brunch Dishes 246

Breads, Rolls & Coffee Cakes 256

Cookies & Candies 270

Desserts 298

Pies & Pastries 322

Cakes 338

Acknowledgments &
Photo Credits 360

Index 361

Your Guide to Great Cooking

GREAT AMERICAN BRAND NAME RECIPES COOKBOOK is just that—a great collection of recipes developed and tested by the great American food companies, using their brand-name products. Expert home economists at top American food companies have developed, tested, and written these recipes to help you use their products. We have selected the most popular recipes for this book, many of which have been collected from the pages of our best-selling FAVORITE RECIPES™ Magazine. Now you have a convenient volume containing all of your favorites.

The variety of these recipes is apparent as you glance through the book. You'll find recipes for any occasion. We've included appetizers, beverages, soups and salads, main dishes of all kinds, breads and rolls, and a variety of desserts. From breakfast to supper and even midnight snacks, there are recipes for any time of day. For busy days, you'll find terrific recipes that get you out of the kitchen in a hurry. When you have time to be creative, choose one of the gourmet specialties. Recipes with the international flair of Italy, the Orient, Mexico, and France are included, along with home-style dishes that represent American cooking from every region. You can try new ideas for family meals, or present something elegant for a special occasion.

When looking through this book, you'll notice that a large number of these recipes can be prepared in your microwave oven. Some have been developed especially for microwave cooking. Although these recipes have been thoroughly tested, the microwave cooking times given must be considered approximate. Higher-wattage microwave ovens cook foods more quickly than those with low wattage. In addition, the starting temperature of the food, the shape and size of the pieces, and the food's depth in the cooking utensil can affect cooking time. Most recipes will give a test for doneness. It's best to use the cooking times in the recipe as a guideline; check to see if the food is done before adding more time.

Some recipes in this book are followed by a nutritional analysis, giving numeric values for the number of calories and amount of protein, fat, carbohydrate, sodium, and cholesterol in each serving of the recipe. This information is based on the ingredients listed in the recipe. For cases in which a choice of ingredients is given, the first option was used in computing the nutritional analysis. If the ingredient list calls for "2 tablespoons butter or margarine," for example, the nutritional information applies to the recipe made with butter, not margarine. Ingredients listed as "optional" or "if desired" were not included in the analysis. If a range of servings is given in the recipe, the analysis was computed for the largest number of servings. Please remember that, just as individual foods of the same type are different, their nutrition content can vary. Consequently, these figures should be viewed as approximations.

As wonderful as these recipes are, you'll also find that this book is appealing to browse through. You'll get great ideas for menu-planning by looking at the large full-color photographs throughout the book. And with a collection of recipes this comprehensive, you'll always have just the right recipe at your fingertips. So start cooking—and enjoy the delicious results!

APPETIZERS

Good friends and good times call for these tempting appetizers. Look for easy dips and spreads to welcome impromptu guests, elegant first courses to set the tone for an important meal, and wonderful party fare for gatherings large and small. You'll find a variety of sensational starters to let your hospitality shine.

Cracked Black Pepper and Herb Spread

- **1 package (8 ounces) cream cheese, softened**
- **6 ounces goat cheese (Montrachet, Chèvre or feta)**
- **¼ cup WISH-BONE® Italian Dressing**
- **½ cup chopped red onion**
- **1 teaspoon fresh chopped thyme leaves***
- **1 teaspoon fresh chopped sage leaves****
- **1 teaspoon cracked black pepper**

In food processor or blender, process all ingredients until blended; cover and chill. Garnish, if desired, with additional cracked black pepper and serve with assorted fresh vegetables, crackers and breads.
Makes about 2 cups spread.
   ***Substitution:** Use ½ teaspoon dried thyme leaves.
   ****Substitution:** Use ½ teaspoon dried sage leaves.
   Note: Also terrific with Wish-Bone® Robusto Italian, Herbal Italian Blended Italian, Lite Italian or Lite Classic Dijon Vinaigrette Dressing.

Curried Peanut Dip

- **1 pouch CAMPBELL'S® Onion Soup and Recipe Mix**
- **1 cup sour cream**
- **1 cup plain yogurt**
- **¼ cup creamy peanut butter**
- **2 teaspoons curry powder**
  Chopped peanuts for garnish
  Fresh pear slices for garnish

1. In medium bowl, blend soup mix, sour cream, yogurt, peanut butter and curry powder. Cover; chill until serving time, at least 2 hours.
2. Garnish with chopped peanuts and pear slices. Serve with vegetable or fruit dippers.
Makes 2¼ cups.

Colorful Carrot Dip

- **1 8-ounce package *Light* PHILADELPHIA BRAND Neufchâtel Cheese, softened**
- **½ cup finely shredded carrot**
- **1 teaspoon parsley flakes**
- **⅛ teaspoon salt**
  Dash of pepper

Combine neufchâtel cheese, carrots and seasonings, mixing until well blended. Chill. Serve with vegetable dippers.
1 cup.
   Variations: Substitute freeze-dried chopped chives for parsley flakes.
   Substitute ½ teaspoon dried basil leaves, crushed, for parsley flakes.
   Substitute ¼ teaspoon dill weed or lemon pepper for parsley flakes.

Bacon-Horseradish Dip

- **1 pouch CAMPBELL'S® Onion Soup and Recipe Mix**
- **2 cups sour cream**
- **5 slices bacon, cooked and crumbled**
- **1 tablespoon prepared horseradish**
- **1 teaspoon Dijon-style mustard**
  Cooked bacon curl for garnish

1. In medium bowl, combine soup mix, sour cream, crumbled bacon, horseradish and mustard; mix well. Cover; chill until serving time, at least 2 hours.
2. Garnish with bacon curl. Serve with chips or crackers.
Makes 2 cups.

Colorful Carrot Dip

Baked Cream Cheese Appetizer

1 4-ounce package refrigerated crescent dinner rolls
1 8-ounce package PHILADELPHIA BRAND Cream Cheese
½ teaspoon dill weed
1 egg yolk, beaten

Unroll dough on lightly floured surface; press together seams to form 12×4-inch rectangle. Sprinkle top of cream cheese with half of dill; lightly press dill into cream cheese. Place cream cheese, dill-side down, in center of dough. Sprinkle cream cheese with remaining dill. Enclose cream cheese in dough by bringing sides of dough together, pressing edges to seal. Place on lightly greased cookie sheet; brush with egg yolk. Bake at 350°, 15 to 18 minutes or until lightly browned. Serve with assorted crackers and apple slices.
8 servings.

Variations: Substitute combined ½ teaspoon dried rosemary leaves, crushed, and ½ teaspoon paprika for dill weed.

Substitute *Light* PHILADELPHIA BRAND Neufchâtel Cheese for Cream Cheese.

Baked Cream Cheese Appetizer

Blue Cheese Walnut Spread

1 envelope KNOX® Unflavored Gelatine
¾ cup cold water
½ cup sour cream
⅓ cup milk
1 tablespoon lemon juice
1 teaspoon Worcestershire sauce
4 ounces blue cheese, crumbled
1 package (8 ounces) cream cheese, softened
½ cup walnuts

In small saucepan, sprinkle unflavored gelatine over ¼ cup cold water; let stand 1 minute. Stir over low heat until gelatine is completely dissolved, about 3 minutes.

In blender, process sour cream, remaining ½ cup water, milk, lemon juice, Worcestershire sauce and cheeses until blended. While processing, through feed cap, gradually add gelatine mixture, then walnuts; process until blended. Pour into 7½×3¾×2¼-inch loaf pan or 4-cup bowl; chill until firm, about 3 hours. Unmold onto lettuce-lined platter and serve, if desired, with crackers, party-size breads and fruits.
Makes about 3¾ cups spread.

Eggplant Caviar

1 large eggplant, unpeeled
¼ cup chopped onion
2 tablespoons lemon juice
1 tablespoon olive or vegetable oil
1 small clove garlic
½ teaspoon salt
¼ teaspoon TABASCO® pepper sauce
Sieved egg white (optional)
Lemon slice (optional)

Preheat oven to 350°F. Place eggplant in shallow baking dish. Bake 1 hour or until soft, turning once. Trim off ends; slice eggplant in half lengthwise. Place cut-side-down in colander and let drain 10 minutes. Scoop out pulp; reserve pulp and peel. In blender or food processor combine eggplant peel, onion, lemon juice, oil, garlic, salt and Tabasco® sauce. Cover; process until peel is finely chopped. Add eggplant pulp. Cover; process just until chopped. Place in serving dish. Garnish with egg white and lemon slice, if desired. Serve with toast points.
Makes about 1½ cups.

Garlic Spread

1 8-ounce package PHILADELPHIA BRAND Cream Cheese, softened
½ cup PARKAY Margarine, softened
2 tablespoons chopped parsley
2 tablespoons chopped onion
1 garlic clove, minced

Combine cream cheese and margarine, mixing until well blended. Add remaining ingredients; mix well. Chill.
Approximately 1⅔ cups.

Chili con Queso

2 tablespoons CRISCO® Oil
¼ cup minced onion
1 can (7½ ounces) whole tomatoes, drained and finely chopped
1 can (4 ounces) chopped green chilies, undrained
¼ teaspoon salt
2 cups shredded Cheddar or Monterey Jack cheese (about 8 ounces)
⅓ cup whipping cream
Nacho chips

Heat Crisco® Oil in 1-quart saucepan. Add onion. Cook over medium-high heat, stirring occasionally, until onion is tender. Add tomatoes, chilies and salt. Stir to blend and break apart tomatoes. Heat to boiling. Reduce heat to medium-low. Cook, stirring occasionally, 15 minutes. Remove from heat. Stir in cheese and cream. Cook over low heat, stirring constantly, until cheese melts. Serve with nacho chips.
About 1¾ cups.

Variation: Hot Chili con Queso. Follow recipe above, substituting jalapeño peppers (drained) for green chilies.

Toasted Sesame Cheese Spread

2 tablespoons KIKKOMAN Soy Sauce
1 package (3 oz.) cream cheese
4 teaspoons sesame seed, toasted
Assorted crackers

Pour soy sauce over cream cheese block in small dish, turning over several times to coat all sides. Cover; refrigerate 2 hours, turning cheese block over often. Remove cheese block from soy sauce and roll in sesame seed. Refrigerate until ready to serve with crackers.
Makes 4 to 6 appetizer servings.

Creamy Chili Dip

2 packages (8 ounces each) cream cheese or reduced-calorie cream cheese, softened
¾ cup V8® Vegetable Juice
1 can (4 ounces) chopped chilies
½ cup VLASIC® or EARLY CALIFORNIA® Chopped Pitted Ripe Olives
½ cup chopped sweet red pepper
2 teaspoons grated onion
¼ teaspoon hot pepper sauce
Fresh cilantro for garnish

1. In medium bowl with mixer at medium speed, beat cream cheese until smooth and fluffy.
2. Gradually beat in V8 juice until smooth and thoroughly blended.
3. Stir in chilies, olives, red pepper, onion and hot pepper sauce. Cover; refrigerate until serving time, at least 4 hours.
4. Garnish with fresh cilantro. Serve with fresh vegetables or chips for dipping.
Makes 4 cups.

Per tablespoon: 28 calories, 0 g protein, 3 g fat, 1 g carbohydrate, 50 mg sodium, 8 mg cholesterol.

Vegetable Dip Verde

1 cup cottage cheese
1 cup firmly packed parsley sprigs
½ cup chopped green onions
⅓ cup capers, drained
2 hard-cooked eggs, peeled, quartered
2 cloves garlic
1 tablespoon lemon juice
¼ teaspoon salt
¼ teaspoon TABASCO® pepper sauce

In container of blender or food processor combine all ingredients. Cover; process until smooth. Remove to serving bowl. Cover; refrigerate at least 1 hour. Serve with cut-up fresh vegetables.
Makes about 1½ cups.

Tropical Fruit Dip

½ cup mayonnaise
¼ cup sour cream
3 tablespoons lime juice
1 teaspoon honey
½ teaspoon ground cumin
¼ teaspoon TABASCO® pepper sauce
½ cup shredded coconut

In medium bowl combine mayonnaise, sour cream, lime juice, honey, cumin and Tabasco® sauce; mix well. Stir in coconut. Cover, refrigerate at least 1 hour. Serve with cut-up fresh fruit.
Makes about 1 cup.

Manhattan Clam Dip

1 (3-ounce) package cream cheese, softened
¼ cup mayonnaise or salad dressing
1 (8-ounce) container BORDEN® or MEADOW GOLD® Sour Cream
½ cup BENNETT'S® Cocktail Sauce
1 or 2 (6½-ounce) cans SNOW'S® or DOXSEE® Minced Clams, drained
2 tablespoons chopped green onion
1 teaspoon REALEMON® Lemon Juice from Concentrate

In small mixer bowl, beat cheese and mayonnaise until smooth. Stir in remaining ingredients. Chill. Garnish as desired. Serve with assorted fresh vegetables or WISE® COTTAGE FRIES® Potato Chips. Refrigerate leftovers.
Makes about 2 cups.

Manhattan Clam Dip

Chicken with Oriental Dipping Sauce

Chicken with Oriental Dipping Sauce

> **2 packages (12 ounces each) SWANSON® Frozen Fried Plump & Juicy® Chicken Dipsters® or 1 package (28 ounces) SWANSON® Frozen Fried Chicken Nibbles®**
> **¾ cup V8® Vegetable Juice**
> **¼ cup packed light brown sugar**
> **2 tablespoons rice vinegar or dry sherry**
> **1 tablespoon soy sauce**
> **1 tablespoon cornstarch**
> **¼ teaspoon grated fresh ginger**

To Microwave:
1. Prepare chicken dipsters according to package directions.
2. In medium microwave-safe bowl, stir together remaining ingredients. Cover with waxed paper; microwave on HIGH 3 minutes or until hot and bubbling, stirring once during cooking. Serve chicken with sauce for dipping.
Makes 1 cup sauce.
   Note: This sauce is also great to use for dipping MRS. PAUL'S® fish sticks, fried eggplant, zucchini sticks and onion rings.

Eggplant Spread

> **¼ cup olive oil**
> **1 medium eggplant, peeled and coarsely chopped (about 1 pound)**
> **½ cup chopped onion**
> **1 clove garlic, minced**
> **¾ cup V8® Vegetable Juice**
> **¼ cup toasted chopped pine nuts**
> **2 tablespoons chopped fresh parsley**
> **2 teaspoons soy sauce**
> **1 teaspoon sugar**
> **⅛ teaspoon pepper**
> **Pita bread wedges**

1. In 10-inch skillet over medium heat, in hot oil, cook eggplant, onion and garlic about 15 minutes or until eggplant is tender, stirring often.
2. In covered blender or food processor, blend eggplant mixture until smooth.
3. In medium bowl, combine eggplant mixture, V8 juice, pine nuts, parsley, soy sauce, sugar and pepper. Stir until thoroughly mixed. Cover; refrigerate until serving time, at least 2 hours. Serve with pita bread wedges.
Makes 3 cups.

Per tablespoon: 18 calories, 0 g protein, 2 g fat, 1 g carbohydrate, 28 mg sodium, 0 mg cholesterol.

Quick Paté Mold

> **½ pound liverwurst, cut into small pieces**
> **1 (8-ounce) package cream cheese, softened**
> **2 tablespoons finely chopped onion**
> **1 teaspoon WYLER'S® or STEERO® Chicken-Flavor Instant Bouillon**
> **Parsley, optional**
> **Melba rounds**

In small mixer bowl, combine liverwurst, cheese, onion and bouillon; beat until smooth. Turn into well-oiled 2-cup mold. Chill. Unmold; garnish with parsley if desired. Serve with Melba rounds. Refrigerate leftovers.
Makes 1 appetizer mold.

Chicken Liver Pâté

> **2 packages (8 ounces each) SWANSON® Frozen Chicken Livers**
> **¼ cup water**
> **1 pouch CAMBPELL'S® Onion Soup and Recipe Mix**
> **2 slices bacon, chopped**
> **¼ cup butter or margarine, cut up**
> **2 tablespoons brandy**
> **½ teaspoon dry mustard**
> **¼ teaspoon dried thyme leaves, crushed**
> **¼ teaspoon pepper**
> **Fresh parsley for garnish**
> **Chopped hard-cooked egg for garnish**

To Microwave:
1. Remove frozen livers from boxes but do not remove from pouches. Place in 2-quart microwave-safe casserole. Microwave, uncovered, at 50% power 5 minutes, turning pouches over once during cooking. Let stand 5 minutes. Remove livers from pouches and place in same casserole.

2. Add water, soup mix and bacon. Cover with lid; microwave on HIGH 5 minutes, stirring twice during cooking. Reduce power to 50%. Cover; microwave 4 minutes or until livers are no longer pink, stirring once during cooking.

3. In covered blender or food processor, combine liver mixture, butter, brandy, mustard, thyme and pepper. Blend until smooth.

4. Spoon mixture into 3-cup crock. Cover; refrigerate 4 hours or overnight. Garnish with parsley and egg. Serve with crackers.
Makes about 3 cups.

Guacamole

3 ripe medium avocados, seeded and peeled
2 tablespoons REALIME® Lime Juice from Concentrate *or* REALEMON® Lemon Juice from Concentrate
½ teaspoon garlic salt
½ teaspoon sugar
¼ teaspoon pepper

In blender container or food processor, mash avocados. Add remaining ingredients; mix well. Chill to blend flavors. Garnish as desired. Serve with WISE® BRAVOS® or LA FAMOUS® Tortilla Chips or fresh vegetables. Refrigerate leftovers.
Makes about 2 cups.

Variations: Add 1 or more of the following: sour cream, cooked crumbled bacon, chopped water chestnuts, chopped fresh tomato, chopped chilies.

Cool and Creamy Cucumber Spread

3 medium cucumbers
1 (8-ounce) *plus* 1 (3-ounce) package cream cheese, softened
½ cup sour cream
¼ cup snipped fresh dill*
1½ teaspoons lemon juice
1 envelope LIPTON® Vegetable Recipe Soup Mix

Thinly slice 1 cucumber and arrange in bottom of lightly oiled 4-cup ring mold; set aside.

Peel, seed and coarsely chop remaining cucumbers. With food processor or electric mixer, combine cream cheese, 1 cup chopped cucumber, sour cream, dill, lemon juice and vegetable recipe soup mix until smooth. Stir in remaining chopped cucumber. Turn into prepared mold; chill until firm, at least 3 hours. To serve, unmold onto serving platter and fill center, if desired, with cherry tomatoes and leaf lettuce. Serve with assorted crackers.
Makes about 3½ cups spread.

***Substitution:** Use 2 tablespoons dried dill weed.

Molded Cheese

2 packages (4-serving size) or 1 package (8-serving size) JELL-O® Brand Orange or Lemon Flavor Gelatin
1½ cups boiling water
½ pound (2½ cups) finely grated sharp Cheddar cheese
1 package (8 ounces) cream cheese, softened
1 cup (½ pint) sour cream
½ cup chopped scallions
¼ cup chopped parsley
3 tablespoons prepared horseradish
1 tablespoon Worcestershire sauce

Dissolve gelatin in boiling water. Combine remaining ingredients in large bowl; with electric mixer at medium speed, beat until well blended. Gradually blend into gelatin. Pour into 6-cup mold. Chill until firm, about 3 hours. Unmold. Garnish with fresh fruit or vegetables, if desired. Serve as an appetizer with assorted crackers.
Makes 5½ cups or 11 servings.

Cool and Creamy Cucumber Spread

Garden Vegetable Spread

1 8-ounce container Soft PHILADELPHIA BRAND Cream Cheese
½ cup shredded carrot
½ cup shredded zucchini
1 tablespoon chopped parsley
¼ teaspoon garlic salt
Dash of pepper

Combine ingredients; mix well. Chill. Serve with party rye or pumpernickel bread slices or assorted crackers. *1⅓ cups.*

Variation: Serve with LENDER'S Pre-Sliced Frozen Plain Bagelettes, toasted.

Florentine Dip

1 8-ounce package *Light* PHILADELPHIA BRAND Neufchâtel Cheese, softened
½ cup plain yogurt
2 tablespoons milk
1 10-ounce package frozen spinach, thawed, well-drained, chopped
2 hard-cooked eggs, finely chopped
¼ teaspoon pepper
¼ teaspoon salt

Combine neufchâtel cheese, yogurt and milk, mixing until well blended. Stir in remaining ingredients. Serve with vegetable dippers. *2½ cups.*

Florentine Dip

Hearty Herbed Cheese Spread

1 pouch CAMPBELL'S® Onion Soup and Recipe Mix
2 packages (8 ounces each) cream cheese, softened
2 cups shredded sharp Cheddar cheese (8 ounces), at room temperature
½ cup chopped fresh parsley
2 tablespoons milk
1 teaspoon dried basil leaves, crushed
1 teaspoon dried tarragon leaves, crushed
½ teaspoon dried dill weed, crushed
2 tablespoons cracked pepper
Paprika for garnish

1. In medium bowl, combine soup mix, cheeses, parsley, milk, basil, tarragon and dill; beat with wooden spoon until well blended.
2. Line 9-inch pie plate with plastic wrap, letting wrap hang over edge. Spoon cheese mixture into pie plate, packing down firmly. Cover; chill until serving time, at least 4 hours.
3. Invert pie plate over serving dish and remove pie plate and plastic from cheese. Smooth surface of cheese with a knife to remove any wrinkles. Press cracked pepper into sides of cheese; sprinkle top with paprika. Serve with crackers.
Makes 3¼ cups.

Note: To make a fancy design on cheese spread, first cut a piece of cardboard into desired shape (flower, Christmas tree, etc.), and lay cardboard on cheese spread. Sprinkle paprika around design. Carefully remove cardboard to leave a stenciled design in paprika.

Warm Herb Cheese Spread

3 (8-ounce) packages cream cheese, softened
¼ cup BORDEN® or MEADOW GOLD® Milk
¼ cup REALEMON® Lemon Juice from Concentrate
½ teaspoon *each* basil, oregano, marjoram and thyme leaves
¼ teaspoon garlic powder
½ pound cooked shrimp, chopped (1½ cups), optional

Preheat oven to 350°. In large mixer bowl, beat cheese until smooth. Gradually beat in milk then ReaLemon® brand. Stir in remaining ingredients. Pour into 9-inch quiche dish or pie plate. Cover; bake 15 minutes or until hot. Garnish as desired. Serve warm with crackers or fresh vegetables. Refrigerate leftovers.
Makes about 4 cups.

Microwave: In 9-inch pie plate, prepare cheese spread as above. Cook on 50% power (medium) 5 to 6 minutes or until hot. Stir before serving.

Hot Crabmeat Appetizer

1 8-ounce package PHILADELPHIA BRAND Cream Cheese, softened
1 7½-ounce can crabmeat, drained, flaked
2 tablespoons finely chopped onion
2 tablespoons milk
½ teaspoon KRAFT Cream Style Horseradish
¼ teaspoon salt
Dash of pepper
⅓ cup sliced almonds, toasted

Combine all ingredients except almonds, mixing until well blended. Spoon mixture into 9-inch pie plate; sprinkle with almonds. Bake at 375°, 15 minutes. Serve with crackers. *Approximately 1½ cups.*

Variations: Substitute 8-ounce can minced clams, drained, for crabmeat.

Omit almonds; sprinkle with dill weed.

Hot Beef Dip

¼ cup chopped onion
1 tablespoon PARKAY Margarine
1 cup milk
1 8-ounce package
   PHILADELPHIA BRAND
   Cream Cheese, cubed
1 3-ounce package smoked
   sliced beef, chopped
1 4-ounce can mushrooms,
   drained
¼ cup (1 ounce) KRAFT Grated
   Parmesan Cheese
2 tablespoons chopped parsley

Saute onions in margarine. Add milk and cream cheese; stir over low heat until cream cheese is melted. Add remaining ingredients; heat thoroughly, stirring occasionally. Serve hot with French bread slices, if desired.
2½ cups.

Variation: Substitute 2½-ounce package smoked sliced turkey for 3-ounce package smoked sliced beef.

Serving Suggestion: For a colorful variety, serve with French, whole-wheat or rye bread cubes.

Hot Artichoke Dip

1 package (9 ounces) frozen
   artichoke hearts, thawed
½ pint (8 ounces) sour cream
¼ cup grated Parmesan cheese
1 envelope LIPTON® Golden
   Onion Recipe Soup Mix
Buttered bread crumbs
Suggested Dippers*

Preheat oven to 350°

In food processor or blender, puree artichokes. Add sour cream and cheese; process until smooth. Stir in golden onion recipe soup mix. Turn into 2½-cup casserole, then top with bread crumbs. Bake uncovered 30 minutes or until heated through. Serve with Suggested Dippers.
Makes about 2¼ cups dip.

***Suggested Dippers:** Use carrot or celery sticks, whole mushrooms or sliced zucchini.

Microwave Directions: Omit bread crumbs. Prepare mixture as above. Heat at HIGH (Full Power), turning casserole occasionally, 8 minutes or until heated through. Let stand covered 5 minutes. Serve as above.

Mexican-Style Appetizer

Mexican-Style Appetizer

1 can (11½ ounces)
   CAMPBELL'S® Condensed
   Bean with Bacon Soup
1 package (1¼ ounces) taco
   seasoning mix
¼ teaspoon hot pepper sauce
1 cup sour cream
1 can (4 ounces) chopped green
   chilies, drained
½ cup VLASIC® or EARLY
   CALIFORNIA® Sliced
   Pimento-Stuffed Olives
1 cup shredded longhorn
   cheese (4 ounces)
½ cup alfalfa sprouts
½ cup chopped CAMPBELL'S
   FRESH® Tomato
Tortilla chips

1. In small bowl, combine soup, taco seasoning mix and hot pepper sauce; stir until blended. On large serving plate, spread mixture into a 6-inch round. Spread sides and top of bean mixture with sour cream to cover.
2. Layer chilies, olives, cheese, alfalfa sprouts and tomato over sour cream. Cover; refrigerate until serving time, at least 4 hours. Surround with tortilla chips.
Makes 10 appetizer servings.

Layered Crab Spread

2 (8-ounce) packages cream cheese, softened
2 tablespoons REALEMON® Lemon Juice from Concentrate
1 teaspoon Worcestershire sauce
¼ teaspoon garlic powder
2 tablespoons finely chopped green onion
¾ cup BENNETT'S® Chili Sauce
1 (6-ounce) can ORLEANS® White Crab Meat, drained

In large mixer bowl, beat cheese, ReaLemon® brand, Worcestershire and garlic powder until fluffy; stir in onion. Spread evenly on 10-inch plate. Top with chili sauce then crabmeat. Cover; chill thoroughly. Garnish as desired. Serve with assorted crackers. Refrigerate leftovers.
Makes 10 to 12 servings.

Nutty Blue Cheese Vegetable Dip

Party Cheese Ball

2 8-ounce packages PHILADELPHIA BRAND Cream Cheese, softened
2 cups (8 ounces) shredded CRACKER BARREL Brand Sharp Natural Cheddar Cheese
1 tablespoon chopped pimento
1 tablespoon chopped green pepper
1 tablespoon finely chopped onion
2 teaspoons worcestershire sauce
1 teaspoon lemon juice
Dash of ground red pepper
Dash of salt
Chopped pecans

Combine cream cheese and cheddar cheese, mixing at medium speed on electric mixer until well blended. Add all remaining ingredients except pecans; mix well. Chill several hours. Shape into ball; roll in pecans. Serve with crackers.
Approximately 2 cups.
Variation: Omit pecans. Roll in finely chopped parsley, dried beef or toasted chopped almonds.

Nutty Blue Cheese Vegetable Dip

1 cup mayonnaise or salad dressing
1 (8-ounce) container BORDEN® or MEADOW GOLD® Sour Cream
¼ cup (1 ounce) crumbled blue cheese
1 tablespoon finely chopped onion
2 teaspoons WYLER'S® or STEERO® Beef-Flavor Instant Bouillon
½ to ¾ cup coarsely chopped walnuts
Assorted fresh vegetables

In medium bowl, combine mayonnaise, sour cream, blue cheese, onion and bouillon; mix well. Stir in nuts; cover and chill. Stir before serving. Garnish as desired. Serve with vegetables. Refrigerate leftovers.
Makes about 2 cups.

Pine Nut Cheese Spread

1 8-ounce package PHILADELPHIA BRAND Cream Cheese, softened
2 tablespoons KRAFT Grated Parmesan Cheese
¼ cup chopped green pepper
1 tablespoon finely chopped onion
2 teaspoons chopped pimento
Dash of ground red pepper
⅓ cup pine nuts or slivered almonds, toasted

Combine all ingredients except pine nuts, mixing until well blended. Chill. Shape into log. Coat with pine nuts just before serving.
1 cup.
Variation: Substitute *Light* PHILADELPHIA BRAND Neufchâtel Cheese for Cream Cheese. Increase Parmesan cheese to ¼ cup (1 ounce). Spoon into serving container. Top with pine nuts just before serving.
Hint: Homemade cheese spreads in colorful containers make great hostess gifts. Include the recipe for an added personal touch.

Savory Cheddar Spread

1 8-ounce package PHILADELPHIA BRAND Cream Cheese, softened
1/2 cup MIRACLE WHIP Salad Dressing
1 cup (4 ounces) 100% Natural KRAFT Shredded Mild Cheddar Cheese
2 tablespoons green onion slices
8 crisply cooked bacon slices, crumbled
1/2 cup crushed buttery crackers

Combine cream cheese and salad dressing, mixing until well blended. Add cheddar cheese and onions; mix well. Spoon into 9-inch pie plate; sprinkle with combined bacon and crumbs. Bake at 350°, 15 minutes. Serve with additional crackers.
2 cups.
Variation: Substitute 1/4 cup bacon flavored bits for crumbled bacon.
Microwave: Microwave cream cheese on Medium (50%) 30 seconds. Assemble recipe as directed except for sprinkling with bacon and crumbs. Microwave on High 4 minutes or until thoroughly heated, turning dish every 2 minutes. Sprinkle with combined bacon and crumbs. Serve as directed.

Refreshing Cucumber Dip

1 8-ounce package PHILADELPHIA BRAND Cream Cheese, softened
1/2 cup sour cream
1 tablespoon milk
1 teaspoon grated onion
1/4 teaspoon worcestershire sauce
1/3 cup finely chopped cucumber

Combine all ingredients except cucumbers, mixing until well blended. Stir in cucumbers. Chill several hours or overnight. Serve with chips or vegetable dippers.
1 2/3 cups.

Pineapple-Almond Cheese Spread

2 cans (8 ounces each) DOLE® Crushed Pineapple
1 package (8 ounces) cream cheese, softened
4 cups shredded sharp Cheddar cheese
1/2 cup mayonnaise
1 tablespoon soy sauce
1 cup DOLE™ Chopped Natural Almonds, toasted
1/2 cup finely chopped DOLE™ Green Bell Pepper
1/4 cup minced green onion or chives
DOLE™ Celery stalks or assorted breads

Drain pineapple. In large bowl, beat cream cheese until smooth; beat in Cheddar cheese, mayonnaise and soy sauce until smooth. Stir in pineapple, almonds, green pepper and onion. Refrigerate, covered. Use to stuff celery stalks or serve as dip with assorted breads. Serve at room temperature.
Makes 4 cups.

Hawaiian Coconut Spread

1 8-ounce container Soft PHILADELPHIA BRAND Cream Cheese
2 tablespoons KRAFT Apricot, Pineapple or Peach Preserves
1/3 cup flaked coconut

Combine cream cheese and preserves, mixing until well blended. Add coconut; mix well. Chill. Serve with nut bread slices.
1 1/3 cups.
Variations: Add 1/8 teaspoon anise seed.
Substitute 1/4 cup whole berry cranberry sauce for KRAFT Preserves.

Zucchini Chive Dip

1 8-ounce container Soft PHILADELPHIA BRAND Cream Cheese
3 tablespoons milk
1 small zucchini, shredded
3 tablespoons chopped chives
1/8 teaspoon salt

Combine cream cheese and milk, mixing until well blended. Add remaining ingredients; mix well. Chill. Serve with vegetable dippers or chips.
1 cup.

Quick Mexican Spread

1 8-ounce package *Light* PHILADELPHIA BRAND Neufchâtel Cheese, softened
1 4-ounce can chopped green chilies, drained

Combine neufchâtel cheese and chilies, mixing until well blended. Chill. Serve with tortilla chips or spread over warm tortillas or corn bread.
1 cup.

Piña Pepper Spread

1 can (8 ounces) DOLE® Crushed Pineapple, drained
1/2 cup bottled taco sauce
1 package (8 ounces) cream cheese, softened
Taco chips or crackers

Combine pineapple and taco sauce in small bowl. Place cream cheese on serving plate in block or cut into individual servings. Spoon pineapple mixture over top. Serve with taco chips or crackers.
Makes 4 servings.

Piña Pepper Spread

Peppy Bean Dip

- 1 pouch CAMPBELL'S® Onion Soup and Recipe Mix
- ½ cup sour cream
- 1 can (16 ounces) refried beans
- ½ cup salsa
- 1 large clove garlic, minced
  VLASIC® or EARLY CALIFORNIA® Sliced Pitted Ripe Olives for garnish

1. In medium bowl, combine soup mix, sour cream, beans, salsa and garlic; mix well. Cover; chill until serving time, at least 2 hours.
2. Garnish with olives. Serve with corn chips or vegetable dippers.
Makes 2½ cups.

Mustard Sauce

- 2 tablespoons CRISCO® Oil
- 2 tablespoons all-purpose flour
- 2 tablespoons dry mustard
- ½ teaspoon salt
- 1 cup milk

Blend Crisco® Oil, flour, mustard and salt in small saucepan. Cook over medium-high heat 1 minute. Stir in milk. Cook, stirring constantly, until sauce thickens and bubbles.
About 1 cup.

Roasted Red Pepper Mousse Spread

- 1 envelope KNOX® Unflavored Gelatine
- ½ cup cold water
- 2 cups (1 pint) whipping or heavy cream
- 1 jar (8 ounces) roasted red peppers, drained and coarsely chopped
- ½ cup mayonnaise
- 1 cup loosely packed basil leaves*
- ¼ cup grated Parmesan cheese
- 1 small clove garlic, finely chopped
- ½ teaspoon salt
- ⅛ teaspoon pepper

In small saucepan, sprinkle unflavored gelatine over cold water; let stand 1 minute. Stir over low heat until gelatine is completely dissolved, about 3 minutes. Remove from heat and let stand until lukewarm, about 2 minutes.

In large bowl, with electric mixer, beat cream until soft peaks form. Gradually add red peppers, mayonnaise, basil, cheese, garlic, salt and pepper. While beating, gradually add lukewarm gelatine mixture and beat until blended. Pour into 7-cup mold or bowl; chill until firm, about 3 hours. Unmold and serve, if desired, with sliced Italian bread, toasted.
Makes about 6 cups spread.

*Substitution: Use 1 cup chopped fresh parsley plus 1 teaspoon dried basil leaves.

Shrimp Spread

- 2 (8-ounce) packages cream cheese, softened
- ½ cup REALEMON® Lemon Juice from Concentrate
- 2 (4¼-ounce) cans ORLEANS® Shrimp, drained and soaked as label directs
- 1 to 2 tablespoons finely chopped green onion
- 1 tablespoon prepared horseradish
- 1 teaspoon Worcestershire sauce
- ¼ teaspoon pepper
- ⅛ teaspoon garlic powder

In small mixer bowl, beat cheese until fluffy; gradually beat in ReaLemon® brand. Stir in remaining ingredients. Chill to blend flavors. Garnish as desired. Serve with crackers or fresh vegetables. Refrigerate leftovers.
Makes about 3 cups.

Salmon Mousse

- 2 envelopes KNOX® Unflavored Gelatine
- 1 can (15½ ounces) salmon, drained (reserve liquid)*
- 1 stalk celery, cut into 3-inch pieces
- 1 small onion, quartered
- ½ medium cucumber, peeled, seeded and quartered
- 1 cup (½ pint) whipping or heavy cream
- ¾ cup mayonnaise
- ¼ cup lemon juice
- 1 teaspoon dried dill weed
- ½ teaspoon salt (optional)

In medium saucepan, sprinkle unflavored gelatine over reserved salmon liquid blended with enough water to equal 1 cup; let stand 1 minute. Stir over low heat until gelatine is completely dissolved, about 5 minutes.

In blender or food processor, process gelatine mixture, vegetables, cream, mayonnaise and lemon juice until blended. Add salmon, dill and salt; process until blended. Pour into 6-cup mold or bowl; chill until firm, about 3 hours. Unmold and serve with assorted crackers.
Makes about 5½ cups spread.

*Substitution: Use 2 cans (6½ ounces each) tuna, drained (reserve liquid).

Shrimp Spread

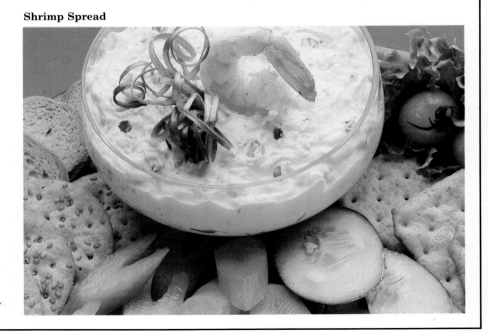

Spicy Appetizer Dip

- 1 (8-ounce) can crushed pineapple in its own juice
- 1 cup COLLEGE INN® Chicken or Beef Broth
- 3 tablespoons cornstarch
- 2 tablespoons soy sauce
- 2 tablespoons white wine vinegar
- 2 tablespoons firmly packed light brown sugar
- ¼ teaspoon crushed red pepper Cocktail franks, ham cubes or fresh vegetables

Drain pineapple, reserving juice. In small saucepan, blend reserved juice, broth, cornstarch, soy sauce, vinegar, brown sugar and red pepper. Cook and stir until mixture thickens and boils. Stir in pineapple. Serve hot or cold with cocktail franks, ham cubes or vegetables.
Makes 2 cups.

Mini Monte Cristo Sandwiches

- 2 tablespoons butter or margarine, softened
- 2 tablespoons prepared mustard
- 8 slices white bread
- 4 slices fontina or Swiss cheese (about 4 ounces)
- 4 slices cooked ham (about 4 ounces)
- 3 eggs
- ½ cup milk
- 1 envelope LIPTON® Golden Onion Recipe Soup Mix
- ¼ cup butter or margarine

Blend 2 tablespoons butter with mustard; evenly spread on each bread slice. Equally top 4 bread slices with cheese and ham; top with remaining bread, buttered side down. Cut each sandwich into 4 triangles.

Beat eggs, milk and golden onion recipe soup mix until well blended. Dip sandwiches in egg mixture, coating well.

In large skillet, melt ¼ cup butter and cook sandwiches over medium heat, turning once, until golden.
Makes about 16 mini sandwiches.

Spicy Appetizer Dip

Country Pâté

- 4 slices bacon
- 1 pound ground beef
- ½ pound cooked ham, cut into ¼-inch pieces
- ½ pound raw skinless boneless chicken breast, cut into ¼-inch pieces
- 2 eggs
- 1 pouch CAMPBELL'S® Onion Soup and Recipe Mix
- 2 tablespoons brandy
- ½ teaspoon pepper
- ¼ teaspoon ground nutmeg Watercress for garnish Cherry tomatoes for garnish

To Microwave:

1. Arrange bacon slices ½ inch apart across bottom and up sides of 9- by 5-inch microwave-safe loaf dish; set aside.

2. In medium bowl, thoroughly mix beef, ham, chicken, eggs, soup mix, brandy, pepper and nutmeg. Spoon meat mixture into bacon-lined dish, packing down firmly. Fold ends of bacon over filling.

3. Cover with waxed paper; microwave on HIGH 8 minutes, rotating once during cooking. Carefully pour off fat. Cover; microwave on HIGH 8 minutes or until center is firm, rotating dish twice during cooking. Let stand, covered, 10 minutes. Pour off fat. Invert onto serving plate. Cover; refrigerate until serving time, at least 4 hours.

4. Cut loaf into thin slices. Garnish with watercress and cherry tomatoes. Serve with crackers and mustard.
Makes 18 appetizer servings.

Note: If you are using a temperature probe, cook pâté to an internal temperature of 175° to 185°F.

Herbed Cheese Pinwheel Canapes

1 8-ounce package
  PHILADELPHIA BRAND
  Cream Cheese, softened
2 tablespoons chopped parsley
2 teaspoons lemon juice
½ teaspoon dried basil leaves,
  crushed
⅛ teaspoon pepper
⅛ teaspoon garlic powder
1 1-pound unsliced whole-wheat
  bread loaf, crusts trimmed
  Soft PARKAY Margarine
¼ cup finely chopped pecans
¼ cup sesame seed
1 tablespoon worcestershire
  sauce

Combine cream cheese, parsley, juice and seasonings, mixing until well blended. Slice bread lengthwise into ½-inch slices. Roll each slice to ¼-inch thickness. Evenly spread each bread slice with cream cheese mixture; roll up, starting at narrow end. Spread bread rolls with margarine, excluding ends. In small skillet, combine remaining ingredients; cook 3 minutes or until worcestershire sauce evaporates. Cool. Coat bread rolls with pecan mixture. Cover; chill at least 30 minutes. Cut each bread roll crosswise into ½-inch slices.
Approximately 2½ dozen.

Herbed Cheese Pinwheel Canapes

Cheese & Nut Stuffed Bread Slices

1 loaf Italian or French bread
  (about 16 inches long)
1 (8-ounce) *plus* 1 (3-ounce)
  package cream cheese,
  softened
4 tablespoons butter or
  margarine, softened
1 cup shredded Cheddar cheese
  (about 4 ounces)
1 envelope LIPTON® Vegetable
  Recipe Soup Mix
½ cup chopped walnuts

Trim ends of bread, then cut bread crosswise into 4 pieces. Hollow out center of each piece, leaving ½-inch shell; reserve shells (save bread for fresh bread crumbs).

With food processor or electric mixer, combine cream cheese with butter until smooth. Add Cheddar cheese, vegetable recipe soup mix and walnuts; process until blended. Pack into reserved shells. Wrap in plastic wrap or wax paper, then chill at least 4 hours. To serve, cut into ½-inch slices.
Makes about 2 dozen slices.

Note: Store any remaining cheese mixture, covered, in refrigerator and serve as a spread with crackers.

Mexican Shrimp Cocktail

½ cup WISH-BONE® Italian
  Dressing
½ cup chopped tomato
1 can (4 ounces) chopped green
  chilies, undrained
¼ cup chopped green onions
1½ teaspoons honey
¼ teaspoon hot pepper sauce
1 pound medium shrimp,
  cleaned and cooked
2 teaspoons finely chopped
  coriander (cilantro) or
  parsley

In medium bowl, combine Italian dressing, tomato, chilies, green onions, honey and hot pepper sauce. Stir in shrimp. Cover and marinate in refrigerator, stirring occasionally, at least 2 hours. Just before serving, stir in coriander.
Makes about 6 servings.

Note: Also terrific with Wish-Bone® Robusto Italian, Lite Italian, Blended Italian or Herbal Italian Dressing.

Cheese Stuffed Tomatoes

1 cup BORDEN® or MEADOW
  GOLD® Cottage Cheese
¼ cup (1 ounce) crumbled blue
  cheese
1 teaspoon celery seed
1 teaspoon prepared mustard
¼ teaspoon onion powder
30 cherry tomatoes, tops
  removed and seeded

In medium bowl, combine cheeses and seasonings; mix well. Spoon cheese mixture into tomatoes; cover and chill. Refrigerate leftovers.
Makes 30 appetizers.

Cheesy Potato Skins

    4 large baking potatoes, baked
      Oil
 1/4 lb. VELVEETA Pasteurized
      Process Cheese Spread,
      cubed
    2 tablespoons chopped red or
      green pepper
    2 crisply cooked bacon slices,
      crumbled
    1 tablespoon green onion slices
      Sour cream

Cut potatoes in half lengthwise; scoop out centers, leaving 1/4-inch shell. Fry shells, a few at a time, in deep hot oil, 375°, 2 to 3 minutes or until golden brown; drain. Place on cookie sheet. Top with process cheese spread; broil until process cheese spread begins to melt. Top with remaining ingredients. *8 appetizers.*

Preparation time: 60 minutes
Cooking time: 10 minutes

Beer Batter Fried Veggies 'n Things

      Oil
    1 envelope LIPTON® Golden
      Onion Recipe Soup Mix
    1 cup all-purpose flour
    1 teaspoon baking powder
    2 eggs
 1/2 cup beer
    1 tablespoon prepared mustard
      Suggested Veggies 'n Things*

In deep-fat fryer, heat oil to 375°.
   Meanwhile, in large bowl, beat golden onion recipe soup mix, flour, baking powder, eggs, beer and mustard until smooth and well blended. Let batter stand 10 minutes. Dip Suggested Veggies 'n Things into batter, then carefully drop into hot oil. Fry, turning once, until golden brown; drain on paper towels. Serve warm.
Makes about 4 cups veggies 'n things.
   Suggested Veggies 'n Things: Use any of the following to equal 4 to 5 cups—broccoli florets, cauliflowerets, sliced mushrooms or zucchini, or chilled mozzarella sticks.

Herb Appetizer Cheesecake

    1 cup dry bread crumbs
 1/4 cup PARKAY Margarine,
      melted
 1/4 cup olive oil
    2 cups fresh basil leaves
 1/2 teaspoon salt
    1 garlic clove, cut in half
    2 8-ounce packages
      PHILADELPHIA BRAND
      Cream Cheese, softened
    1 cup ricotta cheese
    3 eggs
 1/2 cup (2 ounces) KRAFT Grated
      Parmesan Cheese
 1/2 cup pine nuts

Combine crumbs and margarine; press onto bottom of 9-inch springform pan. Bake at 350°, 10 minutes.
   Place oil, basil, salt and garlic in blender container. Cover; process on high speed until smooth. Combine basil mixture, cream cheese and ricotta cheese, mixing at medium speed on electric mixer until well blended. Add eggs, one at a time, mixing well after each addition. Blend in parmesan cheese; pour over crust. Top with pine nuts. Bake at 325°, 1 hour and 15 minutes. Loosen cake from rim of pan; cool before removing rim of pan. Serve warm or at room temperature.

Garnish with tomato rose and fresh basil, if desired. Chill any remaining cheesecake.
16 servings.
   Variation: Substitute 1 cup chopped parsley and 1 tablespoon dried basil leaves for fresh basil leaves.

Beef Kushisashi

 1/2 cup KIKKOMAN Soy Sauce
 1/4 cup chopped green onions
      and tops
    2 tablespoons sugar
    1 tablespoon vegetable oil
 1 1/2 teaspoons cornstarch
    1 clove garlic, pressed
    1 teaspoon grated fresh ginger
      root
 2 1/2 pounds boneless beef sirloin
      steak

Blend soy sauce, green onions, sugar, oil, cornstarch, garlic and ginger in small saucepan. Simmer, stirring constantly, until thickened, about 1 minute; cool. Cover and set aside. Slice beef into 1/8-inch-thick strips about 4 inches long and 1 inch wide. Thread onto bamboo or metal skewers keeping meat as flat as possible; brush both sides of beef with sauce. Place skewers on rack of broiler pan; broil to desired degree of doneness.
Makes 10 to 12 appetizer servings.

Beef Kushisashi

Baked Stuffed Shrimp

Baked Stuffed Shrimp

    1 pound jumbo raw shrimp
        (about 12 to 16), peeled,
        leaving tails on
    1 cup chopped mushrooms
    1/3 cup chopped onion
    1 clove garlic, finely chopped
    1 teaspoon WYLER'S® or
        STEERO® Chicken-Flavor
        Instant Bouillon
    1/4 cup margarine or butter
    1 1/2 cups soft bread crumbs
        (3 slices bread)
    1 tablespoon chopped pimiento
        Melted margarine or butter
        Chopped parsley, optional

Preheat oven to 400°. In large skillet, cook mushrooms, onion, garlic and bouillon in margarine until tender. Remove from heat; stir in crumbs and pimiento. Cut a slit along underside of each shrimp; do not cut through. Remove vein; brush entire shrimp with margarine. Mound stuffing mixture in hollow of each shrimp. Place in greased shallow baking dish. Bake 10 to 12 minutes or until hot. Garnish with parsley if desired. Refrigerate leftovers.

Makes 6 to 8 servings.

Microwave: In 1-quart glass measure, microwave margarine on full power (high) 45 seconds or until melted. Add mushrooms, onion, garlic and bouillon. Microwave on full power (high) 3 minutes or until onion is tender. Stir in crumbs and pimiento. Prepare shrimp as above. Place in 2 greased 12×7-inch shallow baking dishes or 1 (12-inch) round glass platter. Microwave on full power (high) 3 minutes or until hot. Proceed as above.

Baked Stuffed Clams

    12 clams, well scrubbed*
        Water
    1 envelope LIPTON® Vegetable
        Recipe Soup Mix
    2 cups fresh bread crumbs
    1 teaspoon oregano
    1/8 teaspoon pepper
    2 tablespoons oil
    2 tablespoons grated Parmesan
        cheese

In large skillet, arrange clams, then add 1/2 inch water. Cook covered over medium-high heat 5 minutes or until clams open. Remove clams, reserving 3/4 cup liquid; strain liquid. (Discard any unopened clams.) Remove clams from shells, then chop clams; reserve 12 shell halves.

Preheat oven to 350°. In small bowl, combine vegetable recipe soup mix, bread crumbs, oregano and pepper. Stir in clams and reserved liquid. Stuff reserved shells with clam mixture. Arrange on baking sheet; drizzle with oil, then sprinkle with cheese. Bake 15 minutes or until golden.

Makes 12 stuffed clams.

*Substitution: Use 2 cans (6 1/2 ounces each) minced or chopped clams, drained (reserve 1/4 cup liquid). Mix reserved liquid with 1/2 cup water. Shells can be purchased separately.

Microwave Directions: Omit oil. Cook and stuff clams as above. On plate, arrange clams and heat uncovered at HIGH (Full Power) 5 minutes or until heated through, rearranging clams once.

Baked Artichoke Squares

    3 tablespoons CRISCO® Oil
    1 cup chopped fresh
        mushrooms
    1/4 cup thinly sliced celery
    1 clove garlic, minced
    1 can (14 ounces) artichoke
        hearts, drained and chopped
    1/3 cup chopped green onion
    1/2 teaspoon dried marjoram
        leaves
    1/4 teaspoon dried oregano leaves
    1/4 teaspoon cayenne
    1 cup shredded Cheddar cheese
        (about 4 ounces)
    1 cup shredded Monterey Jack
        cheese (about 4 ounces)
    2 eggs, slightly beaten
Pastry:
    1 1/2 cups all-purpose flour
    1/2 teaspoon salt
    1/2 cup CRISCO® Oil
    1/4 cup milk

Preheat oven to 350°F. Heat Crisco® Oil in medium skillet. Add mushrooms, celery and garlic. Sauté until celery is tender. Remove from heat. Stir in artichoke hearts, onion, marjoram, oregano and cayenne. Add Cheddar cheese, Monterey Jack cheese and eggs. Mix well. Set aside.

For pastry, combine flour and salt in medium mixing bowl. Blend Crisco® Oil and milk in small mixing bowl. Add to flour mixture. Stir with fork until mixture forms a ball. Press dough in bottom and 1 1/2 inches up sides of 13×9-inch pan. Bake at 350°F, 10 minutes.

Spread cheese mixture on baked crust. Bake at 350°F, about 20 minutes, or until center is set. Cool slightly. Cut into 24 squares. Serve warm.

2 dozen appetizers.

Appetizer Ham Logs

2 cups ground ham
1 egg, beaten
¼ teaspoon pepper
¼ cup seasoned fine dry bread crumbs
½ cup horseradish sauce
1 tablespoon prepared mustard
⅛ teaspoon celery salt
Vegetable oil for frying
Pimiento strips

Combine ham, egg and pepper in medium bowl; mix well. Shape into 1-inch logs or balls. Roll in bread crumbs. Refrigerate, covered, 1 hour.

To make mustard sauce, combine horseradish sauce, mustard and celery salt in small bowl until well blended. Refrigerate, covered, until serving time.

Heat 3 inches oil in heavy, large saucepan over medium-high heat until oil is 365°F; adjust heat to maintain temperature. Fry ham logs, a few at a time, 2 to 3 minutes or until golden. Drain on paper towels. Garnish with pimiento strips. Serve with mustard sauce.
Makes about 24 appetizers.

*Favorite recipe from **National Pork Producers Council***

Ham-Wrapped Oysters

3 tablespoons prepared horseradish
½ pound ham, cut into 3×1×¼-inch strips
2 dozen fresh oysters, shucked
3 tablespoons butter or margarine, melted
1 tablespoon lemon juice
¼ teaspoon garlic powder

Spread horseradish on 1 side of each ham strip. Place 1 oyster on each ham strip; roll up and secure with wooden pick. Arrange on broiler pan. Combine butter, lemon juice and garlic powder in small cup. Brush each ham roll with some of the lemon-butter. Broil, 5 inches from heat, 10 to 15 minutes or until edges of oysters curl, brushing occasionally with the remaining lemon-butter.
Makes 24 appetizers.

*Favorite recipe from **National Pork Producers Council***

Top: Appetizer Ham Logs, Miniature Teriyaki Pork Kabobs (page 23); bottom: Ham-Wrapped Oysters, Rumaki (page 22)

Buffalo-Style Chicken Wings

    Oil
**12 chicken wings (about
    2 pounds)**
½ cup all-purpose flour
**2 tablespoons butter or
    margarine**
¼ cup sliced green onions
**1 medium clove garlic, finely
    chopped**
**1 cup (8 ounces) WISH-BONE®
    Sweet 'n Spicy® French
    Dressing**
1 teaspoon thyme leaves
1 teaspoon oregano leaves
1 teaspoon ground cumin
½ teaspoon hot pepper sauce *
**   WISH-BONE® Chunky Blue
    Cheese Dressing**
**   Celery sticks**

In deep-fat fryer or large heavy skillet, heat oil to 375°.

Cut tips off chicken wings (save tips for soup). Halve chicken wings at joint. Lightly coat chicken with flour, then carefully drop chicken, a few pieces at a time, into hot oil. Fry, turning occasionally, 15 minutes or until golden brown; drain on paper towels.

Meanwhile, in large skillet, melt butter and cook green onions with garlic over medium heat, stirring occasionally, 3 minutes or until onions are tender. Remove from heat and stir in sweet 'n spicy French dressing, thyme, oregano, cumin and hot pepper sauce. Add chicken and toss to coat. Serve with chunky blue cheese dressing and celery sticks.
Makes 24 appetizers.
    *Variations: First Alarm Chicken Wings: Add 1 teaspoon hot pepper sauce.
    Second Alarm Chicken Wings: Add 1½ teaspoons hot pepper sauce.
    Third Alarm Chicken Wings: Add 2 teaspoons hot pepper sauce.
    Note: Also terrific with Wish-Bone® Lite Sweet 'n Spicy French, Russian or Lite Russian Dressing.

Marinated Mushrooms

**½ cup WISH-BONE® Italian &
    Cheese Dressing**
2 pounds fresh mushrooms
2 teaspoons lemon juice

In large saucepan, heat Italian & cheese dressing and cook mushrooms over medium heat, stirring occasionally, 5 minutes. Add lemon juice. Remove mushrooms with dressing to large shallow baking dish. Cover and marinate in refrigerator, stirring occasionally, 4 hours or overnight.
Makes about 4 cups mushrooms.
    Note: Also terrific with Wish-Bone® Italian, Robusto Italian, or Lite Italian Dressing.

Marinated Antipasto

**1½ pounds medium raw shrimp,
    peeled, deveined and
    cooked**
**6 ounces Provolone cheese, cut
    into cubes**
**1 (6-ounce) can pitted ripe
    olives, drained**
½ cup sliced green onions
1 cup vegetable oil
**⅔ cup REALEMON® Lemon Juice
    from Concentrate**
**2 tablespoons Dijon-style
    mustard**
2 teaspoons sugar
1½ teaspoons thyme leaves
1 teaspoon salt
**4 ounces Genoa salami, cut into
    cubes**
**1 large red pepper, seeded and
    cut into squares**

Place shrimp, cheese, olives and onions in large shallow dish. In small bowl or jar, combine remaining ingredients except salami and pepper; mix well. Pour over shrimp mixture.

Cover; refrigerate 6 hours or overnight, stirring occasionally. Add salami and pepper; toss. Drain; serve with toothpicks. Refrigerate leftovers.
Makes about 8 cups.

Rumaki

16 slices bacon
**1 pound chicken livers, cut into
    quarters**
**1 can (8 ounces) sliced water
    chestnuts, drained**
⅓ cup soy sauce
**2 tablespoons packed brown
    sugar**
**1 tablespoon Dijon-style
    mustard**

Cut bacon slices in half crosswise. Wrap ½ slice bacon around piece of chicken liver and water chestnut slice. Secure with wooden pick. (Reserve any remaining water chestnut slices for another use.) Arrange on broiler pan. Combine soy sauce, brown sugar and mustard in small bowl. Brush over bacon rolls. Broil, 6 inches from heat, 15 to 20 minutes or until bacon is crisp and chicken livers are done, turning and brushing with soy sauce mixture occasionally.
Makes about 32 appetizers.

Favorite recipe from **National Pork Producers Council**

Marinated Antipasto

Chicken Wings with Honey & Orange Sauce

**12 chicken wings (about
  2 pounds)**
**1 envelope LIPTON® Golden
  Onion Recipe Soup Mix**
⅓ cup honey
¼ cup water
**¼ cup frozen concentrated
  orange juice, partially
  thawed and undiluted**
¼ cup sherry
1 tablespoon prepared mustard
2 teaspoons soy sauce
¼ teaspoon ground ginger
3 dashes hot pepper sauce

Preheat oven to 350°.

Cut tips off chicken wings (save tips for soup). Halve remaining chicken wings at joint.

In 13×9-inch baking dish, blend remaining ingredients; add chicken and turn to coat. Bake uncovered, basting occasionally, 40 minutes or until chicken is done and sauce is thickened.
Makes 24 appetizers.

Microwave Directions: In 13×9-inch baking dish, prepare chicken wings and sauce as above. Heat uncovered at HIGH (Full Power), basting and rearranging chicken occasionally, 20 minutes or until chicken is done and sauce is thickened. Let stand uncovered 5 minutes.

Chicken Wings with Honey & Orange Sauce

Miniature Teriyaki Pork Kabobs

**1 pound boneless pork, cut into
  4×1×½-inch strips**
**1 can (11 ounces) mandarin
  oranges**
**1 small green bell pepper, cut
  into 1×¼×¼-inch strips**
¼ cup teriyaki sauce
1 tablespoon honey
1 tablespoon vinegar
⅛ teaspoon garlic powder

Soak 24 (8-inch) bamboo skewers in water 10 minutes. Thread pork strips accordion-style with mandarin oranges on skewers. Place 1 pepper strip on end of each skewer. Arrange on broiler pan.

For sauce, combine teriyaki sauce, honey, vinegar and garlic powder in small bowl; mix well. Brush sauce over kabobs. Broil, 6 inches from heat, about 15 minutes or until pork is done, turning and basting with sauce occasionally.
Makes about 24 appetizers.

Favorite recipe from **National Pork Producers Council**

Thai Chicken Strips

**½ cup WISH-BONE® Italian
  Dressing**
¼ cup dry white wine
1 tablespoon sugar
1 tablespoon soy sauce
**1 tablespoon finely chopped
  coriander (cilantro) or
  parsley**
½ teaspoon ground ginger
½ teaspoon ground cumin
¼ teaspoon paprika
**¼ cup sesame seeds, well
  toasted**
**1½ pounds boneless chicken
  breasts, cut into lengthwise
  strips**

In food processor or blender, process Italian dressing, wine, sugar, soy sauce, coriander, ginger, cumin and paprika until blended. In large shallow baking dish, combine dressing mixture, sesame seeds and chicken. Cover and marinate in refrigerator, stirring occasionally, at least 3 hours.

Remove chicken and marinade to large shallow baking pan or aluminum foil-lined broiler rack. Broil chicken with marinade, turning occasionally, 10 minutes or until done. Garnish as desired.
Makes about 20 appetizers.

Note: Also terrific with Wish-Bone® Robusto Italian, Classic Dijon Vinaigrette, Herbal Italian, Lite Italian, Blended Italian or Lite Classic Dijon Vinaigrette Dressing.

Filled New Potatoes

**2 pounds (18) small new
  potatoes**
**1 8-ounce container Soft
  PHILADELPHIA BRAND
  Cream Cheese**
Caviar
Chopped chives

Cook potatoes in boiling salted water 15 to 20 minutes or until tender; drain. Cut thin slice from bottom to form base; scoop out top with melon ball cutter. Fill with cream cheese; top with caviar or chives. Serve warm.
1½ dozen.

Golden Mini Quiches

- 1 envelope LIPTON® Golden Onion Recipe Soup Mix
- 1½ cups light cream or half and half
- 3 eggs, beaten
  Pastry for double-crust pie*
- 1 cup shredded Swiss cheese (about 4 ounces)

Preheat oven to 400°.

In medium bowl, thoroughly blend golden onion recipe soup mix, cream and eggs; set aside.

On lightly floured board, roll pastry ⅛ inch thick; cut into 36 (2½-inch) circles. Press into 7½×9¾-inch muffin pans. Evenly fill prepared pans with cheese, then egg mixture. Bake 25 minutes or until knife inserted in center comes out clean and pastry is golden. Serve warm.
Makes 3 dozen mini quiches.

Variation: For one 9-inch quiche, bake one 9-inch unbaked pastry shell at 375°, 10 minutes. Fill pastry shell with cheese, then egg mixture. Bake 40 minutes or until quiche tests done and pastry is golden.
Makes about 7 servings.

Freezing/Reheating Directions: Mini quiches can be baked, then frozen. Simply wrap in heavy-duty aluminum foil; freeze. To reheat, unwrap and bake at 350°, 15 minutes or until heated through. **OR,** place 12 quiches on plate and microwave at HIGH (Full Power) 4 minutes or until heated through, turning plate once.

Deviled Stuffed Eggs

- 12 hard-cooked eggs
- ⅓ cup finely chopped VLASIC® Country Classic Sweet Gherkins
- ⅓ cup MARIE'S® Refrigerated Buttermilk Spice Ranch Style Salad Dressing
- 2 tablespoons finely chopped onion
- ¼ teaspoon salt
  Finely chopped VLASIC® Country Classic Sweet Gherkins for garnish

1. Remove egg shells. Cut eggs in half lengthwise. Remove and chop egg yolks. Dice 1 egg white.
2. To make filling: In medium bowl, combine yolks, diced egg white, ⅓ cup gherkins, salad dressing, onion and salt.

3. Spoon about 1 tablespoon filling into each remaining egg white half. Cover; refrigerate until serving time, at least 4 hours.
4. To serve: Top each filled half with chopped gherkins.
Makes 22 appetizers.

Grilled Cheese

- 1 piece raclette cheese* (12 to 16 ounces)
- 1 tablespoon olive or vegetable oil
- ½ teaspoon ground oregano
  Sliced crusty French bread or large crackers

Place cheese in 10-inch iron skillet; brush with oil. Sprinkle oregano on top. Place bread slices around cheese in skillet.

Grill cheese, on covered grill, over medium-hot **KINGSFORD® Charcoal Briquets** 10 minutes or until cheese is very soft. Remove to table; spread cheese on bread slices.
Makes 6 servings.

*Raclette cheese is available at specialty cheese shops. You can try another soft cheese, such as Swiss, but cooking time may vary.

Crispy Fried Mushrooms

- ½ cup all-purpose flour
- ½ teaspoon salt
- ¼ teaspoon dry mustard
- ¼ teaspoon paprika
  Dash pepper
- ½ cup buttermilk
- 8 ounces whole fresh mushrooms
  CRISCO® Oil for frying

Mix flour, salt, mustard, paprika and pepper in large plastic food storage bag. Set aside. Place buttermilk in small bowl. Dip a few mushrooms at a time in buttermilk. Place in bag with flour mixture. Shake to coat.

Heat 2 to 3 inches Crisco® Oil in deep-fryer or heavy saucepan to 375°F. Fry a few mushrooms at a time, 2 to 3 minutes, or until deep golden brown, turning over several times. Drain on paper towels. Serve hot with *catsup*, if desired.
4 to 6 servings.

Crispy Fried Mushrooms

Spring Rolls

- ½ **pound ground pork**
- 1 **teaspoon KIKKOMAN Soy Sauce**
- 1 **teaspoon dry sherry**
- ½ **teaspoon garlic salt**
- 2 **tablespoons vegetable oil**
- 3 **cups fresh bean sprouts**
- ½ **cup sliced onion**
- 1 **tablespoon KIKKOMAN Soy Sauce**
- 1 **tablespoon cornstarch**
- ¾ **cup water, divided**
- 8 **sheets egg roll skins**
- ½ **cup prepared biscuit mix**
- 1 **egg, beaten**
  Vegetable oil for frying
  Hot mustard, tomato catsup and KIKKOMAN Soy Sauce

Combine pork, 1 teaspoon soy sauce, sherry and garlic salt; mix well. Let stand 15 minutes. Heat 2 tablespoons oil in hot wok or large skillet over medium-high heat; brown pork mixture in hot oil. Add bean sprouts, onion and 1 tablespoon soy sauce. Stir-fry until vegetables are tender-crisp; drain and cool. Dissolve cornstarch in ¼ cup water. Place about ⅓ cupful pork mixture on lower half of egg roll skin. Moisten left and right edges with cornstarch mixture. Fold bottom edge up to just cover filling. Fold left and right edges ½ inch over; roll up jelly-roll fashion. Moisten top edge with cornstarch mixture and seal. Complete all rolls. Combine biscuit mix, egg and remaining ½ cup water in small bowl; dip each roll in batter. Heat oil for frying in wok or large saucepan over medium-high heat to 370°F. Deep fry rolls, a few at a time, in hot oil 5 to 7 minutes, or until golden brown, turning often. Drain on paper towels. Slice each roll into 4 pieces. Serve with mustard, catsup and soy sauce as desired.
Makes 8 appetizer servings.

Grilled Oysters

- 12 to 16 **fresh oysters in shells**
- ½ **cup butter or margarine**
- 2 **tablespoons lemon juice**
- 2 **tablespoons chopped parsley**

Thoroughly scrub oysters. Arrange oysters on grill grid; do not open shells. Grill oysters, on uncovered grill, over medium-hot **KINGS-FORD® Charcoal Briquets** 12 to 15

"Philly" Stuffed Mushrooms

minutes or until shells steam open. (Discard any oysters that do not open.)

Meanwhile, in saucepan, combine butter, lemon juice and parsley. Heat butter mixture on edge of grill until butter is melted, stirring frequently.

Carefully remove cooked oysters from grill and serve hot with lemon-butter mixture spooned over.
Makes 4 appetizer servings.

Cantonese Meatballs

- 1 **can (20 oz.) pineapple chunks in syrup**
- 3 **tablespoons brown sugar, packed**
- 5 **tablespoons KIKKOMAN Teriyaki Sauce, divided**
- 1 **tablespoon vinegar**
- 1 **tablespoon tomato catsup**
- 1 **pound lean ground beef**
- 2 **tablespoons instant minced onion**
- 2 **tablespoons cornstarch**
- ¼ **cup water**

Drain pineapple; reserve syrup. Combine syrup, brown sugar, 3 tablespoons teriyaki sauce, vinegar and catsup; set aside. Mix beef with remaining 2 tablespoons teriyaki sauce and onion; shape into 20 meatballs. Brown meatballs in large skillet;

drain off excess fat. Pour syrup mixture over meatballs; simmer 10 minutes, stirring occasionally. Dissolve cornstarch in water; stir into skillet with pineapple. Cook and stir until sauce thickens and pineapple is heated through.
Makes 6 to 8 appetizer servings.

"Philly" Stuffed Mushrooms

- 2 **pounds medium mushrooms**
- 6 **tablespoons PARKAY Margarine**
- 1 **8-ounce package PHILADELPHIA BRAND Cream Cheese, softened**
- ½ **cup (2 ounces) crumbled KRAFT Natural Blue Cheese**
- 2 **tablespoons chopped onion**

Remove mushroom stems; chop enough stems to measure ½ cup. Cook half of mushroom caps in 3 tablespoons margarine over medium heat 5 minutes; drain. Repeat with remaining mushroom caps and margarine. Combine cream cheese and blue cheese, mixing until well blended. Stir in chopped stems and onions; fill mushroom caps. Place on cookie sheet; broil until golden brown.
Approximately 2½ dozen.

Cajun-Style Chicken Nuggets

- 1 envelope LIPTON® Onion or Onion-Mushroom Recipe Soup Mix
- ½ cup plain dry bread crumbs
- 1½ teaspoons chili powder
- 1 teaspoon ground cumin
- 1 teaspoon thyme leaves
- ¼ teaspoon red pepper
- 2 pounds boneless chicken breasts, cut into 1-inch pieces
  Oil

In large bowl, combine onion recipe soup mix, bread crumbs, chili powder, cumin, thyme and pepper. Dip chicken in bread crumb mixture, coating well.

In large skillet, heat ½ inch oil and cook chicken over medium heat, turning once, until done; drain on paper towels. Serve warm and, if desired, with assorted mustards.

Makes about 5 dozen nuggets.

Microwave Directions: Prepare chicken as above. In 13×9-inch baking dish, arrange chicken, then drizzle with 2 to 3 tablespoons oil. Heat uncovered at HIGH (Full Power) 6 minutes or until chicken is done, rearranging chicken once; drain on paper towels. Serve as above.

Curried Chicken Puffs

Curried Chicken Puffs

- ½ cup water
- ⅓ cup PARKAY Margarine
- ⅔ cup flour
  Dash of salt
- 2 eggs
- 1 8-ounce package PHILADELPHIA BRAND Cream Cheese, softened
- ¼ cup milk
- ¼ teaspoon salt
  Dash of curry powder
  Dash of pepper
- 1½ cups chopped cooked chicken
- ⅓ cup slivered almonds, toasted
- 2 tablespoons green onion slices

Bring water and margarine to boil. Add flour and salt; stir vigorously over low heat until mixture forms ball. Remove from heat; add eggs, one at a time, beating until smooth after each addition. Place level measuring tablespoonfuls of batter on ungreased cookie sheet. Bake at 400°, 25 minutes. Cool.

Combine cream cheese, milk, salt, curry powder and pepper, mixing until well blended. Add chicken, almonds and onions; mix lightly. Cut tops from cream puffs; fill with chicken mixture. Replace tops. Place puffs on cookie sheet. Bake at 375°, 5 minutes or until warm.

Approximately 1½ dozen.

Note: Unfilled cream puffs can be prepared several weeks in advance and frozen. Place puffs on a jelly roll pan and wrap securely in plastic wrap.

Empress Chicken Wings

- 1½ pounds chicken wings (about 8 wings)
- 3 tablespoons KIKKOMAN Soy Sauce
- 1 tablespoon dry sherry
- 1 tablespoon minced fresh ginger root
- 1 clove garlic, minced
- 2 tablespoons vegetable oil
- ¼ to ⅓ cup cornstarch
- ⅔ cup water
- 2 green onions and tops, cut diagonally into thin slices
- 1 teaspoon slivered fresh ginger root

Disjoint chicken wings; discard tips (or save for stock). Combine soy sauce, sherry, minced ginger and garlic in large bowl; stir in chicken. Cover and refrigerate 1 hour, stirring occasionally. Remove chicken; reserve marinade. Heat oil in large skillet over medium heat. Lightly coat chicken pieces with cornstarch; add to skillet and brown slowly on all sides. Remove chicken; drain off fat. Stir water and reserved marinade into same skillet. Add chicken; sprinkle green onions and slivered ginger evenly over chicken. Cover and simmer 5 minutes, or until chicken is tender.

Makes 4 to 6 appetizer servings.

Mini Cocktail Meatballs

- 1 envelope LIPTON® Onion, Onion-Mushroom, Beefy Mushroom or Beefy Onion Recipe Soup Mix
- 1 pound ground beef
- ½ cup plain dry bread crumbs
- ¼ cup dry red wine or water
- 2 eggs, slightly beaten

Preheat oven to 375°.

In medium bowl, combine all ingredients; shape into 1-inch meatballs.

In shallow baking pan, arrange meatballs and bake 18 minutes or until done. Serve, if desired, with assorted mustards or tomato sauce.

Makes about 4 dozen meatballs.

Flaky Ham Puffs

1 recipe Mustard Sauce (see Index)
Pastry:
1²/₃ cups all-purpose flour
¹/₃ cup yellow cornmeal
¹/₄ cup grated Parmesan cheese
¹/₄ teaspoon salt
¹/₂ cup CRISCO® Oil
3 tablespoons ice water
Filling:
³/₄ cup ground fully cooked ham (about 4 ounces)
¹/₄ cup dairy sour cream
¹/₂ teaspoon prepared mustard
¹/₈ teaspoon onion powder
¹/₈ teaspoon pepper

Prepare Mustard Sauce as directed. Cover and refrigerate.

For pastry, combine flour, cornmeal, Parmesan cheese and salt in medium mixing bowl. Add Crisco® Oil. Stir with fork until moistened. Add water. Mix well. Divide dough in half. Form each half into a ball. Place 1 ball between 2 large sheets waxed paper. Roll dough ¹/₈ inch thick. Remove top sheet waxed paper. Cut dough into 2-inch circles. Repeat with remaining dough.

For filling, mix all ingredients in small mixing bowl. Preheat oven to 375°F.

To assemble puffs, place one pastry circle on ungreased baking sheet. Place 1 scant teaspoon filling in center of circle. Top with another pastry circle. Press edges of circles together with fork. Repeat with remaining pastry circles and filling.

Bake puffs at 375°F, 10 to 15 minutes, or until light golden brown. Remove to wire rack. Serve hot with Mustard Sauce.

About 2¹/₂ dozen appetizers.

Variation: Flaky Crab Puffs. Follow recipe above, substituting crab filling for ham filling. For crab filling, mix 1 can (6 to 6¹/₂ ounces) crab meat (rinsed and drained), 2 tablespoons grated Parmesan cheese, 1 tablespoon mayonnaise or salad dressing, 1 tablespoon minced green onion and ¹/₈ teaspoon hot pepper sauce in small mixing bowl.

Crispy Wontons

³/₄ pound ground pork
8 water chestnuts, finely chopped
¹/₄ cup finely chopped green onions and tops
1 tablespoon KIKKOMAN Soy Sauce
¹/₂ teaspoon salt
1 teaspoon cornstarch
¹/₂ teaspoon grated fresh ginger root
1 package (1 lb.) wonton skins
Vegetable oil for frying
Tomato catsup and hot mustard *or* KIKKOMAN Sweet & Sour Sauce

Combine pork, water chestnuts, green onions, soy sauce, salt, cornstarch and ginger in medium bowl; mix well. Place ¹/₂ teaspoonful pork mixture in center of each wonton skin. Fold wonton skin over filling to form a triangle. Turn top of triangle down to meet fold. Turn over; moisten 1 corner with water. Overlap opposite corner over moistened corner; press firmly. Heat oil in wok or large saucepan over medium-high heat to 375°F. Deep fry wontons, a few at a time, 2 to 3 minutes, or until brown and crispy. Drain on paper towels. Serve warm with catsup and mustard or sweet & sour sauce, as desired.

Makes 10 appetizer servings.

Salmon Canapes

1 (6¹/₂-ounce) can salmon, drained and flaked
1 tablespoon low-calorie mayonnaise
1 tablespoon REALEMON® Lemon Juice from Concentrate
¹/₈ teaspoon dill weed
24 Melba rounds
6 slices LITE-LINE® Process Cheese Product,* any flavor, quartered
24 thin slices cucumber
Parsley

In small bowl, combine salmon, mayonnaise, ReaLemon® brand and dill; mix well. On each Melba round, place a Lite-line piece, cucumber slice, 2 teaspoons salmon mixture and parsley. Serve immediately. Refrigerate leftovers.

Makes 24 appetizers; 36 calories per appetizer.

*"¹/₂ the calories"—8% milk fat version.

Calories by product analyses and recipe calculation.

Crispy Wontons

Seafood Cocktails with Watercress Sauce

sels open, stirring occasionally. Discard any mussels that do not open.
3. With slotted spoon, remove mussels from pan; remove and discard top halves of shells. Arrange mussels on serving platter; pour sauce over mussels.
Makes about 5 dozen appetizers.

Note: To make sure raw mussels are safe to eat, tap on any open shells. If the mussel closes its shell, it will be safe to eat after cooking. Discard those that remain open. After cooking, discard any mussels with closed shells, because they were not alive before cooking and are not safe to eat.

Per appetizer: 10 calories, 1 g protein, 1 g fat, 1 g carbohydrate, 34 mg sodium, 3 mg cholesterol.

Seafood Cocktails with Watercress Sauce

- **1 large bunch watercress, stems removed (about 2 cups loosely packed)***
- **1 small bunch parsley, stems removed (about 1 cup loosely packed)***
- **1 medium clove garlic, finely chopped**
- **1 envelope LIPTON® Golden Onion Recipe Soup Mix**
- **½ pint (8 ounces) sour cream**
- **¼ cup mayonnaise**
- **⅛ teaspoon pepper**
  Suggested Seafood**

In food processor or blender, combine watercress, parsley and garlic until blended. Add golden onion recipe soup mix, sour cream, mayonnaise and pepper; process until smooth. Chill at least 2 hours. Serve with Suggested Seafood. Garnish as desired.
Makes about 2 cups sauce or about 8 appetizer servings.

*Variation: Omit watercress. Use 2 small bunches parsley, stems removed (about 2 cups loosely packed).
(continued)

**Suggested Seafood: Use about 2 pounds cooked and chilled butterflied shrimp, scallops, crab claws and legs, lobster meat or clams.

Herbed Mussels in Wine

- **3 pounds mussels (about 5 to 6 dozen)**
- **2 tablespoons butter or margarine**
- **⅓ cup chopped green onions**
- **1 large clove garlic, minced**
- **¼ teaspoon dried Italian seasoning, crushed**
- **¾ cup V8® Vegetable Juice**
- **¼ cup Chablis or other dry white wine**
  Generous dash pepper

1. Discard any open mussels that do not close when tapped with fingers. Scrub mussels; clip off beards with kitchen shears.
2. In 4-quart saucepan over low heat, in hot butter, cook onions with garlic and Italian seasoning until onions are tender, stirring often. Add mussels, V8 juice, wine and pepper. Heat to boiling; reduce heat to low. Cover; simmer 6 to 8 minutes or until mus-

Beer-Batter Shrimp

- **1 cup flour**
- **1 tablespoon paprika**
- **½ teaspoon salt**
- **1 (12-ounce) can or bottle beer**
- **½ teaspoon Worcestershire sauce**
- **¼ teaspoon TABASCO® pepper sauce**
  Vegetable oil
- **2 pounds shrimp, peeled, deveined**
  Flour for dredging
  Creole Tartar Sauce (recipe follows)

In medium bowl combine 1 cup flour, paprika and salt. Whisk in beer, Worcestershire sauce and Tabasco® sauce. Cover; let stand at room temperature at least 1 hour. In large heavy saucepot or deep-fat fryer, heat about 3 inches oil over medium-high heat to 375°F. Dredge shrimp in flour, then dip in batter. Fry shrimp, a few at a time, 2 to 3 minutes or until golden. Drain on paper towels. Serve immediately with Creole Tartar Sauce.
Makes 8 servings.

Creole Tartar Sauce

- **¼ cup finely chopped green onions**
- **¼ cup finely chopped celery**
- **¼ cup finely chopped parsley**
- **3 tablespoons tomato paste**
- **2 tablespoons Dijon-style mustard**
- **2 tablespoons olive or vegetable oil**

1 tablespoon white wine vinegar
¾ teaspoon TABASCO® pepper
   sauce
½ teaspoon paprika

In small bowl combine all ingredients until well blended.
Makes about 1 cup.

Sausage Antipasto Platter

Pesto Spread (recipe follows)
1 large tomato
6 ounces thinly sliced Genoa
   salami
6 ounces thinly sliced ham
   cappicola
6 ounces thinly sliced pepperoni
1 loaf (8 ounces) French bread,
   cut into ¼-inch slices
1 pound unpared cooked new
   potatoes, cut into ¼-inch
   slices
4 ounces pea pods, trimmed,
   strings removed
1 red bell pepper, cut into strips
1 small zucchini, cut diagonally
   into ¼-inch slices
4 ounces mushrooms, sliced
½ cup dry cured olives (optional)

Prepare Pesto Spread. Cut ½-inch slice from top of tomato; zigzag edge. Scoop out pulp. Fill tomato with Pesto Spread; place in center of large serving platter. Arrange remaining ingredients around tomato. To serve, spread slices of bread or potatoes with Pesto Spread and top with sliced meat and vegetables.
Makes 8 servings.
PESTO SPREAD: Combine ¾ cup tightly packed fresh basil leaves, 2 teaspoons crushed fresh rosemary or ¾ teaspoon dried rosemary, crushed, ¼ cup tightly packed Italian parsley and 2 quartered garlic cloves in food processor. Cover and process until blended. Add ⅓ cup French bread crumbs, ¼ cup grated Parmesan cheese, 1 teaspoon lemon juice, ½ teaspoon salt, and dash pepper. With motor running, slowly pour in ⅓ cup light cream and ¼ cup olive oil through feed tube. Process until blended. Pour into small bowl. Refrigerate, covered, 1½ to 2 hours to blend flavors.
Makes about 1 cup.

*Favorite recipe from **National Live Stock and Meat Board***

Sausage Antipasto Platter

Party Quiche Squares

1 (11-ounce) package pie crust
   mix
1 (10-ounce) package frozen
   chopped broccoli, thawed
   and well drained
1½ cups shredded Swiss cheese
   (6 ounces)
2 tablespoons all-purpose flour
1 cup COLLEGE INN® Chicken
   Broth
¾ cup heavy cream
5 eggs
2 tablespoons GREY POUPON®
   Dijon Mustard

Prepare pie crust mix according to package directions; roll out on floured surface to 16×11-inch rectangle. Arrange on bottom of ungreased 15½×10½×1-inch baking pan, trimming to fit.

Combine broccoli, cheese and flour; arrange evenly over pastry. Blend chicken broth, cream, eggs and mustard; pour evenly over broccoli mixture. Bake at 350°F for 35 to 40 minutes or until knife inserted in center comes out clean. Cool slightly. To serve, cut into squares. Garnish as desired.
Makes 60 appetizers.

Spiced Apple Party Mix

**½ teaspoon ground cinnamon
¼ teaspoon ground nutmeg
1 cup SUN-MAID® Raisins
¾ cup coarsely chopped dried
    apples
1 cup DIAMOND® Walnut pieces**

In medium bowl, combine cinnamon and nutmeg. Add raisins and apples; toss to coat with spices. Add walnuts; toss. Store in airtight container. *Makes 2½ cups.*

Curried Popcorn Mix

**6 cups unseasoned popped corn
2 cups pretzel sticks
1½ cups DIAMOND® Walnut pieces
¼ cup butter or margarine,
    melted
2 teaspoons curry powder
¼ teaspoon hot pepper sauce
    Salt to taste
1½ cups SUN-MAID® Golden
    Raisins**

In large, deep baking or roasting pan, combine popped corn, pretzels and walnuts. In small bowl, mix butter, curry powder and pepper sauce; drizzle over popcorn mixture and toss to coat evenly. Bake in 300°F oven about 30 minutes, tossing twice. Remove from oven. Mix in salt. Cool completely. Store in airtight container. Mix in raisins before serving. *Makes about 2 quarts.*

Sesame Cheese Crackers

**1 cup all-purpose flour
½ teaspoon salt
⅛ teaspoon ground red pepper
    (cayenne)
6 tablespoons cold butter or
    margarine
1 cup (4 oz.) finely grated
    Cheddar cheese
¼ cup sesame seed, toasted
½ teaspoon KIKKOMAN Soy
    Sauce
4½ to 7½ teaspoons ice-cold
    water**

Combine flour, salt and pepper in medium bowl; cut in butter until mixture resembles coarse crumbs. Stir in cheese and sesame seed. Combine soy sauce and 3 teaspoons water; stir into dry ingredients. Add more water, a little at a time, mixing lightly until dough begins to stick together. Turn out dough and press together on lightly floured board or pastry cloth; roll out to ⅛-inch thickness. Cut dough into 2×1-inch rectangles with pastry wheel or knife. Place on lightly greased baking sheets and bake at 400°F. 8 to 10 minutes, or until lightly browned. Remove crackers to rack to cool. *Makes 8 appetizer servings.*

Onion Party Puffs

**⅓ cup LIPTON® Onion Butter
    (recipe follows)
1 package (8 ounces)
    refrigerator biscuits**

Prepare Lipton® Onion Butter. Cut each biscuit into 4 sections. Arrange on ungreased baking sheet; dot with onion butter. Bake in preheated 400°F oven 8 minutes or until golden. *Makes 40 puffs.*
LIPTON® ONION BUTTER: Thoroughly blend 1 envelope **LIPTON® Onion Soup Mix** with ½ pound butter or margarine in medium bowl. Refrigerate, covered, any unused portion. Use on baked potatoes and cooked vegetables. *Makes 1¼ cups.*

Toasty Onion Sticks

**⅓ cup LIPTON® Onion Butter
    (see recipe above)
12 slices white bread**

Prepare Lipton® Onion Butter. Trim crust from bread. Spread onion butter on bread; cut each slice into 5 strips. Arrange strips on ungreased baking sheet. Bake in preheated 375°F oven 10 minutes or until golden. *Makes 5 dozen appetizers.*

Crispy Bagel Chips

**1 envelope LIPTON® Golden
    Onion Recipe Soup Mix
½ cup butter or margarine,
    melted
1 teaspoon basil leaves
½ teaspoon oregano
¼ teaspoon garlic powder
4 to 5 plain bagels, cut into
    ⅛-inch slices**

Preheat oven to 250°.
  In small bowl, thoroughly blend all ingredients except bagels; generously brush on both sides of bagel slices. On two ungreased baking sheets, arrange bagel slices and bake 50 minutes or until crisp and golden. Store in airtight container up to 1 week. *Makes about 28 chips.*

Curried Popcorn Mix (left), Spiced Apple Party Mix (right)

Peppered Pecans

3 tablespoons butter or margarine
3 cloves garlic, minced
1½ teaspoons TABASCO® pepper sauce
½ teaspoon salt
3 cups pecan halves

Preheat oven to 250°F. In small skillet melt butter. Add garlic, Tabasco® sauce and salt; cook 1 minute. Toss pecans with butter mixture; spread in single layer on baking sheet. Bake 1 hour or until pecans are crisp; stir occasionally.
Makes 3 cups.

Mongolian Almonds

1 cup whole natural almonds
2 tablespoons KIKKOMAN Teriyaki Sauce
1 teaspoon brown sugar
⅛ to ¼ teaspoon TABASCO® pepper sauce
1 tablespoon water
½ teaspoon vegetable oil

Toast almonds on ungreased baking sheet in preheated 350°F oven 10 minutes without stirring. Remove pan from oven and cool almonds in pan on wire rack. *Reduce oven temperature to 250°F.* Combine teriyaki sauce, brown sugar, pepper sauce and water in narrow 1-quart saucepan. Bring to boil over medium-low heat. Stir in almonds and boil about 5 minutes, or until sauce is absorbed by almonds, stirring frequently. Add oil and toss almonds until coated; turn out onto baking sheet, separating almonds. Bake 5 minutes; stir and turn almonds over. Bake 5 minutes longer. Remove almonds from pan to large plate; cool in single layer. Store in loose-fitting container or plastic bag.
Makes 1 cup.

Onion-Buttered Popcorn

In large bowl, combine **1 pouch CAMPBELL'S® Onion Soup and Recipe Mix** with **½ cup melted butter or margarine.** Toss with **4 quarts hot popped popcorn** to coat well. Serve immediately.
Makes 4 quarts.

Party Scramble

Party Scramble

½ cup butter or margarine, cut up
1 pouch CAMPBELL'S® Onion Soup and Recipe Mix
1 cup bite-size wheat cereal squares
1 cup bite-size corn cereal squares
1 bag (6 ounces) PEPPERIDGE FARM® Cheddar Cheese Goldfish® Crackers
1 bag (5½ ounces) PEPPERIDGE FARM® Pretzel Goldfish® Crackers
2 cups unsalted peanuts

To Microwave:
1. Place butter in 2-cup glass measure. Cover with waxed paper; microwave on HIGH 45 seconds or until melted. Stir in soup mix.
2. In 4-quart microwave-safe bowl, combine remaining ingredients. Pour butter mixture over cracker mixture; toss to coat well. Microwave, uncovered, on HIGH 5 minutes or until hot, stirring twice during heating.
3. Cool. Store mixture in airtight container.
Makes about 10 cups.

Hell-Fire Crispy Balls

1 cup flour
2 teaspoons baking powder
¼ teaspoon salt
1 egg
⅓ cup tomato juice, heated
1 small onion, finely chopped
1 teaspoon TABASCO® pepper sauce
Vegetable oil

In medium bowl combine flour, baking powder and salt. Stir in egg, tomato juice, onion and Tabasco® sauce. In large skillet over medium-high heat bring 1 inch oil to 350°F. Drop batter by teaspoonfuls into oil; fry, a few at a time, 5 to 7 minutes or until golden brown on all sides. Drain on paper towels. Serve immediately.
Makes 2 dozen balls.

BEVERAGES

A plentiful collection of drinks for all occasions. You'll find favorite standbys and new ideas for festive punches and party drinks, midday pick-me-ups, cool refreshers to soothe a summer thirst, and bracing hot mugs for a winter evening.

Banana Shake

2 ripe bananas, cut up (about 2 cups)
⅓ cup REALEMON® Lemon Juice from Concentrate
1 cup cold water
1 (14-ounce) can EAGLE® Brand Sweetened Condensed Milk (NOT evaporated milk)
2 cups ice cubes

In blender container, combine all ingredients except ice; blend well. Gradually add ice, blending until smooth. Garnish as desired. Refrigerate leftovers. (Mixture stays thick and creamy in refrigerator.)
Makes about 5 cups.
  Mixer Method: Omit ice cubes. In large mixer bowl, mash bananas; gradually beat in ReaLemon® brand, sweetened condensed milk and 2½ cups cold water. Chill before serving.
  Strawberry-Banana Shake: Reduce bananas to ½ cup; add 1½ cups fresh strawberries *or* 1 cup frozen unsweetened strawberries, partially thawed.
  Banana-Orange Shake: Reduce bananas to 1 cup; use 1 cup orange juice instead of water.

Beefy Mary

2 (10-ounce) cans tomato and chile cocktail
1 (13¾-fluid ounce) can COLLEGE INN® Beef Broth
¼ cup lemon juice
Ice
Celery or cucumber sticks

Combine tomato and chile cocktail, beef broth and lemon juice. Serve over ice; garnish with celery or cucumber sticks.
Makes 6 servings.

Hot Tomato Sipper

1 tablespoon WYLER's® or STEERO® Beef-Flavor Instant Bouillon *or* 3 Beef-Flavor Bouillon Cubes
1 (46-ounce) can tomato juice
2 teaspoons prepared horseradish
4 drops hot pepper sauce

In large saucepan, combine all ingredients; over low heat, simmer 10 minutes or until bouillon dissolves. Serve hot.
Makes about 1½ quarts.
Microwave: In 2-quart glass measure, combine ingredients. Microwave on full power (high) 12 to 14 minutes or until hot and bouillon dissolves, stirring after 6 minutes.

Toro

½ cup Spicy Hot V8® Vegetable Juice *or* No Salt Added V8® Vegetable Juice
½ cup prepared CAMPBELL'S® Condensed Consommé
½ cup ice cubes
Green onion brushes for garnish (see Note below)

1. In covered blender or food processor, blend all ingredients except green onion brushes until smooth.
2. To serve: Pour into chilled 8-ounce glasses. Garnish with green onion brushes.
Makes 1½ cups or 2 servings.
  Note: To make green onion brushes, slice off the roots and tops of green onions. Leaving at least 3 inches in the center, make lengthwise cuts from center to one or both ends to make a fringe. Place the green onions in ice water for a few hours. The ends will curl to look like brushes.

Per serving: 25 calories, 2 g protein, 0 g fat, 4 g carbohydrate, 592 mg sodium (No Salt Added V8® Juice: 400 mg sodium), 0 mg cholesterol.

Clockwise from top: Rosé Wine Cooler (page 40), Banana-Orange Shake, Bourbon Slush (page 38), Hot Tomato Sipper, Melon Citrus Cooler (page 39)

Pineapple Passion

2 cups DOLE® Pineapple Juice
8 pineapple juice cubes

Combine pineapple juice and juice cubes in blender; blend until slushy. Garnish as desired.
Makes 2 servings.
PINEAPPLE JUICE CUBES: Pour unsweetened, canned pineapple juice into your ice cube trays. Freeze and use just like regular ice cubes. Juice cubes add an intriguing tart-sweet flavor to iced tea, mineral water, lemonade, wine coolers (especially sangria), fruit juices and punch.

Pineapple Mint Tulip

1 cup DOLE® Pineapple Juice
2 tablespoons powdered sugar
1 tablespoon grenadine syrup
1 sprig fresh mint
Ice cubes or pineapple juice cubes (see recipe above)

In 1-quart measure, combine pineapple juice, sugar and grenadine; stir well. Rub mint sprig around inside of tall glass. Partially fill glass with ice cubes; pour in juice mixture.
Makes 1 serving.

Checkmate

3 cups DOLE® Pineapple Juice
1½ cups carrot pieces
1½ teaspoons minced fresh ginger root
6 pineapple juice cubes (see recipe above) or ice cubes
1 tablespoon frozen orange juice concentrate

Puree pineapple juice, carrots and ginger in blender. Strain through a sieve. Pour strained juice back into blender; add juice cubes and juice concentrate. Blend until smooth.
Makes 4 servings.

Left to right: Checkmate, Pineapple Passion, Pineapple Mint Tulip

Island Fruit Cooler

¾ cup DOLE® Pineapple Juice
½ cup guava, papaya or mango juice
¼ cup lemon-lime soda
Ice cubes
Fresh fruit for garnish

In pitcher, combine pineapple and guava juices and soda. Pour over ice cubes in glass. Garnish with fresh fruit.
Makes 2 servings.

Lemon Tea Sparkler

2 cups brewed tea
½ cup REALEMON® Lemon Juice from Concentrate
½ cup sugar
1 (32-ounce) bottle ginger ale, chilled
Ice

In pitcher, combine tea, ReaLemon® brand and sugar; stir until sugar dissolves. Just before serving, add ginger ale. Serve over ice.
Makes about 7 cups.

Low Calorie Lemonade

3¼ cups cold water
½ cup REALEMON® Lemon Juice
    from Concentrate
4 to 8 envelopes sugar
    substitute or 1½ teaspoons
    liquid sugar substitute

Combine ingredients; mix well. Serve over ice. Garnish as desired.
Makes about 1 quart.
    To make 1 serving: Combine ¾ cup cold water, 2 tablespoons ReaLemon® brand and 1 to 2 envelopes sugar substitute or ½ teaspoon liquid sugar substitute.

Lemonade Syrup Base

2 cups sugar
½ cup water
2 cups REALEMON® Lemon
    Juice from Concentrate

In medium saucepan, combine sugar and water. Over low heat, cook until sugar dissolves, stirring occasionally; add ReaLemon® brand. Cool. Store covered in refrigerator.
Makes about 3⅔ cups.
    For 1 (8-ounce) serving: Pour ⅓ cup lemonade syrup into glass; add ⅔ cup cold water. Stir; add ice.
    For 1 quart: In pitcher, combine 1⅓ cups lemonade syrup and 2⅔ cups cold water; stir. Add ice.

Zesty V8

3 cups V8® Vegetable Juice *or*
    No Salt Added V8®
    Vegetable Juice, chilled
½ teaspoon prepared
    horseradish
½ teaspoon Worcestershire
    sauce

In small pitcher, combine all ingredients. To serve: Pour into chilled 8-ounce glasses.
Makes 3 cups or 4 servings.

Per serving: 36 calories, 1 g protein, 0 g fat, 9 g carbohydrate, 628 mg sodium (No Salt Added V8® Juice: 53 mg sodium), 0 mg cholesterol.

Tonic Thyme

1½ cups V8® Vegetable Juice *or*
    No Salt Added V8®
    Vegetable Juice
1 tablespoon lime juice
⅛ teaspoon dried thyme leaves,
    crushed
¼ cup tonic water, chilled
    Fresh thyme sprigs or lime
    wedges for garnish

1. In small pitcher, stir together V8 juice, lime juice and dried thyme. Add tonic water; stir.
2. To serve: Pour over ice cubes in 10-ounce glasses. Garnish with fresh thyme.
Makes 1¾ cups or 2 servings.

Per serving: 49 calories, 0 g protein, 0 g fat, 11 g carbohydrate, 609 mg sodium (No Salt Added V8® Juice: 48 mg sodium), 0 mg cholesterol.

City Slicker

¾ cup DOLE® Pineapple Juice
    Pineapple juice cubes (see
    page 34) *or* ice cubes
    Ginger ale
    Dash ground ginger
    Cucumber slice, cherry tomato
    and lemon slice for garnish

Pour pineapple juice over juice cubes in glass. Fill with ginger ale. Add ginger and stir. Garnish with cucumber slice, cherry tomato and lemon slice.
Makes 1 serving.

Sparkling V8

3 cups V8® Vegetable Juice *or*
    No Salt Added V8®
    Vegetable Juice
2 bottles (6½ ounces each)
    sparkling mineral water,
    chilled
    Mint leaves for garnish

1. In small pitcher, mix V8 juice and sparkling mineral water.
2. To serve: Pour over ice cubes in 10-ounce glasses. Garnish with mint leaves.
Makes 4¾ cups or 6 servings.

Per serving: 24 calories, 0 g protein, 0 g fat, 6 g carbohydrate, 414 mg sodium (No Salt Added V8® Juice: 30 mg sodium), 0 mg cholesterol.

Quick Wink Breakfast Drink

1 ripe, medium DOLE™ Banana,
    frozen*
¾ cup milk
1 tablespoon wheat germ
2 teaspoons honey
¼ teaspoon ground cinnamon

Slice banana; puree with remaining ingredients in blender.
Makes 1 to 2 servings.
    *Peel banana and freeze overnight in airtight plastic bag.

Quick Banana Malt

1 ripe, medium DOLE™ Banana,
    frozen*
¾ cup milk
3 tablespoons chocolate malted
    milk powder

Slice banana; puree with remaining ingredients in blender.
Makes 1 serving.
    *Peel banana and freeze overnight in airtight plastic bag.

Quick Banana Malt

Frosty Chocolate Shake

- 1 teaspoon KNOX® Unflavored Gelatine
- ½ cup skim milk
- 2 tablespoons chocolate syrup
- 2 packets aspartame sweetener
- ¼ teaspoon vanilla extract
- 1 cup ice cubes (6 to 8)

In small saucepan, sprinkle unflavored gelatine over ¼ cup milk; let stand 1 minute. Stir over low heat until gelatine is completely dissolved, about 5 minutes.

In blender, process remaining ¼ cup milk, syrup, sweetener and vanilla until blended. While processing, through feed cap, gradually add gelatine mixture and process until blended. Add ice cubes, 1 at a time; process at high speed until ice is melted.
Makes 2 servings; 77 calories per serving.

Pineapple Orange Slush

- 3 cups DOLE® Pineapple Orange Juice, chilled
- 1 pint orange sherbet
- 1 cup crushed ice

Combine pineapple orange juice and sherbet in blender. Add ice; blend until slushy.
Makes 6 servings.

Sparkling Harvest Cider

- 2 quarts apple cider, chilled
- 1 cup REALEMON® Lemon Juice from Concentrate
- ½ cup sugar
- 1 (32-ounce) bottle ginger ale, chilled
  Apple slices or cinnamon sticks, optional
  Ice

In punch bowl, combine apple cider, ReaLemon® brand and sugar; stir until sugar dissolves. Just before serving, add ginger ale. Garnish with apple and cinnamon sticks if desired. Serve over ice.
Makes about 3 quarts.

Christmas Carol Punch

Christmas Carol Punch

- 2 medium red apples
- 2 quarts clear apple cider
- 8 cinnamon sticks
- 2 teaspoons whole cloves
- ½ cup SUN-MAID® Raisins
  Orange slices
  Lemon slices
- ¼ cup lemon juice

Core apples; slice into ½-inch rings. In Dutch oven, combine cider, cinnamon, cloves, apple rings and raisins. Bring to boil over high heat; reduce heat to low and simmer 5 to 8 minutes or until apples are just tender. Remove cloves; add orange and lemon slices and lemon juice. Pour into punch bowl. Ladle into large mugs, including an apple ring, some raisins and citrus slices in each serving. Serve with spoons.
Makes about 2 quarts.

Volcano Punch

- 3 quarts DOLE® Pineapple Juice
- 2 cans (6 ounces each) frozen limeade concentrate
- 2 quarts ginger ale
- 2 pints orange or lemon sherbet
  Fresh fruit for garnish

In punch bowl, combine pineapple juice and limeade concentrate. Just before serving, stir in ginger ale and add scoops of sherbet. Garnish with fresh fruit.
Makes about 6 quarts.

Fruit Punch

- 5½ cups DOLE® Pineapple Juice, chilled
- 1 quart apple juice, chilled
- 1 package (10 ounces) frozen strawberries, thawed
- 1 quart ginger ale, chilled
  Fresh strawberry slices, lime slices and fresh mint for garnish

In punch bowl, combine pineapple and apple juices. Puree undrained strawberries in blender; stir pureed strawberries into pineapple juice mixture. Pour in ginger ale. Garnish with strawberry slices, lime slices and fresh mint.
Makes 3 quarts.

Orange Tea Punch

- 4 cups brewed tea
- 2 cups orange juice, chilled
- 1 cup REALEMON® Lemon Juice from Concentrate
- 1 cup sugar
- 1 quart orange sherbet
- 1 (32-ounce) bottle ginger ale, chilled

In pitcher, combine tea, orange juice, ReaLemon® brand and sugar; stir until sugar dissolves. Chill. Just before serving, pour tea mixture into large punch bowl; add scoops of sherbet and ginger ale.
Makes about 4 quarts.

Tropical Cream Punch

1 (14-ounce) can EAGLE® Brand Sweetened Condensed Milk (NOT evaporated milk)
1 (6-ounce) can frozen orange juice concentrate, thawed
1 (6-ounce) can frozen pineapple juice concentrate, thawed
2 (32-ounce) bottles club soda, chilled
Orange slices

In punch bowl, combine sweetened condensed milk and juice concentrates; mix well. Gradually add club soda; stir. Garnish with orange slices. Serve over ice.
Makes about 3 quarts.

Tip: Omit orange juice concentrate and pineapple juice concentrate. Add 1 (12-ounce) can frozen pineapple orange juice drink concentrate, thawed. Proceed as above.

Microwave Hot Cocoa

5 tablespoons sugar
3 tablespoons HERSHEY'S Cocoa
Dash salt
3 tablespoons hot water
2 cups milk
¼ teaspoon vanilla

Combine sugar, cocoa, salt and hot water in 1-quart micro-proof measuring cup. Microwave at HIGH (100%) for 1 to 1½ minutes or until boiling. Add milk; stir and microwave an additional 1½ to 2 minutes or until hot. Stir in vanilla; blend well.
4 servings.

One serving: Place 2 heaping teaspoons sugar, 1 heaping teaspoon HERSHEY'S Cocoa and dash salt in micro-proof cup. Add 2 teaspoons cold milk; stir until smooth. Fill cup with milk; microwave at HIGH (100%) for 1 to 1½ minutes or until hot. Stir to blend.

Hot Cocoa Mix

1 cup CREMORA® Non-Dairy Creamer*
1 cup nonfat dry milk
¾ to 1 cup sugar
½ cup unsweetened cocoa

In medium bowl, combine ingredients; mix well. Store in airtight container. To serve, spoon 3 heaping tablespoons mix into mug; add ¾ cup boiling water. Stir.
Makes about 3 cups.

Mocha: Add ¼ cup instant coffee.
Mexican: Add 1 teaspoon ground cinnamon.
Low-calorie: Omit sugar. Add 15 envelopes low-calorie sweetener with NUTRASWEET® *or* 2 teaspoons (5 envelopes) low-calorie granulated sugar substitute. To serve, spoon 2 heaping tablespoons into mug; add ¾ cup boiling water. Stir.

*Cremora® non-dairy creamer is a coffee whitener and should not be used as a milk replacement.

Creamy Hot Chocolate

1 (14-ounce) can EAGLE® Brand Sweetened Condensed Milk (NOT evaporated milk)
½ cup unsweetened cocoa
1½ teaspoons vanilla extract
⅛ teaspoon salt
6½ cups hot water
CAMPFIRE® Marshmallows, optional

In large saucepan, combine sweetened condensed milk, cocoa, vanilla and salt; mix well. Over medium heat, slowly stir in water; heat through, stirring occasionally. Top with marshmallows if desired.
Makes about 2 quarts.

Tip: Chocolate can be stored in refrigerator up to 5 days. Mix well and reheat before serving.

Microwave: In 2-quart glass measure, combine all ingredients except marshmallows. Microwave on full power (high) 8 to 10 minutes, stirring every 3 minutes. Top with marshmallows if desired.

Spicy Warmer

2 cups V8® Vegetable Juice
1 teaspoon Worcestershire sauce
½ teaspoon prepared horseradish
¼ teaspoon hot pepper sauce

To Microwave: In 4-cup glass measure, stir together all ingredients. Cover with vented plastic wrap; mi-

crowave on HIGH 3 minutes or until boiling.
Makes about 2 cups or 3 servings.

Bullshot

1 cup V8® Vegetable Juice
1 cup SWANSON® Clear Ready to Serve Beef Broth
2 teaspoons lemon juice
¼ teaspoon prepared horseradish

To Microwave: In 4-cup glass measure, stir together all ingredients. Cover with vented plastic wrap; microwave on HIGH 3 minutes or until boiling.
Makes about 2 cups or 2 servings.

Hot Mulled Pineapple Juice

5½ cups DOLE® Pineapple Juice
1 apple, cored and cubed
½ cup DOLE™ Raisins
½ cup brown sugar, packed
2 cinnamon sticks, broken
1 tablespoon grated orange peel
½ teaspoon whole cloves
Quartered orange slices for garnish

In saucepan, combine all ingredients; simmer 15 minutes. Strain before serving. Garnish with quartered orange slices.
Makes 6 servings.

Hot Mulled Pineapple Juice

Spiced Tea

6 cups water
1 cup firmly packed light brown sugar
6 cinnamon sticks
8 whole cloves
8 tea bags
1 cup orange juice
½ cup REALEMON® Lemon Juice from Concentrate

In large saucepan, combine water, sugar, cinnamon and cloves; bring to a boil. Reduce heat; simmer uncovered 10 minutes. Remove spices. Pour over tea bags; steep 5 minutes. Remove tea bags; add fruit juices. Serve hot or cold.
Makes about 1½ quarts.

Hot Spiced Lemonade

3 cups water
⅔ cup firmly packed light brown sugar
½ cup REALEMON® Lemon Juice from Concentrate
8 whole cloves
2 cinnamon sticks
Additional cinnamon sticks for garnish, optional

In medium saucepan, combine all ingredients except garnish. Simmer uncovered 20 minutes to blend flavors; remove spices. Serve hot in mugs with cinnamon sticks if desired.
Makes about 4 cups.
Microwave: In 1-quart glass measure, combine ingredients as above. Microwave on full power (high) 4 to 5 minutes or until heated through. Serve as above.

Hot Cranberry Cider

1 quart apple cider or apple juice
1 (32-ounce) bottle cranberry juice cocktail
½ cup REALEMON® Lemon Juice from Concentrate
⅓ cup firmly packed light brown sugar
8 whole cloves
2 cinnamon sticks

In large saucepan, combine ingredients; bring to a boil. Reduce heat; simmer uncovered 10 minutes. Remove spices. Serve warm.
Makes about 2 quarts.

Hot Buttered Pineapple Smoothie

5½ cups DOLE® Pineapple Juice
¼ cup brown sugar, packed
2 tablespoons butter or margarine
10 whole cloves
3 cinnamon sticks
1 DOLE™ Lemon, sliced

In large saucepan, combine pineapple juice, brown sugar, butter, cloves and cinnamon sticks. Bring to a boil; simmer 5 minutes. Add lemon slices. Serve hot in mugs.
Makes 1½ quarts.

Piña Colada

½ cup DOLE® Pineapple Juice
3 ounces rum
¼ cup canned cream of coconut
2 cups crushed ice

Combine pineapple juice, rum and cream of coconut in blender. Add ice; blend until slushy.
Makes 2 servings.

Party Mai Tais

3 cups pineapple juice, chilled
1 cup light rum
1 (6-ounce) can frozen orange juice concentrate, thawed
½ cup REALEMON® Lemon Juice from Concentrate
Ice
Orange slices and maraschino cherries for garnish, optional

In pitcher, combine all ingredients except ice and garnish; stir to dissolve orange juice concentrate. Serve over ice; garnish with orange and cherries if desired.
Makes about 5 cups.

Bourbon Slush

2 cups brewed tea
1 (6-ounce) can frozen orange juice concentrate, thawed
⅓ cup sugar
2 cups cold water
1 cup bourbon
⅓ cup REALEMON® Lemon Juice from Concentrate

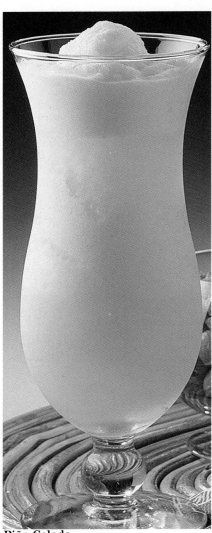

Piña Colada

In large bowl, combine tea, juice concentrate and sugar; stir until sugar dissolves. Add remaining ingredients. Freeze. About 1 hour before serving, remove from freezer; when mixture is slushy, spoon into cocktail glasses. Garnish as desired.
Makes about 6 cups.

Pineapple Margarita

⅓ cup DOLE® Pineapple Juice
1½ ounces tequila
1 ounce triple sec
Juice of 1 lemon
Crushed ice

Combine pineapple juice, tequila, triple sec and lemon juice in blender. Add ice; blend until slushy. Serve in frosted glass. (Do not put salt on rim.)
Makes 1 serving.

Frozen Margaritas

**½ cup REALIME® Lime Juice
   from Concentrate
½ cup tequila
¼ cup triple sec or other orange-
   flavored liqueur
1 cup confectioners' sugar
4 cups ice cubes**

In blender container, combine all ingredients except ice; blend well. Gradually add ice, blending until smooth. Serve immediately.
Makes about 1 quart.

Devilish Daiquiri

**2 ripe, medium DOLE™
   Bananas*
   Grated peel and juice from 1
   lemon
⅓ cup light rum
¼ cup creme de banana liqueur
2 tablespoons powdered sugar
2 cups crushed ice**

Slice bananas; combine bananas, lemon peel and juice, rum, liqueur and sugar in blender. Add ice; blend until slushy.
Makes 2 to 4 servings.
*Frozen bananas can be used. Peel bananas and freeze overnight in airtight plastic bag.

Melon Citrus Cooler

**2 cups orange juice, chilled
½ cup REALEMON® Lemon Juice
   from Concentrate
⅓ cup sugar
2 cups fresh or frozen melon
   balls
½ to 1 cup vodka, optional
2 (12-ounce) cans lemon-lime
   carbonated beverage, chilled
Ice**

In pitcher, combine orange juice, ReaLemon® brand and sugar; stir until sugar dissolves. Just before serving, add melon balls, vodka if desired and lemon-lime carbonated beverage. Serve over ice.
Makes about 2 quarts.

The Death Mix

**Fresh lime wedge
Celery salt (optional)
Ice
6 ounces tomato juice
1¼ ounces vodka
2 tablespoons lemon juice
½ beef bouillon cube, crushed
½ teaspoon horseradish
10 drops TABASCO® pepper
   sauce
4 drops Worcestershire sauce
Pinch each of salt, pepper,
   celery salt
Lemon slice (optional)**

Wet rim of 12-ounce glass with lime wedge; dip into celery salt. Fill glass with ice. Add remaining ingredients except garnish; stir. Garnish with lemon slice, if desired.
Makes 1 serving.

Seaside Mary

**2 cups tomato juice, chilled
1 (8-ounce) bottle DOXSEE® or
   SNOW'S® Clam Juice, chilled
⅓ cup vodka, optional
1 tablespoon REALEMON®
   Lemon Juice from
   Concentrate
1 teaspoon Worcestershire
   sauce
¼ teaspoon celery salt
8 drops hot pepper sauce**

In small pitcher, combine ingredients; stir. Serve over ice. Garnish as desired. Refrigerate leftovers.
Makes about 3½ cups.

Bloody Mary

**3 cups tomato juice, chilled
¾ cup vodka
4 teaspoons REALEMON®
   Lemon Juice from
   Concentrate
2 teaspoons Worcestershire
   sauce
½ teaspoon celery salt
⅛ teaspoon hot pepper sauce
Dash pepper**

In pitcher, combine ingredients; stir. Serve over ice; garnish as desired.
Makes about 1 quart.
Tip: For non-alcoholic Bloody Mary, omit vodka. Proceed as above.
BLOODY MARY GARNISHES
Onion & Olive Pick: Dip cocktail onions in chopped parsley; alternate on toothpick with pimiento-stuffed olives.
Green Onion Firecracker: With small scissors or very sharp knife, cut tips of green onion to end of dark green onion portion. Chill in ice water until curled.

Bloody Mary

Champagne Sherbet Punch

Champagne Sherbet Punch

3 cups pineapple juice, chilled
¼ cup REALEMON® Lemon Juice from Concentrate
1 quart BORDEN® or MEADOW GOLD® Pineapple Sherbet
1 (750 mL) bottle champagne, chilled

In punch bowl, combine pineapple juice and ReaLemon® brand. Just before serving, scoop sherbet into punch bowl; add champagne. Stir gently.
Makes about 2½ quarts.
Tip: For rosy champagne punch, use raspberry sherbet and pink champagne.

Planter's Punch

4 cups orange juice, chilled
4 cups pineapple juice, chilled
¾ cup REALIME® Lime Juice from Concentrate
½ cup grenadine syrup
1½ cups dark rum
Ice

In punch bowl or large pitcher, combine all ingredients except ice; stir. Serve over ice.
Makes about 2½ quarts.

Lemony Light Cooler

3 cups dry white wine *or* white grape juice, chilled
½ to ¾ cup sugar
½ cup REALEMON® Lemon Juice from Concentrate
1 (32-ounce) bottle club soda, chilled
Strawberries, plum, peach or orange slices or other fresh fruit

In pitcher, combine wine, sugar and ReaLemon® brand; stir until sugar dissolves. Just before serving, add club soda and fruit; serve over ice.
Makes about 7 cups.
Tip: Recipe can be doubled.

White Sangria

½ to ¾ cup sugar
½ cup REALEMON® Lemon Juice from Concentrate, chilled
¼ cup REALIME® Lime Juice from Concentrate, chilled
1 (750 mL) bottle sauterne, chilled
¼ cup orange-flavored liqueur
1 (32-ounce) bottle club soda, chilled
Orange, plum or nectarine slices, green grapes or other fresh fruit
Ice

In pitcher, combine sugar and juices; stir until sugar dissolves. Add sauterne and orange-flavored liqueur. Just before serving, add club soda, fruit and ice.
Makes about 2 quarts.

Pina Colada Punch

Ice Ring, optional, or block of ice
1 (20-ounce) can crushed pineapple, undrained
2 (15-ounce) cans COCO LOPEZ® Cream of Coconut
1 (46-ounce) can pineapple juice, chilled
2 cups light rum, optional
1 (32-ounce) bottle club soda, chilled

Prepare ice ring in advance. In blender container, combine crushed pineapple and cream of coconut; blend until smooth. In large punch bowl, combine pineapple mixture, pineapple juice and rum if desired. Just before serving, add club soda and ice.
Makes about 4 quarts.
ICE RING: Fill ring mold with water to within 1 inch of top rim; freeze. Arrange pineapple chunks and maraschino cherries on top of ice. Carefully pour small amount of cold water over fruits; freeze.

Rosé Wine Cooler

Berry Mint Ice Ring, optional, or block of ice
1½ cups sugar
1 cup REALEMON® Lemon Juice from Concentrate
2 (750 mL) bottles rosé wine, chilled
1 (32-ounce) bottle club soda, chilled

Prepare ice ring in advance. In large punch bowl, combine sugar and ReaLemon® brand; stir until sugar dissolves. Just before serving, add wine, club soda and ice.
Makes about 3½ quarts.
BERRY MINT ICE RING: Combine 3 cups water, 1 cup ReaLemon® brand and ¾ cup sugar; stir until sugar dissolves. Pour 3 cups mixture into 6-cup ring mold; freeze. Arrange strawberries and mint leaves on top of ice. Slowly pour remaining ReaLemon® brand mixture over fruit; freeze.

Spirited Egg Nog

1 (32-ounce) can BORDEN® Egg Nog, chilled
½ cup rum, brandy or bourbon
Whipped cream
Ground nutmeg

In pitcher, combine egg nog and liquor. Garnish with whipped cream and nutmeg. Refrigerate leftovers.
Makes about 1 quart.

Syllabub

1 quart BORDEN® or MEADOW GOLD® Half-and-Half
½ cup sugar
⅓ cup REALEMON® Lemon Juice from Concentrate
⅓ cup brandy
3 tablespoons dry or cocktail sherry
Candy lemon sticks, optional

In large mixer bowl, on low speed, beat half-and-half until frothy; gradually beat in sugar then ReaLemon® brand, brandy and sherry. Chill; stir before serving. Garnish with lemon sticks if desired.
Makes about 5 cups.

Lemon Toddy

⅓ cup water
¼ cup REALEMON® Lemon Juice from Concentrate
3 tablespoons honey
3 tablespoons whiskey

In small saucepan, combine ingredients. Over low heat, simmer to blend flavors, stirring occasionally to dissolve honey. Serve hot.
Makes 1 serving.
Microwave: In 2-cup glass measure, combine ingredients. Heat on 100% power (high) for 1 to 1½ minutes or until hot.

Hot Maple Toddy

1 to 1¼ cups whiskey
1 (8-ounce) bottle CARY'S® Pure Maple Syrup
¾ cup REALEMON® Lemon Juice from Concentrate
Butter and cinnamon sticks, optional

In medium saucepan, combine all ingredients except butter and cinnamon sticks. Over low heat, simmer uncovered 10 minutes. Serve hot with butter and cinnamon sticks if desired.
Makes about 3 cups.
Microwave: In 1-quart glass measure, combine ingredients as above. Heat on 100% power (high) 4 to 5 minutes or until heated through. Serve as above.

Simmered Sherry Bouillon

8 cups water
3 tablespoons WYLER'S® or STEERO® Beef-Flavor Instant Bouillon or 9 Beef-Flavor Bouillon Cubes
⅓ cup dry or cocktail sherry
Lemon slices, optional

In large saucepan, bring water and bouillon to a boil; stir until bouillon dissolves. Remove from heat; stir in sherry. Serve hot. Garnish with lemon slices if desired.
Makes about 2 quarts.
Microwave: In 2-quart glass measure, heat water and bouillon on 100% power (high) 10 to 14 minutes or until boiling. Stir until bouillon dissolves. Proceed as above.

Mulled Cider

2 quarts apple cider
¾ to 1 cup REALEMON® Lemon Juice from Concentrate
1 cup firmly packed light brown sugar
8 whole cloves
2 cinnamon sticks
¾ cup rum, optional
Additional cinnamon sticks, optional

In large saucepan, combine all ingredients except rum and additional cinnamon sticks; bring to a boil. Reduce heat; simmer uncovered 10 minutes. Remove spices; add rum just before serving if desired. Serve hot with cinnamon sticks if desired.
Makes about 2 quarts.
Tip: Can be served cold.
Microwave: In deep 3-quart round baking dish, combine ingredients as above. Heat on 100% power (high) 13 to 14 minutes or until hot. Serve as above.

Spirited Coffee Lopez

4 cups hot coffee
½ cup COCO LOPEZ® Cream of Coconut
½ cup Irish whiskey
1 teaspoon vanilla extract
Whipped cream

In heatproof pitcher, combine all ingredients except whipped cream; mix well. Pour into mugs; top with whipped cream. Serve immediately.
Makes 5 cups.

Spirited Coffee Lopez

SOUPS

For satisfying lunches and simple, informal suppers, nothing beats a hearty bowl of soup. Try robust soups, rich with meat and vegetables, or refreshing clear soups that whet the appetite. Along with traditional, long-simmering soups with their wonderful flavor and aroma, you'll discover tasty fuss-free creations prepared with convenience foods.

Lentil and Brown Rice Soup

- **1 envelope LIPTON® Onion, Beefy Onion or Beefy Mushroom Recipe Soup Mix**
- **4 cups water**
- **3/4 cup lentils, rinsed and drained**
- **1/2 cup uncooked brown or regular rice**
- **1 can (14 1/2 ounces) whole peeled tomatoes, undrained and coarsely chopped**
- **1 medium carrot, coarsely chopped**
- **1 large stalk celery, coarsely chopped**
- **1/2 teaspoon basil leaves**
- **1/2 teaspoon oregano**
- **1/4 teaspoon thyme leaves (optional)**
- **1 tablespoon finely chopped parsley**
- **1 tablespoon apple cider vinegar**
- **1/4 teaspoon pepper**

In large saucepan or stockpot, combine onion recipe soup mix, water, lentils, uncooked rice, tomatoes, carrot, celery, basil, oregano and thyme. Bring to a boil, then simmer covered, stirring occasionally, 45 minutes or until lentils and rice are tender. Stir in remaining ingredients.
Makes about 3 (2-cup) servings.

Microwave Directions: In 3-quart casserole, combine onion recipe soup mix, water, tomatoes, carrot, celery, basil, oregano and thyme. Heat covered at HIGH (Full Power) 12 minutes or until boiling. Stir in lentils and uncooked brown rice* and heat covered at MEDIUM (50% Full Power), stirring occasionally, 60 minutes or until lentils and rice are tender. Stir in remaining ingredients. Let stand covered 5 minutes.

*If using uncooked regular rice, decrease 60-minute cooking time to 30 minutes.

Spinach-Rice Soup

- **1 can (13 3/4 oz.) ready-to-serve chicken broth**
- **1 package (11 oz.) BIRDS EYE® Creamed Spinach, thawed**
- **1/4 cup MINUTE® Rice**
- **Dash of pepper**
- **Dash of nutmeg**

Bring broth and spinach to a full boil in medium saucepan. Stir in rice. Cover; remove from heat. Let stand 5 minutes. Season with pepper and nutmeg.
Makes 3 servings.
Note: Recipe may be doubled.

Fresh Spinach Soup

- **1 tablespoon butter or margarine**
- **2 cups loosely packed chopped spinach leaves**
- **1 can (10 3/4 ounces) CAMPBELL'S® Condensed Cream of Potato Soup**
- **1 soup can milk**
- **2 tablespoons dry sherry or vermouth**
- **Dash ground nutmeg**

To Microwave:
1. In 2-quart microwave-safe casserole, combine butter and spinach. Cover with lid; microwave on HIGH 2 minutes or until spinach is wilted.
2. Stir in soup until smooth; stir in milk, sherry and nutmeg until well blended. Cover; microwave on HIGH 6 minutes or until hot and bubbling, stirring once during cooking.
Makes about 3 cups or 3 servings.

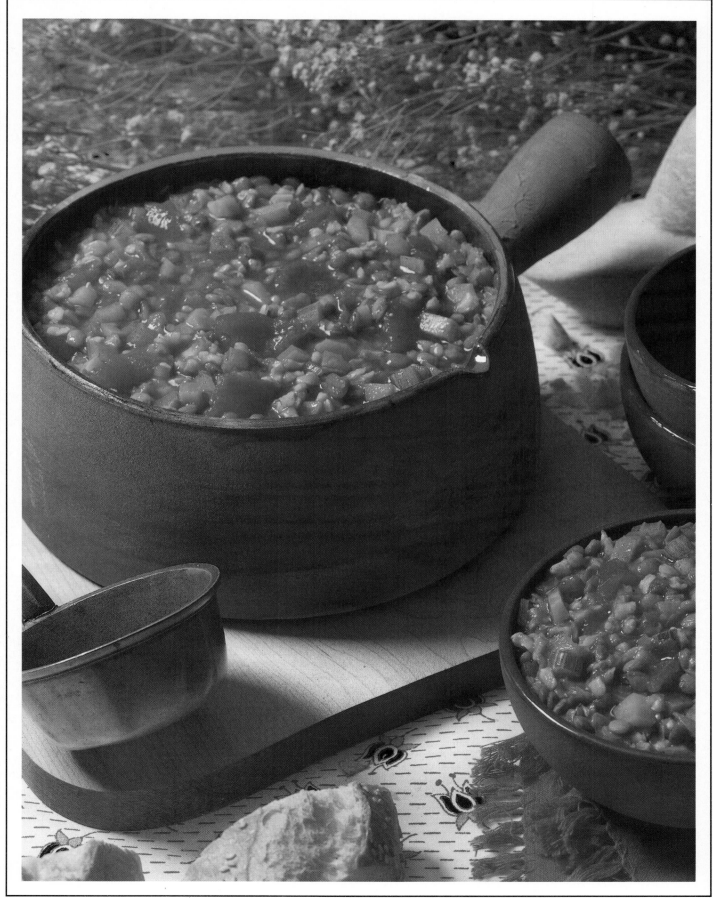

Lentil and Brown Rice Soup

Creamed Corn Chowder

- **6 slices bacon, cut in ¹/₂-inch pieces**
- **¹/₂ cup chopped onion**
- **¹/₃ cup chopped green pepper**
- **2 (17-ounce) cans cream style sweet corn**
- **2 (13³/₄-fluid ounce) cans COLLEGE INN® Chicken Broth**
- **¹/₈ teaspoon ground black pepper**

In large saucepan, over medium-high heat, cook bacon until crisp; remove and crumble bacon. Pour off all but 2 tablespoons drippings. Cook onion and green pepper in reserved drippings 2 to 3 minutes. Add corn, chicken broth and pepper. Heat to a boil; reduce heat. Cover and simmer 15 minutes. Serve garnished with bacon.
Makes 6 servings.

Creamed Corn Chowder

California Bisque

- **1 tablespoon butter or margarine**
- **¹/₄ cup thinly sliced celery**
- **¹/₂ teaspoon chili powder**
  Generous dash ground cinnamon
- **1 can (11 ounces) CAMPBELL'S® Condensed Tomato Bisque**
- **1 soup can water**
- **2 teaspoons lemon juice**
- **¹/₂ cup chopped avocado**

To Microwave:

1. In 1¹/₂-quart microwave-safe casserole, combine butter, celery, chili powder and cinnamon. Cover with lid; microwave on HIGH 3 minutes or until celery is tender, stirring once during cooking.
2. Stir in soup, water and lemon juice. Cover; microwave on HIGH 3 minutes or until hot and bubbling. Stir in avocado.
Makes about 3 cups or 3 servings.

Extra-Good Mushroom Cream Soup

- **2 tablespoons butter or margarine**
- **¹/₂ cup chopped onion**
- **1 cup sliced CAMPBELL'S FRESH® Mushrooms**
- **¹/₂ teaspoon dried thyme leaves, crushed**

- **1 can (10³/₄ ounces) CAMPBELL'S® Condensed Cream of Mushroom Soup**
- **¹/₂ cup light cream**
- **³/₄ cup milk**
  PEPPERIDGE FARM® Goldfish® Crackers

1. In 2-quart saucepan over medium heat, in hot butter, cook onion, mushrooms and thyme until mushrooms are tender, stirring occasionally.
2. Stir in soup, cream and milk. Heat through, stirring occasionally. Ladle into bowls; serve with crackers.
Makes about 3¹/₂ cups or 4 servings.

To Microwave: In 2-quart microwave-safe casserole, combine butter, onion, mushrooms and thyme. Cover with lid; microwave on HIGH 7 to 9 minutes until vegetables are tender, stirring once. Stir in soup, cream and milk. Cover; microwave on HIGH 5 to 7 minutes until heated through, stirring occasionally. Ladle into bowls; serve with crackers.

Oriental Vegetable Soup

- **2 cans (14¹/₂ ounces each) SWANSON® Clear Ready to Serve Chicken Broth**
- **1 tablespoon soy sauce**
- **1 tablespoon dry sherry**
- **¹/₈ teaspoon grated fresh ginger**
- **¹/₂ cup fresh or frozen cut green beans**
- **¹/₄ cup thinly sliced carrot**
- **¹/₄ cup cubed tofu**

To Microwave:

1. In 2-quart microwave-safe casserole, stir together broth, soy sauce, sherry and ginger. Stir in beans and carrot. Cover with lid; microwave on HIGH 10 minutes or until soup is boiling and vegetables are tender-crisp.
2. Stir in tofu. Let stand, covered, 2 minutes.
Makes about 5 cups or 6 servings.

Clear Japanese Soup

1½ quarts chicken broth
⅓ cup dry sherry
4½ teaspoons KIKKOMAN Soy Sauce
1 lemon, thinly sliced
Garnishes:
5 to 6 fresh mushrooms, sliced
2 green onions and tops, sliced diagonally
1 carrot, very thinly sliced

Bring broth to simmer in large saucepan. Add sherry and soy sauce; simmer 2 to 3 minutes. Ladle soup into small bowls; float a lemon slice in each bowl. Arrange garnishes on tray and add to soup as desired.
Makes about 6 cups.

Double Onion Soup Gratinée

1 tablespoon butter or margarine
2 green onions, thinly sliced
1 can (10½ ounces) CAMPBELL'S® Condensed French Onion Soup
1 soup can water
2 tablespoons dry vermouth
1 cup PEPPERIDGE FARM® Onion & Garlic Croutons
1 cup shredded Swiss cheese (4 ounces)

To Microwave:
1. In 4-cup glass measure, combine butter and onions. Microwave, uncovered, on HIGH 1 minute or until onions are wilted.
2. Stir in soup, water and vermouth. Microwave, uncovered, on HIGH 5 minutes or until boiling, stirring once during cooking.
3. Ladle soup into three 10-ounce bowls. Sprinkle croutons over soup; sprinkle with cheese. Let stand, uncovered, 1 minute or until cheese is melted.
Makes about 3 cups or 3 servings.

Chilled Carrot Soup

2 tablespoons vegetable oil
1 large onion, chopped
1½ teaspoons curry powder
3½ cups chicken broth
1 pound carrots, sliced
2 stalks celery, sliced

1 bay leaf
½ teaspoon ground cumin
½ teaspoon TABASCO® pepper sauce
1 cup milk
1 cup cottage cheese

In large saucepan heat oil; cook onion and curry 3 to 5 minutes. Add broth, carrots, celery, bay leaf, cumin and Tabasco® sauce; mix well. Cover; simmer 25 minutes or until vegetables are tender. Remove bay leaf.

Spoon carrot mixture, milk and cottage cheese in several batches into container of blender or food processor. Cover; process until smooth. Pour into serving bowl. Cover; refrigerate until chilled. Serve with additional Tabasco® sauce, if desired.
Makes 8 servings.

Blushing Onion Soup

4 cups thinly sliced onions
1 clove garlic, finely chopped
¼ cup margarine or butter
1 (46-ounce) can tomato juice
1 cup water

2 teaspoons WYLER'S® or STEERO® Beef-Flavor Instant Bouillon or 2 Beef-Flavor Bouillon Cubes
2 teaspoons parsley flakes
8 slices French bread, toasted
2 cups (8 ounces) shredded Mozzarella cheese

In large kettle or Dutch oven, cook onions and garlic in margarine until tender. Stir in tomato juice, water, bouillon and parsley. Bring to a boil; reduce heat. Simmer 20 to 30 minutes, stirring occasionally. Ladle into 8 ovenproof soup bowls. Top with bread slices and sprinkle generously with cheese. Broil 2 to 3 minutes or until cheese melts. Serve immediately.
Makes 8 servings.

Microwave: In 2-quart glass measure, melt margarine on 100% power (high) 1 minute. Add onions and garlic; cook covered on 100% power (high) 5 to 6 minutes or until onions are tender. Add tomato juice, water, *instant bouillon* and parsley. Cook covered on 100% power (high) 15 to 17 minutes or until boiling. Proceed as above.

Blushing Onion Soup

Southern Tomato-Bean Soup

- **1 tablespoon vegetable oil or bacon drippings**
- **1/2 cup chopped celery**
- **1/2 cup chopped onion**
- **1 clove garlic, minced**
- **1/4 teaspoon dried thyme leaves, crushed**
- **1 can (16 ounces) CAMPBELL'S® Pork & Beans in Tomato Sauce**
- **1 can (14 1/2 ounces) tomatoes, undrained, cut up**
- **1/8 teaspoon black pepper**
- **1/8 teaspoon ground red pepper (cayenne)**

To Microwave:

1. In 2-quart microwave-safe casserole, combine oil, celery, onion, garlic and thyme. Cover with lid; microwave on HIGH 3 minutes or until vegetables are tender, stirring once during cooking.

2. Stir in pork and beans, tomatoes with their liquid, black pepper and red pepper. Cover; microwave on HIGH 8 minutes or until hot and bubbling, stirring once during cooking.
Makes about 4 cups or 4 servings.

Norwegian Pea Soup

- **3 1/2 quarts water, divided**
- **1 package (1 pound) whole dry yellow peas or split yellow peas, rinsed**
- **1 1/2 cups finely chopped carrots**
- **1 1/2 cups finely chopped onions**
- **1/4 teaspoon ground cumin**
- **2 1/2-pound shank end fully cooked ham**
- **KAVLI Croutons (recipe follows)**
- **1 cup thinly sliced celery**
- **2 tablespoons olive oil**

Place 7 cups of the water and the peas in heavy, large saucepan. Bring to a boil over high heat; boil 2 minutes. Remove from heat. Cover and let soak 1 hour. Drain peas; discard water. (If using split peas, omit this step.)

Return peas to heavy, large saucepan. Add remaining 7 cups water, the carrots, onions and cumin. Bring to a boil over high heat. Reduce heat to low. Cover and simmer 1 hour, stirring occasionally. Add ham; cook 1 hour more, stirring occasionally. Meanwhile, prepare Kavli Croutons. Add celery to soup mixture and cook until peas mash easily, stirring occasionally. Remove ham; cut into cubes. Brown ham in hot oil in large skillet over medium-high heat. Return to soup; heat through. Serve topped with Kavli Croutons.
Makes about 6 servings.

KAVLI CROUTONS: Melt 1/3 cup butter or margarine in large skillet over medium heat. Add 1 small garlic clove. Cook and stir several minutes. Add 1 1/2 cups coarsely broken KAVLI Norwegian Thick-Style Crispbreads. Cook and stir until croutons are lightly browned. Stir in 2 tablespoons chopped parsley.

Italian Vegetable Soup

- **1 pound bulk Italian sausage**
- **2 cups chopped onion**
- **2 cloves garlic, finely chopped**
- **7 cups water**
- **4 medium carrots, pared and sliced**
- **1 (28-ounce) can tomatoes, undrained and broken up**
- **2 tablespoons WYLER'S® or STEERO® Beef-Flavor Instant Bouillon or 6 Beef-Flavor Bouillon Cubes**
- **1 teaspoon Italian seasoning**
- **1/4 teaspoon pepper**
- **1 1/2 cups coarsely chopped zucchini**
- **1 (15-ounce) can garbanzo beans, drained**
- **1 cup uncooked CREAMETTE® Rotini or Elbow Macaroni**

In large kettle or Dutch oven, brown sausage, onion and garlic; pour off fat. Add water, carrots, tomatoes, bouillon, Italian seasoning and pepper; bring to a boil. Reduce heat; cover and simmer 30 minutes. Add zucchini, beans and rotini. Cover; cook 15 to 20 minutes or until rotini is tender. Garnish as desired. Refrigerate leftovers.
Makes about 2 1/2 quarts.

Broccoli Cheese Soup

- **1/2 cup chopped onion**
- **1/4 cup margarine or butter**
- **1/4 cup unsifted flour**
- **3 cups water**
- **2 (10-ounce) packages frozen chopped broccoli, thawed and well drained**
- **4 teaspoons WYLER'S® or STEERO® Chicken-Flavor Instant Bouillon or 4 Chicken-Flavor Bouillon Cubes**
- **1 teaspoon Worcestershire sauce**
- **3 cups (12 ounces) shredded Cheddar cheese**
- **2 cups (1 pint) BORDEN® or MEADOW GOLD® Coffee Cream or Half-and-Half**

In large saucepan or Dutch oven, cook onion in margarine until tender; stir in flour. Gradually stir in water then broccoli, bouillon and Worcestershire. Over medium heat, cook and stir until thickened and broccoli is tender, about 10 minutes. Add cheese and cream. Cook and stir until cheese melts and soup is hot *(do not boil)*. Garnish as desired. Refrigerate leftovers.
Makes about 2 quarts.

Broccoli Cheese Soup (left), Italian Vegetable Soup (right)

Lentil-Pasta Soup

- **1 tablespoon olive or vegetable oil**
- **1 cup chopped onion**
- **2 cloves garlic, minced**
- **1 can (19 ounces) CAMPBELL'S® Home Cookin'® Hearty Lentil Soup**
- **1 can (14½ ounces) SWANSON® Clear Ready to Serve Beef Broth**
- **½ cup chopped fresh parsley**
- **½ teaspoon dried basil leaves, crushed**
- **½ teaspoon dried oregano leaves, crushed**
- **½ cup small shell pasta, uncooked**

To Microwave:

1. In 3-quart microwave-safe casserole, combine oil, onion and garlic. Cover with lid; microwave on HIGH 3 minutes or until onion is tender, stirring once during cooking.

2. Stir in soup and broth. Cover; microwave on HIGH 8 minutes or until very hot. Stir in parsley, basil, oregano and pasta. Cover; microwave on HIGH 13 minutes or until pasta is tender, stirring twice during cooking. Let stand, covered, 5 minutes.

Makes about 4 cups or 4 servings.

Minestrone

- **3 medium carrots**
- **3 stalks celery**
- **2 medium onions**
- **1 large potato**
- **¼ pound green beans**
- **2 medium zucchini**
- **½ pound cabbage**
- **1 medium clove garlic**
- **⅓ cup olive oil**
- **3 tablespoons butter**
- **3½ cups beef broth**
- **1½ cups water**
- **1 can (28 ounces) Italian plum tomatoes**
- **½ teaspoon salt**
- **½ teaspoon dried basil, crumbled**
- **¼ teaspoon dried rosemary, crumbled**
- **¼ teaspoon pepper**
- **1 bay leaf**
- **1 can (1 pound) cannellini beans**

1. Pare carrots; chop coarsely. Chop celery coarsely. Chop onions. Pare potato; cut into ¾-inch cubes. Trim green beans; cut into 1-inch pieces.

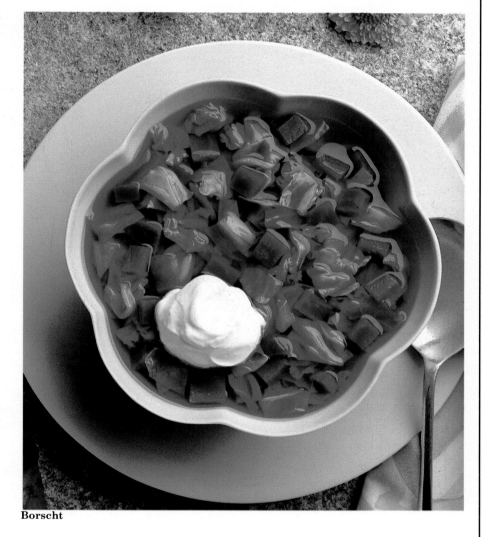

Borscht

Trim zucchini; cut into ½-inch cubes. Coarsely shred cabbage. Mince garlic.

2. Heat oil and butter in 5-quart Dutch oven over medium heat. Add onions; sauté, stirring occasionally, until soft and golden but not brown, 6 to 8 minutes. Stir in carrots and potato; sauté 5 minutes. Stir in celery and green beans; sauté 5 minutes. Stir in zucchini; sauté 3 minutes. Stir in cabbage and garlic; cook 1 minute.

3. Add broth, water and liquid from tomatoes to pan. Chop tomatoes coarsely; add to pan. Stir in salt, basil, rosemary, pepper and bay leaf. Heat to boiling; reduce heat to low. Simmer, covered, stirring occasionally, 1½ hours.

4. Rinse and drain cannellini beans; add beans to soup. Cook, uncovered, over medium-low heat, stirring occasionally, until soup is thick, 30 to 40 minutes longer. Remove bay leaf.

Makes about 12 cups; 8 to 10 servings.

Note: Serve sprinkled with grated Parmesan cheese, if desired.

Borscht

- **3 cups chopped cabbage**
- **¼ cup BLUE BONNET® Margarine**
- **1 (16-ounce) can sliced beets**
- **1 (46-fluid ounce) can COLLEGE INN® Beef Broth**
- **2 tablespoons lemon juice**
- **½ teaspoon ground black pepper**
- **1 cup dairy sour cream**

In large saucepan, over medium-high heat, cook cabbage in margarine until tender. Drain beets, reserving liquid; chop beets. Stir in beef broth, beets with liquid, lemon juice and pepper. Heat to a boil; reduce heat. Simmer 15 minutes. Serve with dollop of sour cream.

Makes 8 servings.

Gazpacho

- 1 (14½-ounce) can stewed tomatoes
- 1 (13¾-fluid ounce) can COLLEGE INN® Chicken or Beef Broth
- 1 medium cucumber, coarsely chopped
- ½ cup sliced scallions
- ¼ cup red wine vinegar
- ¼ teaspoon liquid hot pepper seasoning

Drain tomatoes, reserving liquid; coarsely chop tomatoes. In medium bowl, combine chopped tomatoes, reserved liquid, broth, cucumber, scallions, vinegar and liquid hot pepper seasoning. Refrigerate 2 to 3 hours. Serve cold.
Makes 4 servings.

Wisconsin Cheese 'n Beer Soup

- 2 tablespoons butter or margarine
- 2 tablespoons all-purpose flour
- 1 envelope LIPTON® Golden Onion Recipe Soup Mix
- 3 cups milk
- 1 teaspoon Worcestershire sauce
- 1 cup shredded Cheddar cheese (about 4 ounces)
- ½ cup beer
- 1 teaspoon prepared mustard

In medium saucepan, melt butter and cook flour over medium heat, stirring constantly, 3 minutes or until bubbling. Stir in golden onion recipe soup mix thoroughly blended with milk and Worcestershire sauce. Bring just to the boiling point, then simmer, stirring occasionally, 10 minutes. Stir in remaining ingredients and simmer, stirring constantly, 5 minutes or until cheese is melted. Garnish, if desired, with additional cheese, chopped red pepper and parsley.
Makes about 4 (1-cup) servings.

Creamy Tomato Bisque

- 2 cups water
- 1 (14½-ounce) can tomatoes, undrained
- ½ cup chopped celery
- 2 tablespoons chopped onion

Tortellini Soup

- 5 teaspoons WYLER'S® or STEERO® Chicken-Flavor Instant Bouillon *or* 5 Chicken-Flavor Bouillon Cubes
- 2 medium tomatoes, pared and diced
- ¼ cup margarine or butter
- 3 tablespoons flour
- 2 cups (1 pint) BORDEN® or MEADOW GOLD® Light or Coffee Cream
- 1 tablespoon sugar

In large saucepan, combine water, canned tomatoes, celery, onion and bouillon; cover and simmer 20 minutes. Place in blender container; blend until smooth. In same pan, cook fresh tomatoes in *2 tablespoons* margarine about 5 minutes; remove from pan. In same pan, melt remaining *2 tablespoons* margarine; stir in flour. Add cream; over low heat, cook and stir until thickened. Stir in bouillon mixture, tomatoes and sugar; heat through *(do not boil)*. Garnish as desired. Refrigerate leftovers.
Makes about 2½ quarts.

Tortellini Soup

- 2 cloves garlic, crushed
- 1 tablespoon BLUE BONNET® Margarine
- 2 (13¾-fluid ounce) cans COLLEGE INN® Chicken or Beef Broth
- 8 ounces frozen or fresh cheese tortellini
- 1 (15-ounce) can chopped spinach, undrained
- 1 (14½-ounce) can stewed tomatoes, undrained and cut up
- Grated Parmesan cheese

In large saucepan, over medium-high heat, cook garlic in margarine for 2 to 3 minutes. Add broth and tortellini. Heat to a boil; reduce heat; simmer 10 minutes. Add spinach and tomatoes; simmer 5 minutes more. Serve with cheese.
Makes 6 servings.

Golden Cauliflower Soup

> 2 (10-ounce) packages frozen cauliflower *or* 1 small head fresh cauliflower, separated into small flowerets (about 4 cups)
> 2 cups water
> ½ cup chopped onion
> ⅓ cup margarine or butter
> ⅓ to ½ cup unsifted flour
> 2 cups BORDEN® or MEADOW GOLD® Milk
> 1 tablespoon WYLER'S® or STEERO® Chicken-Flavor Instant Bouillon *or* 3 Chicken-Flavor Bouillon Cubes
> 2 cups (8 ounces) shredded mild Cheddar cheese
> ⅛ to ¼ teaspoon ground nutmeg
> Chopped green onion or parsley

In medium saucepan, cook cauliflower in *1 cup* water until tender. Reserve *1 cup* cooked flowerets. In blender or food processor, blend remaining cauliflower and liquid; set aside. In large heavy saucepan, cook onion in margarine until tender; stir in flour. Gradually add remaining *1 cup* water, milk and bouillon; cook and stir until well blended and slightly thickened. Add cheese, pureed cauliflower, reserved flowerets and nutmeg; cook and stir until cheese melts and mixture is hot (do not boil). Garnish with green onion. Refrigerate leftovers.
Makes 1½ to 2 quarts.

Two-Bean Soup

> 1 tablespoon olive oil
> ½ cup chopped onion
> 2 large cloves garlic, minced
> 1 teaspoon dried basil leaves, crushed
> 4 cups V8® Vegetable Juice *or* No Salt Added V8® Vegetable Juice
> 1 can (16 ounces) chick peas, drained
> 1 cup thinly sliced carrots
> 1 cup green beans, cut into 1-inch pieces
> 1 cup sliced CAMPBELL'S FRESH® Mushrooms (4 ounces)
> 1 large bay leaf

1. In 4-quart saucepan over medium heat, in hot oil, cook onion, garlic and basil until onion is tender, stirring frequently.
2. Stir in remaining ingredients. Heat to boiling. Reduce heat to low. Simmer 30 minutes or until vegetables are tender. Discard bay leaf.
Makes 6½ cups or 8 side-dish servings.

Per serving: 126 calories, 4 g protein, 3 g fat, 23 g carbohydrate, 591 mg sodium (No Salt Added V8® Juice: 208 mg sodium), 0 mg cholesterol.

Clear Vegetable Soup

> 1 can (10¾ ounces) CAMPBELL'S® Condensed Chicken Broth
> 1 soup can water
> ½ cup sliced carrot
> ½ cup sliced celery
> ¼ cup rotelle or other macaroni
> 1 teaspoon chopped fresh parsley

1. In 2-quart saucepan over high heat, heat chicken broth, water, carrot and celery to boiling. Add rotelle. Reduce heat to low. Cover; simmer until macaroni is done, about 20 minutes.
2. Ladle soup into bowls; top with parsley.
Makes about 3 cups or 3 servings.

Tortilla Soup

> 1 (4-ounce) jar sliced or diced pimientos
> ½ cup chopped onion
> ½ teaspoon ground cumin
> 1 tablespoon BLUE BONNET® Margarine
> 2 (13¾-fluid ounce) cans COLLEGE INN® Chicken or Beef Broth
> 1 (8¾-ounce) can whole kernel sweet corn, undrained
> 2 tablespoons chopped parsley
> 2 cups coarsely broken tortilla chips
> 1 cup shredded Monterey Jack, Cheddar or Monterey Jack with jalapeño pepper cheese (4 ounces)

Drain pimientos, reserving liquid. In medium saucepan, over medium-high heat, cook onion and cumin in margarine for 2 to 3 minutes, stirring occasionally. Stir in reserved pimiento liquid, broth, corn and parsley. Heat to a boil; reduce heat. Cover; simmer 10 minutes.

Meanwhile, arrange tortilla chips, cheese and pimientos in individual serving bowls. Ladle hot soup into bowls. Serve immediately.
Makes 6 to 8 servings.

Clear Vegetable Soup

Curried Zucchini Soup

- **1 tablespoon butter or margarine**
- **2 cups coarsely chopped zucchini**
- **2 tablespoons sliced green onion**
- **1 teaspoon curry powder**
- **1 can (10³/₄ ounces) CAMPBELL'S® Condensed Cream of Potato Soup**
- **1³/₄ cups milk PEPPERIDGE FARM® Croutons for garnish**

To Microwave:

1. In 2-quart microwave-safe casserole, combine butter, zucchini, onion and curry powder. Cover with lid; microwave on HIGH 7 minutes or until zucchini is very tender, stirring once during cooking.
2. Stir soup into zucchini mixture. In covered blender or food processor, blend soup mixture until smooth. Return to casserole. Stir in milk.
3. Cover; refrigerate until serving time, at least 4 hours. Thin chilled soup to desired consistency with additional milk. Ladle into bowls and garnish with croutons.

Makes about 4 cups or 4 servings.

Note: To serve this soup hot, prepare as above through step 2. Cover; microwave on HIGH 4 minutes or until hot and bubbling.

Curried Zucchini Soup

White Gazpacho

- **4 teaspoons WYLER'S® or STEERO® Chicken-Flavor Instant Bouillon *or* 4 Chicken-Flavor Bouillon cubes**
- **2 cups boiling water**
- **3 medium cucumbers, pared, seeded and cut into cubes (about 3 cups)**
- **1 (16-ounce) container BORDEN® or MEADOW GOLD® Sour Cream**
- **2 tablespoons REALEMON® Lemon Juice from Concentrate**
- **¹/₄ teaspoon garlic powder**
- **¹/₄ teaspoon pepper**

In small saucepan, dissolve bouillon in water. Cool completely. In blender or food processor, blend cucumber with ¹/₂ cup bouillon liquid until smooth. In medium bowl, combine cucumber mixture, remaining bouillon liquid, sour cream, ReaLemon® brand, garlic powder and pepper; mix well. Chill thoroughly. Garnish as desired. Serve with condiments. Refrigerate leftovers.

Makes about 1¹/₂ quarts.

Suggested Condiments: Chopped fresh tomato, chopped green onions, chopped green pepper, toasted slivered almonds and toasted croutons.

Spinach-Potato Soup

- **2 tablespoons butter or margarine**
- **1 cup sliced leeks**
- **1¹/₂ pounds potatoes, peeled and cubed (4 cups)**
- **2 cans (14¹/₂ ounces each) SWANSON® Clear Ready to Serve Chicken Broth or 3 cans (10¹/₂ ounces each) CAMPBELL'S® Ready to Serve Low Sodium Chicken Broth**
- **¹/₄ cup water**
- **4 cups coarsely chopped spinach leaves**
- **1 teaspoon lemon juice**
- **¹/₈ teaspoon pepper Sour cream or plain low-fat yogurt for garnish**

1. In 3-quart saucepan over medium heat, in hot butter, cook leeks until tender, stirring often.
2. Add potatoes, broth and water. Heat to boiling; reduce heat to low.

Cover; simmer 25 minutes or until potatoes are tender, stirring occasionally.
3. Stir in spinach, lemon juice and pepper; simmer 5 minutes. Garnish with sour cream.

Makes 6¹/₂ cups or 7 side-dish servings.

Per serving: 121 calories, 3 g protein, 5 g fat, 18 g carbohydrate, 587 mg sodium (Low Sodium Chicken Broth: 97 mg sodium), 9 mg cholesterol.

Black Bean Soup with Rice and Sherry

- **1 cup dry black beans, rinsed**
- **4 cups beef broth**
- **4 cups chicken broth**
- **¹/₂ pound smoked ham hock**
- **1 large yellow onion, sliced**
- **1 carrot, sliced**
- **4 sprigs parsley**
- **2 cloves garlic**
- **1 teaspoon ground thyme Salt Pepper**
- **3 cups hot cooked rice**
- **¹/₂ cup dry sherry**
- **1 small red onion, chopped**

Place beans in large bowl. Cover with water; soak overnight. Drain beans; discard water. Place beans in large stockpot. Add broths, ham hock, yellow onion, carrot, parsley, garlic and thyme. Bring to a boil over high heat. Reduce heat to low. Cover and simmer 6 to 8 hours, stirring occasionally. Strain soup into large saucepan, reserving bean mixture and discarding ham hock. Puree bean mixture, in batches, in blender or food processor. Stir bean mixture into broth. Cook over low heat 2 hours more, stirring occasionally. Season to taste with salt and pepper. Ladle soup into bowls. Top with rice, sherry and red onion.

Makes 6 servings.

*Favorite recipe from **Rice Council***

Bavarian Pea Soup

Greek Lemon Soup

**2 cans (14½ ounces each)
SWANSON® Clear Ready to
Serve Chicken Broth
¼ cup orzo or regular long-grain
rice, uncooked
2 eggs
2 tablespoons lemon juice
Thin lemon slices for garnish**

To Microwave:
1. In 2-quart microwave-safe casserole, combine broth and orzo. Cover with lid; microwave on HIGH 8 minutes or until boiling. Stir soup.
2. Reduce power to 50%. Cover; microwave 18 minutes or until orzo is tender, stirring once during cooking.
3. In small bowl, beat eggs with lemon juice. Slowly beat ½ cup hot soup into egg mixture. Return egg mixture to broth, stirring constantly until soup is slightly thickened. Garnish with lemon slices.
Makes about 4 cups or 4 servings.
   Note: Orzo is a small rice-shaped pasta that is traditional in this classic soup.

Hot & Sour Soup

**1 can (10½ oz.) condensed
chicken broth
2 soup cans water
1 can (4 oz.) sliced mushrooms
2 tablespoons cornstarch
2 tablespoons KIKKOMAN Soy
Sauce
2 tablespoons distilled white
vinegar
½ teaspoon TABASCO® pepper
sauce
1 egg, beaten
2 green onions and tops,
chopped**

Combine chicken broth, water, mushrooms, cornstarch, soy sauce, vinegar and pepper sauce in medium saucepan. Bring to boil over high heat, stirring constantly, until slightly thickened. Gradually pour egg into boiling soup, stirring constantly in 1 direction. Remove from heat; stir in green onions. Garnish with additional chopped green onions or cilantro, as desired. Serve immediately.
Makes about 5 cups.

Bavarian Pea Soup

**1 tablespoon butter or
margarine
½ cup shredded cabbage
¼ teaspoon caraway seed
1 can (19 ounces) CAMPBELL'S®
Home Cookin'® Split Pea
with Ham or Chunky Split
Pea 'n Ham Soup
Pumpernickel bread, torn into
pieces for garnish
Shredded Swiss cheese for
garnish**

To Microwave:
1. In 1-quart microwave-safe casserole, combine butter, cabbage and caraway. Cover with lid; microwave on HIGH 3 minutes or until cabbage is tender, stirring once during cooking.
2. Stir in soup. Cover with lid; microwave on HIGH 4 minutes or until heated through, stirring once during cooking.
3. Pour soup into 2 microwave-safe soup bowls; top with bread and cheese. Microwave, uncovered, on HIGH 1 minute or until cheese is melted.
Makes 2 servings.

Egg Drop Soup

**2 cans (14½ ounces each)
SWANSON® Clear Ready to
Serve Chicken Broth
1 tablespoon cornstarch
1 tablespoon rice vinegar or dry
sherry
2 teaspoons soy sauce
½ cup cooked ham cut into thin
strips
½ cup snow peas
3 green onions, sliced
2 eggs, beaten**

To Microwave:
1. In 2-quart microwave-safe casserole, stir together broth, cornstarch, vinegar and soy sauce until smooth; stir in ham, snow peas and onions. Cover with lid; microwave on HIGH 10 minutes or until boiling, stirring twice during cooking.
2. With fork, stir broth in swirling motion. Without stirring, slowly pour eggs into swirling broth; then stir just until eggs are set in long strands.
Makes about 4 cups or 4 servings.

Chicken & Rice Gumbo

Chicken & Rice Gumbo

> 1 (46-fluid ounce) can COLLEGE
>   INN® Chicken Broth
> 1 pound boneless chicken, cut
>   in bite-size pieces
> 1 (17-ounce) can whole kernel
>   sweet corn, drained
> 1 (14½-ounce) can stewed
>   tomatoes, undrained and
>   chopped
> 1 (10-ounce) package frozen
>   okra, thawed and chopped
> ½ cup uncooked rice
> 1 teaspoon ground black pepper

In large saucepan, over medium-high heat, heat chicken broth, chicken, corn, tomatoes, okra, rice and pepper to a boil. Reduce heat; simmer, uncovered, 20 minutes or until rice is cooked.
Makes 10 servings.

Chicken-Vegetable Soup

> 2½ cups water
> 1 pouch CAMPBELL'S® Chicken
>   Rice Soup Mix
> 1 cup frozen mixed vegetables
>   Generous dash dried thyme
>   leaves, crushed

1. In 2-quart saucepan, stir together all ingredients. Over medium-high heat, heat to boiling, stirring occasionally.
2. Reduce heat to low; simmer 5 minutes or until chicken and vegetables are tender.
Makes 2 servings.

Lettuce and Chicken Soup

> 2½ cups water
> 1 pouch CAMPBELL'S Chicken
>   Noodle Soup Mix
> ½ cup shredded carrot
> ¼ cup sliced green onions
> 2 teaspoons lemon juice
> 1 cup shredded lettuce

To Microwave:

1. Pour water into 2-quart microwave-safe casserole. Cover with lid; microwave on HIGH 6 minutes or until boiling.
2. Stir in soup mix, carrot, onions and lemon juice. Microwave, uncovered, on HIGH 4 minutes or until chicken is tender. Stir in lettuce. Let stand, covered, 5 minutes.
Makes about 3 cups or 3 servings.

Chicken-Corn Soup Santa Fe

> 1 tablespoon butter or
>   margarine
> 1 clove garlic, minced
> 1 can (10¾ ounces)
>   CAMPBELL'S® Condensed
>   Chicken Broth
> 1 soup can water
> 1 can (8 ounces) cream-style
>   golden corn
> 1 can (5 ounces) SWANSON®
>   Premium Chunk White
>   Chicken, undrained
> ½ teaspoon finely chopped
>   VLASIC® Hot Jalapeno
>   Peppers
> ¼ teaspoon ground cumin
>   Tortilla chips

To Microwave:

1. In 2-quart microwave-safe casserole, combine butter and garlic. Cover with lid; microwave on HIGH 30 seconds or until butter is melted.
2. Stir in broth, water, corn, chicken, peppers and cumin. Cover; microwave on HIGH 5 minutes or until hot and bubbling. Place a few tortilla chips in each of four 10-ounce soup bowls. Ladle hot soup over chips.
Makes about 4 cups or 4 servings.

Chicken Noodle Chowder

> 1 pouch CAMPBELL'S® Chicken
>   Noodle Soup Mix
> 2 cups water
> ½ cup shredded zucchini
> 1 can (about 8 ounces) whole
>   kernel corn, drained
> ¼ cup chopped onion
> ¼ teaspoon dried rosemary
>   leaves, crushed
> 1 cup milk
> ½ cup shredded Swiss cheese
>   (2 ounces)

1. In 2-quart saucepan, stir together soup mix, water, zucchini, corn, onion and rosemary. Over high heat, heat to boiling.
2. Reduce heat to low. Cover; simmer 8 to 10 minutes until chicken in soup is tender, stirring occasionally.
3. Stir in milk and cheese; cook until cheese is melted and soup is heated through, stirring often. Serve at once.
Makes 3 servings.

Chicken and Pasta Soup

1 (2½-pound) chicken, cut up
1 (46-fluid ounce) can COLLEGE INN® Chicken Broth
1 (16-ounce) can cut green beans
1 (6-ounce) can tomato paste
1 cup uncooked small shell macaroni
1 teaspoon dried basil leaves

In large saucepan, over medium-high heat, heat chicken and chicken broth to a boil; reduce heat. Cover; simmer 25 minutes or until chicken is tender. Remove chicken; cool slightly. Add remaining ingredients to broth. Heat to a boil; reduce heat. Cover; simmer 20 minutes or until macaroni is cooked. Meanwhile, remove chicken from bones and cut into bite-size pieces. Add to soup; cook 5 minutes more.
Makes 6 servings.

Quick Deli Turkey Soup

½ pound BUTTERBALL® Deli Turkey Breast, cubed
1 can (13¾ ounces) ready-to-serve chicken broth
1 can (14½ ounces) stewed tomatoes, undrained
1 small zucchini, cut up (about 1 cup)
¼ teaspoon dried basil leaves
½ cup cooked chili-mac pasta or macaroni

Combine broth, tomatoes with juice, zucchini and basil in large saucepan. Bring to a boil over high heat. Reduce heat to medium; simmer 10 minutes or until zucchini is tender. Stir in turkey and pasta. Continue heating until turkey is hot.
Makes 4 servings.

New England Style Turkey Chowder

2 cups diced cooked BUTTERBALL® turkey (¾ pound)
2 cans (17 ounces each) cream-style corn
2½ cups milk
1 cup chicken broth
1 cup diced potato
½ cup finely shredded carrot

½ cup finely chopped onion
1 teaspoon salt
¼ teaspoon ground black pepper

Combine all ingredients in large saucepan. Bring to boil over high heat; reduce heat to low. Cover and simmer 20 minutes, stirring occasionally.
Yield: 6 to 8 servings (9 cups).

Turkey Vegetable Soup

BUTTERBALL® turkey carcass
1 large onion, sliced
3 ribs celery, coarsely chopped
2 teaspoons salt
1 teaspoon dried rosemary leaves
½ teaspoon ground white pepper
2 bay leaves
6 sprigs fresh parsley
12 cups water
3 cubes chicken bouillon
2 cups sliced carrots
½ cup uncooked rice
1 package (10 ounces) frozen peas

Place turkey carcass, onion, celery, salt, rosemary, pepper, bay leaves and parsley in water in Dutch oven. Bring to boil over high heat; reduce heat to low. Cover and simmer 2 hours. Remove carcass. Strip turkey from bones; reserve turkey. Discard carcass. Strain broth and discard vegetables. Bring broth to boil over high heat; add bouillon cubes, carrots and rice. Reduce heat to low; simmer 10 to 12 minutes. Add peas and reserved turkey. Continue to cook 5 to 10 minutes or until vegetables and rice are tender, stirring occasionally.
Yield: 6 to 8 servings (10 cups).

Chicken Noodle Soup

1 (46-fluid ounce) can COLLEGE INN® Chicken Broth
½ pound boneless chicken, cut in bite-size pieces
1½ cups uncooked medium egg noodles
1 cup sliced carrots
½ cup chopped onion
⅓ cup sliced celery
1 teaspoon dried dill weed
¼ teaspoon ground black pepper

In large saucepan, over medium-high heat, heat chicken broth, chicken, noodles, carrots, onion, celery, dill and pepper to a boil. Reduce heat; simmer 20 minutes or until chicken and noodles are cooked.
Makes 8 servings.

Chicken Noodle Soup

Turkey-Barley Soup

2 quarts chicken or turkey stock
2 medium onions, chopped
½ cup sliced carrots
½ cup sliced celery
⅓ cup uncooked barley, rinsed
4 sprigs parsley
1 bay leaf
1 teaspoon salt
½ teaspoon poultry seasoning
1 can (16 ounces) tomatoes,
**   undrained, chopped**
2 cups cubed cooked turkey
¼ teaspoon TABASCO® pepper
**   sauce**
2 tablespoons chopped parsley
**   (optional)**

In large saucepot combine chicken stock, onions, carrots, celery, barley, parsley sprigs, bay leaf, salt and poultry seasoning. Cover; bring to a boil. Reduce heat; simmer 45 minutes or until barley is tender. Add tomatoes, turkey and Tabasco® sauce. Cook until heated through. Remove bay leaf. Garnish with chopped parsley, if desired.
Makes 8 servings.

Apple-Cheese Soup

2 apples, peeled and chopped
1 tablespoon water
¼ teaspoon ground nutmeg
¼ teaspoon cinnamon
1 can (11 ounces) CAMPBELL'S®
**   Condensed Cheddar Cheese**
**   Soup/Sauce**
¾ cup milk
**   Sour cream or plain yogurt for**
**   garnish**

To Microwave:

1. In 2-quart microwave-safe casserole, combine apples, water, nutmeg and cinnamon. Cover with lid; microwave on HIGH 5 minutes or until apples are very tender, stirring once during cooking.
2. Stir soup into apple mixture. In covered blender or food processor, blend soup mixture until smooth. Return to casserole. Stir in milk. Cover; microwave on HIGH 3 minutes or until hot and bubbling. Garnish with sour cream and additional nutmeg.
Makes about 3 cups or 3 servings.

   Note: This soup is equally delicious served hot or cold.

Scandinavian Raspberry Soup

2 (10-ounce) packages frozen
**   red raspberries in syrup,**
**   thawed**
½ cup orange juice
¼ cup REALEMON® Lemon Juice
**   from Concentrate**
1 tablespoon cornstarch
¾ cup chablis or other dry white
**   wine**
**   Fresh orange sections**
**   Raspberries, orange rind**
**   twists or mint leaves for**
**   garnish**
**   Sour cream**

In blender container, puree *1 package* raspberries; strain to remove seeds. In medium saucepan, combine pureed raspberries, orange juice, ReaLemon® brand and cornstarch; mix well. Over medium heat, cook and stir until slightly thickened and clear; cool. Stir in remaining package raspberries and chablis. Chill. To serve, place several orange sections in each bowl; add soup. Garnish as desired; serve with sour cream. Refrigerate leftovers.
Makes 8 to 10 servings.

Light and Lively Turkey Soup

2 cups cubed cooked
**   BUTTERBALL® turkey**
**   (¾ pound)**
1 cup uncooked instant rice
½ cup chopped celery
¼ cup minced fresh parsley
½ stick (¼ cup) butter or
**   margarine**
1 can (46 ounces) chicken broth
1 teaspoon finely shredded
**   lemon peel**
1 tablespoon lemon juice

Cook and stir rice, celery and parsley in butter in large saucepan over medium heat until celery is tender. Stir in remaining ingredients. Bring soup to boil over high heat. Reduce heat to low and simmer 15 minutes, stirring occasionally.
Yield: 5 to 6 servings (7 cups).

Scandinavian Raspberry Soup

Shrimp Creole Soup

½ cup sliced celery
½ cup sliced green onions
1 clove garlic, minced
1 tablespoon vegetable oil
1 pouch CAMPBELL'S® Chicken
    Rice Soup Mix
1 can (about 15 ounces)
    tomatoes, undrained, cut up
1 cup water
1 small bay leaf
¼ teaspoon sugar
⅛ teaspoon dried thyme leaves,
    crushed
⅛ teaspoon pepper
    Generous dash hot pepper
    sauce
½ pound medium shrimp, peeled
    and deveined

1. In 2-quart saucepan over medium-high heat, cook celery, green onions and garlic in oil until celery is tender, stirring often.
2. Stir in soup mix, tomatoes with their liquid, water, bay leaf, sugar, thyme, pepper and hot pepper sauce. Heat to boiling, stirring occasionally.
3. Reduce heat to low. Cover; simmer 5 minutes. Stir in shrimp. Cover; simmer 5 minutes more or until shrimp are opaque. Remove bay leaf before serving.
Makes 3 servings.

Shrimp Creole Soup

Fish Soup Florentine

1 pouch CAMPBELL'S® Noodle
    Soup and Recipe Mix
2½ cups water
1 cup chopped fresh spinach
¼ teaspoon dried oregano
    leaves, crushed
    Dash crushed red pepper
½ pound flounder or other fish
    fillets, cut into ½-inch
    pieces
2 tablespoons Chablis or other
    dry white wine

1. In 2-quart saucepan, stir together soup mix, water, spinach, oregano and red pepper. Over high heat, heat to boiling. Reduce heat to low. Cover; simmer 5 minutes.
2. Stir in fish and wine. Cover; simmer 5 minutes more or until fish flakes easily when tested with a fork. Serve at once.
Makes 4 servings.

Skillet Seafood Bisque

¼ cup butter or margarine
1 cup sliced CAMPBELL'S
    FRESH® Mushrooms
2 tablespoons chopped fresh
    chives
1 clove garlic, minced
3 tablespoons all-purpose flour
1 can (10¾ ounces)
    CAMPBELL'S® Condensed
    Chicken Broth
1 pound medium shrimp, shelled
    and deveined
½ cup Chablis or other dry white
    wine
½ cup heavy cream
1 tablespoon chopped fresh
    parsley
    Fresh dill sprigs

1. In 10-inch skillet over medium heat, in hot butter, cook mushrooms, chives and garlic until tender, stirring occasionally. Stir in flour until smooth. Gradually stir in chicken broth. Heat to boiling, stirring constantly.
2. Add shrimp. Reduce heat to low. Cover; simmer about 5 minutes or until shrimp are done. Stir in wine, cream and parsley; heat through. Ladle into bowls; top with dill sprigs.
Makes about 4½ cups or 6 servings.

Shrimp Bisque Orleans

¼ cup butter or margarine
1 large onion, chopped
½ cup chopped celery
2 cloves garlic, minced
2 tablespoons flour
2 tablespoons tomato paste
3 cups milk
2 cups clam or fish broth
1 bay leaf
½ teaspoon dried basil leaves
½ teaspoon TABASCO® pepper
    sauce
¼ teaspoon salt
1 pound shrimp, peeled,
    deveined
¼ cup sliced green onions

In large saucepot melt butter; add chopped onion, celery and garlic. Cook 5 minutes or until tender. Stir in flour and tomato paste; cook 1 minute. Remove from heat. Gradually stir in milk and broth; add bay leaf, basil, Tabasco® sauce and salt. Bring to a boil. Reduce heat; simmer 10 minutes. Add shrimp and green onions; simmer 5 minutes longer or until shrimp turn pink. Remove bay leaf.
Makes 6 servings.

Fisherman's Bouillabaisse

- **¼ cup olive or vegetable oil**
- **2 cloves garlic, finely chopped**
- **1 cup water**
- **½ cup dry white wine**
- **1 envelope LIPTON® Onion or Onion-Mushroom Recipe Soup Mix**
- **1 tablespoon finely chopped parsley**
- **1 teaspoon thyme leaves**
- **1 can (14½ ounces) whole peeled tomatoes, undrained and chopped**
- **3 lobster tails (about 1½ pounds), cut into 3-inch pieces**
- **1 pound red snapper, cod, halibut or haddock, cut into pieces**
- **6 clams, well scrubbed**
- **6 mussels, well scrubbed**

In large saucepan or stockpot, heat oil and cook garlic over medium heat until golden. Add water, wine, onion recipe soup mix, parsley and thyme; blend thoroughly. Stir in tomatoes. Bring to a boil, then simmer covered 15 minutes. Add lobster and snapper and simmer 10 minutes. Add clams and mussels and simmer an additional 5 minutes or until shells open. (Discard any unopened shells.) Serve, if desired, with bread or rolls.
Makes about 4 (2-cup) servings.

Seafood Bisque

- **½ pound shrimp, shelled, deveined and cut in half crosswise**
- **½ pound sea scallops, coarsely chopped**
- **1 (16-ounce) can whole new potatoes, drained and diced**
- **1 clove garlic, crushed**
- **¼ cup BLUE BONNET® Margarine**
- **⅔ cup all-purpose flour**
- **2 (13¾-fluid ounce) cans COLLEGE INN® Chicken Broth**
- **½ teaspoon ground white pepper**
- **1 cup light cream or half-and-half**

In large saucepan, over medium heat, cook shrimp, scallops, potatoes and garlic in margarine until seafood is done. Stir in flour until blended. Gradually add chicken broth and pep-

per. Heat to a boil, stirring constantly. Boil 1 minute. Stir in light cream; heat through. (Do not boil.)
Makes 6 servings.

Mussel Rice Soup

- **1 cup coarsely chopped onion**
- **1 tablespoon butter or margarine**
- **3 ribs celery, sliced**
- **5 cups chicken broth**
- **½ cup uncooked rice**
- **½ teaspoon salt**
- **½ teaspoon dried basil, crushed**
- **¼ teaspoon pepper**
- **2 medium tomatoes, peeled, seeded, chopped**
- **2 cans (4 ounces each) mussels,* drained**
- **2 cups torn spinach**

Cook and stir onion in melted butter in Dutch oven over medium-high heat until crisp-tender. Add celery; cook 1 minute more. Add broth, rice and seasonings. Bring to a boil over high heat. Reduce heat to low. Cover and simmer 10 minutes. Stir in tomatoes and mussels; simmer 5 minutes more or until rice is tender. Add spinach. Serve immediately.

***Substitution:** Use 1 can (10 ounces) whole clams, drained, for the mussels.

*Favorite recipe from **Rice Council***

Mussel Rice Soup

Tomato-Shrimp Soup

- **2 tablespoons butter or margarine**
- **½ cup thinly sliced onion**
- **¼ cup chopped green pepper**
- **1 medium clove garlic, minced**
- **3 cups V8® Vegetable Juice**
- **1 small bay leaf**
- **¾ pound medium shrimp, shelled and deveined**
- **½ pound flounder or other whitefish fillets, cut into 2-inch pieces**
- **Toasted PEPPERIDGE FARM® Fully Baked French-Style Bread slices**

1. In 2-quart saucepan over medium heat, in hot butter, cook onion, green pepper and garlic until vegetables are tender.
2. Stir in V8 juice and bay leaf. Heat to boiling. Reduce heat to low; simmer, uncovered, 10 minutes.
3. Add shrimp and fish. Cook until shrimp are pink and opaque and fish flakes easily with fork. Discard bay leaf. To serve: Ladle soup over toasted bread in bowls.
Makes 5 cups or 5 main-dish servings.

Per serving: 177 calories, 21 g protein, 7 g fat, 9 g carbohydrate, 663 mg sodium, 119 mg cholesterol.

Split Pea and Meatball Soup

- **1 cup dry green split peas, rinsed and drained**
- **1 can (10½ ounces) CAMPBELL'S® Condensed Beef Broth**
- **2 cups water**
- **1 cup chopped onion**
- **½ teaspoon summer savory leaves, crushed**
- **⅛ teaspoon pepper**
- **½ pound ground beef**
- **¼ cup soft bread crumbs**
- **1 egg**
- **1 tablespoon chopped fresh parsley**
- **1 clove garlic, minced**
- **1 cup chopped carrots**
- **1 cup sliced celery**
- **1 can (14½ ounces) stewed tomatoes**

1. In 4-quart Dutch oven over high heat, combine peas, beef broth, water, onion, savory and pepper. Heat to boiling; reduce heat to low. Cover; simmer 1 hour.

2. Meanwhile, for meatballs, in medium bowl, combine ground beef, bread crumbs, egg, parsley and garlic. Mix lightly, but well. Shape into 36 balls, using 1 rounded teaspoonful for each. Set aside.

3. Add carrots, celery and tomatoes to soup mixture. Over high heat, heat to boiling. Add meatballs; reduce heat to low. Cover; simmer 30 minutes until vegetables are tender and meat is done.

Makes about 8 cups or 6 servings.

Creamy Clam Bisque

- **¼ cup chopped onion**
- **2 tablespoons margarine or butter**
- **3 tablespoons flour Dash pepper**
- **½ cup dry white wine**
- **2 (6½-ounce) cans SNOW'S® or DOXSEE® Chopped Clams, drained, reserving liquid**
- **2 cups (1 pint) BORDEN® or MEADOW GOLD® Half-and-Half**
- **1 egg yolk Paprika, optional**

Hearty Vegetable Soup

In medium saucepan, cook onion in margarine until tender. Gradually stir in flour and pepper; add wine and reserved clam liquid. Cook and stir until thickened; remove from heat. Blend half-and-half with egg yolk; stir into wine mixture along with clams. Heat through *(do not boil)*. Garnish with paprika if desired. Refrigerate leftovers.

Makes about 1 quart.

Sausage Corn Chowder

- **1 package (8 ounces) SWIFT PREMIUM® BROWN 'N SERVE™ Microwave Sausage Links, thawed, cut into ½-inch slices**
- **2 cups cubed potatoes**
- **¾ cup chopped onion**
- **½ cup chopped celery**
- **¼ cup water**
- **1 can (12 ounces) corn with red and green bell peppers**
- **1 can (17 ounces) cream-style corn**
- **2 cups milk**
- **1 teaspoon salt**
- **⅛ teaspoon ground thyme Dash ground white pepper**

Microwave Directions: Place potatoes, onion, celery and water in 2-quart microwave-safe bowl. Cover with vented plastic wrap and *microwave* on High (100%) 9 to 10 minutes or until vegetables are tender, stirring twice. Stir in sausage, corn, cream-style corn, milk, salt, thyme and pepper. Cover and *microwave* on High 7 to 8 minutes or until hot, stirring twice.

Makes 6 servings.

Hearty Vegetable Soup

- **3 pounds beef shanks, cracked**
- **8 cups water**
- **3 tablespoons WYLER'S® or STEERO® Beef-Flavor Instant Bouillon or 9 Beef-Flavor Bouillon Cubes**
- **2 bay leaves**
- **1 (28-ounce) can whole tomatoes, undrained**
- **1 cup pared, sliced carrots**
- **½ cup chopped celery**
- **½ cup chopped onion**
- **1 teaspoon thyme leaves**
- **1 cup uncooked CREAMETTES® Elbow Macaroni**
- **2 cups sliced zucchini (2 small)**

In large kettle or Dutch oven, combine shanks, water, bouillon and bay leaves. Bring to a boil; simmer covered 1½ hours or until meat is tender. Remove shanks and bay leaves; cut meat into cubes. Discard bones. Cool stock; skim fat from surface. Add meat, tomatoes, carrots, celery, onion and thyme; simmer covered 20 minutes. Add macaroni and zucchini. Cook 10 minutes longer or until tender. Refrigerate leftovers.

Makes about 3 quarts.

Hot and Sour Soup

Sopa de Sonora

7½ cups water, divided
1 cup dry pinto beans, rinsed
1 pound boneless lean pork shoulder, trimmed, cut into 1-inch cubes
1 tablespoon vegetable oil
1 can (14½ ounces) ready-to-serve beef broth
1½ tablespoons LAWRY'S® Minced Onion with Green Onion Flakes
¼ teaspoon LAWRY'S® Garlic Powder with Parsley
1 package (1⅝ ounces) LAWRY'S® Chili Seasoning Mix
2 cups thinly sliced carrots LAWRY'S® Seasoned Salt Condiments*

Place 3 cups of the water and the beans in 3-quart saucepan. Bring to a boil over high heat; boil 2 minutes. Remove from heat. Cover and let soak 1 hour. Drain beans; discard water.

Brown pork in hot oil in Dutch oven over medium-high heat. Add beans, remaining 4½ cups water, the broth, minced onion, garlic powder and chili seasoning mix. Bring to a boil over high heat. Reduce heat to low. Cover and simmer 1½ hours. Add carrots; simmer, covered, about 30 minutes or until carrots are tender. Season to

taste with seasoned salt. Ladle into bowls. Serve with condiments.
Makes 6 to 8 servings.

Condiments: Cherry tomato quarters, sliced green onions, chopped cilantro, lime wedges, sour cream or LAWRY'S® Chunky Taco Sauce.

Frank and Vegetable Soup

1 package (16 ounces) ECKRICH® Franks, cut into ¼-inch slices
1½ cups chopped onions
1 cup sliced carrots
½ cup sliced celery
1 tablespoon butter or margarine
1 can (14½ ounces) whole tomatoes, undrained
1 package (10 ounces) frozen cut green beans, thawed
5 cups beef broth or bouillon Grated Parmesan cheese

Saute onions, carrots and celery in butter in large saucepan over medium heat 5 minutes. Add tomatoes with juice; break up tomatoes. Mix in beans and broth. Bring to a boil over high heat. Reduce heat to low; simmer 15 minutes. Add franks and simmer 5 minutes more. Top each serving with cheese.
Makes 8 servings.

Hot and Sour Soup

1 ounce dried Oriental mushrooms
2 cans (13¾ ounces each) chicken broth or 3⅓ cups chicken stock
2 cups orange juice
¾ pound boneless pork, cut into julienne strips
1 cup carrots, cut into julienne strips
1 can (8 ounces) sliced water chestnuts, drained
1 tablespoon soy sauce
¼ teaspoon salt
½ pound tofu, drained and cut into ½-inch cubes
3 tablespoons white wine vinegar
¾ teaspoon TABASCO® pepper sauce
¼ cup cornstarch
⅓ cup water

In small bowl pour enough boiling water over mushrooms to cover. Let stand 30 minutes; drain. In large saucepot combine mushrooms, broth, orange juice, pork, carrots, water chestnuts, soy sauce and salt. Bring to a boil. Reduce heat; simmer 3 minutes or until pork is cooked. Add tofu, vinegar and Tabasco® sauce. Combine cornstarch and water until smooth; add to soup. Stir constantly, bring to a boil over medium heat and boil for 1 minute.
Makes 8 servings.

Corned Beef & Cabbage Chowder

2 tablespoons butter or margarine
½ cup thinly sliced celery
½ cup finely chopped onion
2 cups water
2 cups coarsely shredded cabbage
1 cup thinly sliced carrots
1 envelope LIPTON® Noodle Soup Mix with Real Chicken Broth
1 teaspoon dry mustard
1½ tablespoons all-purpose flour
2 cups milk
¼ pound thinly sliced cooked corned beef, cut into thin strips

In large saucepan or stockpot, melt butter and cook celery and onion over medium heat until tender. Stir in water, cabbage and carrots. Bring to a boil, then simmer covered, stirring occasionally, 15 minutes or until vegetables are almost tender. Stir in noodle soup mix, then mustard and flour blended with milk. Bring just to the boiling point, then simmer, stirring constantly, until chowder is thickened, about 5 minutes. Stir in corned beef and heat through, but do not boil.

Makes about 3 (1¾-cup) servings.

Microwave Directions: In 3-quart casserole, heat butter at HIGH (Full Power) 1 minute. Add celery and onion and heat 5 minutes or until vegetables are tender, stirring once. Add water, cabbage and carrots. Heat covered, stirring occasionally, 15 minutes or until vegetables are tender. Stir in noodle soup mix, then mustard and flour blended with milk. Heat covered, stirring occasionally, 7 minutes or until chowder is thickened. Stir in corned beef. Let stand covered 5 minutes.

Albóndingas Soup

- **1 pound ground beef**
- **¼ cup seasoned dry bread crumbs**
- **2 tablespoons minced onion**
- **2 tablespoons water**
- **1 egg**
- **½ teaspoon salt**
- **¾ teaspoon TABASCO® pepper sauce, divided**
- **1 large green pepper**
- **2 tablespoons olive or vegetable oil**
- **1 medium onion, chopped**
- **1 clove garlic, minced**
- **4 cups beef broth**
- **1 can (16 ounces) tomatoes, undrained**
- **¼ teaspoon saffron threads, crumbled**

In medium bowl combine beef, crumbs, minced onion, water, egg, salt and ¼ teaspoon Tabasco® sauce; mix well. Shape into 1-inch meatballs. Cover; refrigerate. Coarsely chop enough green pepper to yield ½ cup; cut remainder into thin strips for garnish.

In large saucepot heat oil; cook ½ cup chopped green pepper, chopped onion and garlic 3 minutes or until tender. Stir in broth, tomatoes, saffron and remaining ½ teaspoon Tabasco® sauce. Bring to a boil, reduce heat and simmer uncovered 30 minutes; stir occasionally. Add meatballs;

simmer covered 20 minutes longer or until meatballs are cooked. Garnish with green pepper strips.

Makes 6 servings.

Microwave Directions: Prepare meatballs as directed above. Chop and cut green pepper as directed above. In 3-quart microwave-safe casserole place *1 tablespoon* oil, chopped green pepper, chopped onion and garlic. Cover loosely with plastic wrap; cook on High 2 to 4 minutes or until vegetables are softened. Stir in broth, *drained* canned tomatoes, saffron and remaining ½ teaspoon Tabasco® sauce. Cook uncovered on High 10 minutes. Add meatballs and continue to cook uncovered on High 15 to 18 minutes or until meatballs are cooked; stir twice during cooking. Garnish with green pepper strips.

Beefy Vegetable Soup

- **1 tablespoon vegetable oil**
- **2 pounds boneless beef chuck, cut into 1-inch cubes**
- **2 medium onions, chopped**
- **1 can (16 ounces) tomatoes, undrained**
- **½ cup uncooked barley, rinsed**
- **10 cups water**
- **⅓ cup soy sauce**
- **2 teaspoons dried thyme leaves**
- **½ teaspoon salt**
- **¼ pound fresh spinach leaves**
- **4 large carrots, shredded**
- **2 medium potatoes, pared, cubed**
- **2 large celery stalks, sliced**
- **¼ pound green beans, cut into pieces**
- **½ teaspoon TABASCO® pepper sauce**

In large heavy saucepot or Dutch oven heat oil over medium-high heat; add beef and brown on all sides. Remove and set aside. In same pot over medium heat, cook onions 3 minutes or until tender. Return meat to pot; add tomatoes, barley, water, soy sauce, thyme and salt. Cover. Bring to a boil. Reduce heat; simmer 1 hour. Add spinach, carrots, potatoes, celery, beans and Tabasco® sauce. Simmer covered 45 minutes longer or until meat and vegetables are tender.

Makes 10 to 12 servings.

Albóndingas Soup

BLT Soup

**6 slices bacon, cut in ¹/₂-inch
    pieces
1 medium onion, sliced
2 (13³/₄-fluid ounce) cans
    COLLEGE INN® Chicken or
    Beef Broth
1 (14¹/₂-ounce) can peeled
    tomatoes, undrained and cut
    up
2 tablespoons A.1.® Steak Sauce
2 cups shredded iceberg lettuce**

In large saucepan, cook bacon until
crisp; remove and crumble bacon.
Pour off all but 2 tablespoons drippings. Cook onion in reserved drippings for 2 to 3 minutes. Add broth,
tomatoes and steak sauce. Heat to a
boil; reduce heat. Cover and simmer
10 minutes. Add lettuce; simmer 2
minutes. Stir in bacon.
Makes 4 to 6 servings.

BLT Soup

Ham and Pea Noodle Soup

**1 cup diced cooked ham
    (6 ounces)
1 tablespoon butter or
    margarine
1 pouch CAMPBELL'S® Noodle
    Soup and Recipe Mix
2¹/₂ cups water
¹/₂ cup frozen peas**

1. In 2-quart saucepan over medium
heat, cook ham in butter until
browned.
2. Stir in soup mix, water and peas.
Heat to boiling. Reduce heat to low.
Cover; simmer 7 to 10 minutes until
noodles and peas are tender, stirring
occasionally. Serve at once.
Makes 2 servings.

Vermont Vegetable Stew

**1 pound ECKRICH® Smoked
    Sausage, sliced thin
1 medium onion, chopped
1 tablespoon vegetable oil
3 cups water
2 teaspoons beef bouillon
    granules
1 bay leaf
¹/₂ teaspoon dried thyme leaves
3 carrots, sliced
3 ribs celery, sliced**

**¹/₄ head green cabbage, cut into
    1-inch pieces
2 tablespoons uncooked rice
1 can (8 ounces) tomato sauce
1 can (14¹/₂ ounces) red kidney
    beans
1 can (28 ounces) whole
    tomatoes, undrained, cut up**

Saute onion in oil in Dutch oven until
tender. Add remaining ingredients.
Bring to a boil over high heat. Reduce
heat to low; cover and simmer 30 minutes or until vegetables are tender.
Makes 8 servings.

Octoberfest Sausage Soup

**¹/₂ pound ECKRICH® Smoked
    Sausage
1 cup beef broth
1 cup chicken broth
¹/₄ cup coarsely chopped celery
¹/₄ cup coarsely chopped onion
¹/₄ cup coarsely chopped green
    bell pepper
1 medium potato, pared, diced**

**2 tablespoons cornstarch,
    dissolved in 2 tablespoons
    water
1 cup (4 ounces) shredded
    Swiss cheese
1 can (8 ounces) sauerkraut,
    drained
2 cups half and half
¹/₄ teaspoon ground white pepper
2 green onions, sliced**

Combine broths, celery, onion, green
pepper and potato in large saucepan;
bring to a boil over high heat. Reduce
heat to low; simmer until vegetables
are crisp-tender, about 15 minutes.
Add dissolved cornstarch; cook and
stir until soup thickens. Cut sausage
into quarters lengthwise, then cut
crosswise into ¹/₄-inch pieces. Add sausage, cheese, sauerkraut, half and
half and white pepper. Stir. Continue
heating until mixture is hot. DO NOT
BOIL. Serve immediately. Garnish
with green onions.
Makes 4 to 6 servings.

Sausage and Lentil Soup

1 package (10 ounces)
   ECKRICH® SMOK-Y-LINKS®
   Sausages, cut into ½-inch
   slices
½ cup chopped onion
½ cup sliced carrot
½ cup sliced celery
1 clove garlic, minced
2 tablespoons vegetable oil
1 cup lentils, sorted, rinsed
6 cups water
3 teaspoons beef bouillon
   granules
1 can (14½ ounces) whole
   tomatoes, undrained, cut up
   Dash ground black pepper
2 teaspoons lemon juice

Cook onion, carrot, celery and garlic
in oil in Dutch oven over medium heat
5 minutes. Add lentils, water and
bouillon granules. Bring to a boil over
high heat. Reduce heat to low; cover
and simmer 30 minutes or until lentils are tender. Add sausage, tomatoes
with juice and pepper to lentil mixture. Simmer 10 minutes. Stir in
lemon juice.
Makes 6 to 8 servings.

Chili Soup Jarlsberg

1 pound beef round steak, diced
2 tablespoons vegetable oil
2 cans (14½ ounces each)
   ready-to-serve beef broth
1 can (15 ounces) dark red
   kidney beans
1 can (14½ ounces) tomatoes,
   chopped, undrained
1 medium green bell pepper,
   chopped
1 medium red bell pepper,
   chopped
1 large onion, chopped
1 large clove garlic, minced
3¼ teaspoons chili powder,
   divided
¼ teaspoon ground cumin
1½ cups (6 ounces) shredded
   JARLSBERG cheese, divided
¼ cup butter or margarine,
   softened
1 small clove garlic, minced
12 KAVLI Norwegian Thick-Style
   Crispbreads

Brown beef in hot oil in large, deep
saucepan over medium-high heat.
Add broth. Bring to a boil over high

heat. Reduce heat to low. Cover and
simmer 1 hour. Add beans, tomatoes,
peppers, onion, large garlic clove, 3
teaspoons of the chili powder and the
cumin. Simmer, covered, 30 minutes.
Gradually blend in ½ cup of the
cheese. Heat just until cheese melts.

Blend butter, small garlic clove and
remaining ¼ teaspoon chili powder in
small bowl. Spread on crispbreads; arrange on cookie sheet. Bake in preheated 375°F oven several minutes or
until butter is melted. Sprinkle with
½ cup of the cheese. Bake just until
cheese is melted.

Ladle soup into bowls. Garnish with
remaining ½ cup cheese. Serve with
crispbreads.
Makes 6 servings.

Favorite recipe from **Norseland Foods, Inc.**

Chunky Beef Barley Soup

1½ pounds beef stew meat, cut
   into ½-inch cubes
2 tablespoons all-purpose flour
2 cloves garlic, minced
¼ cup vegetable oil
2 quarts water

1 can (14½ ounces) tomatoes,
   coarsely chopped,
   undrained
1 cup coarsely chopped onion
½ cup QUAKER® Scotch® Brand
   Pearled Barley*
1 tablespoon salt (optional)
1 teaspoon dried basil, crushed
⅛ teaspoon pepper
1 package (16 ounces) frozen
   vegetable medley

Dredge meat in flour. Brown meat
with garlic in hot oil in 4-quart Dutch
oven over medium-high heat. Add water, tomatoes, onion, barley, salt, basil
and pepper. Bring to a boil over high
heat. Reduce heat to low. Cover and
simmer 1 hour or until meat and barley are tender. Add frozen vegetables.
Return to a boil over high heat. Reduce heat to low. Simmer 5 minutes or
until vegetables are tender. Additional water may be added if soup becomes too thick upon standing.
Makes about 12 servings.

Substitution: Use ¾ cup Quaker®
Scotch® Quick Barley for the pearled
barley. Add quick barley with frozen
vegetables. Return to a boil; cover and
simmer 10 to 12 minutes or until barley is tender.

Chili Soup Jarlsberg

SALADS

Crisp vegetables, luscious fruits, substantial potatoes or pasta—along with meats, poultry or fish—combine to make salads of dazzling variety. Add to your salad repertoire with creations that complement a main course or make satisfying meals by themselves.

Classic Spinach Salad

½ **pound fresh spinach leaves (about 10 cups)**
1 **cup sliced mushrooms**
1 **medium tomato, cut into wedges**
⅓ **cup seasoned croutons**
¼ **cup chopped red onion**
4 **slices bacon, crisp-cooked and crumbled**
½ **cup WISH-BONE® Classic Dijon Vinaigrette or Lite Classic Dijon Vinaigrette Dressing**
1 **hard-cooked egg, sliced**

In large salad bowl, combine spinach, mushrooms, tomato, croutons, red onion and bacon. Add classic Dijon vinaigrette dressing and toss gently. Garnish with egg.
Makes about 6 side-dish servings.

Tomato and Onion Salad

6 **tablespoons vegetable oil**
3 **tablespoons tarragon or cider vinegar**
1 **clove garlic, halved**
1 **tablespoon chopped parsley**
¼ **teaspoon dry mustard**
¼ **teaspoon dried oregano leaves**
¼ **teaspoon salt**
¼ **teaspoon TABASCO® pepper sauce**
3 **tomatoes, sliced**
1 **large onion, sliced**

In small bowl combine oil, vinegar, garlic, parsley, mustard, oregano, salt and Tabasco® sauce; mix well. Cover; let stand at least 30 minutes. Remove garlic. Arrange tomato slices alternately with onion rings on serving platter. Top with salad dressing.
Makes 6 servings.

Firecracker Salad

1 **tablespoon sesame seed, toasted**
2 **tablespoons distilled white vinegar**
2 **teaspoons sugar**
1 **teaspoon minced fresh ginger root**
4 **teaspoons KIKKOMAN Soy Sauce**
1 **cup julienne-stripped radishes**
1 **cup julienne-stripped cucumber**
4 **cups finely shredded iceberg lettuce**
1½ **teaspoons minced fresh cilantro or parsley**

Measure sesame seed, vinegar, sugar, ginger and soy sauce into jar with screw-top lid; cover and shake well until sugar dissolves. Combine radishes, cucumber and 3 tablespoons dressing; cover and refrigerate 30 minutes, stirring occasionally. Toss lettuce with cilantro in large bowl. Pour radish mixture and remaining dressing over lettuce. Toss lightly to combine.
Makes 6 servings.

Cheese and Red Bean Salad

1 **(16-ounce) container BORDEN® or MEADOW GOLD® Cottage Cheese**
1 **(15½-ounce) can kidney beans, drained**
½ **cup chopped green pepper**
½ **cup sliced pimiento-stuffed olives**
½ **cup chopped onion**
¼ **teaspoon seasoned pepper Lettuce leaves**

In large bowl, combine all ingredients except lettuce; mix well. Chill. Serve on lettuce. Refrigerate leftovers.
Makes 6 to 8 servings.

Celery Seed Dressing (page 92)

Fresh Vegetable Salad

½ cup WISH-BONE® Italian
    Dressing
1 tablespoon chopped fresh
    tarragon leaves*
1 teaspoon lemon juice
¼ teaspoon pepper
    Assorted Fresh Vegetables**
½ cup sliced green onions
    Salt to taste

In large salad bowl, blend Italian
dressing, tarragon, lemon juice and
pepper. Toss with Assorted Fresh Vegetables and green onions; add salt.
Cover and marinate in refrigerator,
stirring occasionally, 3 hours.
Makes about 6 side-dish servings.
  ***Substitution:** Use 1 teaspoon
dried tarragon leaves.
  ****Assorted Fresh Vegetables:** Use
any combination of the following to
equal 6 cups—broccoli florets, cauliflowerets, sliced red, green or yellow
pepper, carrots, yellow squash, zucchini or snow peas.
  Hint: For crisp-tender vegetables,
cook vegetables in boiling water
about 1 minute, then immediately
drain and rinse with very cold water
until completely cool.
  Note: Also terrific with Wish-
Bone® Robusto Italian, Herbal Italian, Italian & Cheese, Blended Italian
or Classic Dijon Vinaigrette Dressing.

Lynn's Salad

1 head DOLE™ Cauliflower, cut
    into flowerets
1 bunch DOLE™ Broccoli, cut
    into flowerets
1 jar (6 ounces) marinated
    artichoke hearts, drained
8 ounces mozzarella cheese,
    cubed
2 cups pitted ripe olives
    Dash garlic salt
1 bottle (8 ounces) Italian salad
    dressing

In large bowl, combine cauliflower,
broccoli, artichokes, cheese, olives and
garlic salt. Pour salad dressing over
vegetable mixture. Refrigerate, covered, overnight. Drain salad dressing
(save for another use, if desired).
Makes 6 servings.

Marinated Tomatoes & Cucumbers

Marinated Tomatoes & Cucumbers

2 large tomatoes, sliced
1 small cucumber, sliced
1 small onion, sliced
⅓ cup vegetable oil
⅓ cup REALEMON® Lemon Juice
    from Concentrate
1 tablespoon sugar
¼ teaspoon basil leaves
½ teaspoon salt
1 clove garlic, finely chopped
    Lettuce leaves
    Imitation bacon or cooked
    crumbled bacon

In 2-quart shallow baking dish, arrange tomatoes, cucumber and onion.
In small bowl, combine remaining ingredients except lettuce and imitation
bacon; pour over tomatoes. Chill several hours. Line platter with lettuce;
arrange tomatoes, cucumbers and onion on top and sprinkle with imitation
bacon.
Makes 4 to 6 servings.

Pennsylvania Dutch Chow Chow

1 cup cauliflowerets
1 cup whole kernel corn
1 cup green beans cut into
    1½-inch pieces
1 jar (16 ounces) VLASIC®
    Country Classic Sweet
    Chunky Relish
½ cup cooked or canned kidney
    beans, drained
¼ cup thinly sliced celery

1. In 2-quart saucepan over medium
heat, in boiling water, cook cauliflower, corn and green beans 4 minutes or until tender-crisp. Drain.
2. In medium bowl, combine cooked
vegetables, relish, kidney beans and
celery. Cover; refrigerate until serving time, at least 4 hours, stirring occasionally.
Makes 5 cups or 10 servings.
  To Microwave: In 1-quart microwave-safe casserole, combine cauliflower, corn, green beans and 2
tablespoons water. Microwave, covered, on HIGH 5 minutes or until vegetables are tender-crisp, stirring
twice. Proceed as above.

Bean Sprout & Spinach Salad

Boiling water
1 pound fresh spinach, washed
1/2 pound fresh bean sprouts
1 tablespoon sugar
4 teaspoons distilled white vinegar
1 tablespoon KIKKOMAN Soy Sauce
1 teaspoon sesame seed, toasted

Pour boiling water over spinach in colander; rinse immediately with cold water. Drain thoroughly and place in medium serving bowl. Repeat procedure with bean sprouts and place in same bowl. Combine sugar, vinegar, soy sauce and sesame seed; pour over vegetables and toss to combine. Cover and refrigerate at least 1 hour before serving.
Makes 4 servings.

Simple Salad Élégante

1/4 cup WISH-BONE® Italian or Lite Italian Dressing
10 small snow peas (about 1½ ounces)
1/2 cup sliced mushrooms
1/2 small red pepper, cut into rings
2 cups mixed salad greens

In small bowl, combine all ingredients except salad greens. Cover and marinate in refrigerator, stirring occasionally, 4 hours or overnight. To serve, arrange marinated vegetables on salad greens.
Makes about 2 side-dish servings.

Sunflower Seed Cole Slaw

1 can (20 ounces) DOLE® Pineapple Tidbits
1/2 pound DOLE™ Carrots, shredded
1/4 pound DOLE™ Green Cabbage, shredded
1/4 pound red cabbage, shredded
1/2 cup sunflower seeds, lightly toasted
1/2 cup mayonnaise
2 tablespoons DOLE® Frozen Pineapple Orange Juice Concentrate

1/4 teaspoon salt
Pinch white pepper

Drain pineapple; reserve 2 tablespoons juice. In bowl, combine pineapple, carrots, green and red cabbage and sunflower seeds. To make dressing, in 1-quart measure, combine mayonnaise, juice concentrate, reserved pineapple juice, salt and pepper. Pour over salad mixture and toss. Refrigerate, covered, until ready to serve.
Makes 8 servings.

Dilly Bean Salad

1 envelope LIPTON® Onion Recipe Soup Mix
3/4 cup water
1/4 cup red wine vinegar
1/4 cup oil
1/4 cup snipped fresh dill*
1 tablespoon finely chopped parsley
1 small clove garlic, finely chopped
1 pound green beans, cooked**
1 can (16 ounces) chick peas (garbanzos) or red kidney beans, rinsed and drained (optional)
2 cups fresh or canned sliced mushrooms

In medium bowl, blend onion recipe soup mix, water and vinegar. Stir in oil, dill, parsley and garlic. Toss with remaining ingredients; chill.
Makes about 6 cups salad.

   *Substitution: Use 1 tablespoon dried dill weed.

   **Substitution: Use 2 cans (16 ounces each) cut green beans, drained.

Dole's Summer Vegetable Salad

1 head DOLE™ Lettuce
2 DOLE™ Tomatoes
1 cucumber
1/2 DOLE™ Red Bell Pepper
1/4 red onion
1 cup sliced DOLE™ Celery
1 cup snow peas, ends and strings removed
1 cup sliced DOLE™ Cauliflower Dill Dressing (recipe follows)

Tear lettuce into bite-size pieces. Cut tomatoes into wedges. Slice cucumber, red pepper and red onion. Place all vegetables in salad bowl; toss with Dill Dressing.
Makes 4 servings.
DILL DRESSING: In 1-quart measure, combine 1/2 cup *each* dairy sour cream and mayonnaise, 1 tablespoon vinegar, 1 teaspoon *each* dried dill weed and onion powder, 1 teaspoon Dijon mustard, 3/4 teaspoon garlic salt and cracked pepper to taste. Refrigerate, covered, until ready to serve.

Corn Relish Salad

3/4 cup sugar
1/2 cup CRISCO® Oil
1/4 cup white vinegar
1/2 teaspoon celery seed
1/4 teaspoon whole mustard seed
1 can (17 ounces) whole kernel corn, drained
1 can (16 ounces) sauerkraut, pressed to remove excess liquid
1/2 cup chopped green pepper
1/3 cup chopped onion
1 jar (2 ounces) diced pimiento, drained

Combine sugar, Crisco® Oil, vinegar, celery seed and mustard seed in medium serving bowl. Stir until sugar dissolves. Add remaining ingredients. Mix well. Cover and refrigerate at least 8 hours or overnight. Drain and stir before serving.
6 to 8 servings.

Corn Relish Salad

Spinach Salad with Raspberry Dressing

½ cup plain nonfat yogurt
¼ cup fresh or frozen red
    raspberries, thawed if frozen
1 tablespoon skim milk
1½ teaspoons chopped fresh mint
    or ½ teaspoon dried mint,
    crushed
4 to 6 cups fresh spinach,
    washed, drained and
    trimmed
2 large fresh mushrooms, sliced
1 tablespoon sesame seeds,
    toasted
4 to 6 red onion rings
6 slices ARMOUR® Lower Salt
    Bacon, cooked crisp and
    crumbled

Carefully combine yogurt, raspberries, milk and mint in small bowl; set aside. Combine spinach, mushrooms and sesame seeds in medium bowl; mix well. Arrange spinach mixture evenly on 2 individual salad plates; top with red onion rings. Drizzle yogurt dressing over salads; sprinkle with bacon. Garnish with fresh raspberries and mint sprig, if desired. *Makes 2 servings.*

Nutrition Information Per Serving: 200 calories, 15.8 g protein, 10.1 g fat, 14.1 g carbohydrates, 19.1 mg cholesterol, 556 mg sodium.

Citrus, Avocado & Bacon Salad

3 tablespoons orange juice
    concentrate, thawed
2 tablespoons vegetable oil
1 tablespoon lime juice
1 tablespoon honey
1 tablespoon white vinegar
3 cups mixed salad greens,
    washed and drained
½ avocado, peeled, pitted and
    sliced
6 slices ARMOUR® Lower Salt
    Bacon, cut in half and
    cooked crisp
1 (11-ounce) can mandarin
    oranges, drained

Combine orange juice concentrate, oil, lime juice, honey and vinegar in small bowl; set aside. Divide mixed salad greens evenly between 2 individual

Spinach Salad with Raspberry Dressing (top); Citrus, Avocado & Bacon Salad (bottom)

salad plates. Arrange avocado and bacon spoke-fashion over greens. Arrange mandarin oranges on top of greens. Drizzle with dressing. Garnish with chopped unsalted peanuts, if desired.
Makes 2 servings.

Nutrition Information Per Serving:
496 calories, 9.4 g protein, 30.6 g fat, 51.5 g carbohydrates, 18 mg cholesterol, 398 mg sodium.

Eggplant Salad

⅓ **cup CRISCO® Oil**
1 **tablespoon lemon juice**
½ **teaspoon dried oregano leaves**
2 **cloves garlic, minced**
1 **medium eggplant (about
    1 pound), peeled and cut
    into ½-inch cubes**
1 **medium onion, thinly sliced
    and separated into rings**
1 **medium zucchini, halved
    lengthwise and thinly sliced**
1 **cup sliced fresh mushrooms**
1 **medium tomato, peeled,
    seeded and chopped**
¼ **teaspoon salt**

Combine Crisco® Oil, lemon juice, oregano and garlic in large skillet. Cook over moderate heat, stirring occasionally, until garlic is lightly browned. Add eggplant and onion. Stir to coat. Cook, stirring occasionally, about 10 minutes, or until eggplant is tender. Remove from heat. Transfer to medium serving bowl. Stir in zucchini, mushrooms, tomato and salt. Cover and refrigerate at least 8 hours or overnight. Stir before serving. Sprinkle with *grated Parmesan cheese,* if desired.
6 to 8 servings.

Eggplant Salad

Italian-Style Cauliflower Salad

1 **head DOLE™ Cauliflower, cut
    into flowerets**
½ **cup olive or vegetable oil**
¼ **cup vinegar**
1 **clove garlic, pressed**
½ **teaspoon salt**
½ **teaspoon cracked black
    pepper**
¼ **teaspoon dried basil,
    crumbled**
1 **cup sliced DOLE™ Green or
    Red Bell Pepper**
1 **cup sliced DOLE™ Celery**
1 **cup sliced DOLE™ Carrots**
½ **cup sliced pimento-stuffed
    olives**
¼ **cup chopped parsley**

In large saucepan, cook cauliflower in steamer basket over boiling water 8 minutes or until tender-crisp. Drain; transfer to large bowl. To make dressing, in 1-quart measure, combine oil, vinegar, garlic, salt, pepper and basil. Pour dressing over warm cauliflower. Add remaining ingredients; toss to coat. Refrigerate, covered, overnight.
Makes 6 servings.

Watercress-Carrot Salad

2 **medium bunches watercress**
6 **medium carrots**
¾ **cup CRISCO® Oil**
¼ **cup lemon juice**
1 **tablespoon sugar**
¾ **teaspoon salt**
¼ **teaspoon paprika**
¼ **teaspoon dry mustard**
⅛ **teaspoon pepper**

Remove and discard tough ends and bruised leaves from watercress. Tear remaining watercress into bite-size pieces. Cut carrots in half lengthwise and crosswise. With a vegetable peeler, cut carrot pieces into ribbon-like strips. Combine watercress and carrots in salad bowl.

Blend remaining ingredients in small mixing bowl. Pour over vegetables. Toss to coat. Serve immediately.
6 to 8 servings.

Sprout-Green Bean Salad

3 **packages (9 ounces each)
    frozen French-cut green
    beans**
½ **cup CRISCO® Oil**
¼ **cup white vinegar**
2 **teaspoons sugar**
½ **teaspoon salt**
¼ **teaspoon pepper**
1 **can (16 ounces) bean sprouts,
    rinsed and drained**
1 **cup thinly sliced celery**
¾ **cup chopped green onion**
1 **jar (2 ounces) diced pimiento,
    drained**

Cook beans in 3-quart saucepan according to package directions. Drain and cool. Blend Crisco® Oil, vinegar, sugar, salt and pepper in small mixing bowl. Set aside.

Mix green beans, bean sprouts, celery, onion and pimiento in large serving bowl. Stir dressing. Pour over bean mixture. Toss to coat. Cover and refrigerate at least 3 hours. Stir before serving. Garnish with *cherry tomatoes,* if desired.
10 to 12 servings.

Zesty Mushroom Salad

1 **cup vegetable oil**
⅓ **cup wine vinegar**
1 **tablespoon lemon juice**
1 **tablespoon chopped chives**
½ **teaspoon salt**
¼ **teaspoon TABASCO® pepper
    sauce**
1 **small clove garlic, minced**
6 **cups torn iceberg lettuce**
2 **cups torn spinach leaves**
¼ **pound mushrooms, sliced**
⅓ **cup sliced pitted ripe olives**

In jar with tightly fitting lid combine oil, vinegar, lemon juice, chives, salt, Tabasco® sauce and garlic; shake well. In large bowl combine lettuce, spinach, mushrooms and olives. Add ¾ cup dressing and toss lightly to mix well. Refrigerate remaining dressing in covered jar for later use.
Makes 8 servings.

Spinach Salad

1/4 **pound sliced bacon**
1/2 **cup sliced scallions**
2 **tablespoons all-purpose flour**
1 **cup COLLEGE INN® Beef or Chicken Broth**
1/3 **cup red wine vinegar**
8 **cups spinach leaves, torn**
2 **cups sliced fresh mushrooms**

In large skillet, over medium-high heat, cook bacon until crisp. Drain, reserving 1/4 cup drippings. Crumble bacon; set aside. In reserved drippings, over medium heat, cook scallions until tender. Stir in flour; cook 1 minute. Stir in broth and vinegar; heat to a boil. Reduce heat; cook until slightly thickened.

In large bowl, mix spinach leaves and mushrooms. Pour hot dressing over salad, tossing to coat well. Sprinkle with reserved bacon pieces. Serve immediately.
Makes 8 servings.

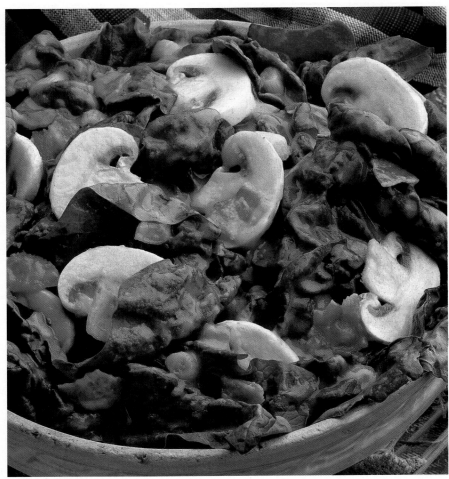

Spinach Salad

Mexican Tossed Salad

3 **large ripe avocados, seeded, peeled and sliced**
1/2 **cup BORDEN® or MEADOW GOLD® Sour Cream**
1/4 **cup REALEMON® Lemon Juice from Concentrate**
1 **tablespoon finely chopped onion**
1 **tablespoon water**
1/4 **teaspoon salt**
1/4 **teaspoon hot pepper sauce**
6 **cups torn mixed salad greens**
1 **large tomato, seeded and chopped**
1 **cup (4 ounces) shredded mild Cheddar or Monterey Jack cheese**
1/2 **cup sliced pitted ripe olives**
1 **cup coarsely crushed tortilla chips**

In medium bowl, mash *1 avocado;* stir in sour cream, *3 tablespoons* of the ReaLemon® brand, onion, water, salt and hot pepper sauce. Chill to blend flavors. In large salad bowl, sprinkle remaining *2 avocados* with remaining *1 tablespoon* ReaLemon® brand. Top with salad greens, tomato, cheese and olives; chill. Just before serving, toss with avocado dressing and tortilla chips.
Makes 8 servings.

Warm Bean Salad

1 **tablespoon vegetable oil**
3/4 **cup chopped celery**
2 **green onions, thinly sliced**
1 **can (16 ounces) CAMPBELL'S® Home Style Beans**
1 **tablespoon chopped fresh parsley**
1 **tablespoon red wine vinegar**
1/8 **teaspoon pepper**
1 **CAMPBELL'S FRESH® Tomato, chopped**

To Microwave:
1. In 1 1/2-quart microwave-safe casserole, combine oil, celery and onions. Cover with lid; microwave on HIGH 1 1/2 minutes or until celery is tender-crisp.
2. Stir in beans, parsley, vinegar and pepper. Cover; microwave on HIGH 2 1/2 minutes or until heated through, stirring once during cooking. Stir in tomato.
Makes about 3 cups or 3 servings.

Country Pineapple Slaw

1 **can (20 ounces) DOLE® Pineapple Chunks**
1 **package (16 ounces) DOLE® Cole Slaw Mix**
1/2 **cup sunflower seeds**
Zesty Dressing (recipe follows)

Drain pineapple. In large bowl, combine pineapple with cole slaw mix and sunflower seeds. Toss with Zesty Dressing. Refrigerate, covered, until ready to serve.
Makes 6 servings.
ZESTY DRESSING: In 1-quart measure, combine 1/2 cup *each* mayonnaise and dairy sour cream, 2 tablespoons lemon juice, 1 tablespoon Dijon mustard and 1/2 teaspoon caraway seeds. Blend well.

Piñata Salad

- 1 head DOLE™ Iceberg Lettuce, torn
- 1 avocado, diced
- 1 can (16 ounces) garbanzo beans, drained
- 1 cup diced DOLE™ Tomatoes
- 1 cup ripe olives, cut into wedges or sliced
- 1 cup sliced DOLE™ Celery
- 1 cup sliced jicama or radishes
- 4 ounces sharp Cheddar cheese, shredded
  Gazpacho Dressing (recipe follows)
  Chile Dressing (recipe follows)

Place lettuce in salad bowl. Place avocado, garbanzo beans, tomatoes, olives, celery, jicama and cheese in individual bowls for a choice of toppings. Serve with either Gazpacho or Chile Dressing.
Makes 6 to 8 servings.
GAZPACHO DRESSING: In screw-top jar, combine ½ cup olive or vegetable oil, ¼ cup vinegar, 3 sliced green onions, ¾ cup diced tomato, ¼ cup diced green bell pepper, 1 pressed garlic clove, 3 tablespoons chopped cilantro or parsley, 1 teaspoon salt and 6 drops liquid hot pepper seasoning. Shake well to combine.
CHILE DRESSING: Puree 7 ounces (1 can) diced green chiles, 1 cup mayonnaise and ¼ cup dairy sour cream in blender. Refrigerate, covered, until ready to serve.

Cucumber Salad

- 3 medium cucumbers, scored lengthwise with tines of fork and thinly sliced
- ¾ teaspoon salt, divided
- ⅓ cup chopped onion
- ⅓ cup cider vinegar
- 3 tablespoons CRISCO® Oil
- 2 tablespoons sugar
- 1½ teaspoons caraway seeds
- ½ teaspoon paprika
- ⅛ teaspoon pepper

Place cucumbers in medium mixing bowl. Sprinkle with ¼ teaspoon salt. Let stand about 1 hour. Drain.

Blend remaining ingredients and remaining ½ teaspoon salt in small mixing bowl. Pour over cucumbers. Toss to coat. Cover and refrigerate at least 3 hours. Stir before serving.
6 to 8 servings.

Marinated Vegetables

- 4 cups assorted fresh vegetables*
- ¼ cup REALEMON® Lemon Juice from Concentrate
- ¼ cup vegetable oil
- 1 tablespoon sugar
- 1 teaspoon salt
- ½ teaspoon oregano or thyme leaves
- ⅛ teaspoon pepper

Place vegetables in 1½-quart shallow baking dish. In small bowl or jar, combine remaining ingredients; mix well. Pour over vegetables. Cover; refrigerate 6 hours or overnight, stirring occasionally. Serve as appetizer or on lettuce leaves as salad.
Makes 4 cups.
Suggested Vegetables: Cauliflowerets, carrots, mushrooms, cherry tomatoes, broccoli flowerets, zucchini, onion or cucumber.

Tip: Recipe can be doubled.

Tangy Coleslaw

- 1 tablespoon BLUE BONNET® Margarine
- 2 tablespoons all-purpose flour
- 2 tablespoons sugar
- ¼ teaspoon ground black pepper
- 2 tablespoons GREY POUPON® Dijon Mustard
- 1½ cups COLLEGE INN® Chicken Broth
- ⅓ cup white wine vinegar
- 8 cups shredded red or green cabbage
- ½ cup chopped red onion

In medium saucepan, over medium heat, melt margarine. Blend in flour; cook 1 minute. Add sugar, pepper, mustard and chicken broth; cook until mixture thickens and boils. Stir in vinegar. Cover; refrigerate 1 hour.

In large bowl, mix together cabbage and onion. Pour dressing over salad, tossing to coat well. Refrigerate at least 1 hour to blend flavors.
Makes about 9 cups.

Tangy Coleslaw

Snack Cups

> 1 package (4-serving size)
>   JELL-O® Brand Orange,
>   Lemon or Lime Flavor Sugar
>   Free Gelatin
> 3/4 cup boiling water
> 1/2 cup cold water
>   Ice cubes
> 1 tablespoon lemon juice
>   (optional)
> 1/2 cup each sliced celery,
>   chopped cabbage and
>   shredded carrot*

Completely dissolve gelatin in boiling water. Combine cold water and ice cubes to make 1¼ cups. Add to gelatin with lemon juice, stirring until slightly thickened. Remove any unmelted ice. Fold in vegetables; spoon into individual glasses. Chill until set, about 30 minutes. Garnish with parsley, if desired.
Makes about 3 cups or 6 servings.

Additional Vegetable Combinations: Use sliced celery with grated carrots and golden raisins.

Use sliced celery with chopped cabbage, chopped apple or sliced ripe or green pitted olives.

Use sliced celery with chopped cucumber and chopped pimiento.

Use sliced celery with drained mandarin orange sections and chopped green pepper.

Snack Cups

Winter Fruit Bowl

> 2 packages (4-serving size) or
>   1 package (8-serving size)
>   JELL-O® Brand Lemon
>   Flavor Gelatin
> 1½ cups boiling water
> 1 can (12 fluid ounces) lemon-
>   lime carbonated beverage,
>   chilled
>   Ice cubes
> 3 cups diced or sliced fresh
>   fruits* (bananas, oranges,
>   apples, pears, grapes)

Dissolve gelatin in boiling water. Combine beverage and ice cubes to make 2½ cups. Add to gelatin, stirring until slightly thickened. Remove any unmelted ice. Chill until thickened, about 10 minutes. Fold in fruits. Pour into 8-cup serving bowl. Chill until set, about 3 hours. Garnish with whipped topping and orange sections, if desired.
Makes about 6½ cups or 12 servings.

*Do not use fresh pineapple, kiwifruit, mango, papaya or figs.

Creamy Nectarine Mold with Strawberry Sauce

> 1 envelope unflavored gelatin
> 1/2 cup cold water
> 1 8-ounce package
>   PHILADELPHIA BRAND
>   Cream Cheese, softened
> 1/2 cup sugar
> 1/2 cup milk
> 2 tablespoons orange flavored
>   liqueur
> 1 cup whipping cream, whipped
> 1 nectarine, sliced
> 1 pint strawberries, sliced
> 1/4 cup sugar
> 1 tablespoon orange flavored
>   liqueur

Soften gelatin in water; stir over low heat until dissolved. Combine cream cheese and sugar, mixing until well blended. Gradually add gelatin, milk and liqueur, mixing until blended. Fold in whipped cream. Spoon ¼ cup cream cheese mixture into lightly oiled 1-quart mold. Arrange nectarines on cream cheese mixture; top with remaining cream cheese mixture. Chill until firm. Unmold onto serving plate.   *(continued)*

Combine strawberries, sugar and liqueur; let stand 10 minutes. Serve with mold.
6 to 8 servings.

Variation: Substitute orange juice for orange flavored liqueur. Add 1 teaspoon grated orange peel to cream cheese mixture.

Classic Tomato Aspic

> 3 envelopes KNOX® Unflavored
>   Gelatine
> 3 cups cold tomato juice
> 2 cups tomato juice, heated to
>   boiling
> 1/4 cup lemon juice
> 2 tablespoons sugar
> 1½ teaspoons Worcestershire
>   sauce
> 4 to 6 dashes hot pepper sauce

In large bowl, sprinkle unflavored gelatine over 1 cup cold juice; let stand 1 minute. Add hot juice and stir until gelatine is completely dissolved, about 5 minutes. Stir in remaining 2 cups cold juice, lemon juice, sugar, Worcestershire sauce and hot pepper sauce. Pour into 5½-cup ring mold or bowl; chill until firm, about 4 hours. To serve, unmold and fill, if desired, with salad greens and your favorite cut-up fresh vegetables.
Makes about 10 servings.

Cherry Waldorf Gelatin

> 2 cups boiling water
> 1 (6-ounce) package cherry
>   flavor gelatin
> 1 cup cold water
> 1/4 cup REALEMON® Lemon Juice
>   from Concentrate
> 1½ cups chopped apples
> 1 cup chopped celery
> 1/2 cup chopped walnuts or
>   pecans
>   Lettuce leaves
>   Apple slices and celery leaves,
>   optional

In medium bowl, pour boiling water over gelatin; stir until dissolved. Add cold water and ReaLemon® brand; chill until partially set. Fold in apples, celery and nuts. Pour into lightly oiled 6-cup mold or 9-inch square baking pan. Chill until set, 4 to 6 hours or overnight. Serve on lettuce. Garnish with celery leaves and apple if desired.
Makes 8 to 10 servings.

Muffin Pan Snacks

**1 package (4-serving size)
JELL-O® Brand Lemon
Flavor Gelatin**
1/2 teaspoon salt
1/8 teaspoon garlic powder
1 1/2 cups boiling water
2 teaspoons vinegar
1 teaspoon vegetable oil
1/8 teaspoon black pepper
**1/8 teaspoon dried oregano,
crumbled**
Snack combinations*

Dissolve gelatin, salt and garlic powder in boiling water. Add vinegar, oil, pepper and oregano. Place aluminum-foil baking cups in muffin pans. Place different snack combinations in each cup, filling each about 2/3 full. Then fill with gelatin mixture. Chill until firm, about 2 hours. Unmold carefully from foil cups. Serve with crisp salad greens, if desired.
Makes 4 cups or 8 to 10 servings.

Snack Combinations: Use cauliflower florets with diced pimiento.
Use cucumber slices with tomato slices.
Use chopped hard-cooked egg with chopped cucumber and pickle.
Use shredded carrot with raisins.
Use drained canned button or sliced mushrooms with pimiento strips.
Use diced apple with chopped nuts.
Use sliced hard-cooked egg with anchovies.
Use cubed cream cheese with chopped nuts.
Use diced pimiento with diced green pepper and tomato.
Use sliced celery with sliced ripe or stuffed green olives.

Neapolitan Vegetable Mold

**2 packages (4-serving size) or
1 package (8-serving size)
JELL-O® Brand Lemon
Flavor Gelatin**
1 teaspoon salt
2 cups boiling water
1 1/2 cups cold water
3 tablespoons vinegar
1 1/2 cups shredded carrots
1/2 cup mayonnaise
1 cup finely chopped cabbage
1 1/2 cups finely chopped spinach
1 teaspoon grated onion

Dissolve gelatin and salt in boiling water. Add cold water and vinegar. Measure 1 1/3 cups of the gelatin into bowl. Place bowl in larger bowl of ice and water; stir until slightly thickened. Stir in carrots and pour into 6-cup ring mold or 9×5-inch loaf pan. Chill until set but not firm.

Measure 1 cup of the remaining gelatin; blend in mayonnaise. Chill over ice until thickened. Stir in cabbage; spoon over carrot layer in mold. Chill.

Chill remaining gelatin over ice until slightly thickened. Add spinach and onion. Spoon over mayonnaise layer in mold. Chill until firm, about 3 hours. Unmold. Garnish with chicory and carrot curls, if desired.
Makes 5 1/2 cups or 10 servings.

Holiday Fruit Salad

**3 packages (3 ounces each)
strawberry flavor gelatin**
3 cups boiling water
2 ripe DOLE™ Bananas
**1 package (16 ounces) frozen
strawberries**
**1 can (20 ounces) DOLE®
Crushed Pineapple**
**1 package (8 ounces) cream
cheese, softened**
**1 cup dairy sour cream or plain
yogurt**
1/4 cup sugar
Crisp DOLE™ Lettuce leaves

In large bowl, dissolve gelatin in boiling water. Slice bananas into gelatin mixture. Add frozen strawberries and undrained pineapple. Pour half the mixture into 13×9-inch pan. Refrigerate 1 hour or until firm. In mixer bowl, beat cream cheese with sour cream and sugar; spread over chilled layer. Gently spoon remaining gelatin mixture on top. Refrigerate until firm, about 2 hours. Cut into squares; serve on lettuce-lined salad plates. Garnish with additional pineapple, if desired.
Makes 12 servings.

Golden Salad

**1 package (4-serving size)
JELL-O® Brand Lemon or
Orange Flavor Gelatin**
1/2 teaspoon salt
1 1/4 cups boiling water
**1 can (8 1/4 ounces) crushed
pineapple in juice**
**1 tablespoon lemon juice or
vinegar**

Holiday Fruit Salad

1 1/2 cups shredded carrots
1/3 cup chopped pecans

Dissolve gelatin and salt in boiling water. Stir in undrained pineapple and lemon juice. Chill until thickened. Stir in carrots and nuts and pour into individual molds. Chill until firm, about 3 hours. Unmold. Serve with crisp salad greens and mayonnaise, if desired.
Makes about 3 cups or 6 servings.

Melon Wedges

**1 cantaloupe or honeydew
melon**
**1 package (4-serving size)
JELL-O® Brand Apricot or
Orange Flavor Sugar Free
Gelatin**
1 cup boiling water
3/4 cup cold water
**1 banana, sliced, 1/2 cup sliced
strawberries or 1 can
(8 1/4 ounces) crushed
pineapple in juice, well
drained**

Cut melon in half lengthwise; scoop out seeds and drain well. Dissolve gelatin in boiling water. Add cold water. Chill until slightly thickened. Stir in fruit. Pour into melon halves. Chill until firm, about 3 hours. Cut in wedges. Serve with additional fresh fruit, cottage cheese and crisp greens, if desired.
Makes 6 servings.

Note: Chill any excess fruited gelatin in dessert dishes.

Sparkling Berry Salad

Sparkling Berry Salad

- **2 envelopes KNOX® Unflavored Gelatine**
- **2 cups cranberry-raspberry juice***
- **1/3 cup sugar**
- **1 cup club soda**
- **1/4 cup creme de cassis (black currant) liqueur (optional)**
- **1 teaspoon lemon juice**
- **1 teaspoon fresh grated orange peel (optional)**
- **3 cups assorted blueberries, raspberries or strawberries**

In medium saucepan, sprinkle unflavored gelatine over 1 cup cranberry-raspberry juice; let stand 1 minute. Stir over low heat until gelatin is completely dissolved, about 5 minutes. Stir in sugar until dissolved.

In large bowl, blend remaining 1 cup cranberry-raspberry juice, soda, gelatine mixture, liqueur, lemon juice and orange peel. Chill, stirring occasionally, until mixture is consistency of unbeaten egg whites, about 60 minutes. Fold in berries. Pour into 6-cup mold or bowl; chill until firm, about 3 hours. Unmold and serve, if desired, with sour cream.
Makes about 8 servings.

***Substitution:** Use 2 cups cranberry juice cocktail and increase sugar to 1/2 cup.

Clam & Tomato Molded Salad

- **4 envelopes unflavored gelatine**
- **4 cups tomato juice**
- **1/2 cup chopped celery**
- **1/4 cup chopped green onions**
- **2 (6 1/2-ounce) cans SNOW'S® or DOXSEE® Minced Clams, drained, reserving 1/2 cup liquid**
- **1 (4-serving size) package lemon flavor gelatin**
- **1 (16-ounce) container BORDEN® or MEADOW GOLD® Cottage Cheese**
- **Lettuce leaves**

In medium saucepan, sprinkle unflavored gelatine over 1 1/2 cups tomato juice; let stand 1 minute. Over low heat, stir until gelatine dissolves. Remove from heat; add celery, *2 tablespoons* onions and remaining 2 1/2 cups tomato juice. Chill until partially set, about 45 minutes; stir in drained clams. Meanwhile, in small saucepan, heat reserved clam liquid; add lemon gelatin, stirring until dissolved. Remove from heat; add cheese and remaining *2 tablespoons* onions. Chill until partially set, about 30 minutes; stir. In lightly oiled 9×5-inch loaf pan, spoon half the tomato mixture; spread cheese mixture evenly over tomato layer. Top with remaining tomato mixture. Chill 6 hours or until set. Unmold onto lettuce. Garnish as desired. Refrigerate leftovers.
Makes 10 to 12 servings.

Mediterranean Orange and Red Onion Salad

- **2 envelopes KNOX® Unflavored Gelatine**
- **1 cup cold water**
- **2 1/2 cups orange juice**
- **2 tablespoons sugar**
- **1 tablespoon lemon juice**
- **2 teaspoons red wine vinegar**
- **4 medium oranges, peeled, sectioned and chopped (about 1 cup)**
- **1/2 cup finely chopped celery**
- **1/4 cup finely chopped red onion**

In medium saucepan, sprinkle unflavored gelatine over cold water; let stand 1 minute. Stir over low heat until gelatine is completely dissolved, about 5 minutes.

In large bowl, blend gelatine mixture, orange juice, sugar, lemon juice and vinegar. Chill, stirring occasionally, until mixture is consistency of unbeaten egg whites, about 40 minutes. Fold in remaining ingredients. Pour into 6-cup ring mold or bowl; chill until firm, about 4 hours. Unmold and garnish, if desired, with celery leaves.
Makes about 8 servings.

Buffet Slaw

- **2 cans (8 1/4 ounces each) crushed pineapple in juice**
- **2 packages (4-serving size) or 1 package (8-serving size) JELL-O® Brand Lemon Flavor Gelatin**
- **1 1/2 cups boiling water Ice cubes**
- **3 tablespoons vinegar**
- **1/2 teaspoon celery salt**

1 cup each finely shredded
green and red cabbage
¼ cup chopped parsley
1 tablespoon finely chopped
onion

Drain pineapple, reserving juice. Add water to juice to make 1 cup; set aside. Completely dissolve gelatin in boiling water. Combine measured liquid and ice cubes to make 2½ cups. Add to gelatin with vinegar and celery salt, stirring until slightly thickened. Remove any unmelted ice. Chill until thickened, about 10 minutes. Fold in pineapple, cabbage, parsley and onion. Pour into 8-cup bowl. Chill until set, about 3 hours. Garnish with cabbage leaves, parsley and onion rings, if desired.
Makes 6 cups or 12 servings.

Minted Melon Mold

1½ cups boiling water
1 (3-ounce) package lemon
flavor gelatin
1 (3-ounce) package lime flavor
gelatin
¾ cup REALIME® Lime Juice
from Concentrate
½ cup cold water
⅛ teaspoon peppermint extract
2 cups melon balls (cantaloupe,
honeydew, etc.)
Lettuce leaves
Coconut Cream Dressing
Mint leaves and additional
melon balls, optional

In medium bowl, pour boiling water over gelatins; stir until dissolved. Add ReaLime® brand, cold water and extract; chill until partially set. Fold in melon. Pour into lightly oiled 5-cup ring mold. Chill until set, about 3 hours or overnight. Unmold onto lettuce. Serve with Coconut Cream Dressing; garnish with mint and melon balls if desired.
Makes 8 to 10 servings.

Coconut Cream Dressing

½ cup BORDEN® or MEADOW
GOLD® Sour Cream
3 tablespoons flaked coconut
1 tablespoon honey
1 tablespoon REALIME® Lime
Juice from Concentrate

In small bowl, combine all ingredients; mix well. Chill before serving. Refrigerate leftovers.
Makes about ½ cup.

Layered Peach Salad

1 can (8 ounces) sliced peaches,
drained
¼ cup sliced celery
¾ cup boiling water
1 package (4-serving size)
JELL-O® Brand Gelatin, any
red flavor
½ cup cold water
Ice cubes

Arrange peach slices and celery in 8×4-inch loaf pan. Pour boiling water into blender. Add gelatin. Cover and blend at low speed until gelatin is completely dissolved, about 30 seconds. Combine cold water and ice cubes to make 1 cup. Add to gelatin and stir until ice is partially melted; then blend at high speed for 30 seconds. Pour into pan. Chill until firm, about 3 hours. Salad layers as it chills. Unmold. Garnish with celery leaves and additional peach slices, if desired.
Makes about 4 cups or 8 servings.
Layered Carrot-Pineapple Salad: Prepare Layered Peach Salad as directed, substituting 1 can (8¼ ounces) pineapple slices, drained and cut in half, ¼ cup shredded carrot and orange flavor gelatin for the peaches, celery and red flavor gelatin. Garnish with chicory and carrot curls, if desired.

Ginger Pineapple Mold

1 can (20 ounces) pineapple
slices in juice
2 packages (4-serving size) or
1 package (8-serving size)
JELL-O® Brand Lime or
Apricot Flavor Gelatin
1½ cups boiling water
1 cup ginger ale or cold water
¼ teaspoon ginger

Drain pineapple, reserving juice. Cut 4 pineapple slices in half; set aside. Cut remaining pineapple slices into chunks. Dissolve gelatin in boiling water. Add reserved juice, ginger ale and ginger. Chill until slightly thickened. Measure 1 cup of the gelatin. Arrange some of the pineapple chunks in 6-cup ring mold; top with measured gelatin. Chill until set but not firm, about 10 minutes. Fold remaining pineapple chunks into remaining gelatin; spoon over gelatin in mold. Chill until firm, about 4 hours. Unmold. Garnish with halved pineapple slices, halved cherry tomatoes and crisp greens, if desired.
Makes 5 cups or 10 servings.

Ginger Pineapple Mold

Autumn Pear 'n Apple Salad

>   2 envelopes KNOX® Unflavored
>   Gelatine
>   2½ cups apple juice
>   ¼ cup light brown sugar
>   1¼ cups pear nectar
>   ¼ teaspoon ground cinnamon
>   ⅛ teaspoon ground nutmeg
>   1 small pear, chopped
>   1 small apple, chopped
>   6 dried Calimyrna figs,
>   quartered
>   ¼ cup chopped pecans or
>   walnuts (optional)

In medium saucepan, sprinkle unflavored gelatine over 1 cup apple juice; let stand 1 minute. Stir over low heat until gelatine is completely dissolved, about 5 minutes. Stir in sugar until dissolved.

In large bowl, blend remaining 1½ cups apple juice, pear nectar, gelatine mixture, cinnamon and nutmeg. Chill, stirring occasionally, until mixture is consistency of unbeaten egg whites, about 60 minutes. Fold in remaining ingredients. Pour into 6-cup mold; chill until firm, about 3 hours. Unmold onto serving platter.
Makes about 12 servings.

Creamy Garden Salad

>   2 envelopes unflavored gelatine
>   1½ cups water, divided
>   2 cups mayonnaise
>   ⅓ cup lemon juice
>   ¾ teaspoon TABASCO® pepper
>   sauce
>   1½ cups diced cucumber
>   1 cup shredded carrot
>   ½ cup thinly sliced radishes
>   ½ cup thinly sliced green onions

In medium saucepan sprinkle gelatine over 1 cup water; let stand 1 minute. Stir over low heat until gelatine is completely dissolved. Add remaining ½ cup water, mayonnaise, lemon juice and Tabasco® sauce; mix well. Chill until slightly thickened. Stir in cucumber, carrot, radishes and green onions. Turn into 6-cup mold. Cover; refrigerate 3 hours or until firm. Unmold onto serving plate.
Makes 6 to 8 servings.

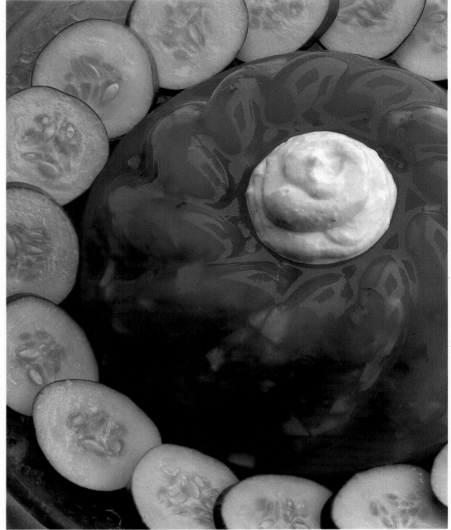

Tomato-Garden Aspic with Horseradish Cream

Tomato-Garden Aspic with Horseradish Cream

>   1 (13¾-fluid ounce) can
>   COLLEGE INN® Beef or
>   Chicken Broth
>   2 (3-ounce) or 1 (6-ounce)
>   package ROYAL® Lemon
>   Gelatin
>   2 cups tomato juice
>   1 tablespoon A.1.® Steak Sauce
>   ½ cup finely chopped celery
>   ½ cup finely chopped cucumber
>   ⅓ cup finely chopped onion
>   Lettuce
>   Horseradish Cream (recipe
>   follows)

Refrigerate broth; remove fat. In saucepan, over high heat, heat broth to a boil; stir in gelatin until dissolved. Stir in tomato juice and steak sauce. Refrigerate until slightly thickened. Stir in celery, cucumber and onion. Pour into 5- to 6-cup mold. Refrigerate until firm, about 3 hours. To serve, unmold onto lettuce-lined serving plate. Serve with Horseradish Cream. Garnish as desired.
Makes 6 to 8 servings.
HORSERADISH CREAM: In small bowl, beat together ½ cup prepared whipped topping, ¼ cup mayonnaise *or* salad dressing and 1 tablespoon horseradish. Refrigerate until serving time.

Rainbow Fruit Salad

**2 peaches, peeled, pitted and
sliced
2 DOLE™ Oranges, peeled and
sliced
2 cups DOLE™ Strawberries,
hulled and sliced
1 cup DOLE™ Seedless Grapes
1 cup melon balls
Pineapple Lime Dressing
(recipe follows)**

In large bowl, combine fruit. Add
Pineapple Lime Dressing; stir gently
to coat.
Makes 8 servings.
PINEAPPLE LIME DRESSING: In
small bowl, combine ½ cup Dole®
Pineapple Juice, ½ teaspoon grated
lime peel, 3 tablespoons *each* lime
juice and honey and 1 tablespoon
chopped crystallized ginger. Whisk
until blended.

Ambrosia

**1 can (20 ounces) DOLE®
Pineapple Chunks
1 can (11 ounces) DOLE®
Mandarin Orange Segments
in Syrup
1 firm, large DOLE™ Banana,
sliced, optional
1½ cups DOLE™ Seedless Grapes
1 cup miniature marshmallows
1 cup flaked coconut
½ cup pecan halves or coarsely
chopped nuts
1 cup dairy sour cream or plain
yogurt
1 tablespoon brown sugar**

Drain pineapple and orange segments. In large bowl, combine pineapple, mandarin oranges, banana,
grapes, marshmallows, coconut and
nuts. In 1-quart measure, combine
sour cream and brown sugar. Stir into
fruit mixture. Refrigerate, covered, 1
hour or overnight.
Makes 4 servings.

Carrot Pineapple Salad

**1 DOLE™ Fresh Pineapple
1 honeydew melon
3 large DOLE™ Carrots, thinly
sliced
½ cup thinly sliced DOLE™ Pitted
Dates
Honey-Lime Vinaigrette (recipe
follows)**

Twist crown from pineapple. Cut pineapple lengthwise into quarters. Remove fruit from shells with curved
knife. Trim off core and cut fruit into
chunks. Cut melon in half; scoop out
seeds and cut fruit into 1-inch pieces.
In salad bowl, combine pineapple,
melon, carrots and dates. Toss with
Honey-Lime Vinaigrette; garnish
with lime slices, if desired.
Makes 6 servings.
HONEY-LIME VINAIGRETTE: In
small bowl, combine ¼ cup honey, 2
tablespoons *each* white wine vinegar
and lime juice, 1 tablespoon vegetable
oil, and 2 teaspoons grated lime peel.
Whisk until blended.

Minted Fruit Salad

**½ cup sugar
⅓ cup orange juice
⅓ cup REALEMON® Lemon Juice
from Concentrate
⅓ cup water
¼ teaspoon peppermint extract
8 cups assorted fresh fruits
Sherbet**

In medium bowl, combine sugar, orange juice, ReaLemon® brand, water
and peppermint extract; stir until
sugar dissolves. Place fruit in 3-quart
shallow baking dish; pour juice mixture over. Cover; chill 3 to 4 hours to
blend flavors. Arrange drained fruit
on platter; top with sherbet and garnish as desired.
Makes 4 servings.

Creamy Topped Fruit Salad

**1 8-ounce package *Light*
PHILADELPHIA BRAND
Neufchâtel Cheese, softened
2 tablespoons lemon juice
1 teaspoon grated lemon peel
½ cup whipping cream
¼ cup powdered sugar
2 cups peach slices
2 cups blueberries
2 cups strawberry slices
2 cups grapes**

Combine neufchâtel cheese, juice and
peel, mixing until well blended. Beat
whipping cream until soft peaks form;
gradually add sugar, beating until
stiff peaks form. Fold into neufchâtel
cheese mixture; chill. Layer fruit in
2½-quart glass serving bowl. Top
with neufchâtel cheese mixture.
Sprinkle with nuts, if desired. Chill.
8 servings.
Variation: Substitute PHILADEL-
PHIA BRAND Cream Cheese for
Neufchâtel Cheese.

Creamy Topped Fruit Salad

Mai Tai Compote

Mai Tai Compote

- 1 medium DOLE™ Fresh Pineapple
- 1 DOLE™ Orange, peeled and sliced
- 1 kiwifruit, peeled and sliced
- 1 cup halved DOLE™ Strawberries
- ½ cup DOLE™ Seedless Red Grapes
- ¼ cup fresh lime juice
- 3 tablespoons honey
- 1 tablespoon light rum
- 1 tablespoon orange-flavored liqueur
- ½ teaspoon grated lime peel
- 1 firm DOLE™ Banana

Cut pineapple in half lengthwise through crown. Remove fruit with curved knife, leaving shells intact. Trim off core and cut fruit into chunks. In large bowl, combine pineapple, orange, kiwi, strawberries and grapes. To make dressing, in 1-quart measure, combine remaining ingredients, except banana. Pour dressing over fruit. Toss gently to coat. Refrigerate, covered, 1 hour. Just before serving, slice banana into fruit salad. Toss gently. Spoon salad into pineapple shells and serve.
Makes 6 to 8 servings.

Indian Fruit Salad

- 1 DOLE™ Fresh Pineapple
- 2 firm DOLE™ Bananas
- 1 head DOLE™ Iceberg Lettuce, torn
- 1 DOLE™ Orange, peeled and sliced

- 2 cups melon balls or diced melon
- ½ cup cashew nuts
- 1 cup mayonnaise
- ¼ cup dairy sour cream
- 1 tablespoon fresh lime juice
- 1 tablespoon sugar
- 1 teaspoon curry powder
- ½ teaspoon grated lime peel
- ½ teaspoon salt

Twist crown from pineapple. Cut pineapple lengthwise into quarters. Remove fruit from shells with curved knife. Trim off core and dice fruit. Slice bananas into large bowl. Add 2½ cups pineapple (reserve remaining pineapple for another use), lettuce, orange, melon and nuts. To make dressing, in 1-quart measure, combine remaining ingredients; refrigerate, covered, until ready to serve. Pour dressing over salad and toss.
Makes 6 to 8 servings.

Fruit Salad with Poppy Seed Dressing

- 1 pear, cored and sliced
- 1 apple, cored and sliced
- 1 banana, peeled and sliced
- 1 orange, peeled and sectioned
- ⅓ cup CRISCO® Oil
- 2 tablespoons lime juice
- 2 tablespoons honey
- ½ teaspoon soy sauce
- ½ teaspoon poppy seed
- ¼ teaspoon ground ginger
- ¼ teaspoon dry mustard
  Dash salt

Combine pear, apple, banana and orange in medium serving bowl. Blend remaining ingredients in small mixing bowl. Pour over fruit. Toss to coat. Serve immediately.

Tip: Toss your own combination of fresh fruits with poppy seed dressing. Create a refreshing summertime salad with seasonal fruits like grapes, strawberries, peaches and melon. Add variety to this tangy salad with any of your favorites.
4 to 6 servings.

Luau Fruit Salad

- 1 can (20 ounces) DOLE® Pineapple Chunks
- 3 DOLE™ Oranges, peeled and sectioned
- 2 apples, cored and chopped

- 1 papaya, peeled, seeded and cut into chunks
- 1 teaspoon cornstarch
- ¼ cup vegetable oil
- 2 tablespoons sugar
- 2 tablespoons white vinegar
- 1 tablespoon poppy seeds
- 1 teaspoon grated orange peel
- ½ teaspoon paprika
- ¼ teaspoon salt
- 5 quarts torn DOLE™ Romaine Lettuce
- ½ cup DOLE™ Blanched Slivered Almonds, toasted

Drain pineapple; reserve juice. In large bowl, combine pineapple, oranges, apples and papaya. For dressing, in saucepan, combine reserved pineapple juice and cornstarch. Cook, stirring, until mixture boils and thickens. Cool. Combine pineapple mixture with oil, sugar, vinegar, poppy seeds, orange peel, paprika and salt in blender. Blend until smooth. Pour dressing over fruit and toss; refrigerate, covered. Just before serving, toss with lettuce and sprinkle with almonds.
Makes 12 servings.

Fruit Salad with Orange Almond Dressing

- 1 head DOLE™ Leaf Lettuce
- 1 DOLE™ Orange, peeled and sectioned
- 1 peach, sliced
- ½ cantaloupe, cut into chunks
- 2 cups DOLE™ Fresh Pineapple chunks
- 1 cup sliced DOLE™ Strawberries
- 1 cup DOLE™ Grapes
- ½ cup DOLE™ Whole Natural Almonds, toasted
  Orange Almond Dressing (recipe follows)

Line large salad bowl with lettuce leaves. Arrange fruit on top; sprinkle with almonds. Serve with Orange Almond Dressing.
Makes 6 to 8 servings.
ORANGE ALMOND DRESSING: In 1-quart measure, combine 1 cup dairy sour cream, ½ cup mayonnaise, ¼ cup toasted Dole™ Chopped Natural Almonds, 2 tablespoons lemon juice and 2 teaspoons grated orange peel. Refrigerate, covered, until ready to serve.

Hot Potato Salad

- **7 to 8 SIZZLEAN® Breakfast Strips, cut into ½-inch pieces**
- **2 medium onions, chopped fine**
- **1 tablespoon all-purpose flour**
- **4 teaspoons sugar**
- **1½ teaspoons salt**
- **1 teaspoon paprika**
- **½ cup vinegar**
- **1 cup water**
- **6 medium potatoes, pared, cooked, sliced thin**

Cook Sizzlean® pieces in medium skillet over medium-low heat until they begin to look crisp. Add onions; cook and stir until tender. Combine flour, sugar, salt and paprika in small cup. Add to Sizzlean® pieces, mixing well. Pour in vinegar and water. Cook and stir until mixture thickens. Add potatoes; reduce heat to low. Heat 10 to 15 minutes or until hot.
Makes 6 servings.

Marinated Potato and Mushroom Salad

- **1½ pounds new potatoes, cooked and cubed (about 4 cups)**
- **1 cup sliced fresh mushrooms (about 4 ounces)**
- **⅓ cup sliced celery**
- **¼ cup sliced green onions**
- **⅓ cup vegetable oil**
- **¼ cup REALEMON® Lemon Juice from Concentrate**
- **1½ teaspoons Dijon-style mustard**
- **1 teaspoon sugar**
- **1 teaspoon WYLER'S® or STEERO® Chicken-Flavor Instant Bouillon**
- **Cracked black pepper, optional**

In shallow baking dish, combine potatoes, mushrooms, celery and onions. In 1-pint jar with tight-fitting lid or cruet, combine remaining ingredients, except pepper; shake well. Pour over potato mixture; mix well. Cover; chill 3 to 4 hours to blend flavors. Serve with pepper if desired. Refrigerate leftovers.
Makes 6 to 8 servings.

Creamy Red Potato Salad

- **½ cup WISH-BONE® Italian Dressing**
- **¾ cup mayonnaise**
- **½ cup sliced green onions**
- **2 tablespoons snipped fresh dill***
- **1 teaspoon Dijon-style mustard**
- **1 teaspoon lemon juice**
- **⅛ teaspoon pepper**
- **3 pounds red bliss or new potatoes, cooked and cut into large chunks**

In large salad bowl, thoroughly combine all ingredients except potatoes. Toss with warm potatoes; cover and chill.
Makes about 10 side-dish servings.
*Substitution: Use 1 teaspoon dried dill weed.
Notes: Recipe can be halved.
Also terrific with Wish-Bone® Herbal Italian, Italian & Cheese, Robusto Italian or Blended Italian Dressing.

Fresh and Creamy Potato Salad

- **4 cups cubed cooked potato**
- **½ cup celery slices**
- **¼ cup chopped green pepper**
- **2 tablespoons green onion slices**
- **1 teaspoon salt**
- **1 8-ounce package PHILADELPHIA BRAND Cream Cheese, softened**
- **½ cup sour cream**
- **2 tablespoons milk**

Combine potatoes, celery, green peppers, onions and salt; mix lightly. Combine cream cheese, sour cream and milk, mixing until well blended. Add to potato mixture; mix lightly. Chill.
6 to 8 servings.

Bacon & Egg Potato Salad

- **5 cups cooked, peeled and cubed potatoes (about 2 pounds)**
- **¼ cup chopped green onions**
- **⅓ cup REALEMON® Lemon Juice from Concentrate**
- **⅓ cup water**
- **¼ cup vegetable oil**
- **1½ teaspoons celery salt**
- **1 teaspoon Worcestershire sauce**
- **½ teaspoon dry mustard**
- **¼ teaspoon pepper**
- **4 slices bacon, cooked and crumbled**
- **3 hard-cooked eggs, chopped**
- **¼ cup grated Parmesan cheese**
- **3 tablespoons chopped parsley**

In large bowl, combine potatoes and onions. In small saucepan, combine ReaLemon® brand, water, oil, celery salt, Worcestershire, mustard and pepper; bring to a boil. Pour over potato mixture; mix well. Cover; chill overnight to blend flavors. Remove from refrigerator 30 minutes before serving; stir in bacon, eggs, Parmesan cheese and parsley. Refrigerate leftovers.
Makes 10 to 12 servings.

Marinated Potato and Mushroom Salad

Zesty Potato Salad

4 large potatoes
1 pouch CAMPBELL'S® Onion Soup and Recipe Mix
¾ cup mayonnaise
¼ cup VLASIC® Sweet Relish
2 teaspoons prepared mustard
¼ teaspoon pepper
1½ cups chopped celery
2 hard-cooked eggs, diced
2 tablespoons chopped pimento (optional)

1. Place potatoes in large saucepan; add enough water to cover potatoes. Over high heat, heat to boiling. Reduce heat to medium-low. Cover; simmer 30 to 40 minutes until potatoes are tender.
2. Drain potatoes; cool, peel and cut into cubes.
3. In large bowl, stir together soup mix, mayonnaise, relish, mustard and pepper. Stir in potatoes, celery, eggs and pimento.
4. Cover; chill until serving time, at least 2 hours.
Makes 8 servings.

German-Style Potato Salad

2 pounds small new potatoes
2 hard-cooked eggs, sliced
½ teaspoon dill weed, crushed
2 tablespoons vegetable oil
½ pound kielbasa, diced
½ cup chopped onion
2 tablespoons all-purpose flour
2 tablespoons sugar
⅓ cup cider vinegar
1 can (10¾ ounces) CAMPBELL'S® Condensed Chicken Broth
⅓ cup water
Dash pepper
VLASIC® or EARLY CALIFORNIA® Sliced Pimento-Stuffed Olives

1. In 4-quart saucepan, place potatoes; add water to cover. Over high heat, heat to boiling. Reduce heat to low. Cover; simmer 20 to 30 minutes until fork-tender. Drain. Cool slightly; cut potatoes into slices.
2. In large bowl, combine potatoes, eggs and dill weed; set aside.
3. In 10-inch skillet over medium heat, in hot oil, cook kielbasa and onion until meat is well browned, stirring occasionally. Remove meat and onion with slotted spoon; add to potato mixture. Reserve drippings in skillet.
4. Stir flour into drippings. Cook 1 minute, stirring constantly. Add sugar, vinegar, broth, water and pepper. Cook until mixture boils, stirring constantly. Pour over potato mixture; toss gently to mix well. Sprinkle with olives. Serve warm.
Makes about 6 cups or 8 servings.

Pasta Vegetable Medley

1 package (12 ounces) bows egg noodles
1¼ cups WISH-BONE® Italian or Robusto Italian Dressing
½ cup mayonnaise
½ teaspoon basil leaves
Assorted Fresh Vegetables*

Cook noodles according to package directions; drain and rinse with cold water until completely cool.

In large salad bowl, blend Italian dressing, mayonnaise and basil; stir in Assorted Fresh Vegetables. Add noodles and toss well; cover and chill.
Makes about 8 side-dish servings.

***Assorted Fresh Vegetables:** Use any combination of the following to equal 5 cups—chopped cucumber, tomato, celery and red, green or yellow pepper; sliced mushrooms and carrots.

Potluck Pasta Salad

8 ounces spiral pasta
½ cup vegetable oil
¼ cup white vinegar
1 large clove garlic, pressed or minced
2 tablespoons lemon juice
2 teaspoons prepared mustard
2 teaspoons Worcestershire sauce
1 teaspoon salt
Dash pepper
¼ pound snow peas, ends and strings removed
2 cups DOLE™ Broccoli flowerets
2 cups sliced fresh mushrooms
1 cup DOLE™ Cauliflower flowerets
1 cup halved cherry tomatoes

Cook pasta according to package directions. Drain. Meanwhile, in screw-top jar, combine oil, vinegar, garlic, lemon juice, mustard, Worcestershire, salt and pepper. Shake well. In large bowl, combine hot pasta with dressing. Mix well. Add vegetables; toss to coat. Refrigerate, covered.
Makes 8 servings.

German-Style Potato Salad

Italian Pasta Salad

**8 ounces uncooked mostaccioli
  or ziti macaroni
2 large tomatoes, coarsely
  chopped
1½ cups broccoli florets, cooked
1 medium green pepper,
  chopped
1 cup (8 ounces) WISH-BONE®
  Robusto Italian Dressing
1 tablespoon chopped fresh
  basil leaves*
1 package (8 ounces) mozzarella
  cheese, diced
¼ cup grated Parmesan cheese**

Cook macaroni according to package directions; drain and rinse with cold water until completely cool.

In large salad bowl, combine tomatoes, broccoli, green pepper, robusto Italian dressing and basil. Add cheeses and macaroni, then toss lightly; cover and chill.
Makes about 10 side-dish servings.

*Substitution: Use 1 teaspoon dried basil leaves.

Garden Macaroni Salad

Chilled Rigatoni Salad

**1 clove garlic, halved
1½ to 2 cups cooked rigatoni
1 can (14 ounces) artichoke
  hearts, drained and cut into
  bite-size pieces
½ cup chopped sweet red
  pepper or green pepper
½ cup bite-size cubes mozzarella
  cheese
1 medium carrot, cut into
  julienne strips
¼ cup sliced pitted black olives
2 ounces salami, cut into thin
  strips
¼ cup CRISCO® Oil
2 tablespoons white wine
  vinegar
1 tablespoon olive oil
½ teaspoon salt
½ teaspoon sugar
½ teaspoon dry mustard
¼ to ½ teaspoon dried oregano
  leaves
¼ to ½ teaspoon dried basil
  leaves**

Rub inside of medium serving bowl with cut sides of garlic. Discard garlic. Mix rigatoni, artichoke hearts, red pepper, mozzarella cheese, carrot, olives and salami in prepared bowl.

Blend remaining ingredients in small bowl. Pour over rigatoni mixture. Toss to coat. Cover and refrigerate 2 to 3 hours. Stir before serving.
4 to 6 servings.

Garden Macaroni Salad

**¼ cup KRAFT Real Mayonnaise
1 8-ounce package
  PHILADELPHIA BRAND
  Cream Cheese, softened
¼ cup sweet pickle relish,
  drained
1 tablespoon KRAFT Pure
  Prepared Mustard
2 cups (7 ounces) elbow
  macaroni, cooked, drained
1 cup chopped cucumber
½ cup chopped green pepper
½ cup radish slices
2 tablespoons chopped onion
½ teaspoon salt**

Gradually add mayonnaise to cream cheese, mixing until well blended. Stir in relish and mustard. Add remaining ingredients; mix lightly. Spoon into lightly oiled 9-inch springform pan with ring insert. Chill several hours or overnight. Unmold. Garnish with cucumber slices and radish roses, if desired.
6 to 8 servings.

Variation: Add ½ cup (2 ounces) KRAFT Grated Parmesan Cheese to cream cheese mixture.

Three Bean Rice Salad

**1 can (16 oz.) cut wax beans,
  drained
1 can (16 oz.) French-style green
  beans, drained
1 can (8¾ oz.) red kidney
  beans, drained
½ cup prepared GOOD
  SEASONS® Italian Salad
  Dressing
¼ cup thinly sliced onion rings
1 teaspoon salt
⅛ teaspoon pepper
1½ cups water
1½ cups MINUTE® Rice**

Mix beans, salad dressing, onion, ½ teaspoon of the salt and the pepper in large bowl; set aside to allow flavors to blend.

Meanwhile, bring water and remaining ½ teaspoon salt to a full boil in medium saucepan. Stir in rice. Cover; remove from heat. Let stand 5 minutes. Fold rice into bean mixture. Cover and chill thoroughly. Serve on lettuce.
Makes 6 servings.

Wild Rice Salad

Rice Pilaf Salad

    1 package (6 ounces) ECKRICH®
        Ham, cut into thin strips
    1 package (9 ounces) rice pilaf
        mix
    3 tablespoons vegetable oil
    1 tablespoon vinegar
    1 cup chopped zucchini
    ½ cup cooked peas
    ¼ cup chopped fresh parsley
    ½ cup cherry tomato halves
    6 lemon wedges
    ⅓ cup plain yogurt

Cook rice pilaf according to package directions, omitting butter. Combine oil and vinegar; pour over warm rice pilaf in large bowl. Mix in ham, zucchini, peas and parsley. Cool to room temperature. Garnish each serving with tomatoes and lemon wedges; top with about 1 tablespoon yogurt.
Makes 6 servings.

South-of-the-Border Salad

    1½ cups V8® Vegetable Juice *or*
        No Salt Added V8®
        Vegetable Juice
    2 tablespoons wine vinegar
    2 tablespoons chopped fresh
        parsley
    1 clove garlic, minced
    3 cups cooked rice (1 cup
        uncooked)
    1 can (4 ounces) chopped
        chilies
    ½ cup frozen whole kernel corn,
        thawed and drained
    3 tablespoons chopped pimento

1. In medium bowl, stir together V8 juice, vinegar, parsley and garlic.
2. Add rice, chilies, corn and pimento; mix well. Cover; refrigerate until serving time, at least 4 hours.
Makes 5 cups or 6 side-dish servings.

Per serving: 143 calories, 3 g protein, 1 g fat, 32 g carbohydrate, 327 mg sodium (No Salt Added V8® Juice: 136 mg sodium), 0 mg cholesterol.

Wild Rice Salad

    1 (13¾-fluid ounce) can
        COLLEGE INN® Beef or
        Chicken Broth
    1 (6-ounce) package long-grain
        and wild rice
    1 (11-ounce) can mandarin
        oranges, drained
    1 (8-ounce) can CHUN KING®
        Sliced Water Chestnuts,
        drained
    ¼ cup sliced scallions
    ⅓ cup mayonnaise
        Lettuce leaves

Reserve 2 tablespoons broth. Add enough water to remaining broth to substitute for water in rice package directions. Cook rice according to directions omitting butter or margarine; cool. Stir in oranges, water chestnuts and scallions. Blend reserved broth and mayonnaise; stir into rice mixture. Cover and refrigerate 2 to 3 hours. Serve on lettuce leaves.
Makes 6 to 8 servings.

Tabbouleh

    ¾ cup bulgur, rinsed and drained
        Boiling water
    2 cups seeded, chopped
        cucumber
    1 large tomato, seeded and
        chopped
    1 cup snipped fresh parsley
    ⅓ cup CRISCO® Oil
    ⅓ cup chopped green onion
    2 tablespoons lemon juice
    1 teaspoon dried mint leaves
    2 cloves garlic, minced
    ½ teaspoon salt
    ⅛ teaspoon white pepper
    ⅛ teaspoon cayenne

Place bulgur in medium mixing bowl. Add enough boiling water to just cover bulgur. Let stand about 1 hour, or until bulgur is rehydrated. Drain.

Combine bulgur, cucumber, tomato and parsley in large serving bowl. Set aside. Blend remaining ingredients in small mixing bowl. Pour over bulgur mixture. Toss to coat. Cover and refrigerate at least 3 hours. Stir before serving.
10 to 12 servings.

Hot Chicken Salad

- **2 cups cubed cooked chicken or turkey**
- **1 cup chopped celery**
- **1 (8-ounce) can water chestnuts, drained and coarsely chopped**
- **2 tablespoons finely chopped onion**
- **1 cup mayonnaise or salad dressing**
- **3 tablespoons REALEMON® Lemon Juice from Concentrate**
- **1 teaspoon WYLER'S® or STEERO® Chicken-Flavor Instant Bouillon**
- **2 tablespoons sliced almonds, toasted**
- **2 tablespoons chopped parsley**

Preheat oven to 350°. In large bowl, combine all ingredients except almonds and parsley. Turn into 1½-quart baking dish; top with almonds. Bake 20 minutes or until hot. Garnish with parsley. Refrigerate leftovers.
Makes 4 to 6 servings.
Microwave: Prepare salad as above in 1½-quart baking dish. Microwave on full power (high) 5 to 6 minutes or until hot. Stir before serving. Garnish with parsley.

Chicken Salad Supreme

- **1 cup mayonnaise or salad dressing**
- **¼ cup REALIME® Lime Juice from Concentrate**
- **1 teaspoon salt**
- **¼ teaspoon ground nutmeg**
- **4 cups cubed cooked chicken or turkey**
- **1 (11-ounce) can mandarin orange segments, drained**
- **1 cup seedless green grape halves**
- **¾ cup chopped celery**
- **½ cup slivered almonds, toasted**

In large bowl, combine mayonnaise, ReaLime® brand, salt and nutmeg. Add remaining ingredients; mix well. Chill. Serve on lettuce. Refrigerate leftovers.
Makes 4 to 6 servings.

Cantonese Chicken Salad

- **3 chicken breast halves**
- **2 cups water**
- **5 tablespoons KIKKOMAN Soy Sauce, divided**
- **4 cups shredded iceberg lettuce**
- **1 medium carrot, peeled and shredded**
- **½ cup finely chopped green onions and tops**
- **⅓ cup distilled white vinegar**
- **2 tablespoons sesame seed, toasted**
- **2 teaspoons sugar**
- **½ teaspoon ground ginger**
- **2 tablespoons minced fresh cilantro or parsley**

Simmer chicken in mixture of water and 1 tablespoon soy sauce in covered saucepan 15 minutes, or until chicken is tender. Remove chicken and cool. (Refrigerate stock for another use, if desired.) Skin and bone chicken; shred meat with fingers into large mixing bowl. Add lettuce, carrot and green onions. Combine vinegar, remaining 4 tablespoons soy sauce, sesame seed, sugar and ginger; stir until sugar dissolves. Pour over chicken and vegetables; toss to coat all ingredients. Cover and refrigerate 1 hour. Just before serving, add cilantro and toss to combine. Garnish as desired.
Makes 6 servings.

Cobb Salad

- **½ cup vegetable oil**
- **¼ cup REALEMON® Lemon Juice from Concentrate**
- **1 tablespoon red wine vinegar**
- **2 teaspoons sugar**
- **½ teaspoon dry mustard**
- **½ teaspoon salt**
- **½ teaspoon Worcestershire sauce**
- **¼ teaspoon garlic powder**
- **¼ teaspoon pepper**
- **6 cups finely shredded lettuce**
- **2 cups finely chopped cooked chicken**
- **3 hard-cooked eggs, finely chopped**
- **2 medium tomatoes, seeded and chopped**
- **1 ripe avocado, seeded, peeled and chopped**
- **¼ cup (1 ounce) blue cheese, crumbled**
- **¼ cup imitation bacon or cooked crumbled bacon**

In 1-pint jar with tight-fitting lid or cruet, combine oil, ReaLemon® brand, vinegar, sugar and seasonings; shake well. Chill to blend flavors. In large salad bowl, arrange remaining ingredients; chill. Just before serving, toss with dressing. Refrigerate leftovers.
Makes 4 servings.

Cobb Salad

Stay Slim Salad

- 2 cups shredded DOLE™ Iceberg Lettuce
- ¼ cup chopped green onion
- ½ pound sliced cooked chicken
- 2 small DOLE™ Bananas, sliced
- 1 large DOLE™ Pink Grapefruit, peeled and sectioned
- 1 cup halved cherry tomatoes
- ½ cup sliced DOLE™ Celery Low-Calorie Dressing (recipe follows)

In medium bowl, combine lettuce and onion. Arrange on 2 salad plates. Arrange chicken in center of each. Arrange bananas, grapefruit, tomatoes and celery around chicken. Serve with Low-Calorie Dressing.
Makes 2 servings.
LOW-CALORIE DRESSING: In screwtop jar, combine ¼ cup lime juice, 2 tablespoons vegetable oil, 2 teaspoons sugar, ½ teaspoon paprika and ¼ teaspoon *each* salt and dry mustard. Shake until well blended.

Festive Chicken Salad

- 1 8¼-ounce can crushed pineapple, undrained
- 1 8-ounce container Soft PHILADELPHIA BRAND Cream Cheese
- 2 cups chopped cooked chicken
- 1 8-ounce can water chestnuts, drained, sliced
- ½ cup celery slices
- ½ cup slivered almonds, toasted
- ¼ cup green onion slices
- ¼ teaspoon salt
  Dash of pepper
- 4 medium tomatoes
  Lettuce

Drain pineapple, reserving ¼ cup liquid. Combine reserved liquid and cream cheese, mixing until well blended. Add pineapple, chicken, water chestnuts, celery, ¼ cup almonds, onions, salt and pepper; mix lightly. Chill. Cut each tomato into six wedges, almost to stem end. Fill with chicken mixture. Sprinkle with remaining almonds. Serve on lettuce-lined plates.
4 servings.
  Variations: Omit tomatoes; serve salad over honeydew or cantaloupe wedges or in lettuce cups.
  Substitute chopped pecans for almonds.

Waldorf Chicken Salad

- 1 cup uncooked CREAMETTE® Medium Macaroni Shells, cooked as package directs, rinsed and drained
- 2 cups cubed cooked chicken or turkey
- 2 cups coarsely chopped apple
- 1 cup (4 ounces) cubed mild Cheddar cheese
- ¾ cup sliced celery
- ½ cup mayonnaise or salad dressing
- ¼ cup applesauce
- 2 teaspoons WYLER'S® or STEERO® Chicken-Flavor Instant Bouillon
- ½ cup chopped pecans

In large bowl, combine ingredients; mix well. Chill thoroughly. Garnish as desired. Refrigerate leftovers.
Makes about 7½ cups.

Deluxe Chicken Walnut Salad

- ½ cup WISH-BONE® Chunky Blue Cheese or Lite Chunky Blue Cheese Dressing
- 2 cups cut-up cooked chicken (about 12 ounces)
- ½ cup green or red seedless grapes
- ½ cup chopped walnuts
- 2 tablespoons sliced green onion

In medium bowl, combine all ingredients and toss well; cover and chill. Serve, if desired, on croissants.
Makes about 2 main-dish servings.

Turkey Pineapple Salad

- 1½ cups (½ pound) cubed BUTTERBALL® SLICE 'N SERVE® Oven Prepared Breast of Turkey
- 1½ cups (½ pound) thin strips BUTTERBALL® SLICE 'N SERVE® Turkey Ham
- 2 cups fresh or canned pineapple chunks
- 1 cup diced unpared red apple
- ½ cup sliced celery
- ¾ cup pecan halves
- ¼ cup sour cream
- ¼ cup mayonnaise
- ½ teaspoon sugar
- ¼ teaspoon ground ginger
- ¾ teaspoon prepared mustard
  Lettuce leaves or pineapple shells

Combine turkey breast, turkey ham, pineapple, apple, celery and pecans in medium bowl. Stir together sour cream, mayonnaise, sugar, ginger and mustard in small bowl. Spoon dressing over salad and toss to blend. Serve immediately on lettuce leaves or pineapple shells.
Makes 6 servings.
  To Make Pineapple Shells: Cut pineapple lengthwise into quarters keeping top attached. Core and remove fruit from each quarter.

Turkey Pineapple Salad

Lemony Chicken Mold

1 (13³/₄-fluid ounce) can COLLEGE INN® Chicken Broth
2 (3-ounce) or 1 (6-ounce) package ROYAL® Lemon Gelatin
1 cup cold water
2 tablespoons white wine vinegar
1 (8-ounce) can crushed pineapple in its own juice, undrained
2 cups chopped cooked chicken
¹/₃ cup sliced celery
1 (2-ounce) jar diced pimientos, well drained

Refrigerate chicken broth; remove fat. In small saucepan, over high heat, heat broth to a boil; stir in gelatin until dissolved. Stir in water, vinegar and pineapple. Refrigerate until slightly thickened. Stir in chicken, celery and pimientos. Pour into 6-cup mold. Refrigerate until firm, about 3 hours. To serve, unmold onto serving plate. Garnish as desired.
Makes 6 to 8 servings.

Layered Chicken Salad

1 8-ounce package *Light* PHILADELPHIA BRAND Neufchâtel Cheese, softened
2 medium avocados, peeled, mashed
¹/₄ cup milk
1 tablespoon lemon juice
1 tablespoon chopped onion
¹/₂ teaspoon salt
4 cups shredded lettuce
1 cup chopped red or green pepper
2 cups chopped cooked chicken
1 11-ounce can mandarin orange segments, drained
4 crisply cooked bacon slices, crumbled

Combine neufchâtel cheese, avocados, milk and juice, mixing until well blended. Add onions and salt; mix well. In 2¹/₂-quart glass serving bowl, layer lettuce, peppers, chicken and oranges. Spread neufchâtel cheese mixture over oranges to cover. Chill. Top with bacon just before serving.
6 to 8 servings.

Lemony Chicken Mold

Apple & Tarragon Salad with Watercress

2 envelopes KNOX® Unflavored Gelatine
2 cups white grape juice
1¹/₂ cups apple juice
1 tablespoon lemon juice
1 medium apple, thinly sliced
1 cup loosely packed watercress leaves, chopped
1 cup seedless green grapes, halved
¹/₄ cup chopped green onions (about 2 medium)
1 tablespoon chopped fresh tarragon*
Grilled or broiled boneless chicken breasts, cut into strips

In medium saucepan, sprinkle unflavored gelatine over 1 cup grape juice; let stand 1 minute. Stir over low heat until gelatine is completely dissolved, about 5 minutes.

In large bowl, blend remaining 1 cup grape juice, apple juice, gelatine mixture and lemon juice. Chill, stirring occasionally, until mixture is consistency of unbeaten egg whites, about 30 minutes. Into 6-cup ring mold, spoon 1 cup gelatine mixture. Arrange apple slices, slightly overlapping, in bottom of mold. Fold watercress, grapes, green onions and tarragon into remaining gelatine mixture; carefully spoon over apple slices. Chill until firm, about 4 hours. To serve, unmold onto serving platter, then fill center with chicken and, if desired, additional watercress leaves. Serve, if desired, with WISH-BONE® Chunky Blue Cheese Dressing.
Makes about 8 servings.
Substitution: Use ¹/₂ teaspoon dried tarragon leaves.

Curried Pineapple Pasta Salad

- **1 can (20 ounces) DOLE® Pineapple Chunks**
- **2 cups cooked, shredded chicken**
- **8 ounces macaroni or other small pasta, cooked**
- **2 cups sliced DOLE™ Celery**
- **½ cup sliced green onion**
- **½ cup julienne-cut DOLE™ Red Bell Pepper**
- **½ cup sliced ripe olives**
- **¾ cup mayonnaise**
- **⅓ cup chopped chutney**
- **¼ cup dairy sour cream**
- **2 teaspoons curry powder**
- **1 teaspoon salt**

Drain pineapple. In salad bowl, combine pineapple, chicken, pasta, celery, onion, red pepper and olives. To make dressing, in 1-quart measure, combine remaining ingredients; toss with salad. Refrigerate, covered, until ready to serve.
Makes 8 servings.

Turkey Salad with Pita Bread

- **3 cups cubed cooked BUTTERBALL® turkey (1 pound)**
- **1 cup sour cream**
- **3 green onions, sliced**
- **1 tablespoon dried dill weed**
- **1 teaspoon seasoned salt**
- **1 medium cucumber, sliced thin**
- **1 small red onion, sliced thin**
- **12 small cherry tomatoes, cut into halves**
- **12 small fresh mushrooms, sliced thin**
  Lettuce leaves
- **6 pita breads, 6½-inch diameter, cut into halves**

Blend sour cream, green onions, dill weed and salt in medium bowl. Add turkey and vegetables except lettuce; toss to combine. Serve on lettuce with pita bread. Or fill pita bread halves with turkey mixture and serve as sandwiches.
Yield: 6 servings.

Garden Chicken Salad

Garden Chicken Salad

- **½ cup olive or vegetable oil**
- **¼ cup red wine vinegar**
- **1 tablespoon Dijon-style mustard**
- **1 tablespoon finely chopped onion**
- **1 tablespoon chopped fresh parsley**
- **¼ teaspoon salt**
- **¼ teaspoon pepper**
- **½ pound small potatoes**
- **¼ pound green beans, trimmed**
- **¼ cup water**
- **2 cans (5 ounces each) SWANSON® Premium Chunk White Chicken, drained**
  CAMPBELL'S FRESH® Butterhead Lettuce Leaves
- **2 hard-cooked eggs, sliced**
- **1 CAMPBELL'S FRESH® tomato, cut into wedges**
  VLASIC® or EARLY CALIFORNIA® Pitted Ripe Olives for garnish

To Microwave:

1. To prepare dressing: In small bowl or shaker jar, combine first 7 ingredients; shake or stir until well blended. Set aside.

2. Pierce potatoes with fork in several places. Arrange potatoes in corners of 8- by 8-inch microwave-safe baking dish; arrange green beans in center. Add water. Cover with vented plastic wrap; microwave on HIGH 6 minutes or until vegetables are nearly tender, rearranging vegetables once during cooking. Let stand, covered, 5 minutes. Drain.

3. Cut potatoes into slices. In medium bowl, toss potatoes and beans with ¼ cup of the dressing. In another small bowl, toss chicken with 2 tablespoons of the dressing. Cover; chill if desired.

4. Arrange lettuce on platter. Mound chicken in center and arrange potatoes, beans, eggs and tomato wedges around chicken. Garnish with olives. Serve with remaining dressing.
Makes 4 servings.

Curried Smoked Turkey Salad

½ cup mayonnaise
¼ cup WISH-BONE® Italian Dressing
2 tablespoons milk
1 teaspoon curry powder
¼ teaspoon ground ginger
⅛ teaspoon pepper
2 cups cut-up cooked smoked or unsmoked turkey breast (about 12 ounces)
2 cups broccoli florets
½ cup chopped red pepper
¼ cup sliced green onions

In large bowl, thoroughly blend mayonnaise, Italian dressing, milk, curry, ginger and pepper. Stir in remaining ingredients; cover and chill. Serve, if desired, over fresh spinach leaves.
Makes about 4 main-dish servings.
Notes: Recipe can be doubled.
Also terrific with Wish-Bone® Robusto Italian, Herbal Italian, Blended Italian, Lite Italian, Classic Dijon Vinaigrette or Lite Classic Dijon Vinaigrette Dressing.

French Quarter Rice Salad

1 package (6 ounces) long grain and wild rice mix
⅔ cup vegetable oil
⅓ cup white wine vinegar
1 tablespoon Dijon-style mustard
1 clove garlic, minced
½ teaspoon TABASCO® pepper sauce
2 cups diced cooked chicken or turkey
1 large carrot, shredded
½ cup raisins
⅓ cup chopped green onions
½ cup pecans, toasted

Cook rice according to package directions. Cool slightly. In large bowl combine oil, vinegar, mustard, garlic and Tabasco® sauce. Add rice, chicken, carrot, raisins and green onions; mix well. Cover; refrigerate 2 to 4 hours to blend flavors. Just before serving, stir in pecans.
Makes 4 servings.

Marinated Beef Salad

½ pound sliced PETER ECKRICH DELI® Roast Beef, cut into strips
½ cup picante salsa
2 tablespoons vegetable oil
3 teaspoons vinegar
¼ cup chopped red onion
1 avocado, peeled, cubed
4 lettuce leaves
1 tomato, cut into wedges
Tortilla chips, optional

Combine salsa, oil, vinegar and red onion in medium bowl. Add roast beef; stir to coat meat with salsa mixture. Cover and refrigerate 1 hour. Just before serving, add avocado and toss. To serve, place beef mixture on lettuce leaves and garnish with tomato. Serve with tortilla chips.
Makes 4 servings.

Shaved Ham Salad

8 ounces shaved fully cooked ham, coarsely chopped
1½ cups coarsely chopped fresh mushrooms
¾ cup bite-size cubes mozzarella cheese
½ cup quartered pimiento-stuffed olives
⅓ cup chopped green onion
1 medium tomato, seeded and chopped
⅓ cup CRISCO® Oil
2 tablespoons red wine vinegar
¼ teaspoon pepper

Mix ham, mushrooms, mozzarella cheese, olives, onion and tomato in medium serving bowl. Blend remaining ingredients in small mixing bowl. Pour over ham mixture. Toss to coat. Serve immediately, or refrigerate and stir before serving.
6 to 8 servings.

Confetti Beef Salad

½ pound PETER ECKRICH DELI® Roast Beef, cut into julienne strips
3 ounces uncooked thin spaghetti (about 2 cups cooked)
1 medium zucchini, cut into pieces
1 small yellow squash, cut into pieces

½ red bell pepper, cut into strips
½ cup coarsely shredded carrot
⅓ cup vinaigrette dressing with Dijon mustard
¼ teaspoon coarsely ground black pepper

Break spaghetti in half. Cook according to package directions. Rinse with cold water; drain. Combine all ingredients in large bowl. Cover and refrigerate at least 1 hour.
Makes 5 servings.

Pineapple and Ham Pasta Salad

1 can (20 ounces) DOLE® Pineapple Tidbits
1 pound cooked ham, diced
1 DOLE™ Red or Green Bell Pepper, seeded and diced
2 cups frozen peas, thawed
2 cups diced DOLE™ Celery
8 ounces elbow macaroni, cooked
1¼ cups mayonnaise
1 tablespoon vinegar
1 teaspoon onion powder
¼ teaspoon pepper
¼ teaspoon dried dill weed

Drain pineapple. In large bowl, combine pineapple, ham, red pepper, peas, celery and macaroni. To make dressing, in 1-quart measure, combine mayonnaise, vinegar, onion powder, pepper and dill weed. Stir dressing into pineapple mixture. Refrigerate 3 to 4 hours before serving to allow flavors to blend.
Makes 8 servings.

Pineapple and Ham Pasta Salad

Individual Taco Salads

Steak Salad in Red-Wine Dressing

½ cup WISH-BONE® Italian
    Dressing
½ cup dry red wine
1 tablespoon Worcestershire
    sauce
1 tablespoon rosemary leaves
2 teaspoons Dijon-style mustard
½ pound beef flank or round
    steak, thinly sliced
1 medium red onion, sliced
1 large tomato, coarsely
    chopped
1 cup sliced carrots
1 cup sliced zucchini

In large shallow baking dish, thoroughly blend Italian dressing, wine, Worcestershire sauce, rosemary and mustard. Add beef and red onion; turn to coat. Cover and marinate in refrigerator, stirring occasionally, at least 3 hours.

Remove beef, onion and marinade to large shallow heavy-duty aluminum-foil-lined baking pan or broiler rack. Broil beef with marinade, turning occasionally, 3 minutes or until done; cover and chill. To serve, toss beef mixture with tomato, then arrange on serving platter with carrots, zucchini and, if desired, watercress.

Makes about 4 main-dish servings.

Note: Also terrific with Wish-Bone® Robusto Italian, Italian & Cheese, Herbal Italian, Blended Italian, Lite Italian or Classic Dijon Vinaigrette Dressing.

Individual Taco Salads

⅓ cup French Dressing (see
    page 93)
    CRISCO® Oil for frying
4 to 6 eight-inch flour tortillas
1 pound ground beef
¼ cup chopped onion
1 can (15½ ounces) kidney
    beans, rinsed and drained
1½ teaspoons chili powder
1 teaspoon cumin
½ teaspoon salt
⅛ teaspoon pepper
4 to 6 cups shredded lettuce
1 cup shredded Cheddar cheese
    (about 4 ounces)

Prepare French Dressing as directed. Cover and refrigerate.

Heat 3 inches Crisco® Oil in deep-fryer or heavy saucepan to 375°F.

Place 1 tortilla in oil. Let float 5 to 10 seconds. Press center of tortilla into oil with metal ladle (tortilla will form a bowl shape). While pressing with metal ladle, fry 1 to 2 minutes longer, or until golden brown. Drain on paper towels. Repeat with remaining tortillas.

Combine ground beef and onion in large skillet. Brown over medium-high heat. Drain. Add beans, chili powder, cumin, salt and pepper. Cook over moderate heat, stirring constantly, for 5 minutes, or until flavors are blended. Stir in ⅓ cup French Dressing.

Divide shredded lettuce equally among fried tortillas. Top with meat mixture. Sprinkle with Cheddar cheese. Serve with *dairy sour cream, chopped tomato, chopped black olives* or *taco sauce,* if desired.

4 to 6 servings.

Ham-Pasta Salad Vinaigrette

1 cup V8® Vegetable Juice
1 tablespoon vegetable oil
1 tablespoon wine vinegar
1 teaspoon dried basil leaves,
    crushed
1 large clove garlic, minced
1½ cups corkscrew macaroni,
    cooked and drained (2 cups
    cooked)
¾ cup cooked ham cut into
    matchstick-thin strips
    (4 ounces)
½ cup cubed part-skim
    mozzarella cheese
2 tablespoons VLASIC® or
    EARLY CALIFORNIA® Sliced
    Pitted Ripe Olives
4 green onions, sliced

1. In medium bowl, stir together V8 juice, oil, vinegar, basil and garlic until well blended.

2. Add macaroni, ham, cheese, olives and onions; toss to coat well.

3. Cover; refrigerate until serving time, at least 2 hours.

Makes 4¹/₂ cups or 4 main-dish servings.

Per serving: 221 calories, 13 g protein, 10 g fat, 21 g carbohydrate, 732 mg sodium, 25 mg cholesterol.

Layered Salad Extraordinaire

 1 8-ounce package *Light* PHILADELPHIA BRAND Neufchâtel Cheese, softened
 ³/₄ cup (3 ounces) crumbled KRAFT Natural Blue Cheese
 ¹/₄ cup KRAFT Light Reduced Calorie Mayonnaise
 ¹/₄ cup milk
 2 tablespoons lemon juice
 1 tablespoon chopped chives
 2 quarts torn assorted greens
 1 cup shredded carrot
 2¹/₂ cups ham cubes
 1 cup chopped green pepper
 2 cups chopped tomato

Combine neufchâtel cheese and blue cheese, mixing until well blended. Add mayonnaise, milk, juice and chives; mix well.

Combine greens and carrots. Combine meat and green peppers. In 3-quart bowl, layer greens mixture, tomatoes and meat mixture. Spread neufchâtel cheese mixture over meat mixture to seal. Cover; chill several hours.

8 servings.

Summer Kielbasa Salad

 ¹/₂ pound ECKRICH® Polska Kielbasa, cut into ¹/₈-inch slices
 1 cup shredded red cabbage
 1 medium cucumber, sliced thin
 4 red radishes, sliced thin
 ¹/₂ cup mayonnaise
 ¹/₂ cup sour cream
 2 tablespoons Dijon mustard
 1 tablespoon prepared horseradish

 ¹/₂ teaspoon dried dill weed
 ¹/₂ teaspoon garlic salt
 ¹/₄ cup crumbled feta cheese
 1 teaspoon chopped fresh parsley

Saute kielbasa in 10-inch skillet over medium heat until lightly browned. Drain on paper towels. Cool. Place kielbasa, cabbage, cucumber and radishes in large bowl. Combine mayonnaise, sour cream, mustard, horseradish, dill weed and garlic salt in small bowl. Whisk to blend; stir in cheese. Pour dressing over kielbasa and vegetables. Cover and refrigerate 20 minutes. Sprinkle with parsley and serve.

Makes 4 to 6 servings.

Marinated Oriental Beef Salad

 1 (1- to 1¹/₄-pound) flank steak
 ¹/₃ cup REALEMON® Lemon Juice from Concentrate
 ¹/₄ cup catsup
 ¹/₄ cup vegetable oil
 1 tablespoon brown sugar

Marinated Oriental Beef Salad

 ¹/₄ teaspoon garlic powder
 ¹/₄ teaspoon ground ginger
 ¹/₄ teaspoon pepper
 8 ounces fresh mushrooms, sliced (about 2 cups)
 1 (8-ounce) can sliced water chestnuts, drained
 1 medium sweet onion, sliced and separated into rings
 1 (6-ounce) package frozen pea pods, thawed, or 4 ounces fresh pea pods
 Lettuce leaves
 Tomato wedges

Broil meat 5 minutes on each side or until desired doneness; slice diagonally into thin strips. Meanwhile, in large bowl, combine ReaLemon® brand, catsup, oil, sugar, garlic powder, ginger and pepper; mix well. Add sliced meat, mushrooms, water chestnuts and onion; mix well. Cover; refrigerate 8 hours or overnight, stirring occasionally. Before serving, add pea pods. Serve on lettuce; garnish with tomato. Refrigerate leftovers.

Makes 4 servings.

Garden Patch Salad

6 ounces SWIFT PREMIUM® Deli Hard Salami, cut into julienne strips
⅓ cup olive oil
2 tablespoons fresh lemon juice
1 tablespoon minced fresh parsley
1 tablespoon grated Parmesan cheese
1 clove garlic, minced
6 ounces mozzarella cheese, cubed
1 pint cherry tomatoes, cut into halves
1 medium zucchini, cut lengthwise into halves, sliced thin
1 small onion, cut into quarters, sliced thin

Place oil, lemon juice, parsley, Parmesan cheese and garlic in jar with tight-fitting lid. Shake ingredients together and let stand 1 hour for flavors to blend. Combine salami, mozzarella cheese, tomatoes, zucchini and onion in salad bowl. Pour dressing over salad and toss to blend before serving. *Makes 6 servings.*

Salad Taverna

Chef's Salad

6 cups torn lettuce
6 ounces spinach, rinsed, drained, trimmed and torn into bite-size pieces
8 ounces cooked turkey, cut into thin strips
8 ounces fully cooked ham, cut into thin strips
6 ounces Swiss cheese, cut into thin strips
1 cup broken melba cracker rounds
8 cherry tomatoes, halved
8 pitted black or green olives, halved
3 green onions, chopped

Combine all ingredients in large salad bowl or divide ingredients among individual salad bowls. Garnish with *hard-cooked egg slices*, if desired. Serve with desired dressing (see pages 92–93).
6 to 8 servings.

Favorite recipe from **CRISCO® Oil/Procter & Gamble**

Salada di Antipasto

2 quarts mixed salad greens
½ pound salami, cut into strips
1 package (8 ounces) mozzarella cheese, cut into strips
1 package (10 ounces) frozen artichoke hearts, cooked and drained
1 cup pitted ripe olives
1 medium tomato, cut into wedges
⅓ cup roasted red peppers, cut into strips
1 cup (8 ounces) WISH-BONE® Robusto Italian Dressing

In large salad bowl, arrange all ingredients except robusto Italian dressing; cover and chill. Just before serving, toss with dressing. Serve, if desired, with Italian bread.
Makes about 4 main-dish servings.
Note: Also terrific with Wish-Bone® Italian, Italian & Cheese, or Lite Italian Dressing.

Salad Taverna

⅓ cup olive or vegetable oil
3 tablespoons lemon juice
1 clove garlic, minced
½ teaspoon TABASCO® pepper sauce
½ teaspoon anise seed
¼ teaspoon salt
8 ounces spinach egg noodles, cooked, drained
½ pound feta cheese, crumbled or 1 cup ricotta or cottage cheese
2 tomatoes, coarsely chopped
½ cup sliced pitted ripe olives
¼ cup chopped parsley (optional)
¼ cup pine nuts (optional)

In large bowl combine oil, lemon juice, garlic, Tabasco® sauce, anise seed and salt; mix well. Add noodles, cheese, tomatoes, olives, parsley and pine nuts; toss to coat evenly. Cover; refrigerate at least 1 hour. Serve with additional Tabasco® sauce, if desired.
Makes 4 to 6 servings.

Wild Rice and Seafood Salad

- ½ cup WISH-BONE® Lite Classic Creamy Dijon Dressing
- 1 pound medium shrimp, cleaned, cooked and coarsely chopped*
- 2 cups cooked wild or regular white rice
- 1 small red or green pepper, chopped
- ½ cup halved seedless grapes
- ¼ cup sliced almonds, toasted
- 1 teaspoon lemon juice
- 3 dashes hot pepper sauce
  Lettuce leaves

In large bowl, combine all ingredients except lettuce; cover and chill. To serve, line bowl or individual serving dishes with lettuce; fill with shrimp mixture. Garnish, if desired, with lemon slices.
Makes about 6 main-dish servings.
   Substitution: Use 2 packages (6 ounces each) frozen crabmeat, thawed and drained. Increase dressing to ¾ cup.
   Note: Also terrific with Wish-Bone® Creamy Italian or Lite Creamy Italian Dressing.

Potato-Tuna Salad

- ½ cup olive or vegetable oil
- ¼ cup white wine vinegar
- 2 tablespoons lemon juice
- 1 clove garlic, minced
- ¾ teaspoon TABASCO® pepper sauce
- ¼ teaspoon salt
- 2 pounds cooked small red potatoes, cubed
- 2 cans (6½ or 7 ounces each) tuna, drained, separated into large chunks
- 1 cup sliced celery
- ⅓ cup sliced green onions
  Fresh spinach leaves (optional)

In large bowl combine oil, vinegar, lemon juice, garlic, Tabasco® sauce and salt; mix well. Add potatoes, tuna, celery and green onions; toss lightly. Cover; refrigerate at least 1 hour. Serve over fresh spinach leaves, if desired.
Makes 6 to 8 servings.

Sea Salad

- 1 bunch DOLE™ Broccoli, cut into flowerets (2 cups)
- 4 ounces snow peas, ends and strings removed
- 8 ounces shell-shaped pasta
- 2 cups sliced DOLE™ Celery
- 2 cups sliced fresh mushrooms
- ½ cup sliced DOLE™ Red Bell Pepper
- 8 ounces cooked, shelled shrimp
  Lemon-Mustard Dressing (recipe follows)

To blanch vegetables, cover broccoli and snow peas with boiling water. Let stand 5 minutes. Rinse under cold water to stop cooking; drain. Cook pasta according to package directions; drain. In large bowl, combine vegetables, pasta and shrimp; toss with Lemon-Mustard Dressing. Refrigerate, covered, at least 2 hours before serving.
Makes 4 servings.
LEMON-MUSTARD DRESSING: In 1-quart measure, combine ½ cup olive or vegetable oil, 3 tablespoons lemon juice, 1 tablespoon wine vinegar, 2 teaspoons Dijon mustard, 1 teaspoon dried dill weed, ¼ teaspoon pepper and salt to taste. Blend well.

Dilled Crab Salad Mold

- 1 envelope unflavored gelatin
- 1 cup water
- ½ cup MARIE'S® Refrigerated Sour Cream and Dill Salad Dressing
- 1 tablespoon finely chopped onion
  Dash hot pepper sauce
- 2 cups crabmeat, flaked
- ½ cup chopped VLASIC® Mild Banana Pepper Rings
- 1 cup heavy cream, whipped
  CAMPBELL'S FRESH® Butterhead Lettuce Leaves

1. In medium saucepan, sprinkle gelatin over water to soften; let stand 1 minute. Over low heat, heat until gelatin is dissolved, stirring constantly. Do not boil.
2. In medium bowl, combine salad dressing, onion and hot pepper sauce. Gradually stir in gelatin mixture. Cover; refrigerate about 40 minutes or until mixture mounds slightly when dropped from spoon.
3. Gently fold crabmeat and peppers into gelatin mixture. Fold in whipped cream. Pour into 4-cup mold. Cover; refrigerate until set, at least 2 hours.
4. To serve: Unmold onto lettuce-lined serving platter. Serve with crackers.
Makes 4 cups.

Potato-Tuna Salad

Tuna & Cracked Wheat Salad

    2½ cups water
    1 package (8 ounces) wheat
        pilaf mix
    ¼ cup lemon juice
    ¼ cup vegetable oil
    2 cans (6½ or 7 ounces each)
        tuna, drained, separated into
        chunks
    1 cucumber, pared, seeded and
        diced
    1 medium carrot, chopped
    ⅓ cup sliced green onions
    ¼ pound mushrooms, sliced
    1 tomato, chopped
    ½ cup sliced pitted ripe olives
    ½ cup chopped parsley
    ½ teaspoon salt
    ½ teaspoon TABASCO® pepper
        sauce
        Lettuce leaves
        Yogurt Dressing (recipe
        follows)

In medium saucepan bring water to a boil. Add pilaf mix; reduce heat, cover and simmer 15 minutes. Remove from heat; stir in lemon juice and oil. Let stand at room temperature until cool. Stir in remaining ingredients except lettuce leaves and Yogurt Dressing. Cover; refrigerate 4 hours. Turn into lettuce-lined serving dish. Serve with Yogurt Dressing.
Makes 6 to 8 servings.

Yogurt Dressing

    2 containers (8 ounces each)
        plain yogurt
    4 teaspoons chopped fresh mint
        or ¼ teaspoon dried dill
        weed
    ⅛ teaspoon TABASCO® pepper
        sauce

In small bowl combine yogurt, mint and Tabasco® sauce; mix well. Cover; refrigerate.
Makes 2 cups.

Cashew-Shrimp Salad

    ¾ cup V8® Vegetable Juice
    1 tablespoon soy sauce
    1 teaspoon vegetable oil
    ½ teaspoon grated lemon peel
    ½ teaspoon grated fresh ginger
    ¾ pound medium shrimp,
        cooked, shelled and
        deveined

    1½ cups cucumber slices cut in
        half
    1 large carrot, cut into
        matchstick-thin strips
        (1¼ cups)
    3 green onions, sliced (½ cup)
    ¼ cup coarsely chopped dry
        roasted unsalted cashews
        (1 ounce)
        CAMPBELL'S FRESH®
        Butterhead Lettuce Leaves
    4 slices PEPPERIDGE FARM®
        Fully Baked French-Style
        Bread

1. In medium bowl, combine V8 juice, soy sauce, oil, lemon peel and ginger.
2. Add shrimp, cucumbers, carrot and onions; toss to coat well. Cover; refrigerate until serving time, at least 2 hours.
3. Before serving, add cashews; toss to coat well. To serve: On 4 lettuce-lined salad plates, arrange shrimp mixture. Serve with French bread.
Makes 4 cups or 4 servings.

Per serving: 268 calories, 19 g protein, 7 g fat, 32 g carbohydrate, 739 mg sodium, 107 mg cholesterol.

Marinated Shrimp & Vegetables

    1 pound medium raw shrimp,
        deveined and cooked
    1 cup fresh cauliflowerets
    4 ounces small whole fresh
        mushrooms
    1 cup sliced zucchini
    1 large red or green pepper, cut
        into squares
    ¾ cup REALEMON® Lemon Juice
        from Concentrate
    1 tablespoon chopped green
        onion
    2 teaspoons sugar
    1 teaspoon salt
    ¼ to ½ teaspoon dill weed
    5 drops hot pepper sauce
    ¾ cup vegetable oil

Place shrimp and vegetables in shallow dish. In small bowl or jar, combine remaining ingredients except oil; mix well. Add oil; mix well. Pour over shrimp and vegetables. Cover; refrigerate 6 hours or overnight, stirring occasionally. Refrigerate leftovers.
Makes about 5 cups.

Cashew-Shrimp Salad

Fisherman's Favorite Cioppino Salad

1 cup WISH-BONE® Italian
   Dressing
1/4 cup dry white wine
1 teaspoon chopped fresh basil
   leaves*
2 cups cooked crabmeat or sea
   legs (about 3/4 pound)
3/4 pound large shrimp, cleaned
   and cooked
2 quarts mixed salad greens
3 medium tomatoes, coarsely
   chopped
10 artichoke hearts, halved**
1 medium red onion, cut into
   rings

In large shallow baking dish, blend Italian dressing, wine and basil; add crabmeat and shrimp. Cover and marinate in refrigerator, stirring occasionally, at least 2 hours.

Meanwhile, in large salad bowl, arrange salad greens, tomatoes, artichoke hearts and onion; cover and chill. Just before serving, add seafood with marinade and toss. Garnish, if desired, with chopped parsley.
Makes about 6 main-dish servings.
   ***Substitution:** Use 1/4 teaspoon dried basil leaves.
   ****Substitution:** Use 1 can (15 ounces) artichoke hearts, drained and halved.
   Note: Also terrific with Wish-Bone® Robusto Italian or Lite Italian Dressing.

Linguine Tuna Salad

1/2 1-pound package
   CREAMETTE® Linguine,
   broken in half
1/4 cup REALEMON® Lemon Juice
   from Concentrate
1/4 cup vegetable oil
1/4 cup chopped green onions
2 teaspoons sugar
1 teaspoon Italian seasoning
1 teaspoon seasoned salt
1 (12 1/2-ounce) can tuna, drained
1 (10-ounce) package frozen
   green peas, thawed
2 firm medium tomatoes,
   chopped

Cook linguine according to package directions; drain. Meanwhile, in large bowl, combine ReaLemon® brand, oil, onions, sugar, Italian seasoning and salt; mix well. Add *hot* linguine; toss. Add remaining ingredients; mix well.

Cover; chill to blend flavors. Serve on lettuce; garnish as desired. Refrigerate leftovers.
Makes 6 servings.

Calypso Shrimp Salad

1 cantaloupe, peeled and sliced
   into 4 rings
   Crisp DOLE™ Lettuce leaves
1 pound frozen salad shrimp,
   thawed
2 firm DOLE™ Bananas, sliced
1 DOLE™ Orange, peeled and
   sliced
1 pound DOLE™ Red Grapes, cut
   into clusters
   Banana Chutney Dressing
   (recipe follows)

Arrange each cantaloupe ring on lettuce-lined salad plate. Fill centers with shrimp. Arrange banana slices, orange slices and grapes around cantaloupe. Serve with Banana Chutney Dressing.
Makes 4 servings.
BANANA CHUTNEY DRESSING: Puree 1 ripe Dole™ Banana in blender. Add 1/2 cup mayonnaise, 2 tablespoons chutney and 1 tablespoon lemon juice. Process until blended. Refrigerate, covered, until ready to serve.

Creamy Shrimp 'n Yogurt Salad with Dill

1 envelope KNOX® Unflavored
   Gelatine
1/2 cup cold water
1/2 pint (8 ounces) plain yogurt
1/2 cup mayonnaise
1 pound shrimp, cleaned,
   cooked and coarsely
   chopped (about 2 1/2 cups)
1/2 cup chopped celery
1/4 cup grated Parmesan cheese
2 tablespoons snipped fresh
   dill*
1 tablespoon snipped chives
   (optional)
1 tablespoon Dijon-style
   prepared mustard
1/2 teaspoon salt
1/4 teaspoon pepper

In small saucepan, sprinkle unflavored gelatine over cold water; let stand 1 minute. Stir over low heat until gelatine is completely dissolved, about 3 minutes.

Calypso Shrimp Salad

In large bowl, with wire whisk or rotary beater, thoroughly blend gelatine mixture, yogurt and mayonnaise. Stir in remaining ingredients. Turn into 4-cup mold or bowl; chill until firm, about 3 hours. Unmold and garnish, if desired, with additional fresh dill.
Makes about 4 main-dish servings.
   ***Substitution:** Use 1 1/2 teaspoons dried dill weed.

Pacific Salad

1 pouch CAMPBELL'S® Onion
   Soup and Recipe Mix
1 cup mayonnaise
3/4 cup ketchup
1/4 cup VLASIC® Sweet Relish
   CAMPBELL'S FRESH®
   Butterhead Lettuce Leaves
1/2 pound asparagus spears,
   cooked and drained
1/2 pound whole green beans,
   cooked and drained
1 pound shrimp, cooked and
   peeled
2 hard-cooked eggs, cut into
   wedges
1 can (about 16 ounces) beets,
   drained and diced

1. To make dressing: In medium bowl, combine soup mix, mayonnaise, ketchup and relish; mix well. Cover; chill until serving time, at least 2 hours.
2. Arrange lettuce on 4 salad plates. Arrange asparagus, green beans, shrimp, eggs and beets in rows on greens.
3. Stir dressing and spoon over salad; reserve any remaining dressing for use on tossed salads.
Makes 4 servings.

Creamy V8 Dressing

1 package (8 ounces) Neufchâtel or reduced-calorie cream cheese, softened
1 cup reduced-calorie mayonnaise
1 cup V8® Vegetable Juice
3 cloves garlic, minced
1 teaspoon lemon juice

1. In medium bowl, blend Neufchâtel until smooth. Gradually stir in mayonnaise until well blended.
2. Stir in V8 juice, garlic and lemon juice. Cover; refrigerate until serving time, at least 2 hours. Use as a salad dressing, for dipping or as a sandwich spread.
Makes 2 1/2 cups.

Per tablespoon: 34 calories, 0 g protein, 3 g fat, 1 g carbohydrate, 89 mg sodium, 7 mg cholesterol.

Ginger-Soy Dressing

3/4 cup V8® Vegetable Juice
1/3 cup vegetable oil
2 tablespoons soy sauce
2 tablespoons red wine vinegar
1 tablespoon sugar
1 tablespoon grated fresh ginger
1 tablespoon dry sherry

In covered jar, combine all ingredients. Shake until well blended. Cover; refrigerate until serving time, at least 2 hours. Shake again just before using. Serve over salad greens or pasta salads.
Makes 1 1/2 cups.

Per tablespoon: 33 calories, 0 g protein, 3 g fat, 2 g carbohydrate, 112 mg sodium, 0 mg cholesterol.

Rosy Blue Cheese Dressing

3/4 cup V8® Vegetable Juice
3 tablespoons vegetable oil
2 tablespoons crumbled blue cheese
1 tablespoon lemon juice
1 tablespoon finely chopped onion
1 small clove garlic, minced

In covered jar, combine all ingredients. Shake until well blended. Cover; refrigerate until serving time, at least

2 hours. Shake again before using. Serve over salad greens or vegetable salads.
Makes 1 cup.

Per tablespoon: 29 calories, 0 g protein, 3 g fat, 1 g carbohydrate, 54 mg sodium, 1 mg cholesterol.

Celery Seed Dressing

1/2 cup sugar
1/4 cup REALEMON® Lemon Juice from Concentrate
2 teaspoons cider vinegar
1 teaspoon dry mustard
1/2 teaspoon salt
1/2 cup vegetable oil
1 teaspoon celery seed or poppy seed

In blender container, combine all ingredients except oil and celery seed; blend until smooth. On low speed, continue blending, slowly adding oil. Stir in celery seed. Chill to blend flavors. Refrigerate leftovers.
Makes about 1 cup.

Golden Fruit Dressing

1/2 cup sugar
1 tablespoon cornstarch
1/4 teaspoon salt
2/3 cup orange juice
1/4 cup REALEMON® Lemon Juice from Concentrate
1 teaspoon grated orange rind
2 eggs, beaten
1 (8-ounce) container BORDEN® LITE-LINE® or VIVA® Plain Lowfat Yogurt

In small saucepan, combine sugar, cornstarch and salt; stir in juices and orange rind. Over medium heat, cook and stir until thickened and clear; remove from heat. Gradually stir about *1/4 cup* hot mixture into eggs; stir into remaining juice mixture. Over low heat, cook and stir until slightly thickened. Cool. Fold in yogurt. Chill. Serve with fresh fruit. Refrigerate leftovers.
Makes about 2 cups.

Clockwise from top: Creamy V8 Dressing, Ginger-Soy Dressing, Rosy Blue Cheese Dressing

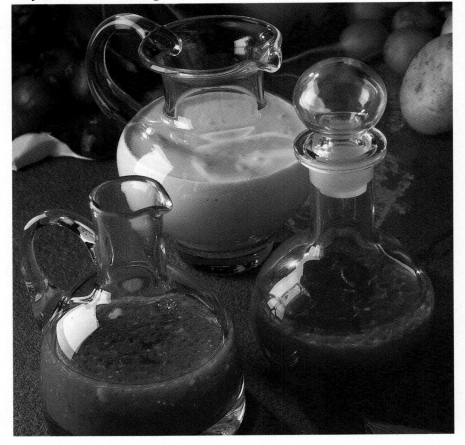

Onion Green Goddess Dressing

    1 pouch CAMPBELL'S® Onion
      Soup and Recipe Mix
 1½ cups mayonnaise
 ¾ cup chopped fresh parsley
 ⅓ cup milk
    1 tablespoon lemon juice
    1 tablespoon anchovy paste
    2 teaspoons dried basil leaves,
      crushed
 ½ teaspoon dried tarragon
      leaves, crushed

1. In medium bowl, combine all ingredients. Stir until well blended. Cover; chill until serving time, at least 2 hours. Thin with additional milk to desired consistency.
2. Serve over salad greens or as a dip for raw vegetables.
Makes 2 cups.

Blue Cheese Dressing

    1 pouch CAMPBELL'S® Onion
      Soup and Recipe Mix
    1 cup sour cream
 ½ cup mayonnaise
 ½ cup crumbled blue cheese
 ½ cup milk

1. In medium bowl, combine all ingredients. Stir until well blended. Cover; chill until serving time, at least 2 hours. Thin with additional milk to desired consistency.
2. Serve over salad greens or as a dip for raw vegetables.
Makes 2 cups.

Vinaigrette Dressing

 ¾ cup CRISCO® Oil
 ⅓ cup red wine vinegar
    1 tablespoon snipped fresh
      parsley
    1 teaspoon Worcestershire
      sauce
 ½ teaspoon salt
 ¼ teaspoon dry mustard
 ¼ teaspoon pepper
    1 clove garlic, minced

Combine all ingredients in jar. Cover tightly and shake until blended.
 Store covered in refrigerator. Shake before serving.
About 1 cup.

Garlic Dressing

    7 cloves garlic, divided
 ¾ cup CRISCO® Oil, divided
    3 tablespoons white wine
      vinegar
 ½ teaspoon salt
 ½ teaspoon freeze-dried chives
 ¼ teaspoon dry mustard
 ⅛ teaspoon pepper

Cut 6 garlic cloves in half. Mince remaining clove and set aside.
 Heat ¼ cup Crisco® Oil in small skillet. Add halved garlic cloves. Cook over low heat, stirring occasionally, about 5 minutes, or until garlic is golden brown. Remove from heat. Cool. Remove and discard garlic.
 Transfer garlic-flavored oil to jar. Add remaining ingredients, including remaining ½ cup Crisco® Oil and minced garlic. Cover tightly and shake until blended. Refrigerate at least 2 hours. Shake before serving. Store covered in refrigerator.
About 1 cup.

French Dressing

 ⅔ cup CRISCO® Oil
 ½ cup catsup
    2 tablespoons white wine
      vinegar
    1 tablespoon sugar
    1 teaspoon paprika
 ½ teaspoon dry mustard

Combine all ingredients in blender pitcher. Blend at medium to high speed until smooth (at least 2 minutes), stopping to scrape pitcher, if necessary.
 Cover and store in refrigerator. Stir before serving.
1¼ cups.

Honey Dressing for Fruit

 ½ cup CRISCO® Oil
 ⅓ cup honey
    3 tablespoons port wine

Combine all ingredients in blender pitcher. Blend at medium speed until smooth. Serve immediately over fruit salad or grapefruit.
About 1 cup.
 Variation: Honey-Apple Dressing. Follow recipe above, substituting apple juice for wine.

Herbed Buttermilk Dressing

    1 cup BORDEN® or MEADOW
      GOLD® Buttermilk
    1 cup mayonnaise or salad
      dressing
    1 teaspoon basil leaves
 ½ teaspoon garlic salt
 ½ teaspoon thyme leaves
 ¼ teaspoon pepper
 ¼ teaspoon onion powder

In small bowl, combine ingredients; mix well. Chill to blend flavors. Serve with salads or as a vegetable dip. Refrigerate leftovers.
Makes about 2 cups.

Parmesan Dressing

    1 pouch CAMPBELL'S® Onion
      Soup and Recipe Mix
 1½ cups mayonnaise
 ½ cup grated Parmesan cheese
 ⅓ cup milk
    1 tablespoon anchovy paste
 ½ teaspoon curry powder
    1 clove garlic, minced

1. In medium bowl, combine all ingredients. Stir until well blended. Cover; chill until serving time, at least 2 hours. Thin with additional milk to desired consistency.
2. Serve over salad greens or as a dip for raw vegetables.
Makes 2 cups.

Lemony Low Cal Dressing

 ¼ cup REALEMON® Lemon Juice
      from Concentrate
 ⅔ cup plus 2 tablespoons water
    1 (1.3-ounce) package low
      calorie Italian salad dressing
      mix

In 1-pint jar with tight-fitting lid or cruet, combine ingredients; shake well. Chill to blend flavors.
Makes about 1 cup: 8 calories per tablespoon.

MEATS

Hearty main dishes of beef, pork, lamb or veal are always favorites. Try new ideas for appetizing family meals or sophisticated entrees for a memorable evening. Serve steaks and chops hot from the grill, or sample the zesty flavors of international specialties.

Beef Tenderloin Dijon

1 beef tenderloin roast (about 2 pounds)
1½ teaspoons salt, divided
¾ teaspoon pepper, divided
2 tablespoons olive oil
2 cloves garlic, minced
4 cups water
2 cans (10¾ ounces each) condensed beef broth
1 bay leaf
½ teaspoon dried thyme leaves
2 whole cloves
1 tablespoon *each* cornstarch and Dijon-style mustard

Tie beef tenderloin roast with heavy string at 2-inch intervals. Combine 1 teaspoon of the salt and ½ teaspoon of the pepper; rub on surface of roast. Heat oil in Dutch oven over medium-high heat. Add roast and garlic; cook until evenly browned, about 6 minutes. Remove roast from pan; pour off drippings. Add water, broth, bay leaf, thyme and cloves; bring to a boil. Add roast; reduce heat to medium-low. Cover and simmer about 20 minutes. Check temperature with instant-read thermometer; temperature should register 130°F for rare. Do not overcook. Remove roast to serving platter. Cover tightly with plastic wrap or foil and allow to stand 10 minutes before carving. (Roast will continue to rise about 10°F in temperature to 140°F for rare.)

Strain cooking liquid; reserve 2 cups. Remove Dutch oven from heat; add cornstarch and mustard, mixing to form a thick paste. Gradually add reserved cooking liquid, stirring constantly. Place Dutch oven over medium heat; add remaining ½ teaspoon salt and ¼ teaspoon pepper. Cook until slightly thickened, about 7 minutes. Remove strings from roast. Carve into thin slices. Serve with sauce and steamed vegetables, if desired.

Note: A beef tenderloin roast will yield four 3-ounce cooked servings per pound.

(continued)

Nutrient data per 3-ounce cooked, trimmed serving: 213 calories; 11 g fat; 70 mg cholesterol; 841 mg sodium; 3.4 mg iron.

*Favorite recipe from **National Live Stock and Meat Board***

Rouladen

6 slices bacon, partially cooked, reserving 2 tablespoons drippings
4 cups sliced onions
6 beef tip steaks (about ¼ pound each), pounded
Dijon-style mustard
6 dill pickle spears
Flour
2 tablespoons vegetable oil
1⅓ cups plus 2 tablespoons water
2 teaspoons WYLER'S® or STEERO® Beef-Flavor Instant Bouillon *or* 2 Beef-Flavor Bouillon Cubes
1 teaspoon thyme leaves
1 bay leaf
1 tablespoon flour
Hot cooked noodles

In large skillet, cook onions in reserved drippings until tender. Remove onions from skillet. On each steak, spread mustard; top with 1 slice bacon, about ½ cup onions and 1 pickle spear. Roll up. Secure with wooden picks. Coat with flour. In same skillet, brown meat in oil. Add *1⅓ cups* water, bouillon, thyme and bay leaf; bring to a boil. Cover and simmer 30 minutes or until tender. Remove meat from skillet; remove bay leaf. Mix remaining *2 tablespoons* water and *1 tablespoon* flour; stir into liquid in skillet. Cook and stir until slightly thickened. Remove picks; serve meat with noodles. Garnish as desired. Refrigerate leftovers.
Makes 6 servings.

Beef Tenderloin Dijon

German Beef Roulade

1½ **pounds flank steak**
4 **teaspoons GREY POUPON®**
Dijon Mustard
6 **slices bacon, diced**
¾ **cup chopped onion**
⅓ **cup chopped dill pickle**
¼ **cup all-purpose flour**
1 **(13¾-fluid ounce) can**
COLLEGE INN® Beef Broth

With meat mallet or rolling pin, flatten meat to approximately a 10×8-inch rectangle. Spread mustard over meat.

In large skillet, over medium-high heat, cook bacon and onion until bacon is crisp; pour off fat, reserving ¼ cup. Spread bacon mixture over meat; sprinkle with pickle. Roll up meat from short end; secure with string.

In large skillet, over medium-high heat, brown beef roll in reserved fat; place in 13×9×2-inch baking dish. Stir flour into fat in skillet until smooth; gradually stir in beef broth. Cook and stir over medium heat until thickened. Pour sauce over beef roll. Cover; bake at 325°F for 1½ hours or until done. Let stand 10 minutes before slicing. Skim fat from sauce; strain and serve with meat.
Makes 6 servings.

German Beef Roulade

Old-Fashioned Pot Roast

3- **to 3½-pound boneless pot**
roast (rump, chuck or round)
1 **envelope LIPTON® Onion,**
Beefy Onion, Beefy
Mushroom or Onion-
Mushroom Recipe Soup Mix
2¼ **cups water**

In Dutch oven, brown roast over medium heat. Add onion recipe soup mix blended with water. Simmer covered, turning occasionally, 2½ hours or until tender. If desired, thicken gravy.
Makes about 6 servings.

Try some of these delicious international variations!

French-Style Pot Roast: Decrease water to 1¼ cups. Add 1 cup dry red wine and 1 teaspoon thyme leaves.

German-Style Pot Roast: Decrease water to ¾ cup. Add 1½ cups beer, 1 teaspoon brown sugar and ½ teaspoon caraway seeds.

Italian-Style Pot Roast: Decrease water to 1 cup. Add 1 can (14½ ounces) whole peeled tomatoes, un-

drained and chopped, 1 teaspoon basil leaves and 1 bay leaf. (Remove bay leaf before serving.)

Microwave Directions: Decrease water to 1¼ cups. In 3-quart casserole, blend onion recipe soup mix with water and heat at HIGH (Full Power) 5 minutes. Add roast and heat uncovered 10 minutes, turning once. Heat covered at DEFROST (30% Full Power), turning occasionally, 50 minutes or until tender. Let stand covered 10 minutes.

Islander's Beef Barbecue

1 **boneless beef chuck roast**
(3 to 3½ pounds)
¾ **cup apricot-pineapple jam**
2 **tablespoons soy sauce**
1 **teaspoon ground ginger**
1 **teaspoon grated lemon peel**

Slice roast across grain into ¼-inch-thick slices. In bowl, combine remaining ingredients. Grill beef slices, on uncovered grill, over medium-hot **KINGSFORD® Charcoal Briquets** 8 to 10 minutes. Turn and baste often with jam mixture.
Makes 4 to 6 servings.

Eight Flavors Pot Roast

1 **can (20 ounces) DOLE®**
Pineapple Chunks
2½ **pounds boneless beef chuck**
1 **tablespoon vegetable oil**
1 **small yellow onion, chopped**
2 **cloves garlic, pressed**
1½ **cups water**
½ **cup soy sauce**
¼ **cup dry sherry**
2½ **tablespoons brown sugar**
2 **cinnamon sticks**
1 **tablespoon minced fresh**
ginger root
1 **teaspoon allspice**
1 **head Chinese cabbage, cut**
into quarters*
4 **teaspoons cornstarch**
2 **tablespoons water**

Drain pineapple; reserve juice. Trim excess fat from beef. Heat large pot until hot. Add oil, swirling to coat sides. Cook onion and garlic in hot oil, stirring, 1 minute. Add beef; brown 2 minutes on each side.

In medium bowl, combine reserved pineapple juice, 1½ cups water, soy sauce, sherry, sugar, cinnamon, ginger and allspice; pour over beef. Bring to boil; reduce heat and simmer, covered, turning meat occasionally, 1¼ hours. Add cabbage; cook 30 minutes longer, adding pineapple last 5 minutes.

Remove meat, cabbage and pineapple from pot. Slice meat and arrange on serving platter with cabbage and pineapple. Strain remaining broth. Pour 1 cup into saucepan. Dissolve cornstarch in 2 tablespoons water; add to broth. Cook, stirring, until sauce boils and thickens. Pour over beef to serve.

Makes 6 servings.

*Or use green cabbage (about 2 pounds).

Standing Rib Roast with Madeira Sauce

2 large cloves garlic, finely chopped
1 teaspoon marjoram leaves (optional)
1 teaspoon thyme leaves
1 teaspoon salt
¼ teaspoon pepper
5-pound standing rib roast (about 3 ribs)
¼ cup butter or margarine
2 cups thinly sliced mushrooms
¼ cup Madeira or dry red wine
1 tablespoon tomato paste
1 envelope LIPTON® Onion, Onion-Mushroom or Beefy Mushroom Recipe Soup Mix
1 tablespoon all-purpose flour
1½ cups water
1 tablespoon finely chopped parsley
Pepper to taste

Preheat oven to 500°. In small bowl, combine garlic, marjoram, thyme, salt and pepper; set aside.

Trim fat from roast. In roasting pan, on rack, place roast; rub with garlic mixture. Roast 10 minutes, then decrease heat to 350° and continue roasting 1½ hours or until meat thermometer reaches 130° (rare) or 150° (medium).

Remove roast to serving platter and keep warm. Skim fat from pan drippings. In medium saucepan, combine pan juices with butter; stir in mushrooms. Cook 5 minutes or until mushrooms are tender. Stir in wine and tomato paste, then onion recipe soup mix and flour blended with water. Bring to a boil, then simmer, stirring frequently, 5 minutes or until sauce is thickened. Stir in parsley and pepper. Serve sauce with roast.

Makes about 6 servings.

Chuckwagon Roast and Vegetables

1 (3-pound) boneless beef chuck roast
3 tablespoons vegetable oil
3 tablespoons flour
1 cup BORDEN® or MEADOW GOLD® Buttermilk
1 cup water
4 teaspoons WYLER'S® or STEERO® Beef-Flavor Instant Bouillon *or* 4 Beef-Flavor Bouillon Cubes
½ teaspoon thyme leaves
¼ teaspoon pepper
4 medium carrots, cut into 1-inch pieces
2 medium onions, cut into wedges
1 (10-ounce) package frozen broccoli spears, thawed and cut into pieces
1 (10-ounce) package frozen cauliflower, thawed

Preheat oven to 350°. In large skillet, brown roast in oil. Place in 3-quart roasting or baking pan. Add flour to drippings in skillet; cook and stir until browned. Add buttermilk, water, bouillon, thyme and pepper. Cook and stir until bouillon dissolves and mixture thickens slightly, about 10 minutes. Place carrots and onions around meat; spoon sauce over meat. Cover; bake 1 hour and 45 minutes or until meat is tender. Add remaining vegetables; bake 10 minutes longer or until tender. Refrigerate leftovers.

Makes 6 to 8 servings.

Chuckwagon Roast and Vegetables

Souper Pot Roast

2 tablespoons all-purpose flour
2½- to 3-pound beef chuck roast
1 can (10¾ ounces) CAMPBELL'S® Condensed Cream of Mushroom Soup
1 bay leaf
4 carrots, peeled and cut into 2-inch lengths
2 large potatoes, cut into quarters

To Microwave:
1. Place flour in 3-quart microwave-safe casserole. Add roast, turning to coat with flour on all sides; discard excess flour. Spread soup over meat; add bay leaf. Cover with lid; microwave on HIGH 20 minutes.
2. Turn roast over, spooning soup over roast. Reduce power to 50%. Cover; microwave 20 minutes.
3. Add carrots and potatoes to casserole. Cover; microwave at 50% power 40 minutes or until meat and vegetables are tender, rotating dish once during cooking. Let stand, covered, 10 minutes. Remove bay leaf.

Makes 6 servings.

Note: The shape of a pot roast can make a big difference in the time needed for cooking it (this is also true for conventional cooking methods). Choose a flatter roast for quicker, more even cooking; a cube-shaped roast will require more time.

Mongolian Beef

- 3/4 **pound boneless tender beef steak (sirloin, rib eye or top loin)**
- 3 **tablespoons cornstarch, divided**
- 4 **tablespoons KIKKOMAN Teriyaki Sauce, divided**
- 1 **tablespoon dry sherry**
- 1 **clove garlic, minced**
- 1 **cup water**
- 1 **teaspoon distilled white vinegar**
- 1/4 **to** 1/2 **teaspoon crushed red pepper**
- 2 **tablespoons vegetable oil, divided**
- 2 **carrots, cut diagonally into thin slices**
- 1 **onion, chunked and separated**
- 1 **green pepper, chunked**

Cut beef across grain into strips, then into 1½-inch squares. Combine 2 tablespoons cornstarch, 1 tablespoon teriyaki sauce, sherry and garlic in medium bowl; stir in beef. Let stand 30 minutes. Meanwhile, combine water, remaining 1 tablespoon cornstarch, 3 tablespoons teriyaki sauce, vinegar and red pepper; set aside. Heat 1 tablespoon oil in hot wok or large skillet over high heat. Add beef and stir-fry 1 minute; remove. Heat remaining 1 tablespoon oil in same pan. Add carrots, onion and green pepper; stir-fry 4 minutes. Add beef and teriyaki sauce mixture; cook and stir until sauce boils and thickens.
Makes 4 servings.

Stuffed Flank Steak

Grilled Tenderloin with Cognac

- 1 **beef tenderloin roast (2 pounds)**
- 1/4 **cup whole green, white or black peppercorns**
  Garlic Mushrooms (recipe follows)
- 1/3 **cup cognac or other brandy**
- 1 **cup whipping cream**
- 2 **tablespoons Dijon-style mustard**
- 1 **tablespoon Worcestershire sauce**
- 2 **teaspoons lemon juice**

Trim excess fat from roast. Crack peppercorns coarsely with mortar and pestle; sprinkle on roast and press into surface.

In grill, arrange medium-hot **KINGSFORD® Charcoal Briquets** around drip pan. Place roast over drip pan. Cover grill and cook, turning once, until meat thermometer registers 140°F for rare (about 45 minutes), 150°F for medium-rare (about 55 minutes), or 170°F for well-done (about 60 minutes). While roast is cooking, prepare Garlic Mushrooms. About 15 minutes before meat is done, place mushrooms next to meat.

When roast is grilled to desired doneness, warm cognac in skillet on range-top. Remove from heat. Place roast in heated skillet. Carefully ignite cognac with match; allow flames to subside, carefully spooning cognac over meat. Remove roast to serving platter; reserve juices.

In saucepan, combine cream, mustard and Worcestershire sauce. Bring to boil. Cook and stir, over medium-low heat, 3 minutes or until slightly thickened. Remove from heat; stir in lemon juice and reserved cognac juices. Carve roast and arrange with Garlic Mushrooms. Pour cream sauce over sliced roast and mushrooms.
Makes 8 servings.

Garlic Mushrooms

- 32 **large fresh mushrooms**
- 1/2 **cup olive or vegetable oil**
- 2 **cloves garlic, minced**

Remove stems from mushrooms; reserve caps. In bowl, combine oil and garlic; add mushroom caps. Gently toss to coat. Remove mushrooms with slotted spoon; place mushroom caps on piece of heavy-duty foil. Seal edges tightly. Grill at side of roast over medium-hot **KINGSFORD® Charcoal Briquets** 10 to 15 minutes or until tender.
Makes 8 servings.

Stuffed Flank Steak

- 1 **(1½-pound) flank steak, pounded**
- 2 **cups herb-seasoned stuffing mix**
- 2 **teaspoons WYLER'S® or STEERO® Beef-Flavor Instant Bouillon or 2 Beef-Flavor Bouillon Cubes**
  Flour
- 3 **tablespoons vegetable oil**
- 1 **cup chopped onion**
- 1 **clove garlic, chopped**
- 2 **(10¾-ounce) cans condensed tomato soup**
- 1/2 **teaspoon basil leaves**
  Hot cooked noodles
  Parsley

Preheat oven to 350°. Prepare stuffing mix according to package directions, dissolving bouillon in liquid. Spread stuffing evenly on top of steak to within 1 inch of edges. Roll up, tucking in ends; tie with string. Coat roll with flour. In large skillet, brown in oil. Place in shallow baking dish. In same skillet, cook onion and garlic until tender. Add soup and basil; cook and stir until smooth. Pour over meat. Cover; bake 1 hour, basting occasionally. Serve with noodles; garnish with parsley. Refrigerate leftovers.
Makes 6 servings.

Grilled Flank Steak Sangrita

- **1 beef flank steak (2¹/₂ to 3 pounds)**
- **1 teaspoon salt**
- **¹/₄ teaspoon pepper**
- **1 teaspoon dried thyme, crushed**
- **¹/₄ cup orange juice concentrate, thawed and undiluted**
- **3 tablespoons vegetable oil Fruity Wine Sauce (recipe follows)**

Lightly score steak and rub with salt, pepper and thyme. In shallow glass dish, combine orange juice concentrate and oil. Add steak; turn to coat with marinade. Cover and refrigerate at least 30 minutes. Drain meat; reserve marinade. Grill steak, on covered grill, over medium-hot **KINGSFORD® Charcoal Briquets** 8 to 10 minutes on each side, turning once and basting often with marinade, until done. Cut meat across grain into diagonal slices. Serve with Fruity Wine Sauce.
Makes 6 servings.

Fruity Wine Sauce

- **1¹/₂ cups red wine**
- **1 orange, thinly sliced**
- **1 lime, thinly sliced**
- **1 apple, thinly sliced**
- **³/₄ cup chopped green onion with tops**
- **¹/₂ cup butter or margarine**
- **2 tablespoons chopped parsley**

In small saucepan, combine red wine, fruit and green onion; bring to boil. Stir in butter and parsley; cook and stir until butter is melted and sauce is hot.
Makes about 2 cups.

Steak with Hearty Mustard Marinade

- **¹/₂ cup Dijon-style mustard**
- **3 tablespoons soy sauce**
- **3 tablespoons dry sherry wine**
- **2 tablespoons brown sugar**
- **1 tablespoon vegetable oil**
- **1 clove garlic, minced**
- **¹/₂ teaspoon TABASCO® pepper sauce**
- **2 pounds round steak, 1¹/₂ inches thick**

Steak with Hearty Mustard Marinade

In medium bowl combine mustard, soy sauce, wine, sugar, oil, garlic and Tabasco® sauce; mix well. Place steak in large shallow dish or plastic bag; add marinade. Cover; refrigerate at least 5 hours; turn meat occasionally.

Remove meat from marinade; place on grill about 5 inches from source of heat. Brush with marinade. Grill 15 minutes; turn meat and brush with marinade. Grill 10 minutes longer or until desired doneness.
Makes 8 servings.

Peppery Rib Steaks

- **¹/₃ cup lemon juice**
- **2 tablespoons vegetable oil**
- **1 clove garlic, crushed**
- **1 teaspoon chili powder**
- **1 teaspoon seasoned salt**
- **¹/₂ teaspoon seasoned or cracked pepper**
- **4 beef rib eye steaks, cut ³/₄ to 1 inch thick (about 6 ounces each)**

In shallow glass dish, combine all ingredients except steaks. Add steaks; turn to coat with marinade. Cover and refrigerate at least 2 hours or overnight. Drain steaks; reserve marinade. Grill steaks, on uncovered grill, over medium-hot **MATCH LIGHT® Charcoal Briquets** about 15 minutes or until cooked, turning and basting often with marinade.
Makes 4 servings.

Pepper-Stuffed Flank Steak

- **2 beef flank steaks (about 1 pound each)**
- **1¹/₄ teaspoons garlic powder**
- **¹/₄ teaspoon black pepper**
- **1 green pepper, cut into strips**
- **1 red pepper, cut into strips**
- **1 onion, cut into thin slices**
- **1 can (15 ounces) tomato sauce**
- **¹/₂ cup finely chopped onion**
- **¹/₄ cup soy sauce**
- **1 tablespoon sugar**
- **1 teaspoon dry mustard**
- **¹/₈ teaspoon cayenne pepper**
- **¹/₄ cup vegetable oil**

With meat mallet, pound each steak to ¹/₄-inch thickness. Sprinkle steaks with ¹/₄ teaspoon of the garlic powder and the pepper. Arrange green and red pepper strips horizontally on steaks. Cover with onion slices. Starting at narrow end of each steak, roll up jelly-roll fashion; tie with kitchen twine. Set aside. In large jar with screw-top lid, combine remaining ingredients except oil. Shake to blend. Brush outsides of beef rolls with oil. Lightly oil grid. Grill steaks, on covered grill, over hot **KINGSFORD® Charcoal Briquets** about 30 minutes, turning often, until done. Brush steaks with tomato-soy mixture during last 10 minutes of grilling.
Makes 6 to 8 servings.

Grilled Steak with Mushroom-Wine Sauce

**4 beef loin T-bone, porterhouse
    or filet mignon steaks, cut
    1 inch thick (8 ounces each)**
**3 tablespoons butter or
    margarine**
**½ pound mushrooms, sliced
    (about 2 cups)**
¼ cup white wine
2 tablespoons minced parsley
**½ teaspoon dried tarragon,
    crushed**
**1 teaspoon instant beef bouillon
    granules**

Slash any fat around edge of steaks every 4 inches. Lightly oil grid. Grill steaks on covered grill, over medium-hot **KINGSFORD® with Mesquite Charcoal Briquets** 8 to 10 minutes on each side for medium-rare, or to desired doneness. While steak is grilling, heat butter in large skillet until hot. Add mushrooms and saute 1 minute or until tender. Add wine, parsley, tarragon and beef bouillon granules; simmer 4 minutes, stirring often. Serve sauce over steak.
Makes 4 servings.

Savory Steak

Flank Steak Bearnaise

**1 8-ounce package
    PHILADELPHIA BRAND
    Cream Cheese, cubed**
¼ cup milk
1 tablespoon green onion slices
**½ teaspoon dried tarragon
    leaves, crushed**
2 egg yolks, beaten
2 tablespoons dry white wine
1 tablespoon lemon juice
1 1½-pound beef flank steak

In saucepan, combine cream cheese, milk, green onions and tarragon; stir over low heat until cream cheese is melted. Stir small amount of hot cream cheese mixture into egg yolks; return to hot mixture. Stir in wine and juice. Cook, stirring constantly, over low heat 1 minute or until thickened. Score steak on both sides. Place on rack of broiler pan. Broil on both sides to desired doneness. With knife slanted, carve steak across grain into thin slices. Serve with cream cheese mixture.
6 servings.

Savory Steak

1½ cups V8® Vegetable Juice
**¼ cup Burgundy or other dry red
    wine**
2 large cloves garlic, minced
**¼ teaspoon coarsely ground
    pepper**
2 pounds top round steak

1. To make marinade: In 12- by 8-inch baking dish, stir together V8 juice, wine, garlic and pepper. Add steak to marinade, turning to coat. Cover; refrigerate at least 4 hours, turning steak occasionally.
2. Remove steak from marinade, reserving marinade. Place steak on grill or on rack in broiler pan. Grill or broil steak 4 inches from heat 15 minutes on each side or until desired doneness, basting occasionally with marinade.
3. Meanwhile, in small saucepan over medium-high heat, heat remaining marinade to boiling. Serve with steak.
Makes 8 servings.

Per serving: 166 calories, 27 g protein, 5 g fat, 3 g carbohydrate, 215 mg sodium, 65 mg cholesterol.

Beer Marinated Steak

1 large onion, thinly sliced
2 cloves garlic, finely chopped
½ cup vegetable oil
1 cup beer
**½ cup REALEMON® Lemon Juice
    from Concentrate**
2 tablespoons light brown sugar
**1 tablespoon Worcestershire
    sauce**
**1 (1- to 1½-pound) flank steak,
    scored**

In medium skillet, cook onion and garlic in *¼ cup* oil until tender; remove from heat. Add remaining ingredients except meat. Place meat in shallow baking dish; pour beer marinade over. Cover; refrigerate 6 hours or overnight, turning occasionally. Remove meat from marinade; grill or broil as desired, basting frequently with marinade. Refrigerate leftovers.
Makes 4 to 6 servings.

Stir-Fried Beef and Vegetables

½ pound boneless beef sirloin steak
1 can (10½ ounces) CAMPBELL'S® Condensed Beef Broth (Bouillon)
1 tablespoon cornstarch
1 tablespoon soy sauce
3 tablespoons vegetable oil
1 clove garlic, minced
4 green onions, cut into 1-inch pieces
1 cup fresh or frozen cut broccoli
1 can (8 ounces) sliced bamboo shoots, drained
Shredded lettuce

1. Freeze steak 1 hour to make slicing easier. Trim and discard excess fat from steak. Cut steak into very thin slices; set aside.
2. In small bowl, combine soup, cornstarch and soy sauce; stir to blend. Set aside.
3. In 10-inch skillet or wok over medium-high heat, in 2 tablespoons hot oil, stir-fry beef strips and garlic until meat is browned; remove from skillet.
4. Add remaining 1 tablespoon oil to skillet. Add green onions and broccoli; stir-fry 1 minute. Add bamboo shoots; stir-fry 30 seconds more.
5. Return beef to skillet. Stir soup mixture; stir into skillet. Heat to boiling; cook 1 minute more. Spoon over shredded lettuce.
Makes about 2½ cups or 2 servings.

Smothered Liver and Onions

2 tablespoons butter or margarine
1 large onion, thinly sliced
1 pound beef liver, ¼ inch thick
1 can (10¾ ounces) CAMPBELL'S® Condensed Cream of Mushroom Soup
¼ cup milk or half-and-half
⅛ teaspoon pepper

To Microwave:
1. In 12- by 8-inch microwave-safe baking dish, combine butter and onion. Cover with vented plastic wrap; microwave on HIGH 5 minutes or until onion is tender, stirring once during cooking.

2. Cut liver into 4 portions. Arrange liver over onions, placing thicker portions toward edges of dish. In small bowl, stir soup until smooth; stir in milk and pepper. Pour over liver. Cover; microwave on HIGH 10 minutes or until liver is no longer pink in center, rearranging liver twice during cooking. Let stand, covered, 5 minutes before serving.
Makes 4 servings.

Liver and Onions

½ cup all-purpose flour
1 teaspoon ground sage
¾ teaspoon salt
½ teaspoon paprika
⅛ teaspoon cayenne
1 pound beef liver, membrane removed, cut into 4×1×¼-inch strips
¼ cup CRISCO® Oil
1 large onion, thinly sliced and separated into rings
⅛ teaspoon instant minced garlic
2 tablespoons snipped fresh parsley
¼ cup dry white wine or chicken broth
1 tablespoon lemon juice

Mix flour, sage, salt, paprika and cayenne in large plastic food storage bag. Add liver. Shake to coat. Remove liver from bag; set aside.

Stir-Fried Beef and Vegetables

Heat Crisco® Oil in medium skillet. Add onion and garlic. Sauté over moderate heat until onion is tender. Push to one side of skillet. Add liver. Fry 6 to 8 minutes, or until no longer pink, turning over 1 or 2 times.

Stir together liver and onion. Sprinkle with parsley. Add wine and lemon juice. Cook, stirring constantly, 1 or 2 minutes longer.
4 servings.

Vegetable-Stuffed Flank Steak

1 tablespoon olive or vegetable oil
1 cup chopped CAMPBELL'S FRESH® Mushrooms
1 package (10 ounces) frozen chopped spinach, thawed and drained
½ cup chopped onion
1 clove garlic, minced
1 cup shredded carrots
½ cup shredded Muenster or Swiss cheese (2 ounces)
½ teaspoon dried basil leaves, crushed
⅛ teaspoon pepper
1½ pounds beef flank steak, pounded to ¼-inch thickness
1 can (10¾ ounces) CAMPBELL'S® Condensed Cream of Mushroom Soup
2 tablespoons dry sherry

To Microwave:
1. In 1½-quart microwave-safe casserole, combine oil, mushrooms, spinach, onion and garlic. Cover with lid; microwave on HIGH 5 minutes or until vegetables are tender, stirring once during cooking. Drain. Stir in carrots, cheese, basil and pepper; mix well.
2. Spread vegetable mixture over steak to within 1 inch of edges. Roll up from long end, jelly-roll fashion, tucking ends of steak into roll. Secure with wooden toothpicks or tie with cotton string. Place rolls, seam side down, in 12- by 8-inch microwave-safe baking dish.
3. In small bowl, stir soup until smooth; stir in sherry. Pour over meat. Cover with vented plastic wrap; microwave on HIGH 10 minutes, rotating dish once during cooking.
4. Spoon pan juices over meat. Reduce power to 50%. Cover; microwave 20 minutes or until meat is tender, rotating dish twice during cooking. Let stand, covered, 10 minutes.
Makes 6 servings.

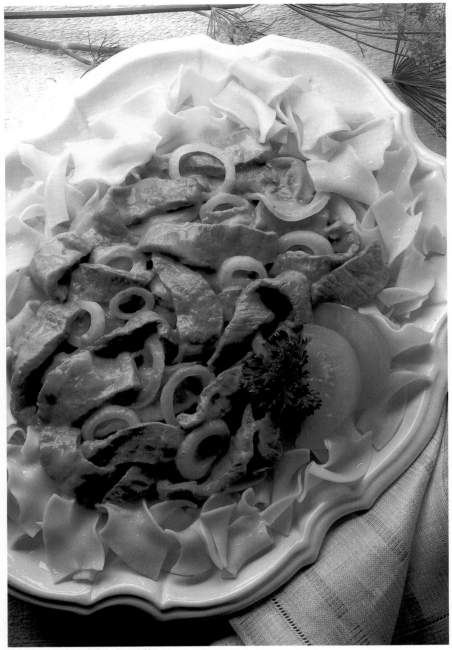

Burgundy Beef Stroganoff

Burgundy Beef Stroganoff

**2 pounds round steak, cut into
    ¼-inch strips
2 tablespoons BLUE BONNET®
    Margarine
4 medium onions, sliced (about
    3 cups)
¼ cup all-purpose flour
1 cup COLLEGE INN® Beef Broth
½ cup Burgundy or other dry red
    wine
3 tablespoons tomato paste
½ teaspoon ground thyme
¾ cup dairy sour cream
    Hot buttered noodles**

In large skillet, over medium heat, brown meat in margarine. Stir in onions and cook for 3 minutes; remove from heat. Sprinkle flour over meat and stir until well combined. Stir in beef broth, Burgundy, tomato paste and thyme until smooth. Cook and stir over medium heat until sauce is thickened and begins to boil. Cover; cook over low heat for 40 to 45 minutes or until tender. Stir sour cream into sauce. (Do not boil.) Serve over hot buttered noodles.
Makes 6 to 8 servings.

Microwave: In 3-quart microwave-proof bowl, place margarine. Microwave, uncovered, on HIGH (100% power) for 1 minute until margarine melts. Toss beef strips with flour; add to margarine. Microwave, uncovered, on HIGH for 6 to 7 minutes, stirring every 2 minutes. Add onions. Microwave, uncovered, on HIGH for 2 to 3 minutes.

Stir in broth, Burgundy, tomato paste and thyme. Cover with plastic wrap; vent. Microwave on HIGH 10 to 12 minutes until sauce is thickened and bubbling. Stir in sour cream. Microwave, uncovered, on HIGH for 1 minute. Let stand 5 minutes before serving. Serve over noodles.

Marinated Flank Steak

**1 envelope LIPTON® Onion or
    Onion-Mushroom Recipe
    Soup Mix
½ cup water
½ cup dry red wine
¼ cup olive or vegetable oil
1 tablespoon finely chopped
    parsley
1 teaspoon oregano
⅛ teaspoon pepper
2-pound beef flank steak**

In large shallow baking dish, thoroughly blend all ingredients except steak; add steak and turn to coat. Cover and marinate in refrigerator, turning steak and piercing with fork occasionally, at least 4 hours. Remove steak, reserving marinade.

Grill or broil steak, turning once, until done. Meanwhile, in small saucepan, bring remaining marinade to a boil, then simmer 5 minutes. If necessary, skim fat from marinade. Serve hot marinade with steak.
Makes about 8 servings.

Beef Stroganoff

**1 pound boneless beef sirloin
    steak
½ cup chopped onion
1 can (10¾ ounces)
    CAMPBELL'S® Condensed
    Cream of Mushroom Soup
½ cup sour cream
½ teaspoon paprika
    Hot cooked noodles**

To Microwave:
1. Freeze steak 1 hour to make slicing easier. Cut steak into very thin slices across the grain.
2. In 2-quart microwave-safe casserole, combine beef and onion. Cover with lid; microwave on HIGH 5 minutes or until beef is no longer pink, stirring once during cooking.
3. In small bowl, stir soup until smooth; stir in sour cream and paprika. Add to beef, stirring to coat. Cover; microwave at 50% power 3 minutes or until heated through. Serve over noodles.
Makes about 3½ cups or 4 servings.

Sauerbraten

1 cup cider vinegar
½ cup dry red wine or beef broth
½ cup water
2 medium onions, thinly sliced
1 carrot, sliced
1 stalk celery, chopped
1 tablespoon salt
12 whole peppercorns
4 whole cloves
2 whole allspice
4-pound boneless beef rump roast
4 tablespoons all-purpose flour, divided
¼ cup CRISCO® Oil
⅓ cup cold water
1 tablespoon sugar
½ cup crushed gingersnap cookies

Mix vinegar, wine, ½ cup water, onions, carrot, celery, salt, peppercorns, cloves and allspice in large bowl or large plastic food storage bag. Add roast. Cover bowl or seal bag. Refrigerate 2 to 3 days, turning roast over each day.

Remove roast from marinade, reserving marinade. Pat roast dry with paper towels. Coat with 2 tablespoons flour. Heat Crisco® Oil in Dutch oven. Add roast. Brown over medium-high heat. Pour reserved marinade over roast. Cover. Reduce heat. Simmer 2½ to 3 hours, or until meat is tender, turning roast over after half the time. Transfer roast to serving platter, reserving liquid and vegetables in Dutch oven.

Strain vegetables and liquid through wire sieve into large bowl, pressing vegetables to remove liquid. Discard vegetables. Skim and discard fat from liquid. Pour 3 cups liquid into saucepan. Discard remaining liquid.

Heat liquid to boiling. Meanwhile, place ⅓ cup cold water in small bowl. Blend in sugar and remaining 2 tablespoons flour. Add to boiling liquid. Cook, stirring constantly, until mixture is thickened. Stir in gingersnaps. Cook 1 to 2 minutes longer, or until heated through. Serve with roast.
8 to 10 servings.

Beef Goulash

¼ cup vegetable oil, divided
2 pounds boneless rump or chuck, cut into 1-inch cubes
3 medium onions, sliced
2 cloves garlic, minced
1 can (16 ounces) tomatoes, undrained, cut into pieces
4 teaspoons paprika
2 beef bouillon cubes
1 teaspoon dried marjoram leaves
1 teaspoon dried thyme leaves
¼ teaspoon TABASCO® pepper sauce
1 bay leaf

In large heavy saucepot or Dutch oven heat 2 tablespoons oil; brown meat in 2 batches. Remove; reserve. In same pot heat remaining 2 tablespoons oil; cook onions and garlic 5 minutes or until lightly browned. Stir in tomatoes, paprika, bouillon cubes, marjoram, thyme, Tabasco® sauce and bay leaf. Return meat to pot. Cover; simmer 1½ to 2 hours or until meat is tender; stir occasionally. Remove bay leaf. Serve over noodles, spaetzle, mashed potatoes or rice.
Makes 8 servings.

Beef Stew

2 pounds beef for stew, cut into 1-inch cubes
¼ cup all-purpose flour
4 tablespoons vegetable oil
2 medium onions, sliced
2 cloves garlic, minced
1 teaspoon dried thyme leaves, crushed
1 bay leaf
1 can (10¾ ounces) CAMPBELL'S® Condensed Beefy Mushroom Soup
½ cup water
3 medium potatoes, peeled and cubed
2 medium carrots, cut into 2- by ½-inch strips
1 cup fresh or frozen cut green beans

1. Coat beef cubes with flour; reserve remaining flour.
2. In 4-quart Dutch oven over medium-high heat, in 2 tablespoons hot oil, cook beef, a few pieces at a time, until browned on all sides. Remove beef as it browns. Reduce heat to medium.
3. Add remaining 2 tablespoons oil to skillet. In hot oil, cook onions, garlic, thyme and bay leaf until onions are tender, stirring occasionally. Stir in reserved flour. Gradually add soup and water; heat to boiling. Return meat to pan. Reduce heat to low. Cover; simmer 1 hour, stirring occasionally.
4. Add potatoes, carrots and green beans. Cover; simmer 25 minutes or until vegetables are tender. Discard bay leaf.
Makes about 6 cups or 8 servings.

Sauerbraten

Oven-Baked Bourguignonne

- **2 pounds boneless beef chuck, cut into 1-inch cubes**
- **¼ cup all-purpose flour**
- **1⅓ cups sliced carrots**
- **1 can (14½ ounces) whole peeled tomatoes, undrained and chopped**
- **1 bay leaf**
- **1 envelope LIPTON® Beefy Onion or Onion Recipe Soup Mix**
- **½ cup dry red wine**
- **1 cup fresh or canned sliced mushrooms**
- **1 package (8 ounces) medium or broad egg noodles**

Preheat oven to 400°.

In 2-quart casserole, toss beef with flour, then bake uncovered 20 minutes. Add carrots, tomatoes and bay leaf, then beefy onion recipe soup mix blended with wine. Bake covered 1½ hours or until beef is tender. Add mushrooms and bake covered an additional 10 minutes. Remove bay leaf.

Meanwhile, cook noodles according to package directions. To serve, arrange bourguignonne over noodles.

Makes about 8 servings.

Microwave Directions: Toss beef with flour; set aside. In 2-quart casserole, combine tomatoes, bay leaf and beefy onion recipe soup mix blended with wine. Heat covered at HIGH (Full Power) 7 minutes, stirring once. Add beef and carrots. Heat covered at DEFROST (30% Full Power), stirring occasionally, 1¼ hours. Add mushrooms and heat covered at DEFROST 30 minutes or until beef is tender. Remove bay leaf. Let stand covered 5 minutes. Cook noodles and serve as above.

Freezing/Reheating Directions: Bourguignonne can be baked, then frozen. Simply wrap covered casserole in heavy-duty aluminum foil; freeze. To reheat, unwrap and bake covered at 400°, stirring occasionally to separate beef and vegetables, 1 hour. **OR,** microwave at HIGH (Full Power), stirring occasionally, 20 minutes or until heated through. Let stand covered 5 minutes.

Mexican Beef Stew

- **2 tablespoons CRISCO® Oil**
- **2 pounds beef stew meat, cut into 1-inch cubes**
- **1 medium onion, chopped**
- **1 clove garlic, minced**
- **1 can (16 ounces) whole tomatoes, undrained, cut up**
- **1 jar (4 ounces) pimiento, drained and mashed**
- **½ to 1 teaspoon ground cumin**
- **½ teaspoon salt**
- **¼ teaspoon pepper**

Heat Crisco® Oil in large skillet. Add beef. Brown over medium-high heat. Remove beef with slotted spoon; set aside. Add onion and garlic to skillet. Sauté over moderate heat until onion is tender. Stir in beef and remaining ingredients. Heat to boiling. Cover. Reduce heat. Simmer, stirring occasionally, about 2 hours, or until beef is tender. Add water during cooking, if necessary.

6 to 8 servings.

Country French Beef Stew

- **2 pounds boneless beef, cut into 1-inch cubes**
- **¼ cup all-purpose flour**
- **2 slices bacon, cut into 1-inch pieces**
- **3 tablespoons oil**
- **¼ cup Cognac (optional)**
- **1 envelope LIPTON® Onion, Beefy Onion, Onion-Mushroom or Beefy Mushroom Recipe Soup Mix**
- **2 cups water**
- **½ cup dry red wine**
- **2 tablespoons Dijon-style prepared mustard**
- **3 carrots, thinly sliced**
- **½ pound mushrooms, halved**
- **1 package (8 ounces) broad egg noodles**

Lightly toss beef with flour; set aside.

In Dutch oven, cook bacon until crisp; remove. Reserve drippings. Heat oil with reserved drippings and brown beef, in three batches, over

Mexican Beef Stew

medium-high heat; remove beef and set aside. Into Dutch oven, add Cognac and cook 1 minute or until only a thin glaze of liquid remains. Stir in onion recipe soup mix blended with water, wine and mustard; bring to a boil. Add beef and bacon and simmer covered, stirring occasionally, 1½ hours or until beef is almost tender. Stir in carrots and simmer covered 25 minutes. Add mushrooms and simmer covered an additional 5 minutes or until beef and vegetables are tender.

Meanwhile, cook noodles according to package directions. To serve, arrange stew over noodles. Garnish, if desired, with chopped parsley. *Makes about 8 servings.*

Wine-Simmered Beef and Vegetables

Beef Burgundy

- ½ **cup all-purpose flour**
- ¾ **teaspoon salt**
- ¼ **teaspoon pepper**
- 1½ **pounds beef round steak, cut into 1-inch pieces**
- 5 **tablespoons CRISCO® Oil, divided**
- 1½ **cups water**
- 1 **cup Burgundy wine**
- 1 **medium onion, thinly sliced**
- ½ **cup snipped fresh parsley**
- 2 **cloves garlic, halved**
- 2 **bay leaves**
- 1½ **teaspoons instant beef bouillon granules**
- 1 **teaspoon dried thyme leaves**
- 8 **ounces fresh mushrooms, sliced**
- ¼ **cup sliced almonds**
  Hot cooked rice or noodles

Mix flour, salt and pepper in large plastic food storage bag. Add beef. Shake to coat. Heat 4 tablespoons Crisco® Oil in Dutch oven. Add beef and any remaining flour mixture. Brown over medium-high heat. Stir in water, wine, onion, parsley, garlic, bay leaves, bouillon granules and thyme. Heat to boiling. Cover. Reduce heat. Simmer 1½ to 2 hours, or until beef is tender, stirring occasionally. Stir in mushrooms; re-cover. Simmer 20 to 30 minutes longer, or until mushrooms are tender. Remove and discard garlic cloves and bay leaves.

Meanwhile, heat remaining 1 tablespoon Crisco® Oil in small skillet. Add almonds. Cook over moderate heat, stirring constantly, until almonds are lightly browned. Stir into beef mixture just before serving. Serve with rice or noodles. *4 to 6 servings.*

Wine-Simmered Beef and Vegetables

- 1½ **to 2 pounds beef round steak**
- 6 **tablespoons all-purpose flour, divided**
- ½ **teaspoon salt**
- ¼ **teaspoon pepper**
- 3 **tablespoons CRISCO® Oil**
- 1 **medium onion, thinly sliced and separated into rings**
- 1 **medium green pepper, cored, seeded and sliced into rings**
- ⅔ **cup julienne carrot strips**
- ½ **teaspoon dried basil leaves**
- ½ **teaspoon dried marjoram leaves**
- ⅔ **cup dry white wine**
- ⅔ **cup cold water**
- ½ **teaspoon instant beef bouillon granules**

Trim bone and fat from beef. Pound trimmed beef with meat mallet. Cut into serving-size pieces. Set aside. Mix 4 tablespoons flour, salt and pepper in large plastic food storage bag. Add beef. Shake to coat.

Heat Crisco® Oil in large skillet. Add beef and any remaining flour mixture. Brown over medium-high heat. Layer onion, green pepper and carrots over beef. Sprinkle with basil and marjoram. Add wine. Heat to boiling. Cover. Reduce heat. Simmer about 1 hour, or until beef is tender. Transfer beef and vegetables to serving platter, reserving drippings in skillet.

Place cold water in 1-cup measure or small bowl. Blend in remaining 2 tablespoons flour. Stir flour mixture into drippings in skillet. Stir in bouillon granules. Cook over medium-high heat, stirring constantly, until thickened and bubbly. Serve with meat and vegetables. *4 to 6 servings.*

Variation: Simmered Beef and Vegetables. Follow recipe above, substituting ⅔ cup water and ¾ teaspoon instant beef bouillon granules for wine.

Stroganoff Superb

- 1 **pound beef sirloin steak, cut into thin strips**
- 3 **tablespoons PARKAY Margarine**
- ½ **cup chopped onion**
- 1 **4-ounce can mushrooms, drained**
- ½ **teaspoon salt**
- ¼ **teaspoon dry mustard**
- ¼ **teaspoon pepper**
- 1 **8-ounce package PHILADELPHIA BRAND Cream Cheese, cubed**
- ¾ **cup milk**
  Hot parsleyed noodles

Brown steak in margarine in large skillet. Add onions, mushrooms and seasonings; cook until vegetables are tender. Add cream cheese and milk; stir over low heat until cream cheese is melted. Serve over noodles. *4 to 6 servings.*

Beef Stew with Dumplings

    **4 pounds lean boneless beef
        chuck, cut into 2-inch cubes**
**¼ cup plus 2 tablespoons
        FILIPPO BERIO Olive Oil,
        divided**
2½ teaspoons salt, divided
¼ teaspoon pepper
3 cups dry red wine
2 cups water
2 tablespoons tomato paste
1 large clove garlic, minced
**½ teaspoon dried thyme,
        crushed**
12 small white onions
4 carrots, cut into quarters
**4 ribs celery, cut into 2-inch
        pieces**
**3 white turnips, cut into
        quarters**
¼ pound small mushrooms
¼ cup chopped parsley
1 cup all-purpose flour
2 teaspoons baking powder
½ teaspoon sugar
1 egg, well beaten
½ cup milk

Brown beef in ¼ cup of the oil in
Dutch oven over medium-high heat.
Season with 2 teaspoons of the salt
and the pepper. Add wine, water, tomato paste, garlic and thyme. Bring
to a boil over high heat. Reduce heat
to low. Cover and simmer 1 hour, stirring occasionally. Add onions, carrots,
celery, turnips, mushrooms and parsley. Simmer, covered, 20 minutes
more.*

Meanwhile, prepare dumplings.
Combine flour, baking powder, remaining ½ teaspoon salt and the
sugar in small bowl. Add egg, milk
and remaining 2 tablespoons oil. Stir
to blend. Drop dumplings by tablespoonfuls onto hot stew. Cook, uncovered, 10 minutes.
Makes 8 servings.

*If stew is too thin, thicken sauce
before cooking dumplings. To thicken,
blend 3 tablespoons all-purpose flour
and ½ cup water in small bowl until
smooth. Gradually stir mixture into
stew. Continue cooking until thickened and smooth, stirring constantly.

Classic Chinese Pepper Steak

Beef Ragoût

    **1 tablespoon butter or
        margarine**
½ cup chopped onion
1 large clove garlic, minced
**1 pound beef for stew, cut into
        1-inch pieces**
1 cup thinly sliced carrots
**1 can (10¼ ounces) FRANCO-
        AMERICAN® Beef Gravy**
**¼ cup Burgundy or other dry red
        wine**
**¼ cup tomato paste
        Hot cooked noodles**

To Microwave:
1. In 2-quart microwave-safe casserole, combine butter, onion and garlic.
Cover with lid; microwave on HIGH 3
minutes or until onion is tender, stirring once during cooking.
2. Stir in beef. Cover; microwave on
HIGH 5 minutes or until beef is no
longer pink, stirring once during
cooking.
3. Stir in carrots, gravy, wine and tomato paste. Cover; microwave on
HIGH 5 minutes or until boiling. Stir
again.
4. Reduce power to 50%. Cover; microwave 30 minutes or until meat is tender, stirring twice during cooking. Let
stand, covered, 5 minutes. Serve over
noodles.
Makes about 3 cups or 4 servings.

Classic Chinese Pepper Steak

    **1 pound boneless beef sirloin
        steak**
**1 tablespoon KIKKOMAN Stir-Fry
        Sauce**
**2 tablespoons vegetable oil,
        divided**
**2 medium-size green, red or
        yellow bell peppers, cut into
        1-inch squares**
**2 medium onions, cut into 1-inch
        squares**
**¼ cup KIKKOMAN Stir-Fry Sauce
        Hot cooked rice (optional)**

Cut beef across grain into thin strips,
then into 1-inch squares; coat with 1
tablespoon stir-fry sauce. Heat 1 tablespoon oil in hot wok or large skillet
over high heat. Add beef and stir-fry 1
minute; remove. Heat remaining 1 tablespoon oil in same pan. Add peppers
and onions; stir-fry 5 minutes. Stir in
beef and ¼ cup stir-fry sauce; cook
and stir just until beef and vegetables
are coated with sauce. Serve immediately with rice.
Makes 4 servings.

Orange-Flavored Grilled Beef

    1 orange
3 tablespoons soy sauce
2 tablespoons brown sugar
2 tablespoons cider vinegar
½ teaspoon pepper
½ teaspoon chili powder
1 clove garlic, minced
1 teaspoon grated fresh ginger
**2 pounds beef round tip roast,
        cut into 3-inch cubes**

Grate peel from orange to equal 1 tablespoon. Squeeze juice from orange
into large bowl. Stir in remaining ingredients except beef. Add beef cubes;
toss to coat with marinade. Cover and
refrigerate 8 hours or overnight.
Drain meat cubes; reserve marinade.
Grill beef cubes, on covered grill, over
medium-hot **KINGSFORD® Charcoal Briquets** 3 minutes. Turn beef
cubes, brush with marinade and cook
5 minutes longer or until done.
Makes 4 servings.

Chinese-Style Beef & Vegetables

⅓ cup WISH-BONE® Italian Dressing
1 tablespoon soy sauce
¼ teaspoon ground ginger
1 cup thinly sliced carrots
1 cup sliced mushrooms
1 cup sliced zucchini
1 (1½-pound) boneless sirloin steak, cut into thin strips
4 cups hot cooked buttered rice

In small bowl, blend Italian dressing, soy sauce and ginger; reserve 2 tablespoons. In large skillet, heat remaining dressing mixture and cook carrots, covered, over medium heat, stirring occasionally, 10 minutes. Add mushrooms and zucchini and cook covered an additional 5 minutes. Remove vegetables and keep warm. Add reserved dressing mixture to skillet, then add beef. Cook uncovered over high heat, stirring constantly, 5 minutes or until beef is done. Return vegetables to skillet and heat through. To serve, arrange beef and vegetables over hot rice.
Makes about 6 servings.

Note: Also terrific with Wish-Bone® Robusto Italian, Blended Italian, Herbal Italian, Lite Italian, Classic Dijon Vinaigrette or Lite Classic Dijon Vinaigrette Dressing.

Broccoli & Beef Stir-Fry

½ pound boneless tender beef steak (sirloin, rib eye or top loin)
1 tablespoon cornstarch
4 tablespoons KIKKOMAN Soy Sauce, divided
1 teaspoon sugar
1 teaspoon minced fresh ginger root
1 clove garlic, minced
1 pound fresh broccoli
1¼ cups water
4 teaspoons cornstarch
3 tablespoons vegetable oil, divided
1 onion, chunked
Hot cooked rice

Cut beef across grain into thin slices. Combine 1 tablespoon *each* cornstarch and soy sauce with sugar, ginger and garlic in small bowl; stir in beef. Let stand 15 minutes. Meanwhile, remove flowerets from broccoli; cut in half lengthwise. Peel stalks; cut crosswise into ⅛-inch slices. Combine water, 4 teaspoons cornstarch and remaining 3 tablespoons soy sauce; set aside. Heat 1 tablespoon oil in hot wok or large skillet over high heat. Add beef and stir-fry 1 minute; remove. Heat remaining 2 tablespoons oil in same pan. Add broccoli and onion; stir-fry 4 minutes. Stir in beef and soy sauce mixture. Cook and stir until mixture boils and thickens. Serve immediately over rice.
Makes 2 to 3 servings.

Oriental Steak Kabobs

1 cup (8 ounces) WISH-BONE® Italian Dressing
¼ cup soy sauce
2 tablespoons brown sugar
½ teaspoon ground ginger
1 green onion, thinly sliced
1 pound boneless beef round, cut into 1-inch pieces
12 large mushrooms
2 cups broccoli florets
1 medium red pepper, cut into chunks

In large shallow baking dish, combine Italian dressing, soy sauce, brown sugar, ginger and onion. Add beef and vegetables; turn to coat. Cover and marinate in refrigerator, stirring occasionally, 4 hours or overnight. Remove beef and vegetables, reserving marinade.

Onto large skewers, alternately thread beef with vegetables. Grill or broil, turning and basting frequently with reserved marinade, 10 minutes or until beef is done.
Makes about 4 servings.

Note: Also terrific with Wish-Bone® Robusto Italian or Lite Italian Dressing.

Red-Cooked Short Ribs

3 pounds beef short ribs
⅓ to ½ cup all-purpose flour
2 tablespoons vegetable oil
1¾ cups water, divided
½ cup KIKKOMAN Teriyaki Sauce
1 clove garlic, pressed
½ teaspoon ground ginger
⅛ teaspoon ground cloves

Coat ribs thoroughly with flour; reserve ¼ cup excess flour. Heat oil in Dutch oven or large saucepan over medium heat. Add ribs and brown slowly on all sides; drain off excess oil. Combine 1¼ cups water, teriyaki sauce, garlic, ginger and cloves; pour over ribs. Cover; simmer 2 hours, or until ribs are tender. Meanwhile, blend reserved flour and remaining ½ cup water. Remove ribs to serving platter; keep warm. Pour pan drippings into large measuring cup; skim off fat. Add enough water to measure 2½ cups; return to pan and bring to boil. Gradually stir in flour mixture. Cook and stir until thickened; serve with ribs.
Makes 4 servings.

Chinese-Style Beef & Vegetables

Lime Kabobs Polynesian

½ cup REALIME® Lime Juice
   from Concentrate
½ cup vegetable oil
3 tablespoons sugar
1 tablespoon BENNETT'S® Chili
   Sauce
½ to 1 teaspoon curry powder
¼ teaspoon garlic powder
1 (1½-pound) sirloin steak
   (about 1 inch thick), cut into
   cubes
1 (8-ounce) can pineapple
   chunks, drained
1 large green pepper, cut into
   squares
2 medium onions, quartered
8 ounces fresh whole
   mushrooms (about 2 cups)
½ pint cherry tomatoes

In small bowl, combine ReaLime® brand, oil, sugar, chili sauce and seasonings; pour over meat. Cover; refrigerate 6 hours or overnight, stirring occasionally. Skewer meat with pineapple and vegetables. Grill or broil as desired, turning and basting frequently with marinade. Serve with rice if desired. Refrigerate leftovers.
Makes 6 servings.

Honey-Mustard Beef Ribs

1 cup butter or margarine
1 bunch green onions with tops,
   finely chopped
1 small yellow onion, finely
   chopped
4 cloves garlic, minced
4 tablespoons prepared mustard
4 tablespoons honey
½ teaspoon liquid smoke,
   optional
1 teaspoon lemon pepper
1 teaspoon brown sugar
5 pounds beef back ribs

In saucepan, combine butter, green onions, yellow onion and garlic. Cook over low heat 15 minutes or until onions are tender. Remove from heat and add remaining ingredients except ribs. Grill ribs, on covered grill, over medium-hot **KINGSFORD® Charcoal Briquets** 30 to 35 minutes, brushing ribs generously with mustard-honey mixture, until meat is tender.
Makes 4 servings.

Beef with Leafy Greens

¾ pound romaine lettuce
½ pound boneless tender beef
   steak (sirloin, rib eye or top
   loin)
4 tablespoons KIKKOMAN Stir-
   Fry Sauce, divided
1 clove garlic, minced
2 tablespoons vegetable oil,
   divided
1 medium onion, chunked
1 teaspoon minced fresh ginger
   root
8 cherry tomatoes, halved *or*
   1 medium tomato, chunked
2 tablespoons chopped unsalted
   peanuts

Separate and rinse lettuce; pat dry. Cut leaves crosswise into 1-inch strips; set aside. Cut beef across grain into thin slices. Combine 1 tablespoon stir-fry sauce and garlic in small bowl; stir in beef to coat. Heat 1 tablespoon oil in hot wok or large skillet over high heat. Add beef and stir-fry 1 minute; remove. Heat remaining 1 tablespoon oil in same pan. Add onion and ginger; stir-fry 2 minutes. Add lettuce; stir-fry 2 minutes longer. Add beef, tomatoes and remaining 3 tablespoons stir-fry sauce; cook and stir until vegetables are coated with sauce and tomatoes are just heated through. Serve immediately with peanuts.
Makes 2 to 3 servings.

Beef with Leafy Greens

Fiery Beef Stir-Fry

½ pound boneless tender beef
   steak (sirloin, rib eye or top
   loin)
1 tablespoon cornstarch
4 tablespoons KIKKOMAN Soy
   Sauce, divided
½ teaspoon sugar
1 clove garlic, minced
1¼ cups water
4 teaspoons cornstarch
1½ teaspoons distilled white
   vinegar
⅛ to ¼ teaspoon ground red
   pepper (cayenne)
3 tablespoons vegetable oil,
   divided
3 cups bite-size cauliflowerets
   Salt
1 onion, chunked and separated
1 green pepper, chunked

Cut beef across grain into thin strips. Combine 1 tablespoon *each* cornstarch and soy sauce with sugar and garlic in small bowl; stir in beef. Let stand 15 minutes. Meanwhile, combine water, remaining 3 tablespoons soy sauce, 4 teaspoons cornstarch, vinegar and red pepper; set aside. Heat 1 tablespoon oil in hot wok or large skillet over high heat. Add beef and stir-fry 1 minute; remove. Heat remaining 2 tablespoons oil in same pan. Add cauliflowerets; lightly sprinkle with salt and stir-fry 2 minutes. Add onion and green pepper; stir-fry 4 minutes. Stir in beef and soy sauce mixture; cook and stir until sauce boils and thickens.
Makes 2 to 3 servings.

Ginger Beef

¾ pound beef flank steak
1 can (11 ounces) CAMPBELL'S®
   Condensed Zesty Tomato
   Soup/Sauce
⅓ cup water
2 tablespoons peanut or
   vegetable oil
1 tablespoon soy sauce
2 teaspoons grated fresh ginger
   or ½ teaspoon ground
   ginger
1 clove garlic, minced
1 medium green pepper, cut into
   1-inch squares
1 cup broccoli flowerets
   Hot cooked rice

To Microwave:

1. Freeze steak 1 hour to make slicing easier. Cut steak across the grain into very thin slices.
2. In 12- by 8-inch microwave-safe baking dish, stir together soup, water, oil, soy sauce, ginger and garlic. Add beef slices; toss to coat well. Cover; refrigerate at least 1 hour.
3. Cover with vented plastic wrap; microwave on HIGH 6 minutes or until beef is no longer pink, stirring twice during cooking.
4. Add green pepper and broccoli. Cover; microwave on HIGH 5 minutes or until vegetables are tender, stirring twice during cooking. Serve over rice.

Makes about 3¹/₂ cups or 4 servings.

Szechuan Beef & Snow Peas

Szechuan Beef & Snow Peas

¹/₂ **pound boneless tender beef steak (sirloin, rib eye or top loin)**
2 **tablespoons cornstarch, divided**
3 **tablespoons KIKKOMAN Soy Sauce, divided**
1 **tablespoon dry sherry**
1 **clove garlic, minced**
³/₄ **cup water**
¹/₄ **to ¹/₂ teaspoon crushed red pepper**
2 **tablespoons vegetable oil, divided**
6 **ounces fresh snow peas, trimmed**
1 **medium onion, chunked**
  Salt
1 **medium tomato, chunked**
  Hot cooked rice

Slice beef across grain into thin strips. Combine 1 tablespoon *each* cornstarch and soy sauce with sherry and garlic in small bowl; stir in beef. Let stand 15 minutes. Meanwhile, combine water, remaining 1 tablespoon cornstarch, 2 tablespoons soy sauce and red pepper; set aside. Heat 1 tablespoon oil in hot wok or large skillet over high heat. Add beef and stir-fry 1 minute; remove. Heat remaining 1 tablespoon oil in same pan. Add snow peas and onion; lightly sprinkle with salt and stir-fry 3 minutes. Add beef, soy sauce mixture and tomato. Cook and stir until sauce boils and thickens and tomato is heated through. Serve immediately with rice.

Makes 2 to 3 servings.

Beef and Bean Sprout Stir-Fry

1 **egg white, slightly beaten**
5 **teaspoons soy sauce, divided**
3 **teaspoons cornstarch, divided**
¹/₈ **teaspoon ground ginger**
¹/₈ **teaspoon garlic powder**
¹/₈ **teaspoon salt**
  Dash white pepper
³/₄ **to 1 pound boneless beef sirloin, cut into thin strips**
¹/₂ **cup cold water**
1 **tablespoon oyster sauce (optional)***
¹/₂ **teaspoon instant chicken bouillon granules**
4 **tablespoons CRISCO® Oil, divided**
1 **cup sliced fresh mushrooms**
¹/₂ **cup green onion slices (1-inch slices)**
1 **can (14 ounces) bean sprouts, drained**
¹/₂ **cup sliced water chestnuts**

Blend egg white, 2 teaspoons soy sauce, 1 teaspoon cornstarch, ginger, garlic powder, salt and pepper in medium mixing bowl. Add beef. Stir to coat. Cover; refrigerate 30 minutes.

Combine cold water, oyster sauce (optional), remaining 3 teaspoons soy sauce, remaining 2 teaspoons cornstarch and bouillon granules in small mixing bowl. Mix well. Set aside.

Heat 2 tablespoons Crisco® Oil in large skillet or wok. Add beef mixture. Stir-fry over medium-high heat until beef is browned. Remove mixture from skillet; set aside. Heat remaining 2 tablespoons Crisco® Oil in large skillet. Add mushrooms and onion. Stir-fry over medium-high heat 1 minute. Add bean sprouts and water chestnuts. Stir-fry 1 minute. Add cornstarch mixture and beef. Cook until thickened and bubbly. Serve with *rice* and additional *soy sauce,* if desired.

4 to 6 servings.

*Available in Oriental foods section of supermarket.

Two-Bean Chili

- 1 pound sweet Italian sausage, removed from casing
- 1 pound ground beef
- 2 medium onions, chopped
- 1 large green pepper, chopped
- 3 cloves garlic, minced
- 1/4 cup flour
- 3 tablespoons chili powder
- 2 teaspoons ground cumin
- 2 teaspoons dried basil leaves
- 2 teaspoons dried oregano leaves
- 1 teaspoon salt
- 2 cans (28 ounces each) Italian-style tomatoes, undrained
- 3 tablespoons Worcestershire sauce
- 1 1/4 teaspoons TABASCO® pepper sauce
- 1 can (20 ounces) chick peas, drained
- 1 can (15 1/2 ounces) red kidney beans, drained
  Sliced ripe olives, chopped onion, chopped green pepper, chopped tomato, shredded cheese and cooked rice (optional)

In large heavy saucepot or Dutch oven cook sausage, beef, onions, green pepper and garlic about 20 minutes or until meats are browned and vegetables are tender; drain off fat. Stir in flour, chili powder, cumin, basil, oregano and salt; cook 1 minute. Add tomatoes; break up with fork. Stir in Worcestershire sauce and Tabasco® sauce. Cover and simmer 1 hour, adding water if necessary; stir occasionally. Stir in chick peas and kidney beans. Cook until heated through. Serve with sliced olives, chopped onion, chopped green pepper, chopped tomato, shredded cheese and rice, if desired.
Makes 8 servings.

Texas-Style Chili

- 3 pounds boneless stew beef, cut into 1/2-inch cubes *or* 3 pounds lean ground beef
- 1 1/2 cups chopped onion
- 1 cup chopped green pepper
- 3 cloves garlic, chopped
- 2 (28-ounce) cans tomatoes, undrained and broken up
- 2 cups water
- 1 (6-ounce) can tomato paste
- 8 teaspoons WYLER'S® or STEERO® Beef-Flavor Instant Bouillon *or* 8 Beef-Flavor Bouillon Cubes
- 2 tablespoons chili powder
- 1 tablespoon ground cumin
- 2 teaspoons oregano leaves
- 2 teaspoons sugar

In large kettle or Dutch oven, brown beef (if using ground beef, pour off fat). Add onion, green pepper and garlic; cook and stir until tender. Add remaining ingredients. Cover; bring to a boil. Reduce heat; simmer 1 1/2 hours (1 hour for ground beef) or until meat is tender. Serve with corn chips and shredded cheese if desired. Refrigerate leftovers.
Makes about 4 quarts.

Cincinnati Chili

- 1 1/2 pounds lean ground beef
- 2 cups chopped onions
- 2 large cloves garlic, minced
- 2 teaspoons chili powder
- 1/4 teaspoon ground cinnamon
  Dash ground cloves
- 4 cups V8® Vegetable Juice
- 2 cans (16 ounces each) kidney beans, drained
  Hot cooked spaghetti

1. In 6-quart Dutch oven over medium heat, cook ground beef, onions and garlic until beef is browned and onions are tender, stirring to separate meat. Spoon off fat.
2. Stir in chili powder, cinnamon and ground cloves; cook 2 minutes. Stir in V8 juice. Heat to boiling; reduce heat to low. Cover; simmer 30 minutes.
3. Stir in beans. Cover; simmer 15 minutes, stirring occasionally. Serve over spaghetti.
Makes 8 3/4 cups or 11 servings.
Note: Unlike Southwestern-style chili, Cincinnati Chili is spiced with cinnamon and cloves, then served over spaghetti.

Per serving: 225 calories, 15 g protein, 10 g fat, 19 g carbohydrate, 628 mg sodium, 38 mg cholesterol.

Meat Loaf Italiano

- 1 egg, beaten
- 1 1/2 lbs. ground beef
- 1 8-oz. can pizza sauce
- 3/4 cup (3 ozs.) VELVEETA Shredded Pasteurized Process Cheese Food
- 3/4 cup old fashioned or quick oats, uncooked
- 1/4 cup cold water
- 1/2 teaspoon dried oregano leaves, crushed

In large bowl, combine all ingredients except 1/4 cup pizza sauce; mix lightly. Shape into loaf in 10×6-inch baking dish. Bake at 350°, 1 hour. Top with remaining sauce. Let stand 10 minutes before serving.
6 servings.

Preparation time: 10 minutes
Baking time: 60 minutes plus standing

Texas-Style Chili

Chili in Tortilla Cups

Chili in Tortilla Cups

Tortilla Cups (recipe follows)
3/4 pound lean ground beef
1/2 cup chopped onion
1 tablespoon chili powder
1 teaspoon ground cumin
1 1/2 cups V8® Vegetable Juice
1 can (16 ounces) kidney beans, drained
Dash hot pepper sauce
1 cup shredded Colby or Monterey Jack cheese (4 ounces)
1/2 cup diced green pepper
3/4 cup diced CAMPBELL'S FRESH® Tomato
2 1/2 cups shredded iceberg lettuce
Chopped green pepper for garnish
Chopped CAMPBELL'S FRESH® Tomato for garnish
Shredded cheese for garnish

1. Prepare Tortilla Cups.
2. In 10-inch nonstick skillet over medium-high heat, cook beef, onion, chili powder and cumin until beef is browned and onion is tender, stirring to separate meat. Spoon off fat.
3. Stir in V8 juice, kidney beans and hot pepper sauce. Heat to boiling. Reduce heat to low; simmer, uncovered, 15 minutes, stirring occasionally.
4. In large bowl, toss cheese, green pepper and tomato with meat mixture.
5. To serve: Divide lettuce among Tortilla Cups. Fill each with about 3/4 cup meat mixture. Garnish with additional green pepper, tomato and cheese.
Makes 6 servings.
TORTILLA CUPS: Preheat oven to 400°F. On baking sheet, place 6 balls of foil (4-inch diameter). Spray 10-inch nonstick skillet with vegetable cooking spray. Over high heat, heat one (8-inch) flour tortilla 5 seconds on each side until tortilla is softened. Drain on paper towels. Immediately drape tortilla over foil ball on baking sheet. Repeat with 5 additional tortillas. Bake 5 minutes or until golden. Remove from oven and cool on foil.

Per serving: 388 calories, 21 g protein, 19 g fat, 36 g carbohydrate, 635 mg sodium, 53 mg cholesterol.

Italian-Style Salisbury Steaks

1 pound ground beef
1/4 cup seasoned dry bread crumbs
1/4 cup water
1 egg, slightly beaten
1/2 teaspoon salt
1/4 teaspoon pepper
1/4 cup WISH-BONE® Italian or Robusto Italian Dressing
2 cups thinly sliced onions
2 cups thinly sliced mushrooms
1 can (8 ounces) tomato sauce
1/2 teaspoon basil leaves

Preheat oven to 350°.

In medium bowl, thoroughly combine ground beef, bread crumbs, water, egg, salt and pepper. Shape into 4 oval patties, then place in 1 1/2-quart oblong baking pan; set aside.

In medium skillet, heat Italian dressing and cook onions with mushrooms over medium heat, stirring occasionally, 5 minutes or until tender. Stir in tomato sauce and basil. Spoon tomato mixture over patties and bake 30 minutes or until done.
Makes 4 servings.

Zesty Meat Loaf

1 1/2 pounds lean ground beef
1 can (11 ounces) CAMPBELL'S® Condensed Zesty Tomato Soup/Sauce
2 eggs, beaten
3/4 cup finely crushed saltine crackers
1 tablespoon Worcestershire sauce
2 tablespoons grated Parmesan cheese

To Microwave:
1. In large bowl, thoroughly blend beef, 1/2 cup of the soup, eggs, crumbs and Worcestershire.
2. In 12- by 8-inch microwave-safe baking dish, firmly shape meat mixture into 8- by 4-inch loaf. Cover with waxed paper; microwave on HIGH 15 minutes or until loaf is firm in center, rotating dish twice during cooking.
3. Spread remaining soup over meat. Microwave, uncovered, on HIGH 2 minutes or until soup is hot. Top with cheese. Let stand, uncovered, 5 minutes before serving.
Makes 6 servings.
Note: If you are using a temperature probe, cook meat loaf to an internal temperature of 170°.

Mini Meat Loaves

1 pouch CAMPBELL'S® Onion
   Soup and Recipe Mix
1½ pounds ground beef
½ pound bulk pork sausage
½ cup fine dry bread crumbs
1 egg
½ cup OPEN PIT® Original Flavor
   Barbecue Sauce
3 small VLASIC® Sweet Pickles,
   halved lengthwise
2 ounces Cheddar cheese, cut
   into thin strips

1. Preheat oven to 350°F. In large bowl, combine soup mix, beef, sausage, bread crumbs, egg and ¼ cup of the barbecue sauce; mix well.
2. Divide meat mixture into 6 equal portions. Flatten each to a 4-inch patty. Place a pickle half on each; fold meat over to enclose pickle. Shape each into a small loaf. Place loaves in large shallow baking pan.
3. Bake 30 minutes. Remove from oven; spoon fat from pan. Spread remaining ¼ cup barbecue sauce over loaves; top with cheese strips. Bake 2 minutes more or until cheese melts.
Makes 6 servings.

Mini Meat Loaves

Easy Cheesy Meat Loaf

1½ pounds lean ground beef
2 cups fresh bread crumbs
   (4 slices bread)
1 cup tomato juice
⅓ cup chopped onion
2 eggs
2 teaspoons WYLER'S® or
   STEERO® Beef-Flavor
   Instant Bouillon
¼ teaspoon pepper
6 slices BORDEN® Process
   American Cheese Food

Preheat oven to 350°. In large bowl, combine all ingredients except cheese food; mix well. In shallow baking dish, shape half the mixture into loaf. Cut *4 slices* cheese food into strips; arrange on meat. Top with remaining meat; press edges together to seal. Bake 1 hour; pour off fat. Top with remaining cheese food slices. Refrigerate leftovers.
Makes 6 to 8 servings.

Meat Loaf Supreme

1 can (10¾ ounces)
   CAMPBELL'S® Condensed
   Cream of Mushroom Soup
1½ pounds ground beef
½ cup chopped onion
½ cup fine dry bread crumbs
1 egg
1 package (8 ounces)
   refrigerated crescent rolls
⅓ cup milk
1 teaspoon honey
¼ teaspoon dill weed, crushed
2 teaspoons Dijon-style mustard

1. In large bowl, thoroughly mix ½ cup of the soup, beef, onion, crumbs and egg. In 12- by 8-inch baking dish, firmly shape mixture into 8- by 4-inch loaf. Bake at 350°F. 1 hour. Remove meat loaf from oven; pour off fat.
2. Unroll and separate crescent roll dough into triangles. Place triangles crosswise over top and down sides of meat loaf, overlapping triangles. Bake 15 minutes or until browned.
3. Meanwhile, prepare sauce: In 1-quart saucepan, stir together remaining soup, milk, honey, dill weed and mustard. Over medium heat, heat to boiling, stirring constantly. Serve with meat loaf.
Makes 6 servings.

Mexican Meatloaf Roll

1½ pounds ground beef
¼ cup old fashioned or quick
   oats, uncooked
2 eggs, beaten
1 tablespoon worcestershire
   sauce
1 teaspoon pepper
1 8-ounce package
   PHILADELPHIA BRAND
   Cream Cheese, softened
1 4-ounce can chopped green
   chilies, drained
¾ cup salsa

Combine meat, oats, eggs, worcestershire sauce and pepper; mix well. On wax paper, press meat mixture into 20×10½-inch rectangle. Combine cream cheese and chilies; mix well. Spread cream cheese mixture over meat mixture to within 1 inch of outer edge. Roll, jelly roll fashion, starting at narrow end. Place in 12×8-inch baking dish. Bake at 350°, 40 minutes. Top with salsa; continue baking 10 minutes. Let stand 10 minutes before serving.
6 to 8 servings.

Picadillo-Stuffed Peppers

4 medium green or sweet red peppers
1 tablespoon water
1 pound lean ground beef
½ cup chopped onion
1 clove garlic, minced
½ teaspoon ground cinnamon
½ teaspoon ground cumin
⅛ teaspoon ground cloves
1 can (11 ounces) CAMPBELL'S® Condensed Zesty Tomato Soup/Sauce
1 small apple, chopped
¼ cup raisins
¼ cup toasted sliced almonds
1 tablespoon vinegar

To Microwave:
1. Cut thin slice from top of each pepper. Chop enough pepper tops to make ⅓ cup; set aside. Remove and discard inner membranes and seeds from peppers. Place pepper shells in 2-quart microwave-safe casserole; add water. Cover with lid; microwave on HIGH 5 minutes or until tender-crisp. Drain and set aside.
2. Crumble beef into same casserole; add onion, garlic, cinnamon, cumin, cloves and chopped pepper tops. Cover; microwave on HIGH 5 minutes or until beef is no longer pink, stirring once during cooking to break up meat. Spoon off fat.
3. Stir in soup, apple, raisins, almonds and vinegar. Divide mixture among peppers. Arrange in 2-quart microwave-safe casserole. Cover; microwave on HIGH 5 minutes or until hot.
Makes 4 servings.

All-American Meat Loaf

8 slices BORDEN® Process American Cheese Food
2 pounds lean ground beef
1¼ cups dry bread crumbs
¾ cup catsup
2 eggs
1 (1.5 ounce) package MRS. GRASS® Onion Recipe, Soup & Dip Mix

Preheat oven to 350° (325° for glass dish). Cut *6 slices* cheese food into small pieces; combine with remaining ingredients. Mix well. In shallow baking pan, shape into loaf. Bake 1 hour. Remove from oven; arrange remaining cheese food slices on top. Return to oven 5 minutes or until cheese food begins to melt. Refrigerate leftovers. *Makes 8 servings.*

Meatza Pizzas

2 pounds lean ground beef
½ cup finely chopped onion
½ cup fresh bread crumbs (1 slice bread)
2 eggs
4 teaspoons WYLER'S® or STEERO® Beef-Flavor Instant Bouillon
¼ teaspoon garlic powder
1 (6-ounce) can tomato paste
½ teaspoon oregano leaves
½ teaspoon sugar
Toppings:
  Sliced mushrooms
  Chopped green pepper
  Sliced pepperoni
  Cooked crumbled bacon
  Shredded Mozzarella cheese

In large bowl, combine meat, onion, crumbs, eggs, bouillon and garlic powder; mix well. Shape into 8 or 10 patties (about 3½ inches each), flattening centers and forming a ½-inch rim around edges. Arrange on broiler pan rack; broil 6 inches from heat 5 to 8 minutes. Meanwhile, stir together tomato paste, oregano and sugar.

Brazilian Beans and Rice

Spread equal portions in center of each patty. Top with your favorite toppings and cheese. Broil 1 to 2 minutes or until hot and bubbly. Serve immediately or cool completely, wrap tightly and freeze. To serve, thaw and reheat in 300° oven 15 to 20 minutes. Refrigerate leftovers.
Makes 8 to 10 servings.
Microwave: Prepare meat patties; top with sauce and desired toppings. Arrange half the patties on a microwave roasting rack in shallow baking dish *or* on a bacon rack. Microwave uncovered on full power (high) 7½ to 8½ minutes or to desired doneness, rotating dish once. Let stand 3 minutes before serving.

Brazilian Beans and Rice

3 green-tip, medium DOLE™ Bananas
1 large onion, chopped
1 large clove garlic, pressed
2 tablespoons minced fresh ginger root
1 tablespoon vegetable oil
½ pound ground beef
½ pound bulk pork sausage
1 teaspoon ground cumin
¼ teaspoon cayenne pepper
1 can (15¼ ounces) kidney beans
1 can (11 ounces) black bean soup
1 can (8 ounces) stewed tomatoes
2 teaspoons minced cilantro or parsley
4 to 6 cups shredded lettuce
3 to 4 cups hot cooked rice

Cut bananas in half crosswise, then lengthwise. In large skillet, saute onion, garlic and ginger in oil; push to side of skillet. Add bananas; saute 30 to 45 seconds. Remove bananas to plate. Add beef, sausage, cumin and cayenne; brown, stirring in onion mixture. Add undrained beans, soup and tomatoes. Cover; simmer 30 minutes, stirring occasionally. Remove from heat. Stir in cilantro. Place bananas on top. Cover; cook 1 minute. Mound 1 cup lettuce on each plate. Top with ½ cup rice, then bean mixture, spooning bananas to side.
Makes 4 to 6 servings.

Meatball Stew

- 1 pound ground beef
- ½ cup soft bread crumbs
- ½ teaspoon dried thyme leaves, crushed
- 1 egg
- 1 clove garlic, minced
- 2 tablespoons vegetable oil
- 1 can (10½ ounces) CAMPBELL'S® Condensed French Onion Soup
- ¼ cup water
- 3 medium potatoes, peeled and quartered
- 3 medium carrots, cut into 1-inch chunks
- 1 medium onion, cut into thin wedges
- 1 tablespoon chopped fresh parsley

1. In medium bowl, combine ground beef, bread crumbs, thyme, egg and garlic; mix thoroughly. Shape into 20 meatballs.
2. In 10-inch skillet over medium heat, in hot oil, cook meatballs until browned on all sides. Pour off fat.
3. Stir soup and water into skillet; stir in potatoes, carrots and onion. Heat to boiling. Reduce heat to low. Cover; simmer 30 minutes or until vegetables are tender, adding more water if needed. Garnish with parsley.
Makes 4 servings.

Meatball Stew

Caribbean Pork Chops

- 1 green-tip, large DOLE™ Banana
- 1 tablespoon vegetable oil
- 2 boneless loin pork chops, 1 inch thick
- 1 large clove garlic, pressed
- 2 tablespoons slivered fresh ginger root
- ½ cup canned coconut milk
- ¼ cup water
- 2 tablespoons chutney
- ⅛ teaspoon cayenne pepper
- 1 tablespoon lime juice
  Shredded lettuce or hot cooked rice, optional

Cut banana in half crosswise, then lengthwise. In skillet, saute banana in oil 30 to 45 seconds, shaking skillet. Remove banana. Add more oil to skillet if necessary. Brown pork chops on each side 2 to 3 minutes. Stir in garlic and ginger; saute lightly. Stir in coconut milk, water, chutney and cayenne. Spoon over pork chops. Cover; simmer 8 to 10 minutes. Stir in lime juice. Remove from heat. Serve over shredded lettuce or with rice, if desired. Generously spoon sauce over pork chops and bananas.
Makes 2 servings.

Pork Chops with Browned Garlic-Butter Sauce

- 1 tablespoon salt
- 1 teaspoon onion powder
- ¾ teaspoon garlic powder
- ½ teaspoon white pepper
- ½ teaspoon dry mustard
- ½ teaspoon rubbed sage
- ½ teaspoon ground cumin
- ½ teaspoon dried thyme leaves
- 12 pork chops, ½ inch thick
- 1¼ cups flour
  Vegetable oil
  Browned Garlic-Butter Sauce (recipe follows)

In small bowl combine salt, onion powder, garlic powder, white pepper, dry mustard, sage, cumin and thyme; mix well. Sprinkle pork chops with 2 tablespoons seasoning mix; pat in with hand. On waxed paper combine remaining mix and flour.

In large skillet over medium-high heat bring ¼ inch oil to 375°F. Dredge chops in seasoned flour; shake off excess. Fry in oil 4 to 5 minutes per side or until chops are done. (Change oil if sediment starts to burn.) Drain on paper towels. Drizzle Browned Garlic-Butter Sauce over pork chops.
Makes 6 to 8 servings.

Browned Garlic-Butter Sauce

- ¾ cup butter or margarine
- 2 cloves garlic, minced
- 2 tablespoons minced parsley
- 1 tablespoon TABASCO® pepper sauce

In small saucepan heat butter until half melted; shake pan constantly. Add garlic and cook 2 to 3 minutes or until butter is melted and foam on surface is barely browned; shake pan occasionally. Stir in parsley and Tabasco® sauce; cook 1 to 2 minutes or until sauce is lightly browned and very foamy. Remove from heat.
Makes ¾ cup sauce.

Sweet and Sour Pork Chops

Preheat oven to 350°. In large oven-proof skillet, brown chops in oil. Remove chops from skillet; pour off fat. In skillet, combine ReaLemon® brand and cornstarch; mix well. Add sugar, onion, soy sauce, bouillon and reserved syrup; cook and stir until slightly thickened and bouillon is dissolved. Add pork chops and carrots. Cover; bake 1 hour or until tender. Add pineapple; cover and bake 10 minutes longer. Garnish with green pepper; serve with rice if desired. Refrigerate leftovers.
Makes 6 servings.

Harvest Pork Chops

- 1 **cup shredded carrots**
- 1 **small apple, cored and chopped**
- ¼ **cup fine dry bread crumbs**
- ¼ **teaspoon dried thyme leaves, crushed**
- 1 **pouch CAMPBELL'S® Onion Soup and Recipe Mix**
- 4 **pork loin rib chops, each cut 1 inch thick**
- 1 **tablespoon vegetable oil**
- ¾ **cup water**
- 1 **tablespoon all-purpose flour**
- ¾ **cup apple juice**

1. To make filling: In medium bowl, stir together carrots, apple, bread crumbs, thyme and 2 tablespoons of the soup mix; mix well.
2. With knife, trim and discard excess fat from edges of pork chops. Make a pocket in each chop by cutting horizontally through each chop almost to the bone. Stuff filling into pockets; secure with toothpicks if needed.
3. In 10-inch ovensafe skillet over medium-high heat, cook pork chops in oil until browned on both sides.
4. Cover skillet; bake at 350°F. 45 minutes or until chops are fork-tender. Transfer chops to serving platter; keep warm. Skim fat from liquid in skillet.
5. In small bowl, whisk water into flour until smooth; stir into skillet along with apple juice and remaining soup mix. Over medium-high heat, heat to boiling, stirring constantly.
6. Reduce heat to low; simmer, uncovered, 5 minutes, stirring occasionally. Serve over pork chops.
Makes 4 servings.

Pork Chops Roma

- ½ **cup WISH-BONE® Italian or Robusto Italian Dressing**
- 6 **pork chops, ½ inch thick (about 2 pounds)**
- 2 **medium green peppers, sliced**
- ¼ **pound mushrooms, sliced**

In large shallow baking dish, pour Italian dressing over pork chops. Cover and marinate in refrigerator, turning occasionally, at least 3 hours. Remove chops, reserving marinade.

In large skillet, heat 2 tablespoons reserved marinade and cook peppers and mushrooms over medium heat, stirring occasionally, until tender; remove. Brown pork chops; drain. Add remaining marinade and simmer covered 15 minutes. Return peppers and mushrooms to skillet and simmer covered an additional 10 minutes or until chops are tender.
Makes about 6 servings.

Sweet and Sour Pork Chops

- 6 **center-cut pork chops (about 1¾ pounds)**
  Vegetable oil
- ½ **cup REALEMON® Lemon Juice from Concentrate**
- 3 **tablespoons cornstarch**
- ½ **cup firmly packed brown sugar**
- ¼ **cup chopped onion**
- 1 **tablespoon soy sauce**
- 1 **teaspoon WYLER'S® or STEERO® Chicken-Flavor Instant Bouillon *or* 1 Chicken-Flavor Bouillon Cube**
- 1 **(20-ounce) can pineapple chunks in heavy syrup, drained, reserving syrup**
- 1 **cup thinly sliced carrots**
  Green pepper rings

Mandarin Pork Chops

Pork Chops and Sauerkraut

2 slices bacon, chopped
½ cup chopped onion
1 jar (32 ounces) VLASIC® Polish Sauerkraut, rinsed and drained
2 apples, peeled and chopped
¼ teaspoon pepper
4 medium pork chops (about 1½ pounds)

To Microwave:
1. In 3-quart microwave-safe casserole, combine bacon and onion. Cover with lid; microwave on HIGH 3½ minutes or until bacon is crisp and onion is tender, stirring once during cooking.
2. Stir in sauerkraut, apples and pepper. Arrange pork chops over sauerkraut, placing thicker portions toward edge of dish. Cover; microwave on HIGH 8 minutes or until very hot. Rearrange pork chops.
3. Reduce power to 50%. Cover; microwave 20 minutes or until pork is no longer pink in center, rearranging chops once during cooking. Let stand, covered, 5 minutes.
Makes 4 servings.

Pork Chops with Sweet Red Peppers

1 cup dry red wine
¼ cup orange juice
1 clove garlic, minced
1 bay leaf, crumbled
1 teaspoon dried savory leaves
1 teaspoon dried marjoram leaves
½ teaspoon salt
½ teaspoon TABASCO® pepper sauce
4 pork chops, about ¾ inch thick
2 tablespoons vegetable oil
2 medium red peppers, cut into strips
½ cup orange sections

In large shallow dish combine wine, orange juice, garlic, bay leaf, savory, marjoram, salt and Tabasco® sauce. Add pork chops. Cover; refrigerate 1½ hours; turn occasionally. Remove chops and pat dry; reserve marinade.

In large skillet heat oil over medium heat. Add chops and brown well on both sides; remove from skillet. Add peppers to skillet; cook 5 minutes or until tender. Return chops to skillet. Add reserved marinade and bring to a boil. Cover. Reduce heat; simmer 20 to 25 minutes or until chops are done. Remove chops and peppers to serving dish. Increase heat to high; boil sauce about 3 minutes or until slightly thickened. Pour sauce over chops; garnish with orange sections.
Makes 4 servings.

Mandarin Pork Chops

4 center-cut pork chops (about 1 pound)
1 tablespoon vegetable oil
½ cup orange juice
¼ cup water
3 tablespoons brown sugar
2 tablespoons REALEMON® Lemon Juice from Concentrate
1 tablespoon cornstarch
2 teaspoons WYLER'S® or STEERO® Chicken-Flavor Instant Bouillon
1 (11-ounce) can mandarin orange segments, drained
1 medium green pepper, sliced

In large skillet, brown chops in oil on both sides; remove from pan. In skillet, add remaining ingredients except orange segments and green pepper; cook and stir until slightly thickened. Add pork chops; cover and simmer 20 minutes or until tender. Add orange segments and green pepper; heat through. Garnish as desired. Refrigerate leftovers.
Makes 4 servings.

Dijon Breaded Pork Chops

¾ cup finely crushed saltine crackers
½ teaspoon salt
½ teaspoon ground thyme
¼ teaspoon pepper
⅛ to ¼ teaspoon ground sage
1 egg
1 tablespoon Dijon mustard
4 pork chops, ½ inch thick
¼ cup CRISCO® Oil

Mix cracker crumbs, salt, thyme, pepper and sage in shallow dish or on sheet of waxed paper. Set aside. Blend egg and mustard in shallow dish. Dip each chop in egg mixture, then in cracker mixture to coat.

Heat Crisco® Oil in large skillet. Add chops. Fry over moderate heat 16 to 20 minutes, or until pork is no longer pink, turning over once.
2 to 4 servings.

Mushroom & Pepper Stuffed Chops

**2 tablespoons butter or
 margarine**
½ pound mushrooms, sliced
**1 small red or green pepper,
 chopped**
½ cup sliced almonds
**1 envelope LIPTON® Onion or
 Onion-Mushroom Recipe
 Soup Mix**
1 cup fresh bread crumbs
⅛ teaspoon pepper
**4 double loin pork or veal
 chops, 2 inches thick (about
 2½ pounds)**

Preheat oven to 350°.

In medium skillet, heat butter and cook mushrooms, red pepper and almonds over medium-high heat 5 minutes or until vegetables are tender. Remove from heat, then stir in onion recipe soup mix combined with bread crumbs and pepper; set aside.

With knife parallel to cutting board, make a deep cut in meaty side of each chop. Evenly stuff each cut with mushroom mixture; secure, if desired, with skewers.

In shallow baking pan, arrange chops and bake 1 hour or until done.
Makes about 4 servings.

Oriental Pork Chops

2 tablespoons vegetable oil
1 clove garlic, minced
4 teaspoons minced ginger root
½ cup dry sherry wine
½ cup soy sauce
¼ cup honey
1 tablespoon grated orange peel
1 tablespoon sesame seeds
**¾ teaspoon TABASCO® pepper
 sauce**
4 pork chops, 1 inch thick
1 teaspoon cornstarch
**2 tablespoons water
 Orange slices, cut into
 quarters**

In medium saucepan heat oil. Add garlic and ginger; cook 1 minute. Remove from heat; add sherry, soy sauce, honey, orange peel, sesame seeds and Tabasco® sauce. Place chops in large shallow dish or plastic bag; add marinade. Cover; refrigerate 1 hour; turn chops occasionally.

Remove chops from marinade; pour marinade into small saucepan. Place chops on grill about 5 inches from source of heat. Grill 10 minutes on each side. Meanwhile, in small bowl combine cornstarch and water; stir into marinade. Stir constantly, bring to a boil over medium heat and boil 1 minute. Brush chops with marinade. Grill 5 to 10 minutes longer or until chops are done; turn and brush frequently with marinade. Serve remaining marinade with chops. Garnish with orange slices.
Makes 4 servings.

Barbecued Pork Leg

**1 boneless pork leg roast, rolled
 and tied (8 to 10 pounds)
 Sam's Mop Sauce (recipe
 follows)
 K.C. MASTERPIECE® Hickory
 Barbecue Sauce**

In grill, arrange medium-hot **KINGS-FORD® Charcoal Briquets** around drip pan. Place prepared pork leg over drip pan; cover grill and cook pork 4 to 4½ hours (adding additional briquets as necessary) or until meat thermometer inserted in thickest portion registers 170°F. Baste pork with Sam's Mop Sauce every 30 minutes, patting a thin coating of sauce on meat with cotton swab mop or pastry brush. Let stand, covered with foil, 10 minutes before serving.

Meanwhile, in saucepan, combine remaining Mop Sauce with an equal amount of barbecue sauce; bring to boil. Slice pork and serve with sauce mixture.
Makes about 20 servings.

Sam's Mop Sauce

1 lemon
1 cup water
1 cup cider vinegar
**1 tablespoon butter or
 margarine**
**1 tablespoon olive or vegetable
 oil**
½ teaspoon cayenne pepper
**1½ to 3 teaspoons hot pepper
 sauce**
**1½ to 3 teaspoons Worcestershire
 sauce**
1½ teaspoons black pepper

With vegetable peeler, remove peel from lemon; squeeze juice from lemon. In heavy saucepan, combine lemon peel, juice and remaining ingredients. Bring to boil. Place saucepan on grill to keep warm, if space permits.
Makes 2¼ cups.

Oriental Pork Chops

Pork Roast with Corn Bread & Oyster Stuffing

    1 (5- to 7-pound) pork loin
        roast*
    2 tablespoons butter or
        margarine
    ½ cup chopped onion
    ½ cup chopped celery
    2 cloves garlic, minced
    ½ teaspoon fennel seeds,
        crushed
    1 teaspoon TABASCO® pepper
        sauce
    ½ teaspoon salt
    2 cups packaged corn bread
        stuffing mix
    1 can (8 ounces) oysters,
        undrained, chopped

Preheat oven to 325°F. Make a deep slit in back of each chop on pork loin. In large saucepan melt butter; add onion, celery, garlic and fennel. Cook 5 minutes or until vegetables are tender; stir in Tabasco® sauce and salt. Add corn bread, oysters and oyster liquid; toss to mix well.

Stuff corn bread mixture into slits in pork. (Any leftover stuffing may be baked in covered baking dish during last 30 minutes of roasting.) Place meat in shallow roasting pan. Cook 30 to 35 minutes per pound or until meat thermometer inserted into meat registers 170°F. Remove to heated serving platter. Allow meat to stand 15 minutes before serving.
Makes 10 to 12 servings.

*Have butcher crack backbone of pork loin roast.

Cider-Glazed Pork Roast

    ½ cup apple cider
    ¼ cup Dijon-style mustard
    ¼ cup vegetable oil
    ¼ cup soy sauce
    1 boneless pork loin roast
        (4 to 5 pounds), tied

In small bowl, combine apple cider, mustard, oil and soy sauce. Insert meat thermometer in center of thickest part of roast. Arrange medium-hot **KINGSFORD® Charcoal Briquets** around drip pan. Place roast over drip pan. Cover grill and cook 2½ to 3 hours or until meat thermometer registers 170°F, adding more briquets as necessary. Brush roast with cider mixture 3 or 4 times during last 30 minutes of cooking.
Makes 6 servings.

Glazed Pork Roast

    1 (3-pound) boneless pork
        shoulder roast (Boston butt)
    1 cup KIKKOMAN Teriyaki Sauce
    3 tablespoons brown sugar,
        packed
    3 tablespoons dry sherry
    1 teaspoon minced fresh ginger
        root
    1 clove garlic, minced
    ¼ cup water
    2 tablespoons sugar
    1 tablespoon cornstarch

Microwave Directions: Pierce meaty parts of roast with fork; place in large plastic bag. Combine teriyaki sauce, brown sugar, sherry, ginger and garlic; pour over roast. Press air out of bag; tie top securely. Refrigerate 8 hours or overnight, turning bag over occasionally. Reserving marinade, remove roast and place, fat side down, in 8×8-inch shallow microwave-safe dish. Brush thoroughly with reserved marinade. Cover roast loosely with waxed paper. Microwave on Medium-high (70%) 30 minutes, or until meat thermometer inserted into thickest part registers 165°F., rotating dish once and brushing with marinade. Remove roast; let stand 10 minutes before slicing. Meanwhile, combine reserved marinade, water, sugar and cornstarch in 2-cup microwave-safe measuring cup. Microwave on High 3 minutes, until mixture boils and thickens, stirring occasionally. Serve teriyaki glaze with roast.
Makes 6 servings.

Herb-Marinated Pork Roast

    3½- to 4-pound bone-in pork loin
        roast
    1 small onion, chopped
    ½ cup CRISCO® Oil
    3 tablespoons cider vinegar
    1 tablespoon lemon juice
    1 teaspoon dried oregano leaves
    2 cloves garlic, minced
    ½ teaspoon dried rosemary
        leaves
    ¼ teaspoon dried dill weed
    ¼ teaspoon salt
    ¼ teaspoon pepper

Place roast in large bowl or large heavy plastic food storage bag. Blend remaining ingredients. Pour over roast. Cover dish or seal bag. Refrigerate 8 hours or overnight, turning roast over occasionally.

Preheat oven to 325°F. Remove roast from marinade. Discard marinade. Place roast in roasting pan. Roast at 325°F, 2 to 3 hours, or until internal temperature registers 170°F. Let stand 15 minutes before carving.
6 to 8 servings.

Pork Roast with Corn Bread & Oyster Stuffing

Pork Roast with Sausage & Spinach Stuffing

Cranberry Glazed Pork Roast

- 1 (3½- to 4-pound) boneless pork loin roast
- Salt and pepper
- 1 (16-ounce) can whole berry cranberry sauce
- ¼ cup REALEMON® Lemon Juice from Concentrate
- 3 tablespoons brown sugar
- 1 teaspoon cornstarch

Preheat oven to 450°. Place meat in shallow baking dish; season with salt and pepper. Roast 20 minutes. Reduce oven temperature to 325°; continue roasting. Meanwhile, in small saucepan, combine remaining ingredients. Over medium heat, cook and stir until slightly thickened, about 5 minutes. After meat has cooked 1 hour, drain off fat; spoon half of the sauce over meat. Continue roasting 1 to 1½ hours or until meat thermometer reaches 170°, basting occasionally. Spoon remaining sauce over meat; return to oven 10 to 15 minutes. Let stand 10 minutes before slicing. Refrigerate leftovers.

To Make Gravy: In small saucepan, combine meat drippings and 2 tablespoons cornstarch. Over medium heat, cook and stir until thickened, about 5 minutes.
Makes about 2 cups.

Pork Roast with Sausage & Spinach Stuffing

- 1 envelope LIPTON® Onion, Onion-Mushroom or Beefy Mushroom Recipe Soup Mix
- 1 package (10 ounces) frozen chopped spinach, cooked and drained
- ½ pound sweet Italian sausage links, removed from casing
- ½ cup fresh bread crumbs
- ½ cup slivered almonds, toasted
- 2 eggs, slightly beaten
- 2 tablespoons finely chopped parsley
- 2 teaspoons thyme leaves
- 1 teaspoon finely chopped garlic (about 1 medium clove)
- ⅛ teaspoon pepper
- 2½-pound boneless center cut pork loin roast
- 1 to 2 tablespoons oil

Preheat oven to 350°.

In large bowl, thoroughly combine onion recipe soup mix, spinach, sausage, bread crumbs, almonds, eggs, parsley, 1 teaspoon thyme, ½ teaspoon garlic and pepper; set aside.

Butterfly roast as directed. Spread spinach mixture evenly on cut side of roast. Roll, starting at long end, jelly-roll style; tie securely with string. In roasting pan, on rack, place pork seam side down. Rub roast with oil, then top with remaining garlic and thyme. Roast for 1½ hours or until meat thermometer reaches 165° (medium) or 180° (well done).
Makes about 8 servings.

How to Butterfly a Pork Loin Roast:
1. Place the boneless roast fat side down. Starting at the thickest edge, slice horizontally through the meat, stopping 1 inch from the opposite edge so that the roast can open like a book.
2. Lightly pound the opened roast and remove any fat thicker than ¼ inch.

Tasty Pork Ragout

- ½ pound boneless pork loin
- 1 small onion, chopped
- 1 large clove garlic, pressed
- ½ teaspoon dried rosemary, crumbled
- 2 tablespoons butter or margarine
- Salt and pepper
- ½ cup water
- 1 head DOLE™ Cauliflower, cut into flowerets (2 cups)
- 1 cup sliced DOLE™ Carrots
- Hot buttered noodles

Cut pork into 1-inch cubes. In large skillet, brown pork with onion, garlic and rosemary in butter. Sprinkle with salt and pepper to taste. Stir in water. Cover; simmer 20 minutes. Add cauliflower and carrots. Cover; simmer 5 minutes longer or until vegetables are tender-crisp. Serve over noodles.
Makes 2 servings.

Tofu & Vegetable Stir-Fry

Crispy Fried Pork and Apples

  6 **butterflied pork chops, ½ inch thick**
  1 **large apple, peeled and cored**
  2 **eggs**
  2 **tablespoons half-and-half**
  1 **cup unseasoned dry bread crumbs**
  1 **teaspoon ground ginger**
  ¾ **teaspoon salt**
  ½ **teaspoon ground coriander (optional)**
  ¼ **teaspoon ground allspice CRISCO® Oil for frying**

Pound each chop with meat mallet. Slice apple into 6 rings. Blend eggs and half-and-half in small mixing bowl. Mix bread crumbs, ginger, salt, coriander (optional) and allspice in shallow dish or on sheet of waxed paper. Set aside.

Heat 2 to 3 inches Crisco® Oil in deep-fryer or large saucepan to 350°F. Dip pork and apple rings in egg mixture, then in bread crumb mixture to coat. Fry 2 pieces of pork at a time, 5 to 7 minutes, or until crust is deep golden brown and pork is no longer pink in center. Drain on paper towels. Fry apple rings 2 to 3 minutes, or until deep golden brown. Drain on paper towels.
6 servings.

Tofu & Vegetable Stir-Fry

  ½ **block tofu**
  1 **pound napa (Chinese cabbage) or romaine lettuce***
  ½ **cup water**
  2 **tablespoons cornstarch, divided**
  4 **tablespoons KIKKOMAN Soy Sauce, divided**
  ¼ **pound boneless lean pork**
  2 **teaspoons minced fresh ginger root**
  1 **clove garlic, minced**
  ½ **teaspoon sugar**
  2 **tablespoons vegetable oil, divided**
  1 **medium onion, chunked**
  2 **medium tomatoes, chunked**

Cut tofu into ½-inch cubes; drain well on several layers of paper towels. Separate and rinse cabbage; pat dry. Cut leaves crosswise into 1-inch strips; set aside. Blend water, 1 tablespoon cornstarch and 3 tablespoons soy sauce; set aside. Cut pork into thin slices, then into thin strips. Combine remaining 1 tablespoon cornstarch and 1 tablespoon soy sauce, ginger, garlic and sugar in small bowl; stir in pork. Heat 1 tablespoon oil in hot wok or large skillet over high heat. Add pork and stir-fry 2 minutes; remove. Heat remaining 1 tablespoon oil in same pan. Add onion; stir-fry 2 minutes. Add cabbage; stir-fry 1 minute. Add tomatoes, pork and soy sauce mixture. Cook and stir gently until sauce boils and thickens. Gently fold in tofu; heat through.
Makes 4 servings.
  *If using romaine, increase water to ⅔ cup.

Pineapple Citrus Glazed Pork Roast

  1 **boneless pork loin roast (3 to 4 pounds)**
    Garlic salt
    Pepper
  1 **can (20 ounces) DOLE® Crushed Pineapple**
  1 **cup orange juice**
  ½ **cup lemon juice**
  ¼ **cup sugar**
  2 **tablespoons cornstarch**
  1 **tablespoon grated orange peel**
  1 **tablespoon grated lemon peel**
  2 **teaspoons dried mint, crushed**

Preheat oven to 400°F. Place pork on rack in shallow roasting pan, fat side up. Sprinkle pork with garlic salt and pepper to taste. Insert meat thermometer. Roast in preheated oven, uncovered, 30 minutes. Reduce oven to 325°F and roast 30 minutes longer.

In saucepan, combine undrained pineapple, orange and lemon juices, sugar and cornstarch. Cook, stirring, until mixture boils and thickens. Stir in orange peel, lemon peel and mint. Spread half of glaze over pork after 1 hour of roasting. Continue roasting and baste with glaze every 30 minutes until thermometer reaches 170°F (about 2 hours total cooking time). Remove pork to serving platter. Let stand 15 minutes before slicing. Serve with remaining glaze.
Makes 8 servings.

Hunan Pork Stir-Fry

  ½ **pound boneless lean pork**
  2 **teaspoons cornstarch**
  6 **teaspoons KIKKOMAN Lite Soy Sauce, divided**
  2 **cloves garlic, minced and divided**
  ¾ **cup water**
  1 **tablespoon cornstarch**
  ⅛ **to ¼ teaspoon crushed red pepper**
  3 **tablespoons vegetable oil, divided**
  3 **cups bite-size cauliflowerets**
  1 **medium-size green pepper, chunked**
  2 **medium tomatoes, cut into eighths**
    Hot cooked rice

Cut pork across grain into thin slices, then into strips. Combine 2 teaspoons *each* cornstarch and lite soy sauce with ½ of the garlic in small bowl; stir in pork. Let stand 30 minutes. Meanwhile, combine water, 1 tablespoon cornstarch, remaining 4 teaspoons lite soy sauce and red pepper; set aside. Heat 1 tablespoon oil in hot wok or large skillet over high heat. Add pork and stir-fry 2 minutes; remove. Heat remaining 2 tablespoons oil in same pan over medium-high heat. Add cauliflowerets and remaining garlic; stir-fry 2 minutes. Add green pepper; stir-fry 3 minutes. Stir in tomatoes, pork and soy sauce mixture. Cook and stir gently until sauce boils and thickens. Serve with rice.
Makes 2 to 3 servings.

Crown Roast of Pork with Cognac Glaze

- **1 cup orange juice**
- **1 jar (12 ounces) red currant or grape jelly**
- **1 envelope LIPTON® Onion or Onion-Mushroom Recipe Soup Mix**
- **½ cup Cognac or brandy**
- **½ teaspoon ground ginger**
- **8- to 9-pound crown roast of pork (about 22 ribs)**
- **Warm Dried Fruit Compote (recipe follows)**

Preheat oven to 200°.

In medium saucepan, heat orange juice, jelly, onion recipe soup mix, Cognac and ginger over low heat, stirring occasionally, 5 minutes or until jelly is melted.

In roasting pan, place crown roast; brush with jelly glaze, then pour remaining glaze over roast. Loosely cover with heavy-duty aluminum foil; roast 2 hours. Increase heat to 350° and continue roasting, basting occasionally, an additional 1½ hours or until meat thermometer reaches 175°. Remove foil and continue roasting, basting occasionally and adding water if needed, 20 minutes or until thermometer reaches 180°.

Remove roast to serving platter and keep warm. Skim fat from pan drippings and serve pan juices with roast. Spoon Warm Dried Fruit Compote into center cavity and around roast. *Makes about 12 servings.*

WARM DRIED FRUIT COMPOTE: In large saucepan, combine 2 cups dried apricots, 2 cups pitted dried prunes, 12 dried figs, halved,* 2 cups orange juice, 2 tablespoons fresh squeezed lemon juice, 3 cinnamon sticks and 1 teaspoon whole cloves. Bring to a boil, then simmer 5 minutes. Stir in 1 cup green or red seedless grapes and simmer 2 minutes or until heated through. Remove cinnamon. *Makes about 8 cups.*

***Substitution:** Use 2 packages (11 ounces each) pitted mixed dried fruit instead of apricots, prunes and figs.

Make-Ahead Directions for Compote: Compote can be prepared up to 2 days ahead. Simply combine as above; bring to a boil, then simmer 5 minutes. Cover and refrigerate. Just before serving, heat through; stir in grapes, then continue as above.

Colorful Stir-Fried Pork

- **⅓ cup KIKKOMAN Stir-Fry Sauce**
- **1 teaspoon distilled white vinegar**
- **¼ to ½ teaspoon crushed red pepper**
- **¾ pound boneless lean pork**
- **1 tablespoon KIKKOMAN Stir-Fry Sauce**
- **3 tablespoons vegetable oil, divided**
- **2 medium carrots, cut into julienne strips**
- **1 medium onion, halved and sliced**
- **¼ pound fresh snow peas, trimmed and cut lengthwise in half**

Combine ⅓ cup stir-fry sauce, vinegar and red pepper; set aside. Cut pork across grain into thin slices, then into strips; coat with 1 tablespoon stir-fry sauce. Heat 1 tablespoon oil in hot wok or large skillet over high heat. Add pork and stir-fry 2 minutes; remove. Heat remaining 2 tablespoons oil in same pan. Add carrots, onion and snow peas; stir-fry 4 minutes. Stir in pork and stir-fry sauce mixture. Cook and stir just until pork and vegetables are coated with sauce. Serve immediately. *Makes 4 servings.*

Hawaiian Roast Pork

- **1 (3-pound) boneless pork shoulder roast (Boston butt)**
- **½ cup KIKKOMAN Soy Sauce**
- **1½ teaspoons liquid smoke seasoning**

Cut pork in half lengthwise. Place halves in large plastic bag. Combine soy sauce and liquid smoke; pour over pork. Press air out of bag; tie top securely. Turn over several times to coat pieces well. Refrigerate 8 hours or overnight, turning bag over occasionally. Remove pork from marinade and place in shallow baking pan; cover with aluminum foil. Bake at 350°F. 30 minutes. Discard foil; turn pieces over. Bake 1 hour longer, or until meat thermometer inserted into thickest part registers 170°F. To serve, cut across grain into thin slices. *Makes 6 servings.*

Colorful Stir-Fried Pork

Oriental Pork

1 teaspoon sesame oil
1 teaspoon vegetable oil
1 teaspoon grated fresh ginger
1 tablespoon soy sauce
1 tablespoon dry sherry
1 clove garlic, minced
1 pound boneless pork, cut into
    2- by 1/4-inch strips
1 can (10 1/2 ounces)
    CAMPBELL'S® Condensed
    Beef Broth (Bouillon)
2 tablespoons cornstarch
1 cup fresh snow peas
1 sweet red pepper, cut into thin
    strips
1 cup sliced CAMPBELL'S
    FRESH® Mushrooms
    Hot cooked rice

To Microwave:
1. In 3-quart microwave-safe casserole, stir together oils, ginger, soy sauce, sherry and garlic. Stir in pork to coat. Cover with lid; refrigerate 1 hour.
2. Microwave, covered, on HIGH 5 minutes or until pork is no longer pink, stirring once during cooking.
3. In small bowl, stir together broth and cornstarch; add to pork mixture along with peas, pepper and mushrooms. Cover; microwave on HIGH 7 minutes or until hot and bubbling, stirring 3 times during cooking. Serve over rice.
Makes about 5 cups or 5 servings.

Oriental Pork

Sweet & Sour Pork Loin

1/2 cup chicken broth or water
1/2 cup catsup
2 tablespoons brown sugar
2 tablespoons cider vinegar
2 tablespoons Worcestershire
    sauce
1 clove garlic, crushed
1/2 teaspoon salt
1/4 teaspoon black pepper
1/8 teaspoon cayenne pepper
1 boneless pork loin roast
    (2 pounds), tied

In saucepan, combine all ingredients except roast. Heat to boiling. Cut roast crosswise into 4 pieces; arrange in shallow glass dish. Pour sweet and sour mixture over pork. Cover and refrigerate overnight. Drain pork; reserve sweet and sour mixture. Grill pork, on uncovered grill, over medium-hot **MATCH LIGHT® Charcoal Briquets** 20 to 25 minutes or until pork is cooked through, turning 3 to 4 times and basting often with sweet and sour mixture.
Makes 4 servings.

Satay Pork

1/2 cup peanut or vegetable oil
1/4 cup soy sauce
2 tablespoons chopped peanuts
1 tablespoon Worcestershire
    sauce
1 tablespoon chopped onion
2 cloves garlic, crushed
2 teaspoons brown sugar
1/4 teaspoon curry powder
1/8 teaspoon coriander
3 pounds boneless pork, cut
    into 1/2-inch cubes

In shallow glass dish, combine all ingredients except pork. Add pork, turning to coat with marinade. Cover and refrigerate 1 to 2 hours, stirring occasionally. Drain pork; reserve marinade. Thread pork on skewers. Grill kabobs, on uncovered grill, over hot **KINGSFORD® Charcoal Briquets** 5 to 6 minutes or until cooked through, turning often and basting with marinade.
Makes 4 to 6 servings.

Cashew Pork Stir-Fry

3/4 pound boneless lean pork
1 tablespoon KIKKOMAN Stir-Fry
    Sauce
3 tablespoons vegetable oil,
    divided
2 stalks celery, cut diagonally
    into 1/2-inch slices
1 onion, chunked
1 large green pepper, chunked
1/4 pound fresh mushrooms,
    sliced
2 medium tomatoes, chunked
1/4 cup KIKKOMAN Stir-Fry Sauce
1/4 cup roasted cashews

Cut pork across grain into thin slices; coat with 1 tablespoon stir-fry sauce. Heat 1 tablespoon oil in hot wok or large skillet over medium-high heat. Add pork and stir-fry 3 minutes; remove. Wipe out pan with paper towel. Heat remaining 2 tablespoons oil in same pan over high heat. Add celery, onion and green pepper; stir-fry 2 minutes. Add mushrooms and stir-fry 2 minutes longer. Add pork, tomatoes and 1/4 cup stir-fry sauce. Cook and stir only until tomatoes are heated through. Just before serving, sprinkle cashews over pork and vegetables.
Makes 4 servings.

Curried Pork

- 1 pound boneless pork, cut into ³/₄-inch cubes
- 2 tablespoons all-purpose flour
- 2 tablespoons butter or margarine, divided
- 1 large onion, chopped
- 1 medium apple, chopped
- 2 cloves garlic, minced
- 2 teaspoons curry powder
- 1½ cups V8® Vegetable Juice
- 2 tablespoons raisins
  Hot cooked rice

1. In medium bowl, toss pork with flour to coat.
2. In 10-inch nonstick skillet over medium heat, in 1 tablespoon hot butter, cook half of the pork until browned on all sides; remove with slotted spoon. Repeat with remaining butter and pork; remove from skillet.
3. In same skillet over medium heat, cook onion, apple, garlic and curry until onion is nearly tender, stirring often. Stir in V8 juice, raisins and pork. Heat to boiling, stirring occasionally; reduce heat to low. Cover; simmer until pork is no longer pink, about 10 minutes. Serve over rice.
Makes 4 cups or 4 servings.

Per serving: 317 calories, 26 g protein, 15 g fat, 20 g carbohydrate, 446 mg sodium, 87 mg cholesterol.

Sweet-and-Sour Pork

- ½ cup all-purpose flour
- 1 teaspoon salt
- ½ teaspoon baking powder
- ½ cup cold water
- 1 pound lean boneless pork, cut into 1-inch cubes
- 1 can (20 ounces) pineapple chunks
- 2 tablespoons white vinegar
- 1 tablespoon cornstarch
  CRISCO® Oil for frying
- 3 carrots, cut into thin diagonal slices
- 1 green pepper, seeded, cored and cut into 1-inch pieces
- 3 tablespoons packed brown sugar
  Hot cooked rice

Mix flour, salt and baking powder in medium mixing bowl. Blend in cold water. Add pork. Stir to coat. Set aside. Drain pineapple chunks, reserving juice. Set aside pineapple chunks. Blend reserved pineapple juice, vinegar and cornstarch in small bowl. Set aside.

Heat 1 inch Crisco® Oil in Dutch oven to 375°F. Remove half the pork from batter with slotted spoon; add to Crisco® Oil. Fry 3 to 5 minutes, or until golden brown. Drain on paper towels. Repeat with remaining pork. Pour off all but 1 tablespoon drippings from Dutch oven. Add carrots. Stir-fry over moderate heat 2 to 3 minutes, or until tender-crisp. Add green pepper. Stir-fry 2 to 3 minutes longer. Add pineapple juice mixture, pineapple chunks and brown sugar. Heat to boiling, stirring constantly. Cook and stir until mixture is clear and thickened. Stir in pork. Cook about 3 minutes, or until hot. Serve with rice.
4 to 6 servings.

Pork and Peanut Stir-Fry

- ¼ pound boneless lean pork
- 4 teaspoons cornstarch, divided
- 3 tablespoons KIKKOMAN Lite Soy Sauce, divided
- 1 teaspoon minced fresh ginger root
- ½ cup water
- 2 teaspoons distilled white vinegar
- ¼ teaspoon garlic powder
- 2 tablespoons vegetable oil, divided
- 1 medium onion, sliced
- 1 medium carrot, cut diagonally into ⅛-inch-thick slices
- 2 medium zucchini, cut diagonally into ⅛-inch-thick slices
- ⅓ cup unsalted roasted peanuts
  Hot cooked rice (optional)

Cut pork across grain into thin slices, then into strips. Combine 2 teaspoons *each* cornstarch and lite soy sauce with ginger in small bowl; stir in pork. Let stand 15 minutes. Meanwhile, combine water, remaining 2 teaspoons cornstarch, 2 tablespoons plus 1 teaspoon lite soy sauce, vinegar and garlic powder; set aside. Heat 1 tablespoon oil in hot wok or large skillet over high heat. Add pork and stir-fry 2 minutes; remove. Heat remaining 1 tablespoon oil in same pan. Add onion and carrot; stir-fry 2 minutes. Add zucchini; stir-fry 2 minutes. Stir in pork and soy sauce mixture. Cook and stir until mixture boils and thickens. Stir in peanuts; serve immediately with rice.
Makes 2 to 3 servings.

Roast Loin of Pork Oriental-Style

- ½ cup WISH-BONE® Italian or Robusto Italian Dressing
- ½ cup honey
- 1 tablespoon finely chopped fresh ginger*
- 1 tablespoon hoisin sauce (optional)
- 2 teaspoons soy sauce
- 1 teaspoon Dijon-style mustard
- 1 (3- to 3½-pound) boneless pork loin roast, tied for roasting

Preheat oven to 375°.

In small bowl, combine all ingredients except pork. In roasting pan, on rack, place pork and roast 45 minutes. Brush pork with ½ of the dressing mixture, then continue roasting, basting occasionally, 35 minutes or until meat thermometer reaches 165° (medium) or 180° (well done). Heat remaining dressing mixture and serve with pork.
Makes about 10 servings.
  *Substitution: Use 1 teaspoon ground ginger.

Curried Pork

Zesty Barbecued Ribs

Glazed Pork Tenderloin

> **2 pork tenderloins, about
>   ³/₄ pound each**
> **¹/₂ cup KIKKOMAN Teriyaki Baste
>   & Glaze**
> **¹/₄ teaspoon anise seed, crushed**
> **¹/₄ teaspoon pepper**
> **¹/₈ teaspoon ground cloves
>   Mustard-Soy Dipping Sauce
>   (recipe follows)**

Place tenderloins on rack in shallow foil-lined baking pan; tuck under thin ends of each tenderloin. Combine teriyaki baste & glaze, anise, pepper and cloves; brush each tenderloin thoroughly with baste & glaze mixture. Bake in 325°F. oven 1 hour, or until meat thermometer inserted into thickest part registers 170°F. Brush occasionally with baste & glaze mixture during baking. Remove from oven and let stand 15 minutes. Cut across grain into thin slices and serve with Mustard-Soy Dipping Sauce.
Makes 4 to 6 servings.
MUSTARD-SOY DIPPING SAUCE:
Blend *2 tablespoons dry mustard* with *1 teaspoon each distilled white vinegar* and *water* to make a smooth paste. Cover and let stand 10 minutes. Thin with enough *KIKKOMAN Soy Sauce* to dipping consistency.

Zesty Barbecued Ribs

> **6 pounds spareribs
>   Water**
> **2 cups catsup**
> **¹/₂ cup REALEMON® Lemon Juice
>   from Concentrate**
> **¹/₂ cup firmly packed brown sugar**
> **1 tablespoon prepared mustard**
> **¹/₂ cup finely chopped onion**
> **¹/₄ cup margarine or butter**
> **¹/₄ cup Worcestershire sauce**
> **1 clove garlic, finely chopped**
> **¹/₄ teaspoon salt**
> **¹/₈ teaspoon hot pepper sauce**

In large pan, cook ribs in boiling water 45 to 60 minutes or until tender. Meanwhile, in medium saucepan, combine remaining ingredients; simmer uncovered 20 minutes, stirring occasionally. Grill or broil ribs as desired, turning and basting frequently with sauce. Refrigerate leftovers.
Makes 6 to 8 servings.
Microwave: To pre-cook ribs, place 1¹/₂ pounds ribs in 12×7-inch shallow baking dish. Add ¹/₄ cup water; cover with vented plastic wrap. Microwave on full power (high) 5 minutes. Reduce to ¹/₂ power (medium); continue cooking 7 minutes. Turn ribs over; cook covered on ¹/₂ power (medium) 7 minutes longer. Repeat with remaining ribs. Proceed as above.

Spicy Country Ribs

> **1 medium onion, finely chopped**
> **3 cloves garlic, crushed**
> **2 tablespoons vegetable oil**
> **1 can (15 ounces) tomato sauce**
> **¹/₂ cup red wine**
> **¹/₄ cup packed brown sugar**
> **³/₄ teaspoon salt**
> **¹/₂ teaspoon dry mustard**
> **¹/₂ teaspoon chili powder**
> **¹/₂ teaspoon hot pepper sauce**
> **¹/₈ teaspoon pepper**
> **5 pounds country-style
>   spareribs**

In medium skillet, saute onion and garlic in oil until onion is soft but not brown. Stir in remaining ingredients except spareribs. Bring to boil; reduce heat and simmer, covered, 20 minutes. Trim any excess fat from ribs. Arrange ribs in shallow glass dish. Cover with plastic wrap, vented. Microwave at 50% power 20 minutes, rearranging ribs once. Remove from oven. Brush ribs with sauce. Lightly oil grid. Grill ribs, on covered grill, over medium-hot **KINGSFORD® Charcoal Briquets** 30 minutes or until cooked through, turning often and basting with sauce.
Makes 6 servings.

Chinese-Style Spareribs

½ cup butter or margarine
1 medium clove garlic, finely chopped
1 envelope LIPTON® Onion, Onion-Mushroom, Beefy Mushroom or Beefy Onion Recipe Soup Mix
1 can (16 ounces) tomato puree
½ cup brown sugar
¼ cup soy sauce
¼ cup white vinegar
¼ cup chili sauce
5 pounds spareribs, country-style ribs or baby back ribs

Preheat oven to 375°.

In large saucepan, melt butter and cook garlic with onion recipe soup mix over medium heat until garlic is golden. Stir in tomato puree, sugar, soy sauce, vinegar and chili sauce. Bring to a boil, then simmer, stirring occasionally, 15 minutes.

Meanwhile, in large aluminum-foil-lined baking pan or on broiler rack, arrange spareribs meaty side up and bake 20 minutes. Brush spareribs generously with sauce, then continue baking, meaty side up, brushing occasionally with remaining sauce, 50 minutes or until spareribs are done.
Makes about 7 main-dish or 12 appetizer servings.

Kamaaina Spareribs

4 pounds lean pork spareribs
Salt and pepper
1 can (20 ounces) DOLE® Crushed Pineapple, drained
1 cup catsup
½ cup brown sugar, packed
⅓ cup red wine vinegar
¼ cup soy sauce
1 teaspoon ground ginger
½ teaspoon dry mustard
¼ teaspoon garlic powder

Have butcher cut across rib bones to make strips 1½ inches wide. Preheat oven to 350°F. Place ribs close together in single layer in baking pan. Sprinkle with salt and pepper to taste. Cover tightly with aluminum foil. Bake in preheated oven 1 hour. Uncover; pour off and discard drippings. In bowl, combine remaining ingredients. Spoon sauce over ribs. Grill over hot coals 15 minutes or bake, uncovered, 30 minutes longer or until ribs are tender and glazed.
Makes 6 servings.

Sweet Jalapeno Ribs

1½ cups OPEN PIT® Original Flavor Barbecue Sauce
½ cup jalapeno jelly
¼ cup cider vinegar
2 tablespoons seeded and chopped VLASIC® Hot Jalapeno Peppers
2 teaspoons garlic powder
6 pounds pork spareribs (2 slabs)

1. To make sauce: In 1-quart saucepan, combine barbecue sauce, jelly, vinegar, peppers and garlic. Over medium heat, heat until jelly melts, stirring often.
2. In covered grill, arrange preheated coals around drip pan; test for medium heat above pan.
3. On grill rack, place ribs, fat side up, over pan but not over coals. Grill, covered, 1½ to 2 hours or until well-done. Adjust vents and add more charcoal as necessary. Turn and brush often with sauce during the last 30 minutes.
Makes 6 servings.

To roast: Place ribs, fat side up, on rack in roasting pan. Roast, uncovered, at 350°F. 1½ to 2 hours or until well-done. Turn and brush often with sauce during the last 30 minutes.

Note: You'll find jalapeno jelly in the Mexican or condiment section of your grocery store. Serve leftover jelly with cream cheese and crackers.

Bake & Glaze Teri Ribs

3 pounds pork spareribs
½ teaspoon garlic powder
½ teaspoon pepper
⅔ cup KIKKOMAN Teriyaki Baste & Glaze
½ teaspoon grated lemon peel

Cut ribs into serving pieces; place, meaty side up, in shallow foil-lined baking pan. Sprinkle garlic powder and pepper evenly over ribs; cover pan loosely with foil. Bake in 350°F. oven 45 minutes. Meanwhile, combine teriyaki baste & glaze and lemon peel. Remove foil and brush both sides of ribs with baste & glaze mixture. Cover and bake 40 minutes longer, or until ribs are tender, brushing with baste & glaze mixture occasionally.
Makes 4 servings.

Barbecued Spareribs

1 pouch CAMPBELL'S® Onion Soup and Recipe Mix
½ cup water
½ cup ketchup
¼ cup packed brown sugar
2 tablespoons vinegar
1 teaspoon chili powder
¼ teaspoon hot pepper sauce
2½ pounds pork spareribs, cut into individual ribs

To Microwave:

1. To prepare sauce, in small bowl, stir together soup mix, water, ketchup, brown sugar, vinegar, chili powder and hot pepper sauce. Arrange ribs in 12- by 8-inch microwave-safe baking dish, placing thicker portions toward edges of dish. Pour sauce over ribs. Cover with vented plastic wrap; microwave on HIGH 5 minutes. Rearrange ribs.
2. Reduce power to 50%. Cover; microwave 40 minutes or until ribs are tender, rearranging ribs and spooning off fat twice during cooking. Let stand, covered, 5 minutes. Spoon off fat.
Makes 4 servings.

Chinese-Style Spareribs

Herbed Pork Sauté

- ¼ **cup all-purpose flour**
- ½ **teaspoon dried basil leaves**
- ½ **teaspoon dried marjoram leaves**
- ½ **teaspoon salt**
- ¼ **teaspoon pepper**
- 1 to 1½ **pounds butterflied pork chops, cut into thin strips**
- 4 **tablespoons CRISCO® Oil, divided**
- 1 **teaspoon instant chicken bouillon granules**
- 1 **teaspoon instant beef bouillon granules**
- 1 **cup hot water**
- ½ **cup coarsely chopped onion**
- ½ **cup chopped carrot**
- 1 **package (10 ounces) frozen Brussels sprouts**

Mix flour, basil, marjoram, salt and pepper in large plastic food storage bag. Add pork. Shake to coat.

Heat 3 tablespoons Crisco® Oil in large skillet. Add pork and any remaining flour mixture. Brown over medium-high heat. Remove pork and drippings from skillet; set aside.

Dissolve chicken and beef bouillon granules in hot water. Set aside. Heat remaining 1 tablespoon Crisco® Oil in large skillet. Add onion and carrot. Sauté over moderate heat until tender. Stir in pork, bouillon mixture and Brussels sprouts. Heat to boiling. Cover. Cook over moderate heat, stirring occasionally, about 10 minutes, or until Brussels sprouts are tender and pork is no longer pink. Serve with *hot mashed potatoes,* if desired. *4 to 6 servings.*

Stuffed Cabbage Leaves

- 1 **pound ground pork or beef**
- ½ **cup chopped onion**
- 1 **can (10½ ounces) CAMPBELL'S® Condensed Beef Broth (Bouillcn)**
- ½ **cup regular rice, uncooked**
- ½ **teaspoon grated lemon peel**
- ½ **cup chopped apple**
- ¼ **cup chopped walnuts**
- ¼ **cup chopped fresh parsley**
- ½ **teaspoon dried mint leaves, crushed (optional)**
- 1 **medium head cabbage**
- 1 **can (10¾ ounces) CAMPBELL'S® Condensed Tomato Soup**
- 1 **tablespoon lemon juice**
- ¼ **teaspoon ground cinnamon**

Stuffed Cabbage Leaves

1. In 10-inch skillet over medium heat, cook pork and onion until pork is well browned, stirring occasionally to break up meat. Pour off fat.

2. Add beef broth, rice and lemon peel. Heat to boiling. Reduce heat to low. Cover; simmer 20 to 25 minutes or until rice is tender (add a little water during cooking if mixture becomes dry). Remove from heat. Stir in apple, walnuts, parsley and mint.

3. Meanwhile, in 4-quart saucepan over high heat, heat about 6 cups water to boiling. Add whole head of cabbage to boiling water. Reduce heat to low. Cover; simmer 1 to 2 minutes or until outer leaves are softened. Remove cabbage from water. Carefully remove 6 outer leaves. Reserve remaining cabbage for another use.

4. Drain cabbage leaves on paper towels. Lay leaves flat on cutting board and cut out any tough stems. Spoon about ¾ cup pork filling into center of one leaf. Fold in sides, then roll up from stem end to form a bundle. Repeat procedure with remaining leaves and filling.

5. In medium bowl, stir together tomato soup, lemon juice and cinnamon. Pour ½ of the soup mixture into 12- by 8-inch baking dish. Place cabbage rolls, seam side down, in prepared dish. Pour remaining soup mixture over all. Cover with foil. Bake at 350°F. 35 minutes or until heated through. *Makes 6 servings.*

Hawaiian Pork Stew

- 2 **pounds boneless pork shoulder (Boston butt)**
- ¼ **cup all-purpose flour**
- 1 **teaspoon ground ginger**
- 2 **tablespoons vegetable oil**
- 1 **can (8 oz.) pineapple chunks in juice**
- 1¾ **cups water, divided**
- ⅓ **cup KIKKOMAN Teriyaki Sauce**
- 1 **pound fresh yams or sweet potatoes, peeled and cut into 2-inch chunks**
- 1 **large onion, cut into eighths Hot cooked rice**

Cut pork into 1½-inch cubes. Coat in mixture of flour and ginger; reserve 2 tablespoons flour mixture. Heat oil in Dutch oven or large pan; brown pork on all sides in hot oil. Drain pineapple; reserve juice. Add juice, 1 cup water and teriyaki sauce to pork. Cover pan; bring to boil. Reduce heat and simmer 1 hour, stirring occasionally. Add yams to pork; simmer, covered, 10 minutes. Stir in onion; simmer, covered, 20 minutes longer, or until pork and yams are tender. Meanwhile, combine reserved flour mixture and remaining ¾ cup water; stir into pork mixture and cook until slightly thickened. Stir in pineapple; cook only until heated through. Serve with rice. *Makes 6 servings.*

Pineapple-Glazed Ham and Sweets

- 1 can (8 ounces) pineapple slices in juice, undrained
- 1 package (12 ounces) MRS. PAUL'S® Frozen Candied Sweet Potatoes
- 1 tablespoon Dijon-style mustard
- ¾ pound cooked ham, cut into 3 slices

To Microwave:

1. To make sauce: Drain pineapple, reserving 2 tablespoons juice; set pineapple aside. To prepare sauce, in small bowl, stir together reserved pineapple juice, contents of sauce packet from sweet potatoes and mustard.

2. Arrange ham slices in center of 10-inch microwave-safe pie plate. Cut pineapple slices in half; arrange pineapple and sweet potatoes around edge of dish. Spoon sauce over.

3. Cover with vented plastic wrap; microwave on HIGH 10 minutes or until potatoes are tender, rotating dish once during cooking. Spoon sauce over ham and sweet potatoes before serving.

Makes 3 servings.

Pineapple-Glazed Ham and Sweets

Golden Glazed Ham Loaf

- 1 pound lean ground ham
- 1 pound ground pork
- 1 cup soft bread crumbs (2 slices bread)
- ⅓ cup chopped onion
- ¼ cup BORDEN® or MEADOW GOLD® Milk
- 1 egg
  Dash pepper
- 1 cup BAMA® Peach Preserves *or* Orange Marmalade
- 2 tablespoons REALEMON® Lemon Juice from Concentrate
- 1 tablespoon prepared mustard

Preheat oven to 350°. In large bowl, combine all ingredients except preserves, ReaLemon® brand and mustard; mix well. In shallow baking dish, shape into loaf. Bake 1½ hours. Meanwhile, stir together preserves, ReaLemon® brand and mustard. Use ⅓ to ½ cup sauce to glaze loaf during last 30 minutes of baking. Heat remaining glaze and serve with loaf. Garnish as desired. Refrigerate leftovers.

Makes 8 servings.   *(continued)*

Microwave: Prepare loaf as above. Cover loosely; microwave on full power (high) 5 minutes. Rotate dish; microwave on ½ power (medium) 20 to 23 minutes or until center is set. Spread with glaze as above; microwave uncovered on ½ power (medium) 3 to 5 minutes. Let stand 5 minutes before serving. Meanwhile, microwave remaining glaze on full power (high) 1 to 2 minutes or until hot, stirring after 1 minute. Serve as above.

Fire and Ice Chili

- 1 can (20 ounces) DOLE® Pineapple Chunks
- 1 can (28 ounces) whole tomatoes
- 1 can (6 ounces) tomato paste
- 1 can (4 ounces) diced green chiles
- 2 medium yellow onions, chopped
- 1 DOLE™ Green Bell Pepper, seeded and chopped
- 3 cloves garlic, pressed or minced
- ¼ cup chili powder
- 4 teaspoons ground cumin
- 1 tablespoon diced jalapeño chiles*
- 2 teaspoons salt
- 2 tablespoons olive oil
- 2 pounds lean boneless pork butt, cut into 1-inch cubes
  Condiments: small bowls of sliced green onions, shredded Cheddar cheese and dairy sour cream

Drain pineapple; reserve juice. Drain and chop tomatoes; reserve juice. In large bowl, combine reserved juices, tomatoes, tomato paste, green chiles, 1 onion, green pepper, 2 cloves garlic, chili powder, cumin, jalapeño chiles and salt.

In Dutch oven, heat oil until very hot. Brown ¼ of the pork in oil. Remove from pot. Repeat with remaining pork. Return browned pork to pot; add remaining 1 onion and 1 clove garlic. Cook until onion is soft. Add tomato mixture to pork mixture. Cover and simmer 2½ hours, stirring occasionally. Stir in pineapple; cover and simmer 30 minutes longer. Serve with condiments.

Makes 8 to 10 servings.

*For more fire, add 2 tablespoons jalapeño chiles.

Pineapple-Orange Glazed Ham

1 ARMOUR® Lower Salt Ham
   Nugget (about 1¾ pounds)
⅔ cup orange marmalade
1 (8-ounce) can pineapple
   chunks, drained and juice
   reserved

Preheat oven to 350°F. Spray roasting pan with nonstick cooking spray; place ham in pan. Combine orange marmalade, 2 tablespoons reserved pineapple juice and pineapple chunks in small bowl. Spoon a third over ham; brush to cover entire surface. Bake, uncovered, for 1 hour and 10 minutes, or until ham reaches an internal temperature of 145°F. Baste with pineapple-marmalade sauce every 10 minutes. Serve with remaining sauce. Garnish with fresh mint leaves or parsley, if desired.
Makes 8 to 10 servings.
   Note: Try apricot-pineapple jam in place of orange marmalade for a different flavor combination.

Nutrition Information Per Serving:
185 calories, 14.1 g protein, 3.9 g fat, 17.2 carbohydrates, 39.2 mg cholesterol, 672 mg sodium.

Pineapple-Orange Glazed Ham

Ham-Sauced Sweet Potatoes

3 sweet potatoes (about
   8 ounces each)
1 can (10¾ ounces)
   CAMPBELL'S® Condensed
   Golden Mushroom Soup
1 cup cooked ham cut into thin
   strips
½ teaspoon grated orange peel
⅓ cup orange juice
¼ cup raisins

To Microwave:
1. Pierce potatoes with fork in several places; arrange in circular pattern on microwave-safe plate. Microwave, uncovered, on HIGH 8 minutes or until tender, rearranging potatoes once during cooking. Let stand, uncovered, while preparing sauce.
2. In medium microwave-safe bowl, combine remaining ingredients. Cover with vented plastic wrap; microwave on HIGH 4 minutes or until hot, stirring once during cooking. Split potatoes; spoon sauce over each.
Makes 3 servings.

Asparagus-Ham Roll-Ups

1 pound fresh asparagus
2 tablespoons water
8 slices (1 ounce each) boiled
   ham
1 can (10¾ ounces)
   CAMPBELL'S® Condensed
   Cream of Celery Soup
½ cup sour cream
¼ cup milk
2 tablespoons chopped fresh
   parsley
1 teaspoon prepared mustard
   Hot cooked rice

To Microwave:
1. Arrange asparagus with tips toward center in 12- by 8-inch microwave-safe baking dish; add water. Cover with vented plastic wrap; microwave on HIGH 4 minutes or until asparagus is tender, rotating dish once during cooking. Drain well.
2. Divide asparagus spears among ham slices; roll ham around asparagus. Secure with wooden toothpicks if necessary. Arrange rolls in same baking dish.

3. In small bowl, stir soup until smooth; stir in sour cream, milk, parsley and mustard until well blended. Pour over ham rolls. Cover with vented plastic wrap; microwave at 50% power 13 minutes or until heated through. Let stand, covered, 5 minutes. Serve over rice.
Makes 4 servings.
   Note: Substitute 1 package (10 ounces) frozen asparagus spears for fresh asparagus. Cook frozen asparagus according to package directions. Drain well, then proceed as above in steps 2 and 3.

Holiday Baked Ham

1 bone-in smoked ham
   (8½ pounds)
1 can (20 ounces) DOLE® Sliced
   Pineapple in Syrup
1 cup apricot preserves
1 teaspoon dry mustard
½ teaspoon ground allspice
   Whole cloves
   Maraschino cherries

Preheat oven to 325°F. Remove rind from ham. Place ham on rack in open roasting pan, fat side up. Insert meat thermometer with bulb in thickest part away from fat or bone. Roast ham in preheated oven about 3 hours.

Drain pineapple; reserve syrup. In small saucepan, combine syrup, preserves, mustard and allspice. Bring to boil; boil, stirring occasionally, 10 minutes. Remove ham from oven, but keep oven hot. Stud ham with cloves; brush with glaze. Using wooden picks, secure pineapple and cherries to ham. Brush again with glaze. Return ham to oven. Roast 30 minutes longer or until thermometer registers 160°F (about 25 minutes per pound total cooking time). Brush with glaze 15 minutes before done. Let ham stand 20 minutes before slicing.
Makes 8 to 10 servings.

Baked Ham with Glazed Vegetables

1 cup apricot nectar
1 cup dried apricot halves
1 cup (8 ounces) WISH-BONE® Deluxe French Dressing
¼ cup honey
¼ teaspoon ground cinnamon
⅛ teaspoon ground nutmeg
½ cup sliced almonds (optional)
1 (5- to 6-pound) fully cooked ham butt end with bone
2 pounds sweet potatoes or yams, peeled and cut into large chunks
1 pound pearl onions, peeled

Preheat oven to 375°.

In medium saucepan, bring nectar to a boil. Add apricots, then remove from heat. Let stand 10 minutes. Stir in deluxe French dressing, honey, cinnamon, nutmeg, then almonds.

On aluminum-foil-lined roasting pan, place ham. With knife, score (lightly cut) fat in diamond pattern. Arrange potatoes and onions around ham. Spoon dressing mixture over ham and vegetables. Loosely cover with heavy-duty aluminum foil and bake, turning vegetables and basting occasionally, 1 hour or until ham is golden and vegetables are tender.
Makes about 10 servings.
Note: Also terrific with Wish-Bone® Lite French Style, Sweet 'n Spicy French or Lite Sweet 'n Spicy French Dressing.

Baked Ham with Wine & Onion Glaze

1 envelope LIPTON® Onion or Onion-Mushroom Recipe Soup Mix
1 cup water
⅓ cup brown sugar
¼ cup Madeira wine or sherry
2 tablespoons butter or margarine, melted
1 tablespoon finely chopped parsley
5- to 6-pound fully cooked ham butt end
1 pound shallots or small onions, peeled and quartered

Preheat oven to 375°.

In small bowl, blend onion recipe soup mix, water, sugar, wine, butter and parsley; set aside.

In roasting pan, place ham. With knife, score (lightly cut) fat in diamond pattern; top with soup mixture. Arrange shallots around ham. Bake, stirring shallots and basting ham occasionally, 60 minutes or until golden brown.
Makes about 8 servings.

Baked Ham with Glazed Vegetables

Ham-Stuffed Peppers

1½ cups cooked unsalted regular rice (½ cup uncooked)
1 cup (5 ounces) diced cooked ham
1 can (16 ounces) whole kernel corn, drained
1 jar (15½ ounces) spaghetti sauce
1 cup (4 ounces) shredded Cheddar cheese
1 can (2.8 ounces) DURKEE French Fried Onions
¼ teaspoon DURKEE Seasoned Salt
¼ teaspoon DURKEE Ground Black Pepper
4 medium green peppers, cut into halves lengthwise and seeded
¼ cup water

Preheat oven to 350°. To hot rice in saucepan, add ham, corn, *1 cup* spaghetti sauce, *½ cup* cheese, *½ can* French Fried Onions and the seasonings; stir well. Spoon rice filling into green pepper halves. Arrange stuffed peppers in 8×12-inch baking dish. In small bowl, combine remaining spaghetti sauce and the water; pour over peppers. Bake, covered, at 350° for 30 minutes or until peppers are done. Top with remaining cheese and onions; bake, uncovered, 5 minutes or until onions are golden brown.
Makes 4 servings.

Glazed Ham Steak

1 (8-ounce) can crushed pineapple, well drained
½ cup BAMA® Peach or Apricot Preserves
2 tablespoons REALEMON® Lemon Juice from Concentrate
1 teaspoon cornstarch
1 (1- to 1½-pound) center cut ham slice

In small saucepan, combine pineapple, preserves, ReaLemon® brand and cornstarch; mix well and bring to a boil. Reduce heat; simmer uncovered 10 to 15 minutes to blend flavors. Broil ham to desired doneness on both sides. Spoon pineapple mixture on top; heat until hot and bubbly. Refrigerate leftovers.
Makes 4 servings.

Barbecued Sausage Kabobs

Barbecued Sausage Kabobs

1 pound ECKRICH® Smoked
    Sausage, cut into 1-inch
    pieces
1 cup dried apricots
1 can (12 ounces) beer
½ red bell pepper
½ green bell pepper
1 Spanish onion, cut into
    wedges
¼ pound fresh medium
    mushrooms, sliced
¾ cup apricot preserves
1 tablespoon prepared mustard
2 tablespoons chili sauce
1 teaspoon Worcestershire
    sauce

Simmer sausage and apricots in beer
in large saucepan over low heat 10
minutes. Cut peppers into 1¼-inch
squares. Add peppers to sausage mixture; let stand off heat 10 minutes.
Assemble kabobs on skewers, alternately threading sausage with onion,
red and green peppers, mushrooms
and apricots. Combine apricot preserves, mustard, chili sauce and
Worcestershire sauce in small saucepan. Heat over medium heat, stirring
until blended. Brush kabobs with
sauce. Grill or broil, 4 inches from
heat, 10 minutes, turning and brushing with more sauce after 5 minutes.
Brush with remaining sauce and
serve.
Makes 4 servings.

Two-Bean Franks

½ cup chopped onion
½ cup chopped celery
1 clove garlic, minced
2 cans (16 ounces each)
    CAMPBELL'S® Pork & Beans
    in Tomato Sauce
1 can (about 15 ounces) kidney
    beans, drained
5 frankfurters, sliced
¼ teaspoon dry mustard

To Microwave:
1. In 3-quart microwave-safe casserole, combine onion, celery and garlic.
Cover with lid; microwave on HIGH 3
minutes or until vegetables are tender, stirring once during cooking.
2. Stir in remaining ingredients.
Cover; microwave on HIGH 10 minutes or until hot and bubbling, stirring twice during cooking. Let stand,
covered, 5 minutes.
Makes about 6 cups or 5 servings.

Bean and Kraut Franks

1 jar (16 ounces) VLASIC® Old
    Fashioned Sauerkraut,
    rinsed and drained
1 can (16 ounces) CAMPBELL'S®
    Pork & Beans in Tomato
    Sauce
1 small onion, chopped
2 tablespoons brown sugar
½ teaspoon caraway seed
1 pound frankfurters or
    knockwurst

To Microwave:
1. In 12- by 8-inch microwave-safe
baking dish, stir together sauerkraut,
pork and beans, onion, brown sugar
and caraway. Cover with vented plastic wrap; microwave on HIGH 5 minutes or until hot, stirring once during
cooking.
2. Arrange frankfurters over sauerkraut mixture. Cover; microwave on
HIGH 5 minutes or until heated
through, rotating dish once during
cooking. Let stand, covered, for 2 minutes.
Makes 4 servings.

Grandpa Snub's Chili

2 tablespoons vegetable oil
2 pounds boneless pork
    shoulder, cut into 1-inch
    cubes
1 medium onion, chopped
1 small green pepper, chopped
2 cloves garlic, minced
3 tablespoons chili powder
1 teaspoon paprika
½ teaspoon celery seed
½ teaspoon salt
½ cup sliced pimiento-stuffed
    green olives
3 tablespoons olive juice (from
    jar)
2 cans (16 ounces each) pinto
    beans, undrained
1 cup water
1 teaspoon TABASCO® pepper
    sauce
    Accompaniments: Cooked
    rice, chopped tomatoes,
    shredded cheese, chopped
    green peppers, chopped
    onion and crackers
    (optional)

In large heavy saucepot or Dutch oven
heat oil. Add pork; cook over medium-
high heat until browned. Add onion,
green pepper, garlic, chili powder, paprika, celery seed and salt. Cook 15
minutes or until vegetables are tender. Stir in olives and olive juice.
Cover. Simmer 1 hour or until meat is
tender; stir occasionally. Stir in
beans, water and Tabasco® sauce.
Cover. Simmer 30 minutes; add more
water if necessary to prevent sticking.
Serve with suggested accompaniments, if desired.
Makes 8 servings.
    Note: This chili is equally delicious
made with beef.

Sausage and Peppers

- **1 pound Italian sausage, cut into 2-inch chunks**
- **2 tablespoons water**
- **2 large green peppers, cut into ½-inch-wide strips**
- **1 medium onion, sliced and separated into rings**
- **2 cloves garlic, minced**
- **1 can (11 ounces) CAMPBELL'S® Condensed Tomato Bisque**
- **½ cup water**
- **½ teaspoon dried basil leaves, crushed**
- **Polenta (recipe follows)**

1. In 10-inch covered skillet over medium heat, cook sausage and 2 tablespoons water 5 minutes. Uncover; cook until sausage is browned on all sides.

2. Add green peppers, onion and garlic; cook until vegetables are tender, stirring frequently.

3. Stir in soup, ½ cup water and basil; reduce heat to low. Cover; simmer 10 minutes. Serve with polenta.

Makes 4 servings.

POLENTA: In heavy 4-quart saucepan, heat 4 cups water to boiling. With wire whisk, gradually stir in 1 cup cornmeal. Reduce heat to low. Simmer 20 to 25 minutes, stirring often. Pour into buttered 9-inch pie plate. Let stand 10 minutes; cut into wedges.

Sausage and Peppers

Mustard Glazed Sausage with Sauteed Cabbage

- **1 pound ECKRICH® Smoked Sausage**
- **2 tablespoons packed brown sugar**
- **1 tablespoon catsup**
- **1 tablespoon prepared mustard**
- **3 tablespoons butter or margarine**
- **½ cup chopped onion**
- **8 cups coarsely chopped green cabbage**
- **¾ teaspoon salt**
- **Dash coarsely ground black pepper**

Preheat oven to 350°F. Place sausage in 12×8×2-inch baking dish. Make several diagonal cuts about ¼ inch deep in sausage. Combine brown sugar, catsup and mustard in small bowl. Spoon over sausage. Bake 20 minutes or until sausage is hot. Meanwhile, melt butter in large skillet over medium-high heat. Add onion and saute until tender. Add cabbage, salt and pepper. Cook, stirring often, until cabbage is crisp-tender. Cut sausage into pieces and serve with cabbage.

Makes 4 to 5 servings.

Grilled Sausage with Apples & Onions

- **1 pound smoked sausage, cut into 1-inch chunks**
- **2 small apples, cored and cut into quarters**
- **2 small onions, cut into quarters**
- **2 tablespoons apple jelly**
- **1 tablespoon butter or margarine**

Thread sausage, apples and onions alternately on 4 skewers. In small saucepan, combine jelly and butter; heat until melted. Brush jelly mixture on sausage kabobs. Grill kabobs, on uncovered grill, over medium-hot **MATCH LIGHT® Charcoal Briquets** 10 to 15 minutes or until cooked through, turning often and basting with jelly mixture.

Makes 4 servings.

Corn-Pepper-Sausage Skillet

- **12 ounces Italian or bulk pork sausage**
- **1 cup chopped green or red pepper**
- **1 cup chopped onion**
- **3 cups fresh whole kernel corn *or* 1 package (16 ounces) frozen whole kernel corn, thawed**
- **½ teaspoon garlic salt**
- **¼ teaspoon pepper**
- **¼ teaspoon chili powder**
- **¼ teaspoon ground cumin**
- **Halved cherry tomatoes (optional)**
- **Herbed cream cheese, softened (optional)**
- **Sprig parsley (optional)**

Crumble sausage into heavy 10-inch skillet or heavy foil pan. Add green pepper and onion. Place skillet, on covered grill, over medium-hot **KINGSFORD® Charcoal Briquets** about 15 minutes or until meat is browned, stirring once or twice. Remove from grill; drain off fat.

Stir in corn, garlic salt, pepper, chili powder and cumin; mix well. Cover skillet with foil. Grill, on covered grill, over medium-hot coals, 10 minutes longer or until heated through. Garnish with tomato halves spread with cream cheese; top with parsley sprig.

Makes 6 servings.

Hunan Stir-Fry with Tofu

- **1 block tofu**
- **½ pound ground pork**
- **1 tablespoon dry sherry**
- **1 teaspoon minced fresh ginger root**
- **1 clove garlic, minced**
- **½ cup regular-strength chicken broth**
- **1 tablespoon cornstarch**
- **3 tablespoons KIKKOMAN Soy Sauce**
- **1 tablespoon vinegar**
- **½ teaspoon crushed red pepper**
- **1 tablespoon vegetable oil**
- **1 onion, cut into ¾-inch pieces**
- **1 green pepper, cut into ¾-inch pieces**
- **Hot cooked rice**

Cut tofu into ½-inch cubes; drain well on several layers of paper towels. Meanwhile, combine pork, sherry, ginger and garlic in small bowl; let stand 10 minutes. Blend broth, cornstarch, soy sauce, vinegar and red pepper; set aside. Heat wok or large skillet over medium-high heat; add pork. Cook, stirring to separate pork, about 3 minutes, or until lightly browned; remove. Heat oil in same pan. Add onion and green pepper; stir-fry 4 minutes. Add pork and soy sauce mixture. Cook and stir until mixture boils and thickens. Gently fold in tofu; heat through. Serve immediately over rice.
Makes 4 servings.

Lamb Stew

- **1½ pounds boneless lamb, cut into ½-inch pieces**
- **1 can (10½ ounces) FRANCO-AMERICAN® Mushroom Gravy**
- **4 small potatoes, cut into quarters**
- **1 tablespoon chopped fresh mint leaves or 1 teaspoon dried mint leaves, crushed**
- **1 cup frozen peas**
- **1 cup quartered CAMPBELL'S FRESH® Mushrooms**
- **1 tablespoon lemon juice**

To Microwave:
1. Place lamb in 3-quart microwave-safe casserole. Cover with lid; microwave on HIGH 6 minutes or until lamb is no longer pink, stirring once during cooking. Spoon off fat.

2. Stir in gravy, potatoes and mint. Cover; microwave on HIGH 5 minutes or until bubbling. Stir again.
3. Reduce power to 50%. Cover; microwave 20 minutes or until meat is nearly tender, stirring twice during cooking.
4. Stir in peas, mushrooms and lemon juice. Cover; microwave at 50% power 10 minutes or until vegetables and meat are tender, stirring once during cooking. Let stand, covered, 5 minutes before serving.
Makes about 6 cups or 6 servings.

Western Lamb Riblets

- **5 pounds lamb riblets, cut into serving-size pieces**
- **¾ cup chili sauce**
- **½ cup honey**
- **½ cup beer**
- **¼ cup Worcestershire sauce**
- **¼ cup finely chopped onion**
- **1 clove garlic, minced**
- **½ teaspoon red pepper flakes**

Trim excess fat from riblets. In saucepan, combine chili sauce, honey, beer, Worcestershire sauce, onion, garlic and red pepper flakes. Heat mixture

Hunan Stir-Fry with Tofu

to boiling. Reduce heat; simmer, covered, 10 minutes. Remove from heat; cool.

Place riblets in plastic bag; set bag in large bowl. Pour marinade over riblets in bag. Close bag securely and refrigerate about 2 hours, turning bag occasionally to distribute marinade evenly.

Drain riblets; reserve marinade. In grill, arrange medium-hot **KINGSFORD® Charcoal Briquets** around drip pan. Place riblets over drip pan. Cover grill and cook 45 minutes, turning riblets and brushing with marinade twice. Bring remaining marinade to boil and serve with riblets.
Makes 6 servings.

Roasted Leg of Lamb with Lemon-Rosemary Glaze

- **5- to 6-pound leg of lamb**
- **6 large cloves garlic, halved**
- **4 large sprigs fresh rosemary, torn into pieces***
- **½ teaspoon pepper**
- **¼ cup butter or margarine, melted**
- **1 can (6 ounces) frozen lemonade concentrate, partially thawed and undiluted**
- **1 envelope LIPTON® Onion or Onion-Mushroom Recipe Soup Mix**

Preheat oven to 325°.

In roasting pan, place lamb fat side up. With knife, make several 1-inch-deep cuts in lamb; stuff cuts with garlic and ½ of the rosemary. Sprinkle with pepper, then drizzle with butter. Roast 1 hour or until meat thermometer reaches 140°.

Meanwhile, in small bowl, blend lemonade concentrate, onion recipe soup mix and remaining rosemary. Pour over lamb, then continue roasting, basting occasionally, 30 minutes or until thermometer reaches 145°.

Remove lamb to serving platter and keep warm. Skim fat from pan drippings and serve pan juices with lamb. Garnish, if desired, with additional rosemary and lemon slices.
Makes about 10 servings.

***Substitution:** Use 1 tablespoon dried rosemary leaves.

Pork Steaks with Peppers

2 tablespoons olive or vegetable oil
1½ pounds pork blade steaks, ½ inch thick (about 4 to 5)
3 medium red, green or yellow peppers, cut into thin strips
1 clove garlic, finely chopped
1 medium tomato, coarsely chopped
1 envelope LIPTON® Onion, Onion-Mushroom or Beefy Mushroom Recipe Soup Mix
1 cup water
½ teaspoon thyme leaves
⅛ teaspoon pepper

In large skillet, heat oil and brown steaks over medium-high heat. Remove steaks. Reduce heat to medium; into skillet, add peppers and garlic and cook 5 minutes or until peppers are crisp-tender. Stir in tomato, then onion recipe soup mix blended with water, thyme and pepper; bring to a boil. Return steaks to skillet and simmer uncovered, stirring sauce occasionally, 25 minutes or until steaks and vegetables are tender.
Makes about 4 servings.

Pork Steaks with Peppers

Lamb Curry

1 tablespoon butter or margarine
1 cup chopped onion
2 tablespoons curry powder
1½ pounds boneless lamb, cut into ½-inch pieces
¼ cup all-purpose flour
1 cup SWANSON® Clear Ready to Serve Chicken Broth
2 apples, peeled and chopped
1 can (8 ounces) tomatoes, drained and cut up (optional)
¼ cup chutney
½ cup sour cream or plain yogurt
Chopped peanuts for garnish
Hot cooked rice

To Microwave:
1. In 3-quart microwave-safe casserole, combine butter, onion and curry. Cover with lid; microwave on HIGH 4 minutes or until onion is tender, stirring once during cooking.
2. In large bowl, toss lamb with flour. Stir lamb and flour into casserole. Cover; microwave on HIGH 6 minutes or until meat is no longer pink, stirring once during cooking.
3. Stir in broth, apples, tomatoes and chutney. Cover; microwave on HIGH 7 minutes or until boiling, stirring once during cooking. Stir again.
4. Reduce power to 50%. Microwave 30 minutes or until meat is tender, stirring 3 times during cooking. Let stand, covered, 5 minutes.
5. Stir in sour cream. Garnish with peanuts; serve over rice.
Makes about 5 cups or 6 servings.

Note: Add tomatoes for a more robust flavor and color; leave them out for creamier curry.

Grilled Smoked Sausage

1 cup apricot or pineapple preserves
1 tablespoon lemon juice
1½ pounds smoked sausage

In small suacepan, heat preserves. Strain; reserve fruit pieces. Combine strained preserve liquid with lemon juice. Grill whole sausage, on uncovered grill, over low **KINGSFORD® Charcoal Briquets** 5 minutes. Brush with glaze; grill sausage about 5 minutes longer, turning and brushing with glaze occasionally. Garnish with fruit pieces.
Makes 6 servings.

Apricot-Stuffed Lamb Chops

4 double loin lamb chops, 2 inches thick (about 2 pounds)
4 dried apricots, halved
1 envelope LIPTON® Onion or Onion-Mushroom Recipe Soup Mix
1 cup water
¼ cup olive or vegetable oil
¼ cup honey
2 tablespoons Dijon-style prepared mustard
2 teaspoons rosemary leaves
½ teaspoon ground ginger

With knife parallel to cutting board, make a 1-inch-wide by 1-inch-deep cut in meaty side of each chop. Stuff each cut with 2 apricot halves; press firmly to close.

In shallow glass baking dish, combine remaining ingredients; add chops and turn to coat. Cover and marinate in refrigerator, turning occasionally, at least 2 hours.

Preheat oven to 425°. Bake chops with marinade, basting and turning chops occasionally, 35 minutes or until meat thermometer reaches 145° (rare), 155° (medium) or 165° (well done).
Makes about 4 servings.

Marinated Kabobs

1 pouch CAMPBELL'S® Onion
    Soup and Recipe Mix
1½ cups water
¼ cup Burgundy or other dry red
    wine
2 tablespoons vegetable oil
1 large clove garlic, minced
1 teaspoon dried basil leaves,
    crushed
2 small bay leaves
¼ teaspoon black pepper
1 pound boneless lamb, cut into
    1-inch pieces
1 green pepper, cut into 1-inch
    squares
1 sweet red pepper, cut into 1-
    inch squares
1 yellow pepper, cut into 1-inch
    squares
2 tablespoons chutney
    Hot cooked rice

1. To make marinade: In 2-cup measure, combine soup mix, ½ cup of the water, wine, oil, garlic, basil, bay leaves and black pepper; mix well with a fork.
2. Place lamb in shallow dish or bowl; pour marinade over lamb. Cover; refrigerate several hours or overnight.
3. Drain meat, reserving marinade. On each of four 8-inch skewers, alternately thread meat and pepper squares. Arrange skewers on rack in broiler pan. Broil 6 inches from heat 10 minutes or until meat is desired doneness, turning occasionally and brushing with reserved marinade.
4. To make sauce: Pour remaining marinade into 1-quart saucepan. Add remaining 1 cup water and chutney. Over medium-high heat, heat to boiling, stirring often. Reduce heat to low; simmer, uncovered, 5 minutes. Remove bay leaves.
5. Serve kabobs on rice with sauce.
Makes 4 servings.
   Note: You can use boneless beef sirloin instead of lamb.

Lemon and Garlic Lamb Chops

1 tablespoon all-purpose flour
1 tablespoon grated lemon peel
½ teaspoon garlic powder
¼ teaspoon salt
⅛ teaspoon pepper
4 lamb shoulder chops
¼ cup CRISCO® Oil

Marinated Kabobs

Mix flour, lemon peel, garlic powder, salt and pepper in large plastic food storage bag. Add chops. Shake to coat. Set aside.

   Heat Crisco® Oil in large skillet. Add chops and any remaining flour mixture. Fry over medium-high heat about 10 minutes, or until chops are golden brown, turning over once. Drain on paper towels.
4 servings.

Lamb Chops with Lemony Apple Glaze

½ cup BAMA® Apple Jelly
¼ cup REALEMON® Lemon Juice
    from Concentrate
¼ cup steak sauce
8 loin lamb chops, 1 inch thick

In small saucepan, melt jelly; stir in ReaLemon® brand and steak sauce. Heat through. Grill or broil chops as desired, basting frequently with sauce. Refrigerate leftovers.
Makes 4 servings.

Lamb Pilaf

3 tablespoons CRISCO® Oil
1 pound boneless leg of lamb or
    lamb shoulder, cut into
    ¾-inch cubes
½ cup chopped onion
⅓ cup chopped green pepper
2½ cups hot water
1½ cups uncooked long grain rice
2 teaspoons dried parsley flakes
2 teaspoons instant chicken
    bouillon granules
1½ teaspoons curry powder
1 bay leaf
¼ teaspoon pepper
¼ teaspoon salt

Heat Crisco® Oil in medium skillet. Add lamb. Brown over medium-high heat. Remove with slotted spoon; set aside. Add onion and green pepper to drippings in skillet. Cook over moderate heat, stirring occasionally, until tender. Stir in lamb and remaining ingredients. Heat to boiling. Cover. Reduce heat. Simmer 20 to 25 minutes, or until lamb and rice are tender and liquid is absorbed. Fluff with fork and remove bay leaf before serving.
4 to 6 servings.

Basque Lamb

¾ cup fresh lemon juice
1 cup dry sherry
½ cup olive or vegetable oil
1 clove garlic, crushed
1 boneless lamb shoulder
    (3 pounds), left untied
1 bunch chives, chopped
1 clove garlic, chopped
1 bunch parsley, chopped
    Salt and pepper

In small bowl, combine lemon juice, sherry, oil and crushed garlic. Let stand 1 hour. Sprinkle inside of roast with an even layer of chives, chopped garlic and parsley. Season with salt and pepper to taste. Roll up meat and tie securely with kitchen twine. In grill, arrange medium-hot **KINGS-FORD® Charcoal Briquets** around drip pan. Fill pan with water. Add hickory chips to coals, if desired. Place roast over drip pan. Cover grill and cook 45 to 60 minutes or until medium-rare, basting often with lemon juice mixture. Remove roast from grill; let stand 15 minutes. Carve into 1-inch-thick slices.
Makes 4 to 6 servings.

Lamb Curry

1 cup diced onions
1 large tart cooking apple, cored and diced
2 to 3 teaspoons curry powder
¼ teaspoon ground ginger
¼ teaspoon ground black pepper
3 tablespoons BLUE BONNET® Margarine
3 tablespoons all-purpose flour
1 (13¾-fluid ounce) can COLLEGE INN® Chicken Broth
¼ cup heavy cream
3½ cups diced cooked lamb or other cooked meat
    Curry Accompaniments*

In large saucepan, over medium heat, cook onions, apple, curry powder, ginger and pepper in margarine until tender, about 5 minutes. Blend in flour; gradually stir in chicken broth until smooth. Cook and stir until sauce is thickened and begins to boil. Stir in cream and lamb; cook until heated through. (Do not boil.) Serve with Curry Accompaniments. Garnish as desired.
Makes 6 servings.   *(continued)*

Curry Accompaniments: If desired, this curry can be served over hot cooked rice with a selection of the following: chutney, raisins, flaked coconut, salted peanuts, crumbled cooked bacon, hard-cooked eggs, sliced avocado and grated orange peel.
Microwave: In 2-quart microwave-proof bowl, combine onions, apple, curry powder, ginger, pepper and margarine. Microwave, uncovered, on HIGH (100% power) for 4 to 5 minutes, stirring every 2 minutes. Blend in flour; gradually stir in broth until smooth. Microwave, uncovered, on HIGH for 6 to 7 minutes until thickened and bubbling, stirring every 2 minutes. Stir in cream and meat. Microwave on MEDIUM (50% power) for 6 to 7 minutes until heated through, stirring after 3 minutes. Let stand 5 minutes before serving. Serve as above.

Aegean Lamb Stew

1 tablespoon vegetable oil
2 pounds lamb with bones for stew, cut into large pieces
1 large onion, sliced
2 cloves garlic, minced
1 can (28 ounces) tomatoes, undrained
½ teaspoon ground cinnamon
½ teaspoon turmeric
½ teaspoon TABASCO® pepper sauce
¼ teaspoon salt
    Pinch ground cloves
6 new potatoes, cut into chunks
1 small eggplant, cut into 1-inch pieces
1 zucchini, cut into ¾-inch pieces

Preheat oven to 350°F. In large skillet heat oil over medium-high heat. Add lamb, a few pieces at a time; brown on all sides. Arrange lamb in 3-quart casserole. Drain off all but 1 tablespoon fat from skillet; cook onion and garlic 5 minutes or until tender. Add tomatoes; stir up bits from bottom of skillet. Stir in cinnamon, turmeric, Tabasco® sauce, salt and cloves. Pour mixture over lamb. Stir in potatoes. Cover; bake 30 minutes. Stir in eggplant and zucchini. Cover; cook 45 minutes longer or until meat and vegetables are tender.
Makes 6 servings.

Apple and Veal Scallop

2 large all-purpose apples, peeled, cored and sliced
¼ cup REALEMON® Lemon Juice from Concentrate
½ cup unsifted flour
1 teaspoon salt
    Fresh ground pepper
8 veal scallops (about 12 ounces)
¼ cup margarine or butter
½ cup apple cider or apple juice
1 cup (½ pint) BORDEN® or MEADOW GOLD® whipping cream, unwhipped

In medium bowl, combine apples and ReaLemon® brand; set aside. In paper or plastic bag, combine flour, salt and pepper. Add veal, a few pieces at a time; shake to coat. In large skillet, brown veal on both sides in margarine; remove from skillet and set aside. Stir in apple mixture and cider, scraping bottom of skillet. Cook 3 to 5 minutes. Slowly add cream, stirring constantly. Simmer 5 to 10 minutes or until slightly thickened. Add veal; heat through. Refrigerate leftovers.
Makes 4 servings.

Lamb Curry

Country-Style Veal

- ¼ cup all-purpose flour
- 3 tablespoons water
- 2 tablespoons dry white wine
- 1½ teaspoons instant beef bouillon granules
- ½ teaspoon dried basil leaves
- ½ teaspoon dried thyme leaves
- ¼ teaspoon dried marjoram leaves
- ¼ teaspoon salt
- ⅛ teaspoon pepper
- ⅛ teaspoon garlic powder
- 3 tablespoons CRISCO® Oil
- 1 to 1½ pounds veal round steak, cut into serving-size pieces
- 1 medium onion, halved and thinly sliced
- 8 ounces whole fresh mushrooms
- 2 tomatoes, peeled, seeded and cut into chunks
- 2 slices lemon
- 1 bay leaf

Mix flour, water, wine, bouillon granules, basil, thyme, marjoram, salt, pepper and garlic powder in small mixing bowl. Set aside. Heat Crisco® Oil in large skillet. Add veal. Fry over medium-high heat until no longer pink. Remove veal from skillet; set aside.

Add onion to drippings in skillet. Sauté over moderate heat until tender. Reduce heat to low. Stir in remaining ingredients and the veal. Add flour mixture. Stir. Cover. Simmer, stirring once, 25 to 30 minutes, or until mushrooms are tender. Remove and discard bay leaf.
4 to 6 servings.

Veal Scallopini with Brandy Cream Sauce

- 1 pound veal scallopini, pounded ¼ inch thick (about 4 cutlets)
- ¼ cup all-purpose flour
- 3 tablespoons butter or margarine
- 1 medium apple, thinly sliced
- 1 envelope LIPTON® Golden Onion Recipe Soup Mix
- 1½ cups water
- 2 tablespoons brandy
- ½ cup light cream or half and half
- 1 tablespoon light brown sugar

Lightly coat veal with flour.

In large skillet, melt butter and cook veal over medium heat until tender. Remove veal to serving platter and keep warm. Reserve 1 tablespoon drippings. Add apple, then golden onion recipe soup mix thoroughly blended with water and brandy to reserved drippings. Bring to a boil, then simmer, stirring occasionally, 10 minutes. Stir in cream and sugar and heat through. Serve sauce over veal.
Makes about 4 servings.

Stuffed Veal Cutlets

- 1 package (3 ounces) cream cheese, softened
- 2 teaspoons grated Parmesan cheese
- 1 teaspoon Dijon mustard
- ½ teaspoon dried parsley flakes
- ⅛ teaspoon garlic powder
- ½ cup all-purpose flour
- ¼ teaspoon salt
- ⅛ teaspoon pepper
- 1 cup seasoned dry bread crumbs
- 2 eggs
- 8 thin slices fully cooked ham
- 8 veal cutlets, pounded thin
- 8 thin slices Swiss cheese (each about 4 inches square), halved
- CRISCO® Oil for frying

Combine cream cheese, Parmesan cheese, mustard, parsley flakes and garlic powder in small mixing bowl. Mix well. Set aside. Mix flour, salt and pepper in shallow dish. Place bread crumbs on sheet of waxed paper. Beat eggs slightly in another shallow dish. Set aside.

Place ham slice on top of each cutlet. Trim ham to within ½ inch of cutlet edge. Spread each ham slice with one-eighth of cream cheese mixture (a scant tablespoon). Top each with 2 pieces Swiss cheese. Brush top edges of cutlets with egg. Fold in half. Press and pound edges of cutlets together with meat mallet to seal. Carefully coat both sides with flour mixture. Dip stuffed cutlets in egg, and then in bread crumbs, pressing to coat thoroughly. Cover and refrigerate about 1 hour.

Heat 2 inches Crisco® Oil in deep-fryer or large saucepan to 350°F. Fry 1 stuffed cutlet at a time, about 2½ minutes, or until deep golden brown, turning over once. Drain on paper towels.
4 to 8 servings.

Country-Style Veal

Veal Parmesan

- 2 tablespoons CRISCO® Oil
- 1 small onion, thinly sliced and separated into rings
- ½ cup chopped green pepper
- 1 clove garlic, minced
- 1 can (15 ounces) tomato sauce
- 2 tablespoons dry white wine
- ¾ teaspoon dried basil leaves
- ½ teaspoon sugar
- ¼ teaspoon fennel seed
- ¼ teaspoon salt
- ⅛ teaspoon pepper
- 1 cup seasoned dry bread crumbs
- ¾ cup grated Parmesan cheese, divided
- ¼ teaspoon pepper
- 2 eggs
- 1 pound veal cutlets, ¼ inch thick
  CRISCO® Oil for frying

For sauce, heat 2 tablespoons Crisco® Oil in medium saucepan. Add onion, green pepper and garlic. Sauté over moderate heat until tender. Stir in tomato sauce, wine, basil, sugar, fennel, salt and ⅛ teaspoon pepper. Heat to boiling. Reduce heat. Simmer, uncovered, for 30 minutes, or until sauce is thickened.

Mix bread crumbs, ¼ cup Parmesan cheese and ¼ teaspoon pepper in shallow dish. Beat eggs slightly in another shallow dish. Dip veal into eggs, then in bread crumb mixture to coat.

Preheat oven to 350°F. Heat ¼ inch Crisco® Oil in large skillet. Add veal. Fry over moderate heat, 3 to 4 minutes, or until golden brown, turning over once. Drain on paper towels. Arrange cutlets in 13×9-inch baking dish. Pour sauce over veal. Sprinkle with remaining ½ cup Parmesan cheese. Bake at 350°F, 15 to 20 minutes or until cheese melts.
4 to 6 servings.

Veal Stew

- 1 pound veal for stew, cut into ½-inch pieces
- 1 tablespoon all-purpose flour
- 1 can (10½ ounces) CAMPBELL'S® Chunky Creamy Mushroom Soup
- 1 cup frozen baby carrots or fresh carrots cut into sticks
- ½ cup fresh or frozen pearl onions
- ¼ teaspoon dried thyme leaves, crushed
- 1 teaspoon lemon juice

To Microwave:
1. In 3-quart microwave-safe casserole, stir together veal and flour. Cover with lid; microwave on HIGH 5 minutes or until veal is no longer pink, stirring once during cooking.
2. Stir soup into meat mixture until smooth. Stir in carrots, onions and thyme. Cover; microwave at 50% power 25 minutes or until veal is tender, stirring 3 times during cooking. Stir in lemon juice. Let stand, covered, 5 minutes.
Makes about 3½ cups or 4 servings.

Veal Chops Stuffed with Fontina

- 4 loin veal chops, 1 inch thick (about 3 pounds)
- 2 ounces thinly sliced fontina or Swiss cheese
- 2 ounces thinly sliced prosciutto or ham
- 4 tablespoons all-purpose flour
- ½ cup WISH-BONE® Italian or Robusto Italian Dressing
- ½ cup finely chopped onion
- ¾ cup water
- ¾ cup beef broth
- ¼ cup Marsala wine
- 1 tablespoon fresh or dried rosemary leaves, crumbled
- ⅛ teaspoon pepper
- ¼ cup whipping or heavy cream

With knife parallel to cutting board, make a 2-inch-wide by 2-inch-deep cut in meaty side of each chop. Evenly stuff each cut with cheese and prosciutto; secure, if desired, with skewers. Lightly coat chops with 2 tablespoons flour, then dip in ¼ cup Italian dressing. On aluminum-foil-lined broiler rack or in large shallow baking pan, arrange chops and broil, turning once, 10 minutes or until done. Remove to serving platter and keep warm.

Meanwhile, in medium skillet, heat remaining ¼ cup Italian dressing and cook onion over medium heat, stirring occasionally, 5 minutes or until tender. Add water, broth and wine thoroughly blended with rosemary, pepper and remaining 2 tablespoons flour. Bring to a boil, then simmer, stirring occasionally, 3 minutes or until thickened. Stir in cream; heat through. Serve over chops.
Makes about 4 servings.

Veal Marengo

Veal Marengo

- 1 tablespoon olive or vegetable oil
- 1½ pounds veal for stew, cut into 1½-inch cubes
- ½ pound small mushrooms
- 2 medium onions, chopped
- 2 cloves garlic, minced
- 2 tablespoons flour
- 1 cup dry white wine
- ½ cup orange juice
- ¼ cup tomato paste
- ½ teaspoon dried basil leaves
- ½ teaspoon dried thyme leaves
- ¼ teaspoon TABASCO® pepper sauce
- 1 chicken bouillon cube
  Hot cooked rice or noodles

In large heavy saucepot or Dutch oven, heat oil; brown meat in 2 batches. Remove; reserve. In same pot cook mushrooms, onions and garlic 5 minutes or until tender. Return meat to pot; sprinkle with flour. Stir constantly; cook 3 minutes. Stir in wine, orange juice, tomato paste, basil, thyme, Tabasco® sauce and bouillon cube. Cover; simmer 1 hour or until meat is tender; stir occasionally. Serve over rice or noodles.
Makes 6 servings.

POULTRY

Versatile, economical poultry can be prepared in so many different ways that you can enjoy it often. For a quick meal, try any one of the tasty stir-fry recipes; when more time is available, choose a slow-simmering stew. And you'll discover new ideas for serving turkey all year round.

Versatile Chicken

    1 (2½- to 3-pound) broiler-fryer
        chicken, cut up
    ¾ cup BORDEN® or MEADOW
        GOLD® Buttermilk
    1 tablespoon WYLER'S® or
        STEERO® Chicken-Flavor
        Instant Bouillon
    ½ teaspoon oregano leaves,
        optional
    1 cup unsifted flour
    1 teaspoon paprika
    ¼ cup margarine or butter,
        melted

In 1-cup measure, combine buttermilk, bouillon and oregano if desired; mix well. Let stand 10 minutes; stir. Place chicken in large bowl. Pour bouillon mixture over chicken; toss to coat. Let stand 30 minutes to blend flavors. In paper or plastic bag, combine flour and paprika. Add chicken, a few pieces at a time; shake to coat. Place in 13×9-inch baking dish. Drizzle with margarine. Bake uncovered in preheated 350° oven 1 hour or until golden. Refrigerate leftovers.
Makes 4 to 6 servings.

Tip: To fry chicken, omit melted margarine; fry in vegetable oil.

Oven-Baked Buttermilk Chicken

    1 envelope LIPTON® Golden
        Onion Recipe Soup Mix
    1 cup all-purpose flour
    2 eggs
    ½ cup buttermilk*
    2½- to 3-pound chicken, cut into
        serving pieces
    ¼ cup butter or margarine,
        melted

Preheat oven to 425°.
  Combine golden onion recipe soup mix with flour; set aside.
  Beat eggs with buttermilk. Dip chicken in buttermilk mixture, then flour mixture, coating well. Place in large shallow baking pan, on rack, and chill 30 minutes. Drizzle with butter, then bake 45 minutes or until done.
Makes about 4 servings.
  *Substitution: Blend 1½ teaspoons lemon juice with enough milk to equal ½ cup; let stand 5 minutes.

Chicken Paprika

    2½- to 3-pound broiler-fryer
        chicken, cut up
    1 teaspoon salt, divided
    ¼ teaspoon pepper, divided
    ¼ cup CRISCO® Oil
    1 medium onion, chopped
    1 can (8 ounces) tomato sauce
    ½ cup water, divided
    1½ to 2 tablespoons paprika
    1 cup dairy sour cream
    ¼ cup all-purpose flour
        Hot cooked narrow egg
        noodles

Sprinkle chicken with ½ teaspoon salt and ⅛ teaspoon pepper. Heat Crisco® Oil in large skillet. Add chicken pieces. Brown over medium-high heat. Remove chicken from skillet; set aside.
  Pour off all but 1 tablespoon drippings. Add onion. Sauté over moderate heat until tender. Stir in tomato sauce, ¼ cup water, paprika, remaining ½ teaspoon salt and remaining ⅛ teaspoon pepper. Add chicken. Heat to boiling. Cover. Reduce heat. Simmer, stirring occasionally, 35 to 40 minutes, or until chicken is tender and meat near bone is no longer pink. Remove chicken from skillet; keep warm.
  Blend sour cream, remaining ¼ cup water and flour in small mixing bowl. Blend into mixture in skillet. Cook over low heat, stirring constantly, until thickened. Serve with chicken and egg noodles. Garnish with *fresh parsley sprigs*, if desired.
4 servings.

Versatile Chicken

Country Chicken and Peppers

1 (2½- to 3-pound) chicken, cut up
1 pound hot Italian sausage, cut in 1-inch pieces
4 medium potatoes, unpared, cut in bite-size pieces
4 red or green peppers, cut in bite-size pieces
4 medium onions, quartered
1 (13¾-fluid ounce) can COLLEGE INN® Chicken Broth
¼ cup red wine vinegar with garlic
2 teaspoons Italian seasoning
3 tablespoons cornstarch

Cut each chicken breast into 2 pieces. In large roasting pan, combine chicken, sausage and potatoes. Bake at 425°F for 20 minutes; stir in peppers and onions. In small bowl, combine 1 cup chicken broth, vinegar and Italian seasoning; pour over meat and vegetables in pan. Cover; bake for 40 to 45 minutes more or until chicken is done, stirring occasionally.

Spoon meat and vegetables into serving dish. In 1-quart measuring cup, combine cornstarch with remaining broth until smooth; add enough pan liquid to equal 3 cups. Discard any remaining pan liquid. Return cornstarch mixture to roasting pan; cook and stir over medium heat until mixture thickens and boils. Pour over meat and vegetables.
Makes 6 servings.

Country Chicken and Peppers

Creamy Chicken Tarragon

2 tablespoons oil
2½- to 3-pound chicken, cut into serving pieces
1 envelope LIPTON® Onion, Onion-Mushroom or Golden Onion Recipe Soup Mix
½ teaspoon tarragon leaves
1 cup water
½ cup dry white wine
2 tablespoons all-purpose flour
½ cup whipping or heavy cream

In large skillet, heat oil and brown chicken over medium-high heat; drain. Add onion recipe soup mix and tarragon blended with water and wine. Simmer covered 45 minutes or until chicken is done. Remove chicken to serving platter and keep warm. Into skillet, stir in flour blended with cream. Bring just to the boiling point, then simmer, stirring constantly, until sauce is thickened, about 5 minutes. Serve sauce over chicken.
Makes about 4 servings.

Microwave Directions: Omit oil. In 3-quart casserole, heat chicken, uncovered, at HIGH (Full Power) 12 minutes, rearranging chicken once; drain. Add onion recipe soup mix and tarragon blended with water and wine. Heat covered 14 minutes or until chicken is done, rearranging chicken once. Remove chicken to serving platter and keep warm. Into casserole, stir flour blended with cream and heat uncovered 4 minutes or until sauce is thickened, stirring once. Serve as above.

Baked Apricot Chicken

1 (10-ounce) jar BAMA® Apricot or Peach Preserves (1 cup)
¼ cup REALEMON® Lemon Juice from Concentrate
2 teaspoons soy sauce
½ teaspoon salt
1 (2½- to 3-pound) broiler-fryer chicken, cut up
1 cup dry bread crumbs
¼ cup margarine or butter, melted

Preheat oven to 350°. In shallow dish, combine preserves, ReaLemon® brand, soy sauce and salt. Coat chicken with apricot mixture; roll in bread crumbs. Set aside remaining apricot mixture. In greased 13×9-inch baking dish, arrange chicken; drizzle with margarine. Bake uncovered 1 hour or until tender. Heat remaining apricot mixture; serve with chicken. Refrigerate leftovers.
Makes 4 to 6 servings.

Chicken Cacciatore

1/3 cup all-purpose flour
2 1/2- to 3-pound broiler-fryer
    chicken, cut up
1/4 cup CRISCO® Oil
1 medium onion, thinly sliced
    and separated into rings
1/2 cup chopped green pepper
2 cloves garlic, minced
1 can (16 ounces) whole
    tomatoes, undrained
1 can (8 ounces) tomato sauce
1 can (4 ounces) sliced
    mushrooms, drained
3/4 teaspoon salt
1/2 teaspoon dried oregano leaves
    Hot cooked noodles

Place flour in large plastic food storage bag. Add a few chicken pieces. Shake to coat. Remove chicken from bag. Repeat with remaining chicken. Heat Crisco® Oil in large skillet. Add chicken. Brown over medium-high heat. Remove chicken from skillet; set aside. Add onion, green pepper and garlic to skillet. Sauté over moderate heat until tender. Add tomatoes, tomato sauce, mushrooms, salt and oregano, stirring to break apart tomatoes. Place chicken pieces on top of tomato mixture. Cover. Reduce heat. Simmer 30 to 40 minutes, or until chicken is tender and meat near bone is no longer pink. Serve with noodles.
4 servings.

Dan D's Chicken BBQ

1/3 cup white Zinfandel wine
1/3 cup olive or vegetable oil
1 tablespoon Dijon-style
    mustard
1 teaspoon dried rosemary,
    crushed
1 clove garlic, minced
    Salt and pepper
1 broiler-fryer chicken (2 to
    3 pounds), quartered

In shallow glass dish, combine all ingredients except chicken. Add chicken; turn to coat with marinade. Cover and refrigerate several hours or overnight, basting occasionally. Drain chicken; reserve marinade. Grill chicken, on covered grill, over medium-hot **KINGSFORD® Charcoal Briquets** about 15 minutes on each side or until fork-tender, basting often with marinade.
Makes 4 servings.

Chicken Livers in Wine Sauce

1/4 cup CRISCO® Oil
1 medium onion, cut into
    8 pieces
1/2 cup chopped celery
1/4 cup snipped fresh parsley
1 clove garlic, minced
1/3 cup all-purpose flour
3/4 teaspoon salt
1/4 teaspoon pepper
1 pound chicken livers, drained
1/2 cup water
1/2 cup milk
3 tablespoons dry white wine
3/4 teaspoon instant chicken
    bouillon granules
1/2 teaspoon dried rosemary
    leaves
    Hot cooked egg noodles

Heat Crisco® Oil in large skillet. Add onion, celery, parsley and garlic. Sauté over moderate heat until onion is tender. Set aside.

Mix flour, salt and pepper in large plastic food storage bag. Add livers. Shake to coat. Add livers and any remaining flour mixture to onion mixture. Brown livers over medium-high heat, stirring occasionally. Stir in water, milk, wine, bouillon granules and rosemary. Heat to boiling, stirring constantly. Cover. Reduce heat. Simmer, stirring occasionally, 7 to 10 minutes, or until livers are no longer pink. Serve with noodles.
4 to 6 servings.

Spicy Orange Chicken

Grilled Curried Chicken

1 cup (8 ounces) WISH-BONE®
    Classic Dijon Vinaigrette
    Dressing
1/2 cup finely ground unsalted
    peanuts
1/2 cup orange marmalade
2 teaspoons curry powder
1/2 teaspoon tarragon leaves
2 whole chicken breasts (about
    1 pound each), split and
    skinned

In large shallow baking dish, thoroughly blend all ingredients except chicken. Add chicken and turn to coat. Cover and marinate in refrigerator, turning occasionally, 4 hours or overnight. Remove chicken, reserving marinade.

Grill or broil chicken, turning and basting frequently with reserved marinade, until done. If chicken browns too quickly, loosely cover with aluminum foil.
Makes about 4 servings.
   Note: Also terrific with Wish-Bone® Lite Classic Creamy Dijon, Blended Italian, Creamy Italian or Lite Creamy Italian Dressing.

Spicy Orange Chicken

1 cup water
1 medium onion, chopped
1 can (6 ounces) frozen orange
    juice concentrate, thawed,
    undiluted
1/4 cup catsup
3 medium cloves garlic, minced
1 teaspoon ground cinnamon
1 teaspoon TABASCO® pepper
    sauce
1/4 teaspoon salt
2 (2 1/2- to 3-pound) broiler-fryer
    chickens, cut up

In medium bowl combine water, onion, orange concentrate, catsup, garlic, cinnamon, Tabasco® sauce and salt; mix well. Place chicken in large shallow dish or plastic bag; add marinade. Cover; refrigerate at least 4 to 6 hours; turn chicken occasionally.

Remove chicken from marinade; place on grill 4 to 5 inches from source of heat. Grill 25 to 30 minutes or until done; turn frequently and brush each time with marinade. Heat any remaining marinade to a boil and serve with chicken.
Makes 8 servings.

Country Captain

Country Captain

2½ pounds chicken parts (breasts, legs, wings), skinned
1 can (11 ounces) CAMPBELL'S® Condensed Zesty Tomato Soup/Sauce
1 green pepper, cut into ½-inch pieces
¼ cup raisins
1 teaspoon curry powder
¼ cup toasted slivered almonds
Hot cooked rice

To Microwave:
1. Arrange chicken in 12- by 8-inch microwave-safe baking dish, placing thicker portions toward edges of dish.
2. In small bowl, stir together soup, green pepper, raisins and curry powder. Spoon soup mixture over chicken.
3. Cover with waxed paper; microwave on HIGH 22 minutes or until chicken is no longer pink in center, rearranging chicken and basting with pan juices once during cooking. Let stand, covered, 5 minutes. Sprinkle with almonds; serve over rice.
Makes 6 servings.

Lemon Herbed Chicken

½ cup butter or margarine
½ cup vegetable oil
⅓ cup lemon juice
2 tablespoons finely chopped parsley
2 tablespoons garlic salt
1 teaspoon dried rosemary, crushed
1 teaspoon dried summer savory, crushed
½ teaspoon dried thyme, crushed
¼ teaspoon coarsely cracked black pepper
6 chicken breast quarters with wings attached

In saucepan, combine all ingredients except chicken. Heat until butter melts. Place chicken in shallow glass dish and brush with sauce; let stand 10 to 15 minutes before cooking. Lightly oil grid. Grill chicken, skin-side up, on uncovered grill, over medium-hot **KINGSFORD**® **Charcoal Briquets** 30 to 45 minutes or until fork-tender, turning and basting with sauce every 10 minutes.
Makes 6 servings.

Elegant Chicken Piccata

⅓ cup plus 1 tablespoon unsifted flour
½ teaspoon paprika
4 skinned chicken breast halves
3 tablespoons margarine or butter
¼ cup water
2 cups (1 pint) BORDEN® or MEADOW GOLD® Coffee Cream or Half-and-Half
1 tablespoon WYLER'S® or STEERO® Chicken-Flavor Instant Bouillon *or* 3 Chicken-Flavor Bouillon Cubes
2 tablespoons dry sherry
2 tablespoons REALEMON® Lemon Juice from Concentrate
½ to ¾ cup shredded Swiss cheese
Hot cooked rice

Preheat oven to 350°. In paper or plastic bag, combine ⅓ cup flour and paprika. Add chicken, a few pieces at a time; shake to coat. In large skillet, over medium heat, brown chicken in margarine on both sides until golden brown. Add water; cover and simmer 20 minutes. Remove chicken; arrange in 12×7-inch baking dish. Stir remaining *1 tablespoon* flour into drippings. Gradually add cream and bouillon. Over low heat, cook and stir until slightly thickened and bouillon is dissolved, about 5 to 10 minutes. Add sherry and ReaLemon® brand; pour over chicken. Bake covered 20 minutes. Uncover; top with cheese. Bake 5 minutes longer. Serve with rice. Refrigerate leftovers.
Makes 4 servings.

Orange-Honey Chicken

**1½ cups V8® Vegetable Juice
2 tablespoons lemon juice
4 teaspoons honey
½ teaspoon grated orange peel
¼ teaspoon garlic powder
⅛ teaspoon pepper
2½- to 3-pound broiler-fryer
    chicken, cut up**

1. To make marinade: In 12- by 8-inch baking dish, stir together V8 juice, lemon juice, honey, orange peel, garlic powder and pepper. Add chicken to marinade, turning to coat. Cover; refrigerate at least 2 hours, turning chicken occasionally.
2. Remove chicken from marinade, reserving marinade. Arrange chicken on rack in broiler pan; broil 6 inches from heat 35 minutes or until chicken is fork-tender, basting chicken with marinade and turning occasionally. *Makes 6 servings.*

Per serving: 233 calories, 25 g protein, 13 g fat, 4 g carbohydrate, 180 mg sodium, 81 mg cholesterol.

Chicken Roma

**2 tablespoons oil
2½- to 3-pound chicken, cut into
    serving pieces
1 can (14½ ounces) whole
    peeled tomatoes, undrained
    and chopped
½ cup sliced pitted ripe olives
1 clove garlic, finely chopped
1 envelope LIPTON® Onion,
    Onion-Mushroom, Beefy
    Mushroom or Beefy Onion
    Recipe Soup Mix
¼ cup dry red wine
1 package (8 ounces) broad egg
    noodles**

In large skillet, heat oil and brown chicken over medium-high heat; drain. Add tomatoes, olives and garlic, then onion recipe soup mix blended with wine. Simmer covered 40 minutes or until chicken is done.

Meanwhile, cook noodles according to package directions. If necessary, skim fat from sauce. To serve, arrange chicken and sauce over hot noodles. *Makes about 4 servings.*

Microwave Directions: Omit oil. In 2-quart casserole, heat chicken at HIGH (Full Power) 12 minutes, rearranging chicken once; drain. Add tomatoes, olives and garlic, then onion recipe soup mix blended with wine. Heat covered 14 minutes or until chicken is done, rearranging chicken once. Let stand covered 5 minutes. Serve as above.

Fried Chicken

**⅓ cup all-purpose flour
½ teaspoon salt
½ teaspoon paprika
¼ teaspoon garlic powder
¼ teaspoon pepper
1 can (5.3 ounces) evaporated
    milk
2½- to 3-pound broiler-fryer
    chicken, cut up
¼ cup CRISCO® Oil**

Mix flour, salt, paprika, garlic powder and pepper in large plastic food storage bag. Set aside. Pour evaporated milk into bowl. Dip chicken in evaporated milk. Add a few chicken pieces to food storage bag. Shake to coat. Remove chicken from bag. Repeat with remaining chicken.

Heat Crisco® Oil in large skillet. Add chicken. Brown over medium-high heat. Cook over moderate heat about 25 minutes, or until meat near bone is no longer pink and juices run clear, turning pieces over frequently. *4 servings.*

Chicken Marinated with Orange & Tarragon

**1 envelope LIPTON® Onion or
    Onion-Mushroom Recipe
    Soup Mix
1 jar (12 ounces) orange
    marmalade
1 cup orange juice
1 teaspoon tarragon leaves
2½- to 3-pound chicken, cut into
    serving pieces
    Hot cooked rice**

In 13×9-inch glass baking dish, thoroughly blend onion recipe soup mix, marmalade, orange juice and tarragon; add chicken and turn to coat. Cover and marinate in refrigerator, turning chicken occasionally, at least 4 hours.

Preheat oven to 400°. Bake chicken with marinade, basting and turning chicken occasionally, 1 hour or until done. To serve, arrange chicken over hot rice. If necessary, skim fat from sauce. Serve sauce with chicken. *Makes about 4 servings.*

Microwave Directions: Marinate chicken as above. Remove chicken from marinade; reserve marinade. In 3-quart casserole, heat chicken, covered, at MEDIUM (50% Full Power) 15 minutes, rearranging chicken once; drain. Add reserved marinade and heat uncovered at HIGH (Full Power) 20 minutes or until chicken is done. Serve as above.

Orange-Honey Chicken

Sauteed Chicken Livers

¼ cup butter or margarine
1 pound chicken livers
1 medium onion, coarsely chopped
2 tablespoons all-purpose flour
1 can (10¾ ounces) CAMPBELL'S® Condensed Chicken Broth
½ cup water
Dash pepper
8 slices PEPPERIDGE FARM® Wheat Bread, toasted

1. In 10-inch skillet over medium-high heat, in hot butter, cook livers and onion 8 to 10 minutes or until livers are done, stirring frequently.
2. With slotted spoon, remove livers and onion from skillet. Into pan drippings, stir flour. Gradually add chicken broth, water and pepper, stirring constantly. Over medium heat, heat to boiling, stirring occasionally. Cook 1 minute more.
3. Add liver mixture; heat through. Serve over toast.
Makes about 3 cups or 4 servings.

Oven Barbecued Chicken

1 (2½- to 3-pound) broiler-fryer chicken, cut up
1 cup unsifted flour
1 teaspoon salt
6 tablespoons margarine or butter, melted
¼ cup chopped onion
1 clove garlic, finely chopped
1 cup catsup
¼ cup firmly packed light brown sugar
¼ cup REALEMON® Lemon Juice from Concentrate
¼ cup water
2 tablespoons Worcestershire sauce

Preheat oven to 350°. In paper or plastic bag, combine flour and salt. Add chicken, a few pieces at a time; shake to coat. Place in greased 13×9-inch baking dish; drizzle with *¼ cup* margarine. Bake 30 minutes. Meanwhile, in small saucepan, cook onion and garlic in remaining *2 tablespoons* margarine until tender. Add remaining ingredients; simmer uncovered 10 minutes. Pour over chicken; bake 30 minutes longer or until tender. Refrigerate leftovers.
Makes 4 to 6 servings.

Chicken with Potatoes & Peppers

¼ cup WISH-BONE® Italian Dressing
1 (2½- to 3-pound) chicken, cut into serving pieces
1 can (28 ounces) whole peeled tomatoes, undrained and chopped
1 pound all-purpose potatoes, cut into chunks
2 medium onions, cut into quarters
2 medium red, green or yellow peppers, cut into thin strips
1 tablespoon fresh rosemary leaves*
1 teaspoon thyme leaves
1 teaspoon salt
¼ teaspoon pepper

Preheat oven to 375°.

In large skillet, heat Italian dressing and brown chicken over medium-high heat; set aside.

In 13×9-inch baking pan, combine remaining ingredients; add chicken and turn to coat. Bake uncovered, stirring occasionally, 50 minutes or until chicken is done and vegetables are tender. Serve, if desired, with French or Italian bread.
Makes about 4 servings.

*Substitution: Use 1 teaspoon dried rosemary leaves.

Note: Also terrific with Wish-Bone® Robusto Italian, Blended Italian, Lite Italian, Herbal Italian, Italian & Cheese, Classic Dijon Vinaigrette or Lite Classic Dijon Vinaigrette Dressing.

Chicken Breasts in Wine Sauce

⅓ cup plus 2 tablespoons all-purpose flour, divided
½ teaspoon onion salt
¼ teaspoon pepper
2 whole chicken breasts, skinned and halved lengthwise
3 tablespoons CRISCO® Oil
2 small onions, cut into thirds
⅔ cup dry white wine
1 teaspoon instant chicken bouillon granules
½ teaspoon dried tarragon leaves
¾ cup half-and-half

Mix ⅓ cup flour, onion salt and pepper in large plastic food storage bag. Add chicken. Shake to coat.

Heat Crisco® Oil in large skillet. Add chicken. Brown over medium-high heat. Add onion, wine, bouillon granules and tarragon. Heat to boiling. Cover. Reduce heat. Simmer about 20 minutes, or until juices run clear and meat near bone is no longer pink. Transfer chicken to serving platter. Cover to keep warm. Remove and discard onion.

Place half-and-half in small bowl. Blend in remaining 2 tablespoons flour. Stir into drippings in large skillet. Cook over medium-low heat, stirring constantly, until thickened and bubbly. Serve with chicken.
4 servings.

Chicken with Potatoes & Peppers

Brunswick Stew

- 1 (14½-ounce) can peeled tomatoes
- 1 (17-ounce) can green lima beans
- 1 (2½-pound) chicken, cut up
- 1 (13¾-fluid ounce) can COLLEGE INN® Chicken Broth
- 2 (6-ounce) cans tomato paste
- 2 tablespoons red wine vinegar
- 2 tablespoons Worcestershire sauce
- ¼ teaspoon ground red pepper
- 2 cups cubed cooked pork

Drain tomatoes and lima beans, reserving liquid; coarsely chop tomatoes. In large heavy pot, over medium-high heat, combine chicken, chicken broth, tomato paste, tomato liquid, lima bean liquid, red wine vinegar, Worcestershire sauce and pepper; heat to a boil. Reduce heat; cover and simmer 20 minutes. Add tomatoes, lima beans and pork; cover. Simmer 20 to 25 minutes more or until chicken is done.
Makes 6 servings.

Microwave: In 5-quart microwave-proof casserole, combine first 8 ingredients as above. Cover with waxed paper. Microwave on MEDIUM (50% power) for 28 to 30 minutes, stirring twice during cooking time. Add tomatoes, lima beans and pork; cover. Microwave on LOW (30% power) for 18 to 20 minutes. Let stand, covered, 10 minutes before serving.

Brunswick Stew

Chicken Kyoto

- 1 cup apple cider
- ½ cup soy sauce
- ½ cup vegetable oil
- ¼ cup sugar
- 2 teaspoons ground ginger
- 1 broiler-fryer chicken (2 to 3 pounds), quartered

In small saucepan, combine all ingredients except chicken. Simmer over medium heat 5 to 8 minutes or until sugar is dissolved. Place chicken in shallow glass dish. Pour marinade over chicken; cover and refrigerate about 6 hours. Drain chicken; reserve marinade. Grill chicken, on uncovered grill, over medium-hot **KINGSFORD® Charcoal Briquets**, about 25 minutes on each side or until fork-tender, basting often with marinade.
Makes 4 servings.

Italian Chicken

- 2½ pounds chicken parts (breasts, legs, wings), skinned
- 1 cup sliced CAMPBELL'S FRESH® Mushrooms
- ½ cup chopped onion
- 1 jar (15½ ounces) PREGO® Spaghetti Sauce

To Microwave:
1. Arrange chicken in 12- by 8-inch microwave-safe baking dish, placing thicker portions toward edges of dish. Top with mushrooms and onion. Pour spaghetti sauce over chicken.
2. Cover with waxed paper; microwave on HIGH 22 minutes or until chicken is no longer pink in center, rearranging chicken parts once during cooking. Let stand, covered, 5 minutes.
Makes 6 servings.

Chicken Adobo

- 3 pounds frying chicken pieces
- ½ cup KIKKOMAN Soy Sauce
- ½ cup distilled white vinegar
- 2 tablespoons sugar
- 1 teaspoon pepper
- 6 large cloves garlic, pressed

Microwave Directions: Rinse chicken pieces and pat dry with paper towels. Combine soy sauce, vinegar, sugar, pepper and garlic in large microwave-safe casserole with lid; add chicken pieces, skin side down. Cover and microwave on High 10 minutes. Turn chicken pieces over; rearrange in dish. Cover and microwave on High 13 minutes longer, or until chicken is tender, rearranging pieces once. Serve immediately.
Makes 4 servings.

Sweet and Spicy Chicken Barbecue

Tequila-Orange Chicken

½ cup orange juice
¼ cup tequila
2 tablespoons seeded and finely chopped VLASIC® Hot Jalapeno Peppers
½ teaspoon grated orange peel
1 can (10½ ounces) FRANCO-AMERICAN® Chicken Gravy
3 whole chicken breasts, split

1. To make sauce: In 1-quart saucepan, combine juice, tequila, peppers and peel. Over high heat, heat to boiling. Reduce heat to low; simmer, uncovered, 10 minutes. Add gravy; heat through, stirring constantly.
2. On grill rack, place chicken, skin side up, directly above medium coals. Grill, uncovered, 1 hour or until tender and juices run clear, turning and brushing often with sauce during the last 30 minutes.
Makes 6 servings.

To broil: Arrange chicken, skin side up, on rack in broiler pan. Broil 6 inches from heat 40 minutes or until tender and juices run clear, turning and brushing often with sauce during the last 20 minutes.

Grilled Capon

1 capon or whole roasting chicken (6 to 7 pounds)
Salt
¼ teaspoon poultry seasoning
1½ medium onions, quartered
1 tablespoon rubbed sage
2 stalks celery with leaves, cut into 1-inch pieces
2 medium carrots, cut into ½-inch pieces
2 tablespoons butter or margarine, melted
K.C. MASTERPIECE® Barbecue Sauce

Wash capon thoroughly under cold running water; pat dry with paper toweling. Rub cavity lightly with salt and poultry seasoning. Insert a few onion quarters in neck and fold neck skin over onion. Fold wings across back with tips touching to secure neck skin. Sprinkle 1 teaspoon of the sage in body cavity and stuff with remaining onion quarters, the celery and carrots. Tie legs and tail together with kitchen twine. Insert meat thermometer in center of thigh muscle, not touching bone. Brush skin with melted butter. Rub with remaining 2 teaspoons sage.

Sweet and Spicy Chicken Barbecue

1½ cups DOLE® Pineapple Orange Juice
1 cup orange marmalade
⅔ cup teriyaki sauce
½ cup brown sugar, packed
½ teaspoon ground cloves
½ teaspoon ground ginger
4 frying chickens (about 2 pounds each), halved or quartered
Salt and pepper
DOLE™ Pineapple slices
4 teaspoons cornstarch

In saucepan, combine juice, marmalade, teriyaki sauce, brown sugar, cloves and ginger. Heat until sugar dissolves; let cool. Sprinkle chicken with salt and pepper to taste. Place in glass baking pan. Pour juice mixture over chicken; turn to coat all sides. Marinate, covered, 2 hours in refrigerator, turning often.

Preheat oven to 350°F. Light charcoal grill. Drain chicken; reserve marinade. Bake chicken in preheated oven 20 minutes. Arrange chicken on lightly greased grill 4 to 6 inches above glowing coals. Grill, turning and basting often with reserved marinade, 20 to 25 minutes or until meat near bone is no longer pink. Grill pineapple slices 3 minutes or until heated through.

In small saucepan, dissolve cornstarch in remaining marinade. Cook over medium heat until sauce boils and thickens. Spoon over chicken.
Makes 8 servings.

Arrange medium-hot **KINGS-FORD® Charcoal Briquets** around drip pan. Place capon, breast-side up, over drip pan; cover grill and cook 1½ to 2 hours or until thermometer registers 185°F. Tent with heavy-duty foil to prevent overbrowning, if necessary. Brush capon with barbecue sauce during last 10 minutes of cooking. Garnish with parsley; serve with additional heated barbecue sauce, if desired.
Makes 6 servings.

Golden Glazed Stuffed Chicken

Golden Glazed Stuffed Chicken

      1 (3- to 4-pound) whole broiler-fryer chicken
        Vegetable oil
        Salt and pepper
      4 cups prepared corn bread stuffing
    ½ cup BAMA® Peach *or* Apricot Preserves
      1 tablespoon margarine or butter, melted
      1 tablespoon REALEMON® Lemon Juice from Concentrate

Preheat oven to 375°. Brush chicken with oil; sprinkle lightly with salt and pepper. Stuff neck and body cavities loosely with stuffing. Place breast-side up on rack in shallow roasting pan. Bake 1 hour and 15 minutes. Turn remaining stuffing into greased 1-quart baking dish; bake 30 minutes. Meanwhile, stir together preserves, margarine and ReaLemon® brand. Spoon glaze over chicken; return to oven and bake 15 minutes longer. Refrigerate leftovers.
Makes 4 to 6 servings.

Microwave: Prepare chicken and stuffing as above. Place chicken breast-side down on microwave rack in 12×7-inch baking dish; cover loosely. Microwave on full power (high) 15 minutes. Turn chicken breast-side up; cover loosely. Microwave on full power (high) 10 to 15 minutes or until tender. Meanwhile, prepare glaze as above. Spoon glaze over chicken during last 5 minutes of cooking time. Turn remaining stuffing into 1-quart round baking dish. Cover; microwave on full power (high) 2 to 3 minutes or until hot.

Mexican Chicken with Spicy Bacon

      2 serrano chili peppers
      2 cloves garlic
        Dash ground cloves
        Dash ground cinnamon
      4 slices bacon, partially cooked
      1 whole roasting chicken (3½ to 4 pounds)

Remove stems from peppers. Slit open; remove seeds and ribs. Finely chop peppers and garlic. Place in small bowl. Stir in cloves and cinnamon. Cut bacon into 1-inch pieces.

Lift skin layer of chicken at neck cavity. Insert hand, lifting skin from meat along breast, thigh and drumstick. Using small metal spatula, spread pepper mixture evenly over meat under skin. Place layer of bacon pieces over pepper mixture. Skewer neck skin to back. Tie legs securely to tail with kitchen twine; twist wing tips under back of chicken. Insert meat thermometer in center of thigh muscle, not touching bone.

Arrange medium-hot **KINGS-FORD® Charcoal Briquets** around drip pan. Place chicken, breast-side up, over drip pan. Cover grill and cook about 1 hour or until meat thermometer registers 185°F. Garnish with grilled cherry tomatoes and additional serrano chili peppers, if desired.
Makes 4 servings.

Roasted Dill Chicken

    ½ cup WISH-BONE® Italian Dressing
      1 cup loosely packed snipped fresh dill*
    ½ cup coarsely chopped shallots or onions
    ½ teaspoon salt
    ¼ teaspoon pepper
      1 (5- to 5½-pound) roasting chicken
      2 pounds all-purpose potatoes, cut into chunks

Preheat oven to 375°.

In food processor or blender, process Italian dressing, dill, shallots, salt and pepper until blended.

In roasting pan, on rack, place chicken; spread dill mixture inside cavity, then under and over skin. Close cavity with skewers or wooden toothpicks; tie legs together with string. Arrange potatoes around chicken. Loosely cover with heavy-duty aluminum foil, then roast 1½ hours, turning potatoes occasionally. Remove foil and continue roasting 15 minutes or until meat thermometer reaches 185° and potatoes are done.
Makes about 4 servings.

***Substitution:** Use 2 tablespoons dried dill weed.

Note: Also terrific with Wish-Bone® Robusto Italian, Herbal Italian, Italian & Cheese, Blended Italian or Lite Italian Dressing.

Herb-Roasted Chicken

2½- to 3-pound broiler-fryer chicken
2 cloves garlic, quartered
¼ cup CRISCO® Oil
1 tablespoon lime juice
1 teaspoon dried tarragon leaves
1 teaspoon dried chervil leaves
½ teaspoon dried thyme leaves
Pepper

Preheat oven to 375°F. Lift skin from chicken breast and place 6 pieces garlic between skin and meat. Cut small slit in each drumstick. Insert a piece of garlic into each slit.

Blend Crisco® Oil and lime juice in small bowl. Brush on chicken. Mix tarragon, chervil and thyme in another small bowl. Rub onto chicken. Sprinkle chicken with pepper.

Place chicken, breast-side up, in roasting pan. Bake at 375°F, 1¼ to 1½ hours, or until juices run clear and meat near bone is no longer pink, brushing with lime juice mixture several times during roasting. Let stand 10 minutes before carving.
4 servings.

Corn-Stuffed Chicken

¼ cup butter or margarine
½ cup chopped onion
½ cup sliced celery
½ teaspoon dried thyme leaves, crushed
4 cups fresh bread cubes
1 cup whole kernel corn, cooked
2 cans (10½ ounces *each*) FRANCO-AMERICAN® Chicken Gravy
¼ teaspoon pepper
5-pound roasting chicken

1. To make stuffing: In 1½-quart saucepan over medium heat, in hot butter, cook onion, celery and thyme until vegetables are tender, stirring often. In large bowl, combine onion mixture, bread, corn, ¼ cup of the gravy and pepper; toss gently to coat.
2. Remove neck and giblets from inside bird. Remove excess fat. Cut off and discard neck skin. Rinse bird with cold running water; drain well. Spoon stuffing loosely into body cavity. Fold skin over stuffing; secure with skewer. With breast side up, lift wings toward neck, then fold tips under back of bird to balance. Tie legs.

3. In covered grill, arrange preheated coals around drip pan; test for medium heat above pan. Insert meat thermometer into thickest part of meat between breast and thigh, without touching fat or bone.
4. On grill rack, place chicken, breast side up, over pan but not over coals. Grill, covered, 2 to 2½ hours or until well-done or 180°F. Adjust vents and add more charcoal as necessary.
5. To make sauce: Remove chicken from grill, reserving 2 tablespoons drippings. In 1-quart saucepan, combine remaining gravy and reserved drippings. Over medium heat, heat through, stirring constantly. Serve sauce with chicken.
Makes 8 to 10 servings.

To roast: Place stuffed bird, breast side up, on rack in roasting pan. Roast, uncovered, at 325°F. 2½ to 3 hours or until well-done or 180°F.

Spinach & Pesto Stuffed Chicken Breasts

¼ cup *plus* 2 tablespoons WISH-BONE® Italian Dressing
¼ cup chopped fresh basil leaves*
¼ cup grated Parmesan cheese
⅛ teaspoon pepper
1 package (10 ounces) frozen chopped spinach, cooked and squeezed dry**
1 cup fresh bread crumbs
4 whole boneless chicken breasts (about 2 pounds), halved

In food processor or blender, process ¼ cup Italian dressing with basil, cheese and pepper until blended. In medium bowl, thoroughly combine dressing mixture, spinach and bread crumbs.

With knife parallel to cutting board, make deep, 3-inch-long cut in center of each chicken breast half to form pocket. Evenly stuff pockets with spinach mixture.

In aluminum-foil-lined large shallow baking pan or on broiler rack, arrange chicken, then brush with remaining 2 tablespoons dressing. Broil, turning once, 7 minutes or until chicken is done.
Makes about 8 servings.

*Substitution: Use 1 tablespoon dried basil leaves. *(continued)*

**Substitution: Use 1 pound fresh spinach leaves, cooked, squeezed dry and chopped (about 1½ cups).
Note: Also terrific with Wish-Bone® Robusto Italian, Herbal Italian, Blended Italian, Italian & Cheese or Lite Italian Dressing.

Special Lemony Chicken

¼ cup unsifted flour
1 teaspoon salt
¼ teaspoon pepper
6 skinned boneless chicken breast halves
¼ cup margarine or butter
¼ cup REALEMON® Lemon Juice from Concentrate
8 ounces fresh mushrooms, sliced (about 2 cups)
Hot cooked rice
Chopped parsley

In paper or plastic bag, combine flour, salt and pepper. Add chicken, a few pieces at a time; shake to coat. In large skillet, brown chicken in margarine on both sides until golden brown. Add ReaLemon® brand and mushrooms. Reduce heat; cover and simmer 20 minutes or until tender. Serve with rice; garnish with parsley. Refrigerate leftovers.
Makes 6 servings.

Spinach & Pesto Stuffed Chicken Breasts

Apple-Raisin Stuffed Chicken Breasts

- 1 (13¾-fluid ounce) can COLLEGE INN® Chicken Broth
- ⅓ cup BLUE BONNET® Margarine
- 1 cup herb-seasoned stuffing mix
- ⅓ cup chopped apple
- ¼ cup seedless raisins
- 2 whole boneless chicken breasts, split and pounded (1 pound)
- 3 tablespoons all-purpose flour
- 1 teaspoon dried tarragon leaves

In saucepan, over medium-high heat, heat ⅓ cup chicken broth and 2 tablespoons margarine until margarine melts. Stir in stuffing mix, apple and raisins. Divide mixture evenly among 4 chicken pieces. Roll up; secure with toothpicks.

In skillet, over medium-high heat, melt remaining margarine. Brown chicken on all sides; remove. Blend flour and tarragon into margarine in skillet. Gradually add remaining broth, stirring constantly until mixture thickens and boils. Return chicken to skillet; reduce heat. Cover; simmer 20 minutes or until done. Garnish as desired.
Makes 4 servings.

Microwave: In 1-quart microwave-proof bowl, place ⅓ cup broth and 2 tablespoons margarine. Microwave, uncovered, on HIGH (100% power) for 1 to 2 minutes until margarine melts. Stir in stuffing mix, apple and raisins. Stuff chicken breasts as above.

In 9-inch microwave-proof pie plate, place remaining margarine. Microwave on HIGH for 35 to 40 seconds until melted. Stir in flour and tarragon. Gradually add remaining broth. Microwave, uncovered, on HIGH for 4 to 5 minutes until mixture thickens and boils, stirring every 2 minutes. Place stuffed chicken in pie plate, turning to coat with sauce; cover with waxed paper. Microwave on HIGH for 8 to 9 minutes until done, rotating dish ¼ turn after 4 minutes. Let stand, covered, 5 minutes.

Apple-Raisin Stuffed Chicken Breasts

Shantung Chicken

- 1 whole chicken breast, skinned and boned
- 2 tablespoons cornstarch, divided
- 3 tablespoons KIKKOMAN Soy Sauce, divided
- 1 tablespoon dry sherry
- 1 clove garlic, minced
- 1 cup water
- 3 tablespoons vegetable oil, divided
- ½ pound fresh bean sprouts
- ¼ pound green onions and tops, cut into 1½-inch lengths, separating whites from tops
- 1 tablespoon slivered fresh ginger root
- 1 tablespoon sesame seed, toasted
- Hot cooked noodles

Cut chicken into narrow strips. Combine 1 tablespoon *each* cornstarch and soy sauce with sherry and garlic in small bowl; stir in chicken. Let stand 5 minutes. Meanwhile, blend water, remaining 1 tablespoon cornstarch and 2 tablespoons soy sauce; set aside. Heat 1 tablespoon oil in hot wok or large skillet over high heat. Add chicken and stir-fry 2 minutes; remove. Heat remaining 2 tablespoons oil in same pan; add bean sprouts, white parts of green onions and ginger; stir-fry 3 minutes. Stir in chicken, soy sauce mixture, green onion tops and sesame seed. Cook and stir until mixture boils and thickens. Serve immediately over noodles.
Makes 4 servings.

Quick Chicken Curry

- **3 cups cubed cooked chicken *or* turkey**
- **1 cup chopped onion**
- **1 clove garlic, finely chopped**
- **¼ cup margarine or butter**
- **¼ cup unsifted flour**
- **2½ cups BORDEN® or MEADOW GOLD® Milk**
- **¾ cup COCO LOPEZ® Cream of Coconut**
- **1 tablespoon curry powder**
- **1 tablespoon WYLER'S® or STEERO® Chicken-Flavor Instant Bouillon *or* 3 Chicken-Flavor Bouillon Cubes**
- **¼ cup REALEMON® Lemon Juice from Concentrate**
- **Hot cooked rice**
- **Condiments**

In large skillet, cook onion and garlic in margarine until tender; stir in flour. Gradually add milk; stir until smooth. Add cream of coconut, curry and bouillon. Over medium heat, cook and stir until thickened. Add RealLemon® brand; reduce heat and simmer 10 minutes. Add chicken. Cook 10 minutes longer. Serve over rice with condiments. Refrigerate leftovers.
Makes 6 servings.

Suggested condiments: Toasted flaked coconut, cashews, pecans or peanuts, chopped green onion, chopped hard-cooked eggs, chutney, crumbled bacon, raisins or sunflower meats.

Microwave: Increase flour to ⅓ *cup;* reduce milk to *2 cups.* In 2-quart round baking dish, microwave margarine on full power (high) 45 seconds to 1 minute or until melted. Add onion and garlic. Cover; microwave on full power (high) 4 minutes or until onion is tender. Proceed as above to add flour, milk, cream of coconut, curry and bouillon. Microwave on ⅔ power (medium-high) 9 to 12 minutes or until slightly thickened, stirring every 2 minutes. Add RealLemon® brand; microwave on ½ power (medium) 5 minutes. Add chicken; microwave on ½ power (medium) 5 minutes or until chicken is heated through. Let stand 5 minutes before serving. Proceed as above.

Rolled Chicken Breasts Florentine

Rolled Chicken Breasts Florentine

- **4 skinless boneless chicken breast halves (about 1 pound)**
- **4 thin slices (1 ounce each) cooked ham**
- **4 thin slices (1 ounce each) Swiss cheese**
- **1 package (10 ounces) frozen chopped spinach, thawed and well drained**
- **1 can (10¾ ounces) CAMPBELL'S® Condensed Golden Mushroom or Cream of Chicken Soup**
- **⅓ cup water**
- **¼ cup sliced green onions**
- **⅛ teaspoon dried thyme leaves, crushed**

To Microwave:
1. With flat side of meat mallet, pound chicken to ¼-inch thickness. Place a ham slice, cheese slice and ¼ of the spinach on each chicken piece. Roll up chicken from short end, jelly-roll fashion. Secure with wooden toothpicks if needed.
2. Place chicken, seam side down, in 12- by 8-inch microwave-safe baking dish. Cover with vented plastic wrap; microwave on HIGH 5 minutes.
3. In small bowl, stir soup until smooth; stir in water, onions and thyme. Pour over chicken. Cover; microwave on HIGH 10 minutes or until chicken is fork-tender, rotating dish once during cooking. Let stand, covered, 5 minutes.
Makes 4 servings.

Note: To thaw 1 package (10 ounces) frozen spinach: Place frozen spinach in 1½-quart microwave-safe casserole. Cover with lid; microwave on HIGH 5 minutes, stirring once during heating. Drain thoroughly.

Chicken-Vegetable Kabobs

½ cup WISH-BONE® Italian & Cheese Dressing
¼ cup dry white wine
1 pound boneless chicken breasts, cubed
1 medium zucchini, cut into ½-inch pieces
1 large green pepper, cut into chunks

In large shallow baking dish, blend Italian & cheese dressing with wine. Add chicken and vegetables and turn to coat. Cover and marinate in refrigerator, turning occasionally, at least 2 hours. Remove chicken and vegetables, reserving marinade.

Onto skewers, alternately thread chicken and vegetables. Grill or broil, turning and basting frequently with reserved marinade, until chicken is done.
Makes about 4 servings.

Chicken Breasts Florentine

2 pounds boneless chicken breasts
¼ cup all-purpose flour
2 eggs, well beaten
⅔ cup seasoned dry bread crumbs
¼ cup oil
1 medium clove garlic, finely chopped
½ cup dry white wine
1 envelope LIPTON® Golden Onion Recipe Soup Mix
1½ cups water
2 tablespoons finely chopped parsley
⅛ teaspoon pepper
Hot cooked rice pilaf or white rice
Hot cooked spinach

Dip chicken in flour, then eggs, then bread crumbs.

In large skillet, heat oil and cook chicken over medium heat until almost done. Remove chicken. Reserve 1 tablespoon drippings. Add garlic and wine to reserved drippings and cook over medium heat 5 minutes. Stir in golden onion recipe soup mix thoroughly blended with water; bring to a boil. Return chicken to skillet and simmer covered 10 minutes or until chicken is done and sauce is slightly thickened. Stir in parsley and pepper. To serve, arrange chicken over hot rice and spinach; garnish as desired.
Makes about 6 servings.

Microwave Directions: Omit oil and decrease wine to ¼ cup. Dip chicken in flour, eggs and bread crumbs as above. In 3-quart casserole, heat chicken, uncovered, at HIGH (Full Power) 4 minutes, rearranging chicken once. Stir in garlic, then golden onion recipe soup mix thoroughly blended with water and wine. Heat uncovered 5 minutes or until boiling, stirring once. Decrease heat to MEDIUM (50% Full Power) and heat uncovered, stirring occasionally, 7 minutes or until chicken is done and sauce is slightly thickened. Stir in parsley and pepper. Let stand covered 5 minutes. Serve as above.

Tandoori-Style Chicken Kabobs

½ pint (8 ounces) plain yogurt
½ cup WISH-BONE® Italian Dressing
1 tablespoon chopped fresh ginger*
1 teaspoon cumin seeds**
1 teaspoon coriander seeds (optional)
½ teaspoon paprika
1 pound boneless chicken breasts, cut into 1-inch pieces

Chicken Breasts Florentine

In food processor or blender, process all ingredients except chicken until blended. In large shallow baking dish, combine chicken with dressing mixture. Cover and marinate in refrigerator, stirring occasionally, at least 3 hours. Remove chicken, reserving marinade.

Onto skewers, thread chicken, then grill or broil, turning and basting occasionally with reserved marinade, 5 minutes or until chicken is done. Serve, if desired, with Tandoori Rice and assorted grilled vegetables.
Makes about 8 servings.

Substitution: Use ½ teaspoon ground ginger.

****Substitution:** Use ½ teaspoon ground cumin.

Note: Also terrific with Wish-Bone® Robusto Italian, Blended Italian, Herbal Italian, Lite Italian, Classic Dijon Vinaigrette or Lite Classic Dijon Vinaigrette Dressing.

Try this unusual side dish as an authentic tandoori accompaniment:
TANDOORI RICE: In medium saucepan, bring 2 cups water, ¼ cup chopped onion, 2 tablespoons butter or margarine, 2 tablespoons brown sugar, ½ teaspoon salt, ½ teaspoon ground cinnamon, ½ teaspoon coriander seeds (optional), ½ teaspoon cardamom and ¼ teaspoon ground cloves to a boil. Stir in 1 cup uncooked regular rice and simmer covered 20 minutes or until rice is tender.

Cashew Chicken

- ³/₄ **pound skinless boneless chicken breasts**
- 2 **tablespoons cornstarch**
- 1 **tablespoon dry sherry**
- 1 **tablespoon soy sauce**
- 1 **teaspoon grated fresh ginger**
- 3 **cups broccoli flowerets**
- 3 **tablespoons peanut or vegetable oil**
- 1 **cup snow peas, each cut in half**
- 1½ **cups water**
- 1 **pouch CAMPBELL'S® Noodle Soup Mix**
- 1 **cup sliced radishes**
- ½ **cup roasted cashews**

1. Cut chicken crosswise into ⅛-inch-wide strips. In medium bowl, combine cornstarch, sherry, soy sauce and ginger; mix well. Add chicken strips; stir to coat well.

2. In 10-inch skillet over high heat, stir-fry broccoli in 1 tablespoon of the oil 1 minute. Add snow peas; stir-fry 3 minutes or until vegetables are tender-crisp. Remove vegetables to plate.

3. In same skillet, stir-fry chicken in remaining 2 tablespoons oil until all pieces change color.

4. Stir in water and soup mix. Heat to boiling, stirring constantly. Reduce heat to low. Cover; simmer 5 minutes or until noodles are tender, stirring occasionally.

5. Return cooked vegetables to skillet; add radishes and cashews. Cook until heated through.
Makes 4 servings.

Cashew Chicken

Mongolian Pot

- 2 **whole chicken breasts, skinned and boned**
- 4 **tablespoons KIKKOMAN Soy Sauce, divided**
- 2 **teaspoons minced fresh ginger root**
- ½ **teaspoon sugar**
- 2 **cans (10¼ oz. each) condensed chicken broth**
- 4 **soup cans water**
- 1 **large clove garlic, minced**
- ½ **pound cabbage, cut into ³/₄-inch chunks (about 4 cups)**
- ³/₄ **pound fresh spinach, trimmed, washed and drained**
- 3 **green onions and tops, cut into 1-inch lengths and slivered**
- 4 **ounces vermicelli or thin spaghetti, cooked and drained**
- ¼ **pound fresh mushrooms, sliced**

Cut chicken into thin strips. Combine 2 tablespoons soy sauce, ginger and sugar in medium dish; stir in chicken. Let stand 15 minutes. Meanwhile, combine chicken broth, water, remaining 2 tablespoons soy sauce and garlic in deep electric skillet or electric wok; bring to boil. Reduce heat; keep broth mixture hot. Arrange cabbage, spinach, green onions, vermicelli and mushrooms on platter. Using chopsticks or tongs, let individuals select and add chicken, vegetables and vermicelli to hot broth. Cook chicken until tender, vegetables to desired doneness and vermicelli until heated through. Serve in individual bowls with additional soy sauce, as desired. When all foods are cooked, serve broth as soup.
Makes 4 to 6 servings.

Sweet-and-Sour Chicken

- 1 **can (16 ounces) whole tomatoes**
- ½ **cup plum jelly**
- ¼ **cup cider vinegar**
- 1 **tablespoon sugar**
- 1 **tablespoon cornstarch**
- 1 **tablespoon soy sauce**
- 1 **teaspoon instant chicken bouillon granules**

Batter:
- ½ **cup water**
- ⅓ **cup all-purpose flour**
- ⅓ **cup cornstarch**
- 1 **teaspoon salt**
- ⅛ **teaspoon garlic powder**
- ⅛ **teaspoon pepper**

- 1 **whole boneless chicken breast, skinned, cut into 1- to 1½-inch pieces**
- **CRISCO® Oil for frying**
- 1 **large green pepper, cored, seeded and cut into 1-inch pieces**
- 4 **green onions, cut into 1-inch pieces**
- 1 **can (8 ounces) pineapple chunks, drained**
- **Hot cooked rice**

Drain tomatoes, reserving ¼ cup juice. Cut up tomatoes and set aside. Blend reserved juice, plum jelly, vinegar, sugar, 1 tablespoon cornstarch, soy sauce and bouillon granules in small mixing bowl. Set aside.

For batter, blend all ingredients in small mixing bowl. Add chicken. Stir to coat. Heat 2 to 3 inches Crisco® Oil in large saucepan to 350°F. Remove several chicken pieces from batter with slotted spoon. Fry in hot Crisco® Oil 3 to 4 minutes, or until light golden brown. Drain on paper towels. Repeat with remaining chicken.

Discard Crisco® Oil, reserving 2 tablespoons in saucepan. Add green pepper and onions. Stir-fry over medium-high heat about 3 minutes, or until tender. Stir in tomato juice mixture. Heat to boiling, stirring constantly. Continue to boil 1 minute, stirring constantly. Stir in pineapple chunks, chicken and tomatoes. Cook 1 to 2 minutes longer. Serve with rice.
2 to 4 servings.

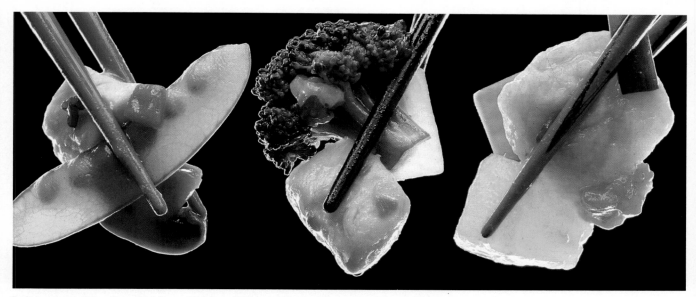

Left to right: Moo Goo Gai Pan, Chicken Walnut Stir-Fry, Sweet-and-Sour Chicken

Chicken Walnut Stir-Fry

5 tablespoons CRISCO® Oil, divided
5 teaspoons soy sauce, divided
3 teaspoons cornstarch, divided
2 whole boneless chicken breasts, skinned, cut into 1-inch pieces
½ cup chicken broth
½ teaspoon ground ginger
½ teaspoon dried crushed red pepper
1 medium onion, cut into 1-inch pieces
1 clove garlic, minced
½ pound fresh broccoli, cut into 1-inch pieces
½ cup coarsely chopped walnuts
Hot cooked rice

Mix 1 tablespoon Crisco® Oil, 2 teaspoons soy sauce and 1 teaspoon cornstarch in small mixing bowl. Add chicken. Stir to coat. Cover and refrigerate about 30 minutes.

Mix chicken broth, ginger, remaining 3 teaspoons soy sauce and remaining 2 teaspoons cornstarch in small bowl. Set aside.

Heat remaining 4 tablespoons Crisco® Oil in large skillet or wok. Add refrigerated chicken mixture and red pepper. Stir-fry over medium-high heat until chicken is no longer pink. Remove chicken from skillet; set aside. Add onion and garlic to skillet. Stir-fry over medium-high heat until onion is tender. Add broccoli. Stir-fry until tender. Add chicken and chicken broth mixture. Cook, stirring constantly, until thickened. Stir in walnuts. Serve with rice.
4 servings.

Jade & Ruby Stir-Fry

1 whole chicken breast, skinned and boned
1 pound fresh broccoli
2 tablespoons vegetable oil
1 medium onion, chunked
2 tablespoons water
2 medium-size red bell peppers, chunked
½ pound fresh mushrooms, quartered
⅓ cup KIKKOMAN Stir-Fry Sauce
¼ teaspoon crushed red pepper

Cut chicken into 1-inch square pieces. Remove flowerets from broccoli; cut into bite-size pieces. Peel stalks; cut into thin slices. Heat oil in hot wok or large skillet over high heat. Add chicken; stir-fry 1 minute. Add broccoli and onion; stir-fry 1 minute. Add water; cover and cook 2 minutes, stirring once. Add bell peppers and mushrooms; stir-fry 2 minutes. Stir in stir-fry sauce and crushed red pepper. Cook and stir until chicken and vegetables are coated with sauce. Serve immediately.
Makes 4 servings.

Moo Goo Gai Pan

2 tablespoons cornstarch
2 tablespoons water
3 whole boneless chicken breasts, skinned, cut into 1-inch pieces
½ teaspoon salt
⅛ teaspoon pepper
¼ cup CRISCO® Oil
¼ cup chopped green onion
2 cups sliced fresh mushrooms
1 jar (2 ounces) sliced pimiento, drained
1 teaspoon ground ginger
1 can (14½ ounces) chicken broth
2 packages (6 to 7 ounces each) frozen pea pods
Hot cooked rice

Blend cornstarch and water in small bowl until smooth. Set aside.

Sprinkle chicken with salt and pepper. Heat Crisco® Oil in large skillet or wok. Add chicken. Stir-fry over medium-high heat until no longer pink. Remove chicken from skillet. Add onion to skillet. Stir-fry over medium-high heat 1 minute. Stir in mushrooms, pimiento and ginger. Cook, stirring constantly, 2 to 3 minutes, or until mushrooms are tender. Add chicken broth and pea pods. Heat to boiling, stirring to break apart pea pods. Add cornstarch mixture. Heat to boiling, stirring constantly. Boil 1 minute. Remove from heat. Stir in chicken. Serve with rice. Sprinkle with *toasted almonds* and serve with *soy sauce*, if desired.
6 to 8 servings.

Mushroom-Stuffed Chicken Breasts

- **4 tablespoons butter or margarine**
- **1½ cups chopped CAMPBELL'S FRESH® Mushrooms**
- **¼ cup chopped green onions**
- **¼ cup finely chopped celery**
- **¼ teaspoon dried marjoram leaves, crushed**
- **2 cups PEPPERIDGE FARM® Herb Seasoned Stuffing Mix, coarsely crushed**
- **4 skinless boneless chicken breast halves (about 1 pound)**
- **1 egg**
- **2 tablespoons milk**
- **1 teaspoon paprika**

To Microwave:

1. To make stuffing: In 2-quart microwave-safe casserole, combine 2 tablespoons of the butter, mushrooms, onions, celery and marjoram. Cover with lid; microwave on HIGH 4 minutes or until vegetables are tender, stirring once during cooking. Stir in ½ cup of the stuffing mix until blended; set aside.
2. With flat side of meat mallet, pound chicken to ¼-inch thickness. Divide stuffing among breast halves. Roll up chicken from short end, jelly-roll fashion. Secure with wooden toothpicks if needed.
3. In small bowl, beat egg and milk. In pie plate, combine remaining 1½ cups stuffing mix and paprika. Dip rolled breasts in egg mixture, then in paprika mixture. Place chicken, seam side down, in 12- by 8-inch microwave-safe baking dish.
4. Place remaining 2 tablespoons butter in small microwave-safe bowl. Microwave on HIGH 30 seconds or until melted. Drizzle over chicken.
5. Cover with waxed paper; microwave on HIGH 8 minutes or until chicken is no longer pink in center, rotating dish once during cooking. Let stand, covered, 5 minutes.
Makes 4 servings.

Note: For even crisper chicken, prepare as directed above. Transfer cooked chicken to broiler pan; broil 4 inches from heat 1 to 2 minutes or until top is browned.

Golden Chicken Stir-Fry

Golden Chicken Stir-Fry

- **1 whole chicken breast, skinned and boned**
- **1 tablespoon cornstarch**
- **5 tablespoons KIKKOMAN Teriyaki Sauce, divided**
- **1 clove garlic, minced**
- **1¼ cups regular-strength chicken broth**
- **4 teaspoons cornstarch**
  Boiling water
- **½ pound fresh bean sprouts**
- **2 cups finely shredded lettuce**
- **2 tablespoons vegetable oil, divided**
- **2 medium carrots, cut into julienne strips**
- **1 onion, chunked**
- **2 teaspoons slivered fresh ginger root**

Cut chicken into thin strips. Combine 1 tablespoon *each* cornstarch and teriyaki sauce with garlic in small bowl; stir in chicken. Let stand 15 minutes. Meanwhile, combine chicken broth, remaining 4 tablespoons teriyaki sauce and 4 teaspoons cornstarch; set aside. Pour boiling water over bean sprouts in bowl; let stand 1 minute. Drain; rinse under cold water and drain thoroughly. Toss sprouts with lettuce. Line serving platter with mixture; set aside. Heat 1 tablespoon oil in hot wok or large skillet over high heat. Add chicken and stir-fry 2 minutes; remove. Heat remaining 1 tablespoon oil in same pan. Add carrots, onion and ginger; stir-fry 4 minutes. Add chicken and teriyaki sauce mixture. Cook and stir until sauce boils and thickens. Turn out onto lined platter; toss to combine before serving.
Makes 4 servings.

Colorful Dragon Stir-Fry

- **1 whole chicken breast, skinned and boned**
- **1 pound fresh broccoli**
- **5 tablespoons KIKKOMAN Stir-Fry Sauce, divided**
- **3 tablespoons vegetable oil, divided**
- **1 medium onion, cut into thin wedges**
- **1 medium carrot, cut diagonally into thin slices**
- **2 tablespoons water**

Cut chicken into ½-inch strips. Remove flowerets from broccoli; set aside. Peel stalks; cut into thin slices. Coat chicken with 1 tablespoon stir-fry sauce. Heat 1 tablespoon oil in hot wok or large skillet over high heat. Add chicken and stir-fry 3 minutes; remove. Heat remaining 2 tablespoons oil in same pan. Add onion; stir-fry 1 minute. Add broccoli and carrot; stir-fry 2 minutes longer. Pour water into pan. Reduce heat and simmer, covered, 3 minutes; stir once. Add remaining 4 tablespoons stir-fry sauce and chicken. Cook and stir just until chicken and vegetables are coated. Serve immediately.
Makes 4 servings.

Crunchy Almond Chicken Cutlets

- **1 cup fresh bread crumbs**
- **1 cup blanched slivered almonds, toasted and finely chopped**
- **2 tablespoons chopped parsley**
- **½ teaspoon ground ginger**
- **¼ teaspoon salt**
- **⅛ teaspoon pepper**
- **3 whole boneless chicken breasts (about 1½ pounds), halved**
- **1 cup (8 ounces) WISH-BONE® Creamy Italian or Lite Creamy Italian Dressing**

Preheat oven to 350°.
In medium bowl, combine bread crumbs, almonds, parsley, ginger, salt and pepper. Dip chicken in creamy Italian dressing, then bread crumb mixture, coating well. In large shallow baking pan, arrange chicken. Bake uncovered 20 minutes or until done.
Makes about 6 servings.

Lemon Chicken

- **1¼ pounds boneless chicken breasts, skinned and cut into bite-size pieces**
- **1 egg, slightly beaten**
- **3 tablespoons cornstarch**
- **2 tablespoons soy sauce**
- **½ cup sugar**
- **2 teaspoons WYLER'S® or STEERO® Chicken-Flavor Instant Bouillon**
- **½ teaspoon garlic powder**
- **1 cup water**
- **½ cup REALEMON® Lemon Juice from Concentrate**
- **2 tablespoons catsup**
  Additional cornstarch
  Vegetable oil
  Shredded lettuce *or* hot cooked rice

In medium bowl, combine egg, *1 tablespoon* cornstarch and soy sauce; mix well. Add chicken, stirring to coat; marinate 10 minutes. Meanwhile, in medium saucepan, combine remaining *2 tablespoons* cornstarch, sugar, bouillon and garlic powder. Gradually add water, ReaLemon® brand and catsup; mix well. Over high heat, cook and stir until mixture comes to a boil. Reduce heat; continue cooking and stirring until mixture thickens. Keep sauce warm. Coat chicken with additional cornstarch. In large skillet, cook chicken in ½ inch hot oil until tender and golden. Arrange chicken on shredded lettuce; pour warm sauce over chicken. Garnish as desired. Serve immediately. Refrigerate leftovers.
Makes 4 servings.

Colorful Dragon Stir-Fry

Baked Chicken Breasts with Rice & Vegetable Stuffing

- **1 envelope LIPTON® Vegetable Recipe Soup Mix**
- **1½ cups water**
- **½ cup uncooked regular rice**
- **1 package (10 ounces) frozen chopped spinach, cooked and squeezed dry**
- **½ medium tomato, coarsely chopped**
- **½ cup shredded mozzarella cheese (about 1½ ounces)**
- **¼ cup grated Parmesan cheese**
- **1 small clove garlic, finely chopped**
- **4 whole boneless chicken breasts (about 2 pounds), skinned and halved**

In medium saucepan, blend vegetable recipe soup mix with water; bring to a boil. Stir in uncooked rice and simmer covered 20 minutes or until tender. Stir in spinach, tomato, cheeses and garlic; set aside.
Preheat oven to 350°. With knife parallel to cutting board, make deep, 3-inch-long cut in center of each chicken breast half to form pocket. Evenly stuff pockets with rice mixture.
In lightly greased baking dish, arrange chicken and bake uncovered, basting occasionally, 40 minutes or until done. Sprinkle, if desired, with paprika.
Makes about 8 servings.

Chicken and Broccoli

- 1 pound skinned boneless chicken breasts, cut into bite-size pieces
- 3 cups broccoli flowerets, cooked
- 1 egg white, beaten
- 5 teaspoons soy sauce
- 2 teaspoons cornstarch
- ¼ cup vegetable oil
- 8 ounces fresh mushrooms, sliced (about 2 cups)
- 2 tablespoons REALEMON® Lemon Juice from Concentrate
- 2 tablespoons dry sherry
- 1 tablespoon chopped pimiento, optional
- Hot cooked rice

In medium bowl, combine egg white, *3 teaspoons* soy sauce and cornstarch; mix well. Add chicken; stir to coat. Refrigerate 1 hour. In large skillet, over high heat, brown chicken in oil; remove. Add mushrooms; cook and stir until tender. Add chicken, broccoli and remaining ingredients except rice; heat through. Serve with rice. Refrigerate leftovers.
Makes 4 to 6 servings.

Chicken Parisian

- ¼ cup unsifted flour
- ¼ teaspoon *each* paprika and pepper
- 6 boneless chicken breast halves, skinned
- 3 tablespoons margarine or butter
- 8 ounces fresh mushrooms, sliced (about 2 cups)
- ½ cup water
- ¼ cup dry white wine
- 2 teaspoons WYLER'S® or STEERO® Chicken-Flavor Instant Bouillon *or* 2 Chicken-Flavor Bouillon Cubes
- 2 teaspoons chopped parsley
- ¼ teaspoon thyme leaves

In paper or plastic bag, combine flour, paprika and pepper. Add chicken, a few pieces at a time; shake to coat. In large skillet, brown chicken in margarine on both sides; remove from pan. In skillet, add remaining ingredients; simmer 3 minutes. Add chicken; simmer covered 20 minutes or until tender. Refrigerate leftovers.
Makes 6 servings.

Chicken and Broccoli

Chicken Breasts with Artichoke-Cheese Stuffing

- 4 whole boneless chicken breasts, skinned and halved lengthwise
- 1½ cups shredded Monterey Jack cheese (about 6 ounces)
- ¼ cup mayonnaise
- 1 tablespoon finely chopped onion
- 1 tablespoon dried parsley flakes
- 1 teaspoon Dijon mustard
- 1 jar (6 ounces) marinated artichoke hearts, drained
- ⅓ cup all-purpose flour
- ¼ teaspoon salt
- ⅛ teaspoon pepper
- 1 egg
- 2 tablespoons water
- 1 cup seasoned dry bread crumbs
- ⅓ cup CRISCO® Oil

Pound chicken breasts to ¼-inch thickness. Set aside. Mix cheese, mayonnaise, onion, parsley flakes and mustard in small mixing bowl. Cut artichoke hearts into bite-size pieces.

Stir into cheese mixture. Spread about ¼ cup cheese mixture down center of each piece of chicken. Roll up and secure ends with wooden picks. Mix flour, salt and pepper in shallow dish. Dip rolled chicken in flour mixture to coat. Set aside.

Mix egg and water in shallow dish. Place bread crumbs in another shallow dish or on sheet of waxed paper. Dip rolled chicken in egg mixture then in bread crumbs, pressing to coat thoroughly. Cover and refrigerate coated chicken about 1 hour.

Preheat oven to 350°F. Place Crisco® Oil in 13×9-inch baking pan. Place in oven 10 minutes. Remove from oven. Using tongs, roll coated chicken in hot Crisco Oil. Arrange chicken in pan. Bake at 350°F, 35 minutes, or until golden brown.
8 servings.

Chicken Cordon Bleu with Golden Cream Sauce

- 3 whole boneless chicken breasts (about 2½ pounds), halved and lightly pounded
- 6 slices Swiss cheese
- 6 slices cooked ham
- 2 tablespoons butter or margarine
- ¼ teaspoon ground nutmeg
- ⅛ teaspoon pepper
- 1 envelope LIPTON® Golden Onion Recipe Soup Mix
- 2 cups (1 pint) light cream or half and half
- ¼ cup water
- Hot cooked noodles

Top each chicken breast half with slice of cheese and ham; roll up and secure with wooden toothpicks.

In large skillet, melt butter and brown chicken over medium heat; drain. Add nutmeg and pepper, then golden onion recipe soup mix blended with cream and water. Bring just to the boiling point, then simmer covered, basting occasionally, 20 minutes or until chicken is done. To serve, arrange chicken and sauce over hot noodles.
Makes about 6 servings.

Orange-Cashew Chicken

- **1 pound boneless chicken breasts**
- **1/2 cup KIKKOMAN Teriyaki Baste & Glaze**
- **2 tablespoons orange juice**
- **2 tablespoons dry white wine**
- **2 tablespoons vegetable oil**
- **1 green pepper, cut into thin strips**
- **1/2 cup diagonally sliced celery**
- **1 can (11 oz.) mandarin orange segments, drained**
- **1/2 cup roasted cashews**

Cut chicken into thin slices. Combine teriyaki baste & glaze, orange juice and wine; set aside. Heat oil in hot wok or large skillet over medium heat. Add chicken, green pepper and celery; stir-fry 3 to 4 minutes. Pour in baste & glaze mixture; cook and stir until chicken and vegetables are coated with sauce. Remove from heat; stir in orange segments and cashews. Serve immediately.
Makes 4 servings.

Chicken 'n Vegetable Stir Fry

- **3 tablespoons oil**
- **1 pound boneless chicken breasts, cut into thin strips**
- **1/2 cup broccoli florets**
- **2 ounces snow peas (about 1/2 cup)**
- **1 medium carrot, thinly sliced**
- **1/2 medium red or green pepper, cut into thin strips**
- **1 envelope LIPTON® Golden Onion Recipe Soup Mix**
- **1 teaspoon cornstarch**
- **1/2 teaspoon ground ginger**
- **1 1/2 cups water**
- **2 teaspoons soy sauce**
- **1 teaspoon white or rice vinegar Hot cooked rice**

In large skillet, heat oil and cook chicken with vegetables over medium-high heat, stirring constantly, 10 minutes or until chicken is golden and vegetables are crisp-tender. Thoroughly blend golden onion recipe soup mix, cornstarch, ginger, water, soy sauce and vinegar; stir into chicken mixture. Bring to a boil, then simmer uncovered 5 minutes or until sauce is thickened. Serve

Chicken 'n Vegetable Stir Fry

over hot rice and garnish, if desired, with sliced green onion and toasted sesame seeds.
Makes about 4 servings.

Microwave Directions: Omit oil and decrease ginger to 1/4 teaspoon. In 2-quart casserole, heat chicken, uncovered, at HIGH (Full Power) 4 minutes or until almost done; remove chicken and drain. Add vegetables to casserole and heat uncovered 5 minutes. Thoroughly blend golden onion recipe soup mix, cornstarch, ginger, water, soy sauce and vinegar; stir into vegetables. Heat uncovered 5 minutes or until sauce is thickened, stirring once. Return chicken to casserole and heat 1 minute or until heated through. Let stand covered 5 minutes. Serve and garnish as above.

Spicy Smoked Duck

- **1 (4- to 5-pound) frozen duckling, thawed**
- **1/4 cup KIKKOMAN Lite Soy Sauce**
- **1 teaspoon liquid smoke seasoning**
- **1/2 teaspoon fennel seed, well crushed**
- **1/4 teaspoon pepper**
- **1/8 teaspoon ground cloves**

Remove and discard giblets and neck from duckling cavity. Wash duckling; drain and gently pat dry with paper towels. Combine lite soy sauce, liquid smoke, fennel, pepper and cloves. Brush body cavity with sauce mixture. Place duckling, breast side up, on rack in roasting pan. Roast at 425°F. 1 hour. *Reduce oven temperature to 350°F.* Continue roasting 45 minutes, or until tender. Brush skin of duckling several times with sauce mixture during last 30 minutes of cooking time. Let stand 15 minutes before carving.
Makes 4 servings.

Grilled Game Hens, Texas-Style

- **1 can (8 ounces) tomato sauce**
- **1/4 cup vegetable oil**
- **1 1/2 teaspoons chili powder**
- **1 teaspoon paprika**
- **1/4 teaspoon garlic powder**
- **1/4 teaspoon cayenne pepper**
- **4 Cornish game hens (1 to 1 1/2 pounds each), cut into halves**

In small bowl, combine all ingredients except game hens. Brush hens generously with tomato mixture. Grill hens, on covered grill, over medium-hot **KINGSFORD® with Mesquite Charcoal Briquets** 45 to 50 minutes or until fork-tender, brushing frequently with tomato mixture.
Makes 4 servings.

Glazed Stuffed Cornish Hens

Braised Chinese Duckling

    1 (4- to 5-pound) frozen
        duckling, thawed and
        quartered
    3 tablespoons KIKKOMAN Lite
        Soy Sauce, divided
    1 tablespoon vegetable oil
    2 tablespoons dry sherry
    1 clove garlic, minced
    1 teaspoon ginger juice*
    4 green onions and tops, cut
        into 2-inch lengths
    ⅓ cup water
    2 teaspoons cornstarch

Wash duckling quarters; dry with paper towels. Rub thoroughly with 2 tablespoons lite soy sauce. Let stand 30 minutes. Heat oil in Dutch oven or large skillet over medium heat. Brown duckling slowly in hot oil; drain off fat. Add sherry and garlic. Cover and cook over low heat 45 minutes, or until tender, turning quarters over once. Remove from pan; keep warm. Spoon off and discard excess fat from pan juices; return ⅓ cup juices to pan. Add remaining 1 tablespoon lite soy sauce, ginger juice and green onions; cook 1 minute. Combine water with cornstarch; stir into pan. Cook and stir until sauce boils and thickens. To serve, spoon sauce over duckling quarters.
Makes 4 servings.
 *Peel fresh ginger root, then squeeze through garlic press.

Glazed Stuffed Cornish Hens

    2 Cornish hens (1½ pounds
        each)
    ¼ cup butter or margarine
    ½ cup chopped onion
    ½ cup sweet red pepper cut into
        matchstick-thin strips
    ½ cup green pepper cut into
        matchstick-thin strips
    1 package (8 ounces)
        PEPPERIDGE FARM® Herb
        Seasoned Stuffing Mix
    1 cup SWANSON® Clear Ready
        to Serve Chicken Broth
    ½ cup apricot preserves

To Microwave:
1. Remove giblets and neck from inside hens (reserve for another use if desired). Rinse hens; pat dry. Split hens along backbone and breastbone; set aside.
2. In 3-quart microwave-safe casserole, combine butter, onion and peppers. Cover with lid; microwave on HIGH 3 minutes or until tender, stirring once during cooking. Add stuffing and broth; toss to mix well.
3. Pat stuffing mixture into bottom of 12- by 8-inch microwave-safe baking dish. Arrange hen halves, skin side up, over stuffing; set aside.
4. Place preserves in small microwave-safe bowl. Microwave, uncovered, on HIGH 45 seconds or until melted. Brush preserves over hens. Cover with waxed paper; microwave on HIGH 17 minutes or until hens are no longer pink in center, rotating dish twice and rearranging hens once during cooking. Let stand, covered, 5 minutes.
Makes 4 servings.

Oriental Game Hens

    4 Cornish game hens (1 to
        1½ pounds each)
      Salt
    ½ cup peanut or vegetable oil
    ½ cup soy sauce
    2 tablespoons brown sugar
    1 tablespoon wine vinegar
    ½ teaspoon grated fresh ginger
      Dash ground cloves

Remove giblets from hens. Remove fatty portion from neck and tail area of hens. Rinse hens under cold running water. Pat hens dry with paper toweling. Sprinkle cavities with salt. Close neck and body openings with skewers. Tie legs together; tuck wings under back and tie with kitchen twine. Arrange hens in shallow microwaveable dish and cover with vented plastic wrap. Microwave at 50% power

10 minutes. For basting sauce, in small bowl, combine remaining ingredients. Lightly oil grid. Grill hens, on uncovered grill, over medium-hot **KINGSFORD® Charcoal Briquets** 20 minutes or until thigh moves easily and juices run clear, basting often with sauce.
Makes 4 servings.

Roasted Duckling with Orange & Plum Sauce

- 1 (3-pound) duckling
- 1 medium orange, halved
- 1 medium onion, halved
- ½ cup WISH-BONE® Deluxe French or Lite French Style Dressing
- ½ cup orange juice
- 2 tablespoons brown sugar
- 1 teaspoon grated orange peel (optional)
- ¼ teaspoon ground cinnamon
- ⅛ teaspoon ground cloves
- ⅛ teaspoon ground nutmeg
- 1 tablespoon butter or margarine
- ½ cup chopped onion
- 1 teaspoon finely chopped garlic
- 2 tablespoons brandy
- 2 medium plums, pitted and cut into wedges
- 2 small oranges, peeled, sectioned and seeded

Preheat oven to 400°.

Stuff duckling with orange and onion halves. Close cavity with skewers or wooden toothpicks; tie legs together with string. With pin or fork, pierce skin. In roasting pan, on rack, arrange duckling breast side up. Roast 40 minutes, turning duckling every 10 minutes.

Meanwhile, in small bowl, blend deluxe French dressing, orange juice, sugar, orange peel, cinnamon, cloves and nutmeg. Pour ½ of the dressing mixture over duckling; loosely cover with heavy-duty aluminum foil. Continue roasting, basting occasionally, 30 minutes or until meat thermometer reaches 185°. Remove to serving platter and keep warm.

Meanwhile, in medium saucepan, melt butter and cook onion with garlic over medium heat, stirring occasionally, 5 minutes or until onion is tender. Add brandy, the plums and orange sections and cook, stirring occasionally, 5 minutes. Stir in remaining dressing mixture and heat through. Serve with duckling.
Makes about 2 servings.

Thai Hens

- 3 fresh or thawed Rock Cornish hens (1¼ to 1½ pounds each)
- ½ cup KIKKOMAN Teriyaki Sauce
- 1 tablespoon grated lemon peel
- 1 tablespoon lemon juice
- 2 cloves garlic, pressed
- ¼ to ½ teaspoon ground red pepper (cayenne)
- 1 tablespoon minced fresh cilantro

Remove and discard giblets and necks from hens. Split hens lengthwise. Rinse halves under cold running water; drain well and pat dry with paper towels. Place in large plastic bag. Combine teriyaki sauce, lemon peel and juice, garlic and red pepper; pour over hens. Press air out of bag; tie top securely. Turn bag over several times to coat halves. Refrigerate 8 hours or overnight, turning bag over occasionally. Reserving marinade, remove hens and place on rack of broiler pan. Broil about 7 inches from heat source 45 to 50 minutes, or until tender, turning over frequently and brushing with reserved marinade. Remove to serving platter and immediately sprinkle cilantro over hens.
Makes 4 to 6 servings.

Lemon Herb Cornish Hens

- 2 (1½-pound) Rock Cornish hens, split in half lengthwise
  Salt and pepper
- 2 tablespoons finely chopped onion
- 1 clove garlic, finely chopped
- ¼ cup vegetable oil
- ¼ cup REALEMON® Lemon Juice from Concentrate
- 2 teaspoons WYLER'S® or STEERO® Chicken-Flavor Instant Bouillon *or* 2 Chicken-Flavor Bouillon Cubes
- 1 teaspoon chopped parsley
- 1 teaspoon rosemary leaves, crushed

Season hens lightly with salt and pepper. In small saucepan, cook onion and garlic in oil until tender. Add remaining ingredients; simmer 10 minutes. Grill hens until tender and crisp, about 1 hour, turning and basting frequently with sauce. Refrigerate leftovers.
Makes 4 servings.

Oven Method: Place hens on rack in roasting pan. Bake at 375° for 1 hour and 15 minutes, basting frequently.

Lemon Herb Cornish Hens

Raisin-Stuffed Cornish Game Hens with Apples

    1 envelope LIPTON® Onion
        Recipe Soup Mix
 1¼ cups apple cider or juice
    2 cups unseasoned cube
        stuffing mix
 ⅓ cup raisins
 ⅓ cup coarsely chopped walnuts
    4 Cornish hens (1 to 1½ pounds
        each)
    2 large apples, cored and halved
 ¼ cup brown sugar
 ½ teaspoon ground cinnamon

Preheat oven to 375°.

In medium bowl, blend onion recipe soup mix with cider. Pour ½ mixture into medium bowl; stir in stuffing mix, raisins and walnuts. Stuff hens with raisin mixture; secure cavities with poultry pins or skewers. In shallow baking pan, arrange hens and apples.

To remaining cider mixture, blend in sugar and cinnamon; brush hens and apples with ½ mixture. Bake, brushing occasionally with remaining glaze mixture, 1 hour or until hens are done. To serve, on large serving platter, arrange hens and apples, sliced.

Makes 4 servings.

Microwave Directions: Prepare hens and glaze mixture as above. Slice apples in quarters. In 3-quart oblong baking dish, arrange hens and apples; brush with ½ glaze. Heat at HIGH (Full Power), brushing occasionally with remaining glaze and turning dish occasionally, 45 minutes or until hens are done. Let stand covered 5 minutes. Serve as above.

Grilled Cornish Game Hens

    2 Cornish game hens (1 to
        1½ pounds each)
    3 tablespoons olive or vegetable
        oil
 ⅓ cup lemon juice
    1 tablespoon black peppercorns,
        coarsely crushed
 ½ teaspoon salt
        Sprig fresh rosemary

Split hens lengthwise. Rinse under cold running water; pat dry with paper toweling. Place hens in large plastic bag; set in bowl. In small bowl, combine oil, lemon juice, peppercorns and salt. Pour marinade over hens in bag. Close bag securely and refrigerate several hours or overnight, turning hens occasionally to coat with marinade.

Arrange medium-hot **KINGS-FORD® Charcoal Briquets** around drip pan. Just before grilling, add rosemary sprig to coals. Drain hens; reserve marinade. Place hens, skin-side up, over drip pan. Cover grill and cook 45 minutes or until thigh moves easily and juices run clear. Baste with marinade occasionally. Garnish with fresh rosemary, if desired.

Makes 4 servings.

Turkey with Garlic and Chili Pepper Stuffing

 14- to 16-pound BUTTERBALL®
        Turkey, thawed if frozen
    2 medium red bell peppers,
        chopped
 ½ cup chopped onion
    4 to 5 large cloves garlic,
        minced
 ⅓ cup butter or margarine
    2 cans (4 ounces each) diced
        green chili peppers, drained
 ¼ cup chopped fresh parsley
 ¼ teaspoon salt
 ¼ teaspoon ground red pepper
    8 cups unseasoned dried whole
        wheat or white bread cubes
 1½ cups (6 ounces) shredded
        Cheddar cheese
 ¾ to 1 cup chicken broth

Preheat oven to 325°F. To make stuffing, saute red bell peppers, onion and garlic in butter in medium saucepan over medium-high heat until crisp-tender. Stir in chili peppers, parsley, salt and ground red pepper. Combine bread cubes, cheese and vegetable mixture in large bowl. Add enough broth to moisten. Toss to mix.

Prepare turkey for roasting, stuffing neck and body cavities lightly. Roast immediately according to package directions, or roast turkey unstuffed and place stuffing in greased 2½-quart casserole. Cover casserole and bake alongside turkey 1 hour or until hot.

12 to 14 servings (10 cups stuffing).

Turkey with Garlic and Chili Pepper Stuffing

Cornish Hens with Chestnut-Sausage Stuffing

 ¼ cup WISH-BONE® Italian or
        Robusto Italian Dressing
    1 medium onion, chopped
    1 cup chopped celery
    1 pound sweet Italian sausage
        links, removed from casing
    1 cup cooked chestnuts,
        chopped
    2 cups fresh bread crumbs
 ½ cup pine nuts or slivered
        almonds, toasted
 ½ teaspoon marjoram leaves
 ½ teaspoon thyme leaves
 ⅛ teaspoon pepper
    4 Cornish hens (1 to 1½ pounds
        each)*

Apple & Herb Stuffing

til tender. Cut up oysters; reserve liquid. Stir oysters into skillet with ½ teaspoon thyme, oregano and ½ teaspoon Tabasco® sauce. Cook 5 minutes longer. Remove bay leaves. Add rice and oyster liquid.

Wash Cornish hens; pat dry. Stuff cavity of each hen with oyster stuffing. (Bake remaining stuffing in greased, covered baking dish during last half hour of roasting time.) Arrange hens on rack in shallow roasting pan. Melt remaining ¼ cup butter; stir in salt, remaining ¼ teaspoon thyme and remaining ¼ teaspoon Tabasco® sauce. Brush hens with butter mixture. Bake 1½ hours or until hens are cooked; baste often with pan drippings.

To serve, spoon extra stuffing onto serving platter; arrange hens on stuffing. To make gravy, pour excess fat from roasting pan; add flour to pan and stir. Place pan on stove-top burner over medium heat; gradually add broth, scraping up bits from bottom of pan. Stir constantly, bring to a boil and boil 1 minute. Serve with hens.

Makes 6 servings.

Preheat oven to 350°.

In large skillet, heat Italian dressing and cook onion with celery over medium-high heat, stirring occasionally, 3 minutes or until tender. Add sausage and cook, stirring occasionally, 5 minutes or until lightly browned. Stir in chestnuts, bread crumbs, pine nuts, marjoram, thyme and pepper. Stuff hens with sausage mixture. Close cavities with skewers or wooden toothpicks; tie legs together with string. In roasting pan, on rack, place stuffed hens. Loosely cover with heavy-duty aluminum foil, then roast 1 hour. Remove foil and continue roasting 15 minutes or until meat thermometer reaches 185°. Serve, if desired, with cooked carrots and green beans.

Makes 4 servings.

*Substitution: Use 1 (5- to 6-pound) roasting chicken. Adjust cooking temperature and times as needed.

Cornish Hens with Oyster Stuffing

  ¾ **cup butter or margarine, divided**
  1 **large onion, chopped**
  1 **cup chopped celery**
  ½ **cup chopped shallots**
  1 **small red pepper, chopped**
  1 **small green pepper, chopped**
  2 **medium cloves garlic, minced**
  2 **bay leaves**
  2 **dozen fresh oysters, shucked, liquid reserved**
  ¾ **teaspoon dried thyme leaves, divided**
  ½ **teaspoon dried oregano leaves**
  ¾ **teaspoon TABASCO® pepper sauce, divided**
  5 **cups cooked rice**
  6 **Cornish game hens**
  ¼ **teaspoon salt**
  1 **tablespoon flour**
  1 **cup chicken broth**

Preheat oven to 350°F. In large skillet melt ½ cup butter. Add onion, celery, shallots, red and green peppers, garlic and bay leaves; cook 5 minutes or un-

Apple & Herb Stuffing

  2 **cups sliced celery**
  1½ **cups chopped onion**
  ½ **cup margarine or butter**
  1¾ **cups hot water**
  1 **tablespoon WYLER'S® or STEERO® Chicken-Flavor Instant Bouillon or**
  3 **Chicken-Flavor Bouillon Cubes**
  12 **cups dry bread cubes (about 16 slices bread)**
  3 **cups coarsely chopped red apples**
  1 **cup slivered almonds, toasted**
  1 **tablespoon chopped parsley**
  2 **teaspoons poultry seasoning**
  ¼ **teaspoon rubbed sage**

In large skillet, cook celery and onion in margarine until tender. Add water and bouillon; cook until bouillon dissolves. In large bowl, combine remaining ingredients; add bouillon mixture. Mix well. Loosely stuff turkey just before roasting. Place remaining stuffing in greased baking dish; bake at 350° for 30 minutes or until hot. Refrigerate leftovers.

Makes about 2½ quarts.

Turkey with Sausage and Orange Corn Bread Stuffing

Turkey with Sausage and Orange Corn Bread Stuffing

**½ roll (8 ounces) ECKRICH®
    Country Sausage
12- to 14-pound BUTTERBALL®
    Turkey, thawed if frozen
    Orange Corn Bread (recipe
    follows)
1 cup chopped onion
½ cup chopped green bell
    pepper
½ cup chopped celery
2 eggs, beaten
1 teaspoon dried thyme leaves
½ teaspoon salt
1 to 1¼ cups turkey or chicken
    broth**

Prepare Orange Corn Bread. Cool and crumble; set aside. Preheat oven to 325°F. To make stuffing, cook sausage, onion, green pepper and celery in large skillet until meat is browned and vegetables are tender. Drain thoroughly. Combine sausage mixture, eggs, thyme and salt in large bowl. Add corn bread; toss to mix. Add enough broth to moisten; toss. Prepare turkey for roasting; stuff neck and body cavities lightly. Roast immediately according to package directions, or roast turkey unstuffed and place stuffing in greased 2½-quart casserole. Cover casserole and bake alongside turkey 1 hour or until hot. *Makes 10 to 12 servings (8 cups stuffing).*

(continued)

ORANGE CORN BREAD: Preheat oven to 400°F. Combine 1½ cups yellow cornmeal, ½ cup all-purpose flour, 2 tablespoons sugar, 4 teaspoons baking powder and ½ teaspoon salt in medium bowl. Stir in 1 cup milk, 1 beaten egg, ⅓ cup vegetable oil and 2 teaspoons finely shredded orange peel (zest) until just blended. (Do not overmix.) Pour into greased 9×9×2-inch baking pan. Bake 20 to 25 minutes or until wooden pick inserted near center comes out clean.
Makes 9 servings.

Traditional Gravy

**Drippings
Fat
Turkey, chicken or giblet broth
½ cup all-purpose flour
Salt and ground black pepper,
    to taste
Cooked giblets, chopped fine,
    optional**

Conventional Directions: Pour drippings from roasting pan into large measuring cup. Place ¼ cup fat from drippings into medium saucepan or roasting pan. Discard any remaining fat from drippings. To drippings, add enough broth to make 4 cups. Stir flour into fat in saucepan. Gradually blend in drippings. Bring to boil over medium-high heat, stirring constantly. Reduce heat to low; continue cooking 3 to 5 minutes. Season with salt and pepper. Add cooked giblets, if desired.
Yield: 4 cups.

Microwave Directions: Pour drippings from roasting pan into large measuring cup. Place ¼ cup fat from drippings into medium microwave-safe bowl. Discard any remaining fat from drippings. To drippings, add enough broth to make 4 cups. Stir flour into fat in bowl. Gradually blend in drippings. Microwave, uncovered, on HIGH 7 to 10 minutes or until mixture comes to boil and thickens, stirring every 2 minutes. Season with salt and pepper. Add cooked giblets, if desired.

Gravy Additions: Add 1 or 2 of the following: 2 tablespoons chopped fresh parsley, 2 tablespoons sherry, ½ cup sour cream or 1 jar (2½ ounces) sliced mushrooms, drained.

*Favorite recipe from **Swift-Eckrich, Inc.***

Harvest Sausage Stuffing

- 1 pound bulk sausage
- 2 cups chopped celery
- 8 ounces fresh mushrooms, sliced (about 2 cups)
- 1½ cups chopped onion
- 4 teaspoons WYLER'S® or STEERO® Chicken-Flavor Instant Bouillon *or* 4 Chicken-Flavor Bouillon Cubes
- 1 to 1½ cups boiling water
- 2 (7-ounce) packages herb-seasoned stuffing mix
- 1⅓ cups (one-half jar) NONE SUCH® Ready-to-Use Mincemeat
- 1 (8-ounce) can sliced water chestnuts, coarsely chopped
- 2 teaspoons poultry seasoning

In large skillet, brown sausage; pour off fat. Add celery, mushrooms and onion; cook until onion is tender. Add bouillon and water to sausage mixture; bring to a boil. In large bowl, combine remaining ingredients with sausage mixture; mix well. Use to loosely stuff turkey just before roasting; place remaining stuffing in 2-quart greased baking dish; cover. Bake at 350° for 45 minutes or until hot. Refrigerate leftovers.
Makes about 3 quarts.

Turkey with American Stuffing

- 6- to 8-pound BUTTERBALL® Breast of Turkey
- 3 cups dried bread cubes
- 1 cup (4 ounces) crumbled fully cooked sausage
- ¾ cup diced red apple, unpared
- ½ cup chopped onion
- ½ cup chopped walnuts
- 1 teaspoon dried rosemary leaves, crushed
- ½ teaspoon rubbed sage
- ¾ cup water
- ⅓ cup butter or margarine

Roast turkey according to package directions. Meanwhile, prepare stuffing. Combine bread cubes, sausage, apple, onion, walnuts and seasonings in medium bowl. Heat water and butter in small saucepan over medium heat until butter melts. Toss with bread mixture. Spoon into 2-quart casserole.

Cover and bake alongside turkey last 45 minutes of roasting time. Slice turkey and serve with stuffing.
Yield: 8 servings.

Savory Corn Bread Stuffing

- 1 pound fresh mushrooms, sliced (about 4 cups)
- 1 cup chopped celery
- ¾ cup chopped onion
- ½ cup margarine or butter
- 4 teaspoons WYLER'S® or STEERO® Chicken-Flavor Instant Bouillon *or* 4 Chicken-Flavor Bouillon Cubes
- 1⅔ cups boiling water
- 1 pound bulk sausage, browned and drained
- 1 (16-ounce) package corn bread stuffing mix
- 1½ teaspoons poultry seasoning

In large skillet, cook mushrooms, celery and onion in margarine until tender. In large bowl, dissolve bouillon in water. Add sausage, mushroom mixture and remaining ingredients; mix well. Loosely stuff turkey just before roasting. Place remaining stuffing in greased baking dish; bake at 350° for 30 minutes or until hot. Refrigerate leftovers.
Makes about 3 quarts.

Old-Fashioned Bread Stuffing

- 1½ cups chopped onion
- 1½ cups diced celery
- 1 stick (½ cup) butter or margarine
- 1 teaspoon poultry seasoning
- 1 teaspoon rubbed sage
- 1 teaspoon salt
- Dash ground black pepper
- ½ cup water or chicken broth
- 8 cups dried bread cubes (10 to 12 bread slices, cubed and dried overnight)

Cook and stir onion and celery in butter in medium skillet over medium heat until tender. Stir in seasonings. Add onion mixture and water to bread cubes in large bowl. Toss to mix. Stuff neck and body cavities of turkey. Roast immediately.
Yield: 8 cups (enough for 12- to 14-pound turkey).

Cranberry-Sausage: Cut 1 cup fresh cranberries into halves. Cut 1 package (8 ounces) fully cooked sausage links into pieces. Add to bread cubes.

Bacon and Green Pepper: Substitute 1½ cups chopped green bell pepper for celery. Substitute 1 teaspoon dried thyme leaves, crushed, for poultry seasoning and sage. Reduce salt to ½ teaspoon. Add 12 slices cooked diced bacon to bread cubes.

*Favorite recipe from **Swift-Eckrich, Inc.***

Harvest Sausage Stuffing

Barbecued Turkey with Herbs

1 turkey (9 to 13 pounds), fresh or frozen, thawed
³/4 cup vegetable oil
¹/2 cup chopped fresh parsley
2 tablespoons chopped fresh sage *or* 2 teaspoons dried sage, crushed
2 tablespoons chopped fresh rosemary *or* 2 teaspoons dried rosemary, crushed
1 tablespoon chopped fresh thyme *or* 1 teaspoon dried thyme, crushed
Salt and coarsely cracked black pepper

Remove neck and giblets from turkey. Rinse turkey under cold running water; drain and pat dry with paper toweling. In small bowl, combine remaining ingredients. Brush cavities and outer surface of turkey generously with herb mixture. Pull skin over neck and secure with skewer. Fold wings behind back and tie legs and tail together with kitchen twine. Insert meat thermometer into center of thickest part of thigh, not touching bone.

Arrange medium-hot **KINGS-FORD® Charcoal Briquets** around large drip pan. Position turkey directly over drip pan. Cover grill and cook turkey 11 to 13 minutes per pound or until internal temperature reaches 185°F, basting occasionally with herb mixture. Add more briquets as necessary. Garnish with additional fresh herbs, if desired.
Makes 8 to 10 servings.

Oyster Stuffing

1 cup chopped cooked oysters
1 cup chopped celery
1 medium onion, chopped
¹/2 stick (¹/4 cup) butter or margarine
8 cups fresh bread cubes
1 cup chicken or turkey broth
2 eggs, beaten
¹/2 to 1 teaspoon dried tarragon leaves or parsley flakes
1 to 2 teaspoons lemon juice
¹/2 teaspoon salt

Cook and stir oysters, celery and onion in butter in medium skillet over medium heat until tender. Add to bread cubes in large bowl. Combine remaining ingredients in small bowl. Pour over bread mixture and toss to mix. Stuff neck and body cavities of turkey. Roast immediately. Or, bake in covered 2-quart casserole in preheated 325°F oven 45 minutes or until hot.
Yield: 6 cups (enough for 10- to 12-pound turkey).

*Favorite recipe from **Swift-Eckrich, Inc.***

Parmesan Seasoned Turkey

4 slices BUTTERBALL® SLICE 'N SERVE® Breast of Turkey, cut ³/8 inch thick
2 tablespoons butter or margarine, melted
1¹/2 teaspoons grated Parmesan cheese
Dash coarsely ground black pepper
Dash crushed red pepper
Dash onion powder

Combine butter, cheese, peppers and onion powder in small dish. Brush both sides of turkey with seasoned butter. Grill over medium coals 6 to 8 minutes or until hot. Turn over halfway through heating.
Makes 4 servings.

Note: Turkey may be heated under broiler. Place turkey on broiler pan. Broil, 4 inches from heat, 8 minutes or until hot. Turn turkey over and baste with seasoned butter halfway through heating.

Clove Glazed Turkey

3-pound BUTTERBALL® Boneless Turkey, thawed
20 whole cloves
3 tablespoons red currant jelly
1 pineapple slice, cut into halves
2 maraschino cherries
Spiced Currant Sauce (recipe follows)

Press cloves into turkey. Melt jelly in small saucepan over medium heat. Brush 1¹/2 tablespoons jelly over turkey. Roast turkey according to package directions; omit brushing with oil. About 30 minutes before turkey is done, brush with remaining 1¹/2 tablespoons jelly. Wrap turkey in foil and let stand 10 to 15 minutes. Remove netting from turkey. Garnish with pineapple and maraschino cherries. Slice turkey and serve with Spiced Currant Sauce.
Yield: 8 servings.

Spiced Currant Sauce

¹/2 cup red currant jelly
¹/2 cup pineapple juice
1 tablespoon brown sugar
1 tablespoon cornstarch
¹/4 teaspoon ground cloves

Combine all ingredients in small saucepan, stirring until cornstarch dissolves. Cook and stir over medium heat until sauce comes to boil and thickens. Cook and stir 1 minute more.
Yield: 1 cup.

Clove Glazed Turkey

Turkey Oscar

4 slices cooked BUTTERBALL®
   turkey (1 pound)
2 tablespoons butter or
   margarine
1 can (6 ounces) crab meat,
   drained, warmed
8 hot cooked asparagus spears
   Bearnaise Sauce (recipe
   follows)
   Toast points, optional

Heat turkey slices in butter in medium skillet over medium heat. Place slices on individual plates. Top each slice with crab meat, asparagus spears and Bearnaise Sauce. Serve with toast points.
Yield: 4 servings.

Bearnaise Sauce

2 tablespoons tarragon vinegar
1 tablespoon dried tarragon
   leaves, crushed
2 tablespoons finely chopped
   shallots or green onions
   Dash freshly ground black
   pepper
2 egg yolks
2 tablespoons water
1 stick (½ cup) butter, melted
   and cooled to room
   temperature

Combine vinegar, tarragon, shallots and pepper in small saucepan. Over medium heat, cook and stir until vinegar evaporates and shallots soften. Blend yolks and water in cup; add to shallots, stirring constantly over *low* heat until mixture thickens. Remove from heat. Add butter gradually, stirring briskly after each addition until blended.
Yield: ¾ cup.

Turkey à la Cordon Bleu

6- to 8-pound BUTTERBALL®
   Breast of Turkey
   Cordon Bleu Rice (recipe
   follows)
   Cordon Bleu Sauce (recipe
   follows)

Roast turkey according to package directions. Meanwhile, prepare Cordon Bleu Rice and Cordon Bleu Sauce. Slice turkey and serve with rice and sauce.
Yield: 8 to 10 servings.   (continued)

Turkey Oscar

Cordon Bleu Rice

3 cups cooked rice
2 cups diced fully cooked ham
   or Canadian-style bacon
1½ cups (6 ounces) shredded
   aged Swiss cheese
3 tablespoons chopped fresh
   parsley
3 tablespoons butter or
   magarine, melted

Combine rice, ham, cheese, parsley and butter in medium bowl. Spoon into 2-quart casserole. Cover and bake alongside turkey last 40 minutes of roasting time.
Yield: 5 cups.

Cordon Bleu Sauce

½ stick (¼ cup) butter or
   margarine
¼ cup all-purpose flour
½ teaspoon salt
2½ cups milk
1 package (3 ounces) cream
   cheese, cut into small
   pieces
1½ cups (6 ounces) shredded
   aged Swiss cheese

Melt butter in medium saucepan over medium heat. Blend in flour and salt. Gradually add milk. Bring to boil, stirring constantly. Cook and stir 1 minute more. Reduce heat to low. Add cream cheese and Swiss cheese; stir until melted.
Yield: 3⅓ cups.

Turkey Curry

3 cups cubed cooked
   BUTTERBALL® turkey
   (1 pound)
½ cup finely chopped onion
2 tablespoons butter or
   margarine
1 tablespoon curry powder
1 gravy packet (8 ounces)
   included with turkey
⅔ cup water
½ cup whipping cream or half
   and half
1½ teaspoons honey
½ teaspoon salt
¼ teaspoon ground black pepper
   Hot cooked rice
   Toasted almonds, shredded
   coconut and/or chopped
   dried fruit, optional

Cook and stir onion in butter in medium saucepan over low heat 5 minutes or until tender. Add curry powder and cook 2 minutes, stirring occasionally. Stir in contents of gravy packet and water. Bring to boil over high heat, stirring constantly. Reduce heat to low; simmer 3 to 5 minutes, stirring occasionally. Blend in cream, honey, salt and pepper. Stir turkey into sauce and heat 3 to 5 minutes or until heated through. Serve over rice with almonds, coconut and/or dried fruit as a garnish or accompaniment.
Yield: 4 servings.

Turkey Florentine

6- to 8-pound BUTTERBALL®
Breast of Turkey
1 package (6 ounces) long grain
and wild rice mix
1 package (10 ounces) frozen
chopped spinach, thawed,
drained
¾ cup diced fully cooked ham

Roast turkey according to package directions. Prepare rice according to package directions. Stir in spinach and ham. Place in buttered 1½-quart casserole. Bake alongside turkey last 45 minutes of roasting time. Slice turkey and serve with Florentine rice.
Yield: 8 servings.

Turkey Orloff

Turkey Hash

2 cups cubed cooked
BUTTERBALL® turkey
(³/₄ pound)
½ cup chopped celery
⅓ cup chopped onion
⅓ cup chopped green bell
pepper
½ stick (¼ cup) butter or
margarine
3 cups diced cooked potatoes
½ teaspoon poultry seasoning
¼ teaspoon salt
⅛ teaspoon ground black pepper
½ to 1 cup turkey gravy

Cook and stir celery, onion and green pepper in butter in heavy skillet over medium heat until tender. Stir in potatoes, turkey and seasonings. Cook over low heat, about 5 minutes, stirring frequently. Add gravy; cook and stir until mixture is hot.
Yield: 4 servings (4½ cups).

Turkey Orloff

3-pound BUTTERBALL®
Boneless Breast of Turkey
Orloff Rice (recipe follows)
Orloff Sauce (recipe follows)

Roast turkey according to package directions. Wrap in foil. Let stand 10 to 15 minutes. Meanwile, prepare Orloff Rice and Orloff Sauce. Remove netting from turkey. Slice turkey and place rice between slices. Spoon some sauce over turkey. Serve remaining sauce with turkey.
Yield: 8 servings.   *(continued)*

Orloff Rice

⅓ cup long grain rice
8 cups water
½ stick (¼ cup) butter
1 medium onion, chopped fine
1 egg, beaten

Cook rice, uncovered, 5 minutes in boiling water. Drain. Melt butter in 2-quart baking dish. Stir in onion and rice. Cover and bake alongside turkey 1 hour, stirring after 30 minutes. Blend egg into cooked rice; keep warm.
Yield: 1 cup.

Orloff Sauce

½ stick (¼ cup) butter or
margarine
⅓ cup all-purpose flour
2 cups chicken broth
½ cup cottage cheese, pureed
2 egg yolks, beaten
½ cup (2 ounces) shredded
Monterey Jack cheese

Melt butter in medium saucepan over medium-low heat. Blend in flour and cook 2 minutes, stirring frequently. Gradually stir in broth. Bring to boil over medium heat, stirring constantly. Cook 2 minutes more. Remove from heat. Add cottage cheese, egg yolks and Monterey Jack cheese, stirring until smooth.
Yield: 2½ cups.

Kensington Crepes

Filling:
2 cups finely diced cooked
BUTTERBALL® turkey
(³/₄ pound)
¼ cup chopped onion
½ stick (¼ cup) butter or
margarine
¼ cup all-purpose flour
½ teaspoon salt
2 cups milk
1 cup chopped nuts
½ teaspoon curry powder
1 egg, beaten
3 tablespoons (³/₄ ounce)
shredded Cheddar cheese
Crepes:
6 eggs
¼ cup all-purpose flour
2 tablespoons water
¼ teaspoon salt

To make filling: Cook and stir onion in butter in small saucepan over medium heat until tender. Blend in flour and salt. Remove from heat. Gradually add milk. Cook over medium heat until mixture thickens, stirring constantly. Pour 1½ cups sauce into medium bowl. Add turkey, nuts and curry powder. Combine well. Add egg and cheese to remaining sauce in pan. Bring to boil over medium-low heat, stirring constantly until cheese melts. Set aside.

To make crepes: Combine eggs, flour, water and salt in medium bowl. Beat thoroughly. Spoon 2 tablespoons batter into seasoned 6-inch crepe pan or skillet. Cook over medium heat until lightly browned. Remove from pan and stack between paper towels.

To fill crepes: Preheat oven to 325°F. Spread about ¼ cup filling across center of each crepe. Roll edges over filling and place in 13×9-inch baking dish. Spoon cheese sauce over top. Heat in oven about 10 minutes. For a golden top, place under broiler about 2 to 3 minutes.
Yield: 6 servings, 2 crepes each.

Note: Or assemble crepes and refrigerate if not to be served immediately. Spoon sauce over crepes just before heating. Allow 15 to 20 minutes to heat if taken directly from refrigerator.

Shanghai Turkey Stir-Fry

- **1 small turkey thigh, skinned and boned**
- **3 tablespoons cornstarch, divided**
- **4 tablespoons KIKKOMAN Soy Sauce, divided**
- **1 tablespoon dry sherry**
- **1 tablespoon minced fresh ginger root**
- **1 clove garlic, minced**
- **1 cup water**
- **3 tablespoons vegetable oil, divided**
- **1 large carrot, cut into julienne strips**
- **1 onion, sliced**
- **1 package (10 oz.) frozen French-style green beans, thawed and drained**

Cut turkey into thin, narrow strips; set aside. Combine 2 tablespoons *each* cornstarch and soy sauce with sherry, ginger and garlic in medium bowl; stir in turkey. Let stand 30 minutes. Meanwhile, combine water, remaining 1 tablespoon cornstarch and 2 tablespoons soy sauce; set aside. Heat 2 tablespoons oil in hot wok or large skillet over high heat. Add turkey and stir-fry 3 minutes, or until tender; remove. Heat remaining 1 tablespoon oil in same pan. Add carrot and onion; stir-fry 2 minutes. Add green beans; stir-fry 1 minute longer. Stir in turkey and soy sauce mixture. Cook and stir until mixture boils and thickens. Serve immediately.
Makes 6 servings.

Turkey Parmigiana

- **4 to 6 slices (³⁄₈ inch thick) cooked BUTTERBALL® turkey (1 pound)**
- **2 eggs, slightly beaten**
- **1 tablespoon water**
- **2 teaspoons vegetable oil**
- **½ cup seasoned dried bread crumbs**
- **¾ cup grated Parmesan cheese, divided**
  Vegetable oil
- **2½ cups spaghetti or marinara sauce**
- **2 teaspoons dried oregano leaves, crushed**
- **¾ cup (3 ounces) shredded mozzarella cheese**

Preheat oven to 350°F. Combine eggs, water and 2 teaspoons oil in shallow dish; set aside. Combine bread crumbs and ½ cup Parmesan cheese in another shallow dish. Dip turkey slices into egg mixture, then coat with bread crumb mixture. Heat oil in heavy skillet over medium heat. Brown turkey slices 2 to 4 minutes per side. Layer turkey in 11×7-inch baking dish. Combine spaghetti sauce and oregano; pour over turkey. Top each turkey slice with mozzarella cheese and remaining ¼ cup Parmesan cheese. Bake in oven 20 to 25 minutes or until cheese melts.
Yield: 4 servings.

Glazed Turkey Kabobs

Glazed Turkey Kabobs

- **16 cubes (1 inch each) cooked BUTTERBALL® turkey (1 pound)**
  Water
- **1 can (20 ounces) pineapple chunks, drained; reserve juice**
- **½ cup packed brown sugar**
- **2 tablespoons soy sauce**
- **16 slices bacon, cut into halves**
- **2 large red bell peppers, cut into 24 (1½-inch) triangles**
- **3 large green bell peppers, cut into 32 (1½-inch) triangles**
  Hot cooked rice

Preheat broiler. Add water to pineapple juice to make 1 cup. Combine juice, brown sugar and soy sauce in small saucepan. Bring to boil over high heat. Reduce heat to low; simmer 2 to 3 minutes. Set glaze aside. Cook bacon in large skillet over medium-high heat until done, but not crisp. Dip turkey and pineapple into glaze. Assemble each kabob as follows: red pepper, green pepper, pineapple, bacon piece folded in half, turkey, bacon piece folded in half, pineapple and green pepper. Repeat. Complete kabob with additional red pepper. Brush kabobs with glaze. Broil 4 to 5 inches from heat 4 to 5 minutes. Turn kabobs, brush with glaze and broil 4 to 5 minutes more or until heated through. Serve kabobs on rice.
Yield: 4 servings, 2 kabobs each.

Turkey Schnitzel

- **4 slices (¼ inch thick) cooked BUTTERBALL® turkey (¾ pound)**
- **¼ cup lemon juice**
- **1 egg**
- **2 teaspoons milk**
- **¾ cup seasoned dried bread crumbs**
  Butter or margarine
  Hot cooked noodles
  Lemon wedges

Marinate turkey slices in lemon juice in plastic bag in refrigerator 1 hour; drain. Blend egg and milk in shallow dish. Dip turkey slices into egg mixture; coat with bread crumbs. Brown turkey in butter in large skillet over medium heat 2 to 4 minutes per side. Serve with noodles and lemon wedges.
Yield: 4 servings.

Turkey Paprikash

Turkey Paprikash

3-pound BUTTERBALL®
 Boneless Breast of Turkey
Vegetable oil
5 teaspoons paprika, divided
 Dash salt and ground black
 pepper
2 tablespoons butter or
 margarine
¾ cup chopped onion
1 tablespoon all-purpose flour
1 cube chicken bouillon
 dissolved in 1 cup hot water
1 cup sour cream
 Hot cooked spaetzle or
 noodles

Brush turkey with oil. Combine 1 teaspoon paprika, salt and pepper in cup; sprinkle on turkey. Roast turkey according to package directions. Remove from pan. Wrap in foil and let stand 10 to 15 minutes. Melt butter in medium saucepan over medium heat. Add onion; cook and stir until tender. Stir in flour. Gradually add remaining 4 teaspoons paprika and bouillon. Bring to boil over high heat. Reduce heat to low; simmer and stir 3 minutes. Blend small amount of hot mixture into sour cream, then add to sauce. Heat gently over low heat to serving temperature. Do not boil. Remove netting from turkey. Slice turkey; serve with sauce and spaetzle.
Yield: 8 servings.

Oriental Turkey Terrine

2½ pounds ground turkey
2 eggs, beaten
¾ cup finely chopped onion
¼ cup chopped fresh cilantro or
 parsley
¼ cup KIKKOMAN Soy Sauce
1½ cups dry bread crumbs
½ teaspoon ground ginger
¼ teaspoon fennel seed, crushed
¼ teaspoon pepper
⅛ teaspoon ground cloves
 Dash ground cinnamon

Combine turkey, eggs, onion, cilantro and soy sauce in large bowl; set aside. Stir together bread crumbs, ginger, fennel, pepper, cloves and cinnamon. Sprinkle evenly over turkey mixture, mixing until thoroughly blended. Press firmly into greased 12-cup Bundt or tube pan. Bake at 375°F. 45 minutes, or until top is lightly browned and starts to pull away from side of pan. Turn out onto serving platter; let stand 5 minutes before cutting into thin slices.
Makes 6 to 8 servings.
 Note: If desired, press turkey mixture into greased 9¼×5¼-inch loaf pan; bake at 375°F. 1 hour, or to doneness described above.

Turkey Fillets in Spicy Cilantro Marinade

1 cup chopped onion
1 large tomato, quartered
⅓ cup soy sauce
¼ cup chopped green pepper
3 tablespoons vegetable oil
3 tablespoons lime juice
2 tablespoons minced cilantro or
 parsley
2 cloves garlic, minced
¾ teaspoon pepper
4 turkey breast fillets (about
 ½ pound each)

Place all ingredients, except turkey, in blender; blend 30 seconds. Place turkey fillets in large plastic bag; place bag in bowl. Pour marinade over turkey in bag. Close bag securely; refrigerate 4 hours, turning occasionally. Drain turkey fillets; reserve marinade. Grill turkey, on uncovered grill, over hot **KINGSFORD® Charcoal Briquets** 5 minutes on each side or until tender, brushing often with marinade.
Makes 4 servings.

Turkey with Wine-Glazed Vegetables

3-pound BUTTERBALL®
 Boneless Breast of Turkey or
 Boneless Turkey, thawed if
 frozen
 Vegetable oil
1 teaspoon dried rosemary
 leaves, divided
1 teaspoon dried thyme leaves,
 divided
8 carrots, cut into ½-inch slices
8 small red potatoes, unpared,
 cut into quarters
4 small onions, cut into halves
1 cup chicken broth
⅓ cup white wine
1 medium clove garlic, minced
2 bay leaves
4 ribs celery, cut into 1-inch
 pieces
4 teaspoons cornstarch,
 dissolved in 1 tablespoon
 white wine

Brush turkey with oil; sprinkle with ½ teaspoon of the rosemary and ¼ teaspoon of the thyme. Roast according to package directions.

Meanwhile, place carrots, potatoes and onions in 2-quart casserole. Combine broth, 1/3 cup wine, garlic, bay leaves, remaining 1/2 teaspoon rosemary and remaining 3/4 teaspoon thyme in small saucepan. Bring to a boil over high heat. Reduce heat to low; simmer 3 minutes. Pour over vegetables; cover. Bake alongside turkey during last hour of roasting time. After 45 minutes, add celery.

When done, remove turkey from oven, wrap in foil and let stand 15 minutes before removing netting. Remove vegetables from oven and discard bay leaves. Drain broth into small saucepan. Add turkey pan drippings. Gradually stir dissolved cornstarch into broth mixture. Cook and stir over medium heat until clear and thickened. Pour over hot vegetables and serve with sliced turkey.
Makes 8 servings.

Turkey Marengo

**3-pound BUTTERBALL®
    Boneless Breast of Turkey,
    thawed
    Vegetable oil
1/2 teaspoon parsley flakes
1/4 teaspoon ground black pepper
1/4 cup white wine
1 jar (15 1/2 ounces) spaghetti
    sauce
1/4 cup water
1 jar (2 1/2 ounces) sliced
    mushrooms, drained
1 can (2 1/4 ounces) sliced black
    olives, drained
2 tablespoons brandy
    Hot cooked rice**

Brush turkey with oil. Combine parsley and pepper in cup; sprinkle over turkey. Roast turkey according to package directions. Remove turkey from pan. Wrap in foil and let stand 10 to 15 minutes. Pour wine into roasting pan, stirring to combine with pan juices. Cook juices down to half amount over medium heat. Add spaghetti sauce, water, mushrooms, olives and brandy. Simmer over low heat until heated through. Remove netting from turkey. Slice turkey and serve on rice with sauce.
Yield: 8 servings.

Creamed Turkey Stack-Ups

**2 cups cubed cooked turkey or
    chicken
1/4 cup margarine or butter
1/4 cup unsifted flour
2 cups BORDEN® or MEADOW
    GOLD® Milk
1 tablespoon WYLER'S® or
    STEERO® Chicken-Flavor
    Instant Bouillon *or* 3
    Chicken-Flavor Bouillon
    Cubes
1 (2 1/2-ounce) jar sliced
    mushrooms, drained
1/4 cup chopped green pepper
1 (2-ounce) jar sliced pimientos,
    drained
12 pancakes**

In medium saucepan, melt margarine; stir in flour. Add milk and bouillon; cook and stir until bouillon dissolves and mixture thickens. Stir in remaining ingredients except pancakes; heat through. Serve over pancakes. Refrigerate leftovers.
Makes 4 to 6 servings.

Tip: Turkey mixture can be served in patty shells or as a crepe filling.

Turkey Marengo

Turkey Cutlets with Ginger & Lime Sauce

**1 pound boneless turkey cutlets
3/4 cup all-purpose flour
3 eggs, slightly beaten
1/2 cup WISH-BONE® Italian
    Dressing
1/2 cup chopped green onions
1/2 cup chicken broth
1 tablespoon butter or
    margarine
1 teaspoon lime juice
1/4 teaspoon ground ginger
1/8 teaspoon pepper**

Dip turkey in flour, then eggs, then again in flour. In large skillet, heat 1/4 cup Italian dressing and cook 1/2 of the turkey over medium heat, turning once, 5 minutes or until done; drain on paper towels and keep warm. Heat remaining 1/4 cup Italian dressing and repeat with remaining turkey.

Into skillet, add green onions and cook 1 minute. Stir in remaining ingredients, then bring to a boil to heat through. Serve over turkey.
Makes about 4 servings.

Note: Also terrific with Wish-Bone® Robusto Italian, Herbal Italian or Blended Italian Dressing.

Turkey Parmesan

**1 teaspoon diet margarine
1 (2-ounce) slice raw turkey
    breast
3 tablespoons prepared
    spaghetti sauce
1 teaspoon grated Parmesan
    cheese
1 slice LITE-LINE® Mozzarella
    Flavor Process Cheese
    Product***

In small skillet, over medium heat, melt margarine. Add turkey breast slice. Cook 2 minutes; turn. Reduce heat to low; top turkey with remaining ingredients. Cover; cook 2 to 3 minutes longer. Garnish as desired.
Makes 1 serving; 198 calories.

*"1/2 the calories"—8% milkfat product. Caloric values by product analyses and recipe calculation.

FISH & SHELLFISH

Increasingly popular for its nutritional value, seafood has always been prized for its flavor. Serve sole in a delicate sauce, or try a Creole specialty bursting with tomatoes and spices. For a special occasion, create a splendid lobster or swordfish dish. An added benefit—most seafood cooks quickly, so in very little time you can produce an impressive, delicious meal.

Salmon Steaks in Dill Sauce

- **1 tablespoon butter or margarine**
- **½ cup chopped green onions**
- **1 can (10¾ ounces) CAMPBELL'S® Condensed Cream of Celery Soup**
- **½ cup half-and-half**
- **¼ cup Chablis or other dry white wine**
- **2 tablespoons chopped fresh dill weed or 1 teaspoon dried dill weed, crushed**
- **4 salmon steaks, ¾ inch thick (about 6 ounces each)**

To Microwave:

1. In 12- by 8-inch microwave-safe baking dish, combine butter and onions. Cover with vented plastic wrap; microwave on HIGH 2 minutes or until onions are tender, stirring once during cooking.

2. Stir in soup until smooth. Stir in half-and-half, wine and dill; blend well.

3. Arrange salmon steaks in sauce with thicker portions toward edges of dish. Cover; microwave on HIGH 9 minutes or until fish flakes easily when tested with fork, rotating dish twice during cooking. Let stand, covered, 5 minutes. Garnish with additional dill weed.
Makes 4 servings.

Bacon-Wrapped Tuna

- **3 pounds fresh tuna**
- **½ cup olive or vegetable oil**
- **¼ cup lime juice**
- **1 cup dry white wine**
- **2 cloves garlic, crushed**
- **1 teaspoon grated fresh ginger**
- **6 slices bacon**

Cut tuna into 6 steaks, each about 1 inch thick. Remove any skin or bone. In shallow glass dish, combine oil, lime juice, wine, garlic and ginger. Add tuna; turn to coat with marinade.

Cover and refrigerate 2 hours. Drain fish; reserve marinade. Wrap 1 slice of bacon around each steak and secure with wooden pick. Lightly oil grid. Grill fish steaks, on uncovered grill, over medium-hot **KINGSFORD® Charcoal Briquets** about 10 minutes or until fish flakes easily when tested with fork. Turn once halfway through cooking time; baste often with marinade.
Makes 6 servings.

Shrimp & Mushroom Stuffed Sole

- **¼ cup *plus* 2 tablespoons WISH-BONE® Italian Dressing**
- **2 cups thinly sliced mushrooms**
- **½ cup sliced green onions**
- **¾ pound uncooked medium shrimp, cleaned and coarsely chopped**
- **2 tablespoons brandy or sherry**
- **½ teaspoon thyme leaves**
- **½ teaspoon salt (optional)**
- **⅛ teaspoon pepper**
- **2 cups fresh bread crumbs**
- **4 sole or flounder fillets (1 to 1½ pounds)**

Preheat oven to 400°.

In large skillet, heat ¼ cup Italian dressing and cook mushrooms with green onions over medium heat, stirring occasionally, 3 minutes. Add shrimp and cook, stirring constantly, 2 minutes or until shrimp turn pink. Stir in brandy, thyme, salt and pepper, then bread crumbs.

In large shallow baking pan, evenly divide shrimp mixture into 4 mounds. Place 1 fillet over each mound; brush fillets with remaining 2 tablespoons dressing. Bake 10 minutes or until fish flakes. Garnish, if desired, with chopped parsley and paprika.
Makes about 4 servings.

Note: Also terrific with Wish-Bone® Robusto Italian, Herbal Italian, Blended Italian or Classic Dijon Vinaigrette Dressing.

Salmon Steaks in Dill Sauce

Grilled Fish with Salsa

½ cup quartered cherry
    tomatoes
½ cup cubed mango or papaya
¼ cup sliced green onion
¼ cup cubed avocado
2 tablespoons chopped cilantro
    or parsley
1 tablespoon olive or vegetable
    oil
2 tablespoons lime juice
1 teaspoon minced jalapeño
    pepper
    Salt and pepper
1¼ pounds white fish fillets (ling
    cod, red snapper or halibut)

In small bowl, combine tomatoes, mango, onion, avocado, cilantro, oil, 1 tablespoon of the lime juice and the jalapeño pepper. Season with salt and pepper to taste; set aside. Measure fish at its thickest part to determine cooking time. Sprinkle both sides of fish with remaining 1 tablespoon lime juice and additional pepper. Lightly oil grid. Grill fillets, on covered grill, over medium-hot **KINGSFORD® Charcoal Briquets** 10 minutes per inch of thickness or until fish flakes easily when tested with fork. Garnish with additional mango or papaya slices, if desired. Serve with salsa.
Makes 4 servings.

Lemony Fish Fillets

1¼ cups crushed cornflakes
2 teaspoons lemon pepper
    seasoning
¼ to ½ teaspoon dried dill weed
⅛ teaspoon garlic powder
¼ cup buttermilk
1 egg
1 pound fish fillets, ½ inch
    thick, cut into serving-size
    pieces
    CRISCO® Oil for frying

Mix cornflake crumbs, lemon pepper seasoning, dill weed and garlic powder in shallow dish or on sheet of waxed paper. Set aside. Blend buttermilk and egg in medium mixing bowl. Dip fish in buttermilk mixture, then in cornflake mixture to coat.

Heat ⅛ inch Crisco® Oil in large skillet. Add fish. Fry 5 to 8 minutes, or until fish flakes easily with fork, turning over once. Drain on paper towels.
4 servings.

Chinese Trout

4 medium trout (about
    2 pounds), dressed
¼ cup KIKKOMAN Soy Sauce
2 tablespoons vegetable oil,
    divided
1 cup water
4 teaspoons cornstarch
1 tablespoon sugar
2 tablespoons tomato catsup
1 tablespoon KIKKOMAN Soy
    Sauce
2½ teaspoons distilled white
    vinegar
⅛ teaspoon crushed red pepper
½ cup sliced green onions and
    tops
2 teaspoons finely chopped
    garlic
2 teaspoons finely chopped
    fresh ginger root

Score both sides of trout with diagonal slashes ¼ inch deep and 1 inch apart; place in large shallow pan. Combine ¼ cup soy sauce and 1 tablespoon oil; pour over trout, turning to coat both sides well. Marinate 45 minutes, turning over once. Reserving marinade, remove trout and place on rack of broiler pan. Broil 3 inches from heat source 5 minutes on each side, or until fish flakes easily when tested with fork; brush occasionally with reserved marinade. Meanwhile, combine water, cornstarch, sugar, catsup, 1 tablespoon soy sauce, vinegar and red pepper; set aside. Heat remaining 1 tablespoon oil in saucepan over medium-high heat. Add green onions, garlic and ginger; stir-fry 2 minutes. Stir in catsup mixture. Cook and stir until sauce boils and thickens. Serve with trout.
Makes 4 servings.

Saucy Fish Fillets

1 can (8 ounces) DOLE®
    Pineapple Tidbits
1 tablespoon cider vinegar
1 tablespoon sugar
1½ teaspoons cornstarch
½ teaspoon instant chicken
    bouillon granules
¼ teaspoon ground ginger
    Pinch cayenne pepper
¼ cup sliced green onions
¼ cup sliced water chestnuts
4 white fish fillets, about ½ inch
    thick
2 tablespoons butter or
    margarine, melted
½ cup flavored cracker crumbs
    Paprika

Microwave: Drain pineapple; reserve juice. To make sauce, add enough water to juice to make ⅔ cup liquid. In 1½-quart microwave-safe bowl, whisk together juice mixture, vinegar, sugar, cornstarch, bouillon, ginger and cayenne. Microwave on HIGH 4 to 5 minutes or until sauce is thickened and clear, whisking after 2 minutes to prevent lumps. Stir in onions, water chestnuts and pineapple. Set aside.

Arrange fish fillets in 12×8×2-inch microwave-safe dish with thickest areas to outside edges of dish. Drizzle with butter; sprinkle with cracker crumbs and paprika. Cover with waxed paper. Microwave on HIGH 5 to 9 minutes, rotating dish after 3 minutes. Fish is done when thin areas flake easily with fork and thick areas are fork-tender. Let fish stand 2 to 3 minutes; serve with sauce.
Makes 4 servings.

Saucy Fish Fillets

Swordfish Steaks with Dill-Mustard Sauce

Swordfish Steaks with Dill-Mustard Sauce

⅓ cup WISH-BONE® Italian
    Dressing
2 swordfish or shark steaks,
    1 inch thick (about 1 pound)
½ cup dry white wine
⅛ teaspoon pepper
1 tablespoon snipped fresh dill*
1 tablespoon Dijon-style
    mustard
½ cup whipping or heavy cream

In large skillet, heat Italian dressing and cook fish over medium heat, turning once, 8 minutes or until fish flakes. Remove to serving platter and keep warm. Into skillet, add wine, then pepper, dill and mustard. Bring to a boil, then simmer, stirring occasionally, 8 minutes. Stir in cream and heat 1 minute or until thickened. Serve over fish. Garnish, if desired, with baby vegetables.
Makes about 2 servings.
  Substitution: Use 1 teaspoon dried dill weed.
  Note: Also terrific with Wish-Bone® Robusto Italian, Blended Italian or Italian & Cheese Dressing.

Crab-Stuffed Trout

⅓ cup butter or margarine,
    divided
2 cups chopped CAMPBELL'S
    FRESH® Mushrooms
½ cup finely chopped onion
½ cup shredded carrot
1 cup crabmeat, flaked
¼ cup fine dry bread crumbs
3 tablespoons chopped fresh
    parsley, divided
1 tablespoon white wine
    Worcestershire sauce
6 brook trout or salmon
    (8 ounces each), pan-
    dressed
2 teaspoons lemon juice
    Arugula for garnish
    Cherry tomatoes for garnish

1. To make filling: In 10-inch skillet over medium heat, in 3 tablespoons hot butter, cook mushrooms, onion and carrot until tender and liquid has evaporated, stirring occasionally. In medium bowl, combine onion mixture, crabmeat, crumbs, 2 tablespoons of the parsley and Worcestershire; toss gently to coat. Spoon ½ cup filling loosely into each fish cavity; secure with toothpicks.
2. Arrange fish in oiled grill basket. In covered grill, arrange preheated coals around drip pan; test for hot coals above pan. On grill rack, place grill basket over pan but not over coals. Cover; grill 16 to 20 minutes or until fish begins to flake when tested with fork, turning once.
3. To make sauce: In 1-quart saucepan, combine remaining butter, remaining parsley and juice. Over medium heat, heat until butter is melted, stirring occasionally.
4. To serve: Garnish with arugula and tomatoes. Serve with sauce.
Makes 6 servings.
  To broil: Arrange fish on rack in broiler pan. Broil 6 inches from heat 16 to 20 minutes or until fish begins to flake when tested with fork, turning once.

Teriyaki Fish Fillets

1 can (20 ounces) DOLE®
    Pineapple Chunks
1 clove garlic, pressed
2 tablespoons slivered fresh
    ginger root
1 tablespoon minced green
    onion
5 teaspoons teriyaki sauce
1 teaspoon white vinegar
1 pound sole fillets
2 teaspoons cornstarch
1 teaspoon minced fresh ginger
    root
1 teaspoon sesame oil

Measure 2 tablespoons juice from pineapple can; mix with garlic, slivered ginger, onion, 3 teaspoons teriyaki sauce and vinegar. Arrange fish in shallow dish. Pour marinade over fish. Refrigerate 10 minutes. Arrange fish on greased broiler rack. Brush with marinade. Broil 6 inches from heat 5 to 6 minutes. In saucepan, combine remaining 2 teaspoons teriyaki sauce, undrained pineapple and remaining ingredients. Cook until sauce boils and thickens. Serve with fish.
Makes 4 servings.

Almondine Fish

1 pound fish fillets, fresh or frozen, thawed
Margarine or butter, melted
REALEMON® Lemon Juice from Concentrate
½ cup margarine or butter
3 tablespoons REALEMON® Lemon Juice from Concentrate
¼ cup sliced almonds, toasted

Preheat broiler. Place fish on oiled cold broiler pan. Brush fish with melted margarine and sprinkle with ReaLemon® brand. Broil 4 to 6 inches from heat 10 to 12 minutes per inch of fish thickness, turning halfway through cooking and basting frequently. Cook until fish flakes with fork. Meanwhile, in small saucepan, melt *½ cup* margarine; stir in *3 tablespoons* ReaLemon® brand and almonds. Serve warm over fish. Refrigerate leftovers.
Makes 4 servings.

Almondine Fish

Vegetable-Stuffed Fish Rolls

½ cup chopped CAMPBELL'S FRESH® Tomato
½ cup chopped CAMPBELL'S FRESH® Mushrooms
¼ cup chopped green onions
1 can (10¾ ounces) CAMPBELL'S® Condensed Cream of Celery Soup
6 haddock fillets (1½ pounds)
¼ cup water
1 cup shredded Muenster cheese (4 ounces)

1. In medium bowl, combine tomato, mushrooms, green onions and ¼ cup of the soup. Place about 3 tablespoons of the mixture on each fish fillet and roll up. Secure with toothpicks if needed.
2. Place fish rolls, seam side down, in 10- by 6-inch baking dish. Bake at 350°F. 25 minutes or until fish flakes easily when tested with fork. Discard any liquid in baking dish.
3. Meanwhile, in 2-quart saucepan, combine remaining soup and water. Over medium heat, heat through. Pour sauce over fish rolls; sprinkle with cheese.
4. Bake 2 minutes more or until cheese is melted.
Makes 6 servings.   *(continued)*

To Microwave: In medium bowl, combine tomato, mushrooms, green onions and ¼ cup of the soup. Fill and roll fish rolls as directed. Place fish rolls, seam side down, in 10- by 6-inch microwave-safe dish. Cover with vented plastic wrap; microwave on HIGH 8 to 14 minutes or until fish flakes easily when tested with fork, rotating dish twice during cooking. Discard any liquid in dish. Let stand, covered, 2 to 3 minutes. Meanwhile, in 2-cup glass measure, combine remaining soup and water. Microwave, uncovered, on HIGH 2 minutes or until hot. Pour sauce over fish rolls; top with cheese. Microwave, uncovered, on HIGH 1 minute more or until cheese melts.

Grilled Trout with Two Sauces

4 whole, cleaned trout or other small whole fish (about 12 ounces each)
Walnut Butter Sauce (recipe follows) *or*
Tarragon Cream Sauce (recipe follows)

Grill fish on well-oiled grid or in well-oiled wire grill basket, on covered grill, over medium-hot **KINGS-FORD® with Mesquite Charcoal Briquets** 3 to 5 minutes or until fish flakes easily when tested with fork; turn once. Serve with Walnut Butter Sauce or Tarragon Cream Sauce.
Makes 4 servings.

Walnut Butter Sauce

½ cup chopped walnuts
½ cup butter or margarine
3 tablespoons Madeira wine

In skillet, saute walnuts in 2 tablespoons of the butter until golden and fragrant. Reduce heat and add remaining 6 tablespoons butter; stir until melted. Stir in Madeira. Serve warm.
Makes about ½ cup.

Tarragon Cream Sauce

¼ cup olive or vegetable oil
¼ cup whipping cream
1 tablespoon red wine vinegar
1 tablespoon finely chopped parsley
1 garlic clove, minced
½ teaspoon dried tarragon, crushed
¼ teaspoon pepper

In medium bowl, combine all ingredients; mix well with wire whisk. Serve cool.
Makes about ½ cup.

Mexican Style Tuna Loaf

4 (6½-ounce) cans tuna, drained
3 cups fresh bread crumbs
    (6 slices bread)
2 eggs, slightly beaten
¼ cup chopped green pepper
¼ cup chopped onion
3 tablespoons REALEMON®
    Lemon Juice from
    Concentrate
2 teaspoons WYLER'S® or
    STEERO® Chicken-Flavor
    Instant Bouillon
    Mexican Sauce

Preheat oven to 350°. In large bowl, combine all ingredients except Mexican Sauce. In greased shallow baking dish, shape into loaf. Bake 30 to 35 minutes. Let stand 10 minutes before serving. Serve with Mexican Sauce. Garnish as desired. Refrigerate leftovers.
Makes 6 to 8 servings.
MEXICAN SAUCE: In small saucepan, combine 1 (15-ounce) can tomato sauce with tomato bits and 2 teaspoons cornstarch; mix well. Stir in 3 tablespoons ReaLemon® Lemon Juice from Concentrate, 1 tablespoon sugar, 1½ teaspoons chili powder and 1 teaspoon Wyler's® or Steero® Chicken-Flavor Instant Bouillon. Over high heat, bring to a boil. Reduce heat; simmer 5 minutes.
Makes about 1½ cups.

Microwave

Tuna Loaf: Mix ingredients as above. Turn into 2½-quart microwave baking ring. Cook on 100% power (high) 12 to 13 minutes or until set and almost firm in center. Let stand 5 minutes. Serve as above.
Sauce: In 1-quart glass measure, combine tomato sauce and cornstarch. Add remaining ingredients. Cook on 100% power (high) 8 minutes or until thickened, stirring every 2 minutes.

Quick and Easy Tuna Rice with Peas

1 package (10 oz.) BIRDS EYE®
    Green Peas
1¼ cups water
1 can (11 oz.) condensed
    cheddar cheese soup
1 can (12½ oz.) tuna, drained
    and flaked
1 chicken bouillon cube
1½ cups MINUTE® Rice

Bring peas, water, soup, tuna and bouillon cube to a full boil in medium saucepan. Stir in rice. Cover; remove from heat. Let stand 5 minutes. Fluff with fork.
Makes 4 servings.

Oriental Steamed Fish

4 white fish steaks, about
    ¾ inch thick
1 tablespoon slivered fresh
    ginger root
¼ cup orange juice
2 tablespoons KIKKOMAN Soy
    Sauce
1½ teaspoons distilled white
    vinegar
½ teaspoon brown sugar
1 teaspoon Oriental sesame oil
2 green onions and tops, minced

Place fish, in single layer, on oiled rack of bamboo steamer; sprinkle ginger evenly over fish. Set rack in large pot or wok of boiling water. (Do not allow water level to reach fish.) Cover and steam 8 to 10 minutes, or until fish flakes easily when tested with fork. Meanwhile, combine orange juice, soy sauce, vinegar and brown sugar in small saucepan; bring to boil. Remove from heat; stir in sesame oil. Arrange fish on serving platter; sprinkle green onions over fish and pour sauce over all.
Makes 4 servings.

Pineapple-Tomato Salsa and Fish

1 DOLE™ Fresh Pineapple
1 cucumber, peeled, seeded and
    diced
1 DOLE™ Green Bell Pepper,
    seeded and diced
1 DOLE™ Tomato, chopped
½ red onion, finely chopped
¼ cup lemon juice
1 clove garlic, pressed
2 tablespoons finely chopped
    cilantro or parsley
2 tablespoons white wine
    vinegar
1 tablespoon vegetable oil
2 teaspoons sugar
1 teaspoon salt
1 teaspoon dried dill weed
4 white fish steaks (½ inch
    thick)
1 tablespoon butter or
    margarine

Twist crown from pineapple. Cut pineapple lengthwise into quarters. Remove fruit from shells with curved knife. Trim off core and cut fruit into bite-size pieces. In medium bowl, combine half of pineapple with next 12 ingredients (reserve remaining pineapple for another use). In skillet, saute fish in butter 2 to 3 minutes. Spread pineapple salsa over fish. Cover; simmer 10 minutes or until fish is tender and flakes with a fork.
Makes 4 servings.

Mexican Style Tuna Loaf

Grilled Oriental Fish Steaks

Grilled Oriental Fish Steaks

4 fish steaks (halibut, salmon or swordfish), about ³/₄ inch thick
¹/₄ cup KIKKOMAN Lite Soy Sauce
3 tablespoons minced onion
1 tablespoon chopped fresh ginger root
1 tablespoon sesame seed, toasted
¹/₂ teaspoon sugar

Place fish in single layer in shallow baking pan. Measure lite soy sauce, onion, ginger, sesame seed and sugar into blender container; process on low speed 30 seconds, scraping sides down once. Pour sauce over fish; turn over to coat both sides. Marinate 30 minutes, turning fish over occasionally. Remove fish and broil or grill 4 inches from heat source or moderately hot coals 5 minutes on each side, or until fish flakes easily when tested with fork. Garnish as desired.
Makes 4 servings.

Seafood Creole

1 tablespoon vegetable oil
3 tomatoes, peeled, coarsely chopped
1 large onion, chopped
1 green pepper, chopped
1 celery stalk, chopped
3 cloves garlic, minced
1¹/₂ cups water
³/₄ cup uncooked rice
1 teaspoon ground cumin
¹/₂ teaspoon dried thyme leaves
¹/₂ teaspoon TABASCO® pepper sauce
1 bay leaf
1¹/₂ pounds red snapper fillets with skin, cut into 2-inch pieces
¹/₄ cup chopped parsley

In large skillet heat oil; cook tomatoes, onion, green pepper, celery and garlic until crisp-tender. Add water, rice, cumin, thyme, Tabasco® sauce and bay leaf. Bring to a boil; reduce heat and simmer covered 10 minutes. Add fish and parsley. Cover; simmer 5 to 10 minutes longer or until liquid is absorbed and fish flakes easily when tested with fork. Remove bay leaf.
Makes 4 servings.

Microwave Directions: In 3-quart microwave-safe casserole place oil, onion, green pepper, celery and garlic. Cover loosely with plastic wrap; cook on High 3 to 4 minutes or until vegetables are crisp-tender. Stir in tomatoes, *1 cup* water, rice, cumin, thyme, Tabasco® sauce and bay leaf. Re-cover; cook on High 20 minutes; stir. Add fish and parsley. Re-cover; cook on High 5 to 7 minutes or until fish flakes easily when tested with fork. Let stand covered 10 minutes before serving. Remove bay leaf.

Poached Red Snapper

2 quarts water
1 cup (8 ounces) WISH-BONE® Italian Dressing
1 cup dry white wine
2 medium carrots, finely chopped
¹/₂ cup chopped shallots or onions
1 tablespoon lemon juice
1 teaspoon grated lemon peel (optional)
3 whole cloves
1 teaspoon salt
¹/₄ teaspoon pepper
1 pound new or all-purpose potatoes, cut into large chunks
1 whole red snapper (about 2¹/₂ to 3 pounds)
1 pound fresh spinach leaves, stems trimmed

Place 13×9×2¹/₂-inch baking pan on 2 stove burners; fill with water, Italian dressing, wine, carrots, shallots, lemon juice, lemon peel, cloves, salt and pepper. Bring to a boil, then simmer uncovered 5 minutes. Add potatoes and simmer, stirring occasionally, 20 minutes. Add snapper and simmer, basting occasionally, 25 minutes or until fish flakes and potatoes are tender. Carefully remove snapper and potatoes to serving platter and keep warm. Add spinach to cooking liquid and simmer 30 seconds; drain. To serve, arrange potatoes and spinach around snapper.
Makes about 4 servings.

Note: Also terrific with Wish-Bone® Robusto Italian, Blended Italian, Herbal Italian, Italian & Cheese, Lite Italian, Classic Dijon Vinaigrette or Lite Classic Dijon Vinaigrette Dressing.

Grilled Salmon Steaks with Watercress Sauce

1 cup (8 ounces) WISH-BONE® Italian Dressing
¹/₂ cup chopped watercress
4 salmon, tuna or swordfish steaks, 1 inch thick (about 2 pounds)
¹/₂ cup whipping or heavy cream
2 tablespoons dry vermouth
Pinch of sugar (optional)

In large shallow baking dish, combine Italian dressing with watercress. Add fish and turn to coat. Cover and marinate in refrigerator, turning fish occasionally, at least 4 hours. Remove fish, reserving marinade. Grill or broil, turning once and basting with reserved marinade, until fish flakes.

Meanwhile, in small saucepan, bring ¹/₄ cup reserved marinade to a boil, then simmer uncovered 5 minutes. Stir in cream, vermouth and sugar. Cook, stirring occasionally, 3 minutes or until slightly thickened. Serve hot sauce over fish.
Makes about 4 servings.

Note: Also terrific with Wish-Bone® Robusto Italian, Lite Italian, Blended Italian, Herbal Italian, Classic Dijon Vinaigrette or Lite Classic Dijon Vinaigrette Dressing.

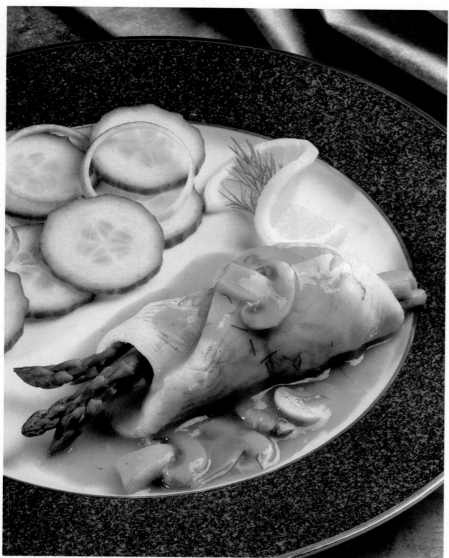

Fish Rolls with Asparagus

Salmon Steaks with Cucumber Sauce

4 salmon steaks, 1 inch thick
2 tablespoons CRISCO® Oil
³/₄ cup peeled, seeded and chopped cucumber
¹/₄ cup finely chopped celery
2 tablespoons chopped green onion
2 tablespoons all-purpose flour
1 teaspoon instant chicken bouillon granules
¹/₈ teaspoon pepper
1 cup half-and-half
1 egg yolk, slightly beaten

Set oven to broil and/or 550°F. Place salmon steaks on broiler pan. Broil 3 to 4 inches from heat, 10 to 15 minutes, or until fish flakes easily with fork, turning over once.

Meanwhile, heat Crisco® Oil in small saucepan. Add cucumber and celery. Sauté over moderate heat until tender-crisp. Add onion. Sauté 30 seconds longer. Stir in flour, bouillon granules and pepper. Blend in half-and-half. Cook, stirring constantly, 5 to 7 minutes, or until thickened and bubbly. Blend small amount of hot mixture into egg yolk. Add back to hot mixture. Cook, stirring constantly, 1 minute. Serve with salmon.
4 servings.

Pacific Coast Barbecued Salmon

4 fresh or frozen salmon steaks, 1 inch thick (about 8 ounces each)
¹/₂ cup butter or margarine
2 tablespoons fresh lemon juice
1 tablespoon Worcestershire sauce

Thaw salmon steaks, if frozen. In saucepan, combine butter, lemon juice and Worcestershire sauce; simmer 5 minutes, stirring frequently. Brush salmon steaks with butter mixture. Place steaks in well-greased wire grill basket.

Grill steaks, on uncovered grill, over medium-hot **KINGSFORD® Charcoal Briquets** 6 to 9 minutes or until lightly browned. Baste steaks with butter mixture and turn; grill 6 to 9 minutes longer, basting often, until fish flakes easily when tested with fork.
Makes 4 servings.

Fish Rolls with Asparagus

¹/₂ pound fresh asparagus, cut into 4-inch spears, or 1 package (10 ounces) frozen asparagus spears
1¹/₂ pounds flounder fillets
2 cups sliced CAMPBELL'S FRESH® Mushrooms
1 cup V8® Vegetable Juice
1 tablespoon fresh dill weed or ¹/₂ teaspoon dried dill weed, crushed
1 tablespoon cornstarch

1. Divide asparagus evenly among fish fillets. Roll up fillets jelly-roll fashion; secure with toothpicks, if necessary. Set aside.

2. Spray 10-inch nonstick skillet with vegetable cooking spray. Over medium heat, cook mushrooms until lightly browned.

3. In small bowl, stir together V8 juice, dill and cornstarch until smooth. Gradually stir into skillet. Cook over medium heat until mixture boils and thickens.

4. Place fish rolls in sauce. Reduce heat to low. Cover; simmer 15 minutes or until fish flakes easily when tested with fork. Before serving, remove toothpicks.
Makes 6 servings.

Per serving: 127 calories, 23 g protein, 3 g fat, 5 g carbohydrate, 263 mg sodium, 55 mg cholesterol.

Poached Sole with Dill Sauce

**1 (13¾-fluid ounce) can
  COLLEGE INN® Chicken
  Broth
6 sole or flounder fillets (about
  1½ pounds)
3 tablespoons lemon juice
1 tablespoon cornstarch
3 tablespoons snipped fresh dill
  or 1 tablespoon dried dill
  weed**

In skillet, over medium-high heat, heat 1¼ cup chicken broth to a boil; reduce heat. Add fish; cover and simmer 2 to 3 minutes or until fish flakes easily with fork. Carefully remove fish with slotted spoon to heated serving platter.

Meanwhile, in small saucepan, blend remaining broth and lemon juice into cornstarch. Cook over medium-high heat, stirring, until mixture thickens and boils. Boil 1 minute; stir in dill. To serve, spoon sauce over fish. Garnish as desired. *Makes 6 servings.*

Microwave: In 2-quart microwave-proof oblong dish, place fish and 1¼ cups broth; cover with plastic wrap. Microwave on HIGH (100% power) for 5 to 6 minutes until fish flakes easily with fork. Remove fish to warm serving platter.

In 1-quart microwave-proof bowl, mix ¼ cup broth, lemon juice and 2 tablespoons cornstarch. Microwave on HIGH for 4 to 5 minutes until mixture thickens and boils; stir in dill. Spoon sauce over fish; serve as above.

Poached Sole with Dill Sauce

Fisherman's Light Fillets

**½ cup WISH-BONE® Lite Italian
  or Italian Dressing
1 small green pepper, cut into
  strips
1 small onion, thinly sliced
1 pound fish fillets
1 medium tomato, coarsely
  chopped
  Hot cooked rice**

In large skillet, heat lite Italian dressing and cook green pepper and onion over medium heat, stirring occasionally, 5 minutes or until tender. Add fish and tomato, then simmer covered 10 minutes or until fish flakes. Serve over hot rice. *Makes about 4 servings.*

Grilled Fish Steaks with Vegetable Butter

**1 envelope LIPTON® Vegetable
  Recipe Soup Mix
½ cup butter or margarine,
  softened
2 tablespoons brandy or sherry
½ teaspoon ground ginger
4 halibut, cod, swordfish,
  salmon or shark steaks
  (about 2 pounds), ½ inch
  thick
½ cup orange juice
¼ cup oil**

In medium bowl, with electric mixer or rotary beater, thoroughly blend vegetable recipe soup mix, butter, brandy and ginger. Turn onto wax paper and shape into 8×2-inch log. Wrap in plastic wrap or wax paper, then chill until firm.

Meanwhile, in large baking dish, arrange fish; add orange juice and oil. Cover and marinate in refrigerator, turning occasionally, at least 1 hour. Remove fish from marinade. Grill or broil until fish flakes. To serve, top each steak with ½-inch slice butter mixture. *Makes 4 servings.*

Microwave Directions: Prepare butter mixture and marinate fish as above. In 13×9-inch baking dish, arrange fish and heat uncovered at HIGH (Full Power), rearranging fish occasionally, 9 minutes or until fish flakes. Top with butter as above. Let stand covered 5 minutes.

Fabulous Fish Terrine

½ cup dry white wine or fish
    broth
¼ teaspoon salt
2 pounds white fish fillets
2 tablespoons butter or
    margarine
⅓ cup chopped onion
1 clove garlic, minced
1 small red pepper, slivered
½ cup chopped celery
3 eggs, lightly beaten
⅔ cup dry bread crumbs
½ to ¾ teaspoon TABASCO®
    pepper sauce
    Lemon slices, parsley and red
    pepper rings for garnish

Preheat oven to 350°F. In medium
skillet combine wine and salt; bring
to a boil. Add fish; cover and cook over
low heat 5 minutes or until fish flakes
easily when tested with fork. Remove
fish and liquid to large bowl; cool.

In same skillet melt butter; cook onion and garlic 5 minutes or until tender. Add red pepper slivers and celery;
cook 5 minutes longer. Add cooked
vegetables to fish and mix well,
breaking up fish into large pieces.
Add eggs, bread crumbs and Tabasco®
sauce; mix well. Press mixture into
greased 9×5×3-inch loaf pan. Bake 45
minutes or until center is firm. Cool
10 minutes. Loosen edges of loaf with
spatula; turn onto serving platter.
Garnish with lemon slices, parsley
and red pepper rings.
Makes 8 servings.

Microwave Directions: In 2-quart
microwave-safe baking dish place ¼
cup wine and fish fillets. Cover loosely
with plastic wrap; cook on High 5 to 7
minutes or until fish flakes easily
when tested with fork. Remove fish
fillets to large bowl; discard liquid. In
same baking dish place *1 tablespoon*
butter, onion, garlic, red pepper slivers and celery. Cover loosely with
plastic wrap; cook on High 5 to 8 minutes or until vegetables are tender.
Add vegetables to bowl with fish. Add
salt, eggs, bread crumbs and Tabasco®
sauce; mix well. Press mixture into
greased 9×5×3-inch microwave-safe
loaf pan. Cover loosely with plastic
wrap; cook on High 10 to 12 minutes
or until mixture is slightly firm on
top. Re-cover; let stand 10 minutes.
Loosen edges of loaf with spatula;
turn onto serving platter. Garnish
with lemon slices, parsley and red
pepper rings.

Ginger Fish Fillets

1 pound fresh or thawed fish
    fillets
½ cup KIKKOMAN Teriyaki Sauce
1 tablespoon vegetable oil
1 teaspoon sugar
1 tablespoon slivered fresh
    ginger root
1 large green onion and top, cut
    into 1-inch lengths and
    slivered
⅓ cup water
1½ teaspoons cornstarch

Place fillets in single layer in shallow
baking pan. Combine teriyaki sauce,
oil and sugar; pour over fish. Turn fillets over to coat well. Marinate 20
minutes, turning fish over occasionally. (If fillets are very thin, marinate
for only 10 minutes.) Sprinkle ginger
and green onion evenly over each fillet. Bake in marinade at 350°F. 6 to
10 minutes, or until fish flakes easily
when tested with fork. Remove to
serving platter and keep warm; reserve ¼ cup pan juices. Blend water
and cornstarch in small saucepan.
Stir in reserved pan juices. Cook and
stir until mixture boils and thickens.
To serve, spoon sauce over fish.
Makes 4 servings.

Tangy Catfish

1½ pounds catfish fillets, fresh or
    frozen*
⅔ cup lemon juice
2 teaspoons TABASCO® pepper
    sauce
⅔ cup flour
⅔ cup yellow cornmeal
1 teaspoon salt
    Vegetable oil

Thaw fish if frozen. Cut fillets crosswise into ¾-inch strips. In shallow
dish combine lemon juice and Ta-
basco® sauce; add fish. Cover; refrigerate 1 hour; turn fish occasionally. On
waxed paper combine flour, cornmeal
and salt. Coat fish with flour mixture.

In large skillet over medium-high
heat bring 1 inch oil to 350°F. Fry fillet strips, a few at a time, 3 to 5 minutes or until golden brown on all
sides. Drain on paper towels. Serve
with additional Tabasco® sauce, if desired.
Makes 6 to 8 appetizer servings.
*Haddock or halibut fillets may be
substituted.

Fabulous Fish Terrine

Skillet Fish Italiano

1 small onion, sliced
2 tablespoons margarine or butter
1 pound fish fillets, fresh or frozen, thawed
¼ cup REALEMON® Lemon Juice from Concentrate
½ teaspoon oregano leaves
2 cups sliced zucchini
1 cup sliced fresh mushrooms (about 4 ounces)
½ cup chopped tomato
½ cup (2 ounces) shredded Swiss cheese

In large skillet, cook onion in margarine until tender. Add fish fillets, ReaLemon® brand, oregano, zucchini and mushrooms; cover and simmer 10 minutes. Top with tomato and cheese; cover and simmer 2 minutes or until cheese melts. Serve immediately. Refrigerate leftovers.
Makes 4 servings.

Microwave: In 2-quart baking dish, melt margarine on full power (high) 45 seconds to 1 minute. Add onion; cover with plastic wrap and microwave on full power (high) 2 to 3 minutes or until tender. Add zucchini and mushrooms; cover and microwave on full power (high) 3 minutes or until zucchini is tender-crisp. Stir; add oregano, fish and ReaLemon® brand. Cover and microwave on full power (high) 5 to 6 minutes or until fish flakes with fork. Sprinkle with tomato and cheese. Microwave on full power (high) 1 to 1½ minutes or until cheese begins to melt. Let stand until cheese melts.

Spanish Stuffed Bell Peppers

9 medium green, red or yellow bell peppers
1½ cups chopped onions
1 tablespoon extra virgin olive oil
1 tablespoon all-purpose flour
1 can (8 ounces) tomato sauce
½ cup PET® Evaporated or PET® Light Evaporated Skimmed Milk
¼ teaspoon saffron
¼ teaspoon ground fennel
¼ teaspoon salt
¼ teaspoon black pepper
1 cup tricolor corkscrew pasta, cooked, drained
½ cup frozen peas
1 can (6½ ounces) STARKIST® Solid White or Solid Light Tuna in Springwater, drained, flaked

Remove top and seeds from peppers. Tops may be reserved for garnish, if desired. Chop 1 pepper; set 8 peppers aside. Cook and stir onions and chopped pepper in hot oil in medium skillet over low heat until vegetables are soft. Stir in flour. Cook 3 minutes, stirring constantly. Gradually stir in tomato sauce, milk and seasonings. Cook until mixture thickens and comes to a boil, stirring constantly. Remove from heat and stir in pasta, peas and tuna. Fill remaining 8 peppers with tuna mixture and arrange in baking pan. Cover with foil. Bake at 350°F 45 minutes. Garnish as desired.
Makes 8 servings.

Halibut Provençale

6 tablespoons CRISCO® Oil, divided
½ cup chopped onion
½ cup chopped green pepper
2 cloves garlic, minced
1 cup sliced fresh mushrooms
1 large tomato, peeled, seeded and chopped
3 pounds halibut fillets, cut into serving-size pieces
¾ cup dry white wine*
2 tablespoons snipped fresh parsley
2 small bay leaves

Heat 2 tablespoons Crisco® Oil in small skillet. Add onion, green pepper and garlic. Sauté over moderate heat until tender. Stir in mushrooms and tomato. Set aside.

Heat remaining 4 tablespoons Crisco® Oil in large skillet. Add fish. Fry over medium-high heat 4 minutes, turning over once. Remove from heat. Spread vegetable mixture over fish. Add wine, parsley and bay leaves. Cover. Cook over low heat, 10 to 15 minutes, or until fish flakes easily with fork. Remove and discard bay leaves.
12 servings.

*For milder flavor, substitute ½ cup water and ¼ cup dry white wine for ¾ cup dry white wine.

Dilled Salmon Loaf

¼ lb. VELVEETA Pasteurized Process Cheese Spread, cubed
¼ cup milk
1 15½-oz. can salmon, drained, skinned, boned, flaked
2 eggs, beaten
⅔ cup dry bread crumbs
½ cup finely chopped celery
½ cup chopped onion
1 tablespoon lemon juice
½ teaspoon dill weed

* * *

½ lb. VELVEETA Pasteurized Process Cheese Spread, cubed
¼ cup milk
1 2¼-oz. can sliced ripe olives, drained

In large saucepan, combine process cheese spread and milk; stir over low heat until process cheese spread is melted. Add salmon, eggs, crumbs, celery, onions, juice and dill; mix well.

Skillet Fish Italiano

Place in greased 8×4-inch loaf pan. Bake at 350°, 40 to 45 minutes or until golden brown.

Combine process cheese spread and milk in saucepan, stirring over low heat until process cheese spread is melted. Stir in olives. Serve over salmon.
6 servings.

Preparation time: 20 minutes
Baking time: 45 minutes

Microwave: Prepare and bake salmon loaf as directed. Microwave process cheese spread and milk in 2-cup microwave-safe measure on High 3 to 4 minutes or until process cheese spread is melted, stirring after 2 minutes. Stir in olives. Microwave on High 30 seconds to 1 minute or until thoroughly heated. Serve over salmon.

Lemon Broiled Fish

Emperor's Sweet & Sour Fish

1½ **pounds fresh or thawed fish**
    fillets, ½ inch thick
 1 **can (6 oz.) unsweetened**
    pineapple juice
¼ **cup KIKKOMAN Soy Sauce**
¼ **cup water**
¼ **cup sugar**
 2 **tablespoons cornstarch**
 3 **tablespoons vinegar**
 2 **tablespoons tomato catsup**
    Dash ground red pepper
    (cayenne)
¼ **cup minced green onions and**
    tops

Microwave Directions: Place fish in single layer in large microwave-safe dish; set aside. Combine pineapple juice, soy sauce, water, sugar, cornstarch, vinegar, catsup and red pepper in 2-cup microwave-safe measuring cup. Microwave on High 5 minutes, or until mixture boils and thickens, stirring occasionally to prevent lumping. Remove ¼ cup sauce and pour over fillets, turning each piece over to coat both sides. Keep remaining sauce warm. Cover fish with waxed paper; microwave on High 8 minutes, or until fish flakes easily when tested with fork, turning dish once. Remove fillets to serving platter with slotted spoon. To serve, drizzle warm sauce over fillets and sprinkle green onions over sauce. Pass remaining sauce.
Makes 4 to 6 servings.

Lemony Stuffed Flounder

 5 **tablespoons butter or**
    margarine
½ **cup water**
 2 **cups PEPPERIDGE FARM®**
    Herb Seasoned Stuffing Mix
½ **teaspoon grated lemon peel**
½ **cup chopped onion**
½ **cup shredded carrot**
 1 **pound flounder fillets**
    Paprika for garnish
    Lemon slices for garnish

To Microwave:
1. In 4-cup glass measure, combine 4 tablespoons of the butter and water. Microwave, uncovered, on HIGH 1½ minutes or until butter is melted. Stir in stuffing mix and lemon peel; set aside.
2. In 10-inch microwave-safe pie plate, combine remaining 1 tablespoon butter, onion and carrot. Cover with waxed paper; microwave on HIGH 3 minutes or until vegetables are tender, stirring once during cooking. Stir into stuffing mixture.
3. Make 4 mounds of stuffing in same pie plate. Divide fish into 4 parts and arrange over stuffing. Sprinkle with

paprika and top with lemon slices. Cover with waxed paper; microwave on HIGH 8 minutes or until fish flakes easily when tested with fork, rotating dish once during cooking. Let stand, covered, 5 minutes.
Makes 4 servings.

Lemon Broiled Fish

½ **cup margarine or butter,**
    melted
¼ **cup REALEMON® Lemon Juice**
    from Concentrate
 2 **cups fresh bread crumbs**
    (about 4 slices)
 1 **tablespoon chopped parsley**
½ **teaspoon paprika**
 1 **pound fish fillets, fresh or**
    frozen, thawed

Combine margarine and ReaLemon® brand. In medium bowl, combine bread crumbs, parsley and ¼ *cup* of the lemon mixture. Add paprika to remaining lemon mixture. Dip fish into paprika mixture; broil until fish flakes with fork. Top with bread crumb mixture. Return to broiler; heat through. Refrigerate leftovers.
Makes 4 servings.

Steamed Trout with Orange & Ginger

- ½ cup WISH-BONE® Italian or Robusto Italian Dressing
- 1 medium red onion, chopped
- ¼ cup orange juice
- 1 tablespoon finely chopped fresh ginger*
- 1 teaspoon grated orange peel (optional)
- ½ teaspoon ground cumin
- ⅛ teaspoon pepper
- 2 whole trout or fresh-water fish (about 1 pound each), boned
- 1 cup coarsely chopped green onions
- 1 cup thinly sliced carrots
- 1 cup thinly sliced yellow squash
- 1 cup thinly sliced snow peas (about 4 ounces)

In large shallow oblong baking dish, thoroughly combine Italian dressing, red onion, orange juice, ginger, orange peel, cumin and pepper. Add trout and turn to coat. Cover and marinate in refrigerator, turning occasionally, at least 3 hours. Remove trout, reserving marinade.

Preheat oven to 450°. For each serving, place 1 trout on 1 piece (18×18-inch) parchment paper or heavy-duty aluminum foil; equally top each with reserved marinade, green onions, carrots, squash and snow peas. Wrap parchment or foil loosely around trout and vegetables, sealing edges airtight with double fold. Bake 20 minutes or until trout flakes. Serve, if desired, with hot cooked wild rice.
Makes 2 servings.

   *Substitution: Use 1 teaspoon ground ginger.

Steamed Mussels in White Wine

- ⅓ cup WISH-BONE® Italian Dressing
- ½ cup chopped shallots or onions
- 3 pounds mussels, well scrubbed
- ⅔ cup dry white wine
- ½ cup chopped parsley
- ¼ cup water
    Generous dash crushed red pepper

In large saucepan or stockpot, heat Italian dressing and cook shallots over medium heat, stirring occasionally, 2 minutes or until tender. Add remaining ingredients. Bring to a boil, then simmer covered 4 minutes or until mussel shells open. (Discard any unopened shells.) Serve, if desired, with Italian or French bread.
Makes about 3 main-dish or 6 appetizer servings.

   Note: Also terrific with Wish-Bone® Robusto Italian or Blended Italian Dressing.

Steamed Mussels in White Wine

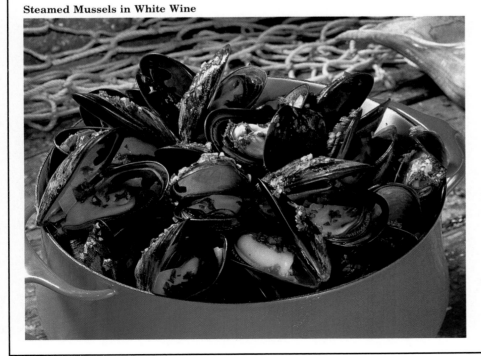

Salmon Cheese Puff Pies

- 1 (15½-ounce) can salmon, drained and flaked
- 1 cup BORDEN® or MEADOW GOLD® Cottage Cheese
- ¼ cup chopped green pepper
- ¼ cup chopped onion
- 3 tablespoons REALEMON® Lemon Juice from Concentrate
- 1 (2-ounce) jar pimientos, drained and chopped
- ¼ cup dill weed
- 1 (10-ounce) package frozen puff pastry patty shells, thawed in refrigerator overnight

Preheat oven to 450°. In large bowl, combine all ingredients except patty shells. On floured surface, roll each shell to an 8-inch circle. Place equal amounts of salmon mixture in center of each circle. Fold over; seal edges with water and press with fork. Place on ungreased baking sheet; cut slit near center of each turnover. Reduce oven temperature to 400°; bake 25 minutes or until golden brown. Refrigerate leftovers.
Makes 6 servings.

Lemon Swordfish

- 1 tablespoon grated lemon peel
- ¾ cup fresh lemon juice
- ¾ cup olive or vegetable oil
- ¼ to ½ cup parsley, chopped
- 2 tablespoons prepared horseradish
- 2 cloves garlic, minced
- 1 teaspoon dried thyme, crushed
- 1 teaspoon salt
- ¼ teaspoon pepper
- 1 bay leaf
- 1½ pounds swordfish steaks

In shallow glass dish, combine all ingredients except fish. Add swordfish; turn to coat with marinade. Cover and refrigerate at least 2 hours, turning fish occasionally. Drain fish; reserve marinade. Grill swordfish, on uncovered grill, over medium-hot **KINGSFORD® Charcoal Briquets** about 7 minutes, basting lightly with marinade. Carefully turn swordfish and grill 5 to 6 minutes longer or until fish flakes easily when tested with fork, basting lightly with marinade.
Makes 4 servings.

Greek-Style Shrimp

Cajun Fish

 1 cup butter or margarine
 2 tablespoons paprika
 2 teaspoons popcorn butter salt
 2 teaspoons onion powder
 2 teaspoons garlic powder
 2 teaspoons cayenne pepper
 1½ teaspoons white pepper
 1½ teaspoons black pepper
 1 teaspoon dried thyme,
   crushed
 1 teaspoon dried oregano,
   crushed
 2 pounds red snapper fillets

Heat iron skillet on grill directly over medium-hot **MATCH LIGHT® Charcoal Briquets** at least 15 minutes. Meanwhile, in small saucepan, melt butter. In small bowl, combine remaining ingredients except fish. Brush fillets with butter; sprinkle seasoning mix evenly on both sides of fillets. Place fillets in hot skillet and ladle melted butter over fillets.* Cook about 2 minutes on each side. Serve immediately with additional melted butter for dipping.
Makes 4 servings.
  Note: This method of grilling produces heavy smoke.

Tuna Loaf

 1 can (6½ ounces) STARKIST®
   Solid White Tuna in
   Springwater, drained
 2 eggs, lightly beaten
 1 cup PET® Evaporated or PET®
   Light Evaporated Skimmed
   Milk
 ½ cup whole wheat bread
   crumbs
 2 tablespoons finely chopped
   green bell pepper
 1 tablespoon finely chopped
   onion
 2 tablespoons lemon juice
 ½ teaspoon salt
 ⅛ teaspoon white pepper
 ¼ teaspoon Worcestershire
   sauce

Combine all ingredients in medium bowl. Transfer to 8½×4½-inch glass loaf pan. Bake at 350°F 30 to 40 minutes or until firm. May be served hot or cold or used as spread for sandwiches or crackers. Garnish as desired.
Makes 4 servings.
  Note: Recipe may be doubled. Bake in 8×8-inch baking dish.

Greek-Style Shrimp

 2 tablespoons olive oil
 1 cup sliced green onions
 4 large cloves garlic, minced
 1 pound large shrimp, shelled
   and deveined
 ¾ cup V8® Vegetable Juice *or* No
   Salt Added V8® Vegetable
   Juice
 ⅓ cup crumbled feta cheese
   (2 ounces)
 2 tablespoons chopped fresh
   parsley
   Dash pepper
 8 slices PEPPERIDGE FARM®
   Fully Baked French-Style
   Bread

In 10-inch skillet over medium heat, in hot oil, cook onions and garlic until onions are tender. Add shrimp; cook until shrimp are pink and opaque, stirring constantly. Stir in V8 juice. Heat to boiling. Reduce heat to low; simmer 2 minutes. Sprinkle with cheese, parsley and pepper. Serve with bread.
Makes 4 servings.
  Note: If desired, use oven-safe skillet. After sprinkling with cheese, broil 3 minutes or until cheese is lightly browned.

Per serving: 420 calories, 28 g protein, 14 g fat, 45 g carbohydrate, 858 mg sodium (No Salt Added V8® Juice: 714 mg sodium), 155 mg cholesterol.

Seafood Cacciatore

- 1 pound shrimp, cleaned
- 1 small onion, chopped
- 2 garlic cloves, minced
- 2 tablespoons oil
- 1 can (14½ oz.) whole tomatoes in juice
- 1 can (8 oz.) tomato sauce
- 1½ cups water
- 1 medium green pepper, cut into thin strips
- ¾ teaspoon dried basil leaves
- ½ teaspoon dried oregano leaves
- ½ teaspoon salt
- ⅛ teaspoon ground red pepper
- 1 chicken bouillon cube
- 1½ cups MINUTE® Rice
- 8 clams, well scrubbed

Cook and stir shrimp with onion and garlic in hot oil in large skillet until shrimp turn pink. Stir in tomatoes with juice, tomato sauce, water, green pepper, seasonings and bouillon cube. Bring to a full boil, breaking up tomatoes with spoon. Stir in rice. Cover; remove from heat. Let stand 5 minutes.

Meanwhile, place clams on rack in pan with water below rack. Bring to a boil. Cover and steam 5 to 10 minutes or until clams open. Discard any unopened clams. Fluff rice mixture with fork and serve topped with clams.
Makes 4 servings.

Microwave Directions: Combine shrimp, onion, garlic and oil in micro-wavable dish. Cover and cook at HIGH 4 minutes. Stir in remaining ingredients, except clams. Break up tomatoes with spoon. Cover and cook at HIGH 7 to 8 minutes longer. Let stand 5 minutes.

Meanwhile, arrange clams in micro-wavable dish. Cover and cook at HIGH 5 to 7 minutes or until shells are open and meat is firm. Discard any unopened clams. Fluff rice mixture with fork and serve topped with clams.
Makes 4 servings.

Shrimp Oriental

- 8 ounces fresh mushrooms, sliced (about 2 cups)
- 1 cup sliced celery
- ½ cup finely chopped onion
- ¼ cup margarine or butter
- ⅓ cup REALEMON® Lemon Juice from Concentrate
- ¼ cup water
- 2 tablespoons brown sugar
- 1 tablespoon soy sauce
- ¼ teaspoon ground ginger
- 2 teaspoons cornstarch
- 12 ounces small raw shrimp, peeled and deveined
- 1 (6-ounce) package frozen pea pods, thawed, or 4 ounces fresh pea pods
- Hot cooked rice

Grilled Lobster with Spicy Sauce

- 4 whole, live lobsters* (1 to 1½ pounds each)
- ¼ cup dry sherry
- 3 tablespoons soy sauce
- 2 to 3 tablespoons sugar
- 2 teaspoons grated fresh ginger *or* ½ teaspoon ground ginger
- 1 teaspoon red pepper flakes
- 2 cloves garlic, minced
- Butter or margarine, melted

Bring large kettle of water to boil. Plunge lobsters into water. Return water to boil; cover and simmer 3 minutes or just until lobsters turn pink. Remove lobsters; rinse under cold running water and drain. Turn lobsters, underside up, and cut through inner shell of tails to expose meat.

For spicy sauce, in small bowl, combine remaining ingredients except butter. Brush lobster shells and meaty underside with sauce, letting sauce soak into meat. Grill lobsters, meat-side up, on covered grill, over medium-hot **KINGSFORD® with Mesquite Charcoal Briquets** 13 to 15 minutes or until meat turns opaque, basting often with sauce. When lobsters are cooked, make a deep cut lengthwise in center of underside with sharp knife. Spread halves enough to remove stomach (near head) and black vein. Crack claw shells with hammer. Serve with melted butter and additional spicy sauce.
Makes 4 servings.

*2 pounds jumbo fresh shrimp can be substituted for lobster. Leave shell on and thread on skewers. Grill as above, reducing cooking time to 5 minutes or until shrimp turn pink.

Shrimp Oriental

Festival Shrimp

1 DOLE™ Fresh Pineapple
1 large DOLE™ Tomato, cut into quarters
1 medium onion, cut into quarters
1 jar (4 ounces) pimentos
¼ cup canned diced green chilies
2 tablespoons lime juice
1½ teaspoons ground coriander
1 teaspoon garlic salt
1 teaspoon sugar
¼ cup butter or margarine
1 pound medium shrimp, cooked and shelled*
1 tablespoon chopped fresh cilantro or parsley
Hot cooked rice

Twist crown from pineapple. Cut pineapple lengthwise into quarters. Remove fruit from shell with curved knife. Trim off core and cut fruit into chunks. Set aside.

In food processor or blender, combine tomato, onion, pimentos, green chilies, lime juice, coriander, garlic salt and sugar. Process until pureed.

In large skillet, melt butter. Add pureed sauce and simmer 5 minutes. Stir in shrimp, pineapple and cilantro. Cook just until heated through. Serve immediately over hot rice.
Makes 4 servings.

*Cook shrimp in simmering water 2 to 3 minutes or until pink and firm. Drain; set aside until cool enough to handle. Remove shells; cut along curve of body with sharp knife to remove back vein.

Beer-Batter Shrimp

½ cup beer
⅓ cup all-purpose flour
⅓ cup cornstarch
1 egg
2 tablespoons CRISCO® Oil
⅛ teaspoon cayenne
⅛ teaspoon garlic powder
CRISCO® Oil for frying
1 pound fresh medium shrimp, peeled, deveined and butterflied

Combine beer, flour, cornstarch, egg, 2 tablespoons Crisco® Oil, cayenne and garlic powder in medium mixing bowl. Mix well. Cover and refrigerate at least 1 hour.

Festival Shrimp

Heat 2 to 3 inches Crisco® Oil in deep-fryer or large saucepan to 375°F. Dip shrimp in batter. Fry a few shrimp at a time, 1 to 1½ minutes, or until golden brown. Drain on paper towels. Serve immediately or keep warm in 175°F oven.
4 to 6 servings.

Seafood Kabobs

2 dozen large sea scallops
1 dozen medium shrimp, shelled and deveined
1 can (8½ ounces) whole small artichoke hearts, drained
2 red or yellow peppers, cut into 2-inch pieces
¼ cup olive or vegetable oil
¼ cup lime juice

In large bowl, combine all ingredients and toss gently. Thread scallops, shrimp, artichoke hearts and peppers alternately on skewers; reserve marinade. Lightly oil grid. Grill kabobs, on uncovered grill, over low **KINGS-FORD® Charcoal Briquets** 6 to 8 minutes or until scallops turn opaque and shrimp turn pink. Turn kabobs carefully at least twice during grilling and brush with marinade.
Makes 6 servings.

Deep-Fried Clams

2 cups oyster crackers, finely crushed
½ teaspoon poultry seasoning
¼ teaspoon salt
¼ teaspoon cayenne
¼ teaspoon garlic powder
¼ teaspoon ground marjoram
2 eggs
1 can (10 ounces) whole baby clams, drained
CRISCO® Oil for frying

Mix cracker crumbs, poultry seasoning, salt, cayenne, garlic powder and marjoram in large plastic food storage bag. Set aside. Beat eggs slightly in small mixing bowl. Gently stir in clams. Remove a few clams with slotted spoon and add to cracker mixture. Shake to coat. Remove clams from cracker mixture; set aside. Repeat with remaining clams.

Heat 2 to 3 inches Crisco® Oil in deep-fryer or large saucepan to 375°F. Fry a few clams at a time, about 30 seconds, or until golden brown. Drain on paper towels. Serve immediately.
2 to 4 servings.

Barbecued Shrimp on a Skewer

- 1 envelope LIPTON® Onion or Onion-Mushroom Recipe Soup Mix
- 1 can (14½ ounces) whole peeled tomatoes, undrained and chopped
- ½ cup vegetable or olive oil
- ¼ cup dry white wine or vermouth
- ¼ cup chopped fresh basil leaves*
- 1 tablespoon lemon juice
- 1 teaspoon cracked peppercorns
- 2 pounds uncooked large shrimp, cleaned
- 4 thin slices cooked ham, cut into strips
- 1 tablespoon finely chopped parsley

In large bowl, combine onion recipe soup mix, tomatoes, oil, wine, basil, lemon juice and peppercorns. Add shrimp. Cover and marinate in refrigerator, stirring occasionally, at least 2 hours. Remove shrimp, reserving marinade.

On skewers, alternately thread shrimp with ham strips, weaving ham around shrimp. Grill or broil, turning and basting frequently with reserved marinade, until shrimp are done. Bring remaining marinade to a boil, then simmer 2 minutes; stir in parsley. Serve as a dipping sauce or, if desired, arrange skewers over hot cooked rice and top with sauce.
Makes about 6 servings.
   ***Substitution:** Use 1½ teaspoons dried basil leaves.

Tangy Cocktail Sauce

- ¾ cup BENNETT'S® Chili Sauce *or* catsup
- 3 tablespoons REALEMON® Lemon Juice from Concentrate
- ½ teaspoon prepared horseradish
- ½ teaspoon Worcestershire sauce

In small bowl, combine ingredients. Chill to blend flavors.
Makes about 1 cup.

Shrimp Creole

- ½ cup WISH-BONE® Italian Dressing
- 1 medium green pepper, cut into chunks
- 1 medium onion, sliced
- 1 can (14½ ounces) whole peeled tomatoes, undrained and chopped
- 1 pound uncooked medium shrimp, cleaned
- ⅛ teaspoon crushed red pepper
- 2 cups hot cooked rice

In medium skillet, heat Italian dressing and cook green pepper and onion over medium heat, stirring occasionally, 5 minutes or until tender. Stir in tomatoes and simmer covered 15 minutes. Add shrimp and red pepper and simmer covered an additional 5 minutes or until shrimp turn pink. To serve, arrange shrimp mixture over hot rice.
Makes about 4 servings.
   Note: Also terrific with Wish-Bone® Robusto Italian, Lite Italian, Italian & Cheese or Herbal Italian Dressing.

Shrimp Creole

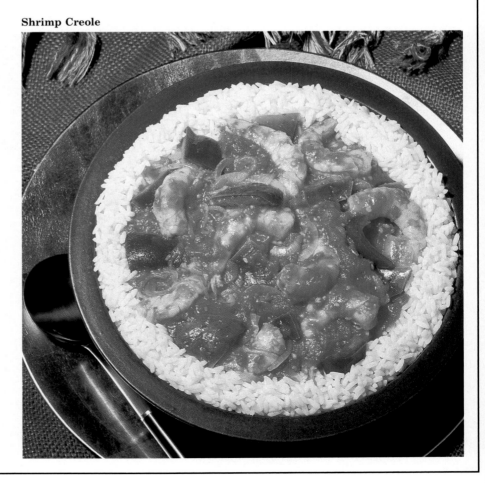

Scallops with Golden Cream Sauce

- 2 tablespoons butter or margarine
- 1 medium red pepper, cut into thin strips
- 1 cup uncooked regular rice
- 1 envelope LIPTON® Golden Onion Recipe Soup Mix
- 2¼ cups water
- 1 tablespoon lime juice
- ¼ cup light cream or half and half
- 1 pound bay scallops
- 2 medium green onions, sliced

In medium skillet, melt butter and cook red pepper over medium heat until crisp-tender. Stir in uncooked rice, then golden onion recipe soup mix thoroughly blended with water and lime juice. Bring to a boil, then simmer covered 30 minutes or until rice is tender. Stir in remaining ingredients and cook covered 5 minutes or until scallops are tender. Serve, if desired, with freshly ground pepper.
Makes about 4 servings.

Shrimp Etouffée

½ cup butter or margarine
2 medium onions, chopped
1 cup chopped celery
1 cup chopped green onions
2 cloves garlic, minced
½ cup flour
4 cups water
2 cans (16 ounces each) tomatoes, drained
2 tablespoons lemon juice
1 teaspoon salt
2 bay leaves
¼ teaspoon dried thyme leaves
2 pounds shrimp, peeled, deveined
½ teaspoon TABASCO® pepper sauce
Hot cooked rice

In large saucepot or Dutch oven melt butter; add onions, celery, green onions and garlic. Cook 5 minutes or until tender. Add flour; stir until well blended. Stir in water, tomatoes, lemon juice, salt, bay leaves and thyme. Bring to a boil, reduce heat and simmer covered 30 minutes; stir occasionally. Add shrimp and Tabasco® sauce. Simmer 5 minutes longer or until shrimp turn pink. Remove bay leaves. Serve over rice.
Makes 8 servings.

Saucy Shrimp over Chinese Noodle Cakes

Crab and Rice Primavera

1½ cups BIRDS EYE® FARM FRESH Broccoli, Green Beans, Pearl Onions and Red Peppers
¼ cup water
1⅓ cups milk
1 pound imitation crabmeat or crabmeat
2 tablespoons butter or margarine
1 teaspoon garlic salt
¾ teaspoon dried basil leaves
1½ cups MINUTE® Rice
½ cup grated Parmesan cheese

Bring vegetables and water to a boil in medium saucepan, stirring occasionally. Reduce heat; cover and simmer 3 minutes.

Add milk, imitation crabmeat, butter, garlic salt and basil. Bring to a full boil. Stir in rice and cheese. Cover; remove from heat. Let stand 5 minutes. Fluff with fork.
Makes 4 servings.

Saucy Shrimp over Chinese Noodle Cakes

Chinese Noodle Cakes (recipe follows)
1¼ cups water
2 tablespoons cornstarch, divided
4 tablespoons KIKKOMAN Soy Sauce, divided
1 teaspoon tomato catsup
½ pound medium-size raw shrimp, peeled and deveined
2 tablespoons vegetable oil, divided
1 clove garlic, minced
½ teaspoon minced fresh ginger root
1 green pepper, chunked
1 medium onion, chunked
2 stalks celery, cut diagonally into thin slices
2 tomatoes, chunked

Prepare Chinese Noodle Cakes. Combine water, 1 tablespoon cornstarch and 3 tablespoons soy sauce with catsup; set aside. Blend remaining 1 tablespoon cornstarch and 1 tablespoon soy sauce in small bowl; stir in shrimp until coated. Heat 1 tablespoon oil in hot wok or large skillet over high heat. Add shrimp and stir-fry 1 minute; remove. Heat remaining 1 tablespoon oil in same pan. Add garlic and ginger; stir-fry until fragrant. Add green pepper, onion and celery; stir-fry 4 minutes. Stir in soy sauce mixture, shrimp and tomatoes. Cook and stir until sauce boils and thickens. Cut Chinese Noodle Cakes into squares and serve with shrimp mixture.
Makes 4 servings.

CHINESE NOODLE CAKES: Cook *8 ounces capellini* (angel hair pasta) according to package directions. Drain; rinse under cold water and drain thoroughly. Heat *1 tablespoon vegetable oil* in large, nonstick skillet over medium-high heat. Add half the capellini; slightly spread to fill bottom of skillet to form noodle cake. Without stirring, cook 5 minutes, or until golden on bottom. Lift cake with wide spatula; add *1 tablespoon oil* to skillet and turn cake over. Cook 5 minutes longer, or until golden brown, shaking skillet occasionally to brown evenly; remove to rack and keep warm in 200°F. oven. Repeat with remaining capellini.

Lemon-Dill Lobster Tails

¾ cup MARIE'S® Refrigerated Sour Cream and Dill Salad Dressing
1 teaspoon grated lemon peel
1 clove garlic, minced
⅛ teaspoon pepper
4 frozen lobster tails (6 ounces each), thawed

1. To make sauce: In small bowl, combine salad dressing, peel, garlic and pepper.
2. With kitchen shears, cut membrane from underside of tails; discard. With sharp knife, loosen meat from shell, leaving meat and shell intact. To prevent tail from curling, bend backwards, breaking at joints.
3. Brush grill rack with oil. On grill rack, place lobster tails, shell side down, directly above medium coals. Grill, uncovered, 18 minutes or until opaque, turning twice and brushing tops with sauce.
4. To serve: With fork, loosen meat from shell, starting at end and pulling forward. Serve with any remaining sauce.
Makes 4 servings.

Paella Olé

½ pound shrimp, cleaned
2 garlic cloves, crushed
2 tablespoons butter or
   margarine
1¼ cups chicken broth
1 tablespoon cornstarch
1 can (14½ oz.) stewed
   tomatoes
½ cup sliced pepperoni
1 package (10 oz.) BIRDS EYE®
   CLASSICS, Peas and Pearl
   Onions, thawed
¼ teaspoon ground red pepper
1½ cups MINUTE® Rice
⅛ teaspoon saffron (optional)

Cook and stir shrimp and garlic in hot
butter in large skillet until shrimp
turn pink. Mix broth and cornstarch
in small bowl; stir into shrimp. Add
tomatoes, pepperoni, vegetables and
red pepper. Cook and stir until mixture thickens and comes to a full boil.
Stir in rice and saffron. Cover; remove
from heat. Let stand 5 minutes. Fluff
with fork.
Makes 4 servings.
Microwave Directions: Reduce butter to 1 tablespoon. Cook garlic and
butter in 2½-quart microwavable dish
at HIGH 1 minute. Mix broth and
cornstarch in small bowl; stir into
garlic mixture. Add remaining ingredients. Cover and cook at HIGH 3
minutes. Stir; cover and cook at HIGH
3 minutes longer. Stir again; cover
and cook at HIGH 2 to 4 minutes
longer or until thickened. Fluff with
fork.
Makes 4 servings.

Shrimp Scampi Italiano

⅓ cup WISH-BONE® Italian or
   Robusto Italian Dressing
1 pound uncooked medium
   shrimp, cleaned

In large shallow nonaluminum
broiler-proof pan, pour Italian dressing over shrimp. Cover and marinate
in refrigerator, turning occasionally,
at least 2 hours. Broil shrimp with
dressing, turning and basting frequently, until pink. Garnish, if desired, with chopped parsley. Serve, if
desired, with hot cooked rice.
Makes about 4 servings.

Stir-Fried Scallops & Vegetables

1 pound scallops
¼ cup REALEMON® Lemon Juice
   from Concentrate
1 cup thinly sliced carrots
3 cloves garlic, finely chopped
⅓ cup margarine or butter
2 cups sliced fresh mushrooms
   (about 8 ounces)
¾ teaspoon thyme leaves
2 teaspoons cornstarch
½ teaspoon salt
¼ cup diagonally sliced green
   onions
1 (6-ounce) package frozen pea
   pods, thawed, or 4 ounces
   fresh pea pods
2 tablespoons dry sherry
   Hot cooked rice

In shallow baking dish, marinate
scallops in ReaLemon® brand 30 minutes, stirring occasionally. In large
skillet, over high heat, cook and stir
carrots and garlic in margarine until
tender-crisp, about 3 minutes. Add
mushrooms and thyme; cook and stir
about 5 minutes. Stir cornstarch and
salt into scallops mixture; add to vegetables. Cook and stir until scallops
are opaque, about 4 minutes. Stir in
onions, pea pods and sherry. Remove
from heat. Serve immediately with
hot cooked rice. Refrigerate leftovers.
Makes 4 servings.

Stir-Fried Scallops & Vegetables

Bacon-Wrapped Shrimp

1 pound fresh or frozen shrimp,
   shelled and deveined
1 small onion, finely chopped
½ cup olive or vegetable oil
½ teaspoon sugar
½ teaspoon cayenne pepper
¼ teaspoon salt
¼ teaspoon dried oregano,
   crushed
½ teaspoon garlic powder
½ pound bacon
   Mexican Fried Rice (recipe
   follows)

Thaw shrimp, if frozen. Place shrimp
in plastic bag; set in bowl. For marinade, in small bowl, combine onion,
oil, sugar, cayenne pepper, salt, oregano and garlic powder. Pour marinade
over shrimp; close bag. Marinate
shrimp 3 hours in refrigerator, turning occasionally.
  Cut bacon slices into halves lengthwise, then crosswise. In large skillet,
partially cook bacon. Drain on paper
toweling. Drain shrimp; reserve marinade. Wrap bacon strips around
shrimp and secure with wooden picks.
Place shrimp in wire grill basket or
on 12×9-inch piece of heavy-duty foil.
(If using foil, puncture foil in several
places.)
  Grill shrimp, on uncovered grill,
over medium-hot **KINGSFORD®
Charcoal Briquets** 6 minutes or until bacon and shrimp are done, turning basket or individual shrimp once
and basting with marinade. Serve
with Mexican Fried Rice.
Makes 6 servings.

Mexican Fried Rice

3 tablespoons vegetable oil
1 cup long grain rice
2 cups water
1 cup chili salsa
½ cup chopped green pepper
1 small onion, chopped
1 clove garlic, minced

In 12-inch skillet, heat oil. Add rice;
cook until golden brown, stirring often. Stir in remaining ingredients.
Bring mixture to boil; reduce heat.
Cover; simmer 15 to 20 minutes or until rice is tender. Season to taste;
serve with additional salsa, if desired.
Makes 6 servings.

Shanghai Shrimp

- **4 scallions, cut in 1-inch pieces**
- **1 teaspoon minced ginger**
- **2 tablespoons peanut oil**
- **1 pound large shrimp, shelled and deveined**
- **1 cup COLLEGE INN® Chicken Broth**
- **1 tablespoon cornstarch**
- **1 (11-ounce) can mandarin oranges, undrained**
- **1 (8-ounce) can CHUN KING® Sliced Water Chestnuts, undrained**
- **Hot cooked rice**

In large skillet, over medium-high heat, cook scallions and ginger in oil for 2 to 3 minutes. Add shrimp; cook for 3 to 4 minutes. Blend chicken broth into cornstarch; stir into skillet with oranges and water chestnuts. Reduce heat; simmer, covered, until slightly thickened and heated through. Serve over rice. Garnish as desired.
Makes 6 servings.

Shanghai Chicken: Substitute 1 pound boneless chicken, cut in 2-inch strips, for shrimp.

Savory Seafood Stew

- **²/₃ cup WISH-BONE® Italian Dressing**
- **¹/₂ cup dry white wine**
- **¹/₄ cup sliced onion**
- **6 clams, well scrubbed**
- **1 lobster, cut into 2-inch pieces (about 1 pound)**
- **¹/₂ pound fish fillets, cut into large pieces**
- **¹/₄ pound scallops**
- **¹/₄ pound uncooked medium shrimp, cleaned**

In large saucepan, combine Italian dressing, wine, onion and clams. Bring to a boil, then simmer covered, stirring occasionally, 5 minutes. Add remaining ingredients, then simmer covered, stirring occasionally, 5 minutes or until seafood is done. (Discard any unopened clam shells.) Serve, if desired, with hot cooked rice or crusty French bread.
Makes about 4 servings.

Note: Also terrific with Wish-Bone® Robusto Italian, Blended Italian, Herbal Italian, Italian & Cheese or Lite Italian Dressing.

Shanghai Shrimp

Shrimp & Vegetable Stir-Fry

- **2 tablespoons cornstarch, divided**
- **4 tablespoons KIKKOMAN Teriyaki Sauce, divided**
- **1 tablespoon minced fresh ginger root**
- **¹/₂ pound medium-size raw shrimp, peeled and deveined**
- **³/₄ cup water**
- **2 tablespoons vegetable oil, divided**
- **2 stalks celery, cut diagonally into ¹/₄-inch-thick slices**
- **1 medium-size red bell pepper, cut into 1-inch squares**
- **¹/₄ pound green onions and tops, cut into 1-inch lengths, separating whites from tops**

Combine 1 tablespoon *each* cornstarch and teriyaki sauce with ginger in small bowl; add shrimp and stir to coat evenly. Let stand 15 minutes. Meanwhile, combine water, remaining 1 tablespoon cornstarch and 3 tablespoons teriyaki sauce; set aside. Heat 1 tablespoon oil in hot wok or large skillet over high heat. Add shrimp and stir-fry 1 minute; remove. Heat remaining 1 tablespoon oil in same pan. Add celery, red pepper and white parts of green onions; stir-fry 2 minutes. Stir in shrimp, teriyaki sauce mixture and green onion tops. Cook and stir until mixture boils and thickens. Serve over rice, if desired.
Makes 4 servings.

MAIN-DISH CASSEROLES

Easy-to-serve casseroles are a mainstay for the busy cook—for a complete meal, just add a crisp green salad. Serve enchiladas or a hearty chicken pot pie for welcome family fare, and work magic with leftovers and pantry-shelf ingredients. For entertaining a group, grace the buffet table with a gourmet cassoulet—a perfect melding of flavors and textures in one dish.

Smoked Sausage Noodle Bake

- 1 pound ECKRICH® Smoked Sausage
- 8 ounces uncooked medium egg noodles
- 2 tablespoons butter or margarine
- ½ cup chopped onion
- ½ cup chopped celery
- 1 can (17 ounces) cream-style corn
- ½ cup sour cream
- ½ teaspoon salt
  Dash ground black pepper

Preheat oven to 350°F. Cook noodles according to package directions. Melt butter in small saucepan over medium-high heat. Saute onion and celery until crisp-tender. Combine noodles, onion, celery, corn, sour cream, salt and pepper in large bowl. Pour into buttered shallow 2-quart baking dish. Cut sausage into serving-size pieces. Arrange on top of noodles and push down partially into noodles. Bake 40 minutes or until hot.
Makes 4 to 6 servings.

Meat 'n' Tater Pie

- 2 cups KELLOGG'S CORN FLAKES® cereal, crushed to make 1 cup, divided
- ½ teaspoon salt
- ¼ teaspoon pepper
- 1 tablespoon prepared mustard
- ⅓ cup milk
- 1 pound ground beef
- 2 eggs
- 2 cups stiff mashed potatoes
- ¼ cup chopped onion
- 2 teaspoons parsley flakes
- 2 tablespoons butter or margarine, melted
- ½ cup shredded American cheese
  Paprika

Combine ½ cup of the crushed cereal, the salt, pepper, mustard and milk in large bowl; beat well. Add ground beef, mixing until combined. Gently press meat mixture in bottom and up side of 9-inch pie pan. Beat eggs lightly in small bowl. Add potatoes, onion and parsley. Stir until combined. Spread potato mixture evenly in meat shell. Place pie pan on baking sheet. Bake at 350°F 35 minutes. Meanwhile, combine remaining ½ cup crushed cereal with melted butter in small bowl; set aside. Sprinkle cheese evenly over potato mixture. Top with cereal mixture. Bake 10 minutes more or until cheese melts. Sprinkle with paprika.
Makes 6 servings.

Ham and Cheese Strata

- 12 white bread slices
- 1½ cups (6 ounces) shredded 100% Natural KRAFT Mild Cheddar Cheese
- 1 10-ounce package frozen chopped broccoli, thawed, well-drained
- 1 cup chopped ham
- 1 8-ounce package PHILADELPHIA BRAND Cream Cheese, softened
- 3 eggs
- 1 cup milk
- ½ teaspoon dry mustard

Place six bread slices on bottom of 12×8-inch baking dish. Cover with 1 cup cheddar cheese, broccoli, ham and remaining bread slices, cut in half diagonally. Beat cream cheese until light and fluffy. Add eggs, one at a time, mixing well after each addition. Blend in milk and mustard; pour over bread. Top with remaining cheddar cheese. Bake at 350°, 45 to 50 minutes or until set. Let stand 10 minutes before serving.
6 servings.

Ham and Cheese Strata

Cheesy Pork Chops 'n Potatoes

- **1 jar (8 ounces) pasteurized processed cheese spread**
- **1 tablespoon vegetable oil**
- **6 thin pork chops, ¼ to ½ inch thick**
- **DURKEE Seasoned Salt**
- **½ cup milk**
- **4 cups frozen cottage fries**
- **1 can (2.8 ounces) DURKEE French Fried Onions**
- **1 package (10 ounces) frozen broccoli spears,* thawed and drained**

Preheat oven to 350°. Spoon cheese spread into 8×12-inch baking dish; place in oven just until cheese melts, 5 minutes. Meanwhile, in large skillet, heat oil. Brown pork chops on both sides; drain. Sprinkle chops with seasoned salt; set aside. Using fork, stir milk into melted cheese until well blended. Stir cottage fries and ½ can French Fried Onions into cheese mixture. Divide broccoli spears into 6 small bunches. Arrange bunches of spears over potato mixture with flowerets around edges of dish. Arrange chops over broccoli *stalks*. Bake, covered, at 350° for 35 to 40 minutes or until pork chops are done. Top chops with remaining onions; bake, uncovered, 5 minutes or until onions are golden brown.
Makes 4 to 6 servings.

Microwave Directions: Omit oil. Reduce milk to ¼ cup. In 8×12-inch microwave-safe dish, place cheese spread and milk. Cook, covered, on HIGH 3 minutes; stir to blend. Stir in cottage fries and ½ *can* onions. Cook, covered, 5 minutes; stir. Top with broccoli spears as above. Arrange *unbrowned* pork chops over broccoli *stalks* with meatiest parts toward edges of dish. Cook, covered, on MEDIUM (50-60%) 24 to 30 minutes or until pork chops are done. Turn chops over, sprinkle with seasoned salt and rotate dish halfway through cooking time. Top with remaining onions; cook, uncovered, on HIGH 1 minute. Let stand 5 minutes.

*1 small head fresh broccoli (about ½ pound) may be substituted for frozen spears. Divide into spears and cook 3 to 4 minutes before using.

Tortilla Lasagna

- **1 tablespoon vegetable oil**
- **1 large onion, chopped**
- **1 medium green pepper, chopped**
- **1 large clove garlic, minced**
- **1 pound ground beef**
- **1 teaspoon dried oregano leaves**
- **1 can (16 ounces) tomatoes, drained, chopped**
- **1 can (8 ounces) tomato sauce**
- **1 cup sour cream**
- **¾ teaspoon TABASCO® pepper sauce**
- **10 corn tortillas, 5 inches in diameter**
- **1 can (16 ounces) pinto beans, drained**
- **2 cups (8 ounces) shredded Cheddar cheese**

Preheat oven to 350°F. In large skillet heat oil; cook onion, green pepper and garlic 3 minutes or until tender. Add ground beef and oregano, breaking up meat with fork as it cooks; cook until browned. Drain off fat; remove from heat.

In medium bowl combine tomatoes, tomato sauce, sour cream and Tabasco® sauce; mix well. Cut each tortilla in half. Arrange 10 halves in shallow 11×7-inch baking dish. Spread half the meat mixture over tortillas. Top with half the pinto beans, half the tomato mixture and 1 cup shredded cheese. Repeat with remaining ingredients. Bake 30 minutes or until heated through. Let stand 10 minutes before serving.
Makes 4 servings.

Country French Cassoulet

- **¼ cup WISH-BONE® Italian Dressing**
- **2 medium onions, chopped**
- **2 medium carrots, chopped**
- **1 pound kielbasa (Polish sausage), sliced diagonally**
- **¼ cup dry white wine**
- **1 cup chicken broth**
- **1 can (8 ounces) tomato puree**
- **1 teaspoon thyme leaves**
- **2 cups cut-up cooked pork or lamb (about 12 ounces)**
- **1 can (16 ounces) cannellini beans, rinsed and drained**
- **½ cup fresh bread crumbs**
- **2 tablespoons butter or margarine, melted**
- **2 tablespoons finely chopped parsley**

Preheat oven to 350°.

In large skillet, heat Italian dressing and cook onions, carrots and kielbasa over medium heat, stirring occasionally, 10 minutes or until vegetables are tender and kielbasa is lightly browned. Stir in wine, then broth, tomato puree, thyme and pork.

In lightly greased deep 2-quart casserole, layer ½ of the tomato mixture, then ½ of the beans; repeat. Top with bread crumbs combined with butter and parsley. Bake 40 minutes or until heated through.
Makes about 8 servings.

Note: Also terrific with Wish-Bone® Robusto Italian, Blended Italian, Lite Italian, Classic Dijon Vinaigrette or Lite Classic Dijon Vinaigrette Dressing.

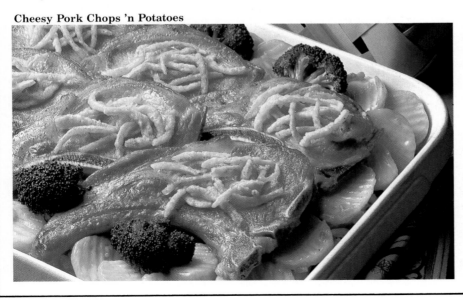
Cheesy Pork Chops 'n Potatoes

American-Style Cassoulet

4½ quarts water, divided
1 package (1 pound) dry green peas, rinsed
2 large onions, cut into wedges
1 bay leaf
2 pounds boneless lamb, cut into 1½-inch cubes
2 pounds boneless pork loin, partially frozen and cut into ½-inch slices
1 pound garlic-flavored sausage links
½ cup FILIPPO BERIO Olive Oil, divided
1 cup coarsely chopped carrots
1 cup chopped onion
1 large clove garlic, minced
1½ cups dry white wine
1 can (14½ ounces) tomatoes
¼ cup tomato paste
⅓ cup chopped parsley
½ teaspoon dried thyme, crushed
Salt
Pepper
½ cup coarse fresh bread crumbs

Place 2 quarts of the water, the peas, onion wedges and bay leaf in large, deep saucepan. Bring to a boil over high heat; boil 2 minutes. Remove from heat. Cover and let soak 1 hour. Drain peas; discard water. Place peas and 2 quarts of the water in same saucepan. Bring to a boil over high heat. Reduce heat to low. Cover and simmer 1 hour or until peas are tender, stirring occasionally. Drain, reserving liquid. Discard bay leaf. Set peas aside; keep warm.

Brown meats, in batches, in ¼ cup of the oil in Dutch oven over medium-high heat. Return meats to Dutch oven; add carrots, chopped onion and garlic. Cook and stir several minutes. Add remaining 2 cups water, the wine, tomatoes, tomato paste, parsley and thyme. Bring to a boil. Reduce heat to low. Cover and simmer 30 minutes, stirring occasionally. Season to taste with salt and pepper. Alternately layer peas and meat mixture in large, deep casserole. Pour 1 cup of the reserved liquid over top. Sprinkle with bread crumbs and drizzle with remaining ¼ cup oil. Bake at 375°F 1 hour. Add additional reserved liquid if casserole becomes dry.
Makes 8 to 10 servings.

Chili Beef and Corn Casserole

Chili Beef and Corn Casserole

1 (13¾-fluid ounce) can COLLEGE INN® Beef Broth
1 (6-ounce) can tomato paste
1 (1¼-ounce) package ORTEGA® Taco Seasoning Mix
¾ cup uncooked rice
1 pound ground beef
1 cup chopped onion
1 (17-ounce) can whole kernel sweet corn, drained
Corn chips, optional
Diced fresh tomato, optional

In small bowl, blend 1 cup beef broth, tomato paste and taco seasoning mix; set aside. In saucepan, over high heat, combine remaining broth and enough water to equal 1¾ cups liquid; heat to a boil. Add rice and cook according to package directions.

In large skillet, over medium-high heat, brown beef and cook onion until done; pour off fat. In 2-quart casserole, layer ⅓ each of the rice, corn, meat mixture and reserved sauce; repeat layers twice, combining the last portion of meat and sauce for the top layer. Cover; bake at 375°F for 40 to 45 minutes or until hot. Garnish with corn chips and diced tomato, if desired.
Makes 4 to 6 servings.

Microwave: Combine first 3 ingredients as above. In 1½-quart microwave-proof bowl, combine remaining broth and enough water to equal 1¾ cups liquid. Stir in rice; cover. Microwave on HIGH (100% power) for 15 to 17 minutes, stirring after 7 minutes.

Crumble beef in 1½-quart microwave-proof bowl. Microwave, uncovered, on HIGH for 2 minutes; stir in onion. Microwave, uncovered, on HIGH for 2 to 3 minutes; pour off fat. In 2-quart microwave-proof casserole, layer as above; cover. Microwave on HIGH for 15 to 17 minutes, rotating casserole ½ turn after 7 minutes. Let stand, covered, for 5 minutes before serving.

Cheese-Stuffed Beef Rolls

        1 jar (15½ ounces) spaghetti
            sauce
        1 egg, slightly beaten
     ¼ teaspoon DURKEE Leaf
            Oregano
     ¼ teaspoon DURKEE Garlic
            Powder
        1 container (15 ounces) ricotta
            cheese
     ¼ cup (1 ounce) grated
            Parmesan cheese
        1 cup (4 ounces) shredded
            mozzarella cheese
        1 can (2.8 ounces) DURKEE
            French Fried Onions
        6 thin slices deli roast beef
            (about ½ pound)
        2 medium zucchini, sliced
            (about 3 cups)

Preheat oven to 375°. Spread ½ cup spaghetti sauce in bottom of 8×12-inch baking dish. In large bowl, thoroughly combine egg, seasonings, ricotta cheese, Parmesan cheese, ½ cup mozzarella cheese and ½ can French Fried Onions. Spoon equal amounts of cheese mixture on 1 end of each beef slice. Roll up beef slices jelly-roll style and arrange, seam-side down, in baking dish. Place zucchini along both sides of dish. Pour remaining spaghetti sauce over beef rolls and zucchini. Bake, covered, at 375° for 40 minutes or until heated through. Top beef rolls with remaining mozzarella cheese and onions. Bake, uncovered, 3 minutes or until onions are golden brown.
Makes 6 servings.
   Microwave Directions: In large microwave-safe bowl, prepare cheese mixture as above. Cook, covered, on HIGH 2 to 4 minutes or until warmed through. Stir cheese mixture halfway through cooking time. Spread ½ cup spaghetti sauce in bottom of 8×12-inch microwave-safe dish. Prepare beef rolls and place in dish as above. Arrange zucchini along both sides of dish. Pour remaining spaghetti sauce over beef rolls and zucchini. Cook, loosely covered, 14 to 16 minutes or until heated through. Rotate dish halfway through cooking time. Top beef rolls with remaining mozzarella cheese and onions; cook, uncovered, 1 minute or until cheese melts. Let stand 5 minutes.

Cheeseburger Pie

Cheeseburger Pie

        1 (9-inch) unbaked pastry shell,
            pricked
        8 slices BORDEN® Process
            American Cheese Food
        1 pound lean ground beef
     ½ cup tomato sauce
     ⅓ cup chopped green pepper
     ⅓ cup chopped onion
        1 teaspoon WYLER'S® or
            STEERO® Beef-Flavor
            Instant Bouillon or 1 Beef-
            Flavor Bouillon Cube
        3 eggs, well beaten
        2 tablespoons flour
            Chopped tomato and shredded
            lettuce, optional

Preheat oven to 425°. Bake pastry shell 8 minutes; remove from oven. Reduce oven temperature to 350°. Cut 6 *slices* cheese food into pieces; set aside. In large skillet, brown meat; pour off fat. Add tomato sauce, green pepper, onion and bouillon; cook and stir until bouillon dissolves. Remove from heat; stir in eggs, flour and cheese food pieces. Turn into prepared shell. Bake 20 to 25 minutes or until hot. Arrange remaining cheese food slices on top. Return to oven 3 to 5 minutes or until cheese food begins to melt. Garnish with tomato and lettuce if desired. Refrigerate leftovers.
Makes one 9-inch pie.

Beef and Wild Rice Casserole

     2⅔ cups boiling water
     ⅔ cup uncooked wild rice, rinsed
            and drained
        4 teaspoons WYLER'S® or
            STEERO® Beef-Flavor
            Instant Bouillon or 4 Beef-
            Flavor Bouillon Cubes
     1½ pounds lean ground beef
        1 cup chopped celery
     ½ cup chopped onion
        1 clove garlic, finely chopped
        1 (10¾-ounce) can condensed
            cream of mushroom soup
     ½ cup uncooked long grain rice
     ⅛ teaspoon pepper

Preheat oven to 350°. In 2-quart baking dish, combine water, wild rice and bouillon; set aside. In large skillet, brown meat; pour off fat. Stir in celery, onion and garlic; cook until tender. Add soup, long grain rice and pepper. Add meat mixture to wild rice mixture; mix well. Cover. Bake 1 hour and 30 minutes. Serve hot. Refrigerate leftovers.
Makes 8 servings.

Chicken Enchiladas

3 cups finely chopped cooked chicken
1 cup chopped onion
¼ cup margarine or butter
¼ cup unsifted flour
2½ cups hot water
1 tablespoon WYLER'S® or STEERO® Chicken-Flavor Instant Bouillon or 3 Chicken-Flavor Bouillon Cubes
1 (8-ounce) container BORDEN® or MEADOW GOLD® Sour Cream, at room temperature
2 cups (8 ounces) shredded Cheddar cheese
1 (4-ounce) can chopped mild green chilies, drained
1 teaspoon ground cumin
12 (6-inch) corn tortillas or 10 (8-inch) flour tortillas
Sour cream, chopped green onions and chopped tomato for garnish

Preheat oven to 350°. In medium saucepan, cook onion in margarine until tender. Stir in flour then water and bouillon; cook and stir until thickened and bouillon dissolves. Remove from heat; stir in sour cream. In large bowl, combine *1 cup* sauce, chicken, *1 cup* cheese, chilies and cumin; mix well. Dip each tortilla into remaining hot sauce to soften; fill each with equal portions of chicken mixture. Roll up. Arrange in greased 13×9-inch baking dish. Spoon remaining sauce over. Sprinkle with remaining cheese. Bake 25 minutes or until bubbly. Garnish as desired. Refrigerate leftovers.
Makes 6 to 8 servings.

Microwave: In 2-quart round baking dish, microwave margarine on full power (high) 1 minute or until melted. Add onion; microwave on full power (high) 3 to 5 minutes or until tender. Stir in flour, then water and bouillon; microwave on full power (high) 8 minutes, or until thickened and bouillon dissolves, stirring every 2 minutes. Stir in sour cream. Proceed as above. Arrange rolled tortillas in greased 12×7-inch baking dish. Microwave on ⅔ power (medium-high) 9 minutes or until bubbly. Let stand 5 minutes before serving.

Turkey Divan

1 pound broccoli, cut into spears, or 1 package (16 ounces) frozen broccoli spears
¼ cup water
1 can (10¾ ounces) CAMPBELL'S® Condensed Cream of Mushroom Soup
¼ cup milk
1 tablespoon dry sherry
Generous dash ground nutmeg
2 cups cubed cooked turkey or chicken
¼ cup shredded Cheddar cheese (1 ounce)

To Microwave:
1. In 10- by 6-inch microwave-safe casserole, combine broccoli and water. Cover with vented plastic wrap; microwave on HIGH 6 minutes or until broccoli is almost tender, rotating dish once during cooking. Let stand, covered, 3 minutes. Drain.
2. In medium bowl, stir soup until smooth. Stir in milk, sherry and nutmeg; stir in turkey. Pour over broccoli. Sprinkle with cheese. Cover with waxed paper; microwave on HIGH 6 minutes or until heated through, rotating dish once during cooking. Let stand, covered, 5 minutes.
Makes 4 servings.

Country-Style Chicken Dinner

3 cups frozen hash brown potatoes
1 can (2.8 ounces) DURKEE French Fried Onions
1 can (10¾ ounces) condensed cream of chicken soup
1 cup milk
6 slices (¾ ounce *each*) processed American cheese
2 to 2½ pounds chicken pieces, fat trimmed, skinned if desired
1 package (10 ounces) frozen mixed vegetables, thawed and drained

Preheat oven to 375°. In 9×13-inch baking dish, combine frozen potatoes and *½ can* French Fried Onions. In small bowl, blend soup and milk; pour *half* over potato mixture. Arrange cheese slices over potato mixture; top with chicken, skin-side down. Pour remaining soup mixture over chicken. Bake, uncovered, at 375° for 35 minutes. Stir vegetables into potatoes and turn chicken pieces over. Bake, uncovered, 20 minutes or until chicken is done. Stir potato mixture and top chicken with remaining onions; bake, uncovered, 3 minutes or until onions are golden brown. Let stand 15 minutes before serving.
Makes 4 to 6 servings.

Country-Style Chicken Dinner

California-Style Chicken

    1 can (15 ounces) tomato sauce
    3 tablespoons red wine vinegar
    1/2 teaspoon DURKEE Sweet Basil
    1/4 teaspoon DURKEE Garlic
        Powder
    12 small red potatoes, thinly
        sliced (about 3 cups)
    1 can (2.8 ounces) DURKEE
        French Fried Onions
    2 1/2 pounds chicken pieces, fat
        trimmed, skinned if desired
    1 package (10 ounces) frozen
        whole green beans, thawed
        and drained

Preheat oven to 375°. In small bowl, combine tomato sauce, vinegar and seasonings. Spread *1/2 cup* tomato mixture in bottom of 9×13-inch baking dish; top with potatoes and *1/2 can* French Fried Onions. Arrange chicken over potatoes and onions. Spoon *1 cup* tomato mixture over chicken and potatoes. Bake, covered, at 375° for 35 minutes. Stir green beans into potatoes. Spoon remaining tomato mixture over chicken. Bake, covered, 10 to 15 minutes or until chicken and beans are done. Top chicken with remaining onions; bake, uncovered, 3 minutes or until onions are golden brown.
Makes 4 to 6 servings.

Old-Fashioned Chicken Pot Pie

    6 tablespoons butter or
        margarine, divided
    3 tablespoons flour
    2 cups chicken broth
    1 1/4 teaspoons dried rosemary
        leaves, divided
    1/4 teaspoon TABASCO® pepper
        sauce
    1/2 pound cubed cooked chicken
    2 medium carrots, sliced and
        cooked
    1 cup frozen peas
    1 1/2 cups packaged dry biscuit mix
    1/2 cup milk

Preheat oven to 400°F. In large saucepan melt 3 tablespoons butter. Stir in flour; cook 1 minute. Remove from heat. Gradually add broth. Stir constantly, bring to a boil over medium heat and boil 1 minute. Stir in 1/2 teaspoon rosemary, Tabasco® sauce, chicken, carrots and peas. Spoon mixture into greased 2-quart shallow baking dish.

In medium bowl combine biscuit mix and remaining 3/4 teaspoon rosemary. Cut in remaining 3 tablespoons butter until mixture resembles coarse crumbs. Stir in milk. On heavily floured surface pat out biscuit dough 1/2 inch thick. Cut into 10 triangles. Arrange triangles on chicken mixture. Bake 25 minutes or until biscuits are browned.
Makes 4 servings.

Turkey Cottage Pie

    1/4 cup butter or margarine
    1/4 cup all-purpose flour
    1 envelope LIPTON® Golden
        Onion Recipe Soup Mix
    2 cups water
    2 cups cut-up cooked turkey or
        chicken
    1 package (10 ounces) frozen
        mixed vegetables, thawed
    1 1/4 cups shredded Swiss cheese
        (about 5 ounces)
    1/8 teaspoon pepper
    5 cups hot mashed potatoes

Preheat oven to 375°.

In large saucepan, melt butter and cook flour over medium-low heat, stirring constantly, 5 minutes or until golden. Stir in golden onion recipe soup mix thoroughly blended with water. Bring to a boil, then simmer 15 minutes or until thickened. Stir in turkey, vegetables, 1 cup cheese and pepper. Turn into lightly greased

2-quart casserole; top with hot potatoes, then remaining cheese. Bake 30 minutes or until bubbling.
Makes about 8 servings.

Microwave Directions: In 2-quart casserole, heat butter at HIGH (Full Power) 1 minute. Stir in flour and heat uncovered, stirring frequently, 2 minutes. Stir in golden onion recipe soup mix thoroughly blended with water. Heat uncovered, stirring occasionally, 4 minutes or until thickened. Stir in turkey, vegetables, 1 cup cheese and pepper. Top with hot potatoes, then remaining cheese. Heat uncovered, turning casserole occasionally, 5 minutes or until bubbling. Let stand uncovered 5 minutes. For additional color, sprinkle, if desired, with paprika.

Scalloped Turkey

    2 cups diced cooked
        BUTTERBALL® turkey
        (3/4 pound)
    1/2 cup chopped celery
    1/4 cup chopped green bell
        pepper
    3 tablespoons butter or
        margarine, divided
    2 tablespoons all-purpose flour
    1/4 teaspoon salt
    1 1/2 cups milk
    1 tablespoon chopped pimiento
    4 cups potato chips, divided

Turkey Cottage Pie

Preheat oven to 350°F. Cook and stir celery and green pepper in 1 tablespoon butter in medium saucepan over medium heat. Remove from pan. Melt remaining 2 tablespoons butter in same saucepan over medium heat. Blend in flour and salt. Remove from heat. Gradually add milk. Cook over medium heat until mixture thickens, stirring constantly. Add turkey, celery, green pepper and pimiento. Crush potato chips lightly to make 2 cups. Put about 1½ cups potato chips in bottom of buttered 1 to 1½-quart baking dish. Add turkey mixture. Sprinkle remaining chips on top. Bake in oven 30 to 40 minutes or until sauce bubbles.

Yield: 4 servings.

Chicken and Ham Supreme

- **1 package (9 ounces) frozen artichoke hearts**
- **1 can (10¾ ounces) CAMPBELL'S® Condensed Cream of Mushroom Soup**
- **½ cup plain yogurt**
- **½ cup shredded Swiss cheese (2 ounces)**
- **1 teaspoon dried basil leaves, crushed**
- **⅛ teaspoon ground red pepper (cayenne)**
- **2 cups cooked rice**
- **1½ cups cubed cooked chicken**
- **1 cup cubed cooked ham Chopped fresh parsley for garnish**

To Microwave:

1. Place artichoke hearts in small microwave-safe bowl. Cover with vented plastic wrap; microwave on HIGH 4 minutes or until heated through, stirring once during cooking. Drain; set aside.
2. In small bowl, stir soup until smooth; stir in yogurt, cheese, basil and pepper.
3. In 8- by 8-inch microwave-safe baking dish, combine rice and ½ cup of the soup mixture; spread evenly in dish. Top with chicken, ham and artichoke hearts. Spoon remaining soup mixture over.
4. Cover with vented plastic wrap; microwave on HIGH 8 minutes or until heated through, rotating dish once during cooking. Let stand, covered, 2 minutes. Garnish with parsley.

Makes 4 servings. *(continued)*

Deep Dish Turkey Pie

Note: You can substitute 1 package (about 10 ounces) frozen asparagus or broccoli spears for the artichoke hearts. Cook vegetables according to package directions; drain, then cut into bite-size pieces. Proceed as above in steps 2 through 4.

Chicken Puff Bravo

- **¾ lb. VELVEETA Mexican Pasteurized Process Cheese Spread with Jalapeño Pepper, cubed**
- **½ cup sour cream**
- **¼ teaspoon garlic salt**
- **2 eggs, separated**
- **2 10-oz. pkgs. frozen chopped spinach, thawed, well-drained**
- **3 cups chopped cooked chicken**
- **¼ cup chopped red or green pepper**
- **1 4-oz. can sliced mushrooms, drained**
- **2 8-oz. cans PILLSBURY Refrigerated Quick Crescent Dinner Rolls**

In 3-quart saucepan, combine process cheese spread, sour cream and garlic salt; stir over low heat until process cheese spread is melted. Remove from heat. Beat egg yolks thoroughly; reserve 1 tablespoon for glaze. Gradually stir remaining egg yolks into cheese mixture. Cool. Beat egg whites until stiff peaks form; fold into cheese mixture. Add remaining ingredients

except dough; mix lightly. Unroll one can dough; press onto bottom and sides of greased 12-inch ovenproof skillet, pressing perforations together to seal. Spread spinach mixture over dough. Unroll second can dough; separate into eight triangles. Loosely twist each triangle at pointed end. Arrange dough triangles on spinach mixture, pointed ends towards center. Seal outer edges to crust. Brush dough with reserved egg yolk. Bake at 375°, 35 to 40 minutes or until egg mixture is set.

8 servings.

Preparation time: 20 minutes
Baking time: 40 minutes

Variation: Substitute 2-oz. jar sliced pimento, drained, for red or green pepper.

Recipe Tip: Substitute 12-inch deep-dish pizza pan for skillet.

Deep Dish Turkey Pie

- **3 cups cubed cooked turkey *or* chicken**
- **1 cup sliced cooked carrots**
- **1 cup cubed cooked potatoes**
- **1 cup frozen green peas, thawed**
- **6 tablespoons margarine or butter**
- **⅓ cup unsifted flour**
- **2 tablespoons WYLER'S® or STEERO® Chicken-Flavor Instant Bouillon *or* 6 Chicken-Flavor Bouillon Cubes**
- **¼ teaspoon pepper**
- **4 cups BORDEN® or MEADOW GOLD® Milk**
- **2¼ cups biscuit baking mix**

Preheat oven to 375°. In large saucepan, melt margarine; stir in flour, bouillon and pepper. Over medium heat, gradually add milk; cook and stir until mixture thickens. Add remaining ingredients except biscuit mix; mix well. Pour into 2½-quart baking dish. Prepare biscuit mix according to package directions for rolled biscuits. Roll out to cover dish; cut slashes in center of dough. Place on top of dish; crimp edges. Bake 40 minutes or until golden. Refrigerate leftovers.

Makes 6 servings.

Creamy Turkey & Broccoli

Creamy Turkey & Broccoli

- 1 package (6 ounces) stuffing mix,* plus ingredients to prepare mix
- 1 can (2.8 ounces) DURKEE French Fried Onions
- 1 package (10 ounces) frozen broccoli spears, thawed and drained
- 1 package (1⅛ ounces) DURKEE Cheese Sauce Mix
- 1¼ cups milk
- ½ cup sour cream
- 2 cups (10 ounces) cubed cooked turkey or chicken

Preheat oven to 350°. In medium saucepan, prepare stuffing mix according to package directions; stir in ½ can French Fried Onions. Spread stuffing over bottom of greased 9-inch round baking dish. Arrange broccoli spears over stuffing with flowerets around edge of dish. In medium saucepan, prepare cheese sauce mix according to package directions using 1¼ cups milk. Remove from heat; stir in sour cream and turkey. Pour turkey mixture over broccoli *stalks*. Bake, covered, at 350° for 30 minutes or until heated through. Sprinkle remaining onions over turkey; bake, uncovered, 5 minutes or until onions are golden brown.
Makes 4 to 6 servings.

Microwave Directions: In 9-inch microwave-safe dish, prepare stuffing mix according to package microwave directions; stir in ½ *can* onions. Arrange stuffing and broccoli spears in dish as above; set aside. In medium microwave-safe bowl, prepare cheese sauce mix according to package microwave directions using 1¼ cups milk. Add turkey and cook, covered, 5 to 6 minutes, stirring turkey halfway through cooking time. Stir in sour cream. Pour turkey mixture over broccoli *stalks*. Cook, covered, 8 to 10 minutes or until heated through. Rotate dish halfway through cooking time. Top turkey with remaining onions; cook, uncovered, 1 minute. Let stand 5 minutes.

*3 cups leftover stuffing may be substituted for stuffing mix. If stuffing is dry, stir in water, 1 tablespoon at a time, until moist but not wet.

Turkey Cassoulet

- 3-pound BUTTERBALL® Boneless Turkey
- 2 cans (15½ ounces each) Great Northern beans, drained
- 1 can (15 ounces) tomato sauce special
- ½ pound fully cooked Polish smoked sausage, cut into ½-inch pieces
- 6 slices cooked bacon, cut into 1-inch pieces
- ¼ cup chopped onion
- 2 cloves garlic, minced
- 1 teaspoon fennel seed
- ¼ teaspoon ground black pepper

Roast turkey according to package directions. Combine remaining ingredients in 2-quart casserole. Cover and bake alongside turkey last hour of roasting time. Wrap turkey in foil and let stand 10 to 15 minutes. Remove netting from turkey; slice turkey. To serve, arrange turkey on bean mixture, spooning some beans over turkey slices.
Yield: 8 servings.

Cheesy Chicken Tetrazzini

- 2 boneless, skinless whole chicken breasts, cut into 1-inch pieces (about 1½ pounds)
- 2 tablespoons butter or margarine
- 1½ cups sliced mushrooms
- 1 small red bell pepper, cut into julienne strips
- ½ cup sliced green onions
- ¼ cup all-purpose flour
- 1¾ cups chicken broth
- 1 cup light cream or half-and-half
- 2 tablespoons dry sherry
- ½ teaspoon salt
- ¼ teaspoon black pepper
- ¼ teaspoon dried thyme, crushed
- 1 package (8 ounces) tricolor corkscrew pasta, cooked, drained
- ¼ cup grated Parmesan cheese
- 2 tablespoons chopped parsley
- 1 cup (4 ounces) shredded NOKKELOST or JARLSBERG cheese

Brown chicken in melted butter in large skillet over medium-high heat. Add mushrooms; cook and stir until tender. Add red pepper and green onions; cook several minutes, stirring occasionally. Stir in flour and cook several minutes over medium heat until blended. Gradually blend in broth, cream and sherry. Cook until thickened and smooth, stirring constantly. Stir in salt, pepper and thyme. Toss with pasta, Parmesan cheese and parsley. Spoon into 1½-quart baking dish. Bake at 350°F 30 minutes. Top with shredded cheese. Bake until cheese is melted.
Makes 6 servings.

Favorite recipe from **Norseland Foods, Inc.**

Turkey Tetrazzini

- **6 slices cooked BUTTERBALL®
  turkey (1 pound)**
- **²/₃ cup sliced onion**
- **½ stick (¼ cup) butter or
  margarine**
- **¼ cup all-purpose flour**
- **1 teaspoon salt**
- **¼ teaspoon ground white pepper**
- **½ teaspoon poultry seasoning**
- **¼ teaspoon dry mustard**
- **2 cups milk**
- **1 cup (4 ounces) shredded
  sharp Cheddar cheese,
  divided**
- **2 tablespoons chopped pimiento**
- **2 tablespoons sherry**
- **1 can (4 ounces) sliced
  mushrooms, undrained**
- **1 package (7 ounces) spaghetti,
  cooked, drained**

Preheat oven to 400°F. Cook and stir onion in butter in medium saucepan over medium heat until tender. Blend in flour and seasonings. Remove from heat. Gradually add milk. Stirring constantly, cook over medium heat until mixture thickens. Add ²/₃ cup cheese and pimiento, stirring until cheese melts. Add sherry and undrained mushrooms to cheese sauce. Place layer of spaghetti in 12×8-inch baking dish. Cover with layer of turkey and layer of sauce. Repeat the layers. Sprinkle remaining ⅓ cup cheese over top. Bake about 25 minutes.
Yield: 6 servings.

Note: Casserole may be assembled in advance and frozen. To serve, heat, covered, in 350°F oven for 1½ hours or until hot.

Sausage-Chicken Creole

Sausage-Chicken Creole

- **1 can (14½ ounces) whole
  tomatoes, undrained and cut
  up**
- **½ cup uncooked regular rice**
- **½ cup hot water**
- **2 teaspoons DURKEE RedHot
  Cayenne Pepper Sauce**
- **¼ teaspoon DURKEE Garlic
  Powder**
- **¼ teaspoon DURKEE Leaf
  Oregano**
- **1 bag (16 ounces) frozen
  vegetable combination
  (broccoli, corn, red pepper),
  thawed and drained**
- **1 can (2.8 ounces) DURKEE
  French Fried Onions**
- **4 chicken thighs, skinned**
- **½ pound link Italian sausage,
  quartered and cooked***
- **1 can (8 ounces) tomato sauce**

Preheat oven to 375°. In 8×12-inch baking dish, combine tomatoes, uncooked rice, hot water, cayenne pepper sauce and seasonings. Bake, covered, at 375° for 10 minutes. Stir vegetables and ½ can French Fried Onions into rice mixture; top with chicken and cooked sausage. Pour tomato sauce over chicken and sausage. Bake, covered, at 375° for 40 minutes or until chicken is done. Top chicken with remaining onions; bake, uncovered, 3 minutes or until onions are golden brown.
Makes 4 servings.

*To cook sausage, simmer in water to cover until done. Or, place in microwave-safe dish and cook, covered, on HIGH 3 minutes or until done.

Jambalaya

2 cloves garlic, crushed
1 tablespoon BLUE BONNET®
    Margarine
1 (14½-ounce) can stewed
    tomatoes, undrained and
    coarsely chopped
1½ cups cubed cooked ham
1 (13¾-fluid ounce) can
    COLLEGE INN® Chicken
    Broth
1 cup uncooked rice
½ teaspoon dried thyme leaves
12 ounces shrimp, shelled and
    deveined

In skillet, over medium-high heat,
cook garlic in margarine for 1 to 2
minutes. Add remaining ingredients
except shrimp; heat to a boil; reduce
heat. Cover; simmer 25 minutes. Add
shrimp; cook, covered, 5 to 10 minutes
or until liquid is absorbed.
Makes 6 servings.

Creole Chicken Jambalaya

¼ cup vegetable oil
2 medium onions, chopped
6 green onions, chopped
2 medium green peppers,
    chopped
1 (2½- to 3-pound) broiler-fryer
    chicken, cut into 8 pieces
½ pound cooked ham, cubed
½ pound smoked or Polish
    sausage, cut into ½-inch
    slices
1 can (16 ounces) tomatoes, cut
    into pieces, undrained
1 can (6 ounces) tomato paste
1 teaspoon salt
1¾ cups uncooked rice
½ cup water
¾ teaspoon TABASCO® pepper
    sauce

In large saucepot or Dutch oven heat
oil. Add onions, green onions and peppers; cook 10 minutes or until tender.
Add chicken and brown on all sides,
about 10 minutes. Add ham, sausage,
tomatoes, tomato paste and salt.
Cover; simmer 10 minutes; stir in
rice. Add water. Cover. Simmer 1 hour
or until chicken is done; stir frequently. Add additional water if rice
begins to stick to bottom of pan. Before serving, stir in Tabasco® sauce.
Makes 8 servings.

Jambalaya

Layered Seafood Quiche

¾ cup finely chopped onion
1 can (12½ ounces) or 2 cans
    (6½ ounces) STARKIST®
    Solid White or Solid Light
    Tuna in Springwater,
    drained, flaked
2 cups (8 ounces) shredded
    Cheddar cheese
3 eggs, lightly beaten
1 can (12 ounces) PET®
    Evaporated or PET® Light
    Evaporated Skimmed Milk
½ teaspoon salt

Cook onion in medium saucepan, covered, over very low heat until soft,
adding water if necessary to prevent
scorching. Line bottom of 9-inch pie
pan with tuna. Sprinkle with cooked
onion; top with cheese. Combine eggs,
milk and salt in small bowl; mix well.
Pour over cheese. Bake in preheated
350°F oven 30 minutes or until set.
Let stand at least 10 minutes before
cutting. Garnish as desired.
Makes 8 servings.

So-Easy Fish Divan

- 1 package (1⅛ ounces) DURKEE Cheese Sauce Mix
- 1⅓ cups milk
- 1 bag (16 ounces) frozen vegetable combination (brussels sprouts, carrots, cauliflower), thawed and drained
- 1 can (2.8 ounces) DURKEE French Fried Onions
- 1 pound unbreaded fish fillets, thawed if frozen
- ½ cup (2 ounces) shredded Cheddar cheese

Preheat oven to 375°. In small saucepan, prepare cheese sauce mix according to package directions using 1⅓ cups milk. In 8×12-inch baking dish, combine vegetables and *½ can* French Fried Onions; top with fish fillets. Pour cheese sauce over fish and vegetables. Bake, covered, at 375° for 25 minutes or until fish flakes easily with fork. Top fish with Cheddar cheese and remaining onions; bake, uncovered, 3 minutes or until onions are golden brown.
Makes 3 to 4 servings.

Tuna-Pasta Casserole

- 1 cup frozen peas
- 1 can (10¾ ounces) CAMPBELL'S® Condensed Cream of Celery Soup
- ½ cup milk
- ½ cup shredded Swiss cheese (2 ounces)
- 1 can (6½ ounces) tuna, drained and flaked
- 2 cups cooked corkscrew or other macaroni (1 cup uncooked)
- 2 hard-cooked eggs, chopped
- ½ cup crushed potato chips

To Microwave:
1. Place peas in 1½-quart microwave-safe casserole. Cover with lid; microwave on HIGH 4 minutes or until tender. Drain; set aside.
2. In same casserole, stir soup until smooth; stir in milk and cheese. Fold tuna, macaroni, eggs and peas into soup mixture. Cover; microwave on HIGH 7 minutes or until hot and bubbling, stirring once during cooking. Let stand, covered, 5 minutes.
3. Sprinkle potato chips over casserole.
Makes 4 servings.

Clam Noodle Florentine

- ½ (1-pound) package CREAMETTE® Egg Noodles, cooked and drained
- ⅓ cup chopped onion
- ¼ cup margarine or butter
- ¼ cup unsifted flour
- ½ teaspoon salt
- ¼ teaspoon pepper
- 2 cups (1 pint) BORDEN® or MEADOW GOLD® Half-and-Half or Milk
- 2 (6½-ounce) cans SNOW'S® or DOXSEE® Minced or Chopped Clams, drained, reserving liquid
- 1 (10-ounce) package frozen chopped spinach, thawed and well drained
- ¼ cup grated Parmesan cheese
- ½ cup buttered bread crumbs

Preheat oven to 350°. In large saucepan, cook onion in margarine until tender. Stir in flour, salt and pepper. Gradually stir in half-and-half and reserved clam liquid. Over medium heat, cook and stir until thickened and bubbly, about 8 minutes. Remove from heat; add noodles, clams, spinach and cheese. Mix well. Turn into greased 2-quart baking dish. Top with crumbs. Bake 25 to 30 minutes or until hot. Refrigerate leftovers.
Makes 6 to 8 servings.

Herb-Baked Fish & Rice

- 1½ cups hot HERB-OX Chicken Bouillon
- ½ cup uncooked regular rice
- ¼ teaspoon DURKEE Italian Seasoning
- ¼ teaspoon DURKEE Garlic Powder
- 1 package (10 ounces) frozen chopped broccoli, thawed and drained
- 1 can (2.8 ounces) DURKEE French Fried Onions
- 1 tablespoon grated Parmesan cheese
- 1 pound unbreaded fish fillets, thawed if frozen
  DURKEE Paprika (optional)
- ½ cup (2 ounces) shredded Cheddar cheese

Preheat oven to 375°. In 8×12-inch baking dish, combine hot bouillon, uncooked rice and seasonings. Bake, covered, at 375° for 10 minutes. Top with broccoli, ½ can French Fried Onions and the Parmesan cheese. Place fish fillets diagonally down center of dish; sprinkle fish lightly with paprika. Bake, covered, at 375° for 20 to 25 minutes or until fish flakes easily with fork. Stir rice. Top fish with Cheddar cheese and remaining onions; bake, uncovered, 3 minutes or until onions are golden brown.
Makes 3 to 4 servings.

Microwave Directions: In 8×12-inch microwave-safe dish, prepare rice mixture as above, except reduce bouillon to 1¼ cups. Cook, covered, on HIGH 5 minutes, stirring halfway through cooking time. Stir in broccoli, ½ can onions and the Parmesan cheese. Arrange fish fillets in single layer on top of rice mixture; sprinkle fish lightly with paprika. Cook, covered, on MEDIUM (50–60%) 18 to 20 minutes or until fish flakes easily with fork and rice is done. Rotate dish halfway through cooking time. Top fish with Cheddar cheese and remaining onions; cook, uncovered, on HIGH 1 minute or until cheese melts. Let stand 5 minutes.

Herb-Baked Fish & Rice

Hasty Shore Dinner

- **1 cup small shell pasta, cooked in unsalted water and drained**
- **½ cup mayonnaise**
- **½ cup milk**
- **1 can (10¾ ounces) condensed cream of celery soup**
- **1 package (8 ounces) frozen imitation crabmeat,* thawed, drained and cut into chunks**
- **1 can (4 ounces) shrimp, drained**
- **1 cup (4 ounces) shredded Swiss cheese**
- **1 can (2.8 ounces) DURKEE French Fried Onions**
- **½ teaspoon DURKEE Dill Weed**
- **¼ teaspoon DURKEE Seasoned Salt**

Preheat oven to 350°. Return hot pasta to saucepan. Stir in mayonnaise, milk, soup, crabmeat, shrimp, *½ cup* cheese, *½ can* French Fried Onions and the seasonings; mix well. Pour into 1½-quart casserole. Bake, covered, at 350° for 35 minutes or until heated through. Top with remaining cheese and onions; bake, uncovered, 5 minutes or until onions are golden brown.
Makes 4 to 6 servings.

Microwave Directions: Prepare pasta mixture as above; pour into 1½-quart microwave-safe casserole. Cook, covered, on HIGH 12 to 15 minutes or until heated through. Stir casserole halfway through cooking time. Top with remaining cheese and onions; cook, uncovered, 1 minute or until cheese melts. Let stand 5 minutes.

*1 can (6 ounces) crabmeat, drained, may be substituted for imitation crabmeat.

All-in-One Tuna Casserole

- **1 envelope LIPTON® Golden Onion Recipe Soup Mix**
- **1½ cups milk**
- **1 package (10 ounces) frozen peas and carrots, thawed**
- **1 package (8 ounces) medium egg noodles, cooked and drained**
- **1 can (6½ ounces) tuna, drained and flaked**
- **½ cup shredded Cheddar cheese (about 2 ounces)**

Preheat oven to 350°.

In large bowl, blend golden onion recipe soup mix with milk; stir in peas and carrots, cooked noodles and tuna. Turn into greased 2-quart oblong baking dish, then top with cheese. Bake 20 minutes or until bubbling.
Makes about 4 servings.

Superb Fillet of Sole & Vegetables

- **1 can (10¾ ounces) condensed cream of celery soup**
- **½ cup milk**
- **1 cup (4 ounces) shredded Swiss cheese**
- **½ teaspoon DURKEE Sweet Basil**
- **¼ teaspoon DURKEE Seasoned Salt**
- **¼ teaspoon DURKEE Ground Black Pepper**
- **1 package (10 ounces) frozen baby carrots, thawed and drained**
- **1 package (10 ounces) frozen asparagus cuts, thawed and drained**
- **1 can (2.8 ounces) DURKEE French Fried Onions**
- **1 pound unbreaded sole fillets, thawed if frozen**

Preheat oven to 375°. In small bowl, combine soup, milk, *½ cup* cheese and the seasonings; set aside. In 8×12-inch baking dish, combine carrots, asparagus and *½ can* French Fried Onions. Roll up fish fillets. (If fillets are wide, fold in half lengthwise before rolling.) Place fish rolls upright along center of vegetable mixture.

Pour soup mixture over fish and vegetables. Bake, covered, at 375° for 30 minutes or until fish flakes easily with fork. Stir vegetables; top fish with remaining cheese and onions. Bake, uncovered, 3 minutes or until onions are golden brown.
Makes 3 to 4 servings.

Microwave Directions: Prepare soup mixture as above; set aside. In 8×12-inch microwave-safe dish, combine vegetables as above. Roll up fish fillets as above; place upright around edges of dish. Pour soup mixture over fish and vegetables. Cook, covered, on HIGH 14 to 16 minutes or until fish flakes easily with fork. Stir vegetables and rotate dish halfway through cooking time. Top fish with remaining cheese and onions; cook, uncovered, 1 minute or until cheese melts. Let stand 5 minutes.

Eggplant Parmesan

- **1 egg**
- **2 tablespoons milk**
- **1 cup Italian-seasoned fine dry bread crumbs**
- **1 medium eggplant, peeled and cut into ¼-inch slices (1 pound)**
- **1 jar (15½ ounces) PREGO® Spaghetti Sauce**
- **2 cups shredded mozzarella cheese (8 ounces)**
- **2 tablespoons grated Parmesan cheese**

To Microwave:

1. In pie plate, beat together egg and milk. Place bread crumbs in another

Superb Fillet of Sole & Vegetables

pie plate. Dip eggplant slices in egg mixture, then in crumbs to coat well.

2. Arrange ½ of the eggplant slices on a 10-inch microwave-safe plate lined with paper towels. Microwave, uncovered, on HIGH 4 minutes or until tender, rearranging slices once during cooking. Repeat with remaining eggplant.

3. Spread ¼ cup of the spaghetti sauce in 8- by 8-inch microwave-safe baking dish. Layer ½ of the eggplant, ½ of the mozzarella and ½ of the remaining spaghetti sauce in dish; repeat layers. Sprinkle with Parmesan cheese.

4. Cover with vented plastic wrap; microwave on HIGH 4 minutes or until hot. Rotate dish. Reduce power to 50%. Microwave, covered, 10 minutes or until hot and bubbling, rotating dish once during cooking. Let stand, covered, 5 minutes.
Makes 4 servings.

Cheese-Mushroom Strata

Smoky Macaroni and Cheese

**1 can (10¾ ounces)
    CAMPBELL'S® Condensed
    Cream of Celery Soup**
¾ cup milk
¼ teaspoon white pepper
**¾ cup shredded mozzarella
    cheese (3 ounces)**
**½ cup shredded smoked
    mozzarella or smoked gouda
    cheese (2 ounces)**
**½ cup shredded white Cheddar
    cheese (2 ounces)**
**8 ounces ziti, cooked and
    drained (6 cups cooked)**
**2 tablespoons grated Parmesan
    cheese**
**2 tablespoons buttered bread
    crumbs**

1. In 3-quart saucepan over medium heat, stir soup. Add milk, pepper, mozzarella, smoked mozzarella and Cheddar cheese; heat until cheeses melt, stirring often. Remove from heat. Add cooked ziti; toss to coat.

2. Spoon ziti mixture into 1½-quart casserole. Sprinkle top with Parmesan cheese. Bake at 350°F. 25 minutes. Sprinkle with bread crumbs. Bake 5 minutes more.
Makes 6 cups or 6 main-dish servings.

Per serving: 329 calories, 14 g protein, 14 g fat, 36 g carbohydrate, 601 mg sodium, 36 mg cholesterol.

Cheese-Mushroom Strata

4 eggs, lightly beaten
**1 (13¾-fluid ounce) can
    COLLEGE INN® Chicken or
    Beef Broth**
½ cup dairy sour cream
**2 teaspoons GREY POUPON®
    Dijon Mustard**
**8 slices white bread, cubed
    (about 4 cups cubes)**
**2 cups shredded Cheddar
    cheese (8 ounces)**
**1 (4½-ounce) can sliced
    mushrooms, drained**

In large bowl, beat together eggs, broth, sour cream and mustard. Stir in bread cubes, cheese and mushrooms. Pour into greased 2-quart oval or 12×8×2-inch baking dish. Cover; refrigerate overnight.

Uncover; bake at 350°F for 50 to 60 minutes or until set. Let stand 5 to 10 minutes before serving. Garnish as desired.
Makes 6 to 8 servings.

PASTA

What can be more heartwarming than a steaming dish of pasta? Tangy tomato sauces enhanced by olives or capers, robust sausage dishes, seafood sauces with a Mediterranean ambience, or distinctly American creations— serve any of these pasta specialties for a friendly, convivial meal.

Pasta with Vegetables

1 teaspoon olive or vegetable oil
2 medium zucchini, cut into
   1½-inch-long sticks
1 sweet red pepper, cut into
   ½-inch squares
½ cup chopped onion
2 cloves garlic, minced
1 can (11 ounces) CAMPBELL'S®
   Condensed Zesty Tomato
   Soup/Sauce
½ cup water
¼ cup Chablis or other dry white
   wine
8 ounces thin spaghetti or other
   pasta, cooked and drained
   Grated Parmesan cheese for
   garnish

To Microwave:
1. In 2-quart microwave-safe casserole, combine oil, zucchini, red pepper, onion and garlic. Cover with lid; microwave on HIGH 4 minutes or until vegetables are tender, stirring once during cooking.
2. Stir in soup, water and wine. Cover; microwave on HIGH 7 minutes or until hot and bubbling, stirring once during cooking. Let stand, covered, 5 minutes. Serve over hot pasta. Garnish with Parmesan cheese.
Makes 8 servings.

Ham Pasta Primavera

3 tablespoons unsalted
   margarine or butter, divided
1 cup pea pods
½ cup shredded carrots
3 green onions, sliced
1 small red pepper, cut into
   strips
¾ cup evaporated skim milk
3 cups (12 ounces) ARMOUR®
   Lower Salt Ham cut into
   small cubes
10 ounces uncooked spaghetti,
   cooked according to
   package directions omitting
   salt and drained

Melt 1 tablespoon of the margarine in medium skillet over medium heat. Add vegetables; sauté until tender. Add remaining 2 tablespoons margarine, milk and ham. Cook over medium-high heat about 3 to 4 minutes, or until mixture thickens slightly. Serve over warm spaghetti. Garnish with fresh basil, cilantro or freshly ground pepper, if desired.
Makes 4 to 6 servings.

Nutrition Information Per Serving: 347 calories, 19 g protein, 9.7 g fat, 43.5 g carbohydrates, 29.1 mg cholesterol, 521 mg sodium.

Tortellini in Cream Sauce

1 teaspoon olive or vegetable oil
2 cloves garlic, minced
½ cup chopped sweet red
   pepper
¼ cup chopped onion
1 can (10¾ ounces)
   CAMPBELL'S® Condensed
   Cream of Mushroom Soup
½ cup half-and-half or milk
¼ cup Chablis or other dry white
   wine
¼ teaspoon dried tarragon
   leaves, crushed
8 ounces cheese tortellini,
   cooked and drained
½ cup crumbled feta or grated
   Parmesan cheese
¼ cup sliced green onions

To Microwave:
1. In 2-quart microwave-safe casserole, combine oil, garlic, red pepper and chopped onion. Cover with lid; microwave on HIGH 2 minutes or until vegetables are tender, stirring once during cooking.
2. Stir in soup until smooth. Stir in half-and-half, wine and tarragon. Cover; microwave on HIGH 5 minutes or until hot and bubbling, stirring once during cooking. Let stand, covered, 5 minutes.
3. Toss with hot tortellini. Sprinkle with cheese and green onions.
Makes 4 servings.

Pasta with Vegetables

Fettuccine with Roasted Red Pepper Sauce

    3 large red peppers*
    ½ cup whipping or heavy cream
    ¼ cup WISH-BONE® Italian
        Dressing
    2 tablespoons chopped fresh
        basil leaves**
      Salt and pepper to taste
    1 package (12 ounces)
        fettuccine or medium egg
        noodles, cooked and
        drained
      Grated Parmesan cheese

In large aluminum-foil-lined baking pan or on broiler rack, place peppers. Broil, turning occasionally, 20 minutes or until peppers turn almost completely black. Immediately place in paper bag; close bag and let cool about 30 minutes. Under cold running water, peel off skin, then remove stems and seeds.

In food processor or blender, process prepared peppers, cream, Italian dressing, basil, salt and pepper until blended. Toss with hot fettuccine and serve with cheese.

Makes about 4 main-dish servings.

    *Substitution: Use 2 cups drained roasted red peppers.
    **Substitution: Use 2 teaspoons dried basil leaves.
    Note: Also terrific with Wish-Bone® Robusto Italian, Blended Italian, Herbal Italian, Lite Italian or Classic Dijon Vinaigrette Dressing.

Fettuccine Alfredo

    ¾ pound uncooked fettuccine
      Boiling salted water
    6 tablespoons unsalted butter
    ⅔ cup whipping cream
    ½ teaspoon salt
      Large pinch ground white
        pepper
      Large pinch ground nutmeg
    1 cup freshly grated Parmesan
        cheese (about 3 ounces)
    2 tablespoons chopped fresh
        parsley

1. Cook fettuccine in large pot of boiling salted water just until al dente, 6 to 8 minutes; drain well. Return to dry pot.
2. While fettuccine is cooking, place butter and cream in 10-inch heavy skillet over medium-low heat. Cook, stirring constantly, until blended and mixture bubbles for 2 minutes. Stir in

salt, pepper and nutmeg. Remove from heat. Gradually stir in Parmesan cheese until thoroughly blended and fairly smooth. Return skillet briefly to heat if necessary to completely blend cheese, but don't let sauce bubble or cheese will become lumpy and tough.
3. Pour sauce over fettuccine in pot. Place over low heat. Stir and toss with 2 forks until sauce is slightly thickened and fettuccine evenly coated, 2 to 3 minutes. Sprinkle with parsley. Serve immediately.
Makes 4 servings.

Smoked Sausage Stuffed Pasta Shells

    ¾ pound ECKRICH® Smoked
        Sausage, chopped fine
    18 large macaroni shells
    1 pound ricotta cheese
    1 egg, beaten
    1½ cups (6 ounces) shredded
        mozzarella cheese
    ½ cup chopped fresh parsley
    ¼ cup grated Parmesan cheese
    ½ teaspoon dried basil leaves
    ½ teaspoon dried oregano leaves
    1 jar (15 ounces) prepared
        spaghetti sauce with
        mushrooms and onions
    ⅓ cup water

Fettuccine with Roasted Red Pepper Sauce

Prepare shells according to package directions. Preheat oven to 375°F. Combine ricotta cheese and egg in medium bowl. Add mozzarella, parsley, Parmesan cheese, basil and oregano. Stir in sausage. Combine spaghetti sauce and water in small bowl. Put ¾ cup of the sauce in bottom of 13×9×2-inch baking pan. Fill shells with sausage-cheese mixture and place in pan. Pour remaining sauce over top. Bake 35 minutes or until stuffed shells are heated through and cheese melts.
Makes 9 servings (2 shells each).

Linguine with Red Seafood Sauce

    3 tablespoons olive or vegetable
        oil
    1 large onion, finely chopped
    2 cloves garlic, minced
    ½ cup dry white wine
    2 cups (16 ounces) canned or
        homemade meatless
        spaghetti sauce
    2 tablespoons chopped parsley
    1 bay leaf, crumbled
    2 teaspoons dried basil leaves
    ¾ teaspoon TABASCO® pepper
        sauce
    ½ teaspoon salt
    ¾ pound medium shrimp,
        peeled, deveined
    ¾ pound sea scallops, quartered
        or bay scallops
    12 ounces linguine, cooked,
        drained

In large heavy saucepot or Dutch oven heat oil; cook onion and garlic 5 minutes or until golden. Add wine; simmer until reduced by half. Stir in spaghetti sauce, parsley, bay leaf, basil, Tabasco® sauce and salt. Cover; simmer 10 minutes. Add shrimp and scallops. Cover; simmer 4 to 5 minutes or until seafood is done. Serve with linguine.
Makes 6 servings.
  Microwave Directions: In 3-quart microwave-safe casserole place oil, onion, garlic and white wine. Cook uncovered on High 5 to 7 minutes or until onion is tender. Stir in spaghetti sauce, parsley, bay leaf, basil, Tabasco® sauce and salt. Cook uncovered on High 5 to 8 minutes or until bubbly. Stir in shrimp and scallops. Cook uncovered on High 7 to 9 minutes or until seafood is done. Serve with linguine.

Santa Fe Pasta

**³/₄ lb. VELVEETA Pasteurized
   Process Cheese Spread
2 tablespoons milk
1 8³/₄-oz. can whole kernel corn,
   drained
1 8-oz. can kidney beans,
   drained
2 cups (8 ozs.) mostaccioli
   noodles, cooked, drained
1 4-oz. can chopped green
   chilies, drained
¹/₂ teaspoon chili powder
1 cup corn chips**

Cube ¹/₂ lb. process cheese spread.
Combine with milk in saucepan; stir
over low heat until process cheese
spread is melted. Add corn, beans,
noodles, chilies and chili powder; mix
lightly. Spoon mixture into 1¹/₂-quart
casserole. Bake at 350°, 20 minutes.
Top with chips and remaining process
cheese spread, sliced. Continue baking until process cheese spread begins
to melt.
6 servings.

Preparation time: 15 minutes
Baking time: 25 minutes

   Microwave: Cube ¹/₂ lb. process
cheese spread. Combine with milk in
2-quart microwave-safe bowl. Microwave on High 2 to 3 minutes or until
process cheese spread is melted, stirring after 2 minutes. Stir in corn,
beans, noodles, chilies and chili powder; microwave on High 5 minutes,
stirring every 2 minutes. Top with
chips and remaining process cheese
spread, sliced. Microwave on High 2
minutes or until process cheese
spread begins to melt.

Creamy Fettucini Alfredo

**1 8-ounce package
   PHILADELPHIA BRAND
   Cream Cheese, cubed
³/₄ cup (3 ounces) KRAFT Grated
   Parmesan Cheese
¹/₂ cup PARKAY Margarine
¹/₂ cup milk
8 ounces fettucini, cooked,
   drained**

In large saucepan, combine cream
cheese, parmesan cheese, margarine
and milk; stir over low heat until
smooth. Add fettucini; toss lightly.
4 servings.

Creamy Fettucini Alfredo

Pesto

**¹/₄ cup plus 1 tablespoon olive oil
2 tablespoons pine nuts
1 cup tightly packed, rinsed,
   drained, stemmed fresh
   basil leaves (do not use
   dried basil)
2 medium cloves garlic
¹/₄ teaspoon salt
¹/₄ cup freshly grated Parmesan
   cheese
1¹/₂ tablespoons freshly grated
   Romano cheese**

1. Heat 1 tablespoon of the oil in
small saucepan or skillet over
medium-low heat. Add pine nuts;
saute, stirring and shaking pan constantly, until nuts are light brown, 30
to 45 seconds. Transfer nuts immediately to paper-towel-lined plate to
drain.

2. Combine pine nuts, basil leaves,
garlic, salt and remaining ¹/₄ cup oil
in food processor or blender container.
Process until mixture is evenly
blended and pieces are very finely
chopped.
3. Transfer basil mixture to small
bowl. Stir in Parmesan and Romano
cheeses. Pesto can be refrigerated,
covered with thin layer of olive oil, up
to 1 week, or pesto can be frozen for
several months. Thaw and bring to
room temperature before using.
Makes about ³/₄ cup pesto.
   Serving Suggestions: Toss pesto
with hot cooked buttered fettuccine or
linguine; this recipe will dress ¹/₂ to
³/₄ pound pasta. Stir small amount of
pesto into broth-based vegetable or
meat soups. Whisk small amount of
pesto into vinaigrette for tossed salads. Mix pesto with softened butter to
be used on steamed vegetables,
poached fish or omelets.

Creamy Tortellini Primavera

- **3 tablespoons olive or vegetable oil**
- **1 medium clove garlic, finely chopped**
- **1 envelope LIPTON® Vegetable Recipe Soup Mix**
- **2 cups (1 pint) light cream or half and half**
- **1 pound egg or spinach tortellini, cooked and drained**
- **¼ cup grated Parmesan cheese**
- **¼ cup finely chopped parsley**
- **¼ teaspoon pepper**

In large skillet, heat oil and cook garlic over medium heat until golden. Stir in vegetable recipe soup mix blended with cream, then hot tortellini. Bring just to the boiling point, then simmer, stirring occasionally, 5 minutes. Stir in remaining ingredients. Garnish, if desired, with additional parsley and cheese.
Makes about 4 appetizer or 2 main-dish servings.

Microwave Directions: In 2-quart casserole, heat oil with garlic at HIGH (Full Power) 2 minutes. Stir in vegetable recipe soup mix blended with cream and heat uncovered 4 minutes, stirring twice. Add hot tortellini and heat uncovered 3 minutes. Stir in remaining ingredients and heat 1 minute. Garnish and serve as above.

Seafood over Angel Hair Pasta

Seafood over Angel Hair Pasta

- **¼ cup WISH-BONE® Italian Dressing**
- **¼ cup chopped shallots or onions**
- **1 cup thinly sliced carrots**
- **1 cup thinly sliced snow peas (about 4 ounces)**
- **1 cup chicken broth**
- **¼ cup sherry**
- **8 mussels, well scrubbed**
- **½ pound sea scallops**
- **½ pound uncooked medium shrimp, cleaned (keep tails on)**
- **¼ cup whipping or heavy cream**
- **2 tablespoons all-purpose flour Salt and pepper to taste**
- **8 ounces angel hair pasta or capellini, cooked and drained**

In 12-inch skillet, heat Italian dressing and cook shallots over medium-high heat 2 minutes. Add carrots and snow peas and cook 2 minutes. Add broth, then sherry. Bring to a boil, then add mussels, scallops and shrimp. Simmer uncovered 3 minutes or until seafood is done and mussel shells open. (Discard any unopened shells). Stir in cream blended with flour and cook over medium heat, stirring occasionally, 2 minutes or until sauce is slightly thickened. Stir in salt and pepper. Serve over hot angel hair pasta and, if desired, with freshly ground pepper.
Makes about 4 main-dish servings.

Note: Also terrific with Wish-Bone® Robusto Italian, Italian & Cheese, Lite Italian, Herbal Italian, Blended Italian, Classic Dijon Vinaigrette or Lite Classic Dijon Vinaigrette Dressing.

Shrimp Milano

- **1 lb. frozen cleaned shrimp, cooked, drained**
- **2 cups mushroom slices**
- **1 cup green or red pepper strips**
- **1 garlic clove, minced**
- **¼ cup PARKAY Margarine**
- **¾ lb. VELVEETA Pasteurized Process Cheese Spread, cubed**
- **¾ cup whipping cream**
- **½ teaspoon dill weed**
- **⅓ cup (1½ ozs.) KRAFT 100% Grated Parmesan Cheese**
- **8 ozs. fettucini, cooked, drained**

In large skillet, saute shrimp, vegetables and garlic in margarine. Reduce heat to low. Add process cheese spread, cream and dill. Stir until process cheese spread is melted. Stir in parmesan cheese. Add fettucini; toss lightly.
4 to 6 servings.

Preparation time: 20 minutes
Cooking time: 15 minutes

Paradise Pasta

- ¼ **cup unsalted butter**
- 1 **can (28 ounces) Italian plum tomatoes**
- ¼ **cup finely shredded carrot**
- ¼ **cup finely chopped celery**
- ¼ **cup finely chopped onion**
- 1 **tablespoon dried basil, crumbled**
- ¼ **teaspoon sugar**
- 6 **tablespoons pine nuts (1½ to 2 ounces), toasted**
- 1 **pound uncooked angel hair pasta**
  Boiling salted water
- 2 **tablespoons unsalted butter, at room temperature**
- 1 **cup whipping cream**
- ¾ **teaspoon salt**
- ¼ **teaspoon ground white pepper**
  Fresh parsley sprigs, if desired

1. Melt ¼ cup butter in 3-quart heavy noncorrosive saucepan over medium heat. Drain liquid from tomatoes into saucepan. Puree tomatoes in blender or food processor and press through sieve into saucepan; discard seeds.
2. Add carrot, celery, onion, basil and sugar to saucepan. Heat to boiling. Reduce heat to low; simmer, uncovered, stirring occasionally, 1 hour.
3. Coarsely chop 3 tablespoons of the pine nuts; keep remaining 3 tablespoons pine nuts whole.

4. Cook angel hair pasta in large kettle of boiling salted water just until al dente, 2 minutes; drain well. Transfer to heated serving bowl. Add 2 tablespoons butter; toss until melted.
5. Just before serving, stir cream, chopped pine nuts, salt and pepper into sauce. Cook over low heat just until sauce is hot; do not boil. Pour sauce over pasta; toss to mix. Sprinkle with remaining whole pine nuts; garnish with parsley. Serve immediately.
Makes 6 servings.

Spinach and Noodles Parmesan

- ½ **cup chopped onion**
- 1 **package (10 ounces) frozen chopped spinach**
- 1 **can (10¾ ounces) CAMPBELL'S® Condensed Cream of Celery Soup**
- ½ **cup sour cream**
- ½ **cup grated Parmesan cheese**
- ⅛ **teaspoon black pepper**
- ⅛ **teaspoon ground nutmeg Generous dash ground red pepper (cayenne)**
- 2 **cups cooked wide egg noodles (6 ounces uncooked)**

To Microwave:
1. Place onion in 2-quart microwave-safe casserole. Cover with lid; microwave on HIGH 3 minutes or until tender, stirring once during cooking.
2. Add spinach. Cover; microwave on HIGH 5 minutes or until spinach is thawed, stirring twice during cooking. Stir in soup; stir in sour cream, cheese, black pepper, nutmeg and red pepper.
3. Cover; microwave at 50% power 8 minutes or until hot, stirring once during cooking. Add hot noodles; toss to coat.
Makes about 5 cups or 8 servings.

Nouvelle Fettucini

- 2 **cups broccoli flowerets**
- 1 **cup carrot slices**
- ¼ **cup PARKAY Margarine**
- 2 **cups summer squash slices**
- ½ **lb. asparagus spears, cut into 1-inch pieces**
- 1 **teaspoon dried oregano leaves, crushed**
- ¾ **lb. VELVEETA Pasteurized Process Cheese Spread, cubed**
- ¾ **cup half and half**
- ¼ **lb. pepperoni, chopped**
- ⅓ **cup (1½ ozs.) KRAFT 100% Grated Parmesan Cheese**
- 8 **ozs. fettucini, cooked, drained**

In large skillet, stir-fry broccoli and carrots in margarine 3 minutes. Add squash, asparagus and oregano; stir-fry until crisp-tender. Reduce heat to low. Add process cheese spread, half and half, pepperoni and parmesan cheese; stir until process cheese spread is melted. Add fettucini; toss lightly.
6 servings.

Preparation time: 25 minutes
Cooking time: 15 minutes

Microwave: Reduce half and half to ½ cup. Microwave broccoli, carrots and margarine in 2½-quart microwave-safe bowl on High 2 minutes, stirring after 1 minute. Stir in squash, asparagus and oregano; microwave on High 2 to 3 minutes or until crisp-tender, stirring after 2 minutes. Add process cheese spread and half and half; mix lightly. Microwave on High 4 to 6 minutes or until process cheese spread is melted, stirring every 2 minutes. Stir in pepperoni and parmesan cheese; microwave on High 2 to 4 minutes or until thoroughly heated, stirring after 2 minutes. Add fettucini; toss lightly.

Spinach and Noodles Parmesan

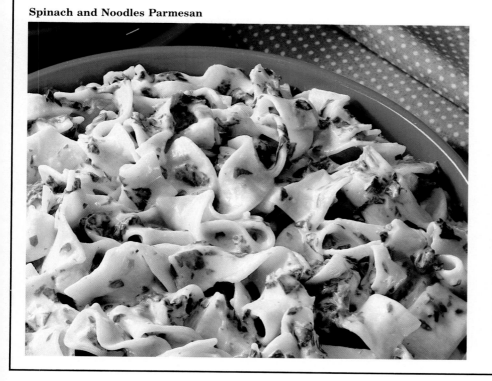

Spaghetti Mediterranean

1½ **pounds fresh tomatoes (about 4 large)**
12 **pitted green olives**
4 to 6 **flat anchovy fillets**
2 **medium cloves garlic**
½ **pound uncooked spaghetti Boiling salted water**
¼ **cup olive oil**
½ **cup chopped fresh parsley**
1 **tablespoon drained capers**
2 **teaspoons chopped fresh basil or ½ teaspoon dried basil, crumbled**
½ **teaspoon dried oregano, crumbled**
½ **teaspoon salt**
¼ **teaspoon dried hot red pepper flakes**

1. Place tomatoes in large saucepan with boiling water to cover 60 seconds to loosen skins. Immediately drain tomatoes and rinse under cold running water. Peel, seed and chop tomatoes coarsely. Slice olives. Chop anchovies. Mince garlic.
2. Cook spaghetti in large kettle of boiling salted water just until al dente, 8 to 12 minutes; drain well.
3. While spaghetti is cooking, heat oil in 10-inch noncorrosive skillet over medium-high heat. Add garlic; cook just until garlic begins to color, 45 to 60 seconds. Stir in tomatoes, parsley, capers, basil, oregano, salt and the pepper flakes.
4. Add olives and anchovies to skillet; cook over medium-high heat, stirring constantly until most of the visible liquid has evaporated and sauce is slightly thickened, about 10 minutes.

Pour sauce over spaghetti in heated serving bowl. Toss lightly and serve immediately.
Makes 3 to 4 servings.

Creamy Spinach Fettucini

1 **small green pepper, chopped**
1 **small red pepper, chopped**
1 **small onion, chopped**
1 **(8-ounce) carton plain nonfat yogurt**
½ **cup canned white sauce**
2 **tablespoons dried Italian seasoning**
1½ **cups (6 ounces) ARMOUR® Lower Salt Ham cut into ½-inch cubes**
12 **ounces uncooked spinach fettucini, cooked according to package directions omitting salt and drained**
6 **slices ARMOUR® Lower Salt Bacon, cooked crisp and crumbled**

Spray large skillet with nonstick cooking spray; place over medium heat. Add vegetables; sauté until tender-crisp. Mix yogurt, white sauce and seasoning in small bowl. Add to vegetables and heat through. Add ham; continue cooking until hot. Spoon over warm fettucini; top with bacon. Garnish with parsley or fresh rosemary, if desired.
Makes 4 to 6 servings.

Nutrition Information Per Serving: 352 calories, 17.7 g protein, 9 g fat, 48 g carbohydrates, 20.6 mg cholesterol, 531 mg sodium.

Summer Spaghetti

1 **pound firm ripe fresh plum tomatoes**
1 **medium onion**
6 **pitted green olives**
2 **medium cloves garlic**
⅓ **cup chopped fresh parsley**
2 **tablespoons finely shredded fresh basil or ¾ teaspoon dried basil, crumbled**
2 **teaspoons drained capers**
½ **teaspoon paprika**
¼ **teaspoon dried oregano, crumbled**
1 **tablespoon red wine vinegar**
½ **cup olive oil**
1 **pound uncooked spaghetti Boiling salted water**

1. Chop tomatoes coarsely. Chop onion and olives. Mince garlic. Combine tomatoes, onion, olives, garlic, parsley, basil, capers, paprika and oregano in medium bowl; toss well. Drizzle vinegar over tomato mixture. Then pour oil over tomato mixture. Stir until thoroughly mixed. Refrigerate, covered, at least 6 hours or overnight.
2. Just before serving, cook spaghetti in large kettle of boiling salted water just until al dente, 8 to 12 minutes; drain well. Immediately toss hot pasta with cold marinated tomato sauce. Serve at once.
Makes 4 to 6 servings.

Spaghetti with Cream Sauce

2 **cups mushroom slices**
1 **cup halved zucchini slices**
1 **garlic clove, minced**
2 **tablespoons PARKAY Margarine**
⅓ **cup half and half**
½ **lb. VELVEETA Pasteurized Process Cheese Spread, cubed**
8 **ozs. spaghetti, cooked, drained**

Sauté vegetables and garlic in margarine until zucchini is crisp-tender. Reduce heat to low. Add half and half and process cheese spread; stir until process cheese spread is melted. Toss with hot spaghetti.
6 servings.

Preparation time: 15 minutes
Cooking time: 10 minutes

Summer Spaghetti

Mediterranean Pasta

- 1 roll (16 ounces) ECKRICH®
    Country Sausage
- 2 medium onions, sliced thin
- 1 small clove garlic, minced
- 1 tablespoon olive oil
- 2 medium zucchini, sliced thin
- ½ teaspoon dried basil leaves
- ¼ teaspoon dried oregano leaves
- ¼ teaspoon salt
    Dash ground black pepper
- 2 large tomatoes, seeded, cut
    into large pieces
    Hot cooked thin spaghetti
    Grated Parmesan cheese,
    optional

Break sausage into pieces and cook in large skillet over medium heat until lightly browned. Drain and set aside. Place onions, garlic and oil in same skillet. Cook and stir over medium heat until onions are quite soft and lightly browned. Add zucchini, basil, oregano, salt and pepper; cook 5 minutes more. Add tomatoes; cover and simmer 10 minutes more, stirring occasionally. Serve over spaghetti with Parmesan cheese.
Makes 4 to 5 servings.

Peanut Noodles

- 1 cup V8® Vegetable Juice
- ½ cup chopped green onions
- ½ cup chopped sweet red
    pepper
- ⅓ cup creamy peanut butter
- 1 clove garlic, minced
- 1 tablespoon soy sauce
- ½ teaspoon grated fresh ginger
    Dash crushed red pepper
- 8 ounces spaghetti, cooked and
    drained
    Chopped unsalted peanuts for
    garnish

In 1-quart saucepan, combine V8 juice, green onions, sweet red pepper, peanut butter, garlic, soy sauce, ginger and crushed red pepper. Over medium heat, heat until hot and smooth, stirring often. In large bowl, combine spaghetti and V8 mixture; toss to coat well. Garnish with peanuts.
Makes 5 cups or 4 main-dish servings.

Per serving: 357 calories, 14 g protein, 12 g fat, 51 g carbohydrate, 566 mg sodium, 0 mg cholesterol.

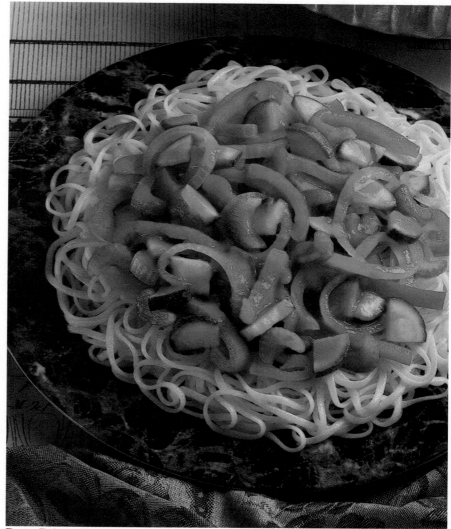

Pasta Primavera

Pasta Primavera

- 2 cups V8® Vegetable Juice
- 1 tablespoon all-purpose flour
- ⅛ teaspoon pepper
- 1 tablespoon olive oil
- 2 large stalks celery, thinly
    sliced
- 1 large onion, thinly sliced
- 2 medium cloves garlic, minced
- 1 teaspoon dried oregano
    leaves, crushed
- ½ teaspoon dried basil leaves,
    crushed
- 1 large sweet red pepper, cut
    into strips
- 1 medium zucchini, cut into
    quarters lengthwise and
    sliced
- 6 cups hot cooked linguini
    Grated Parmesan cheese
    (optional)

1. In small bowl, stir together V8 juice, flour and pepper; set aside. In 10-inch skillet over medium heat, in hot oil, cook celery, onion, garlic, oregano and basil until vegetables are tender, stirring occasionally.
2. Add red pepper and zucchini. Cook until tender, stirring occasionally. Stir V8 mixture into skillet. Cook until mixture boils and thickens, stirring often. Reduce heat to low; simmer, uncovered, 3 minutes.
3. Serve over hot linguini. Top with Parmesan cheese, if desired.
Makes 4 cups sauce or 8 side-dish servings.

Per serving: 164 calories, 4 g protein, 3 g fat, 32 g carbohydrate, 221 mg sodium, 0 mg cholesterol.

Tagliatelle with Creamy Sauce

Tagliatelle with Creamy Sauce

- **7 to 8 ounces tagliatelle pasta, cooked, drained**
- **1 cup GALBANI® Mascarpone cheese**
- **1 package (10 ounces) frozen peas, cooked, drained**
- **2 ounces (½ cup) finely chopped prosciutto**
- **1½ cups (6 ounces) shredded mozzarella cheese**
- **Butter or margarine**

Layer ½ of the tagliatelle in buttered 9×9-inch baking dish. Spoon ½ of the Mascarpone onto tagliatelle. Sprinkle with ½ of the peas and ½ of the prosciutto. Top with ½ of the mozzarella. Repeat layers. Dot with butter. Bake in preheated 350°F oven 20 minutes or until heated through.
Makes 4 to 6 servings.

*Favorite recipe from **Bel Paese Sales Co., Inc.***

Neapolitan Sauce

- **1 can (28 ounces) Italian plum tomatoes**
- **2 tablespoons butter**
- **1 tablespoon olive oil**
- **1 teaspoon dried basil, crumbled**
- **½ teaspoon salt**
- **⅛ teaspoon pepper**
- **3 tablespoons chopped fresh parsley**
- **½ pound spaghetti, cooked**
- **½ cup freshly grated Parmesan cheese, if desired**

Press tomatoes and their liquid through sieve into bowl; discard seeds. Heat butter and oil in 2-quart noncorrosive saucepan over medium heat. Stir in sieved tomatoes, basil, salt and pepper. Heat to boiling; reduce heat to medium-low. Cook, uncovered, stirring frequently, until sauce is reduced and measures 2 cups, 30 to 40 minutes. Stir in parsley. Toss with spaghetti. Serve immediately with Parmesan cheese to sprinkle.
Makes 2 to 3 servings.

Souper Quick "Lasagna"

- **1½ pounds ground beef**
- **1 envelope LIPTON® Onion or Onion-Mushroom Recipe Soup Mix**
- **3 cans (8 ounces each) tomato sauce**
- **1 cup water**
- **½ teaspoon oregano (optional)**
- **1 package (8 ounces) broad egg noodles, cooked and drained**
- **1 package (16 ounces) mozzarella cheese, shredded**

Preheat oven to 375°

In large skillet, brown ground beef over medium-high heat; drain. Stir in onion recipe soup mix, tomato sauce, water and oregano. Simmer covered, stirring occasionally, 15 minutes.

In 2-quart oblong baking dish, spoon enough sauce to cover bottom. Alternately layer noodles, ground beef mixture and cheese, ending with cheese. Bake 30 minutes or until bubbling.
Makes about 6 servings.

Microwave Directions: In 2-quart casserole, heat ground beef, uncovered, at HIGH (Full Power) 7 minutes, stirring once; drain. Stir in onion recipe soup mix, tomato sauce, water and oregano. Heat at MEDIUM (50% Full Power) 5 minutes, stirring once. In 2-quart oblong baking dish, spoon enough sauce to cover bottom. Alternately layer as above. Heat covered at MEDIUM, turning dish occasionally, 10 minutes or until bubbling. Let stand covered 5 minutes.

Pasta with Clam Sauce

- **1 can (10¾ ounces) CAMPBELL'S® Condensed Cream of Mushroom or Cream of Celery Soup**
- **1 can (6½ ounces) minced clams, undrained**
- **¼ cup milk**
- **¼ cup Chablis or other dry white wine**
- **2 tablespoons chopped fresh parsley**
- **2 tablespoons grated Parmesan cheese**
- **1 large clove garlic, minced**
- **8 ounces linguini, cooked and drained**

To Microwave:

1. In 1½-quart microwave-safe casserole, stir soup until smooth; stir in clams with their liquid, milk, wine, parsley, Parmesan and garlic. Cover with lid; microwave on HIGH 8 minutes or until hot and bubbling, stirring once during cooking.

2. Toss with linguini; serve with additional Parmesan.

Makes 4 servings.

Lasagna Deliciousa

- ½ of a 1-pound package uncooked CREAMETTE® Lasagna
- 1 pound bulk Italian sausage
- ½ pound ground beef
- 1 cup chopped onion
- 2 cloves garlic, minced
- 1 can (28 ounces) tomatoes, cut up, undrained
- 2 cans (6 ounces each) tomato paste
- 2 teaspoons sugar
- 2½ teaspoons salt, divided
- 1½ teaspoons dried basil, crushed
- ½ teaspoon fennel seeds
- ¼ teaspoon pepper
- 1 container (15 ounces) ricotta cheese
- 1 egg, beaten
- 1 tablespoon parsley flakes
- 1 cup sliced pitted ripe olives
- 4 cups (1 pound) shredded mozzarella cheese
- ¾ cup grated Parmesan cheese

Prepare lasagna according to package directions; drain. Cook sausage, ground beef, onion and garlic in large skillet over medium-high heat until sausage is no longer pink and onion is tender; drain. Stir in tomatoes, tomato paste, sugar, 2 teaspoons of the salt, the basil, fennel seeds and pepper. Bring to a boil over high heat. Reduce heat to low. Simmer, uncovered, 20 minutes.

In small bowl, blend ricotta, egg, parsley and remaining ½ teaspoon salt. Spoon 1½ cups of the meat sauce into 13×9-inch baking dish. Layer ⅓ *each* of the lasagna, remaining meat sauce, ricotta mixture, olives, mozzarella and Parmesan cheese into dish. Repeat layers. Cover with foil. Bake at 375°F 25 minutes. Uncover. Bake about 20 minutes more or until heated through. Let stand 10 minutes before cutting.

Makes 8 to 10 servings.

Lasagna with White and Red Sauces

- Béchamel Sauce (recipe follows)
- ½ medium onion, sliced
- 1 clove garlic, minced
- 2 to 3 tablespoons vegetable oil
- 1 pound lean ground beef
- 1 can (28 ounces) crushed tomatoes or 1 can (28 ounces) whole tomatoes, chopped, undrained
- ½ cup thinly sliced celery
- ½ cup thinly sliced carrot
- 1 teaspoon dried basil, crushed
- 1 package (1 pound) lasagna noodles, cooked, drained
- 6 ounces BEL PAESE® cheese,* thinly sliced
- 6 hard-cooked eggs, sliced (optional)
- 2 tablespoons butter or margarine, cut into small pieces
- 1 cup (about 2 ounces) freshly grated GALBANI® Parmigiano-Reggiano or Grana Padano cheese

Prepare Béchamel Sauce; set aside. Cook and stir onion and garlic in hot oil in Dutch oven over medium-high heat until tender. Add ground beef and cook until no longer pink, stirring occasionally. Add tomatoes, celery, carrot and basil. Reduce heat to low. Cover and simmer 45 minutes. Remove cover and simmer 15 minutes more.

Arrange ⅓ of the lasagna noodles in bottom of buttered 13½×9-inch baking dish. Add ½ of the Bel Paese® and ½ of the eggs. Spread with meat sauce. Repeat layers of noodles, Bel Paese® and eggs. Spread with Béchamel Sauce. Top with layer of noodles. Dot with butter. Sprinkle with Parmigiano-Reggiano. Bake in preheated 350°F oven 30 to 40 minutes or until heated through. Let stand 10 minutes before cutting.

Makes 6 servings.

*Remove wax coating and moist, white crust from cheese.

BÉCHAMEL SAUCE: Melt 2 tablespoons butter or margarine in small saucepan over medium-low heat. Stir in 2 tablespoons all-purpose flour. Gradually blend in ¾ cup milk. Season to taste with white pepper. Cook until thick and bubbly, stirring constantly.

Makes ¾ cup sauce.

Lasagna with White and Red Sauces

SIDE DISHES

Vegetable, rice, and potato dishes are sensational accompaniments when prepared with the great ideas you'll find here. Serve crisp green beans, carrots, broccoli, and asparagus that sparkle with flavor. Try rice dishes with an international touch or potatoes that are out of the ordinary. These side dishes are alluring enough to steal the limelight.

Homestyle Zucchini & Tomatoes

2 tablespoons oil
1 medium clove garlic, finely chopped*
3 medium zucchini, thinly sliced (about 4½ cups)
1 can (14½ ounces) whole peeled tomatoes, drained and chopped (reserve liquid)
1 envelope LIPTON® Golden Onion or Onion Recipe Soup Mix
½ teaspoon basil leaves

In large skillet, heat oil and cook garlic with zucchini over medium-high heat 3 minutes. Stir in tomatoes, then golden onion recipe soup mix thoroughly blended with reserved liquid and basil. Bring to a boil, then simmer, stirring occasionally, 10 minutes or until zucchini is tender and sauce is slightly thickened.
Makes about 4 servings.
  Substitution: Use ¼ teaspoon garlic powder.
  Microwave Directions: In 2-quart casserole, combine zucchini with tomatoes. Stir in golden onion recipe soup mix thoroughly blended with reserved liquid, garlic and basil. Heat covered at HIGH (Full Power) 5 minutes, stirring once. Remove cover and heat 4 minutes or until zucchini is tender, stirring once. Let stand covered 2 minutes.

Country Bean Barbecue

1 can (16 ounces) lima beans
6 slices bacon, diced
½ cup sliced onion
½ cup diced celery
1 clove garlic, minced
1 cup catsup
1 can (16 ounces) red kidney beans, drained
½ teaspoon TABASCO® pepper sauce

Drain lima beans; reserve ½ cup liquid. In large skillet cook bacon until browned. Drain all but 1 tablespoon bacon fat from skillet. Add onion, celery and garlic; cook 5 minutes or until tender. Stir in catsup, lima beans, reserved lima bean liquid and kidney beans; mix gently. Simmer uncovered 20 minutes; stir occasionally. Stir in Tabasco® sauce.
Makes 6 to 8 servings.

Buffet Bean Bake

6 slices bacon
1 cup packed brown sugar
½ cup vinegar
½ teaspoon salt
1 tablespoon FRENCH'S America's Favorite Mustard or DURKEE Famous Sauce
1 can (16 ounces) butter beans, drained
1 can (16 ounces) French-style green beans, drained
1 can (16 ounces) pork and beans, drained
1 can (16 ounces) lima beans, drained
1 can (15½ ounces) yellow wax beans, drained
1 can (15 ounces) kidney beans, drained
1 can (2.8 ounces) DURKEE French Fried Onions

Preheat oven to 350°. In medium skillet, fry bacon until crisp. Remove from skillet; crumble and set aside. Drain all but about 2 tablespoons drippings from skillet; add sugar, vinegar, salt and mustard. Simmer, uncovered, 10 minutes. In large bowl, combine drained beans, *½ can* French Fried Onions and hot sugar mixture. Spoon bean mixture into 9×13-inch baking dish. Bake, covered, at 350° for 30 minutes or until heated through. Top with crumbled bacon and remaining onions; bake, uncovered, 5 minutes or until onions are golden brown.
Makes 12 to 14 servings.

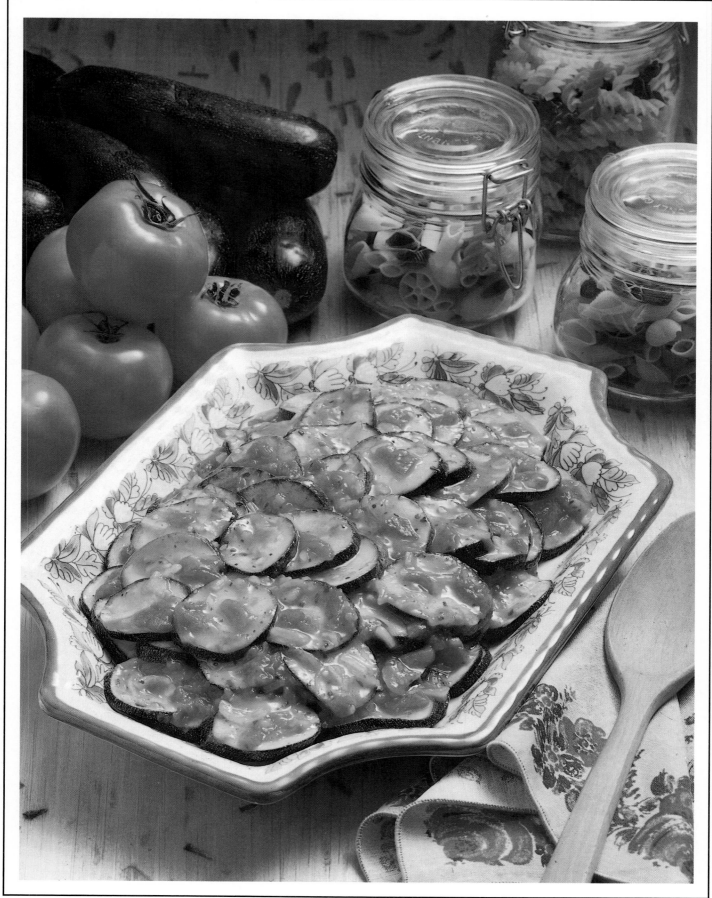

Homestyle Zucchini & Tomatoes

Country-Style Baked Beans

1 envelope LIPTON® Onion, Onion-Mushroom or Beefy Mushroom Recipe Soup Mix
1 can (24 ounces) pork and beans in tomato sauce
1 medium apple, chopped
¼ cup brown sugar
1 tablespoon prepared mustard

In large saucepan, combine all ingredients. Cook uncovered over medium heat, stirring occasionally, 20 minutes.
Makes about 6 servings.
Microwave Directions: In 1½-quart casserole, combine all ingredients. Heat covered at HIGH (Full Power), stirring occasionally, 12 minutes or until bubbling. Let stand covered 5 minutes.

Asparagus in Anchovy Sauce

¾ cup water
¾ teaspoon salt, divided
2 packages (8 to 10 ounces each) frozen asparagus spears
1 cup CRISCO® Oil
3 tablespoons lemon juice
1 tablespoon anchovy paste
1 teaspoon onion powder
1 teaspoon dried chervil leaves
¼ teaspoon garlic powder

Combine water and ½ teaspoon salt in large saucepan. Heat to boiling. Add asparagus. Return to boiling. Cover. Reduce heat to moderate. Cook 3 to 4 minutes, or until asparagus is thawed and warm. Drain. Spread asparagus in shallow baking dish.

Blend remaining ingredients, including remaining ¼ teaspoon salt, in small mixing bowl. Pour over asparagus. Cover and refrigerate 3 to 4 hours, stirring occasionally. Serve chilled or at room temperature.
4 to 6 servings.

Cheddar Broccoli Corn Bake

¼ cup butter or margarine, divided
2 tablespoons all-purpose flour
¼ teaspoon salt
1½ cups milk
1½ cups (6 ounces) shredded Cheddar cheese
1 can (12 ounces) whole kernel corn, drained
2 cups KELLOGG'S CORN FLAKES® cereal, crushed to make 1 cup, divided
2 packages (10 ounces each) frozen broccoli spears, cooked, drained

Melt 2 tablespoons of the butter in large saucepan over medium heat. Stir in flour and salt. Gradually stir in milk. Cook until thickened and bubbly, stirring constantly. Add cheese, stirring until melted. Stir in corn and ¼ cup of the crushed cereal. Remove from heat.

Arrange broccoli in 12×8-inch glass baking dish with florets toward both long edges. Pour cheese sauce over broccoli stalks. Melt remaining 2 tablespoons butter in small saucepan over medium heat. Stir in remaining ¾ cup cereal. Sprinkle over cheese sauce. Bake at 350°F 30 minutes or until heated through.
Makes 8 servings.

Asparagus in Anchovy Sauce

Broccoli and Rice with Walnuts

¼ cup coarsely chopped walnuts or slivered almonds
1 tablespoon oil
½ package (2¼ cups) BIRDS EYE® Broccoli Cuts*
2 tablespoons sliced scallions
1 garlic clove, minced
1 cup chicken broth or water
2 tablespoons dry sherry (optional)
1½ tablespoons soy sauce
1 cup MINUTE® Rice

Cook and stir walnuts in hot oil in large skillet until lightly browned; remove from skillet. Add broccoli, scallions and garlic to oil remaining in skillet. Cook and stir 2 to 3 minutes. Add broth, sherry and soy sauce. Bring to a full boil. Stir in rice. Cover; remove from heat. Let stand 5 minutes. Fluff with fork and sprinkle with walnuts.
Makes 4 servings.
*You may use 1 package (9 oz.) BIRDS EYE® Cut Green Beans for the broccoli.

Brussels Sprouts Amandine

1 tablespoon CRISCO® Oil
¼ cup sliced almonds
¾ cup water
1½ teaspoons instant beef bouillon granules
1 package (16 ounces) frozen Brussels sprouts
Dash pepper

Heat Crisco® Oil in medium saucepan. Add almonds. Sauté over moderate heat until light golden brown. Drain on paper towels.

Combine water and bouillon granules in medium saucepan. Heat to boiling. Add Brussels sprouts. Return to boiling. Cover. Reduce heat. Simmer, stirring once to break apart Brussels sprouts, 8 to 12 minutes, or until tender. Drain. Stir in almonds and pepper.
4 to 6 servings.

Sesame Broccoli

½ bunch DOLE™ Broccoli, cut
   into flowerets
1 tablespoon butter or
   margarine, melted
2 teaspoons sesame seeds,
   toasted
2 teaspoons soy sauce
   Pinch garlic powder
   Pinch ground ginger

In large saucepan, cook broccoli in vegetable steamer basket over boiling water 5 minutes; drain. In small bowl, combine remaining ingredients. In serving bowl, toss broccoli with sesame mixture.
Makes 2 to 3 servings.

Barley with Corn and Red Pepper

½ cup WISH-BONE® Italian
   Dressing
1 medium red pepper, chopped
½ cup chopped onion
1 cup uncooked pearled barley
1¾ cups chicken broth
1¼ cups water
2 tablespoons finely chopped
   coriander (cilantro) or
   parsley
1 tablespoon lime juice
½ teaspoon ground cumin
⅛ teaspoon pepper
1 can (7 ounces) whole kernel
   corn, drained

In large saucepan, heat Italian dressing and cook red pepper with onion over medium heat, stirring occasionally, 5 minutes or until tender. Stir in barley and cook, stirring constantly, 1 minute. Stir in broth, water, coriander, lime juice, cumin and pepper. Simmer covered 50 minutes or until barley is done. (Do not stir while simmering.) Stir in corn.
Makes about 6 servings.

   Note: Also terrific with Wish-Bone® Robusto Italian, Herbal Italian, Lite Italian, Blended Italian, Classic Dijon Vinaigrette or Lite Classic Dijon Vinaigrette Dressing.

Barley with Corn and Red Pepper

Red Cabbage 'n' Apples

¼ cup margarine or butter
⅓ cup REALEMON® Lemon Juice
   from Concentrate
¼ cup firmly packed light brown
   sugar
¼ cup water
½ teaspoon caraway seeds
½ teaspoon salt
4 cups shredded red cabbage
2 medium all-purpose apples,
   cored and coarsely chopped

In large saucepan, melt margarine; stir in ReaLemon® brand, sugar, water, caraway and salt. Add cabbage and apples; bring to a boil. Reduce heat; cover and simmer 25 to 30 minutes.
Makes 6 to 8 servings.

   Microwave: In 2-quart round baking dish, melt margarine on 100% power (high) 45 seconds. Stir in ReaLemon® brand, sugar, water, caraway and salt; add cabbage and apples. Cook covered on 100% power (high) 15 to 20 minutes, stirring every 5 minutes. Let stand for 2 minutes before serving.

Vegetable Stir-Fry

1 8-ounce package *Light*
   PHILADELPHIA BRAND
   Neufchâtel Cheese, cubed
¼ cup sesame seed, toasted
2 cups diagonally cut carrot
   slices
2 cups diagonally cut celery
   slices
¾ cup thin green pepper strips
2 tablespoons PARKAY
   Margarine
¼ teaspoon salt
   Dash of pepper

Coat neufchâtel cheese cubes with sesame seed; chill. In large skillet or wok, stir-fry vegetables in margarine and seasonings until crisp-tender. Remove from heat. Add neufchâtel cheese to vegetables; mix lightly.
6 to 8 servings.

   Variation: Substitute PHILADELPHIA BRAND Cream Cheese for Neufchâtel Cheese.

Broccoli and Pasta

- 1 package (10 ounces) frozen chopped broccoli
- 2 tablespoons CRISCO® Oil
- 2 tablespoons finely chopped onion
- 1 tablespoon snipped fresh parsley
- 1 teaspoon anchovy paste (optional)
- 1 small clove garlic, minced
- 1/4 teaspoon salt
  Dash pepper
- 1 cup cooked small shell macaroni
  Grated Parmesan cheese

Cook broccoli according to package directions. Drain and set aside.

Heat Crisco® Oil in medium skillet. Add onion, parsley, anchovy paste (optional) and garlic. Cook over moderate heat, stirring constantly, about 3 minutes, or until onion is tender. Stir in broccoli, salt and pepper. Cook, stirring occasionally, 2 to 3 minutes longer, or until heated through. Remove from heat. Stir in macaroni. Sprinkle with Parmesan cheese. Serve immediately.
4 to 6 servings.

Spiced Red Cabbage

- 1/4 cup CRISCO® Oil
- 2-pound head red cabbage, cored and chopped
- 1 small onion, thinly sliced and separated into rings
- 1 small apple, cored and chopped
- 1/2 cup raisins
- 1/4 teaspoon ground cloves
- 1/8 teaspoon ground allspice
- 1 tablespoon white wine vinegar
- 2 teaspoons sugar
- 1 teaspoon salt

Heat Crisco® Oil in Dutch oven or large saucepan. Add cabbage, onion, apple, raisins, cloves and allspice. Stir to coat. Cover. Cook over moderate heat, stirring occasionally, about 1 hour, or until cabbage is tender. Stir in vinegar, sugar and salt.
6 to 8 servings.

Sweet 'n Sour Cabbage

- 1 can (11 ounces) DOLE® Mandarin Orange Segments
- 6 cups DOLE® Shredded Cabbage
- 1 medium onion, chopped
- 1 clove garlic, pressed
- 1 tablespoon vegetable oil
- 1/4 cup white wine vinegar
- 1 teaspoon caraway seeds
- 1 teaspoon salt
- 1 cup DOLE™ Fresh Pineapple chunks

Drain oranges; reserve 1/3 cup syrup. In large skillet, saute cabbage, onion and garlic in oil until onion is soft. Stir in reserved syrup, vinegar, caraway seeds and salt. Cover and simmer 10 minutes. Stir in pineapple and oranges. Cover; cook 5 minutes longer.
Makes 4 servings.

Carrot Saute

- 1 small clove garlic, pressed
- 2 tablespoons butter or margarine
- 1 tablespoon soy sauce
- 1 1/2 teaspoons water
- 1/2 teaspoon sugar
- 1 cup sliced DOLE™ Carrots
- 1/2 onion, sliced into chunks
- 1/2 cup sliced DOLE™ Celery
- 1/4 cup DOLE™ Blanched Slivered Almonds, toasted

In large skillet, saute garlic in butter. Stir in soy sauce, water and sugar; bring to a boil. Add carrots, onion and celery; saute until tender-crisp. Sprinkle with nuts.
Makes 2 servings.

Vegetables in Cheese Sauce

- 1 can (11 ounces) CAMPBELL'S® Condensed Cheddar Cheese Soup/Sauce
- 1/3 cup milk
- 1/2 teaspoon dried basil leaves, crushed
- 1 clove garlic, minced
- 2 cups cauliflowerets
- 1 small onion, cut into thin wedges
- 1 1/2 cups diagonally sliced carrots
- 1 package (10 ounces) frozen peas

To Microwave:
1. In 3-quart microwave-safe casserole, stir soup until smooth. Stir in milk, basil and garlic; mix well.
2. Add vegetables; stir to coat well. Cover with lid; microwave on HIGH 15 minutes or until vegetables are tender, stirring twice during cooking. Let stand, covered, 5 minutes.
Makes about 5 1/2 cups or 8 servings.

Broccoli and Pasta

Leeks with Bel Paese®

3 leeks
3 tablespoons butter or margarine
1 tablespoon olive oil
2 cups milk
4 ounces BEL PAESE® cheese,* thinly sliced
Pepper

Trim greens from leeks 2 inches above bulb; discard greens. Remove outer layer of bulb. Wash leeks thoroughly. Cut into large pieces. Melt butter in medium saucepan over medium-low heat. Add oil, milk and leeks. Cover and simmer 20 to 30 minutes or until leeks are tender; drain thoroughly. Place leeks in buttered 1-quart casserole. Cover with cheese. Bake in preheated 350°F oven 10 to 15 minutes or until cheese is melted. Season to taste with pepper. Serve immediately. *Makes 4 servings.*

*Remove wax coating and moist, white crust from cheese.

Dilled Carrots and Parsnips

1 can (10³/₄ ounces) CAMPBELL'S® Condensed Cream of Celery Soup
¹/₂ cup milk
¹/₄ teaspoon dried dill weed, crushed
2 cups carrots cut into 1-inch-long sticks
2 cups parsnips cut into 1-inch-long sticks

To Microwave:
1. In 3-quart microwave-safe casserole, stir soup until smooth. Add milk and dill weed; stir until well blended. Stir in carrots. Cover with lid; microwave on HIGH 6 minutes.
2. Stir in parsnips. Cover; microwave on HIGH 13 minutes or until vegetables are nearly tender, stirring twice during cooking. Let stand, covered, 5 minutes.
Makes 6 servings.

Dilled Carrots: Prepare as above but use 4 cups carrots and omit parsnips. Microwave a total of 19 minutes, stirring twice during cooking.

Onion-Glazed Carrots

1 pound carrots
1 pouch CAMPBELL'S® Onion Soup and Recipe Mix
2 tablespoons butter or margarine
¹/₄ cup packed brown sugar
¹/₄ teaspoon grated orange peel
¹/₄ cup orange juice
¹/₄ teaspoon ground cinnamon Pecan halves for garnish

1. Cut carrots into 2-inch pieces, then cut each piece in half lengthwise.
2. Place carrots in 2-quart saucepan; add enough water to cover carrots. Over high heat, heat to boiling. Reduce heat to medium-low. Cover; simmer 10 minutes or until carrots are tender. Drain carrots in colander.
3. In same saucepan, combine soup mix, butter, brown sugar, orange peel, orange juice and cinnamon. Over medium heat, heat to boiling, stirring constantly.
4. Return carrots to saucepan. Cook 5 minutes more or until carrots are glazed, stirring often. Garnish with pecan halves.
Makes 4 servings.

Note: Sweet potatoes may be prepared in the same way as these carrots. Peel sweet potatoes and cut into bite-size pieces before cooking.

Broccoli and Celery Oriental

1 tablespoon vegetable oil
3 cups broccoli flowerets
1¹/₂ cups thinly sliced celery
¹/₄ cup sliced green onions
2 tablespoons chopped pimento
1 can (10¹/₂ ounces) FRANCO-AMERICAN® Chicken Gravy
1 tablespoon soy sauce Cashews for garnish

To Microwave:
1. In 2-quart microwave-safe casserole, combine oil, broccoli, celery and green onions. Cover with lid; microwave on HIGH 4 minutes or until vegetables are tender-crisp, stirring once during cooking.
2. Stir in pimento, gravy and soy sauce. Cover; microwave on HIGH 3 minutes or until hot and bubbling. Garnish with cashews.
Makes about 3 cups or 4 servings.

Broccoli and Celery Oriental

Lemon Orange Carrots

3 cups pared, sliced carrots, cooked and drained
¹/₂ cup orange marmalade
2 tablespoons REALEMON® Lemon Juice from Concentrate
2 tablespoons margarine or butter

In medium saucepan, combine carrots, marmalade, ReaLemon® brand and margarine; stir to coat evenly. Heat through.
Makes 6 servings.

Hot & Spicy Glazed Carrots

Hot & Spicy Glazed Carrots

2 tablespoons vegetable oil
2 dried red chili peppers
1 pound carrots, peeled and cut diagonally into ⅛-inch slices
¼ cup KIKKOMAN Teriyaki Baste & Glaze

Heat oil in hot wok or large skillet over high heat. Add peppers and stir-fry until darkened; remove and discard. Add carrots; reduce heat to medium. Stir-fry 4 minutes, or until tender-crisp. Stir in teriyaki baste & glaze and cook until carrots are glazed. Serve immediately.
Makes 4 servings.

Carrot Nut Pudding

1 pound carrots, grated
1½ cups milk
½ teaspoon salt
½ cup whipping cream
1 tablespoon all-purpose flour
1 cup ground blanched almonds
½ cup firmly packed brown sugar
¼ cup CRISCO® Oil
¼ cup raisins
½ teaspoon ground turmeric
¼ teaspoon ground nutmeg

Combine carrots, milk and salt in medium saucepan. Blend cream and flour in small mixing bowl. Stir into carrot mixture. Heat to boiling, stirring constantly. Cook, uncovered, over moderate heat, stirring frequently, 40 to 45 minutes, or until liquid cooks away. Stir in remaining ingredients. Cook over low heat, stirring frequently, 10 minutes. Garnish with *slivered almonds*, if desired.
6 servings.

Vegetable Couscous

1 tablespoon olive oil
1½ cups sliced CAMPBELL'S FRESH® Mushrooms (6 ounces)
1 cup chopped onions
¼ cup chopped sweet red pepper
4 cloves garlic, minced
¼ teaspoon dried thyme leaves, crushed
⅛ teaspoon pepper
1¼ cups V8® Vegetable Juice
1 cup shredded zucchini
1 cup quick-cooking couscous, uncooked

1. In 3-quart saucepan over medium heat, in hot oil, cook mushrooms, onions, red pepper, garlic, thyme and pepper until vegetables are tender-crisp, stirring often.

2. Stir in V8 juice and zucchini; heat to boiling. Remove from heat. Stir in couscous. Cover; let stand 5 minutes or until liquid is absorbed.
Makes 4½ cups or 9 side-dish servings.

Per serving: 105 calories, 3 g protein, 2 g fat, 19 g carbohydrate, 117 mg sodium, 0 mg cholesterol.

Corn Fritters

1 can (16 ounces) whole kernel corn, drained
1 cup all-purpose flour
1 cup dairy sour cream
2 eggs
2 tablespoons CRISCO® Oil
2 tablespoons finely chopped onion
1 teaspoon baking powder
1 teaspoon sugar
½ teaspoon salt
¼ teaspoon ground nutmeg
⅛ teaspoon white pepper
CRISCO® Oil for frying

Combine all ingredients except Crisco® Oil for frying in medium mixing bowl. Mix well. Let stand 1 hour.

Heat 2 to 3 inches Crisco® Oil in deep-fryer or large saucepan to 350°F. Drop batter by heaping tablespoonfuls into hot Crisco® Oil. Fry a few at a time 5 to 6 minutes, or until deep golden brown. Drain on paper towels. Repeat with remaining batter. Serve immediately or keep warm in 175°F oven.
14 to 16 fritters.

Cauliflower au Gratin

1 recipe Sesame Vegetable Topping (see Index)
1 cup water
¾ teaspoon salt, divided
2 packages (10 ounces each) frozen cauliflower
1 medium tomato, peeled, seeded and chopped
1 teaspoon dried parsley flakes
2 tablespoons CRISCO® Oil
2 tablespoons all-purpose flour
⅛ teaspoon pepper
1 cup milk
1 cup shredded Cheddar cheese (about 4 ounces)

Prepare Sesame Vegetable Topping as directed. Set aside.

Preheat oven to 350°F. Combine water and ½ teaspoon salt in large saucepan. Heat to boiling. Add cauliflower. Return to boiling. Cover. Reduce heat to moderate. Cook 3 minutes, or until cauliflower is thawed and warm. Drain. Place in 2-quart casserole. Stir in tomato and parsley flakes. Set aside.

Blend Crisco® Oil, flour, remaining ¼ teaspoon salt and pepper in small saucepan. Slowly stir in milk. Cook over moderate heat, stirring constantly, until thickened and bubbly. Add cheese. Stir until cheese melts. Pour over cauliflower mixture. Sprinkle with Sesame Vegetable Topping. Bake at 350°F, 25 to 30 minutes, or until bubbly.
6 to 8 servings.

Baked Celery and Almonds

4 cups diagonally sliced celery
1 (13¾-fluid ounce) can COLLEGE INN® Chicken or Beef Broth
2 tablespoons all-purpose flour
½ cup dairy sour cream
1 (8-ounce) can CHUN KING® Sliced Water Chestnuts, drained
½ cup sliced almonds, toasted
2 tablespoons BLUE BONNET® Margarine
28 RITZ® Crackers, finely rolled (about 1 cup crumbs)

In large covered saucepan, over medium heat, cook celery in ¾ cup broth until tender-crisp, about 10 to 12 minutes; drain in colander. In same saucepan, blend flour into remaining broth until smooth. Cook and stir over medium heat until thickened; blend in sour cream. Stir in celery, water chestnuts and almonds. Pour into shallow 1½-quart baking dish. In small skillet, over medium heat, melt margarine; stir in cracker crumbs. Sprinkle over casserole. Bake at 350°F for 30 minutes or until hot.
Makes 6 servings.

Crunchy Scalloped Celery

3 cups diagonally sliced celery
1 package (10 ounces) frozen peas, thawed and drained
1 can (8 ounces) sliced water chestnuts, drained
1 can (4 ounces) mushroom stems and pieces, drained
1 can (10¾ ounces) condensed cream of celery soup
¼ cup milk
½ teaspoon DURKEE Seasoned Salt
1 can (2.8 ounces) DURKEE French Fried Onions

Preheat oven to 350°. In large saucepan, simmer celery in small amount of boiling water until tender-crisp, about 5 minutes; drain. Stir in peas, water chestnuts, mushrooms, soup, milk, seasoned salt and ½ can French Fried Onions. Pour into 1½-quart casserole. Bake, uncovered, at 350° for 20 minutes or until heated through. Top with remaining onions; bake, uncovered, 5 minutes or until onions are golden brown.
Makes 4 to 6 servings.

Barbecued Garlic

1 whole head of garlic
Olive or vegetable oil for basting

Peel loose, outermost skin from garlic; brush all over with oil. Grill garlic, on covered grill, not directly over medium-hot **KINGSFORD® Charcoal Briquets** 30 to 45 minutes or until garlic cloves are very tender, basting frequently with oil. Press individual cloves between thumb and forefinger to squeeze out garlic. Serve with grilled meats or as a spread for hot fresh bread.
Makes 4 servings.

Baked Celery and Almonds

Corncakes

1⅓ cups all-purpose flour
3 tablespoons sugar
1 tablespoon DAVIS® Baking
    Powder
1 cup COLLEGE INN® Chicken
    Broth
1 egg, slightly beaten
¼ cup BLUE BONNET®
    Margarine, melted
1 (8¾-ounce) can whole kernel
    sweet corn, drained
    Maple syrup

In medium bowl, combine flour, sugar and baking powder. Add chicken broth, egg and margarine, stirring just until blended. Stir in corn. Using ¼ cup batter for each pancake, cook on greased griddle or skillet, over medium heat, turning to brown on both sides. Serve with syrup.
Makes 10 (4-inch) pancakes.

Applecakes: Substitute ½ cup diced apple for corn.

Fresh Corn Maque Choux

2 medium red peppers, halved
    lengthwise
6 ears fresh corn
2 tablespoons butter or
    margarine, divided
2 tablespoons vegetable oil
1 small onion, finely chopped
1 tablespoon sugar
½ teaspoon TABASCO® pepper
    sauce
½ cup chicken broth
⅓ cup heavy cream
1 egg, lightly beaten

In large saucepan over 1 inch boiling water steam pepper halves 8 minutes or until crisp-tender. Drain; reserve. With knife, cut kernels off corn cobs. (You should have about 2½ cups.) In medium skillet heat 1 tablespoon butter with oil. Add corn, onion, sugar and Tabasco® sauce. Cook until corn is almost tender and starts to form a crust on bottom of pan. Gradually stir in broth, scraping up bits on bottom of pan. Stir in remaining 1 tablespoon butter and cream. Cook 5 minutes longer or until almost all liquid evaporates; stir frequently. Remove skillet from heat. Add egg; stir 1 minute or until egg is cooked. Serve in red pepper halves.
Makes 4 servings.

Country Corn Bake

5 slices bacon, fried crisp
1 bag (20 ounces) frozen whole
    kernel corn, thawed and
    drained
1 can (10¾ ounces) condensed
    cream of potato soup
½ cup milk
½ cup thinly sliced celery
1 tablespoon diced pimiento
    (optional)
½ teaspoon DURKEE Seasoned
    Salt
½ cup (2 ounces) shredded
    Cheddar cheese
1 can (2.8 ounces) DURKEE
    French Fried Onions

Preheat oven to 375°. In large bowl, combine corn, soup, milk, celery, pimiento, seasoned salt, *¼ cup* cheese and *½ can* French Fried Onions. Crumble 3 slices bacon; stir into corn mixture. Spoon corn mixture into 8-inch square baking dish. Bake, covered, at 375° for 40 to 45 minutes or until hot and bubbly. Top with remaining bacon slices, cheese and onions; bake, uncovered, 3 minutes or until onions are golden brown.
Makes 4 to 6 servings.

Fried Eggplant

1 cup unseasoned dry bread
    crumbs
¼ cup grated Parmesan cheese
1 teaspoon Italian seasoning
½ teaspoon salt
½ cup all-purpose flour
2 eggs
¼ cup milk
1 pound eggplant, peeled and
    cut into ¼-inch slices
    CRISCO® Oil for frying

Mix bread crumbs, Parmesan cheese, Italian seasoning and salt in shallow dish. Place flour on sheet of waxed paper. Blend eggs and milk in another shallow dish. Dip each slice of eggplant first in flour, then in egg mixture, then in bread crumb mixture to coat.

Corncakes

Heat ¼ inch Crisco® Oil in medium skillet. Fry a few slices eggplant at a time, over moderate heat, 4 to 5 minutes, or until golden brown, turning over once. Drain on paper towels. Serve immediately or keep warm in 175°F oven. Garnish with *grated Parmesan cheese,* if desired.
4 to 6 servings.

Original Green Bean Casserole

Green Beans Napoli

- ³/₄ **pound green beans, cut in half crosswise**
- 2 **tablespoons olive or vegetable oil**
- 1 **tablespoon butter or margarine**
- 3 **tablespoons pine nuts**
- 1 **large clove garlic, minced**
- 1 **tablespoon chopped fresh basil or ½ teaspoon dried basil leaves**
- ¼ **teaspoon TABASCO® pepper sauce**
- ¼ **teaspoon dried rosemary leaves**
- 1 **medium red pepper, cut into strips**
- ½ **teaspoon salt**

In large skillet bring 1 inch water to a boil; add green beans. Cover; cook 8 to 10 minutes or until crisp-tender. Drain; set aside. In same skillet heat oil and butter; add pine nuts, garlic, basil, Tabasco® sauce and rosemary. Cook over medium heat until pine nuts are lightly browned; stir frequently. Add green beans, red pepper strips and salt to skillet. Stir-fry 2 minutes or until pepper strips are crisp-tender.
Makes 4 servings.

Original Green Bean Casserole

- 2 **cans (16 ounces *each*) cut green beans, drained or 2 packages (9 ounces *each*) frozen cut green beans, cooked and drained**
- ³/₄ **cup milk**
- 1 **can (10³/₄ ounces) condensed cream of mushroom soup**
- ⅛ **teaspoon DURKEE Ground Black Pepper**
- 1 **can (2.8 ounces) DURKEE French Fried Onions**

Preheat oven to 350°. In medium bowl, combine beans, milk, soup, pepper and ½ can French Fried Onions; pour into 1½-quart casserole. Bake, uncovered, at 350° for 30 minutes or until heated through. Top with remaining onions; bake, uncovered, 5 minutes or until onions are golden brown.
Makes 6 servings.

Microwave Directions: Prepare green bean mixture as above; pour into 1½-quart microwave-safe casserole. Cook, covered, on HIGH 8 to 10 minutes or until heated through. Stir beans halfway through cooking time. Top with remaining onions; cook, uncovered, 1 minute. Let stand for 5 minutes.

Creamy Green Beans Almondine

- 2 **(9-ounce) packages frozen green beans, cooked and drained**
- 2 **tablespoons margarine or butter**
- 2 **tablespoons flour**
- 2 **teaspoons WYLER'S® or STEERO® Chicken-Flavor Instant Bouillon *or* 2 Chicken-Flavor Bouillon Cubes**
- ³/₄ **cup BORDEN® or MEADOW GOLD® Milk**
- ½ **cup (2 ounces) shredded Mozzarella cheese**
- ¼ **cup sliced almonds, toasted if desired**

In medium saucepan, melt margarine; stir in flour and bouillon. Gradually stir in milk; cook and stir until thickened. Add cheese; stir until melted. Add beans; heat through. Stir in almonds. Serve immediately. Refrigerate leftovers.
Makes 6 servings.

Microwave: In 2-cup glass measure, microwave margarine on full power (high) 30 seconds or until melted. Stir in flour and bouillon. Gradually stir in milk. Microwave on full power (high) 3 to 3½ minutes, stirring after each minute, until thick and bubbly. Add cheese; stir until cheese melts. Add beans; microwave on full power (high) 1 to 2 minutes or until heated through. Stir in almonds.

Cajun-Style Green Beans

- 2 **pounds green beans, trimmed**
- ½ **cup diced salt pork**
- 1 **clove garlic, minced**
- 2 **tablespoons white wine vinegar**
- 1 **tablespoon Dijon-style mustard**
- 1 **teaspoon sugar**
- ½ **teaspoon TABASCO® pepper sauce**
- ¼ **cup chopped celery leaves**

In medium saucepan in 1 inch boiling salted water, cook beans covered 10 minutes or until crisp-tender. Drain. In small skillet over medium-high heat cook salt pork 2 to 3 minutes to render fat. Reduce heat; add garlic and cook 1 minute. Stir in vinegar, mustard, sugar and Tabasco® sauce. Remove from heat; stir in celery leaves. Toss with beans to coat.
Makes 8 servings.

Onion Rings

Spicy Bean Toss

- 1 9-oz. pkg. frozen Italian green beans, thawed, drained
- 1 cup red or green pepper strips
- 1 medium onion, sliced
- 3 tablespoons PARKAY Margarine
- 1 8³/₄-oz. can garbanzo beans, drained
- ¹/₃ cup pitted ripe olive slices
- ³/₄ teaspoon Italian seasoning
- ¹/₂ lb. VELVEETA Pasteurized Process Cheese Spread, cubed
- ¹/₄ cup milk

In large skillet, stir-fry Italian beans, peppers and onions in margarine until crisp-tender. Add garbanzo beans, olives and Italian seasoning; mix lightly. Reduce heat to low. Add process cheese spread and milk; stir until process cheese spread is melted.
4 to 6 servings.

Preparation time: 15 minutes
Cooking time: 15 minutes

Okra-Bacon Casserole

- 1¹/₂ pounds young fresh okra
- 3 large tomatoes, chopped
- 1 medium onion, chopped
- 1 small green pepper, chopped
- ¹/₂ teaspoon TABASCO® pepper sauce
- 5 slices bacon

Preheat oven to 350°F. Slice okra into thin rounds. In greased 2¹/₂-quart casserole arrange okra, tomatoes, onion and green pepper. Season with Tabasco® sauce. Place bacon on top. Bake uncovered 1¹/₂ hours or until okra is tender.
Makes 6 to 8 servings.

Note: Two (10-ounce) packages frozen okra, thawed, may be substituted for fresh okra. Bake casserole 1 hour.

Microwave Directions: In 2¹/₂-quart microwave-safe casserole place bacon; cover with paper towel. Cook on High 4 to 5 minutes or until crisp; remove to paper towel to cool, then crumble and set aside. Into drippings in same casserole place okra, onion and green pepper; season with Tabasco® sauce. Cover loosely with plastic wrap; cook on High 15 to 18 minutes or until okra is just tender. Add tomatoes. Re-cover; cook on High 1 to 2 minutes or until tomatoes are tender. Sprinkle with reserved bacon before serving.

Onion Rings

Batter:
- ³/₄ cup all-purpose flour
- ¹/₂ cup water
- ¹/₂ cup milk
- 6 tablespoons white cornmeal
- 1 tablespoon CRISCO® Oil
- ³/₄ teaspoon seasoned salt
- ¹/₂ teaspoon sugar
- 5 or 6 drops hot red pepper sauce

Onion Rings:
- CRISCO® Oil for frying
- 1 large onion, cut into ¹/₂-inch slices and separated into rings

Combine all batter ingredients in small mixing bowl. Stir until smooth.

Heat 2 to 3 inches Crisco® Oil in deep-fryer or large saucepan to 375°F. Dip a few onion rings in batter. Let excess batter drip back into bowl. Fry a few at a time, 2 to 3 minutes, or until golden brown. Drain on paper towels. Repeat with remaining onion rings. Serve immediately or keep warm in 175°F oven.
4 to 6 servings.

Harvest Vegetable Scallop

4 medium carrots, thinly sliced (about 2 cups)
1 package (10 ounces) frozen chopped broccoli, thawed and drained
1 can (2.8 ounces) DURKEE French Fried Onions
5 small red potatoes, sliced ⅛ inch thick (about 2 cups)
1 jar (8 ounces) pasteurized processed cheese spread
¼ cup milk
DURKEE Ground Black Pepper
DURKEE Seasoned Salt

Preheat oven to 375°. In 8×12-inch baking dish, combine carrots, broccoli and ½ can French Fried Onions. Tuck potato slices into vegetable mixture at an angle. Dot vegetables evenly with cheese spread. Pour milk over vegetables; sprinkle with seasonings as desired. Bake, covered, at 375° for 30 minutes or until vegetables are tender. Top with remaining onions; bake, uncovered, 3 minutes or until onions are golden brown.
Makes 6 servings.

Microwave Directions: In 8×12-inch microwave-safe dish, prepare vegetables as above. Top with cheese spread, milk and seasonings as above. Cook, covered, on HIGH 12 to 14 minutes or until vegetables are tender. Rotate dish halfway through cooking time. Top with remaining onions; cook, uncovered, 1 minute. Let stand 5 minutes.

Creamy Baked Onions

¼ cup butter or margarine
1½ pounds small whole white onions, peeled
1½ cups sliced celery
2 tablespoons flour
1¾ cups milk
2 tablespoons dry sherry wine
¼ to ½ teaspoon TABASCO® pepper sauce
¼ teaspoon salt
½ cup grated Parmesan cheese
Paprika

Preheat oven to 350°F. In large skillet melt butter; add onions. Cook until lightly browned. Stir in celery; cook 1 minute longer. Remove vegetables with slotted spoon to 1½-quart casserole. In same skillet stir in flour; cook

1 minute. Remove from heat. Gradually add milk. Stir in sherry, Tabasco® sauce and salt. Return to heat. Stir constantly, bring to a boil over medium heat and boil 1 minute; stir in cheese. Pour sauce over vegetables. Bake 30 to 40 minutes or until onions are tender. Sprinkle with paprika before serving.
Makes 6 servings.

Blushing Onions

1 (16-ounce) package frozen small whole onions, cooked and drained
½ cup BAMA® Apple Jelly
¼ cup BENNETT'S® Chili Sauce
1 tablespoon margarine or butter
¼ teaspoon salt

In medium saucepan, combine ingredients; mix well. Over medium heat, bring mixture to a boil; reduce heat and simmer 10 to 15 minutes. Refrigerate leftovers.
Makes 6 servings.

Microwave: In 1½-quart baking dish, combine ingredients; mix well. Cook covered on 100% power (high) 3 to 4 minutes; stir.

French Green Peas

4 slices bacon, cooked and crumbled with 2 tablespoons drippings reserved
2 tablespoons CRISCO® Oil
½ cup all-purpose flour
2¼ cups chicken broth
2 packages (10 ounces each) frozen green peas
2 small onions, thinly sliced
2 teaspoons dried parsley flakes
½ teaspoon salt
⅛ teaspoon pepper

Combine reserved bacon drippings and Crisco® Oil in large saucepan. Stir in flour. Cook over moderate heat, stirring constantly, 3 to 4 minutes, or until light brown. Gradually stir in broth. Heat to boiling. Add peas, onions, parsley flakes, salt and pepper. Return to boiling. Cover. Reduce heat. Simmer, stirring occasionally to break apart peas, 20 minutes, or until onion is tender. Sprinkle with crumbled bacon. Garnish with *sliced pimiento*, if desired.
8 servings.

Harvest Vegetable Scallop

Italian-Style Roasted Peppers

Confetti Fried Rice

> 1 can (20 ounces) DOLE®
>   Pineapple Chunks
> 3½ teaspoons vegetable oil
> 1 egg, beaten
> 1 carrot, shredded
> 1 clove garlic, pressed
> 4 cups cooked rice
> 1 can (8 ounces) water
>   chestnuts, chopped
> 4 ounces cooked ham, julienne-
>   cut
> ½ cup frozen peas, thawed
> ⅓ cup chopped green onions
> ¼ cup soy sauce
> ¼ teaspoon ground ginger

Drain pineapple. Heat ½ teaspoon oil in wok or large skillet over low heat. Add egg and swirl around bottom of wok until egg sets in 6-inch pancake. Remove and cool. Cut into ⅛-inch strips. Heat remaining 3 teaspoons oil in wok over high heat. Stir-fry carrot and garlic about 1 minute or until tender. Add rice, stirring until grains separate. Reduce heat slightly. Stir in pineapple, water chestnuts, ham, peas, onions, soy sauce and ginger; increase heat and heat through. Gently stir in egg strips.
Makes 6 servings.

Potato Pancakes

> 4 medium white potatoes,
>   peeled and coarsely
>   shredded
> 1 small onion, grated
> 1 egg
> ⅓ cup all-purpose flour
> 1½ teaspoons salt
> ⅛ teaspoon pepper
> 2 tablespoons CRISCO® Oil

Combine potatoes, onion, egg, flour, salt and pepper in medium mixing bowl. Mix well. Heat Crisco® Oil in large skillet. Spoon ¼ cup potato mixture into skillet for each of 4 pancakes. Flatten with spatula. Cook over moderate heat 10 to 15 minutes, or until golden brown, turning over once. Drain on paper towels. Add additional Crisco® Oil, if necessary. Repeat with remaining potato mixture.
6 to 8 servings.

Note: To keep shredded potatoes from turning brown, place in cold water until ready to use. Drain thoroughly and pat dry between paper towels before using.

Italian-Style Roasted Peppers

> 6 large red, green or yellow
>   peppers
> 1 cup (8 ounces) WISH-BONE®
>   Italian Dressing
> ½ cup chopped fresh basil
>   leaves*
> ⅛ teaspoon pepper

In large aluminum-foil-lined baking pan or on broiler rack, place red peppers. Broil, turning occasionally, 20 minutes or until peppers turn almost completely black. Immediately place in paper bag; close bag and let cool about 30 minutes. Under cold running water, peel off skin, then remove stems and seeds; slice into long thick strips.

In large bowl, combine peppers with remaining ingredients. Cover and marinate in refrigerator, stirring occasionally, at least 4 hours. For best flavor, serve peppers at room temperature and, if desired, with olives, mozzarella cheese and tomatoes.
Makes about 3 cups roasted peppers.

*Substitution: Use 1 tablespoon dried basil leaves.

Note: Also terrific with Wish-Bone® Robusto Italian, Herbal Italian, Italian & Cheese or Lite Italian Dressing.

Homespun Scalloped Potatoes

> 1 8-ounce package
>   PHILADELPHIA BRAND
>   Cream Cheese, cubed
> 1¼ cups milk
> ½ teaspoon salt
> ⅛ teaspoon pepper
> 4 cups thin potato slices
> 2 tablespoons chopped chives

In large saucepan, combine cream cheese, milk, salt and pepper; stir over low heat until smooth. Add potatoes and chives; mix lightly. Spoon into 1½-quart casserole; cover. Bake at 350°, 1 hour and 10 minutes or until potatoes are tender. Stir before serving.
6 servings.

Make Ahead: Prepare as directed except for baking. Cover; refrigerate overnight. When ready to serve, bake as directed.

Garden Medley Rice

 1 can (13¾ oz.) ready-to-serve
   chicken broth
 2 cups assorted vegetables
   (broccoli florets, sliced
   yellow squash, peas, grated
   carrot)
 1 teaspoon onion flakes
 2 teaspoons snipped fresh
   rosemary or 1 teaspoon
   dried rosemary leaves
 ¼ teaspoon garlic powder
 1½ cups MINUTE® Rice
   Freshly ground pepper
   (optional)

Stir together broth, vegetables, onion flakes, rosemary and garlic powder in saucepan and bring to a full boil. Stir in rice. Cover; remove from heat. Let stand 5 minutes. Fluff with fork and sprinkle with pepper. Serve with chicken cutlets or your favorite main dish.
Makes 4 servings.

Microwave Directions: Stir together all ingredients except pepper in microwavable bowl. Cover with plastic wrap and cook at HIGH 4 minutes. Stir; cover and cook at HIGH 3 to 5 minutes longer. Stir again; cover and cook at HIGH 3 minutes. Let stand 5 minutes. Fluff with fork and sprinkle with pepper. Serve with chicken cutlets or your favorite main dish.
Makes 4 servings.

Cajun Dirty Rice

 1 package (8 ounces)
   SWANSON® Frozen Chicken
   Livers, thawed and chopped
 ½ cup chopped green pepper
 ½ cup chopped celery
 1 large clove garlic, minced
 ¼ cup butter or margarine
 1 pouch CAMPBELL'S® Onion
   Soup and Recipe Mix
 2 cups water
 ½ teaspoon hot pepper sauce
 1 cup regular rice, uncooked

1. In 10-inch skillet over medium-high heat, cook livers, green pepper, celery and garlic in butter until vegetables are tender, stirring often.
2. Stir soup mix, water and hot pepper sauce into skillet. Heat to boiling; stir in rice.
3. Reduce heat to low. Cover; simmer 20 minutes or until rice is tender.
Makes 6 servings.

New Year Fried Rice

 3 strips bacon, diced
 ¾ cup chopped green onions
   and tops
 ⅓ cup diced red bell pepper
 ¼ cup frozen green peas, thawed
 1 egg, beaten
 4 cups cold, cooked rice
 2 tablespoons KIKKOMAN Soy
   Sauce

Cook bacon in wok or large skillet over medium heat until crisp. Add green onions, red pepper and peas; stir-fry 1 minute. Add egg and scramble. Stir in rice and cook until heated, gently separating grains. Add soy sauce; cook and stir until heated through. Serve immediately.
Makes 6 to 8 servings.

Louisiana Beans and Rice

 1 tablespoon vegetable oil
 1 cup chopped onion
 1 large green pepper, chopped
 2 cloves garlic, minced
 ½ teaspoon dried thyme leaves,
   crushed
 ¼ teaspoon dried oregano
   leaves, crushed
 2 cans (16 ounces each) red
   beans or pinto beans,
   drained
 1 can (10¾ ounces)
   CAMPBELL'S® Condensed
   Tomato Soup
 1 cup diced cooked ham or
   smoked sausage
 ¼ teaspoon ground red pepper
   (cayenne)
   Hot cooked rice

To Microwave:
1. In 2-quart microwave-safe casserole, combine oil, onion, green pepper, garlic, thyme and oregano. Cover with lid; microwave on HIGH 5 minutes or until vegetables are tender, stirring once during cooking.
2. Stir in beans, soup, ham and red pepper. Cover; microwave on HIGH 5 minutes or until hot. Stir.
3. Reduce power to 50%. Cover; microwave 15 minutes or until flavors are blended. Serve over rice.
Makes about 5 cups or 5 servings.
   Note: Serve as a side dish or in larger servings as a main dish.

Potato and Cheese Casserole

 1 can (10¾ ounces)
   CAMPBELL'S® Condensed
   Cream of Celery Soup
 1 cup shredded Cheddar cheese
   (4 ounces)
 ½ cup milk
   Generous dash pepper
 1 large clove garlic, minced
 4 cups thinly sliced potatoes
 1 cup thinly sliced onions

To Microwave:
1. In medium bowl, stir soup until smooth. Add cheese, milk, pepper and garlic; stir until well blended.
2. In 2-quart microwave-safe casserole layer ½ of the potatoes, ½ of the onions and ½ of the soup mixture. Repeat layers.
3. Cover with lid; microwave on HIGH 23 minutes or until potatoes are tender, rotating dish 3 times during cooking. Let stand, covered, 5 minutes.
Makes 6 servings.

Garden Medley Rice

Galbani® Fontina Potato Surprise

2½ **pounds potatoes**
  3 **tablespoons butter or margarine, melted**
¼ **cup freshly grated imported Parmesan cheese**
  1 **egg**
  1 **egg white**
⅛ **teaspoon salt**
⅛ **teaspoon ground nutmeg**
  4 **tablespoons fine dry bread crumbs, divided**
  8 **ounces GALBANI® Fontina, cut into chunks**
¼ **cup freshly grated sharp Provolone cheese**
¼ **pound prosciutto, cut into small pieces**
  2 **tablespoons butter or margarine, cut into small pieces**

Cook potatoes in boiling water in large saucepan over medium-low heat until tender. Drain. Cool slightly; pare. Press potatoes through food mill or mash until smooth. Combine potatoes, melted butter, Parmesan cheese, egg, egg white, salt and nutmeg in large bowl until smooth; set aside.

Sprinkle ½ of the bread crumbs in well-buttered 9-inch round baking dish. Tilt dish to coat. Spread about ½ of the potato mixture on bottom and sides of dish. Combine Fontina, Provolone and prosciutto in small bowl. Sprinkle over potato mixture in dish. Cover with remaining potato mixture; sprinkle with remaining bread crumbs. Dot with pieces of butter. Bake in preheated 350°F oven 40 minutes or until thin crust forms. Let stand 5 minutes. Invert baking dish onto serving plate, tapping gently to remove. Serve immediately.
Makes 4 to 6 servings.

Favorite recipe from **Bel Paese Sales Co., Inc.**

Classic Spanish Rice

1½ **cups MINUTE® Rice**
  1 **onion, cut into thin wedges**
  1 **garlic clove, minced**
¼ **cup (½ stick) butter or margarine**
1½ **cups water**
  1 **can (8 oz.) tomato sauce**
  1 **small green pepper, diced**
  1 **teaspoon salt**
½ **teaspoon prepared mustard (optional)**
  Sliced stuffed green olives

Cook and stir rice, onion and garlic in hot butter in large skillet over medium heat, stirring frequently until mixture is lightly browned. Stir in remaining ingredients except olives. Bring to a full boil. Cover; remove from heat. Let stand 5 minutes. Fluff with fork. Garnish with olives. Serve with chicken or your favorite main dish.
Makes 4 servings.

Sunny Fries

  1 **14-oz. pkg. frozen cottage fries french fried potatoes**
¼ **lb. VELVEETA Pasteurized Process Cheese Spread, cubed**
  2 **tablespoons milk**
½ **teaspoon dry mustard**

Prepare potatoes as directed on package. Combine process cheese spread, milk and mustard in saucepan; stir over low heat until process cheese spread is melted. Serve over hot cooked potatoes.
4 servings.

Preparation time: 5 minutes
Cooking time: 15 minutes

Microwave: Prepare potatoes as directed on package. Microwave process cheese spread, milk and mustard in 1-quart microwave-safe bowl on High 2½ to 3½ minutes or until process cheese spread is melted, stirring every minute. Serve over hot cooked potatoes.

Cheese & Bacon Potato Bake

Cheese & Bacon Potato Bake

  1 **(13¾-fluid ounce) can COLLEGE INN® Chicken or Beef Broth**
  5 **medium potatoes, pared and thinly sliced (about 5 cups)**
  1 **large onion, thinly sliced**
  6 **slices bacon**
  3 **tablespoons all-purpose flour**
  1 **cup shredded sharp Cheddar cheese (4 ounces)**

In medium saucepan, over medium-high heat, heat broth to a boil; reduce heat. Add potatoes and onion; cover and simmer 5 minutes. Drain, reserving 1½ cups broth. In skillet, over medium-high heat, cook bacon until crisp. Remove and crumble bacon; pour off all but 3 tablespoons drippings. Blend flour into reserved drippings. Gradually add reserved broth; cook over medium heat, stirring constantly, until thickened. Stir in cheese until melted. In greased 2-quart baking dish, layer ⅓ each potato-onion mixture, sauce and bacon. Repeat layers twice. Bake at 400°F for 35 minutes or until done. *Makes 6 servings.*

Risotto with Vegetables

2 tablespoons butter or margarine
2 tablespoons vegetable oil
1 medium onion, chopped
1 clove garlic, minced
1 cup sliced mushrooms
1 cup uncooked Arborio or long grain rice*
Pinch saffron (optional)
2 cups hot chicken broth, divided
¼ teaspoon TABASCO® pepper sauce
1 to 1½ cups hot water, divided
1 package (9 ounces) frozen artichoke hearts, cooked and drained
½ cup fresh or canned roasted red peppers, coarsely chopped**

In medium skillet heat butter and oil; cook onion, garlic and mushrooms 5 minutes or until onions are translucent. Add rice; cook 1 to 2 minutes or until partly translucent. Stir in saffron, if desired.

Add ½ cup hot broth and Tabasco® sauce; stir constantly until rice absorbs broth. Add remaining broth and hot water, ½ cup at a time; stir constantly from bottom and sides of pan and wait until rice just begins to dry out before adding more liquid. Cook and stir until rice is tender but firm to the bite, and is the consistency of creamy rice pudding. (The total amount of liquid used will vary. Watch rice carefully to ensure proper consistency.) Total cooking time is about 30 minutes. Stir in artichokes and roasted peppers. Serve with additional Tabasco® sauce, if desired.
Makes 6 servings.

*Arborio rice gives the best results. Do not use converted rice.

**To roast peppers, hold over source of heat with a fork until skin blisters. Cool slightly; peel and chop.

Skillet Potatoes

Skillet Potatoes

3 tablespoons butter or margarine
1 cup sliced celery
½ cup chopped onion
2 cloves garlic, minced
1 can (10¾ ounces) CAMPBELL'S® Condensed Chicken Broth
¼ cup water
4 cups cubed potatoes
1 cup carrots cut into julienne strips
⅛ teaspoon pepper
Chopped fresh parsley

1. In 10-inch skillet over medium heat, in hot butter, cook celery, onion and garlic until vegetables are tender, stirring occasionally.
2. Add broth, water, potatoes, carrots and pepper to skillet. Heat to boiling; reduce heat to low. Cover; simmer 15 minutes or until potatoes are tender.
3. Uncover; over medium heat, simmer 5 minutes or until broth is slightly thickened, stirring often. Sprinkle with parsley before serving. *Makes about 5 cups or 6 servings.*

Fried Potato Wedges

4 medium white potatoes, baked
CRISCO® Oil for frying

Cut each potato into 6 wedges. Heat 2 to 3 inches Crisco® Oil in deep-fryer or large saucepan to 375°F. Fry half the wedges at a time 2 to 3 minutes, or until golden brown. Drain on paper towels. Serve immediately.
4 to 6 servings.

Tex-Mex Rice and Beans

½ cup chopped onion
1 garlic clove, minced
1 tablespoon oil
1 can (15 oz.) red kidney beans, drained
1 can (10½ oz.) condensed beef bouillon
1 medium green pepper, diced
½ cup barbecue sauce
1½ cups MINUTE® Rice

Cook and stir onion and garlic in hot oil in large skillet until onion is tender but not browned. Stir in beans, bouillon, green pepper and barbecue sauce. Bring to a full boil. Stir in rice. Cover; remove from heat. Let stand 5 minutes. Fluff with fork.
Makes 4 servings.

Microwave Directions: Omit oil. Mix all ingredients in microwavable dish. Cover and cook at HIGH 5 minutes. Stir; cover and cook at HIGH 3 minutes longer. Stir; cover and let stand 5 minutes.
Makes 4 servings.

Pecan-Stuffed Squash

1 (13³/₄-fluid ounce) can COLLEGE INN® Beef or Chicken Broth
2 small acorn squash, halved and seeded
¹/₃ cup BLUE BONNET® Margarine
2 cups dry herb-seasoned stuffing mix
1 (2-ounce) package PLANTERS® Pecan Pieces
¹/₃ cup seedless raisins

Reserve ²/₃ cup broth; pour remaining broth into shallow baking dish. Place squash cut-side down in broth. Bake at 400°F for 25 to 35 minutes. In medium saucepan, over medium-high heat, heat reserved broth and margarine until margarine melts; stir in stuffing mix, pecans and raisins. Turn squash over, cut-side up; spoon stuffing into squash cavities. Bake 20 minutes more or until squash is done, basting with broth after 10 minutes. *Makes 4 servings.*

Microwave: Reserve ²/₃ cup broth. In 2-quart microwave-proof oblong dish, place squash cut-side down in remaining broth. Microwave, uncovered, on HIGH (100% power) for 6 to 7 minutes. In 1-quart microwave-proof bowl, place reserved broth and margarine. Microwave, uncovered, on HIGH for 1 to 2 minutes until margarine melts. Stir in stuffing mix, pecans and raisins. Turn squash over, cut-side up; spoon stuffing into squash cavities. Microwave, uncovered, on HIGH for 5 to 6 minutes until stuffing is heated through and squash is done. Let stand 5 minutes before serving.

Pecan-Stuffed Squash

Golden Squash Bake

8 cups sliced yellow crookneck squash, cooked and drained
6 slices bacon, cooked and crumbled
2 eggs
1 cup BORDEN® or MEADOW GOLD® Cottage Cheese
2 tablespoons flour
2 teaspoons WYLER'S® or STEERO® Chicken-Flavor Instant Bouillon
1 cup (4 ounces) shredded sharp Cheddar cheese

Preheat oven to 350°. In large bowl, combine eggs, cottage cheese, flour and bouillon. Add squash; mix well.

Turn into greased 12×7-inch baking dish. Top with Cheddar cheese and bacon. Bake 20 to 25 minutes. Let stand 5 minutes before serving. Refrigerate leftovers.
Makes 6 to 8 servings.

Southern-Style Squash and Okra

2 small onions, sliced and separated into rings
3 medium crookneck squash, cut into ¹/₄-inch slices
1 package (10 ounces) frozen whole okra, thawed and cut into bite-size pieces
2 tablespoons butter or margarine
1 clove garlic, minced
1 teaspoon salt
¹/₈ teaspoon pepper
¹/₂ teaspoon dried thyme, crushed
1 tablespoon lemon juice
¹/₄ cup grated Cheddar cheese (1 ounce)

Place onion slices, squash and okra on 24×18-inch piece of heavy-duty foil. Dot with butter. Sprinkle with garlic,

salt, pepper, thyme and lemon juice. Fold and seal foil edges tightly. Grill packet, on covered grill, over medium-hot **KINGSFORD® Charcoal Briquets** 25 to 30 minutes or until tender, turning packet over once. To serve, unwrap foil packet and sprinkle with Cheddar cheese.
Makes 4 to 6 servings.

Creamy Baked Mashed Potatoes

1 envelope LIPTON® Vegetable Recipe Soup Mix
4 cups hot mashed potatoes*
1 cup shredded Cheddar or Swiss cheese (about 4 ounces)
¹/₂ cup chopped green onions (optional)
1 egg, slightly beaten
¹/₈ teaspoon pepper

Preheat oven to 375°.
In lightly greased 1¹/₂-quart casserole, thoroughly combine all ingredients except ¹/₄ cup cheese. Bake 40

minutes. Top with remaining cheese and bake an additional 5 minutes or until cheese is melted.
Makes about 8 servings.

*Do not use salt when preparing hot mashed potatoes.

Microwave Directions: In lightly greased 1½-quart casserole, thoroughly combine all ingredients except ¼ cup cheese. Heat covered at HIGH (Full Power), turning casserole occasionally, 7 minutes or until heated through. Top with remaining cheese, then let stand covered 5 minutes.

Crisp Onion-Roasted Potatoes

- 1 envelope LIPTON® Onion or Onion-Mushroom Recipe Soup Mix
- ½ cup olive or vegetable oil
- ¼ cup butter or margarine, melted
- 1 teaspoon thyme leaves (optional)
- 1 teaspoon marjoram leaves (optional)
- ¼ teaspoon pepper
- 2 pounds all-purpose potatoes, cut into quarters

Preheat oven to 450°.

In shallow baking or roasting pan, thoroughly blend all ingredients except potatoes. Add potatoes and turn to coat thoroughly. Bake, stirring potatoes occasionally, 60 minutes or until potatoes are tender and golden brown. Garnish, if desired, with chopped parsley.
Makes about 8 servings.

Chinese Spinach

- 3 tablespoons CRISCO® Oil
- 1 tablespoon soy sauce
- 1 teaspoon lime juice
- ½ teaspoon sugar
- ⅛ teaspoon pepper
- 1 clove garlic, minced
- ½ cup diagonally sliced green onion, 1-inch slices
- 12 ounces fresh spinach, trimmed, washed and torn into bite-size pieces
- ¼ cup sliced water chestnuts
- 1 jar (2 ounces) sliced pimiento, drained

Heat Crisco® Oil, soy sauce, lime juice, sugar and pepper in large skillet. Add garlic. Stir-fry over medium-high heat about 1 minute, or until garlic is light brown. Add onion. Stir-fry 1 minute. Add spinach, water chestnuts and pimiento. Stir-fry 2 to 3 minutes longer, or until spinach is tender.
4 to 6 servings.

Spinach Almond Casserole

- 1 recipe Sesame Vegetable Topping (see Index)
- 2 packages (10 ounces each) frozen chopped spinach, thawed
- 2 tablespoons CRISCO® Oil
- ¼ cup chopped onion
- 2 tablespoons chopped celery
- 2 tablespoons all-purpose flour
- 1 teaspoon salt
- ½ teaspoon dried dill weed
- ⅛ teaspoon pepper
- 1 cup half-and-half
- 1 egg, slightly beaten
- 3 tablespoons chopped almonds

Crisp Onion-Roasted Potatoes

Prepare Sesame Vegetable Topping as directed. Set aside. Preheat oven to 325°F.

Press excess moisture from spinach. Set aside.

Heat Crisco® Oil in medium saucepan. Add onion and celery. Sauté over moderate heat until tender. Remove from heat. Stir in flour, salt, dill weed and pepper. Return to heat. Blend in half-and-half. Cook, stirring constantly, until bubbly. Remove from heat. Blend in egg. Stir in spinach and almonds. Transfer to lightly oiled 1-quart casserole. Sprinkle with Sesame Vegetable Topping. Bake at 325°F, 35 to 40 minutes, or until hot and topping is light brown.
6 to 8 servings.

Saucy Garden Patch Vegetables

- 1 can (11 ounces) condensed Cheddar cheese soup
- ½ cup sour cream
- ¼ cup milk
- ½ teaspoon DURKEE Seasoned Salt
- 1 bag (16 ounces) frozen vegetable combination (broccoli, corn, red pepper), thawed and drained
- 1 bag (16 ounces) frozen vegetable combination (brussels sprouts, carrots, cauliflower), thawed and drained
- 1 cup (4 ounces) shredded Cheddar cheese
- 1 can (2.8 ounces) DURKEE French Fried Onions

Preheat oven to 375°. In large bowl, combine soup, sour cream, milk, seasoned salt, vegetables, ½ cup cheese and ½ can French Fried Onions. Spoon into 8×12-inch baking dish. Bake, covered, at 375° for 40 minutes or until vegetables are done. Top with remaining cheese and onions; bake, uncovered, 3 minutes or until onions are golden brown.
Makes 8 to 10 servings.

Microwave Directions: Prepare vegetable mixture as above; spoon into 8×12-inch microwave-safe dish. Cook, covered, on HIGH 10 to 12 minutes or until vegetables are done. Stir vegetables halfway through cooking time. Top with remaining cheese and onions; cook, uncovered, 1 minute or until cheese melts. Let stand for 5 minutes.

Stuffed Tomatoes

6 to 8 medium tomatoes
2 tablespoons CRISCO® Oil
1/3 cup chopped celery
2 tablespoons chopped onion
2 cups cooked brown rice
1/4 cup grated Parmesan cheese
1 tablespoon snipped fresh
**   parsley**
1 teaspoon dried basil leaves
1/8 teaspoon pepper
1/8 teaspoon garlic powder

Cut thin slice from top of each tomato. Set tops aside. Scoop out center of tomatoes; chop pulp and set aside. Place shells upside down on paper towels to drain.

Preheat oven to 350°F. Heat Crisco® Oil in medium saucepan. Add celery and onion. Sauté over moderate heat until celery is tender. Remove from heat. Add reserved tomato pulp, rice, Parmesan cheese, parsley, basil, pepper and garlic powder. Mix well. Fill tomato shells with rice mixture. Replace tomato tops, if desired.

Lightly oil 9-inch pie plate or round baking dish. Place tomatoes in dish. Cover with aluminum foil. Bake at 350°F, 30 to 45 minutes, or until tomatoes are tender.

6 to 8 servings.

Note: Use 1 lightly oiled custard cup for each tomato instead of pie plate or baking dish, if desired.

Vegetable Sunburst

3 medium carrots, thinly sliced
**   (about 3 cups)**
3 small zucchini, thinly sliced
**   (about 3 cups)**
1 cup (4 ounces) shredded
**   Cheddar cheese**
1 can (2.8 ounces) DURKEE
**   French Fried Onions**
1 can (10 3/4 ounces) condensed
**   cream of celery soup**
1/4 cup milk
1/2 teaspoon DURKEE Seasoned
**   Salt**
1/4 teaspoon DURKEE Garlic
**   Powder**
1/4 teaspoon DURKEE Leaf
**   Oregano**

Preheat oven to 350°. In medium saucepan, cook carrots in boiling water to cover just until tender-crisp. Place hot carrots under cold running water until cool enough to handle; drain. In 1 1/2-quart casserole, arrange *half* the carrots around edge of dish; place *half* the zucchini in center. Sprinkle 1/2 cup cheese and 1/2 can French Fried Onions over vegetables. In small bowl, combine soup, milk and seasonings. Pour *half* the soup mixture over onions. Arrange remaining zucchini around edge of casserole and remaining carrots in center. Pour remaining soup mixture over vegetables. Bake, covered, at 350° for 30 minutes or until vegetables are tender. Top with remaining cheese and onions; bake, uncovered, 5 minutes or until onions are golden brown.

Makes 4 to 6 servings.

Microwave Directions: Place carrots and 1/2 cup water in medium microwave-safe bowl; cook on HIGH 5 to 7 minutes or until carrots are tender-crisp. Stir carrots halfway through cooking time. Drain. Prepare soup mixture as above. In 1 1/2-quart microwave-safe casserole, layer vegetables, cheese, onions and soup mixture as above. Cook, covered, 8 to 10 minutes or until vegetables are tender. Rotate dish halfway through cooking time. Top with remaining cheese and onions; cook, uncovered, 1 minute or until cheese melts. Let stand 5 minutes.

Grilled Tomatoes

2 large tomatoes
2 tablespoons olive or vegetable
**   oil**
1 1/2 teaspoons chopped fresh basil
**   *or* 1/2 teaspoon dried basil,**
**   crushed**
Salt and pepper

In covered grill, arrange medium-hot **KINGSFORD® Charcoal Briquets** on one side of grill. Slice each tomato in half crosswise; remove excess juice and seeds. Drizzle tomato halves with oil. Place in foil pan. Place foil pan on edge of grill not directly over coals. Cook tomatoes, on covered grill, 10 to 14 minutes or until heated through. Sprinkle cut surfaces with basil, salt and pepper. Garnish with fresh basil, if desired.

Makes 4 servings.

Skewered Vegetables

2 medium zucchini, cut into
**   1 1/2-inch slices**
8 small boiling onions
8 fresh medium mushrooms
2 tablespoons butter or
**   margarine, melted**
4 cherry tomatoes
Salt and pepper

In medium saucepan, cook zucchini and onions, covered, in boiling water to cover for 1 minute. Remove with slotted spoon and drain. Alternately thread zucchini, onions and mushrooms on 4 skewers. Brush with melted butter.

Grill vegetables, on covered grill, over medium-hot **KINGSFORD® Charcoal Briquets** 6 minutes or until tender, carefully turning skewers once. Add cherry tomatoes to end of skewers during last minute of grilling. Season to taste with salt and pepper. Serve immediately.

Makes 4 servings.

Vegetable Sunburst

Fresh Vegetable Ring

Fresh Vegetable Ring

- **2 cups broccoli flowerets**
- **2 cups cauliflowerets**
- **1 small zucchini, cut into ¼-inch slices**
- **1 small yellow squash, cut into ¼-inch slices**
- **1 can (10¾ ounces) CAMPBELL'S® Condensed Chicken Broth**
- **6 medium CAMPBELL'S FRESH® Mushrooms, halved**
- **Sweet red pepper strips for garnish**
- **2 teaspoons cornstarch**
- **1 teaspoon chopped fresh basil leaves or ½ teaspoon dried basil leaves, crushed**
- **1 teaspoon wine vinegar**

To Microwave:
1. Arrange broccoli in a circle around rim of a 12-inch round microwave-safe platter. Arrange cauliflower next to broccoli. Arrange alternate slices of zucchini and yellow squash next to cauliflower, leaving space in center of platter. Pour ¼ cup of the broth over vegetables. Cover with vented plastic wrap; microwave on HIGH 5 minutes, rotating dish once during cooking.
2. Place mushrooms in center of platter. Garnish with red pepper strips. Cover; microwave on HIGH 2 minutes or until vegetables are tender-crisp. Let stand, covered, while preparing sauce.
3. To make sauce: In small microwave-safe bowl, combine remaining broth, cornstarch, basil and vinegar; stir until smooth. Cover with vented plastic wrap; microwave on HIGH 2 minutes or until mixture boils, stirring twice during cooking. Spoon over vegetables in platter.
Makes 6 servings.

Swiss Vegetable Medley

- **1 bag (16 ounces) frozen vegetable combination (broccoli, carrots, cauliflower), thawed and drained**
- **1 can (10¾ ounces) condensed cream of mushroom soup**
- **1 cup (4 ounces) shredded Swiss cheese**
- **⅓ cup sour cream**
- **¼ teaspoon DURKEE Ground Black Pepper**
- **1 jar (4 ounces) diced pimiento, drained (optional)**
- **1 can (2.8 ounces) DURKEE French Fried Onions**

Preheat oven to 350°. In large bowl, combine vegetables, soup, ½ cup cheese, the sour cream, pepper, pimiento and ½ can French Fried Onions. Pour into shallow 1-quart casserole. Bake, covered, at 350° for 30 minutes or until vegetables are done. Sprinkle remaining cheese and onions in diagonal rows across top; bake, uncovered, 5 minutes or until onions are golden brown.
Makes 6 servings.
Microwave Directions: Prepare vegetable mixture as above; pour into shallow 1-quart microwave-safe casserole. Cook, covered, on HIGH 8 to 10 minutes or until vegetables are done. Stir vegetables halfway through cooking time. Top with remaining cheese and onions as above; cook, uncovered, 1 minute or until cheese melts. Let stand 5 minutes.

Tangy Blue Cheese Vegetables

- **1 package (3 ounces) cream cheese, softened**
- **¼ cup (2 ounces) crumbled blue cheese**
- **¾ cup milk**
- **1 jar (4½ ounces) whole mushrooms, drained**
- **1 bag (16 ounces) frozen vegetable combination (peas, carrots, cauliflower), thawed and drained**
- **1 can (2.8 ounces) DURKEE French Fried Onions**

Preheat oven to 375°. In medium saucepan, combine cream cheese, blue cheese and milk. Cook and stir over medium heat until smooth. Stir in mushrooms, vegetables and ½ can French Fried Onions; pour into 1-quart casserole. Bake, covered, at 375° for 30 minutes or until vegetables are done. Top with remaining onions; bake, uncovered, 3 minutes or until onions are golden brown.
Makes 4 to 6 servings.
Microwave Directions: In 1-quart microwave-safe casserole, combine cream cheese, blue cheese and milk. Cook, covered, on HIGH 5 to 6 minutes or until cheeses melt, stirring mixture halfway through cooking time. Add mushrooms, vegetables and ½ can onions; cook, covered, 5 to 7 minutes or until vegetables are done. Stir halfway through cooking time. Top with remaining onions; cook, uncovered, 1 minute. Let stand for 5 minutes.

Sweet 'n Sour Stir Fry

Sweet 'n Sour Stir Fry

> 2 tablespoons oil
> 1 cup thinly sliced carrots
> 1 cup snow peas (about
>   4 ounces)
> 1 small green pepper, cut into
>   chunks
> 1 cup sliced water chestnuts
> 1 medium tomato, cut into
>   wedges
> 1/2 cup sliced cucumber, halved
> 3/4 cup WISH-BONE® Sweet 'n
>   Spicy French Dressing
> 2 tablespoons brown sugar
> 2 teaspoons soy sauce

In medium skillet, heat oil and cook carrots, snow peas and green pepper over medium heat, stirring frequently, 5 minutes or until crisp-tender. Add water chestnuts, tomato, cucumber and sweet 'n spicy French dressing blended with brown sugar and soy sauce. Simmer covered 5 minutes or until vegetables are tender. Top, if desired, with sesame seeds. *Makes about 6 servings.*
Note: Also terrific with Wish-Bone® Lite Sweet 'n Spicy French, Russian or Lite Russian Dressing.

Sesame Vegetable Topping

> 2 tablespoons CRISCO® Oil
> 2 tablespoons finely chopped
>   onion
> 2 teaspoons sesame seeds
> 1/2 cup buttery round cracker
>   crumbs

Heat Crisco® Oil in small skillet. Add onion. Sauté over moderate heat until tender-crisp. Add sesame seeds. Cook, stirring constantly, 1 minute. Remove from heat. Stir in cracker crumbs. Use as a topping for vegetable dishes. *About 1/2 cup.*

Almondine Butter Sauce

> 1/2 cup sliced almonds
> 1/3 cup butter or margarine
> 1/4 cup REALEMON® Lemon Juice
>   from Concentrate

In small skillet, over medium low heat, cook almonds in margarine until golden; remove from heat. Stir in ReaLemon® brand. Serve warm over cooked vegetables or fish. *Makes 2/3 cup.*

Easy "Hollandaise" Sauce

> 1/2 lb. VELVEETA Pasteurized
>   Process Cheese Spread,
>   cubed
> 1/4 cup milk
> 1/4 teaspoon paprika
> 1 egg, beaten
> 2 teaspoons lemon juice

Combine process cheese spread, milk and paprika in saucepan; stir over low heat until process cheese spread is melted. Stir small amount of hot mixture into egg; return to hot mixture. Cook, stirring constantly, over low heat until thickened. Stir in juice. Serve over hot cooked vegetables or fish. *1 1/4 cups.*

Preparation time: 5 minutes
Cooking time: 15 minutes

Microwave: Microwave process cheese spread, milk and paprika in 1-quart microwave-safe bowl. Microwave on High 2 1/2 to 3 1/2 minutes or until process cheese spread is melted, stirring every minute. Stir small amount of hot mixture into egg; return to hot mixture. Microwave on Medium (50%) 1 to 1 1/2 minutes or until thickened, stirring every 30 seconds. Stir in juice. Serve over hot cooked vegetables or fish.

Pronto Zucchini

> 4 cups mushroom slices
> 4 cups zucchini slices
> 1/4 cup PARKAY Margarine
> 1/2 cup spaghetti sauce
> 1/4 lb. VELVEETA Pasteurized
>   Process Cheese Spread,
>   cubed
> 2 teaspoons dried oregano
>   leaves, crushed

In large skillet, saute vegetables in margarine until crisp-tender. Drain. Reduce heat to low. Add sauce, process cheese spread and oregano; stir until process cheese spread is melted. *4 to 6 servings.*

Preparation time: 10 minutes
Cooking time: 15 minutes

Variation: Substitute 2 tablespoons chopped fresh oregano leaves for dried oregano leaves.

Stir-Fried Vegetables with Bulgur

- 2 tablespoons vegetable oil
- 2 cups broccoli flowerets
- 1 cup thinly sliced carrots
- 1 cup bulgur wheat
- 1 small clove garlic, minced
- 1 tablespoon sesame seed
- 1 teaspoon dried oregano leaves, crushed
- 1³/₄ cups V8® Vegetable Juice
- 1 cup thinly sliced zucchini
- 1 cup sliced CAMPBELL'S FRESH® Mushrooms (4 ounces)
- ¼ cup sliced green onions
- ½ cup shredded Swiss cheese (2 ounces)

1. In 10-inch skillet or wok over medium-high heat, in hot oil, cook broccoli, carrots, bulgur, garlic, sesame seed and oregano, stirring quickly and frequently (stir-frying), about 2 minutes.
2. Add V8 juice, zucchini, mushrooms and green onions. Heat to boiling; reduce heat to low. Cover; simmer 15 minutes or until all liquid is absorbed, stirring occasionally.
3. Stir in cheese.
Makes 5 cups or 10 side-dish servings.

Per serving: 141 calories, 4 g protein, 5 g fat, 20 g carbohydrate, 173 mg sodium, 6 mg cholesterol.

Citrus Candied Sweet Potatoes

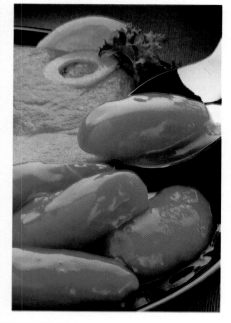

Citrus Candied Sweet Potatoes

- 2 (16- or 18-ounce) cans sweet potatoes, drained
- 1¼ cups firmly packed light brown sugar
- 2 tablespoons cornstarch
- ¾ cup orange juice
- ¼ cup REALEMON® Lemon Juice from Concentrate
- 2 tablespoons margarine or butter, melted

Preheat oven to 350°. In 2-quart shallow baking dish, arrange sweet potatoes. In medium bowl, combine sugar and cornstarch; add orange juice, ReaLemon® brand and margarine. Pour over sweet potatoes. Bake 50 to 55 minutes, basting occasionally with sauce.
Makes 6 to 8 servings.

Microwave: Arrange sweet potatoes as above. Increase cornstarch to 3 tablespoons. In 1-quart glass measure, combine sugar and cornstarch. Add orange juice, ReaLemon® brand and margarine. Cook on 100% power (high) 5 to 8 minutes until slightly thickened, stirring every 2 minutes. Pour over sweet potatoes; cook on 100% power (high) 8 minutes, basting after 4 minutes. Let stand 2 minutes before serving.

Grill-Baked Sweet Potatoes

- 4 medium sweet potatoes
  Vegetable oil
- 4 tablespoons butter or margarine
- 4 tablespoons brown sugar

Tear off four 6×9-inch pieces of heavy-duty foil. Brush sweet potatoes with oil. Pierce several times with fork. Wrap potatoes in foil. Grill potatoes, on uncovered grill, over medium-hot **KINGSFORD® Charcoal Briquets** about 1 hour or until tender, turning once. Remove foil. Open potatoes with tines of fork and push ends to fluff. Top each with 1 tablespoon butter and 1 tablespoon brown sugar.
Makes 4 servings.

Spicy Vegetable Stir-Fry

- ³/₄ to 1 pound fresh broccoli
- ¼ cup CRISCO® Oil
- 1 medium zucchini, cut into julienne strips
- 1 small onion, halved lengthwise and thinly sliced
- ⅛ teaspoon dried crushed red pepper
- 1 cup sliced fresh mushrooms
- 2 tablespoons shelled sunflower seeds
- 2 teaspoons soy sauce

Trim and discard tough ends from broccoli stalks. Cut stalks into thin slices. Separate heads into flowerets.
  Heat Crisco® Oil in large skillet. Add broccoli, zucchini, onion and red pepper. Stir-fry over medium-high heat about 5 minutes, or until broccoli is tender-crisp. Add mushrooms. Stir-fry 1 minute longer, or until mushrooms are tender. Stir in sunflower seeds and soy sauce.
4 to 6 servings.

Italian Vegetable Sauté

- 2 tablespoons CRISCO® Oil
- 1 clove garlic, minced
- ¼ teaspoon dried oregano leaves
- ¼ teaspoon dried marjoram leaves
- 2 cups julienne-cut zucchini
- 1 small onion, thinly sliced and separated into rings
- 1 can (16 ounces) whole tomatoes, drained, cut up
- 2 tablespoons sliced, pitted black olives (optional)
- ½ teaspoon salt
- ⅛ teaspoon pepper
- 2 tablespoons grated Parmesan cheese

Heat Crisco® Oil in large skillet. Add garlic, oregano and marjoram. Sauté over moderate heat until garlic is light brown. Add zucchini and onion. Stir to coat. Sauté 5 to 7 minutes, or until tender. Stir in tomatoes, olives (optional), salt and pepper. Cook until heated through. Stir in Parmesan cheese.
4 to 6 servings.

PIZZA & SANDWICHES

A treasury of ideas for two American classics. Homemade pizza, fresh from the oven, will become a delicious tradition with these easy-to-prepare recipes. Sandwiches with star quality—glamorous enough for company— turn lunches and midnight snacks into delectable feasts. Perk up a casual supper with tacos, fajitas or extra-special burgers.

Classic Pizza

- ½ **tablespoon active dry yeast**
- 1 **teaspoon sugar**
- ½ **cup very warm water (105°F to 115°F)**
- 1¾ **cups all-purpose flour**
- ¾ **teaspoon salt**
- 2 **tablespoons olive oil**
- 1 **medium onion, chopped**
- 1 **medium clove garlic, minced**
- 1 **can (14½ ounces) whole peeled tomatoes, undrained, chopped**
- 2 **tablespoons tomato paste**
- 1 **teaspoon dried oregano, crumbled**
- ½ **teaspoon dried basil, crumbled**
- ⅛ **teaspoon black pepper**
- 1¾ **cups shredded mozzarella cheese**
- ½ **cup grated Parmesan cheese**
- ½ **small red bell pepper, chopped**
- ½ **small green bell pepper, chopped**
- ⅓ **cup pitted ripe olives, cut into halves**
- 4 **fresh medium mushrooms, sliced**
- 1 **can (2 ounces) flat anchovy fillets, drained**

1. Sprinkle yeast and ½ teaspoon of the sugar over warm water in small bowl; stir until yeast is dissolved. Let stand until mixture is bubbly.
2. Place 1½ cups of the flour and ¼ teaspoon of the salt in medium bowl; stir in yeast mixture and 1 tablespoon of the oil, stirring until a smooth, soft dough forms. Knead on floured surface, using as much remaining flour as needed to form stiff elastic dough. Let dough rise, covered, in greased bowl in warm place until doubled in bulk, 30 to 45 minutes.
3. Meanwhile, heat remaining 1 tablespoon oil in medium saucepan over medium heat. Add onion; cook until soft, about 5 minutes. Add garlic; cook 30 seconds. Add tomatoes, tomato paste, oregano, basil, remaining ½ teaspoon sugar, remaining ½ teaspoon salt and the black pepper. Heat to boiling; reduce heat to medium-low.

Simmer, uncovered, stirring occasionally, until sauce is thick, 10 to 15 minutes. Transfer sauce to bowl; let cool.
4. Heat oven to 450°F. Punch dough down. Knead briefly on lightly floured surface to distribute air bubbles; let dough rest 5 minutes. Flatten dough into circle on lightly floured surface. Roll out dough into 10-inch circle. Place circle in greased 12-inch pizza pan; pat dough out to edges of pan. Let stand, covered, 15 minutes.
5. Mix mozzarella and Parmesan cheeses in small bowl. Spread sauce evenly over pizza dough. Sprinkle with two-thirds of the cheeses. Arrange bell peppers, olives, mushrooms and anchovies on top of pizza. Sprinkle remaining cheeses on top of pizza. Bake until crust is golden brown, about 20 minutes. Cut into wedges to serve.
Makes 4 to 6 servings.

Pizza Bread Pronto

- ½ **pound sliced SWIFT PREMIUM® or MARGHERITA® Deli Peperoni**
- **Butter or margarine, softened**
- 4 **mini French rolls, 8 inches long, sliced lengthwise**
- **Grated Parmesan cheese**
- 1 **can (8 ounces) pizza sauce**
- **Sliced mozzarella cheese**
- **Dried oregano leaves**

Spread butter over cut sides of rolls and sprinkle with Parmesan cheese. Broil, 4 inches from heat, until lightly browned. Spread several tablespoons pizza sauce over each. Layer peperoni over sauce. Top with mozzarella cheese and sprinkle with oregano. Broil until cheese melts. Serve hot.
Makes 8 servings.

Classic Pizza

Thick 'n Cheesy Vegetable Pizza

5. Preheat oven to 400°F. Bake crust 5 minutes; remove from oven. Arrange tomato slices and artichoke hearts over crust; sprinkle with cheese. Bake 15 minutes more or until lightly browned.
Makes 4 servings.

Note: Add your favorite pizza toppings, such as anchovies, mushrooms, green pepper strips, roasted red peppers, pepperoni or cooked Italian sausage.

Thick 'n Cheesy Vegetable Pizza

- 2 loaves (1 pound each) frozen bread dough, thawed
- 1 envelope LIPTON® Vegetable Recipe Soup Mix
- 1/4 cup olive or vegetable oil
- 2 tablespoons chopped fresh basil leaves*
- 1 large clove garlic, finely chopped
- 1/4 teaspoon pepper
- 2 cups shredded mozzarella cheese (about 6 ounces)
- 1 cup fresh or canned sliced mushrooms
- 1 medium tomato, coarsely chopped

Preheat oven to 425°.

Into lightly oiled 12-inch pizza pan, press dough to form crust; set aside.

In small bowl, blend vegetable recipe soup mix, oil, basil, garlic and pepper; spread evenly on dough. Top with remaining ingredients. Bake 20 minutes or until cheese is melted and crust is golden brown. To serve, cut into wedges.
Makes about 6 servings.

*Substitution: Use 2 teaspoons dried basil leaves.

Neapolitan Pizza

- 1 pouch CAMPBELL'S® Onion Soup and Recipe Mix
- 2 cups all-purpose flour
- 1 tablespoon sugar
- 1 package active dry yeast
- 3/4 cup very warm water (120° to 130°F.)
- 2 tablespoons olive or vegetable oil
- 2 CAMPBELL'S FRESH® Tomatoes, thinly sliced
- 1 jar (6 ounces) marinated artichoke hearts, drained and cut up
- 2 cups shredded mozzarella cheese (8 ounces)

1. In medium bowl, combine soup mix, 1 cup of the flour, sugar and yeast; mix well. With mixer at low speed, gradually pour warm water and oil into dry ingredients; beat until just mixed. With mixer at medium speed, beat 4 minutes, scraping bowl often.
2. With spoon, stir in about 3/4 cup flour or enough to make a soft dough. Turn dough onto lightly floured surface; knead until smooth and elastic, about 5 minutes, adding more flour as necessary.
3. Grease 14-inch pizza pan or baking sheet. On floured surface, roll dough to 14-inch round. Transfer to pizza pan. Turn edge under to form rim.
4. Let rise in warm place, 20 minutes.

Party Pizza

- 1/2 pound ECKRICH® Beef Smoked Sausage, cut into 1/4-inch slices
- 1 loaf (16 ounces) frozen bread dough, thawed
  Cornmeal
- 2 tablespoons butter or margarine
- 1 1/2 cups green bell pepper strips
- 1 1/2 cups sliced onions
- 8 ounces fresh mushrooms, sliced
- 3 cups (12 ounces) shredded mozzarella cheese, divided
- 1 jar (8 ounces) pizza sauce
- 1 teaspoon dried oregano leaves
- 1/2 teaspoon dried basil leaves
- 1/2 teaspoon fennel seeds
- 1/2 cup grated Parmesan cheese

Let bread dough warm and start to rise. Preheat oven to 425°F. Sprinkle cornmeal in 12-inch circle on buttered pizza pan or baking sheet. Place bread dough on cornmeal; stretch and pull to fit 12-inch circle. Bake 7 minutes. Remove from oven. Melt butter in medium skillet over medium-high heat; add green peppers, onions and mushrooms. Saute until vegetables just begin to lose their crispness. Stir in sausage. Cover bread with 1/2 of the mozzarella cheese. Combine pizza sauce, oregano, basil and fennel seeds in small bowl; spread over mozzarella cheese. Top with sausage mixture. Return to oven and bake 20 to 25 minutes more or until done. Top with remaining 1 1/2 cups mozzarella cheese; sprinkle with Parmesan cheese. Return to oven and bake until mozzarella melts, about 5 minutes more. To serve, cut into wedges or squares.
Makes 1 pizza, 12-inch diameter.

Vegetarian Sandwiches

    Cucumber Sauce (recipe
      follows)
¾ cup V8® Vegetable Juice
¼ cup brown rice, uncooked
2 eggs, beaten
**½ cup shredded mozzarella
    cheese (2 ounces)**
**1 cup canned chick peas,
    drained and mashed**
**¼ cup fresh whole wheat bread
    crumbs**
2 tablespoons chopped walnuts
**1 tablespoon finely chopped
    onion**
1 small clove garlic, minced
    Generous dash ground red
      pepper (cayenne)
**3 whole wheat pita breads
    (sandwich pockets), cut in
    half crosswise**
    CAMPBELL'S FRESH®
      Butterhead Lettuce Leaves

1. Prepare Cucumber Sauce.
2. In small saucepan over high heat, heat V8 juice to boiling. Stir in rice; reduce heat to low. Cover; simmer 45 minutes or until rice is tender and liquid is absorbed, stirring occasionally.
3. In medium bowl, stir together cooked rice, eggs, cheese, chick peas, crumbs, walnuts, onion, garlic and pepper until well mixed. Chill slightly, until firm enough to shape. Shape mixture into 6 patties.
4. Spray 10-inch nonstick skillet with vegetable cooking spray. Over medium heat, cook patties, 3 at a time, 8 minutes or until browned on both sides.

5. In each pita bread half, arrange lettuce and one bean patty; top with Cucumber Sauce.
Makes 6 sandwiches.
CUCUMBER SAUCE: In small bowl, stir together ½ cup plain low-fat yogurt, ½ cup chopped, seeded and peeled cucumber and ⅛ teaspoon dried dill weed, crushed. Cover; refrigerate until serving time.
Makes 1 cup.
Per serving: 268 calories, 12 g protein, 7 g fat, 39 g carbohydrate, 492 mg sodium, 100 mg cholesterol.

Egg Salad Magnifique

**1 8-ounce package
    PHILADELPHIA BRAND
    Cream Cheese, softened**
½ cup KRAFT Real Mayonnaise
**1 tablespoon KRAFT Cream
    Style Prepared Horseradish**
6 hard-cooked eggs, chopped
**1 6-ounce package frozen
    crabmeat, thawed, drained**
½ cup chopped celery
**½ cup chopped red or green
    pepper**
6 croissants, split
    Lettuce

Combine cream cheese, mayonnaise and horseradish, mixing until well blended. Add eggs, crabmeat, celery and peppers; mix lightly. Chill. Fill croissants with lettuce and egg mixture.
6 sandwiches.

Layered Picnic Club Sandwich

**1 loaf unsliced round bread
    (about 9-inch diameter)**
**¾ cup WISH-BONE® Creamy
    Italian Dressing**
    Lettuce leaves
⅓ pound sliced Swiss cheese
**¾ pound sliced cooked roast
    beef**
½ pound sliced cooked turkey
1 large tomato, sliced

Cut bread in half horizontally; hollow out center of each half, leaving ¼-inch shell.

Spread ⅓ cup creamy Italian dressing into each shell; line bottom shell with lettuce. Into bottom shell, layer cheese, roast beef, remaining dressing, turkey, then tomato. Top with lettuce; replace top shell. To serve, cut into wedges.
Makes about 6 servings.
    Note: Also terrific with Wish-Bone® Lite Creamy Italian, Thousand Island, Lite Thousand Island or Chunky Blue Cheese Dressing.

Pineapple Pizza

**2 cans (8 ounces each) DOLE®
    Crushed Pineapple**
½ cup bottled pizza sauce
1 clove garlic, pressed
**1 teaspoon dried oregano,
    crumbled**
**½ loaf frozen bread dough,
    thawed**
**½ pound Italian sausage,
    crumbled, cooked**
**1 small DOLE™ Green Bell
    Pepper, seeded and sliced**
¼ cup chopped green onion
**2 cups shredded mozzarella
    cheese**
**2 tablespoons grated Parmesan
    cheese**

Preheat oven to 500°F. Drain pineapple well, pressing out excess juice with back of spoon. In small bowl, combine pizza sauce, garlic and oregano. Roll and stretch thawed dough to fit greased 12-inch pizza pan. Spread dough with pizza sauce mixture. Top with sausage, green pepper, onion, pineapple and cheeses. Bake in preheated oven 12 to 15 minutes or until pizza is bubbly and crust is browned.
Makes 4 servings.

Layered Picnic Club Sandwich

Grilled Smoked Turkey 'n Muenster Sandwiches

- ¼ cup WISH-BONE® Thousand Island or Lite Thousand Island Dressing
- 6 slices pumpernickel bread (about ¾ inch thick)
- ¼ pound sliced Muenster cheese
- ½ pound sliced smoked or unsmoked cooked turkey breast
- 3 tablespoons butter or margarine, softened

Evenly spread Thousand Island dressing on each bread slice. Equally top 3 bread slices with ½ of the cheese, turkey, then remaining cheese; top with remaining bread slices, dressing side down. Evenly spread butter on outside of bread slices.

In large skillet, cook sandwiches, covered, over medium heat, turning once and pressing down sandwiches occasionally, 8 minutes or until cheese is melted.

Makes 3 hearty sandwiches.

Bacon & Chicken Sandwiches

- 1 (5-ounce) can cooked white meat chicken, drained
- 1 small stalk celery, thinly sliced
- 1 green onion, sliced
- ½ cup plain nonfat yogurt Pepper to taste
- 3 hamburger buns, toasted
- 3 canned pineapple rings, well drained
- 3 slices ARMOUR® Lower Salt Bacon, cooked crisp and crumbled

Combine chicken, celery, onion, yogurt and pepper in small bowl. If desired, place lettuce leaf on bottom of each bun; place pineapple ring on lettuce. Top each with one third of the chicken mixture and bacon.

Makes 3 servings.

Nutrition Information Per Serving: 268 calories, 18.6 g protein, 5.7 g fat, 33.2 g carbohydrates, 40 mg cholesterol, 567 mg sodium.

Beef and Bean Chimichangas

- 1 pound ground beef
- 2 tablespoons CRISCO® Oil
- 1 medium onion, chopped
- 2 cloves garlic, minced
- 1 can (16 ounces) whole tomatoes, drained, cut up
- ⅓ cup salsa
- 1½ teaspoons chili powder
- ¾ teaspoon ground coriander
- ½ teaspoon ground thyme
- ½ teaspoon salt
- ⅛ teaspoon cayenne
- ⅛ teaspoon ground cumin
- 1 cup refried beans CRISCO® Oil for frying
- 6 eight-inch flour tortillas
- ¾ cup shredded Monterey Jack cheese (optional)

Place ground beef in medium skillet. Brown over medium-high heat. Drain. Remove beef from skillet; set aside. Place 2 tablespoons Crisco® Oil in same skillet. Add onion and garlic. Sauté over moderate heat until onion is tender. Stir in ground beef, tomatoes, salsa, chili powder, coriander, thyme, salt, cayenne and cumin. Cook over medium-low heat, stirring occasionally, 10 to 15 minutes, or until mixture is thickened. Remove from heat. Stir in refried beans.

Heat 2 inches Crisco® Oil in deep-fryer or large saucepan to 375°F. Meanwhile, place ½ cup beef mixture in center of each tortilla. Fold opposite sides of tortilla to center over beef mixture. Fold ends toward center; secure with wooden pick.

Fry 1 to 2 chimichangas at a time, 1½ to 2 minutes, or until golden brown. Drain on paper towels. Sprinkle top of each chimichanga with 2 tablespoons Monterey Jack cheese (optional). Serve immediately with *salsa*, if desired.

6 servings.

Beef Fajitas

- ½ cup REALIME® Lime Juice from Concentrate
- ¼ cup vegetable oil
- 2 cloves garlic, finely chopped
- 1 (1- to 1½-pound) flank steak
- 10 (6-inch) flour tortillas, warmed according to package directions
- Garnishes: shredded lettuce, chopped tomatoes, chopped green onion, shredded Cheddar cheese, sliced ripe olives, guacamole, sour cream, picante sauce

In small bowl, combine ReaLime® brand, oil and garlic; pour over meat. Refrigerate 6 hours or overnight, turning occasionally. Remove meat from marinade; grill or broil as desired, basting frequently with marinade. Slice meat diagonally into thin strips; place on tortillas. Top with one or more of the garnishes; fold tortillas. Serve immediately. Refrigerate leftovers.

Makes 10 fajitas.

Bacon & Chicken Sandwiches

Arizona's 7-Layer Taco Sandwich

- 1 pound thinly sliced BUTTERBALL® Deli Turkey Breast
- ½ cup coarsely chopped ripe olives
- ½ teaspoon chili powder
- ½ teaspoon ground cumin
- ¼ teaspoon salt
- ½ cup mayonnaise
- ½ cup sour cream
- ½ cup sliced green onions
- 4 large oval slices French bread, about ½ inch thick
- 1 large tomato, sliced
- 1 ripe avocado, peeled, sliced
- ¾ cup (3 ounces) shredded Cheddar cheese
- ¾ cup (3 ounces) shredded Monterey Jack cheese
- Lettuce leaves
- Salsa

Preheat oven to 350°F. Combine olives, chili powder, cumin and salt in medium bowl; reserve two tablespoons. Stir mayonnaise, sour cream and onions into remaining olive mixture. Using ½ of the mayonnaise mixture, spread on 1 side of each bread slice. Top with tomato and turkey. Spread remaining mayonnaise mixture on top of turkey. Top with avocado slices. Sprinkle with cheeses. Transfer sandwiches to baking sheet. Bake until hot, about 15 minutes. Top with reserved olive mixture. Serve on lettuce leaves with salsa.
Makes 4 open-faced sandwiches.

Arizona's 7-Layer Taco Sandwich

Garden-Fresh Pitas

- 1½ cups cut-up cooked chicken (about 9 ounces)
- ⅓ cup WISH-BONE® Creamy Italian or Lite Creamy Italian Dressing
- ¼ cup finely chopped celery
- 4 small pita breads, split
- Lettuce leaves
- 1 medium tomato, sliced
- ½ cup thinly sliced cucumber

In medium bowl, combine chicken, creamy Italian dressing and celery; cover and chill. To serve, line breads with lettuce, tomato and cucumber; spoon in chicken mixture.
Makes about 4 servings.

Turkey Cranberry Croissant

- Thin-sliced cooked BUTTERBALL® turkey (1 pound)
- 1 package (8 ounces) cream cheese, softened
- ¼ cup orange marmalade
- ½ cup chopped pecans
- 6 croissants or rolls, split
- ¾ cup whole berry cranberry sauce
- Lettuce leaves

Combine cream cheese, marmalade and pecans in small bowl. Spread top and bottom halves of croissants with cream cheese mixture. Layer turkey on bottom halves. Spoon 2 tablespoons cranberry sauce over turkey. Add lettuce and croissant top.
Yield: 6 sandwiches.

Lipton Onion Burgers

- 1 envelope LIPTON® Onion, Onion-Mushroom, Beefy Onion or Beefy Mushroom Recipe Soup Mix
- 2 pounds ground beef
- ½ cup water

In large bowl, combine all ingredients; shape into 8 patties. Grill or broil until done. Serve, if desired, on hamburger rolls.
Makes 8 servings.

Microwave Directions: Prepare patties as above. In oblong baking dish, arrange 4 patties and heat uncovered at HIGH (Full Power) 6 minutes, turning patties once. Repeat with remaining patties. Let stand covered 5 minutes. Serve as above.

Turkey-Topped Biscuits

Turkey-Topped Biscuits

- 1 tablespoon butter or margarine
- ½ pound ground turkey
- 1 tablespoon grated Parmesan cheese
- ½ teaspoon rubbed sage
- ½ teaspoon fennel seed
- ¼ teaspoon garlic powder
- ⅛ teaspoon salt
- ⅛ teaspoon pepper
- ½ cup chopped onion
- 1 medium apple, chopped
- ¾ cup V8® Vegetable Juice
- ¼ cup raisins
- ¼ teaspoon ground cinnamon
- 4 hot biscuits, split

1. In 10-inch skillet over medium heat, in hot butter, cook turkey, Parmesan, sage, fennel, garlic powder, salt and pepper until turkey is browned, stirring to separate turkey.
2. Add onion and apple; cook until tender, stirring often. Stir in V8 juice, raisins and cinnamon. Cook, uncovered, 15 minutes or until slightly thickened.
3. To serve: Spoon turkey mixture onto bottom halves of biscuits; cover with biscuit tops.
Makes 4 servings.

Per serving: 280 calories, 14 g protein, 12 g fat, 31 g carbohydrate, 607 mg sodium, 47 mg cholesterol.

Middle East Pita Pockets

- ½ cup canned chick peas, drained
- ¼ cup water
- 2 tablespoons sesame seeds
- 1 tablespoon lemon juice
- 1 clove garlic
- ½ teaspoon TABASCO® pepper sauce
- ½ teaspoon salt
- ½ cup chopped cucumber
- ½ cup julienne strips yellow squash
- ½ cup julienne strips zucchini
- ¼ cup sliced radishes
- ¼ cup sliced green onions
- 2 pita breads, 6 inches in diameter

In container of blender or food processor combine chick peas, water, sesame seeds, lemon juice, garlic, Tabasco® sauce and salt. Cover; blend until smooth. In medium bowl mix cucumber, yellow squash, zucchini, radishes and green onions. Cut pita breads in half to form pockets. Spoon vegetable mixture into each pocket. Spoon chick pea sauce over vegetables.
Makes 2 servings.

Chili Dogs

- 1 can (11¼ ounces) CAMPBELL'S® Condensed Chili Beef Soup
- 2 tablespoons water
- 2 tablespoons ketchup
- 6 frankfurters
- 6 PEPPERIDGE FARM® Frankfurter Rolls, split
- 3 slices American cheese, cut into triangles

To Microwave:
1. In small microwave-safe bowl, combine soup, water and ketchup. Cover with vented plastic wrap; microwave on HIGH 3 minutes or until very hot, stirring once during cooking.
2. Arrange frankfurters on 10-inch microwave-safe plate lined with paper towels. Microwave, uncovered, on HIGH 2 minutes or until hot.
3. Place cooked frankfurters in rolls. Spoon a heaping tablespoon of soup mixture over each. Arrange cheese triangles over soup mixture.
4. Arrange rolls on same plate lined with clean paper towels. Microwave, uncovered, on HIGH 1 minute or until cheese melts.
Makes 6 servings.

Seafood Salad Sandwiches

- 1 envelope LIPTON® Vegetable Recipe Soup Mix
- ¾ cup sour cream
- ¼ cup mayonnaise
- 1 teaspoon lemon juice
- ½ cup chopped celery
- 1 tablespoon fresh or frozen chopped chives (optional)
- Hot pepper sauce to taste
- ⅛ teaspoon pepper
- 2 packages (6 ounces each) frozen crabmeat, thawed and well drained*
- 4 hard rolls, halved
- Lettuce leaves

In large bowl, blend vegetable recipe soup mix, sour cream, mayonnaise, lemon juice, celery, chives, hot pepper sauce and pepper. Stir in crabmeat;

chill. To serve, line rolls with lettuce, then fill with crab mixture.
Makes 4 hearty sandwiches.

Variations: Use 1 package (12 ounces) frozen cleaned shrimp, cooked and coarsely chopped; OR 2 packages (8 ounces each) sea legs, thawed, drained and chopped; OR 1 can (13 ounces) tuna, drained and flaked; OR 2 cans (4½ ounces each) medium or large shrimp, drained and chopped; OR 2 cans (6½ ounces each) crabmeat, drained and flaked.

Santa Monica Sandwich

**Sliced cooked BUTTERBALL®
  turkey (¾ pound)
4 to 8 slices cooked bacon, cut
  into halves crosswise
4 slices buttered toast
  Avocado Sauce (recipe
  follows)
  Orange sections**

Place 2 to 4 halves of bacon between sliced turkey on each piece of toast. Top with Avocado Sauce and orange sections.
Yield: 4 open-faced sandwiches.

Avocado Sauce

**1 ripe avocado
2 tablespoons mayonnaise
2 teaspoons lemon juice
¼ teaspoon onion powder**

Cut avocado in half; remove pit. Pare. Mash avocado and blend with remaining ingredients in small bowl.
Yield: ⅔ cup.

Chili Burritos

**1 pound ground beef
¼ cup chopped green pepper
1 can (11 ounces) CAMPBELL'S®
  Condensed Zesty Tomato
  Soup/Sauce
1 tablespoon chili powder
1 tablespoon Worcestershire
  sauce
8 (8-inch) flour tortillas
  Guacamole for garnish
  Chopped CAMPBELL'S
  FRESH® Tomatoes for
  garnish
  Shredded Cheddar cheese for
  garnish**

To Microwave:
1. Crumble beef into 2-quart microwave-safe casserole; stir in green pepper. Cover with lid; microwave on HIGH 5 minutes or until beef is no longer pink, stirring once during cooking to break up meat. Spoon off fat.
2. Stir in soup, chili powder and Worcestershire. Cover; microwave on HIGH 5 minutes or until hot and bubbling.
3. Wrap stack of tortillas in damp paper towels. Microwave on HIGH 1 minute or until warm. Spoon heaping ¼ cup meat mixture onto each tortilla. Fold in sides and roll up to make burritos. Garnish with guacamole, tomatoes and cheese.
Makes 8 burritos or 4 servings.

Note: You can also serve the filling mixture on hamburger rolls.

Golden Gate Grill

**¾ pound thinly sliced
  BUTTERBALL® Deli Turkey
  Breast
1 egg, beaten
¼ cup milk or half and half
8 large oval slices sourdough
  French bread
  Grated Parmesan or Romano
  cheese
1 tomato, sliced thin
1 small avocado, peeled, sliced
2 tablespoons chopped fresh
  cilantro
4 slices red onion, separated
  into rings
4 slices Monterey Jack cheese
2 tablespoons butter or
  margarine, softened
1 clove garlic, minced
⅛ to ¼ teaspoon crushed red
  pepper**

Combine egg and milk in shallow dish. Dip 1 side of each bread slice in egg mixture, then in Parmesan cheese. Arrange turkey on undipped side of 4 slices of the bread. Place tomato, avocado, cilantro and red onion on turkey. Top with Monterey Jack cheese and remaining bread, dipped side up. Combine butter, garlic and red pepper. Preheat large skillet over medium heat. Melt 1 tablespoon of the butter mixture in skillet. Brown both sides of 2 sandwiches until crisp. Repeat with remaining butter and sandwiches. Serve immediately.
Makes 4 sandwiches.

Nutty Burgers

**1½ pounds ground beef
1 medium onion, finely chopped
1 clove garlic, minced
1 cup dry bread crumbs
⅓ cup grated Parmesan cheese
⅔ cup pine nuts
⅓ cup chopped parsley
2 eggs
1½ teaspoons salt
1 teaspoon pepper**

In large bowl, combine all ingredients. Shape into 6 thick patties. Grill patties, on covered grill, over medium-hot **KINGSFORD® Charcoal Briquets** 5 minutes on each side or until done. Serve on French bread and garnish with chopped green onion, if desired.
Makes 6 servings.

Golden Gate Grill

Loaf Sandwiches with Bacon & Ham

¼ cup unsalted margarine or butter, melted
1 to 2 teaspoons garlic powder
1 large loaf French bread
3 ounces ARMOUR® Lower Salt Ham, thinly sliced
2 ounces ARMOUR® Lower Salt Monterey Jack Cheese, thinly sliced
6 cherry tomato slices
6 slices ARMOUR® Lower Salt Bacon, cut in half and cooked crisp
12 (¼-inch) zucchini slices

Combine margarine and garlic powder in small bowl; set aside. Make 6 diagonal cuts at equal distances along loaf of bread, cutting ¾ of the way through loaf. Spread margarine mixture on cut sides of bread. Evenly distribute ham and cheese among cuts. Place 1 tomato slice, 2 bacon pieces and 2 zucchini slices in each cut. If desired, wrap entire loaf with foil and bake in 375°F. oven about 15 to 20 minutes, or until cheese is melted. Cut into 6 servings.
Makes 6 servings.

Nutritional Information Per Serving: 380 calories, 14.1 protein, 16.3 g fat, 44 g carbohydrates, 23 mg cholesterol, 701 mg sodium.

Loaf Sandwiches with Bacon & Ham

Sloppy Joes

2 pounds ground beef
1 envelope LIPTON® Onion, Onion-Mushroom, Beefy Mushroom or Beefy Onion Recipe Soup Mix
1 can (15 ounces) tomato sauce
½ cup sweet pickle relish

In large skillet, brown ground beef over medium-high heat; drain. Stir in remaining ingredients. Simmer, stirring occasionally, 10 minutes. Serve, if desired, over toasted hamburger rolls.
Makes about 8 servings.
Microwave Directions: In 2-quart casserole, heat ground beef, uncovered, at HIGH (Full Power) 7 minutes; drain. Stir in remaining ingredients. Heat covered, stirring occasionally, 4 minutes or until heated through. Let stand covered 5 minutes. Serve as above.

Stuffed Cheese Burgers

1½ cups shredded Monterey Jack cheese (about 8 ounces)
1 can (2¼ ounces) chopped black olives
⅛ teaspoon hot pepper sauce
1¾ pounds ground beef
¼ cup finely chopped onion
1 teaspoon salt
½ teaspoon pepper
6 hamburger buns
Butter or margarine, melted

In large bowl, combine cheese, olives and hot pepper sauce. Divide mixture evenly and shape into 6 balls. Mix ground beef with onion, salt and pepper; shape into 12 thin patties. Place 1 cheese ball in center of each of 6 patties and top each with a second patty. Seal edges to enclose cheese balls. Lightly oil grid. Grill patties, on covered grill, over medium-hot **KINGSFORD® Charcoal Briquets** 5 to 6 minutes on each side or until done.
Split buns, brush with butter and place, cut-side down, on grill to heat through. Serve Cheese Burgers on buns.
Makes 6 servings.

Avocado & Bacon Pitas

2 (6-inch) pita breads, cut in half
4 leaves leaf lettuce, washed and drained
12 slices ARMOUR® Lower Salt Bacon, cut in half and cooked crisp
1 avocado, peeled, pitted and sliced
1 (15¼-ounce) can pineapple spears, well drained
4 radishes, thinly sliced
8 tablespoons bottled low sodium, reduced calorie zesty Italian salad dressing

Open sliced edges of pita bread halves. Line with leaf lettuce. Divide bacon, avocado, pineapple and radishes evenly among bread pockets. Before serving, spoon 2 tablespoons of the dressing over top of each sandwich.
Makes 4 sandwiches.

Nutrition Information Per Sandwich: 319 calories, 10.1 g protein, 17.2 g fat, 35.2 g carbohydrates, 18 mg cholesterol, 558 mg sodium.

Barbecue Ham Sandwiches

1 cup catsup
3 tablespoons REALEMON® Lemon Juice from Concentrate
¼ cup chopped onion
¼ cup firmly packed brown sugar
2 tablespoons Worcestershire sauce
1 teaspoon prepared mustard
1 pound thinly sliced cooked ham
Buns or hard rolls

In medium saucepan, combine all ingredients except ham and buns. Simmer uncovered 5 minutes. Add ham; heat through. Serve on buns. Refrigerate leftovers.
Makes 6 to 8 sandwiches.

Microwave: In 2-quart round baking dish, combine ingredients as above. Cover with wax paper; microwave on full power (high) 3 minutes. Stir in ham; cover with wax paper and microwave on full power (high) 3 to 4 minutes or until hot. Serve as above.

Barbecue Ham Sandwiches

Texas-Style Steak on Hot Bread

½ cup olive or vegetable oil
¼ cup lime juice
¼ cup red wine vinegar
1 medium onion, finely chopped
1 clove garlic, minced
1 teaspoon chili powder
½ teaspoon salt
¼ teaspoon ground cumin
1 beef skirt or flank steak (about 1½ pounds)
1 round loaf French or sourdough bread
1 cup salsa
1 cup guacamole

In shallow glass dish, combine oil, lime juice, vinegar, onion, garlic, chili powder, salt and cumin. With meat mallet, pound steak to ¼-inch thickness. Place steak in marinade; turn to coat. Cover and refrigerate several hours or overnight, turning several times. Drain steak; discard marinade. Grill steak, on covered grill, over medium-hot **KINGSFORD® Charcoal Briquets** 4 to 8 minutes on each side, or until done. Cut bread into 1-inch slices and toast on grill. Heat salsa. Carve steak into ¾-inch diagonal strips. Arrange steak on toasted bread. Top with hot salsa and guacamole.
Makes 4 to 6 servings.

The California Classic

¼ cup MIRACLE WHIP Salad Dressing
1 teaspoon KRAFT Pure Prepared Mustard
4 rye bread slices
Alfalfa sprouts
4 cooked turkey slices
¼ lb. VELVEETA Pasteurized Process Cheese Spread, sliced
Thin tomato slices
Peeled avocado slices

Combine salad dressing and mustard; mix well. Spread bread slices with salad dressing mixture. For each sandwich, top one bread slice with sprouts, turkey, process cheese spread, tomatoes, avocados and second bread slice.
2 sandwiches.

Preparation time: 10 minutes

Variation: Substitute salami slices or boiled ham slices for turkey.

Quick 'n Easy Tacos

1 pound ground beef
1 can (14½ ounces) whole peeled tomatoes, undrained and coarsely chopped
1 medium green pepper, finely chopped
1 envelope LIPTON® Onion, Onion-Mushroom or Beefy Mushroom Recipe Soup Mix
1 tablespoon chili powder
3 drops hot pepper sauce
8 taco shells
Taco Toppings*

In medium skillet, brown ground beef over medium-high heat; drain. Stir in tomatoes, green pepper, onion recipe soup mix, chili powder and hot pepper sauce. Bring to a boil, then simmer 15 minutes or until slightly thickened. Serve in taco shells with assorted Taco Toppings.
Makes about 4 servings.

***Taco Toppings:** Use shredded Cheddar or Monterey Jack cheese, shredded lettuce, chopped tomatoes, sliced pitted ripe olives, sour cream or taco sauce.

Microwave Directions: In 2-quart casserole, heat ground beef with green pepper, uncovered, at HIGH (Full Power) 4 minutes, stirring once; drain. Stir in tomatoes, onion recipe soup mix, chili powder and hot pepper sauce. Heat uncovered, stirring occasionally, 7 minutes or until heated through. Let stand uncovered 5 minutes. Serve as above.

EGGS, CHEESE & BRUNCH DISHES

Transform lazy weekend brunches and informal Sunday-night suppers into special events with these innovative ideas for casual dining. Create light and airy souffles, quiches rich with eggs and meat, and waffles and pancakes that rise above the crowd. You'll turn ham and eggs into a gourmet treat.

Tempting Cheese Crepes

- 2/3 cup flour
- 1/2 teaspoon salt
- 3 eggs, beaten
- 1 cup milk
- 2 8-ounce packages *Light* PHILADELPHIA BRAND Neufchâtel Cheese, softened
- 1/4 cup sugar
- 1 teaspoon vanilla
  Strawberry-Banana Topping

Combine flour, salt and eggs; beat until smooth. Gradually add milk, mixing until well blended. For each crepe, pour 1/4 cup batter into hot, lightly greased 8-inch skillet or crepe pan, tilting skillet to cover bottom. Cook over medium-high heat until lightly browned on both sides, turning once.

Combine neufchâtel cheese, sugar and vanilla, mixing until well blended. Spread approximately 1/4 cup neufchâtel cheese mixture onto each crepe. Fold in thirds. Place in 13×9-inch baking dish. Bake at 350°, 15 to 20 minutes or until thoroughly heated. Serve with Strawberry-Banana Topping.
8 servings.

Preparation Tip: Lightly grease and preheat the skillet or crepe pan until a drop of water sizzles when sprinkled on. If the skillet isn't really hot, crepes may be too thick and stick to the pan.

Strawberry-Banana Topping

- 1 10-ounce package frozen strawberries, thawed
- 1 tablespoon cornstarch
- 1 banana, sliced

Drain strawberries, reserving liquid. Add enough water to reserved liquid to measure 1 1/4 cups; gradually add to cornstarch in saucepan, stirring until well blended. Bring to boil over medium heat, stirring constantly. Boil 1 minute. Stir in fruit.
2 cups.

"Philly" Brunch Quiche

- Pastry for 1-crust 10-inch pie
- 1 8-ounce package PHILADELPHIA BRAND Cream Cheese, cubed
- 1 cup milk
- 4 eggs, beaten
- 1/4 cup chopped onion
- 1 tablespoon PARKAY Margarine
- 1 cup finely chopped ham
- 1/4 cup chopped pimento
- 1/4 teaspoon dill weed
  Dash of pepper

On lightly floured surface, roll pastry to 12-inch circle. Place in 10-inch pie plate. Turn under edge; flute. Prick bottom and sides of pastry with fork. Bake at 400°, 12 to 15 minutes or until pastry is lightly browned.

Combine cream cheese and milk in saucepan; stir over low heat until smooth. Gradually add cream cheese mixture to eggs, mixing until well blended. Saute onions in margarine. Add onions and remaining ingredients to cream cheese mixture; mix well. Pour into pastry shell. Bake at 350°, 35 to 40 minutes or until set. Garnish with ham slices and fresh dill, if desired.
8 servings.

Variations: Substitute 1/4 cup finely chopped green pepper for dill weed.

Substitute 10-ounce package frozen chopped spinach, cooked, drained, 1 cup (4 ounces) shredded KRAFT 100% Natural Swiss Cheese and 6 crisply cooked bacon slices, crumbled, for ham, pimento and dill weed.

Substitute 4-ounce package pepperoni slices, chopped, 1/4 cup (1 ounce) KRAFT Grated Parmesan Cheese and 1/2 teaspoon dried oregano leaves, crushed, for ham, pimento and dill weed. Place pepperoni on bottom of baked pastry shell; continue as directed.

"Philly" Brunch Quiche, spinach variation (top); Tempting Cheese Crepes (bottom)

Turkey and Caper Quiche

**3/4 cup diced cooked
BUTTERBALL® turkey
Pastry for single 9-inch pie
crust***
**1/2 cup (2 ounces) shredded
Swiss cheese**
1/3 cup diced tomato
1/4 cup minced onion
1 teaspoon capers
3 eggs, beaten
1 tablespoon Dijon mustard
1 teaspoon seasoned salt
1 cup half and half

Preheat oven to 350°F. Line 9-inch quiche dish or pie pan with pastry. Trim edges and flute. Layer turkey, cheese, tomato, onion and capers in crust. Blend eggs, mustard, salt and half and half in small bowl. Pour mixture into pie crust. Bake in oven 40 to 50 minutes or until knife inserted 1 inch from center comes out clean.
Yield: 4 servings.

*Substitute frozen 9-inch deep dish pie crust, thawed, for pastry. Omit quiche dish; bake directly in foil pan.

Swiss Chicken Quiche

**1 (9-inch) unbaked pastry shell,
pricked**
**2 cups cubed cooked chicken or
turkey**
**1 cup (4 ounces) shredded
Swiss cheese**
2 tablespoons flour
**1 tablespoon WYLER'S® or
STEERO® Chicken-Flavor
Instant Bouillon**
**1 cup BORDEN® or MEADOW
GOLD® Milk**
3 eggs, well beaten
1/4 cup chopped onion
**2 tablespoons chopped green
pepper**
2 tablespoons chopped pimiento

Preheat oven to 425°. Bake pastry shell 8 minutes; remove from oven. Reduce oven temperature to 350°. In medium bowl, toss cheese with flour and bouillon; add remaining ingredients. Mix well. Pour into prepared shell. Bake 40 to 45 minutes or until set. Let stand 10 minutes before serving. Garnish as desired. Refrigerate leftovers.
Makes 6 servings.

Savory Onion Cheese Tart

Savory Onion Cheese Tart

**1 envelope LIPTON® Golden
Onion Recipe Soup Mix**
1 cup milk
1 egg, slightly beaten
1/2 teaspoon rosemary leaves
**1 package (8 ounces) mozzarella
cheese, shredded**
**1 package (15 ounces)
refrigerated pie crusts for
2 (9-inch) crusts**

In small bowl, thoroughly blend golden onion recipe soup mix, milk, egg and rosemary. Stir in cheese. Freeze 1 hour or refrigerate at least 2 hours until mixture is slightly thickened and not runny.

Preheat oven to 375°. On two aluminum-foil-lined baking sheets, unfold pie crusts. Fold crust edges over 1 inch to form rim. Brush, if desired, with 1 egg yolk beaten with 2 tablespoons water. Fill center of each prepared crust with 1/2 soup mixture; spread evenly to rim. Bake 25 minutes or until crusts are golden brown. To serve, cut into wedges.
Makes 2 tarts.

Freezing/Reheating Directions: Tarts can be baked, then frozen. Simply wrap in heavy-duty aluminum foil; freeze. To reheat, unwrap and bake at 350° until heated through.

Quiche Florentine

**1 15-oz. pkg. PILLSBURY All
Ready Pie Crust**
**2 cups (8 ozs.) VELVEETA
Shredded Pasteurized
Process Cheese Food**
**1/3 cup (1 1/2 ozs.) KRAFT 100%
Grated Parmesan Cheese**
**1 10-oz. pkg. frozen chopped
spinach, thawed, well-
drained**
**4 crisply cooked bacon slices,
crumbled**
3/4 cup milk
3 eggs, beaten
1/4 teaspoon pepper

Prepare pie crust according to package directions for filled one-crust pie using 9-inch pie plate. (Refrigerate remaining crust for later use.) In large bowl, combine remaining ingredients; mix well. Pour into unbaked pie crust. Bake at 350°, 35 to 40 minutes or until knife inserted in center comes out clean. Let stand 10 minutes before serving.
6 to 8 servings.

Preparation time: 15 minutes
Baking time: 40 minutes plus standing time

Souper Easy Quiche

4 eggs
**1 can (11 ounces) CAMPBELL'S®
  Condensed Cheddar Cheese
  Soup/Sauce**
½ cup light cream
**1 cup shredded sharp Cheddar
  cheese**
½ cup diced cooked ham
**½ cup drained, cooked
  chopped broccoli**
**1 9-inch unbaked piecrust
  (recipe follows)**
Ground nutmeg

1. In medium bowl, beat eggs until foamy. Gradually add soup and cream, mixing well.
2. Sprinkle cheese, ham and broccoli evenly over piecrust. Pour soup mixture over all. Sprinkle with nutmeg.
3. Bake at 350°F. 50 minutes or until center is set. Let stand 10 minutes before serving.
Makes 6 servings.
PIECRUST: In medium bowl, stir together 1 cup all-purpose flour and ½ teaspoon salt. With pastry blender, cut in ⅓ cup shortening until mixture resembles coarse crumbs. Add 2 to 3 tablespoons cold water, a tablespoon at a time, mixing lightly with fork until pastry holds together. Form into a ball. On lightly floured surface, roll dough to a 13-inch round. Transfer to 9-inch pie plate. Trim edge, leaving ½ inch pastry beyond edge of pie plate. Fold overhang under pastry; pinch a high edge. Flute edge.

Breakfast Pizza

**6 ECKRICH® SMOK-Y-LINKS®
  Sausages, cut into ¼-inch
  slices**
**Pastry for single crust 9-inch
  pie**
**2 cups (8 ounces) shredded
  Swiss cheese**
4 eggs
1½ cups sour cream
2 tablespoons chopped parsley

Preheat oven to 425°F. Roll out pastry and fit into 12-inch pizza pan. Bake, on lowest oven rack, 5 minutes. Cool. Sprinkle sausage and cheese over crust. Lightly beat eggs in medium bowl. Stir in sour cream and parsley until smooth. Pour over sausage and cheese. Bake 20 to 25 minutes more. Cool 5 minutes before cutting.
Makes 4 to 5 servings.

B.L.T.E. Breakfast Pockets

**4 slices bacon, cooked and
  crumbled**
6 eggs
**⅓ cup BORDEN® or MEADOW
  GOLD® Milk**
**1 teaspoon WYLER'S® or
  STEERO® Chicken-Flavor
  Instant Bouillon**
**1 tablespoon margarine or
  butter**
½ cup chopped tomato
**3 (5-inch) pita bread rounds, cut
  in half**
6 lettuce leaves
**6 slices BORDEN® Process
  American Cheese Food**

In medium bowl, beat eggs, milk and bouillon. In medium skillet, melt margarine; add egg mixture. Cook and stir until eggs are set; remove from heat. Stir in bacon and tomato. Fill each pita bread half with lettuce, cheese food slice and *½ cup* egg mixture. Serve immediately. Refrigerate leftovers.
Makes 6 sandwiches.

Southwestern Egg Puff

**1 lb. VELVEETA Mexican
  Pasteurized Process Cheese
  Spread with Jalapeño
  Pepper, cubed**
2 cups cottage cheese
6 eggs, beaten
½ cup picante sauce
**¼ cup PARKAY Margarine,
  melted**
¼ cup flour
½ teaspoon baking powder
½ teaspoon seasoned salt
**1 12-oz. can whole kernel corn
  with sweet peppers, drained**

In large bowl, combine ingredients; mix well. Pour into greased 12×8-inch baking dish. Bake at 350°, 35 to 40 minutes or until golden brown. Top with additional picante sauce, sour cream and avocado slices, if desired.
4 to 6 servings.

Preparation time: 10 minutes
Baking time: 40 minutes

Variation: Substitute VELVEETA Pasteurized Process Cheese Spread for Process Cheese Spread with Jalapeño Pepper.

Souper Easy Quiche

Gingery Banana Waffles

Serve pancakes hot with pancake syrup and additional cooked Sizzlean® strips, if desired.
Makes 5 servings.

Gingery Banana Waffles

    3 cups flour
    4 teaspoons baking powder
    2 teaspoons ground cinnamon
 1½ teaspoons ground ginger
    1 teaspoon salt
    4 eggs
  ²⁄₃ cup brown sugar, packed
    2 extra-ripe, medium DOLE™
      Bananas
 1¼ cups milk
  ½ cup molasses
  ½ cup butter or margarine,
      melted
    4 firm, medium DOLE™ Bananas,
      sliced
      Maple syrup

Preheat waffle iron. In large bowl, combine flour, baking powder, cinnamon, ginger and salt. In medium bowl, beat eggs with brown sugar until light and fluffy. Puree extra-ripe bananas in blender (1 cup). Beat pureed bananas, milk, molasses and butter into egg mixture; add to dry ingredients. Stir until just moistened.

For each waffle, cook ³⁄₄ cup batter in waffle iron until golden brown. Serve with sliced bananas and syrup.
Makes 8 servings.

Mandarin Orange French Toast

    1 can (11 ounces) DOLE®
      Mandarin Orange Segments
    1 tablespoon grated orange peel
  ½ cup orange juice
    1 tablespoon brown sugar
    2 teaspoons cornstarch
    1 teaspoon vanilla extract
      Dash ground nutmeg
    2 eggs, lightly beaten
  ½ cup half-and-half
    4 slices (½ inch thick each)
      stale French bread or thick-
      sliced white bread
    2 tablespoons butter or
      margarine
  ¼ cup DOLE™ Sliced Natural
      Almonds, toasted, optional

Drain syrup from oranges into saucepan. Stir in orange peel and juice, brown sugar, cornstarch, vanilla and nutmeg. Cook over low heat, stirring, until sauce thickens slightly and turns clear. Remove from heat; add orange segments.

In pie plate, combine eggs and half-and-half. Dip bread in egg mixture, saturating both sides. Melt butter in large skillet until hot. Cook soaked bread in skillet until golden brown on each side. Place 2 slices French toast on each plate; top with Mandarin orange sauce. Sprinkle with almonds, if desired.
Makes 2 servings.

Oatmeal Griddlecakes

    8 SIZZLEAN® Breakfast Strips
 1½ cups uncooked rolled oats
    2 cups milk
    1 cup all-purpose flour
    2 tablespoons packed dark
      brown sugar
    2 teaspoons baking powder
    1 teaspoon salt
    3 eggs, lightly beaten
  ¼ cup butter or margarine,
      melted, cooled
      Pancake syrup

Cook Sizzlean® strips according to package directions. Dice and set aside. Mix oats and milk in large bowl and set aside until all milk has been absorbed. Combine flour, brown sugar, baking powder and salt in small bowl. Add eggs and diced Sizzlean® pieces to oat mixture; mix well. Stir in flour mixture. Add butter and stir only long enough to blend batter. Do not overmix.

Lightly grease griddle or heavy skillet and heat over medium heat until water drop flicked onto it "dances" and instantly evaporates. Pour or ladle batter into pan to form 3½-inch-diameter pancakes. Cook 2 to 3 minutes until small bubbles form on pancake surface and begin to break.

Flip over and brown other side. Stack cooked pancakes on heated platter and keep warm. Repeat cooking procedure using remaining batter.

Chocolate Waffles

    1 cup unsifted all-purpose flour
  ³⁄₄ cup sugar
  ½ cup HERSHEY'S Cocoa
  ½ teaspoon baking powder
  ½ teaspoon baking soda
  ¼ teaspoon salt
    1 cup buttermilk
    2 eggs
  ¼ cup butter or margarine,
      melted

Combine flour, sugar, cocoa, baking powder, baking soda and salt in medium bowl. Add buttermilk and eggs; beat with wooden spoon just until blended. Gradually add melted butter, beating until smooth. Bake in waffle iron according to manufacturer's directions. Serve warm with pancake syrup or, for dessert, with ice cream, fruit-flavored syrups and sweetened whipped cream.
10 to 12 four-inch waffles.

Peach Melba Pancakes

Greek-Style Puffy Pancake

Puffy Pancake (recipe follows)
2 cups sliced CAMPBELL'S FRESH® Mushrooms (8 ounces)
1 large onion, sliced
1 cup shredded carrots
³/₄ cup V8® Vegetable Juice
1 teaspoon cornstarch
¹/₂ teaspoon dried basil leaves, crushed
³/₄ cup crumbled feta cheese, divided (4 ounces)
2 tablespoons VLASIC® or EARLY CALIFORNIA® Sliced Pitted Ripe Olives
2 tablespoons chopped fresh parsley

1. Prepare Puffy Pancake.
2. Meanwhile, spray 10-inch nonstick skillet with vegetable cooking spray. Over medium-high heat, cook mushrooms, onion and carrots 5 minutes or until vegetables are tender, stirring often.
3. In small bowl, stir together V8 juice, cornstarch and basil. Stir V8 mixture into skillet; cook 4 minutes or until slightly thickened, stirring often.
4. Sprinkle ¹/₂ of the feta onto pancake. Spoon vegetable mixture over feta. Sprinkle with remaining feta, olives and parsley. Cut into wedges.
Makes 4 servings.
PUFFY PANCAKE: Turn oven to 450°F. Place 10-inch ovenproof skillet on middle rack in oven 5 minutes. Meanwhile, in medium bowl with mixer at medium speed, beat ¹/₂ cup all-purpose flour, ¹/₂ cup skim milk, 2 eggs and ¹/₈ teaspoon salt until well blended. Add 1 tablespoon vegetable oil to skillet, tilting to coat bottom and sides. Pour batter into pan. Bake 10 minutes. Reduce heat to 350°F.; bake 10 minutes more or until puffed and browned.

Per serving: 272 calories, 12 g protein, 16 g fat, 26 g carbohydrate, 637 mg sodium, 163 mg cholesterol.

Cheese Strata

6 slices bread, crusts removed
3 cups (12 ounces) shredded Monterey Jack, Cheddar and/or Swiss cheese, divided
6 eggs
2 cups milk
1 tablespoon LAWRY'S® Minced Onion with Green Onion Flakes
1 teaspoon LAWRY'S® Seasoned Salt

Arrange bread slices in bottom of lightly buttered 13×9-inch baking dish. Sprinkle with 1¹/₂ cups of the cheese. Beat eggs, milk and seasonings in medium bowl until well blended. Pour over cheese. Sprinkle with remaining 1¹/₂ cups cheese. Bake at 350°F 35 minutes or until light golden brown. Let stand 5 minutes before serving.
Makes 6 servings.
Mexican Variation: Pour 1 bottle (8¹/₂ ounces) LAWRY'S® Chunky Taco Sauce over strata 5 minutes before baking time is completed; continue baking.
Herb Variation: Add 2 tablespoons LAWRY'S® Pinch of Herbs to egg mixture; continue as directed.
Mushroom Variation: Cook and stir ¹/₂ pound sliced mushrooms in 2 tablespoons butter or margarine in medium skillet over medium-high heat until mushrooms are soft. Remove from heat; stir in 1 package (0.75 ounces) LAWRY'S® Mushroom Gravy Mix. Add to egg mixture; continue as directed.

Peach Melba Pancakes

1 package (6 ounces) GREAT STARTS® Frozen Pancakes with Sausages
1 tablespoon raspberry preserves
1 teaspoon water
3 fresh or canned peach slices

To Microwave:
1. Prepare pancakes with sausages according to package directions.
2. In microwave-safe custard cup, stir preserves and water. Microwave, uncovered, on HIGH 30 seconds or until hot. Arrange peach slices over hot pancakes; top with raspberry mixture.
Makes 1 serving.

Colorful Ham Omelet

3 tablespoons unsalted margarine or butter, divided
¼ cup finely chopped onion
¼ cup *each* finely chopped red and green pepper
½ cup (2 ounces) ARMOUR® Lower Salt Ham cut into ¼-inch cubes
6 eggs
¼ cup (1 ounce) shredded ARMOUR® Lower Salt Cheddar Cheese

Melt 1 tablespoon of the margarine in small skillet or omelet pan over medium heat. Add onion and red and green peppers; sauté about 3 to 5 minutes, or until tender. Add ham cubes; heat thoroughly. Remove and set aside.

Melt 1 tablespoon of the margarine in same pan over medium heat; add 3 well-beaten eggs. Cook eggs, pulling edges toward center, until almost set. Spoon half of the ham mixture over eggs. Cover and continue cooking until set. *Do not overcook.* Fold half of the omelet over other half. Sprinkle half of the cheese over top. Gently slide onto serving plate. Repeat with remaining ingredients. Serve immediately. Garnish with cilantro, if desired.
Makes 2 servings.

Microwave Directions: Place 1 tablespoon of the margarine, onion, red and green peppers, and ham in small microwave-safe dish. Cook on High power for 3 minutes; set aside. Separate eggs; beat egg whites in medium bowl until soft peaks form. Beat egg yolks with 2 tablespoons water in small bowl. Gently fold yolk mixture into whites. Melt remaining 2 tablespoons margarine in microwave-safe 9-inch pie plate; swirl to coat bottom. Carefully pour half of the egg mixture into pie plate. Cook on Medium power (50%) about 7 to 9 minutes or until almost set. Spoon half of the ham mixture and cheese over eggs. Cook on Medium-High power (70%) for 2 more minutes, or until eggs are set. Fold and remove omelet from pie plate as above. Repeat with remaining ingredients. Garnish as above.

Nutrition Information Per Serving: 497 calories, 27 g protein, 42 g fat, 6.4 g carbohydrates, 851 mg cholesterol, 500 mg sodium.

Pineapple Brunch Casserole

Eggs Arnold

¼ cup butter or margarine
2 medium onions, peeled, thinly sliced
8 eggs
½ cup milk
1 teaspoon TABASCO® pepper sauce
¼ teaspoon salt
2 tablespoons chopped parsley
4 English muffins
1 tablespoon spicy brown mustard
3 ounces thinly sliced salami

In medium skillet melt butter; cook onions over low heat about 15 to 20 minutes or until lightly golden. Meanwhile, in large bowl beat together eggs, milk, Tabasco® sauce and salt. When onions are cooked, stir in egg mixture. When edges begin to set, draw cooked portions toward center so uncooked portion flows to bottom. Stir constantly; cook over low heat about 4 to 6 minutes or until eggs are cooked throughout, but still moist. Gently stir in parsley. Split and toast English muffins; spread with mustard. Top with salami slices and egg mixture. Serve with additional Tabasco® sauce, if desired.
Makes 4 servings.

Pineapple Brunch Casserole

1 can (8 ounces) DOLE® Crushed Pineapple
1 cup biscuit mix
1 cup milk
4 eggs, lightly beaten
6 tablespoons butter or margarine, melted
1 teaspoon Dijon mustard
½ teaspoon onion powder
Pinch ground nutmeg
4 ounces cooked ham, diced
1 cup shredded Monterey Jack or sharp Cheddar cheese
2 green onions, finely chopped

Preheat oven to 350°F. Drain pineapple. Reserve 2 tablespoons pineapple for garnish, if desired. Combine biscuit mix, milk, eggs, butter, mustard, onion powder and nutmeg in blender or in large mixer bowl until smooth. Stir in ham, cheese, onions and pineapple. Pour into greased 9-inch pie plate. Bake in preheated oven 35 to 40 minutes or until set. Garnish with reserved pineapple, if desired.
Makes 6 servings.

Sausage-Asparagus Souffle Sandwiches

6 ounces ECKRICH® Smoked Sausage, cut into 18 slices
Water
¼ teaspoon salt
18 asparagus spears
3 English muffins, split, toasted
3 eggs, separated
½ teaspoon Worcestershire sauce
½ teaspoon Dijon mustard
Dash ground black pepper
¾ cup (3 ounces) shredded Cheddar cheese

Bring ½ inch water and the salt to a boil in large skillet over high heat. Place asparagus in boiling water. Reduce heat to low; cover and simmer 5 minutes or until asparagus is crisp-tender. Meanwhile, arrange muffin halves in 13×9×2-inch baking pan. Arrange 3 asparagus spears on each muffin half.

Preheat oven to 350°F. Beat egg whites in medium bowl until stiff, but not dry. Beat egg yolks with Worcestershire sauce, mustard and pepper in small bowl; fold into whites. Fold in cheese. Top each sandwich with souffle mixture and 3 slices of the sausage. Bake 15 minutes.
Makes 3 servings.

Huevos Rancheros

2 tablespoons vegetable oil
1 small onion, chopped
1 green pepper, chopped
1 tomato, peeled and chopped
1 can (8 ounces) tomato sauce
½ cup water
1 clove garlic, minced
1 teaspoon dried oregano leaves
½ teaspoon salt
½ to 1 teaspoon TABASCO® pepper sauce
6 eggs
Tortillas or toasted English muffins

In large skillet heat oil; add onion and green pepper. Cook 5 minutes or until tender. Add tomato, tomato sauce, water, garlic, oregano, salt and Tabasco® sauce. Cover; simmer 20 minutes. Break eggs, 1 at a time, into cup and slip into sauce. Cover; simmer over low heat 5 minutes or until eggs are set. Serve over tortillas or English muffins.
Makes 6 servings.

Hash-and-Egg Brunch

1 can (12 ounces) corned beef, cut into chunks
3 cups frozen hash brown potatoes, thawed
1 can (10¾ ounces) condensed cream of celery soup
1 can (2.8 ounces) DURKEE French Fried Onions
¼ teaspoon DURKEE Ground Black Pepper
6 eggs
½ cup (2 ounces) shredded Cheddar cheese

Preheat oven to 400°. In large bowl, combine corned beef, potatoes, soup, *½ can* French Fried Onions and the pepper. Spoon evenly into 8×12-inch baking dish. Bake, covered, at 400° for 20 minutes or until heated through. Using back of spoon, make 6 wells in hash mixture. Break 1 egg into each well. Bake, uncovered, 15 to 20 minutes or until eggs are cooked to desired doneness. Sprinkle cheese down center of dish and top with remaining onions. Bake, uncovered, 1 to 3 minutes or until onions are golden brown.
Makes 6 servings.

Microwave Directions: Prepare corned beef mixture as above; spoon into 8×12-inch microwave-safe dish. Do not add eggs. Cook, uncovered, on HIGH 10 minutes. Rotate dish halfway through cooking time. Place eggs in hash as above. Using a toothpick, pierce each egg yolk and white twice. Cook, covered, 5 to 6 minutes or until eggs are cooked to desired doneness. Rotate dish halfway through cooking time. Top with cheese and remaining onions; cook, uncovered, 1 minute or until cheese melts. Let stand for 5 minutes.

Fresh Asparagus Soufflé

1 pound fresh asparagus, cut into 1-inch pieces
¼ cup butter or margarine
¼ cup flour
½ teaspoon dried thyme leaves
½ teaspoon TABASCO® pepper sauce
¼ teaspoon salt
1¼ cups milk
4 eggs, separated
¾ cup grated Parmesan cheese
¼ teaspoon cream of tartar

Preheat oven to 375°F. Prepare collar for 1½-quart greased straight-sided soufflé dish as follows: Fold 26-inch-long sheet of waxed paper in half lengthwise; grease 1 side and wrap around soufflé dish, greased-side-in, so 3 inches extend above top edge of dish. Tie in place with string.

In medium saucepan cook asparagus in 1 inch boiling water 5 minutes or until crisp-tender. Drain; set aside. In same saucepan melt butter; blend in flour, thyme, Tabasco® sauce and salt. Gradually add milk. Stir constantly, bring to a boil over medium heat and boil 1 minute. In medium bowl beat egg yolks. Gradually add ¼ of hot sauce; stir constantly. Gradually stir egg yolk mixture into remaining sauce in pan. Add cheese and asparagus; mix well. Cool slightly.

In large bowl of electric mixer at high speed beat egg whites with cream of tartar until whites are stiff, but not dry. Gently fold in sauce mixture. Spoon into prepared soufflé dish. Bake 40 to 45 minutes or until golden brown. Remove collar. Serve immediately.
Makes 4 servings.

Sausage-Asparagus Souffle Sandwiches

Sausage Omelet

1 package (8 ounces) SWIFT
   PREMIUM® BROWN 'N
   SERVE™ Sausage Links
¼ cup chopped onion
¼ cup chopped green bell
   pepper
5 eggs
¼ cup milk
1 tomato, chopped
1½ tablespoons butter or
   margarine

Heat sausage in heavy 8-inch oven-proof skillet according to package directions. Remove sausage and keep warm. Saute onion and green pepper in same skillet over medium-high heat until vegetables are tender. Combine eggs and milk in medium bowl. Add onion, green pepper and tomato. Melt butter in same skillet over low heat. Add egg mixture and cook until eggs are almost set. Arrange sausage on top of eggs. To finish cooking top of omelet, broil, 4 inches from heat, until center is firm and top is lightly browned. Cut into wedges and serve immediately.
Makes 5 servings.

Cream Cheese Kugel

1 8-ounce package
   PHILADELPHIA BRAND
   Cream Cheese, softened
¼ cup PARKAY Margarine,
   melted
4 eggs, beaten
½ cup milk
¼ cup sugar
½ teaspoon salt
4 cups (8 ounces) fine noodles,
   cooked, drained
½ cup raisins
¼ teaspoon cinnamon

Combine cream cheese and margarine, mixing until well blended. Blend in eggs, milk, sugar and salt. Add noodles and raisins; mix well. Pour mixture into 12×8-inch baking dish. Sprinkle with cinnamon. Bake at 375°, 30 minutes or until set.
6 to 8 servings.
Variation: Substitute 8¼-ounce can crushed pineapple, drained, for raisins.
Microwave: Prepare recipe as directed except for baking. Microwave on High 8 minutes, turning dish after 4 minutes. Microwave on Medium (50%) 9 to 12 minutes or until center is set.

Phyllo Spinach Pie

1 container (15 ounces) ricotta
   cheese
1 package (10 ounces) frozen
   chopped spinach, cooked
   and squeezed dry
2 eggs, slightly beaten
2 tablespoons grated Parmesan
   cheese
1 envelope LIPTON® Vegetable
   Recipe Soup Mix
¼ teaspoon ground nutmeg
2 cups fresh or canned sliced
   mushrooms
15 phyllo strudel sheets
½ cup butter or margarine,
   melted

Preheat oven to 375°.
In large bowl, thoroughly combine ricotta, spinach, eggs, Parmesan cheese, vegetable recipe soup mix and nutmeg; stir in mushrooms and set aside.
Unfold phyllo strudel sheets; cover with wax paper, then damp cloth. Brush 1 sheet at a time with melted butter. Place 6 buttered sheets across 9-inch pie plate, extending sheets over sides; press gently into pie plate. Place an additional 6 buttered sheets in opposite direction across 9-inch pie plate, extending sheets over sides, to form a cross; press gently into pie plate. Turn spinach mixture into prepared pie plate; gently fold sheets over spinach mixture to cover. Form remaining 3 buttered sheets into a ball and place on center of pie; brush with butter. Bake 35 minutes or until golden. Let stand 10 minutes before serving.
Makes about 8 servings.
Freezing Directions: Pie can be frozen up to 1 month. Simply prepare as above, but do not brush with butter or bake. Wrap in heavy-duty aluminum foil; freeze. To serve, unwrap, then brush with butter as above and bake at 375°, 40 minutes or until golden. Let stand as above.

Sausage 'n Egg Brunch Special

½ pound ECKRICH® Smoked
   Sausage
12 ounces frozen shredded hash
   brown potatoes, thawed
½ cup sour cream
¼ cup milk
½ cup (2 ounces) shredded
   sharp Cheddar cheese
1 tablespoon chopped chives
4 eggs

Preheat oven to 350°F. Combine potatoes, sour cream, milk, cheese and chives in medium bowl. Spoon into buttered shallow 2-quart rectangular casserole. Bake 40 minutes. Cut sausage into halves lengthwise, then cut crosswise into bite-sized pieces. Arrange down center of casserole. Bake 10 minutes more. Shape a well in each corner of the potato mixture. Break an egg into each well. Bake 10 to 12 minutes more or until eggs reach desired doneness. Serve immediately.
Makes 4 servings.

Sausage Omelet

Broccoli-Mushroom Omelet

Broccoli-Mushroom Omelet

6 eggs, separated
¼ cup evaporated skim milk
¼ cup grated Parmesan cheese
⅛ teaspoon pepper
**1 cup shredded Swiss cheese
    (4 ounces), divided**
1 cup broccoli flowerets
**1 cup sliced CAMPBELL'S
    FRESH® Mushrooms
    (4 ounces)**
½ cup diced sweet red pepper
**½ teaspoon dried Italian
    seasoning, crushed**
1½ cups V8® Vegetable Juice
1 tablespoon cornstarch

1. Preheat oven to 350°F. In large bowl with mixer at high speed, beat egg whites until stiff but not dry. In small bowl with mixer at high speed, beat egg yolks, milk, Parmesan cheese and pepper until foamy. Carefully fold egg yolk mixture and ½ cup of the Swiss cheese into beaten egg whites.
2. Spray oven-safe 10-inch nonstick skillet with vegetable cooking spray. Over medium heat, heat skillet; add egg mixture. Cook over low heat 5 minutes or until golden on underside. Place skillet in oven; bake 10 minutes or until top is puffed and golden brown.
3. Meanwhile, to prepare sauce: Spray another 10-inch nonstick skillet with vegetable cooking spray. Cook broccoli, mushrooms, red pepper and Italian seasoning until vegetables are tender-crisp, stirring often.
4. In small bowl, stir together V8 juice and cornstarch. Gradually stir V8 mixture into vegetable mixture. Over medium heat, heat until mixture boils and thickens, stirring often.
5. To serve: Running spatula under omelet, slide omelet onto serving plate. Sprinkle with remaining ½ cup Swiss cheese. Spoon sauce over omelet; cut into wedges.
Makes 6 servings.

Per serving: 203 calories, 15 g protein, 15 g fat, 9 g carbohydrate, 407 mg sodium, 295 mg cholesterol.

Frittata Romano

6 eggs
**½ teaspoon TABASCO® pepper
    sauce**
¼ teaspoon salt
**1 cup canned or thawed frozen
    artichoke hearts, drained,
    sliced**
**1 jar (3 ounces) pimiento,
    drained**
⅓ cup grated Parmesan cheese
**2 tablespoons olive or vegetable
    oil**
2 medium cloves garlic, minced

Preheat broiler. In large bowl beat eggs with Tabasco® sauce and salt. Gently fold in artichoke slices, pimiento and cheese. In 8- or 9-inch skillet with ovenproof handle,* heat oil; cook garlic until golden. Pour in egg mixture; cook over low heat. When edges begin to set, draw cooked portions toward center so uncooked portion flows to bottom. Cook until eggs are almost set. Place skillet under broiler 2 to 3 minutes or until eggs are set. To serve, loosen edges with spatula. Place large plate over skillet; invert frittata onto plate. Place serving plate on frittata and invert again so that top is up.
Makes 4 servings.

*If handle is not ovenproof, wrap with a double thickness of heavy-duty aluminum foil.

Savory Sunday Eggs

¼ pound bulk pork sausage
½ cup chopped onion
8 eggs, beaten
½ cup milk
    Dash of pepper
**1 8-ounce package
    PHILADELPHIA BRAND
    Cream Cheese, cubed**
    Chopped chives

Brown sausage in large skillet; drain. Add onions; cook until tender. Add combined eggs, milk and pepper. Cook slowly, stirring occasionally, until eggs begin to set. Add cream cheese; continue cooking, stirring occasionally, until cream cheese is melted and eggs are set. Sprinkle with chives.
6 servings.

BREADS, ROLLS & COFFEE CAKES

Fill your kitchen with the aroma of fresh-baked breads and rolls, and take pride in the delectable results. Your family will rave over homemade doughnuts and coffee cakes for breakfast, fruit-filled muffins for afternoon snacks, and crusty loaves or rolls for any time. And many are surprisingly easy to make!

Golden Oatmeal Muffins

- 1 package DUNCAN HINES® Butter Recipe Golden Cake Mix
- 1 cup quick-cooking oats
- ¼ teaspoon salt
- ¾ cup milk
- 2 large eggs, slightly beaten
- 2 tablespoons butter or margarine, melted
- Honey or jam

1. Preheat oven to 400°F. Grease 24 muffin cups.
2. Combine dry cake mix, oats and salt in bowl. Beat together milk, eggs and butter. Add to dry ingredients, stirring just until moistened. Spoon into muffin cups, filling two-thirds full.
3. Bake at 400°F for 13 minutes or until golden brown. Serve with honey or your favorite jam.
24 muffins.

Honey-Lemon Muffins

- ¾ cup ROMAN MEAL® Original Wheat, Rye, Bran, Flax Cereal
- 1½ cups all-purpose flour
- 1 tablespoon baking powder
- ½ teaspoon salt
- 1 egg, slightly beaten
- 1 cup plain yogurt
- ½ cup vegetable oil
- ½ cup honey
- 2 teaspoons grated lemon peel
- 1 to 2 tablespoons lemon juice

In large bowl, combine cereal, flour, baking powder and salt. In small bowl, mix egg, yogurt, oil, honey, lemon peel and juice. Add liquid mixture to flour mixture; stir just until moistened. Batter will be lumpy; do not overmix. Spoon batter evenly into 12 greased 2½-inch muffin cups. Bake in preheated 375° oven 20 to 25 minutes or until golden brown. Remove to wire rack to cool.
Makes 1 dozen muffins.

Louisiana Corn Muffins

- 1 cup flour
- 1 cup yellow cornmeal
- 2 tablespoons sugar
- 2½ teaspoons baking powder
- ½ teaspoon salt
- 1 cup milk
- ½ cup vegetable oil
- 2 eggs, lightly beaten
- ½ teaspoon TABASCO® pepper sauce
- 1 can (8¾ ounces) whole kernel corn, drained, or 1 cup fresh or thawed frozen corn kernels

Preheat oven to 400°F. Grease twelve 3×1¼-inch muffin cups. In large bowl combine flour, cornmeal, sugar, baking powder and salt. In medium bowl combine milk, oil, eggs and Tabasco® sauce. Make a well in center of dry ingredients; add milk mixture and stir just to combine. Stir in corn. Spoon batter into prepared muffin cups. Bake 15 to 20 minutes or until a cake tester inserted in center comes out clean. Cool 5 minutes on wire rack. Remove from pans. Serve warm.
Makes 12 muffins.

Microwave Directions: Prepare muffin batter as directed above. Spoon approximately ⅓ cup batter into each of 6 paper baking cup–lined 6-ounce custard cups or microwave-safe muffin pan cups. Cook uncovered on High 4 to 5½ minutes or until cake tester inserted in center comes out clean; turn and rearrange cups or turn muffin pan ½ turn once during cooking. Cool 5 minutes on wire rack. Remove from pans. Repeat procedure with remaining batter. Serve warm.

Golden Oatmeal Muffins

Cranberry Muffins and Creamy Orange Spread

- 2 cups flour
- 6 tablespoons sugar
- 2 teaspoons baking powder
- ½ teaspoon salt
- ¾ cup milk
- ½ cup PARKAY Margarine, melted
- 1 egg, beaten
- ¾ cup coarsely chopped cranberries

Creamy Orange Spread:
- 1 8-ounce package PHILADELPHIA BRAND Cream Cheese, softened
- 1 tablespoon sugar
- 1 tablespoon orange juice
- 1 teaspoon grated orange peel

Combine flour, 4 tablespoons sugar, baking powder and salt; mix well. Add combined milk, margarine and egg, mixing just until moistened. Fold in combined remaining sugar and cranberries. Spoon into greased medium-size muffin pan, filling each cup ⅔ full. Bake at 400°, 20 to 25 minutes or until golden brown.

Combine cream cheese, sugar, orange juice and peel, mixing until well blended. Chill. Serve with muffins.
1 dozen.

Variation: Substitute *Light* PHILADELPHIA BRAND Neufchâtel Cheese for Cream Cheese.

Walnut Streusel Muffins

- 3 cups all-purpose flour
- 1½ cups packed brown sugar
- ¾ cup butter or margarine
- 1 cup chopped DIAMOND® Walnuts
- 2 teaspoons baking powder
- 1 teaspoon *each* ground nutmeg and ginger
- ½ teaspoon *each* baking soda and salt
- 1 cup buttermilk or soured milk
- 2 eggs, beaten

In medium bowl, combine 2 cups of the flour and the sugar; cut in butter to form fine crumbs. In small bowl, combine ¾ cup of the crumbs and ¼ cup of the walnuts; set aside. Into remaining crumb mixture, stir in remaining 1 cup flour, the baking powder, spices, soda, salt and remaining ¾ cup walnuts. In another small bowl, combine buttermilk and eggs; stir into dry ingredients just to moisten. Spoon into 18 greased or paper-lined 2¾-inch muffin cups, filling about ⅔ full. Top each with a generous spoonful of reserved crumb-nut mixture. Bake in preheated 350°F oven 20 to 25 minutes or until springy to the touch. Cool in pans 10 minutes. Loosen and remove from pans. Serve warm.
Makes 1½ dozen muffins.

Blueberry Muffins

- 1 package DUNCAN HINES® Deluxe White Cake Mix
- 2 tablespoons all-purpose flour
- 1 teaspoon baking powder
- ⅔ cup milk
- 3 large eggs
- ⅓ cup CRISCO® Oil or PURITAN® Oil
- 1 cup rinsed fresh or well-drained, thawed, frozen blueberries

1. Preheat oven to 375°F. Line 24 muffin cups with paper liners.
2. Combine dry cake mix, flour and baking powder in large bowl. Beat milk, eggs and oil together with fork; add to mixture in bowl and stir just until dry ingredients are moistened. Fold in blueberries.
3. Spoon batter into muffin cups, filling one-third full.
4. Bake at 375°F for 15 to 20 minutes or until golden brown.
24 muffins.

Raisin Scones

- 2 cups all-purpose flour
- 2 tablespoons sugar
- 2 teaspoons baking powder
- ½ teaspoon baking soda
- ½ teaspoon salt
- ½ teaspoon ground nutmeg
- ½ cup butter or margarine, cut into chunks
- 1 cup SUN-MAID® Raisins
- ¾ cup buttermilk
- 1 egg white, lightly beaten, for glaze
- Sugar, for glaze

In large bowl, combine flour, 2 tablespoons sugar, the baking powder, soda, salt and nutmeg. Cut in butter until mixture resembles coarse meal. Mix in raisins, then mix in buttermilk with fork. Gather dough into ball and knead on lightly floured board about 2 minutes. Roll or pat dough out ¾ inch thick. With sharp knife, cut into 3-inch triangles. Space apart on greased baking sheets. Brush tops with egg white; sprinkle with sugar. Bake in preheated 425°F oven for about 15 minutes or until nicely browned. Serve warm with butter or jam.
Makes about 1 dozen scones.

Raisin Scones

Lemon Tea Muffins

Molasses Muffins

    1²/₃ cups unsifted all-purpose flour
      3 tablespoons sugar
      2 teaspoons baking powder
      1 teaspoon ground ginger
    ¹/₂ teaspoon salt
    ¹/₂ cup dark molasses
      2 eggs, slightly beaten
    ¹/₄ cup CRISCO® Oil
    ¹/₄ cup milk

Preheat oven to 400°F. Place paper liners in 12 muffin cups. Set aside.

Mix flour, sugar, baking powder, ginger and salt in medium mixing bowl. Make a well in center of mixture. Set aside. Blend remaining ingredients in small mixing bowl. Pour into well in dry ingredients. Stir just until ingredients are moistened. Pour into lined muffin cups, filling each about two-thirds full. Bake at 400°F, about 15 minutes, or until centers spring back when touched lightly. *1 dozen muffins.*

Variation: *Orange Raisin Muffins.* Follow recipe above, omitting ginger. Add ¹/₂ cup raisins and 2 teaspoons grated orange peel to dry ingredients.

Lemon Tea Muffins

      2 cups unsifted flour
      2 teaspoons baking powder
    ¹/₂ teaspoon salt
      1 cup margarine or butter,
        softened
      1 cup granulated sugar
      4 eggs, separated
    ¹/₂ cup REALEMON® Lemon Juice
        from Concentrate
    ¹/₄ cup finely chopped nuts
      2 tablespoons light brown sugar
    ¹/₄ teaspoon ground nutmeg

Preheat oven to 375°. Stir together flour, baking powder and salt; set aside. In large mixer bowl, beat margarine and granulated sugar until fluffy. Add egg yolks; beat until light. Gradually stir in ReaLemon® brand alternately with dry ingredients (*do not overmix*). In small mixer bowl, beat egg whites until stiff but not dry; fold one-third egg whites into lemon mixture. Fold remaining egg whites into lemon mixture. Fill paper-lined or greased muffin cups ³/₄ full. Combine remaining ingredients; sprinkle evenly over muffins. Bake 15 to 20 minutes. Cool 5 minutes; remove from pan. Serve warm.
Makes about 1¹/₂ dozen.

Treasure Bran Muffins

    1¹/₄ cups whole bran cereal
      1 cup milk
    ¹/₄ cup oil
      1 egg, beaten
    1¹/₄ cups flour
    ¹/₂ cup sugar
      1 tablespoon baking powder
    ¹/₂ teaspoon salt
    ¹/₂ cup raisins

                *   *   *

      1 8-ounce package
        PHILADELPHIA BRAND
        Cream Cheese, softened
    ¹/₄ cup sugar
      1 egg, beaten

Combine cereal and milk; let stand 2 minutes. Add combined oil and egg; mix well. Add combined dry ingredients, mixing just until moistened. Stir in raisins. Spoon into greased and floured medium-size muffin pan, filling each cup ²/₃ full.

Combine cream cheese, sugar and egg, mixing until well blended. Drop rounded measuring tablespoonfuls of cream cheese mixture onto batter. Bake at 375°, 25 minutes.
1 dozen.

Moist Orange Mince Muffins

      2 cups unsifted flour
    ¹/₂ cup sugar
      1 tablespoon baking powder
      1 teaspoon salt
    ¹/₂ teaspoon baking soda
      1 egg, slightly beaten
      1 (8-ounce) container BORDEN®
        LITE-LINE® or VIVA® Orange
        Yogurt
    ¹/₃ cup BORDEN® or MEADOW
        GOLD® Milk
    ¹/₃ cup vegetable oil
      1 (9-ounce) package NONE
        SUCH® Condensed
        Mincemeat, finely crumbled
    ¹/₃ cup BAMA® Orange
        Marmalade, melted, optional

Preheat oven to 400°. In medium bowl, combine dry ingredients; set aside. In medium bowl, combine egg, yogurt, milk, oil and mincemeat; mix well. Stir into flour mixture only until moistened. Fill greased or paper baking cup–lined muffin cups ³/₄ full. Bake 20 to 25 minutes or until golden brown. Immediately turn out of pan. Brush warm muffins with marmalade if desired.
Makes about 1¹/₂ dozen.

French Breakfast Puffs

Paul Bunyan Sticky Buns

    1 package (16 ounces) hot roll
      mix
  1/2 cup butter or margarine,
      melted
    2 tablespoons water
    1 cup packed brown sugar
    1 cup chopped DIAMOND®
      Walnuts
  3/4 cup granulated sugar
    1 tablespoon ground cinnamon

Prepare dough as package directs for rolls. Knead gently on lightly floured board 1 minute. Place dough in lightly greased bowl; turn once to grease surface. Cover; let rise in warm place (85°F) until doubled, about 1 hour. To prepare syrup, in small saucepan, combine 1/4 cup of the butter, the water and brown sugar. Stir over medium heat until sugar dissolves. Bring to boil; reduce heat to low and simmer gently 1 minute. Pour at once into 11×7-inch baking pan, tilting to spread syrup evenly. Sprinkle 1/2 cup of the walnuts over syrup layer; set aside. After dough has risen, turn out onto lightly floured board. Let rest 5 minutes, then stretch and roll into 30×5-inch rectangle. Brush with remaining 1/4 cup butter. In small bowl, combine granulated sugar and cinnamon; sprinkle over butter. Arrange remaining 1/2 cup walnuts on top. Starting from 5-inch side, roll up loosely, jelly-roll fashion, pinching edges to seal. Cut roll into 6 equal pieces. Place cut sides up in prepared pan, spreading pinwheels open a little. Cover; let rise in warm place 35 to 45 minutes or until almost doubled. Cover lower shelf of oven with foil. Bake buns on center shelf of preheated 375°F oven 25 to 35 minutes or until golden. Immediately invert onto tray. Cool 5 minutes. Serve warm.
Makes 6 large buns.

Southern Hush Puppies

      CRISCO® Oil for frying
  3/4 cup yellow cornmeal
  1/3 cup unsifted all-purpose flour
 1 1/2 teaspoons baking powder
  1/2 teaspoon salt
  1/2 cup buttermilk
    1 egg
  1/4 cup finely chopped onion

Heat 2 to 3 inches Crisco® Oil in deep-fryer or large saucepan to 375°F. Mix cornmeal, flour, baking powder and salt in medium mixing bowl. Add remaining ingredients. Mix well. Drop batter by tablespoonfuls into hot Crisco® Oil. Fry a few at a time, 3 to 4 minutes, or until golden brown. Drain on paper towels. Repeat with remaining batter. Serve immediately or keep warm in 175°F oven.
About 1 dozen hush puppies.

Italian Pepperoni Puffs

 2 1/4 to 2 3/4 cups unsifted all-
      purpose flour, divided
    1 package (1/4 ounce) active dry
      yeast
    1 tablespoon sugar
    1 teaspoon garlic salt
  1/2 teaspoon Italian seasoning
  1/4 teaspoon onion powder
  3/4 cup very warm water (120° to
      130°F)
    2 tablespoons CRISCO® Oil
    1 egg
  1/2 cup grated Parmesan cheese
  1/4 cup finely chopped pepperoni
      CRISCO® Oil for frying

Mix 1 1/2 cups flour, yeast, sugar, garlic salt, Italian seasoning and onion powder in large mixing bowl. Add warm water, Crisco® Oil and egg. Beat with electric mixer at low speed until ingredients are moistened, scraping bowl constantly. Beat at medium speed 3 minutes, scraping bowl occasionally. Stir in Parmesan cheese and enough remaining flour to make a slightly stiff dough.

Knead dough on lightly floured surface 5 to 8 minutes, or until smooth and elastic, adding additional flour as necessary. Place in lightly oiled medium mixing bowl. Turn dough over to coat both sides with Crisco® Oil. Cover; let rise in warm place 40 to 50 minutes, or until doubled.

Punch down dough. Place on lightly floured surface. Divide dough in half. Roll each half to 1/8-inch thickness. Cut into 2-inch rounds. Place 1/2 teaspoon chopped pepperoni in center of half of the rounds. Brush edges with water. Top with remaining rounds. Press edges together with fork to seal. Cover; let rise in warm place about 30 minutes, or until doubled.

Heat 2 to 3 inches Crisco® Oil in deep-fryer or large saucepan to 365°F. Fry 3 or 4 puffs at a time, 3 to 4 minutes, or until golden brown, turning

Raised Doughnuts

over several times. Drain on paper towels. Sprinkle with *grated Parmesan cheese*, if desired. Serve warm. *1¹/₂ to 2 dozen puffs.*

French Breakfast Puffs

- **1¹/₂ cups unsifted all-purpose flour**
- **¹/₂ cup confectioners sugar**
- **1 teaspoon baking powder**
- **1 teaspoon salt**
- **³/₄ teaspoon ground nutmeg**
- **¹/₂ cup milk**
- **¹/₂ cup water**
- **¹/₄ cup CRISCO® Oil**
- **1¹/₂ teaspoons grated lemon peel**
- **3 eggs**
  - **CRISCO® Oil for frying**
  - **Confectioners sugar**

Mix flour, ¹/₂ cup confectioners sugar, baking powder, salt and nutmeg in small mixing bowl. Set aside. Combine milk, water, Crisco® Oil and lemon peel in medium saucepan. Heat to rolling boil over medium-high heat. Add flour mixture all at once. Beat with wooden spoon until mixture pulls away from sides of pan into a ball. Remove from heat; cool slightly. Add eggs, one at a time, beating after each addition.

Heat 2 to 3 inches Crisco® Oil in deep-fryer or large saucepan to 350°F.

Drop dough by tablespoonfuls into hot Crisco® Oil. Fry 3 or 4 puffs at a time, 4 to 6 minutes, or until golden brown, turning over several times. Drain on paper towels. Sprinkle top of each puff with confectioners sugar. *About 32 puffs.*

Raised Doughnuts

- **3¹/₂ to 4¹/₂ cups unsifted all-purpose flour, divided**
- **³/₄ cup sugar, divided**
- **2 packages (¹/₄ ounce each) active dry yeast**
- **1 teaspoon salt**
- **1 cup milk**
- **¹/₄ cup vegetable shortening**
- **2 eggs, slightly beaten**
  - **CRISCO® Oil for frying**

Mix 2 cups flour, ¹/₄ cup sugar, yeast and salt in large mixing bowl. Set aside. Combine milk and shortening in small saucepan. Cook over moderate heat until very warm (120° to 130°F). Add to flour mixture. Add eggs. Beat with electric mixer at low speed 1 minute, scraping bowl constantly. Beat at medium speed 3 minutes, scraping bowl occasionally. Stir in enough remaining flour to make a soft dough.

Knead dough on lightly floured surface 5 to 8 minutes, or until smooth and elastic, adding additional flour as necessary (dough will be slightly sticky). Place in lightly oiled medium mixing bowl. Turn dough over to coat both sides with Crisco® Oil. Cover; let rise in warm place 40 to 50 minutes, or until doubled.

Oil baking sheet. Set aside. Punch down dough. Place on lightly floured surface. Divide dough in half. Roll each half to ¹/₂-inch thickness. Cut into 2¹/₂-inch rounds with doughnut cutter. Place doughnuts and holes on prepared baking sheet. Cover; let rise in warm place about 30 minutes, or until doubled.

Heat 2 to 3 inches Crisco® Oil in deep-fryer or large saucepan to 375°F. Fry 2 or 3 doughnuts at a time, 1 to 1¹/₂ minutes, or until golden brown, turning over once. To fry holes, place several at a time in hot Crisco® Oil. Fry 45 to 60 seconds, or until golden brown, turning over occasionally. Drain on paper towels. Place remaining ¹/₂ cup sugar in large plastic food storage bag. Add a few doughnuts and holes at a time; shake to coat. *1¹/₂ dozen doughnuts and 1¹/₂ dozen holes.*

Variation: Glazed Raised Doughnuts. Follow recipe above, except reduce sugar to ¹/₄ cup and do not shake doughnuts in sugar. Before frying doughnuts, combine 1 cup confectioners sugar, 2 tablespoons milk, 1 tablespoon honey and 1 teaspoon grated lemon or orange peel in small mixing bowl. Beat at medium speed with electric mixer until smooth. After frying, dip one side of warm doughnuts in glaze. Cool doughnuts, glazed side up, on wire rack over waxed paper.

Jamaican Sweet Buns

- **2 cups all-purpose flour**
- **¹/₄ cup sugar**
- **4 teaspoons baking powder**
- **2 teaspoons grated lemon peel**
- **¹/₄ teaspoon salt**
- **¹/₂ cup butter or margarine**
- **¹/₂ cup milk**
- **2 egg yolks, lightly beaten**
- **³/₄ cup SUN-MAID® Raisins**
- **³/₄ cup shredded coconut**
- **1 egg white, beaten, for glaze**
  - **Sugar, for glaze**

In medium bowl, combine flour, the ¹/₄ cup sugar, the baking powder, peel and salt. Cut in butter until mixture resembles coarse meal. Combine milk and yolks; mix into flour mixture to form soft dough. Mix in raisins and coconut just to blend. Evenly divide dough into six 4-inch greased tart pans; flatten tops. Brush generously with egg white; sprinkle heavily with sugar (about 2 teaspoons on each). Space apart on baking sheet. Bake in preheated 450°F oven about 15 minutes or until springy to the touch and well browned. Cool in pans. Serve with whipped sweet butter. *Makes 6 buns.*

Crullers

    1 8-ounce package
        PHILADELPHIA BRAND
        Cream Cheese, softened
  1/3 cup PARKAY Margarine
    1 cup flour
      Dash of salt
      Sugar

Combine cream cheese and margarine, mixing until well blended. Add
flour and salt; mix well. Shape dough
into ball; chill 1 hour. On lightly
floured surface, roll dough to 12×6-
inch rectangle. Cut dough into
twenty-four 1/2-inch strips. Fry in deep
hot oil, 375°, 1 to 2 minutes or until
golden brown, turning once using
tongs. Drain on paper towels. Roll in
sugar.
2 dozen.

Easy Apple Kuchen

    2 envelopes active dry yeast
  1/4 cup warm water (about 110°F)
    2 large eggs
    1 package DUNCAN HINES®
        Deluxe Yellow Cake Mix
  1¼ cups all-purpose flour
  1½ cups sugar
    1 tablespoon ground cinnamon
  1/3 cup butter or margarine
    6 medium apples or 2 cans
        (20 ounces each) pie-sliced
        apples, drained

1. Dissolve yeast in warm water in
large mixer bowl. Blend in eggs and
half of dry cake mix. Beat for 1 minute at medium speed. Add remaining
cake mix and beat for 3 minutes at
medium speed. (Batter should be
quite stiff but not doughlike.) Let rest
5 minutes.
2. Sprinkle flour on board. Scrape
batter out onto prepared board.
Knead batter until flour is worked in,
about 100 strokes. Place in greased
bowl, cover, and let rise in warm,
draft-free place for 30 minutes.
3. For topping, mix sugar and cinnamon in bowl; cut in butter with pastry
blender or 2 knives.
4. Preheat oven to 350°F. Grease
13×9×2-inch pan and 8×8×2-inch pan.
Pare, core and slice apples.
5. Punch down dough with greased
fingertips. Spread dough to 1/4- to 1/3-
inch thickness on bottom of pans. Arrange apple slices in rows on top.
Sprinkle with topping. Let rise in
warm place for 30 minutes.

6. Bake at 350°F for 25 to 30 minutes
or until toothpick inserted in center
comes out clean. Serve warm.
24 servings.

Blueberries 'n Cheese Coffeecake

  1/2 cup PARKAY Margarine
  1¼ cups granulated sugar
    2 eggs
  2¼ cups flour
    1 tablespoon baking powder
    1 teaspoon salt
  3/4 cup milk
  1/4 cup water
    2 cups blueberries
    1 8-ounce package
        PHILADELPHIA BRAND
        Cream Cheese, cubed
    1 teaspoon grated lemon peel

* * *

  1/4 cup granulated sugar
  1/4 cup flour
    1 teaspoon grated lemon peel
    2 tablespoons PARKAY
        Margarine
      Powdered sugar

Beat margarine and granulated
sugar until light and fluffy. Add eggs,
one at a time, mixing well after each
addition. Add combined 2 cups flour,
baking powder and salt alternately
with combined milk and water, mixing well after each addition. Toss
blueberries with remaining flour; fold
into batter with cream cheese and
peel. Pour into greased and floured
13×9-inch baking pan.

Combine granulated sugar, flour
and peel; cut in margarine until mixture resembles coarse crumbs. Sprinkle over batter. Bake at 375°, 1 hour.
Cool. Sprinkle with powdered sugar
before serving.
12 servings.

  Variation: Substitute 2 cups frozen
blueberries, thawed, well-drained, for
fresh blueberries.

Fruity Swirl Coffeecake

    1 8-ounce package
        PHILADELPHIA BRAND
        Cream Cheese, softened
    1 cup sugar
  1/2 cup PARKAY Margarine
    2 eggs
  1/2 teaspoon vanilla
  1¾ cups flour
    1 teaspoon baking powder
  1/2 teaspoon baking soda
  1/4 teaspoon salt
  1/4 cup milk
  1/2 cup KRAFT Red Raspberry
        Preserves

Combine cream cheese, sugar and
margarine, mixing until well blended.
Add eggs, one at a time, mixing well
after each addition. Blend in vanilla.
Add combined dry ingredients alternately with milk, mixing well after
each addition. Pour into greased and
floured 13×9-inch baking pan; dot
with preserves. Cut through batter
with knife several times for marble effect. Bake at 350°, 35 minutes.
12 servings.

Easy Apple Kuchen

Cream Cheese Swirl Coffee Cake

Cream Cheese Swirl Coffee Cake

- **2 (3-ounce) packages cream cheese, softened**
- **2 tablespoons confectioners' sugar**
- **2 tablespoons REALEMON® Lemon Juice from Concentrate**
- **2 cups unsifted flour**
- **1 teaspoon baking powder**
- **1 teaspoon baking soda**
- **¼ teaspoon salt**
- **1 cup granulated sugar**
- **½ cup margarine or butter, softened**
- **3 eggs**
- **1 teaspoon vanilla extract**
- **1 (8-ounce) container BORDEN® or MEADOW GOLD® Sour Cream**
- **Cinnamon-Nut Topping***

Preheat oven to 350°. In small bowl, beat cheese, confectioners' sugar and ReaLemon® brand until smooth; set aside. Stir together flour, baking powder, baking soda and salt; set aside. In large mixer bowl, beat granulated sugar and margarine until fluffy. Add eggs and vanilla; mix well. Add dry ingredients alternately with sour cream; mix well. Pour half of batter into greased and floured 10-inch tube pan. Spoon cheese mixture on top of batter to within ½ inch of pan edge. Spoon remaining batter over filling, spreading to pan edge. Sprinkle with Cinnamon-Nut Topping. Bake 40 to 45 minutes or until wooden pick inserted near center comes out clean. Cool 10 minutes; remove from pan. Serve warm.
Makes one 10-inch cake.

Cinnamon-Nut Topping: Combine ¼ cup finely chopped nuts, 2 tablespoons granulated sugar and ½ teaspoon ground cinnamon.

Apricot Crumble Cake

- **1 8-ounce package PHILADELPHIA BRAND Cream Cheese, softened**
- **½ cup PARKAY Margarine**
- **1¼ cups granulated sugar**
- **¼ cup milk**
- **2 eggs**
- **1 teaspoon vanilla**
- **1¾ cups flour**
- **1 teaspoon baking powder**
- **½ teaspoon baking soda**
- **¼ teaspoon salt**
- **1 10-ounce jar KRAFT Apricot or Peach Preserves**
- **2 cups flaked coconut**
- **⅔ cup packed brown sugar**
- **1 teaspoon cinnamon**
- **⅓ cup PARKAY Margarine, melted**

Combine cream cheese, margarine and granulated sugar, mixing at medium speed on electric mixer until well blended. Gradually add milk, mixing well after each addition. Blend in eggs and vanilla. Add combined dry ingredients to cream cheese mixture; mix well. Pour half of batter into greased and floured 13×9-inch baking pan. Dot with preserves; cover with remaining batter. Bake at 350°, 35 to 40 minutes or until wooden pick inserted in center comes out clean.

Combine coconut, brown sugar, cinnamon and margarine; mix well. Spread onto cake; broil 3 to 5 minutes, or until golden brown.
16 servings.

Orange Wake-Up Cake

- **1 package DUNCAN HINES® Butter Recipe Golden Cake Mix**
- **⅔ cup water**
- **3 large eggs**
- **½ cup (1 stick) butter or margarine, softened**
- **2 tablespoons grated orange peel**
- **½ cup chopped pecans**
- **⅓ cup packed brown sugar**
- **¼ cup fine graham cracker crumbs**
- **2 tablespoons butter or margarine, melted**
- **1½ teaspoons ground cinnamon**
- **1 cup confectioners' sugar**
- **2 tablespoons hot water**
- **¼ teaspoon vanilla extract**

1. Preheat oven to 375°F. Grease and flour two 9×1½-inch round layer pans.
2. Combine dry cake mix, water, eggs and ½ cup butter in large mixer bowl. Mix cake as directed on package. Fold in 1 tablespoon of the orange peel. Divide batter evenly in pans.
3. For topping, combine pecans, brown sugar, graham cracker crumbs, 2 tablespoons butter, remaining orange peel and cinnamon; mix well. Sprinkle evenly over batter in pans.
4. Bake at 375°F for 25 to 30 minutes or until toothpick inserted in center comes out clean.
5. For glaze,* mix confectioners' sugar, hot water and vanilla until smooth. Drizzle over warm cakes. Serve warm or cool in pans.
12 to 16 servings.

*Or heat ⅔ cup DUNCAN HINES® Vanilla Frosting in a small saucepan over medium heat, stirring constantly, until thin.

Soda Bread

- 3 cups unsifted all-purpose flour
- 3 tablespoons sugar
- 2 teaspoons baking powder
- 1 teaspoon baking soda
- 1 teaspoon salt
- 1½ cups buttermilk
- 1 egg, slightly beaten
- 3 tablespoons CRISCO® Oil
- ½ cup raisins

Preheat oven to 350°F. Oil 8-inch round baking dish. Set aside.

Mix flour, sugar, baking powder, baking soda and salt in medium mixing bowl. Add buttermilk, egg and Crisco® Oil. Stir with fork until ingredients are moistened. Stir in raisins. Pour into prepared dish.

Bake at 350°F, 35 to 40 minutes, or until wooden pick inserted in center comes out clean. Cool 10 minutes. Remove from dish. Cool completely on wire rack.
One 8-inch round loaf.

Golden Fruit Loaves

Gingerbread

- ¼ cup butter or margarine, softened
- ¼ cup packed brown sugar
- ¼ cup honey
- ¼ cup molasses
- 2 eggs, lightly beaten
- ¾ cup orange juice
- 2 cups all-purpose flour
- 1 teaspoon baking powder
- ¾ teaspoon salt
- ½ teaspoon baking soda
- 1½ teaspoons ground ginger
- 1 teaspoon ground cinnamon
- 1 teaspoon ground nutmeg
- Grated peel of 1 orange
- ¾ cup SUN-MAID® Zante Currants

In large bowl, beat butter and brown sugar until smooth and thick. Add honey and molasses and beat again until smooth. Blend in eggs and then orange juice.

In medium bowl, combine flour, baking powder, salt, baking soda, ginger, cinnamon and nutmeg. Stir in orange peel and currants. Add flour mixture to butter mixture, stirring until blended. Pour the batter into greased 8×8×2-inch pan. Bake in preheated 350°F oven 40 minutes or until pick inserted in the center comes out clean. Cool in pan on wire rack 15 minutes before cutting and serving.
Makes 8 servings.

Golden Fruit Loaves

- 1 package DUNCAN HINES® Butter Recipe Golden Cake Mix
- 1½ cups chopped candied mixed fruit (6 ounces)
- ½ cup all-purpose flour
- ½ teaspoon baking powder
- ½ teaspoon baking soda
- 1 cup milk
- 2 large eggs
- 2 tablespoons butter or margarine, softened

1. Preheat oven to 350°F. Grease and flour two 8½×4½×2½-inch loaf pans.
2. Sprinkle 2 tablespoons dry cake mix over dried fruit; stir to coat.
3. Combine remaining cake mix, flour, baking powder and baking soda in large mixer bowl. Add milk, eggs and butter. Blend at low speed, then beat 2 minutes at medium speed. Fold in fruit. Divide batter evenly in pans.
4. Bake at 350°F for 45 to 50 minutes or until toothpick inserted in center comes out clean. Cool in pans on racks 20 minutes. Remove from pans; cool completely on racks.
2 medium loaves.

Golden Raisin Spice Bread

- 2 cups unsifted flour
- 2 teaspoons baking powder
- 1 teaspoon ground cinnamon
- ½ teaspoon ground nutmeg
- ½ teaspoon salt
- 1 cup sugar
- ½ cup margarine or butter, softened
- 3 eggs
- ½ cup milk
- ½ cup REALEMON® Lemon Juice from Concentrate
- 1 cup golden seedless raisins

Preheat oven to 350°. Stir together flour, baking powder, cinnamon, nutmeg and salt; set aside. In large mixer bowl, beat sugar and margarine until fluffy. Add eggs, 1 at a time; beat well. Add milk alternately with dry ingredients; stir well. Stir in ReaLemon® brand and raisins. Turn into greased and floured 9×5-inch loaf pan. Bake 55 to 60 minutes or until wooden pick inserted near center comes out clean. Cool 10 minutes; remove from pan. Cool completely. Store tightly wrapped.
Makes one 9×5-inch loaf.

Chocolate Chip Banana Bread

2 cups unsifted all-purpose flour
1 cup sugar
1 teaspoon baking powder
1 teaspoon salt
½ teaspoon baking soda
1 cup mashed ripe bananas (about 3 small)
½ cup shortening
2 eggs
1 cup HERSHEY'S MINI CHIPS Semi-Sweet Chocolate
½ cup chopped walnuts

Grease bottom only of 9×5×3-inch loaf pan; set aside. Combine all ingredients except MINI CHIPS Chocolate and walnuts in large mixer bowl; blend well on medium speed. Stir in MINI CHIPS Chocolate and walnuts.

Pour into prepared pan. Bake at 350° for 60 to 70 minutes or until cake tester comes out clean. Cool 10 minutes; remove from pan. Cool completely on wire rack.
1 loaf.

Golden Apple Boston Brown Bread

¼ cup butter or margarine, softened
⅓ cup honey
⅓ cup light molasses
1 cup whole wheat flour
1 cup rye flour
1 cup yellow cornmeal
2 teaspoons baking soda
½ teaspoon salt
2 cups buttermilk
2 cups coarsely chopped Washington Golden Delicious apples

In large bowl, cream butter, honey and molasses. In medium bowl, combine flours, cornmeal, baking soda and salt. Add flour mixture to butter mixture alternately with buttermilk, mixing well after each addition. Stir in apples. Pour batter into 2 greased 8½×4½×2½-inch loaf pans. Bake in preheated 350° oven 1 hour or until toothpick inserted into center comes out clean. Let cool in pans on wire racks 10 minutes. Loosen edges; remove from pans. Cool slightly on wire racks; serve warm.
Makes 2 loaves.
Variation: To steam brown bread, divide batter evenly between 2 greased

1-pound coffee cans, filling cans about three-fourths full. Cover tops of cans with aluminum foil; tie foil to cans with string. Place rack in large kettle; add boiling water to depth of 1 inch. Place cans on rack; cover kettle. Steam over low heat 3 hours or until toothpick inserted near center comes out clean. If necessary, add more boiling water to kettle during steaming. Cool as above.

Favorite recipe from **Washington Apple Commission**

Lemon Bread

2 cups unsifted flour
1 teaspoon baking powder
½ teaspoon baking soda
¼ teaspoon salt
1½ cups sugar
½ cup margarine or butter, softened
3 eggs
½ cup REALEMON® Lemon Juice from Concentrate
½ cup BORDEN® or MEADOW GOLD® Milk
¾ cup chopped pecans, optional Clear Lemon Glaze*

Preheat oven to 350°. Stir together flour, baking powder, baking soda and salt; set aside. In large mixer bowl,

Chocolate Chip Banana Bread

beat sugar and margarine until fluffy. Add eggs, 1 at a time; beat well. Gradually beat in ReaLemon® brand. Add milk alternately with dry ingredients; stir well. Add pecans if desired. Turn into greased and floured 9×5-inch loaf pan. Bake 50 to 55 minutes or until wooden pick inserted near center comes out clean. Remove from oven; drizzle with Clear Lemon Glaze. Cool 15 minutes; remove from pan. Cool completely. Store tightly wrapped.
Makes one 9×5-inch loaf.
*CLEAR LEMON GLAZE: In small saucepan, combine 2 tablespoons sugar and 2 teaspoons ReaLemon® brand; heat until sugar dissolves.

Old-Fashioned Apple Loaf

2 cups unsifted all-purpose flour
2 teaspoons baking powder
1 teaspoon apple pie spice*
½ teaspoon salt
¼ teaspoon baking soda
⅔ cup chunky applesauce
½ cup granulated sugar
2 eggs
¼ cup CRISCO® Oil
2 tablespoons milk
2 tablespoons chopped walnuts
2 teaspoons butter or margarine
1 teaspoon packed brown sugar

Preheat oven to 350°F. Oil and flour 8×4-inch loaf pan. Set aside.

Mix flour, baking powder, apple pie spice, salt and baking soda in medium mixing bowl. Set aside. Combine applesauce, granulated sugar, eggs, Crisco® Oil and milk in large mixing bowl. Mix well. Add flour mixture. Beat at medium speed with electric mixer just until combined, scraping bowl occasionally. Pour into prepared loaf pan.

Combine walnuts, butter and brown sugar in small mixing bowl. Mix with fork until crumbly. Sprinkle down center of loaf. Bake at 350°F, 35 to 45 minutes, or until golden brown and wooden pick inserted in center comes out clean. Immediately remove from pan. Cool on wire rack.
1 loaf.
*Substitute ¾ teaspoon ground cinnamon, dash ground nutmeg and dash ground cloves for apple pie spice, if desired.

Pumpkin Nut Bread

3½ cups unsifted flour
2 teaspoons baking soda
1½ teaspoons ground cinnamon
½ teaspoon baking powder
2 cups sugar
⅔ cup shortening
4 eggs
1 (16-ounce) can pumpkin (about 2 cups)
½ cup water
1 (9-ounce) package NONE SUCH® Condensed Mincemeat, crumbled
1 cup chopped nuts

Preheat oven to 350°. Stir together flour, baking soda, cinnamon and baking powder; set aside. In large mixer bowl, beat sugar and shortening until fluffy. Add eggs, pumpkin and water; mix well. Stir in flour mixture, mincemeat and nuts. Turn into 2 greased 9×5-inch loaf pans. Bake 55 to 60 minutes or until wooden pick inserted near center comes out clean. Cool 10 minutes; remove from pan. Cool completely.
Makes two 9×5-inch loaves.

V8 Cheese Bread

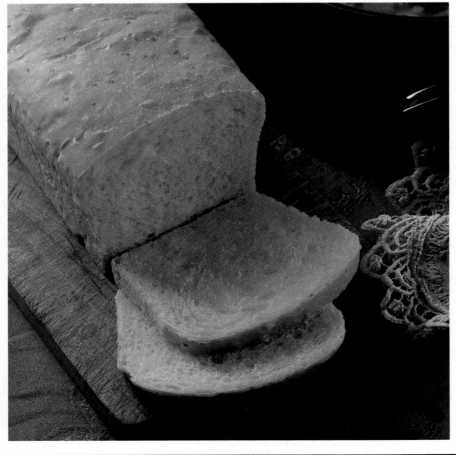

Beer Cheese Bread

1½ cups unsifted all-purpose flour
½ cup whole wheat flour
2 tablespoons sugar
1½ teaspoons baking powder
1 teaspoon instant minced onion
¾ teaspoon baking soda
½ teaspoon salt
2 cups shredded Cheddar cheese (about 8 ounces)
1 cup beer
2 eggs
⅓ cup CRISCO® Oil

Preheat oven to 350°F. Oil and flour 9×5-inch loaf pan. Set aside.
Mix all-purpose flour, whole wheat flour, sugar, baking powder, onion, baking soda and salt in medium mixing bowl. Add remaining ingredients. Beat with electric mixer at medium speed about 1 minute, scraping bowl occasionally. Pour into prepared pan.
Bake at 350°F, 50 to 60 minutes, or until wooden pick inserted in center comes out clean. Immediately remove from pan. Cool on wire rack.
1 loaf.

Mexican Corn Bread

1 cup yellow cornmeal
⅔ cup unsifted all-purpose flour
2 teaspoons baking powder
½ teaspoon salt
¾ cup dairy sour cream
2 eggs
¼ cup CRISCO® Oil
2 cups shredded Cheddar cheese (about 8 ounces), divided
1 can (8¾ ounces) whole kernel corn, drained
1 can (4 ounces) chopped green chilies, drained

Preheat oven to 350°F. Oil 8-inch square baking pan. Set aside.
Mix cornmeal, flour, baking powder and salt in small mixing bowl. Set aside. Blend sour cream, eggs and Crisco® Oil in medium mixing bowl. Add cornmeal mixture, 1½ cups Cheddar cheese, corn and chilies. Mix well. Pour into prepared pan. Sprinkle with remaining ½ cup Cheddar cheese. Bake at 350°F, 30 to 35 minutes, or until wooden pick inserted in center comes out clean. Cut into squares and serve warm.
One 8-inch square pan.

Favorite Banana Bread

1 8-ounce package PHILADELPHIA BRAND Cream Cheese, softened
1 cup sugar
¼ cup PARKAY Margarine
1 cup mashed ripe banana
2 eggs
2¼ cups flour
1½ teaspoons baking powder
½ teaspoon baking soda
1 cup chopped nuts

Combine cream cheese, sugar and margarine, mixing until well blended. Blend in banana and eggs. Add combined remaining ingredients, mixing just until moistened. Pour into greased and floured 9×5-inch loaf pan. Bake at 350°, 1 hour and 10 minutes or until wooden pick inserted near center comes out clean. Cool 5 minutes; remove from pan. Serve with additional cream cheese, if desired.
1 loaf.

V8 Cheese Bread

**5½ to 6 cups all-purpose flour,
        divided
    2 packages active dry yeast
1½ teaspoons salt
    1 cup V8® Vegetable Juice
    ¾ cup water
    3 tablespoons butter or
        margarine
1½ cups shredded Cheddar
        cheese (6 ounces)
    1 egg**

1. In large bowl, combine 2 cups of the
flour, yeast and salt; set aside. In
small saucepan over medium heat,
heat V8 juice, water and butter until
warm (115° to 120°F.)
2. Stir V8 mixture into flour mixture.
With mixer at low speed, beat 30 seconds. Add cheese and egg. With mixer
at high speed, beat 3 minutes. Stir in
2½ cups of the remaining flour.
3. Turn dough onto lightly floured
surface; knead until smooth and elastic, about 6 minutes, adding remaining flour while kneading. Shape
dough into ball; place in large greased
bowl, turning dough to grease top.
Cover; let rise in warm place until
doubled in bulk, about 1 hour.
4. Spray two 8- by 4-inch loaf pans
with vegetable cooking spray. Punch
dough down; divide in half. Shape
into 2 loaves. Place in pans. Cover; let
rise in warm place until doubled,
about 45 minutes.
5. Preheat oven to 375°F. Bake 35
minutes or until golden and loaves
sound hollow when lightly tapped
with fingers. Remove from pans; cool
on wire racks.
Makes 2 loaves, 12 slices each.

Per slice: 79 calories, 2 g protein, 3 g
fat, 12 g carbohydrate, 118 mg sodium, 12 mg cholesterol.

Cinnamon-Raisin Swirl Loaf

**2 cups SUN-MAID® Raisins
        Water
6¾ to 7¼ cups all-purpose flour
    2 packages active dry yeast
    2 cups milk
    ¾ cup granulated sugar
    ¼ cup butter or margarine
    2 teaspoons salt
    3 eggs
    2 teaspoons ground cinnamon
        Powdered Sugar Icing (recipe
        follows)**

Cinnamon-Raisin Swirl Loaf

In small bowl, combine raisins with
enough hot tap water to cover. Plump
5 minutes; drain well. Set aside. In
large bowl, combine 3 cups of the flour
and the yeast. In medium saucepan,
heat milk, ¼ cup of the granulated
sugar, the butter and salt over low
heat just until warm (115° to 120°F)
and until butter is almost melted,
stirring constantly. Add to flour mixture; add eggs. Beat at low speed of
electric mixer for ½ minute, scraping
sides of bowl constantly. Beat 3 minutes at high speed, scraping bowl occasionally. Stir in plumped raisins.
Stir in as much remaining flour as
can be mixed in with a spoon. Turn
out onto lightly floured board. Knead
in enough remaining flour to make a
moderately stiff dough that is smooth
and elastic (6 to 8 minutes total).
Shape into a ball. Place dough in
lightly greased bowl; turn once to
grease surface. Cover; let rise in warm
place (85°F) until doubled, about 1¼
hours.

Punch dough down; divide in half.
Cover; let rest 10 minutes. Roll each
half into 15×7-inch rectangle. Brush
entire surface lightly with water.
Combine remaining ½ cup granulated sugar and the cinnamon; sprinkle ½ of the sugar mixture over each
rectangle. Roll up, jelly-roll fashion,
starting from a 7-inch side; pinch
edges and ends to seal. Place, sealed
edges down, in 2 greased 9×5×3-inch
loaf pans. Cover; let rise in warm
place until nearly doubled, 35 to 45
minutes. Bake in preheated 375°F
oven 35 to 40 minutes or until bread
sounds hollow when tapped, covering
bread with foil the last 15 minutes to
prevent overbrowning. Remove bread
from pans; cool completely on wire
racks. Drizzle with Powdered Sugar
Icing.
Makes 2 loaves.
POWDERED SUGAR ICING: In medium bowl, combine 1 cup sifted powdered sugar, ¼ teaspoon vanilla and
enough milk (about 1½ tablespoons)
to make of drizzling consistency.

Cheese Casserole Bread

Cheese Casserole Bread

2 cups warm milk (105° to 115°)
2 packages active dry yeast
3 tablespoons sugar
1 tablespoon butter
½ teaspoon salt
4½ cups all-purpose flour
6 ounces Cheddar cheese, cut into ½-inch cubes

In large bowl, combine milk and yeast; stir to dissolve yeast. Add sugar, butter and salt; stir until butter is melted. Stir in 3 cups of the flour; beat until smooth. Stir in remaining flour and cheese; mix well. Pour batter into well-buttered 1½-quart round casserole. Cover with waxed paper; let rise in warm place (85°) until doubled, about 1 hour. Remove waxed paper. Bake in preheated 350° oven 50 to 55 minutes or until toothpick inserted into center comes out clean. Let cool in dish on wire rack 10 minutes. Loosen edge; remove from dish. Cool slightly on wire rack; serve warm with butter.
Makes 1 loaf.

Favorite recipe from **American Dairy Association**

Savory Bubble Cheese Bread

6 to 7 cups flour, divided
2 tablespoons sugar
4 teaspoons instant minced onion
2 teaspoons salt
2 packages active dry yeast
½ teaspoon caraway seeds
1¾ cups milk
½ cup water
3 tablespoons butter or margarine
1 teaspoon TABASCO® pepper sauce
2 cups (8 ounces) shredded sharp Cheddar cheese, divided
1 egg, lightly beaten

In large bowl of electric mixer combine 2½ cups flour, sugar, onion, salt, yeast and caraway seeds. In small saucepan combine milk, water and butter. Heat milk mixture until very warm (120°F. to 130°F.); stir in Tabasco® sauce.

With mixer at medium speed gradually add milk mixture to dry ingredients; beat 2 minutes. Add 1 cup flour. Beat at high speed 2 minutes. With wooden spoon stir in 1½ cups cheese and enough flour to make a stiff dough. Turn dough out onto lightly floured surface. Knead 8 to 10 minutes or until dough is smooth and elastic, adding as much remaining flour as needed to prevent sticking. Place in large greased bowl and invert dough to bring greased side up. Cover with towel; let rise in warm place (90°F. to 100°F.) 1 hour or until doubled in bulk.

Punch dough down. Divide dough into 16 equal pieces; shape each piece into a ball. Place ½ the balls in well-greased 10-inch tube pan. Sprinkle with remaining ½ cup cheese. Arrange remaining balls on top. Cover with towel; let rise in warm place 45 minutes or until doubled in bulk. Preheat oven to 375°F. Brush bread with egg. Bake 40 to 50 minutes or until golden brown. Remove from pan. Cool completely on wire rack.
Makes one 10-inch round loaf.

Double-Braided Saffron Bread

4½ to 5½ cups unsifted all-purpose flour, divided
2 tablespoons sugar
1 package (¼ ounce) active dry yeast
1½ teaspoons salt
⅓ cup CRISCO® Oil
1 cup very warm water (120° to 130°F)
⅛ teaspoon powdered saffron
4 eggs
1 teaspoon cold water

Mix 1¼ cups flour, sugar, yeast and salt in large mixing bowl. Stir in Crisco® Oil. Combine warm water and saffron in small bowl. Stir until saffron is dissolved. Add to flour mixture. Beat with electric mixer at medium speed 3 minutes, scraping bowl occasionally. Separate 1 egg; set yolk aside. Add egg white to flour mixture. Add remaining 3 eggs and ½ cup flour. Beat at medium speed 1 minute, scraping bowl occasionally. Stir in enough remaining flour to make soft dough.

Knead dough on lightly floured surface 8 to 10 minutes, or until smooth and elastic, adding additional flour as necessary. Place in lightly oiled large mixing bowl. Turn dough over to coat both sides with Crisco® Oil. Cover; let rise in warm place 1 to 1½ hours, or until doubled.

Oil baking sheet. Set aside. Punch down dough. Place on lightly floured surface. Set aside two thirds of dough. Divide remaining dough into 6 equal portions. Roll each portion with floured fingers into a 10-inch-long piece. Braid 3 pieces together. Braid remaining 3 pieces. Set aside.

Divide remaining dough into 6 equal portions. Roll each portion with floured fingers into a 12-inch-long piece. Braid 3 pieces together. Braid remaining 3 pieces. For each loaf, center 1 small braid on top of 1 large braid. Press ends together to seal. Place both loaves on prepared baking sheet.

Blend reserved egg yolk and cold water in small bowl. Brush on both loaves. Cover; let rise in warm place about 1 hour, or until doubled. Preheat oven to 400°F. Bake loaves at 400°F, 20 to 25 minutes, or until loaves are golden brown and sound hollow when tapped lightly. Cool on wire rack.
2 loaves.

Bohemian Rye Bread

2 packages active dry yeast
4 cups warm water (105° to
115°F)
7 to 8 cups all-purpose flour
2 cups whole wheat flour
1½ cups medium rye flour
3 tablespoons caraway seed
1 tablespoon salt
3 tablespoons light molasses
2 tablespoons LAND O LAKES®
Sweet Cream Butter, melted

In large bowl, combine yeast and warm water; stir to dissolve yeast. Stir in 2 cups of the all-purpose flour, the whole wheat and rye flours, caraway seed, salt and molasses; beat until smooth. Stir in enough of the remaining all-purpose flour to make dough easy to handle. Turn out onto

lightly floured surface. Knead 10 minutes or until dough is smooth and elastic, adding as much remaining flour as needed to prevent sticking. Shape dough into ball. Place in large, greased bowl; turn dough once to grease surface. Cover with towel; let rise in warm place (85°F) until doubled, about 1 hour.

Punch dough down; divide into 4 equal pieces. Shape each piece into ball; place each into greased 2-pound coffee can. Cover; let rise in warm place until doubled, about 45 minutes. Bake in preheated 375°F oven 35 to 45 minutes or until loaves are browned and sound hollow when tapped. Remove from cans to wire racks. Brush tops of hot loaves with butter; cool completely.
Makes 4 loaves.

Oatmeal Dinner Rolls

2 cups old-fashioned oats,
uncooked
1½ cups boiling water
¼ cup LAND O LAKES® Sweet
Cream Butter
2 packages active dry yeast
½ cup warm water (105° to
115°F)
6¼ to 7¼ cups all-purpose flour
1 cup packed brown sugar
⅓ cup light molasses
2 eggs
1½ teaspoons salt

In medium heatproof bowl, combine oats, boiling water and butter; stir until butter is melted. Cool until warm (105° to 115°F). In large bowl, combine yeast and water; stir to dissolve

Cottage Herb Rolls

yeast. Stir in oat mixture, 2 cups of the flour, the sugar, molasses, eggs and salt; beat until smooth. Stir in enough of the remaining flour to make dough easy to handle. Turn out onto lightly floured surface. Knead 10 minutes or until dough is smooth and elastic, adding as much remaining flour as needed to prevent sticking. Shape dough into ball. Place in large, greased bowl; turn dough once to grease surface. Cover with towel; let rise in warm place (85°F) until doubled, about 1½ hours.

Punch dough down; divide in half. With floured hands, shape each half into 18 smooth balls. Place balls in 2 greased 13×9×2-inch pans. Cover; let rise in warm place until doubled, about 1 hour. Bake in preheated 375°F oven 20 to 25 minutes or until golden brown. Remove from pans to wire racks. If desired, brush tops of hot rolls with melted butter; serve warm.
Makes 3 dozen rolls.

Cottage Herb Rolls

1 package active dry yeast
¼ cup warm water
2½ cups unsifted flour
¼ cup sugar
1 teaspoon oregano leaves
1 teaspoon salt
½ cup cold margarine or butter
1 cup BORDEN® or MEADOW
GOLD® Cottage Cheese
1 egg, beaten
Melted margarine or butter

Dissolve yeast in warm water. In large bowl, combine flour, sugar, oregano and salt; mix well. Cut in cold margarine until mixture resembles coarse cornmeal. Blend in cheese, egg and yeast. Turn onto well-floured surface; knead. Shape into ball; place in well-greased bowl. Brush top with melted margarine. Cover; let rise until doubled. Punch down; shape as desired. Brush with melted margarine; cover. Let rise again until nearly doubled. Bake in preheated 375° oven 12 to 15 minutes. Serve warm.
Makes 1½ to 2 dozen.

COOKIES & CANDIES

A batch of ideas for sweet snacking. You'll find crisp lunch-box treats, delicate cookies for the tea table, brownies to cure the "midnight munchies," and lovely frosted cookies for holiday baking. Try these foolproof candies, too—in no time, you can whip up indulgent confections that look professional and taste scrumptious.

Wheat Germ Cookies

**1 package DUNCAN HINES®
   Deluxe Yellow Cake Mix
1 large egg
3 tablespoons brown sugar
¼ cup CRISCO® Oil or PURITAN®
   Oil
2 tablespoons butter or
   margarine, melted
½ cup wheat germ
2 tablespoons water
½ cup chopped nuts**

1. Preheat oven to 375°F.
2. Combine dry cake mix, egg, brown sugar, oil, butter, wheat germ and water in bowl. Mix with spoon. (Dough will be stiff.) Stir in nuts.
3. Drop by teaspoonfuls, 2 inches apart, on ungreased cookie sheets.
4. Bake at 375°F for 10 minutes for chewy cookies, 12 minutes for crispy cookies. Cool 1 minute on cookie sheet, then remove to rack to finish cooling.
About 3 dozen cookies.

Lemon Sugar Cookies

**3 cups unsifted flour
2 teaspoons baking powder
½ teaspoon salt
2 cups sugar
1 cup shortening
2 eggs
¼ cup REALEMON® Lemon Juice
   from Concentrate
Additional sugar**

Preheat oven to 350°. Stir together flour, baking powder and salt; set aside. In large mixer bowl, beat sugar and shortening until fluffy; beat in eggs. Stir in dry ingredients, then ReaLemon® brand; mix well. Chill 2 hours. Shape into 1¼-inch balls; roll in additional sugar. Place 2 inches apart on greased baking sheets; flatten. Bake 8 to 10 minutes or until lightly browned.
Makes about 8 dozen.

Thumbprint Cookies

**1 package (4-serving size)
   JELL-O® Instant Pudding
   and Pie Filling, any flavor
1 package (10 ounces) pie crust
   mix
2 tablespoons butter or
   margarine, melted
4 to 5 tablespoons cold water
1 package (4 ounces) BAKER'S®
   GERMAN'S® Sweet
   Chocolate, broken into
   squares
Whole or chopped toasted
   nuts**

Combine pudding mix and pie crust mix in medium bowl; add butter and 4 tablespoons of the water. Mix with fork until soft dough forms. (If dough is too dry, add 1 tablespoon water.) Shape dough into 1-inch balls. Place 1 inch apart on ungreased baking sheets; press thumb deeply into center of each.

Cut each square of chocolate in half. Press 1 half into center of each cookie. Bake in preheated 350° oven for about 15 minutes or until lightly browned. Immediately press nuts lightly into chocolate centers. Remove from baking sheets and cool on wire racks.
Makes 3 dozen.

Coconut Thumbprints: Prepare Thumbprint Cookies as directed, omitting chocolate and nuts. Mix 1⅓ cups (about) BAKER'S® ANGEL FLAKE® Coconut with ½ cup sweetened condensed milk; spoon into centers of cookies before baking.

Jam Thumbprints: Prepare Thumbprint Cookies as directed, omitting chocolate and nuts. Spoon ½ teaspoon jam into center of each cookie after baking.

Cream Cheese and Jelly Thumbprints: Prepare Thumbprint Cookies as directed, omitting chocolate and nuts. Using 1 package (3 ounces) cream cheese, softened, spoon ½ teaspoon cream cheese into center of each cookie before baking and top each with ½ teaspoon jelly after baking.

Wheat Germ Cookies

Clockwise from top left: Hershey's™ Great American Chocolate Chip Cookies, Reese's Chewy Chocolate Cookies, Chocolate Chip Whole Wheat Cookies and Chocolate Cookie Sandwiches

Chocolate Cookie Sandwiches

- ½ cup shortening
- 1 cup sugar
- 1 egg
- 1 teaspoon vanilla
- 1½ cups unsifted all-purpose flour
- ⅓ cup HERSHEY'S Cocoa
- ½ teaspoon baking soda
- ½ teaspoon salt
- ¼ cup milk
  Creme Filling

Cream shortening, sugar, egg and vanilla in large mixer bowl until light and fluffy. Combine flour, cocoa, baking soda and salt; add alternately with milk to creamed mixture until ingredients are combined.

Drop by teaspoonfuls onto ungreased cookie sheet. Bake at 375° for 11 to 12 minutes or just until soft-set *(do not overbake)*. Cool 1 minute. Remove from cookie sheet; cool completely on wire rack. Prepare Creme Filling. Spread bottom of one cookie with about 1 tablespoon filling; cover with another cookie. Repeat with remaining cookies and filling.
About 15 filled cookies.

Creme Filling

- 2 tablespoons butter or margarine, softened
- 2 tablespoons shortening
- ½ cup marshmallow creme
- ¾ teaspoon vanilla
- ⅔ cup confectioners' sugar

Cream butter and shortening in small mixer bowl; gradually beat in marshmallow creme. Blend in vanilla and confectioners' sugar; beat to spreading consistency.

Chocolate Chip Whole Wheat Cookies

- ¾ cup shortening
- 1½ cups packed light brown sugar
- 1 egg
- ¼ cup water
- 1 teaspoon vanilla
- 1 cup unsifted whole wheat flour
- ½ teaspoon baking soda
- ½ teaspoon salt
- 2 cups quick-cooking oats
- 1 cup chopped dried apricots or raisins
- 1 cup HERSHEY'S MINI CHIPS Semi-Sweet Chocolate

Cream shortening and brown sugar in large mixer bowl until light and fluffy. Add egg, water and vanilla; beat well. Combine whole wheat flour, baking soda and salt; stir into creamed mixture. Stir in oats, dried apricots and MINI CHIPS Chocolate.

Drop by teaspoonfuls onto lightly greased cookie sheet; flatten slightly. Bake at 350° for 10 to 12 minutes or until golden brown. Remove from cookie sheet; cool completely on wire rack.
About 5 dozen cookies.

Reese's Chewy Chocolate Cookies

- 1¼ cups butter or margarine, softened
- 2 cups sugar
- 2 eggs
- 2 teaspoons vanilla
- 2 cups unsifted all-purpose flour
- ¾ cup HERSHEY'S Cocoa
- 1 teaspoon baking soda
- ½ teaspoon salt
- 2 cups (12-ounce package) REESE'S Peanut Butter Chips

Cream butter and sugar in large mixer bowl until light and fluffy. Add eggs and vanilla; beat well. Combine flour, cocoa, baking soda and salt; gradually blend into creamed mixture. Stir in peanut butter chips.

Drop by teaspoonfuls onto ungreased cookie sheet. Bake at 350° for 8 to 9 minutes. *Do not overbake.* (Cookies will be soft; they will puff during baking and flatten upon cooling.) Cool until set, about 1 minute. Remove from cookie sheet; cool completely on wire rack.
About 4½ dozen cookies.

Black-Eyed Susans

Filling:
1 cup chopped SUN-MAID®
    Muscat Raisins
½ cup orange juice
½ teaspoon grated orange peel
¼ cup sugar
    Dash salt
Dough:
½ cup butter or margarine,
    softened
½ cup peanut butter
1 cup sugar
1 egg
1 teaspoon vanilla
1¼ cups all-purpose flour
½ teaspoon baking powder
¼ teaspoon salt

To prepare Filling: In small saucepan, combine all filling ingredients. Cook over medium heat, stirring frequently, until sugar dissolves and mixture thickens slightly. Cool while preparing dough.

To prepare Dough: In medium bowl, cream butter, peanut butter, sugar, egg and vanilla. In small bowl, sift flour with baking powder and salt; stir into creamed mixture. Cover and chill dough several hours. Roll out dough on lightly floured board to ⅛-inch thickness. Cut into 3-inch rounds with cookie cutter. Place 2 teaspoons of filling in centers of *half* the dough rounds. Cut small circles from centers of remaining dough rounds.* Place on top of raisin-filled rounds. Press edges together lightly to seal. Place on greased baking sheets. Bake in preheated 350°F oven 10 to 12 minutes or until golden brown. Cool on baking sheets a few minutes. Remove to wire rack to cool completely.
Makes about 1½ dozen cookies.

*A doughnut cutter works well. Simply cut ½ of dough with holes and ½ without.

Hershey's™ Great American Chocolate Chip Cookies

1 cup butter, softened
¾ cup sugar
¾ cup packed light brown sugar
1 teaspoon vanilla
2 eggs
2¼ cups unsifted all-purpose flour
1 teaspoon baking soda
½ teaspoon salt
2 cups (12-ounce package)
    HERSHEY'S Semi-Sweet
    Chocolate Chips
1 cup chopped nuts (optional)

Cream butter, sugar, brown sugar and vanilla in large mixer bowl until light and fluffy. Add eggs; beat well. Combine flour, baking soda and salt; gradually add to creamed mixture. Beat well. Stir in chocolate chips and nuts.

Drop by teaspoonfuls onto ungreased cookie sheet. Bake at 375° for 8 to 10 minutes or until lightly browned. Cool slightly. Remove from cookie sheet; cool completely on wire rack.
About 6 dozen cookies.

Milk Chocolate Chip Cookies: Substitute 2 cups (11.5-ounce package) HERSHEY'S Milk Chocolate Chips for the semi-sweet chocolate chips.

Easy Peanut Butter Cookies

1 (14-ounce) can EAGLE® Brand
    Sweetened Condensed Milk
    (NOT evaporated milk)
¾ cup peanut butter
2 cups biscuit baking mix
1 teaspoon vanilla extract
    Granulated sugar

Preheat oven to 375°. In large mixer bowl, beat sweetened condensed milk and peanut butter until smooth. Add biscuit mix and vanilla; mix well. Shape into 1-inch balls. Roll in sugar. Place 2 inches apart on ungreased baking sheets. Flatten with fork. Bake 6 to 8 minutes or until *lightly* browned (do not overbake). Cool. Store tightly covered at room temperature. *Makes about 5 dozen.*

Peanut Blossoms: Shape as above; *do not flatten.* Bake as above. Press solid milk chocolate candy in center of each ball immediately after baking.

Peanut Butter & Jelly Gems: Press thumb in center of each ball of dough; fill with jelly, jam or preserves. Bake as above.

Any-Way-You-Like'm Cookies: Stir 1 cup semi-sweet chocolate chips *or* chopped peanuts *or* raisins *or* flaked coconut into dough. Proceed as above.

Easy Peanut Butter Cookies and Peanut Blossoms

Lemon Blossom Cookies

2 cups margarine or butter, softened
1½ cups confectioners' sugar
¼ cup REALEMON® Lemon Juice from Concentrate
4 cups unsifted flour
Finely chopped nuts, optional
Assorted fruit preserves and jams or pecan halves

Preheat oven to 350°. In large mixer bowl, beat margarine and sugar until fluffy. Add ReaLemon® brand; beat well. Gradually add flour; mix well. Chill 2 hours. Shape into 1-inch balls; roll in nuts if desired. Place 1 inch apart on greased baking sheets. Press thumb in center of each ball; fill with preserves or pecan. Bake 14 to 16 minutes or until lightly browned.
Makes about 6 dozen.

Super Chocolate Chunk Cookies

½ cup butter or margarine, softened
½ cup granulated sugar
¼ cup firmly packed brown sugar
1 teaspoon vanilla
1 egg
1 cup flour
½ teaspoon baking soda
½ teaspoon salt
1 package (8 squares) BAKER'S® Semi-Sweet Chocolate, cut into chunks*
¾ cup chopped walnuts

Beat butter, sugars, vanilla and egg until light and fluffy. Mix flour with soda and salt; blend into butter mixture. Stir in chocolate chunks and nuts. Chill 1 hour. Drop 2 inches apart, from heaping tablespoon, onto ungreased baking sheets. Bake at 350° about 15 minutes, or until lightly browned.
Makes 1½ to 2 dozen.

Double-Dip Chocolate Chunk Cookies: Prepare Super Chocolate Chunk Cookies, melting 1 square of the semi-sweet chocolate; cool slightly and add with the butter-sugar mixture; omit the nuts. Melt and cool 4 oz. sweet cooking chocolate; partially dip the cooled baked cookies into the chocolate. Let stand or chill until chocolate is firm. *(continued)*

Super Coconut Chocolate Chunk Cookies: Prepare Super Chocolate Chunk Cookies, adding 1⅓ cups (about) BAKER'S® ANGEL FLAKE® Coconut with the chocolate and nuts.

Super Peanut Butter Chocolate Chunk Cookies: Prepare Super Chocolate Chunk Cookies, adding ½ cup peanut butter with the butter-sugar mixture, increasing the brown sugar to ½ cup and using peanuts instead of walnuts.

*Or use 2 packages (4 ounces each) BAKER'S® GERMAN'S® Sweet Chocolate, cut into chunks.

Note: Recipe may be doubled, tripled or quadrupled. Dough may be chilled 4 hours or overnight; let stand at room temperature about 15 minutes before baking.

Chocolate Kahlúa® Bears

¼ cup KAHLÚA®
2 squares (1 ounce each) unsweetened chocolate
⅔ cup shortening
1⅔ cups sugar
2 eggs
2 teaspoons vanilla
2 cups sifted all-purpose flour
2 teaspoons baking powder
¾ teaspoon salt
½ teaspoon ground cinnamon
Chocolate Icing (recipe follows)

Lemon Blossom Cookies

To Kahlúa® in measuring cup, add enough water to make ⅓ cup liquid. In small saucepan over low heat, melt chocolate; cool. In large bowl, beat shortening, sugar, eggs and vanilla until light and fluffy. Stir in chocolate. In small bowl, combine flour, baking powder, salt and cinnamon. Add dry ingredients to egg mixture alternately with ⅓ cup liquid. Cover; refrigerate until firm. Roll out dough, one fourth at a time, about ¼ inch thick on well-floured surface. Cut out with bear-shaped or other cookie cutters. Place 2 inches apart on ungreased cookie sheets. Bake in preheated 350° oven 8 to 10 minutes. Remove to wire racks to cool. Spread Chocolate Icing in thin, even layer on cookies. Let stand until set; decorate as desired.
Makes about 2½ dozen cookies.

CHOCOLATE ICING: In medium saucepan, combine 6 squares (1 ounce each) semisweet chocolate, ⅓ cup butter or margarine, ¼ cup Kahlúa® and 1 tablespoon light corn syrup. Cook over low heat until chocolate melts, stirring to blend. Add ¾ cup sifted powdered sugar; beat until smooth. If necessary, beat in additional Kahlúa® to make spreading consistency.

Quick Pudding Cookies

1 package (4-serving size) JELL-O® Instant Pudding and Pie Filling, any flavor
1 cup all-purpose biscuit mix
¼ cup vegetable oil
1 egg, slightly beaten
3 tablespoons water

Combine pudding mix and biscuit mix in medium bowl. Stir in oil, egg and water, blending well. Drop from teaspoon 2 inches apart onto ungreased baking sheets. Bake in preheated 375° oven for about 12 minutes, or until lightly browned. Remove from baking sheets and cool on wire racks. Store in tightly covered container.
Makes about 2 dozen.

Note: Cookie dough may be pressed through cookie press, or rolled into 1-inch balls and flattened on baking sheets with fork or glass dipped in flour; reduce water to 2 tablespoons.

Quick Pudding Chip Cookies: Prepare Quick Pudding Cookies as directed, stirring in ½ cup BAKER'S® Semi-Sweet Chocolate Flavored Chips just before baking. Makes 2½ dozen cookies.

On plate: **Coconut Washboards** and **Melting Moments**; on tray: **Coconut Dream Bars** (page 282) and **Coconut Macaroons**

Coconut Washboards

2 cups flour
³/₄ teaspoon CALUMET® Baking Powder
¹/₄ teaspoon cinnamon
¹/₄ teaspoon nutmeg
¹/₈ teaspoon salt
³/₄ cup butter
1 cup firmly packed brown sugar
1 egg
1 teaspoon vanilla
¹/₂ teaspoon almond extract
1¹/₃ cups (about) BAKER'S® ANGEL FLAKE® Coconut

Mix flour with baking powder, spices and salt. Cream butter. Gradually add sugar, beating until light and fluffy. Add egg, vanilla and almond extract; beat well. Add flour mixture, blending well. Stir in coconut. Divide dough into 2 parts. Chill, if necessary, until dough is easily handled. Spread or pat each half into a 10×9-inch rectangle. Cut each rectangle into 4 strips lengthwise. Cut each strip into 10 pieces. Place about 2 inches apart on ungreased baking sheets. Using a floured fork, gently press ridges into cookies. Bake at 375° for 8 to 10 minutes, or until golden brown.
Makes about 6¹/₂ dozen.

Melting Moments

1 cup flour
2 tablespoons cornstarch
¹/₂ cup unsifted confectioners sugar
1 cup butter or margarine, softened
1¹/₃ cups (about) BAKER'S® ANGEL FLAKE® Coconut

Mix flour with cornstarch and sugar in a bowl. Blend in butter to form a soft dough. Cover and chill, if necessary, until dough is firm enough to handle. Shape into small balls, about ³/₄ inch in diameter. Roll in coconut and place on ungreased baking sheets, about 1¹/₂ inches apart. Flatten with lightly floured fork, if desired. Bake at 300° for 20 to 25 minutes, or until lightly browned.
Makes about 3 dozen.

Almond Melting Moments: Prepare Melting Moments as directed, adding 2 teaspoons almond extract with the butter.

Coconut Macaroons

1¹/₃ cups (about) BAKER'S® ANGEL FLAKE® Coconut
¹/₃ cup sugar
3 tablespoons flour
¹/₈ teaspoon salt
2 egg whites
¹/₂ teaspoon almond extract

Combine coconut, sugar, flour and salt in mixing bowl. Stir in egg whites and almond extract; mix well. Drop from teaspoon onto lightly greased baking sheets. Garnish with candied cherry halves, if desired. Bake at 325° for 20 to 25 minutes, or until edges of cookies are golden brown. Remove from baking sheets immediately.
Makes about 18.

Raisin Macaroons: Prepare Coconut Macaroons as directed, adding ¹/₃ cup raisins before baking.

Chip Macaroons: Prepare Coconut Macaroons as directed, adding ¹/₃ cup BAKER'S® Semi-Sweet Chocolate Flavored Chips before baking.

Nut Macaroons: Prepare Coconut Macaroons as directed, adding ¹/₃ cup chopped pecans or almonds before baking.

Fruited Macaroons: Prepare Coconut Macaroons as directed, adding ¹/₃ cup chopped mixed candied fruit before baking. Garnish with candied cherry halves, maraschino cherries or whole almonds, if desired.

Gingerbread People

Pinwheels and Checkerboards

  2 cups flour
  1 teaspoon CALUMET® Baking
      Powder
  ½ teaspoon salt
  ⅔ cup butter or margarine
  1 cup sugar
  1 egg
  1 teaspoon vanilla
  2 squares BAKER'S®
      Unsweetened Chocolate,
      melted

Mix flour, baking powder and salt. Cream butter. Gradually add sugar and continue beating until light and fluffy. Add egg and vanilla; beat well. Gradually add flour mixture, mixing well after each addition. Divide dough in half; blend chocolate into one half. Use prepared doughs to make Pinwheels or Checkerboards.

Pinwheels: Roll chocolate and vanilla doughs separately between sheets of waxed paper into 12×8-inch rectangles. Remove top sheets of paper and invert vanilla dough onto chocolate dough. Remove remaining papers. Roll up as for jelly roll; then wrap in waxed paper. Chill until firm, at least 3 hours (or freeze 1 hour). Cut into ¼-inch slices and place on baking sheets. Bake at 375° about 10 minutes, or until cookies just begin to brown around edges. Cool on racks. *Makes about 4½ dozen.*

Checkerboards: Set out small amount of milk. Roll chocolate and vanilla doughs separately on lightly floured board into 9×4½-inch rectangles. Brush chocolate dough lightly with milk and top with vanilla dough. Using a long sharp knife, cut lengthwise into 3 strips, 1½ inches wide. Stack strips, alternating colors and brushing each layer with milk. Cut lengthwise again into 3 strips, ½ inch wide. Invert middle section so that colors are alternated; brush sides with milk. Press strips together lightly to form a rectangle. Wrap in waxed paper. Chill overnight. Cut into ⅛-inch slices, using a very sharp knife. Place on baking sheets. Bake at 375° for about 8 minutes, or just until white portions begin to brown. Cool on racks. *Makes about 5 dozen.*

Gingerbread People

  1 package DUNCAN HINES®
      Deluxe Spice Cake Mix
  2 teaspoons ground ginger
  2 large eggs
  ⅓ cup CRISCO® Oil or PURITAN®
      Oil
  ⅓ cup dark molasses
  ½ cup all-purpose flour
      Dark raisins

1. Combine all ingredients, except raisins, in large bowl; mix well (mixture will be soft). Refrigerate 2 hours.
2. Preheat oven to 375°F. Roll dough to ¼-inch thickness on lightly floured surface. Cut with 6-inch cookie cutter. Place on ungreased cookie sheets. Press raisins in dough for eyes and buttons.
3. Bake at 375°F for 8 to 10 minutes or until edges just start to brown. Cool several minutes on cookie sheet, then remove to racks to finish cooling.
About 14 six-inch cookies.

Lollipop Cookies

  1 package (3-dozen-size) sugar
      or peanut butter cookie mix
  12 to 14 wooden sticks
      Sugar, for flattening cookies
      SUN-MAID® Raisins
      Dried mixed fruit, snipped

Prepare cookie dough and sheet according to package directions. Roll dough with your hands into 1½-inch balls. Place about 2 inches apart on cookie sheets. Insert wooden stick halfway into each ball of dough. Dip bottom of glass into sugar and flatten cookies. Decorate cookies as desired with raisins and mixed fruit. Bake in preheated oven according to temperature and time on cookie mix package. Remove to wire rack to cool.
Makes about 1 dozen cookies.

Kris Kringle Cookies

1¹/₃ **cups butter or margarine, softened**
1¹/₃ **cups granulated sugar**
2 **eggs**
2²/₃ **cups all-purpose flour**
¹/₄ **teaspoon salt**
1¹/₂ **cups SUN-MAID® Raisins, chopped**
¹/₂ **cup chopped candied ginger***
1 **egg white, beaten, for glaze**
Colored sugars, dragées, candied fruits and DIAMOND® Walnuts, for garnish

In large bowl, cream butter, granulated sugar and eggs. Stir in flour and salt, mixing until blended. Stir in raisins and ginger. Cover and chill dough. Roll out dough on lightly floured board to ¹/₈-inch thickness; cut into desired shapes with sharp-edged cookie cutters. Space apart on greased baking sheets. Brush with beaten white; sprinkle with additional granulated sugar, or decorate with colored sugars, dragées, candied fruits and walnuts, if desired. Bake in preheated 350°F oven 12 to 15 minutes or until golden. Cool 2 to 3 minutes in pan; remove to wire rack to cool completely. *Makes 1¹/₂ to 2 dozen large cookies.*

*An additional ¹/₂ cup of raisins may be substituted for candied ginger; add 1 tablespoon ground ginger.

Confetti Cones

¹/₂ **cup butter or margarine, melted**
¹/₂ **cup granulated sugar**
²/₃ **cup all-purpose flour**
1 **teaspoon vanilla**
2 **egg whites**
¹/₂ **cup DIAMOND® Walnuts, finely chopped**
Colored sugar (about 2 tablespoons)

In medium bowl, combine butter, sugar, flour, vanilla and unbeaten egg whites; beat just until smooth. Stir in walnuts. Drop batter by teaspoonfuls about 4 inches apart onto lightly greased baking sheet and spread slightly.* Sprinkle with colored sugar. Bake in preheated 350°F oven 8 to 10 minutes or until edges are lightly browned. Remove each with broad spatula, quickly shaping into cone.

Set in bottle neck or tiny jar a few minutes to set shape. Store in tightly covered container to keep crisp. *About 2¹/₂ dozen (3-inch) cookies.*

*Bake no more than 6 at a time until you get used to making cones. To speed baking, start second sheet when first one is half baked. Cookies may also be left flat or placed on side of small bottle to make rounded "tiles."

Favorite Butter Cookies

Cookies:
1 **cup LAND O LAKES® Sweet Cream Butter, softened**
1 **cup granulated sugar**
1 **egg**
2¹/₂ **cups all-purpose flour**
1 **teaspoon baking powder**
2 **tablespoons orange juice**
1 **teaspoon vanilla**
Frosting:
4 **cups powdered sugar**
¹/₂ **cup LAND O LAKES® Sweet Cream Butter, softened**
3 to 4 **tablespoons milk**
2 **teaspoons vanilla**
Food coloring (optional)
Colored sugars, flaked coconut and cinnamon candies for decoration

To prepare Cookies: In large bowl, cream butter and granulated sugar. Add egg; beat until light and fluffy. Add flour, baking powder, orange juice and vanilla; beat until well mixed. Cover; refrigerate until firm, 2 to 3 hours. Roll out dough, half at a time, ¹/₄ inch thick on well-floured surface. Cut out with holiday cookie cutters. Place 1 inch apart on ungreased cookie sheets. Bake in preheated 400°F oven 6 to 10 minutes or until edges are lightly browned. Remove to wire racks to cool completely.

To prepare Frosting: In medium bowl, combine all frosting ingredients *except* food coloring and decorations; beat until fluffy. If desired, divide frosting into small bowls and tint with food coloring. Frost cookies and decorate with colored sugars, coconut and candies.
Makes about 3 dozen cookies.

Old-Fashioned Butter Cookies: Prepare and roll out cookie dough as above; cut out with 2-inch round cookie cutter. Place 1 inch apart on ungreased cookie sheets. Press 1 pecan half in center of each cookie. Bake as above.

Top: Kris Kringle Cookies; bottom: Lebkuchen Jewels (page 285)

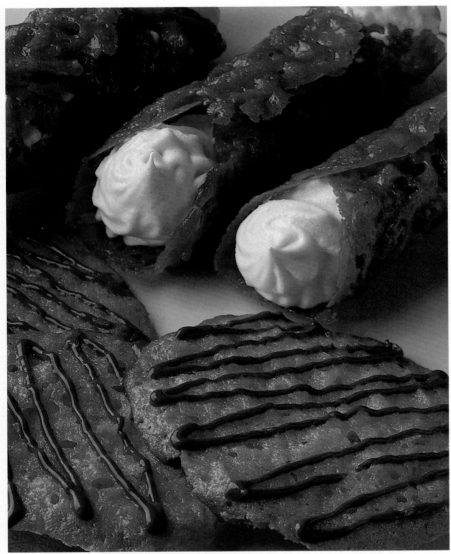

Lacy Chocolate Crisps (top), Florentines (bottom)

Lacy Chocolate Crisps

    ½ cup light corn syrup
    ⅓ cup butter or margarine
    1 package (4 oz.) BAKER'S®
      GERMAN'S® Sweet
      Chocolate
    ½ cup firmly packed light brown
      sugar
    1 cup flour
    ⅔ cup BAKER'S® ANGEL FLAKE®
      Coconut

Bring corn syrup to a boil. Add butter and chocolate. Cook and stir over low heat until smooth. Remove from heat; stir in sugar, flour and coconut. Drop from tablespoon onto lightly greased baking sheets, leaving 3 inches between. Bake at 300° for 15 minutes, or until wafers bubble vigorously and develop lacy holes. Cool on sheets 2 minutes; lift with spatula and finish cooling on racks. (If wafers harden on sheets, return briefly to oven.) If desired, roll warm wafers over wooden spoon handle; cool. Fill with tinted sweetened whipped cream.
Makes 2½ dozen.

Florentines

    ½ cup flour
    ¼ teaspoon baking soda
      Dash of salt
    ¼ cup butter or margarine
    ⅓ cup firmly packed brown sugar
    2 tablespoons light corn syrup
    1 egg, well beaten
    ½ cup BAKER'S® ANGEL FLAKE®
      Coconut
    ½ teaspoon vanilla
    2 squares BAKER'S® Semi-
      Sweet Chocolate
    1 tablespoon butter or
      margarine

Mix flour, soda and salt. Cream ¼ cup butter. Gradually add sugar and beat until light and fluffy. Add corn syrup and egg; blend well. Stir in flour mixture, coconut and vanilla. Drop by half teaspoonfuls onto greased baking sheets, leaving 2 inches between. Bake at 350° about 10 minutes. Cool on baking sheets 1 minute, remove quickly and finish cooling on racks. (If wafers harden on sheets, return briefly to oven.) Melt chocolate and 1 tablespoon butter in saucepan over very low heat, stirring constantly until smooth. Drizzle over wafers.
Makes 4 dozen.

Swiss Cinnamon Cookies

    3 egg whites
    3¼ cups powdered sugar
      (approximately)
    3 cups DIAMOND® Walnuts,
      finely ground
    1 tablespoon ground cinnamon
      Chopped DIAMOND® Walnuts,
      colored sugars, candied
      cherries, dragées, for
      garnish

In medium bowl, beat egg whites until foamy. Gradually beat in 2 cups of the sugar. Beat until mixture holds soft peaks, 3 to 4 minutes; remove ¾ cup of the batter, cover and set aside. Mix the 3 cups walnuts, the cinnamon and ¾ cup more of the sugar into larger egg white-sugar portion. Working with a third of the dough at a time, roll out to ⅛-inch thickness on pastry cloth or board heavily dusted with powdered sugar. Cut into desired shapes with cookie cutters. Place on greased or parchment-lined baking sheets. With tip of knife, spread reserved egg white mixture ⅛ inch thick onto top of each cookie, spreading almost to edges. Decorate immediately, as desired, with chopped walnuts, colored sugars, candied cherries and dragées. Bake in preheated 300°F oven 12 to 14 minutes or until cookies are just set and very lightly browned. Remove to wire racks to cool completely. Store in airtight container. Cookies can be securely wrapped and frozen up to 2 months.
Makes about 3 dozen (3-inch) cookies.

Slice 'n' Bake Lemon Cookies

2¼ cups unsifted flour
¼ teaspoon baking soda
½ cup margarine or butter, softened
½ cup shortening
½ cup granulated sugar
½ cup firmly packed light brown sugar
1 egg
3 tablespoons REALEMON® Lemon Juice from Concentrate
Egg white, beaten
Sliced almonds

Stir together flour and baking soda; set aside. In large mixer bowl, beat margarine, shortening and sugars until fluffy. Add egg; mix well. Gradually add dry ingredients and ReaLemon® brand; mix well. Chill 2 hours; form into two 10-inch rolls. Wrap well; freeze until firm. Preheat oven to 350°. Cut rolls into ¼-inch slices; place 1 inch apart on greased baking sheets. Brush with egg white; top with almonds. Bake 10 to 12 minutes or until lightly browned.
Makes about 5 dozen.

Jelly Jewels

1 package DUNCAN HINES® Deluxe Yellow Cake Mix
¾ cup CRISCO® shortening
2 large egg yolks
1 tablespoon milk
2 large egg whites
2 tablespoons water
1¼ cups ground nuts
Red or green jelly

1. Preheat oven to 375°F. Grease cookie sheets.
2. Combine dry cake mix, shortening, egg yolks and milk; mix well. Shape into 1-inch balls.
3. Combine egg whites and water. Beat with fork until blended. Dip balls in egg white mixture, then roll in nuts. Place 2 inches apart on cookie sheets.
4. Bake at 375°F for 12 to 15 minutes or until golden brown. Immediately press thumb or thimble into center of each cookie making a depression. Cool several minutes on cookie sheets, then remove to racks to finish cooling. Before serving, fill depressions with jelly.
About 4 dozen 2-inch cookies.

Almond Shortbread Cookies

2½ cups unsifted flour
1 teaspoon baking soda
1 teaspoon cream of tartar
1 cup margarine or butter, softened
1½ cups confectioners' sugar
1 egg
1 (9-ounce) package NONE SUCH® Condensed Mincemeat, crumbled
½ cup sliced almonds
½ teaspoon almond extract
Almond Frosting
Additional sliced almonds

Preheat oven to 375°. Stir together flour, baking soda and cream of tartar; set aside. In large mixer bowl, beat margarine and sugar until fluffy. Add egg; mix well. Stir in mincemeat, *½ cup* almonds and extract. Add flour mixture; mix well (dough will be stiff). Roll into 1¼-inch balls. Place on ungreased baking sheets; flatten slightly. Bake 10 to 12 minutes or until lightly browned. Cool. Frost with Almond Frosting and garnish with additional almonds if desired.
Makes about 3 dozen.
ALMOND FROSTING: In small mixer bowl, combine 2¼ cups confectioners' sugar, 3 tablespoons margarine or butter, softened, 3 tablespoons water and ½ teaspoon almond extract; beat well.
Makes about 1 cup.

Granola Cookies

1 cup sugar
½ cup CRISCO® Oil
⅓ cup honey
2 eggs
¼ cup water
2 cups unsifted all-purpose flour
1¾ cups quick-cooking rolled oats
1 teaspoon baking soda
1 teaspoon salt
1 teaspoon ground cinnamon
½ cup chopped dried apricots
½ cup raisins
½ cup chopped nuts
½ cup miniature semisweet chocolate chips
½ cup flaked coconut

Preheat oven to 350°F. Grease baking sheet. Set aside.

Mix sugar, Crisco® Oil, honey, eggs and water in large mixing bowl. Add flour, oats, baking soda, salt and cinnamon. Mix well. Stir in remaining ingredients.

Drop by teaspoonfuls about 2 inches apart onto prepared baking sheet. Bake at 350°F, about 8 minutes, or until almost no indentation remains when touched lightly. Cool on wire rack.
4½ to 5 dozen cookies.

Variation: Granola Bars. Follow recipe above, except spread dough in greased and floured 15×10-inch jelly roll pan. Bake at 350°F, about 15 minutes, or until top is light brown. Cool completely on wire rack. Cut into 48 bars.

Jelly Jewels

"Philly" Apricot Cookies

1½ cups PARKAY Margarine
1½ cups granulated sugar
1 8-ounce package
   PHILADELPHIA BRAND
   Cream Cheese, softened
2 eggs
2 tablespoons lemon juice
1½ teaspoons grated lemon peel
4½ cups flour
1½ teaspoons baking powder
   KRAFT Apricot Preserves
   Powdered sugar

Combine margarine, granulated sugar and cream cheese, mixing until well blended. Blend in eggs, juice and peel. Add combined flour and baking powder; mix well. Chill several hours. Shape level measuring tablespoonfuls of dough into balls. Place on ungreased cookie sheet; flatten slightly. Indent centers; fill with preserves. Bake at 350°, 15 minutes. Cool; sprinkle with powdered sugar.
Approximately 7 dozen.

Raisin Oatmeal Crispies

1 cup butter or margarine,
   softened
1 cup sugar
3 cups rolled oats, uncooked
¾ cup all-purpose flour
1 teaspoon baking soda
½ teaspoon ground cloves
½ teaspoon ground cinnamon
1 cup SUN-MAID® Raisins
¼ cup milk

In large bowl, blend together butter and sugar; add oats. Sift flour with baking soda, cloves and cinnamon.

Add to oats mixture, blending well. Stir in raisins and milk; mix thoroughly. Roll dough into 1-inch balls. Place 3 inches apart on greased baking sheets. Bake in preheated 350°F oven 12 to 15 minutes or until golden brown.
Makes about 4 dozen cookies.

Walnutty Ribbons

2 cups all-purpose flour
½ teaspoon baking powder
½ cup butter or margarine,
   softened
¾ cup sugar
1 egg
2 teaspoons rum flavoring
1 teaspoon vanilla
1 teaspoon grated lemon peel
1 tablespoon milk
1 cup finely chopped DIAMOND®
   Walnuts
⅓ cup orange marmalade (or
   other jam)

In medium bowl, sift flour with baking powder; set aside. In large bowl, cream butter, sugar, egg, rum, vanilla and peel. Blend in flour mixture and milk to make a stiff dough. Divide into 4 equal portions and shape each into a roll about 12 inches long. Transfer to lightly greased cookie sheets, placing rolls about 3 inches apart. Make a wide depression down center of each roll with handle of knife. In small bowl, mix walnuts with marmalade. Spoon ¼ of the mixture down center of each roll. Bake in preheated 350°F oven 15 to 20 minutes or until edges are lightly browned. Slide rolls off onto wire racks to cool. Cut into 1¼-inch slices to serve.
Makes about 3 dozen cookies.

Chocolate Crackles

10 tablespoons butter or
   margarine
6 tablespoons HERSHEY'S
   Cocoa
1 cup sugar
2 teaspoons baking powder
½ teaspoon salt
2 eggs
1 teaspoon vanilla
2 cups unsifted all-purpose flour
½ cup chopped nuts
   Confectioners' sugar

Microwave: Microwave butter in medium micro-proof bowl at HIGH (100%) for 45 to 60 seconds or until melted. Add cocoa; blend well. Beat in sugar, baking powder, salt, eggs and vanilla. Stir in flour and nuts. Refrigerate at least 8 hours or until firm.

Shape dough into 1-inch balls; roll in confectioners' sugar. Cover micro-proof plate with wax paper. Place 8 balls 2 inches apart in circular shape on wax paper. Microwave at MEDIUM (50%) for 1½ to 2 minutes or until surface is dry but cookies are soft when touched. Cool on wax paper on countertop. Repeat cooking procedure with remaining dough. Before serving, sprinkle with additional confectioners' sugar.
About 4 dozen cookies.

Pecan Tassies

1 8-ounce package
   PHILADELPHIA BRAND
   Cream Cheese, softened
1 cup PARKAY Margarine
2 cups flour
2 eggs, beaten
1½ cups packed brown sugar
2 teaspoons vanilla
1½ cups chopped pecans

Combine cream cheese and margarine, mixing until well blended. Add flour; mix well. Chill. Divide dough into quarters; divide each quarter into 12 balls. Press each ball onto bottom and sides of miniature muffin pans. Combine eggs, brown sugar and vanilla; stir in pecans. Spoon into pastry shells, filling each cup. Bake at 325°, 30 minutes or until pastry is golden brown. Cool 5 minutes; remove from pans. Sprinkle with powdered sugar, if desired.
4 dozen.

"Philly" Apricot Cookies

Reese's Cookies

- **1 cup shortening,** *or* **¾ cup butter or margarine, softened**
- **1 cup sugar**
- **½ cup packed light brown sugar**
- **1 teaspoon vanilla**
- **2 eggs**
- **2 cups unsifted all-purpose flour**
- **1 teaspoon baking soda**
- **1 cup REESE'S Peanut Butter Chips**
- **1 cup HERSHEY'S Semi-Sweet Chocolate Chips**

Cream shortening or butter, sugar, brown sugar and vanilla in large mixer bowl until light and fluffy. Add eggs; beat well. Combine flour and baking soda; add to creamed mixture. Stir in peanut butter chips and chocolate chips.

Drop by teaspoonfuls onto ungreased cookie sheet. Bake at 350° for 10 to 12 minutes or until lightly browned. Cool slightly. Remove from cookie sheet; cool completely on wire rack.

About 5 dozen cookies.

Macaroon Almond Crumb Bars

- **1 (18¼- or 18½-ounce) package chocolate cake mix**
- **¼ cup vegetable oil**
- **2 eggs**
- **1 (14-ounce) can EAGLE® Brand Sweetened Condensed Milk (NOT evaporated milk)**
- **½ to 1 teaspoon almond extract**
- **1½ cups coconut macaroon crumbs (about 8 macaroons)**
- **1 cup chopped slivered almonds**

Preheat oven to 350° (325° for glass dish). In large mixer bowl, combine cake mix, oil and *1 egg*. Beat on medium speed until crumbly. Press firmly on bottom of greased 13×9-inch baking pan. In medium mixing bowl, combine sweetened condensed milk, remaining egg and extract; mix well. Add *1 cup* macaroon crumbs and almonds. Spread evenly over prepared crust. Sprinkle with remaining *½ cup* crumbs. Bake 30 to 35 minutes or until lightly browned. Cool thoroughly. Cut into bars. Store loosely covered at room temperature.

Makes 36 bars.

Macaroon Almond Crumb Bars (top), Toffee Bars (bottom)

Rich Lemon Bars

- **1½ cups plus 3 tablespoons unsifted flour**
- **½ cup confectioners' sugar**
- **¾ cup cold margarine or butter**
- **4 eggs, slightly beaten**
- **1½ cups granulated sugar**
- **1 teaspoon baking powder**
- **½ cup REALEMON® Lemon Juice from Concentrate**
- **Additional confectioners' sugar**

Preheat oven to 350°. In medium bowl, combine *1½ cups* flour and confectioners' sugar; cut in margarine until crumbly. Press onto bottom of lightly greased 13×9-inch baking pan; bake 15 minutes. Meanwhile, in large bowl, combine eggs, granulated sugar, baking powder, ReaLemon® brand and remaining *3 tablespoons* flour; mix well. Pour over baked crust; bake 20 to 25 minutes or until golden brown. Cool. Cut into bars. Sprinkle with additional confectioners' sugar. Store covered in refrigerator; serve at room temperature.

Makes 30 bars.

Lemon Pecan Bars: Omit 3 tablespoons flour in lemon mixture. Sprinkle ¾ cup finely chopped pecans over top of lemon mixture. Bake as above.

Coconut Lemon Bars: Omit 3 tablespoons flour in lemon mixture. Sprinkle ¾ cup flaked coconut over top of lemon mixture. Bake as above.

Toffee Bars

- **½ cup margarine or butter**
- **1 cup oats**
- **½ cup firmly packed brown sugar**
- **½ cup unsifted flour**
- **½ cup finely chopped walnuts**
- **¼ teaspoon baking soda**
- **1 (14-ounce) can EAGLE® Brand Sweetened Condensed Milk (NOT evaporated milk)**
- **2 teaspoons vanilla extract**
- **1 (6-ounce) package semi-sweet chocolate chips**

Preheat oven to 350°. In medium saucepan, melt *6 tablespoons* margarine; stir in oats, sugar, flour, nuts and baking soda. Press firmly on bottom of greased 13×9-inch baking pan; bake 10 to 15 minutes or until lightly browned. Meanwhile, in medium saucepan, combine remaining *2 tablespoons* margarine and sweetened condensed milk. Over medium heat, cook and stir until mixture thickens slightly, about 15 minutes. Remove from heat; stir in vanilla. Pour over crust. Return to oven; bake 10 to 15 minutes longer, or until golden brown. Remove from oven; immediately sprinkle chips on top. Let stand 1 minute; spread while still warm. Cool to room temperature; chill thoroughly. Cut into bars. Store tightly covered at room temperature.

Makes 36 bars.

Festive Cookie Bars

Bottom Layer:
- 1¼ cups all-purpose flour
- 1 teaspoon granulated sugar
- 1 teaspoon baking powder
  Dash salt
- ⅔ cup butter or margarine
- 2 tablespoons cold coffee or water
- 1 egg yolk
- 1 package (12 ounces) real semisweet chocolate pieces

Top Layer:
- ½ cup butter or margarine, softened
- 1 cup granulated sugar
- 1 tablespoon vanilla
- 2 eggs plus 1 egg white
- 1 cup SUN-MAID® Raisins
- 1 cup DIAMOND® Walnuts
  Powdered sugar, for garnish

To prepare bottom layer: In large bowl, combine flour, granulated sugar, baking powder and salt. Cut in butter until mixture resembles coarse crumbs. In small bowl, mix coffee and egg yolk to blend; stir into flour mixture to moisten evenly. Form dough into a roll. With floured fingertips, press evenly onto bottom of greased 15×10-inch jelly-roll pan. (Layer will be thin.) Bake in preheated 350°F oven 10 minutes. Sprinkle chocolate pieces evenly over crust; return to oven 2 minutes to melt chocolate. Remove from oven; spread evenly with spatula. Allow to stand several minutes to set.

To prepare top layer: In large bowl, cream butter, granulated sugar and vanilla. Beat in eggs and egg white, one at a time, mixing well after each addition. (Mixture will appear slightly curdled.) Stir in raisins and walnuts. Spread evenly over chocolate layer. Return to oven; bake 20 to 25 minutes or until top is browned. Dust with powdered sugar. Cool in pan; cut into bars.
Makes 3½ to 4 dozen bars.
   Note: Cookies freeze well.

Frosted Toffee Bars

- 2 cups QUAKER® Oats (Quick or Old Fashioned), uncooked
- ½ cup packed brown sugar
- ½ cup margarine, melted
- ½ cup semisweet chocolate chips
- ¼ cup chopped peanuts

In medium bowl, combine oats, sugar and margarine; mix well. Spread in greased 9-inch square pan. Bake in preheated 350° oven 13 minutes or until light golden brown; cool. In small, heavy saucepan over low heat, melt chips. Spread over oat mixture; sprinkle with nuts. Refrigerate until chocolate is set. Cut into 2×1½-inch bars. Store in tightly covered container in refrigerator.
Makes about 2 dozen bars.

Coconut Dream Bars

- 1 cup flour
- ¼ cup firmly packed brown sugar
- ⅓ cup softened butter or margarine
- 2 eggs
- ¾ cup firmly packed brown sugar
- ¼ cup flour
- ½ teaspoon CALUMET® Baking Powder
- 1⅓ cups (about) BAKER'S® ANGEL FLAKE® Coconut
- 1 teaspoon vanilla
- 1 cup chopped walnuts

Combine 1 cup flour and ¼ cup brown sugar. Add butter and mix until blended. Press into ungreased 9-inch square pan; bake at 350° for 15 minutes. Meanwhile, beat eggs until thick and light in color. Gradually beat in ¾ cup brown sugar and continue beating until mixture is light and fluffy. Mix ¼ cup flour with the baking powder; fold into egg mixture. Mix in coconut, vanilla and nuts. Spread over baked crust in pan. Bake 20 to 25 minutes longer or until lightly browned. Cool; cut in bars, triangles or squares.
Makes about 2 dozen.

Chocolate 'n' Oat Bars

- 1 cup unsifted flour
- 1 cup quick-cooking oats
- ¾ cup firmly packed light brown sugar
- ½ cup margarine or butter, softened
- 1 (14-ounce) can EAGLE® Brand Sweetened Condensed Milk (NOT evaporated milk)
- 1 cup chopped nuts
- 1 (6-ounce) package semi-sweet chocolate chips

Preheat oven to 350° (325° for glass dish). In large bowl, combine flour, oats, sugar and margarine; mix well. Reserving ½ cup oat mixture, press remainder on bottom of 13×9-inch baking pan. Bake 10 minutes. Pour sweetened condensed milk evenly over crust. Sprinkle with nuts and chocolate chips. Top with remaining oat mixture; press down firmly. Bake 25 to 30 minutes or until lightly browned. Cool. Cut into bars. Store covered at room temperature.
Makes 36 bars.

Chocolate 'n' Oat Bars

Triple Layer Cookie Bars (left), Pecan Pie Bars (right)

Triple Layer Cookie Bars

½ cup margarine or butter
1½ cups graham cracker crumbs
1 (7-ounce) package flaked coconut (2⅔ cups)
1 (14-ounce) can EAGLE® Brand Sweetened Condensed Milk (NOT evaporated milk)
1 (12-ounce) package semi-sweet chocolate chips
½ cup creamy peanut butter

Preheat oven to 350° (325° for glass dish). In 13×9-inch baking pan, melt margarine in oven. Sprinkle crumbs evenly over margarine. Top evenly with coconut then sweetened condensed milk. Bake 25 minutes or until lightly browned. In small saucepan, over low heat, melt chips with peanut butter. Spread evenly over hot coconut layer. Cool 30 minutes. Chill thoroughly. Cut into bars. Store loosely covered at room temperature.
Makes 36 bars.

Pecan Pie Bars

2 cups unsifted flour
½ cup confectioners' sugar
1 cup cold margarine or butter
1 (14-ounce) can EAGLE® Brand Sweetened Condensed Milk (NOT evaporated milk)
1 egg
1 teaspoon vanilla extract
1 (6-ounce) package almond brickle chips
1 cup chopped pecans

Preheat oven to 350° (325° for glass dish). In medium bowl, combine flour and sugar; cut in margarine until crumbly. Press firmly on bottom of 13×9-inch baking pan. Bake 15 minutes. Meanwhile, in medium bowl, beat sweetened condensed milk, egg and vanilla. Stir in chips and pecans. Spread evenly over crust. Bake 25 minutes or until golden brown. Cool. Cut into bars. Store covered in refrigerator.
Makes 36 bars.

Crunch Bars

5 cups bite-size crispy rice or wheat square cereal
½ cup margarine or butter
1 cup butterscotch *or* peanut butter flavored chips
1 (3½-ounce) can flaked coconut (1⅓ cups)
1 (14-ounce) can EAGLE® Brand Sweetened Condensed Milk (NOT evaporated milk)
1 cup chopped pecans

Preheat oven to 350° (325° for glass dish). Coarsely crush *3 cups* cereal. In 13×9-inch baking pan, melt margarine in oven. Sprinkle crushed cereal over margarine; top evenly with chips, coconut, sweetened condensed milk, nuts and *2 cups* uncrushed cereal. Press down firmly. Bake 25 to 30 minutes or until lightly browned. Cool thoroughly. Cut into bars. Store loosely covered at room temperature.
Makes 36 bars.

Magic Cookie Bars

½ cup margarine or butter
1½ cups graham cracker *or* other
    crumbs*
1 (14-ounce) EAGLE® Brand
    Sweetened Condensed Milk
    (NOT evaporated milk)
1 cup semi-sweet chocolate
    chips *or* other toppings**
1 (3½-ounce) can flaked
    coconut (1⅓ cups)
1 cup chopped nuts***

Preheat oven to 350° (325° for glass dish). In 13×9-inch baking pan, melt margarine in oven. Sprinkle crumbs over margarine; pour sweetened condensed milk evenly over crumbs. Sprinkle with chips then coconut and nuts; press down firmly. Bake 25 to 30 minutes or until lightly browned. Cool. Chill thoroughly if desired. Cut into bars. Store loosely covered at room temperature.
Makes 36 bars.

Crumbs: Vanilla wafer, chocolate wafer, ginger snap cookie, quick-cooking oats, wheat germ.

****Toppings:** Peanut butter flavored chips, butterscotch flavored chips, plain multi-colored candy-coated chocolate pieces, raisins, chopped dried apricots, almond brickle chips, banana chips, chopped candied cherries, small gumdrop candies, miniature marshmallows.

*****Nuts:** Walnuts, pecans, almonds, peanuts, cashews, macadamia nuts.

Flavor Variations:

Mint: Combine ½ teaspoon peppermint extract and 4 drops green food coloring if desired with sweetened condensed milk. Proceed as above.

Mocha: Add 1 tablespoon instant coffee and 1 tablespoon chocolate flavored syrup with sweetened condensed milk. Proceed as above.

Peanut Butter: Combine ⅓ cup peanut butter with sweetened condensed milk. Proceed as above.

Maple: Combine ½ to 1 teaspoon maple flavoring with sweetened condensed milk. Proceed as above.

Seven Layer Magic Cookie Bars: Add 1 (6-ounce) package butterscotch flavored chips after chocolate chips.

Magic Cookie Bars

Apple Raisin Snack Bars

1½ cups old fashioned or quick
    oats, uncooked
¾ cup flour
½ cup packed brown sugar
¼ cup granulated sugar
¾ cup PARKAY Margarine

* * *

2 8-ounce packages
    PHILADELPHIA BRAND
    Cream Cheese, softened
2 eggs
1 cup chopped apple
⅓ cup raisins
1 tablespoon granulated sugar
½ teaspoon cinnamon

Combine oats, flour and sugars; cut in margarine until mixture resembles coarse crumbs. Reserve 1 cup oat mixture; press remaining mixture onto bottom of greased 13×9-inch baking pan. Bake at 350°, 15 minutes.

Combine cream cheese and eggs, mixing until well blended. Pour over crust. Top with combined remaining ingredients; sprinkle with reserved oat mixture. Bake at 350°, 25 minutes. Cool; cut into bars.
Approximately 1½ dozen.

Variation: Substitute *Light* PHILADELPHIA BRAND Neufchâtel Cheese for Cream Cheese.

Chocolate Streusel Bars

1¾ cups unsifted flour
1½ cups confectioners' sugar
½ cup unsweetened cocoa
1 cup cold margarine or butter
1 (8-ounce) package cream
    cheese, softened
1 (14-ounce) can EAGLE® Brand
    Sweetened Condensed Milk
    (NOT evaporated milk)
1 egg
2 teaspoons vanilla extract
½ cup chopped walnuts, optional

Preheat oven to 350°. In large bowl, combine flour, sugar and cocoa; mix well. Cut in margarine until crumbly (mixture will be dry). Reserving 2 cups crumb mixture, press remainder firmly on bottom of 13×9-inch baking pan. Bake 15 minutes. Meanwhile, in large mixer bowl, beat cheese until fluffy. Gradually beat in sweetened condensed milk until smooth. Add egg and vanilla; mix well. Pour evenly over baked crust. Combine reserved crumb mixture with nuts if desired; sprinkle evenly over cheese mixture. Bake 25 minutes or until bubbly. Cool. Chill. Cut into bars. Store covered in refrigerator.
Makes 24 to 36 bars.

Raspberry Oatmeal Bars

1 package DUNCAN HINES®
Deluxe Yellow Cake Mix
2½ cups quick-cooking oats
¾ cup (1½ sticks) butter or
margarine, melted
1 cup (12-ounce jar) raspberry
preserves or jam*
1 tablespoon water

1. Preheat oven to 375°F. Grease 13×9×2-inch pan.
2. Combine dry cake mix and oats in large bowl; add melted butter and stir until crumbly. Measure half of crumb mixture (about 3 cups) into pan. Press firmly to cover bottom. Combine preserves and water; stir until blended. Spread over crumb mixture in pan. Sprinkle remaining crumb mixture over preserves; pat firmly to make top even.
3. Bake at 375°F for 18 to 23 minutes or until top is very light brown. Cool in pan on rack; cut into bars. Store in airtight container.
4 dozen bars.

*Apricot, blackberry or strawberry preserves can be substituted.

Fruit & Nut Snack Bars

½ cup margarine or butter,
softened
1¼ cups granulated sugar
3 eggs
1⅓ cups (one-half jar) NONE
SUCH® Ready-to-Use
Mincemeat (Regular *or*
Brandy & Rum)
½ cup chopped pecans
2 (1-ounce) squares
unsweetened chocolate,
melted
¼ teaspoon salt
1½ cups unsifted flour
Confectioners' sugar
Pecan halves, optional

Preheat oven to 350°. In large mixer bowl, beat margarine and granulated sugar until fluffy. Add eggs; beat well. Stir in mincemeat, chopped pecans, chocolate and salt; mix well. Stir in flour. Spread evenly into lightly greased 13×9-inch baking pan. Bake 30 minutes or until wooden pick inserted near center comes out clean. Cool. Sprinkle with confectioners' sugar. Cut into bars. Garnish with pecan halves if desired.
Makes 24 to 36 bars.

Lebkuchen Jewels

¾ cup packed brown sugar
1 egg
1 cup honey
1 tablespoon grated lemon peel
1 teaspoon lemon juice
2¾ cups all-purpose flour
1 teaspoon *each* ground
nutmeg, cinnamon and
cloves
½ teaspoon *each* baking soda
and salt
1 cup SUN-MAID® Golden
Raisins
½ cup *each* mixed candied fruits
and citron
1 cup chopped DIAMOND®
Walnuts
Lemon Glaze (recipe follows)
Candied cherries and citron,
for garnish

In large bowl, beat sugar and egg until smooth and fluffy. Add honey, lemon peel and juice; beat well. In medium bowl, sift flour with nutmeg, cinnamon, cloves, baking soda and salt; gradually mix into egg-sugar mixture on low speed. Stir in fruits and nuts. Spread batter into greased 15×10-inch jelly-roll pan. Bake in preheated 375°F oven 20 minutes or until lightly browned. Cool slightly in pan; brush with Lemon Glaze. Cool; cut into diamonds. Decorate with candied cherries and slivers of citron, if desired. Store in covered container up to 1 month.
Makes about 4 dozen.
LEMON GLAZE: In small bowl, combine 1 cup sifted powdered sugar with enough lemon juice (1½ to 2 tablespoons) to make a thin glaze.

Jungle Bars

2 ripe, medium DOLE™ Bananas
8 ounces dried figs
8 ounces dried apricots
8 ounces DOLE™ Pitted Dates
8 ounces DOLE™ Raisins
2 cups granola
8 ounces DOLE™ Chopped
Natural Almonds, toasted
1 cup flaked coconut

Coarsely chop bananas, figs, apricots, dates, raisins and granola in food processor or run through food grinder. Stir in almonds. Press mixture into greased 13×9-inch baking dish. Sprinkle with coconut. Cover; refrigerate 24 hours to allow flavors to blend. Cut into squares.
Makes 24 bars.

Raspberry Oatmeal Bars

Pumpkin Cheesecake Bars

- 1 (16-ounce) package pound cake mix
- 3 eggs
- 2 tablespoons margarine or butter, melted
- 4 teaspoons pumpkin pie spice
- 1 (8-ounce) package cream cheese, softened
- 1 (14-ounce) can EAGLE® Brand Sweetened Condensed Milk (NOT evaporated milk)
- 1 (16-ounce) can pumpkin (about 2 cups)
- ½ teaspoon salt
- 1 cup chopped nuts

Preheat oven to 350°. In large mixer bowl, on low speed, combine cake mix, *1 egg,* margarine and *2 teaspoons* pumpkin pie spice until crumbly. Press onto bottom of 15×10-inch jellyroll pan. In large mixer bowl, beat cheese until fluffy. Gradually beat in sweetened condensed milk then remaining *2 eggs,* pumpkin, remaining *2 teaspoons* pumpkin pie spice and salt; mix well. Pour over crust; sprinkle with nuts. Bake 30 to 35 minutes or until set. Cool. Chill; cut into bars. Store covered in refrigerator.
Makes 48 bars.

Pineapple Dream Bars

- ½ cup butter or margarine, softened
- 1 cup dark brown sugar, packed
- 1⅓ cups flour
- 1 can (8¼ ounces) DOLE® Crushed Pineapple
- 2 eggs
- 1 teaspoon baking powder
- 1 teaspoon ground cinnamon
- ¼ teaspoon ground nutmeg
- ¼ teaspoon salt
- 1 teaspoon rum extract
- 1½ cups flaked coconut
- 1 cup chopped walnuts
- ½ cup chopped maraschino cherries

Preheat oven to 350°F. In medium mixer bowl, beat butter and ⅓ cup brown sugar. Blend in 1 cup flour until mixture is crumbly. Pat into bottom of 13×9-inch baking pan. Bake in preheated oven 10 to 15 minutes or until golden. Keep oven hot, but remove pan to cool.

Drain pineapple well, pressing out excess liquid with back of spoon. In large bowl, beat eggs with remaining ⅔ cup brown sugar until thick. In small bowl, combine remaining ⅓ cup flour, baking powder, cinnamon, nutmeg and salt. Stir dry ingredients and extract into egg mixture. Fold in pine-apple, coconut, nuts and cherries. Spread over baked crust. Bake 30 minutes longer or until set. Cool slightly on wire rack before cutting into bars.
Makes 18 bars.

Apple Crumb Squares

- 2 cups QUAKER® Oats (Quick or Old Fashioned), uncooked
- 1½ cups all-purpose flour
- ¾ cup margarine, melted
- 1 cup firmly packed brown sugar
- 1 teaspoon cinnamon
- ½ teaspoon salt (optional)
- ½ teaspoon baking soda
- ¼ teaspoon ground nutmeg
- 1 cup applesauce
- ½ cup chopped nuts

Heat oven to 375°F. Grease 13×9-inch baking pan. Combine all ingredients *except* applesauce and nuts; mix until crumbly. Reserve 1 cup mixture. Press remaining mixture onto bottom of prepared pan. Bake 15 minutes; cool. Spread applesauce over partially baked crust; sprinkle with nuts. Top with reserved 1 cup oat mixture. Bake 13 to 15 minutes or until golden brown. Cool in pan on wire rack; cut into 2-inch squares.
Makes about 2 dozen squares.

Pumpkin Cheesecake Bars

Chocolate Pecan Bars

- 1¼ cups unsifted flour
- 1 cup confectioners' sugar
- ½ cup unsweetened cocoa
- 1 cup cold margarine or butter
- 1 (14-ounce) can EAGLE® Brand Sweetened Condensed Milk (NOT evaporated milk)
- 1 egg
- 2 teaspoons vanilla extract
- 1½ cups chopped pecans

Preheat oven to 350° (325° for glass dish). In large bowl, combine flour, sugar and cocoa; cut in margarine until crumbly. Press firmly on bottom of 13×9-inch baking pan. Bake 15 minutes. Meanwhile, in medium bowl, beat sweetened condensed milk, egg and vanilla. Stir in pecans. Spread evenly over baked crust. Bake 25 minutes or until lightly browned. Cool. Cut into bars. Store covered in refrigerator.
Makes 36 bars.

Marble Squares

1/2 cup PARKAY Margarine
3/4 cup water
1 1/2 1-ounce squares unsweetened
    chocolate
2 cups flour
2 cups sugar
1 teaspoon baking soda
1/2 teaspoon salt
2 eggs, beaten
1/2 cup sour cream

* * *

1 8-ounce package
    PHILADELPHIA BRAND
    Cream Cheese, softened
1/3 cup sugar
1 egg
1 6-ounce package semi-sweet
    chocolate pieces

Combine margarine, water and chocolate in saucepan; bring to a boil. Remove from heat. Stir in combined flour, sugar, baking soda and salt. Add eggs and sour cream; mix well. Pour into greased and floured 15×10×1-inch jelly roll pan.

Combine cream cheese and sugar, mixing until well blended. Blend in egg. Spoon over chocolate batter. Cut through batter with knife several times for marble effect. Sprinkle with chocolate pieces. Bake at 375°, 25 to 30 minutes or until wooden pick inserted in center comes out clean.
Approximately 2 dozen.

Marble Squares

Peanutty Chocolate Snack Squares

5 graham crackers, broken into
    squares
1/2 cup sugar
1 cup light corn syrup
1 cup HERSHEY'S Semi-Sweet
    Chocolate Chips
1 cup peanut butter
1 cup dry roasted peanuts

Microwave: Line bottom of 8-inch square pan with graham cracker squares, cutting to fit as necessary. Combine sugar and corn syrup in 2-quart micro-proof bowl. Microwave at HIGH (100%), stirring every 2 minutes, until mixture boils; boil 3 minutes. Stir in chocolate chips, peanut butter and peanuts. Pour over crackers; spread carefully. Cover; refrigerate until firm. Cut into 2-inch squares.
16 squares.

Cherry Scotchies

2 cups plus 2 tablespoons all-
    purpose flour
3/4 cup packed brown sugar
3/4 cup LAND O LAKES® Sweet
    Cream Butter, softened
1/2 cup flaked coconut
1 egg
1 teaspoon baking powder
1/2 teaspoon salt
2 teaspoons vanilla
1/2 cup chopped maraschino
    cherries, drained
1 package (6 ounces)
    butterscotch chips
Powdered sugar

In large bowl, combine 2 cups flour, the brown sugar, butter, coconut, egg, baking powder, salt and vanilla; beat until well mixed. In small bowl, toss remaining 2 tablespoons flour with drained cherries. Stir cherries and chips into batter. Spread in greased and floured 13×9×2-inch pan. Bake in preheated 375°F oven 20 to 25 minutes or until edges are lightly browned. Cool completely in pan on wire rack. Sprinkle with powdered sugar; cut into bars.
Makes 3 dozen bars.

Minty Chocolate Squares

1 6-ounce package semi-sweet
    chocolate pieces
1 cup PARKAY Margarine
1 3/4 cups graham cracker crumbs
1 cup flaked coconut
1/2 cup chopped nuts
2 8-ounce packages
    PHILADELPHIA BRAND
    Cream Cheese, softened
1 cup sifted powdered sugar
1/2 teaspoon mint extract
    Few drops green food coloring
    (optional)

Melt 1/3 cup chocolate pieces with 3/4 cup margarine over low heat, stirring until smooth. Add combined crumbs, coconut and nuts; mix well. Press onto bottom of ungreased 13×9-inch baking pan; chill. Combine cream cheese, sugar, extract and food coloring, mixing until well blended. Spread over crust; chill. Melt remaining chocolate pieces with remaining margarine over low heat, stirring until smooth. Spread over cream cheese layer; chill. Cut into squares. Serve chilled.
Approximately 3 dozen.

Scrumptious Chocolate Layer Bars

2 cups (12-ounce package) HERSHEY'S Semi-Sweet Chocolate Chips
1 package (8 ounces) cream cheese
1/2 cup plus 2 tablespoons (5-ounce can) evaporated milk
1 cup chopped walnuts
1/4 cup sesame seeds (optional)
1/2 teaspoon almond extract
3 cups unsifted all-purpose flour
1 1/2 cups sugar
1 teaspoon baking powder
1/2 teaspoon salt
1 cup butter or margarine
2 eggs
1/2 teaspoon almond extract

Combine chocolate chips, cream cheese and evaporated milk in medium saucepan. Cook over low heat, stirring constantly, until chips are melted and mixture is smooth. Remove from heat; stir in walnuts, sesame seeds and 1/2 teaspoon almond extract. Blend well; set aside.

Combine remaining ingredients in large mixer bowl; blend well on low speed until mixture resembles coarse crumbs. Press half the mixture in greased 13×9-inch pan; spread with chocolate mixture. Sprinkle rest of crumbs over filling. (If mixture softens and forms a stiff dough, pinch off small pieces to use as topping.) Bake at 375° for 35 to 40 minutes or until golden brown. Cool; cut into bars.

About 3 dozen bars.

Lemon Iced Ambrosia Bars

1 1/2 cups unsifted flour
1/3 cup confectioners' sugar
3/4 cup cold margarine or butter
2 cups firmly packed light brown sugar
4 eggs, beaten
1 cup flaked coconut
1 cup finely chopped pecans
3 tablespoons flour
1/2 teaspoon baking powder
Lemon Icing*

Preheat oven to 350°. In medium bowl, combine flour and confectioners' sugar; cut in margarine until crumbly. Press onto bottom of lightly greased 13×9-inch baking pan; bake 15 minutes. Meanwhile, in large bowl, combine remaining ingredients except icing; mix well. Spread evenly over baked crust; bake 20 to 25 minutes. Cool. Spread with Lemon Icing; chill. Cut into bars. Store covered in refrigerator.

Makes 36 bars.

*LEMON ICING: Combine 2 cups confectioners' sugar, 3 tablespoons REALEMON® Lemon Juice from Concentrate and 2 tablespoons softened margarine; mix until smooth.

Makes about 2/3 cup.

Double-Deck Brownies

2/3 cup flour
1/2 teaspoon CALUMET® Baking Powder
1/4 teaspoon salt
2 eggs
1 cup sugar
1/2 cup butter or margarine, melted and cooled
1/3 cup BAKER'S® ANGEL FLAKE® Coconut
1/4 teaspoon almond extract
2 squares BAKER'S® Unsweetened Chocolate, melted
1 square BAKER'S® Semi-Sweet Chocolate, melted

Mix flour, baking powder and salt. Beat eggs thoroughly. Gradually add sugar and continue beating until light and fluffy. Blend in butter; then

Lemon Iced Ambrosia Bars

stir in flour mixture. Measure 1/2 cup into small bowl. Stir in coconut and almond extract; set aside. Add unsweetened chocolate to remaining batter; spread in greased 8-inch square pan. Drop coconut batter by teaspoonfuls over chocolate batter. Then spread carefully to form a thin layer. Bake at 350° for 30 to 35 minutes or until lightly browned. Cool in pan. Drizzle with semi-sweet chocolate. Cut into squares or bars.

Makes about 20.

Peanut Butter Paisley Brownies

1/2 cup butter or margarine, softened
1/4 cup peanut butter
1 cup sugar
1 cup packed light brown sugar
3 eggs
1 teaspoon vanilla
2 cups unsifted all-purpose flour
2 teaspoons baking powder
1/4 teaspoon salt
1/2 cup (5.5-ounce can) HERSHEY'S Syrup

Blend butter and peanut butter in large mixer bowl. Add sugar and brown sugar; beat well. Add eggs, one at a time, beating well after each addition. Blend in vanilla. Combine flour, baking powder and salt; add to peanut butter mixture.

Spread half the batter in greased 13×9-inch pan. Spoon syrup over top. Carefully spread with remaining batter. Swirl with spatula or knife for marbled effect. Bake at 350° for 35 to 40 minutes or until lightly browned. Cool; cut into squares.

About 3 dozen brownies.

Cheesecake Bars

2 cups unsifted flour
1 1/2 cups firmly packed brown sugar
1 cup cold margarine or butter
1 1/2 cups quick-cooking oats
2 (8-ounce) packages cream cheese, softened
1/2 cup granulated sugar
3 eggs
1/4 cup BORDEN® or MEADOW GOLD® Milk
1 teaspoon vanilla extract
1/4 cup REALEMON® Lemon Juice from Concentrate

Preheat oven to 350°. In bowl, combine flour and brown sugar; cut in margarine until crumbly. Stir in oats. Reserving 1½ cups mixture, press remainder into 15×10-inch jellyroll pan; bake 10 minutes. Meanwhile, in large mixer bowl, beat cheese and granulated sugar until fluffy. Add eggs; beat well. Add milk and vanilla, then ReaLemon® brand; beat well. Pour over crust; sprinkle with reserved mixture. Bake 25 minutes or until lightly browned. Cool. Refrigerate. *Makes 40 bars.*

Lemony Raisin-Coconut Squares

Crust:
- **¼ cup butter or margarine, softened**
- **½ cup packed light brown sugar**
- **1 cup all-purpose flour**
- **¼ cup toasted shredded coconut***

Topping:
- **2 eggs**
- **1 cup packed light brown sugar**
- **1 tablespoon grated lemon peel**
- **¼ cup lemon juice**
- **¼ teaspoon salt**
- **1½ cups SUN-MAID® Raisins**
- **¾ cup toasted shredded coconut***
- **Powdered sugar, for garnish**

To prepare crust: In small bowl, cream butter and the ½ cup brown sugar. Blend in flour and the ¼ cup coconut. Mixture will be dry. Grease 9-inch square cake pan. Line bottom and 2 opposite sides with foil, allowing foil to extend slightly beyond edges; generously grease foil. Press crust mixture evenly into bottom of pan. Bake in preheated 350°F oven about 12 minutes or until edges brown lightly. Remove from oven.

To prepare topping: In medium bowl, beat eggs until foamy with electric mixer. Add the 1 cup brown sugar, the lemon peel and juice, and salt. Beat 2 minutes. Stir in raisins and coconut. Spread topping evenly over crust. Bake 20 to 25 minutes or until top begins to brown. Cool in pan. Loosen edges with sharp knife. Grasp foil edges and lift out of pan. With sharp knife, cut into 16 squares. Dust with powdered sugar, if desired. *Makes 16 squares.*

*To toast 1 cup coconut, spread in shallow baking pan. Bake in 350°F oven about 10 minutes or until lightly browned, stirring occasionally. Cool.

Clockwise from top left: Peanut Butter Paisley Brownies, Scrumptious Chocolate Layer Bars and Best Brownies

Best Brownies

- **½ cup butter or margarine, melted**
- **1 cup sugar**
- **1 teaspoon vanilla**
- **2 eggs**
- **½ cup unsifted all-purpose flour**
- **⅓ cup HERSHEY'S Cocoa**
- **¼ teaspoon baking powder**
- **¼ teaspoon salt**
- **½ cup chopped nuts (optional) Creamy Brownie Frosting**

Blend butter, sugar and vanilla in large bowl. Add eggs; using a wooden spoon, beat well. Combine flour, cocoa, baking powder and salt; gradually blend into egg mixture. Stir in nuts.

Spread in greased 9-inch square pan. Bake at 350° for 20 to 25 minutes or until brownie begins to pull away from edges of pan. Cool; frost with Creamy Brownie Frosting. Cut into squares. *About 16 brownies.*

Creamy Brownie Frosting

- **3 tablespoons butter or margarine, softened**
- **3 tablespoons HERSHEY'S Cocoa**
- **1 tablespoon light corn syrup or honey**
- **½ teaspoon vanilla**
- **1 cup confectioners' sugar**
- **1 to 2 tablespoons milk**

Cream butter, cocoa, corn syrup and vanilla in small mixer bowl. Add confectioners' sugar and milk; beat to spreading consistency. *About 1 cup frosting.*

Dorchester Fudge

Creamy White Fudge

- **1½ pounds white confectioners' coating***
- **1 (14-ounce) can EAGLE® Brand Sweetened Condensed Milk (NOT evaporated milk)**
- **⅛ teaspoon salt**
- **¾ to 1 cup chopped nuts**
- **1½ teaspoons vanilla extract**

In heavy saucepan, over low heat, melt coating with sweetened condensed milk and salt. Remove from heat; stir in nuts and vanilla. Spread evenly into wax paper-lined 8- or 9-inch square pan. Chill 2 hours or until firm. Turn fudge onto cutting board; peel off paper and cut into squares. Store tightly covered at room temperature.

Makes about 2¼ pounds.

Microwave: In 2-quart glass measure, combine coating, sweetened condensed milk and salt. Microwave on full power (high) 3 to 5 minutes or until coating melts, stirring after 3 minutes. Stir in nuts and vanilla. Proceed as above.

Praline Fudge: Omit vanilla. Add 1 teaspoon maple flavoring and 1 cup chopped pecans. Proceed as above.

Confetti Fudge: Omit nuts. Add 1 cup chopped mixed candied fruit. Proceed as above.   *(continued)*

Rum Raisin Fudge: Omit vanilla. Add 1½ teaspoons white vinegar, 1 teaspoon rum flavoring and ¾ cup raisins. Proceed as above.

Cherry Fudge: Omit nuts. Add 1 cup chopped candied cherries.

*White confectioners' coating can be purchased in candy specialty stores.

Raspberry Fudge Balls

- **1 8-ounce package PHILADELPHIA BRAND Cream Cheese, softened**
- **1 6-ounce package semi-sweet chocolate pieces, melted**
- **¾ cup vanilla wafer crumbs**
- **¼ cup KRAFT Raspberry Preserves, strained**
- **Finely chopped almonds**
- **Cocoa**
- **Powdered sugar**

Combine cream cheese and chocolate, mixing until well blended. Stir in crumbs and preserves. Chill several hours or overnight. Shape into 1-inch balls; roll in almonds, cocoa or sugar. *Approximately 3 dozen.*

Dorchester Fudge

- **1 package (8 squares) BAKER'S® Semi-Sweet Chocolate, finely chopped**
- **½ cup marshmallow topping**
- **½ cup chopped nuts* (optional)**
- **¼ cup butter or margarine, at room temperature**
- **½ teaspoon vanilla**
- **1½ cups sugar**
- **⅔ cup evaporated milk**

Place chocolate in a bowl with marshmallow topping, nuts, butter and vanilla; set aside. Combine sugar and milk in 2-quart saucepan. Cook and stir over medium heat until mixture comes to a *full rolling boil.* Keep at full rolling boil 5 minutes, stirring constantly. Carefully pour boiling sugar syrup over chocolate mixture and stir until chocolate is melted. Pour into buttered 8-inch square pan. Chill until firm, about 1 hour. Cut into squares.

Makes 1½ pounds or about 3 dozen pieces.

*Or use 1 cup BAKER'S® ANGEL FLAKE® Coconut.

Mocha Almond Fudge: Prepare Dorchester Fudge as directed, using chopped toasted blanched almonds for the nuts and adding 2 teaspoons MAXWELL HOUSE® or YUBAN® Instant Coffee to milk mixture.

Peanut Butter Fudge: Prepare Dorchester Fudge as directed, substituting ½ cup peanut butter for the nuts and butter.

Fudge Shapes: Prepare Dorchester Fudge as directed, omitting the nuts; cool slightly and pour fudge mixture onto waxed paper on baking sheet. Top with waxed paper and roll with rolling pin until ½ inch thick. Remove top paper; run tines of fork across surface, scoring fudge. Chill until firm; then cut into shapes with small cookie cutters. Garnish with toasted almonds, if desired.

Rich Cocoa Fudge

- **3 cups sugar**
- **⅔ cup HERSHEY'S Cocoa**
- **⅛ teaspoon salt**
- **1½ cups milk**
- **¼ cup butter or margarine**
- **1 teaspoon vanilla**

Butter 8- or 9-inch square pan; set aside. Combine sugar, cocoa and salt in heavy 4-quart saucepan; stir in milk. Cook over medium heat, stirring constantly, until mixture comes to full rolling boil. Boil, without stirring, to soft-ball stage, 234°F on a candy thermometer (or until syrup, when dropped into very cold water, forms a soft ball that flattens when removed from water). Bulb of candy thermometer should not rest on bottom of saucepan.

Remove from heat. Add butter and vanilla; *do not stir.* Cool at room temperature to 110°F (lukewarm). Beat until fudge thickens and loses some of its gloss. Quickly spread in prepared pan; cool. Cut into 1- to 1½-inch squares.
About 3 dozen candies.

Variations: Nutty Rich Cocoa Fudge: Beat cooked fudge as directed. *Immediately* stir in 1 cup broken almonds, pecans or walnuts and quickly spread in prepared pan.

Marshmallow-Nut Cocoa Fudge: Increase cocoa to ¾ cup. Cook fudge as directed. Add 1 cup marshmallow creme with butter and vanilla; *do not stir.* Cool to 110°F (lukewarm). Beat 10 minutes; stir in 1 cup broken nuts and pour into prepared pan. (Fudge does not set until poured into pan).

Chocolate "Philly" Fudge

    4 cups sifted powdered sugar
    1 8-ounce package
        PHILADELPHIA BRAND
        Cream Cheese, softened
    4 1-ounce squares unsweetened
        chocolate, melted
    1 teaspoon vanilla
        Dash of salt
    ½ cup chopped nuts

Gradually add sugar to cream cheese, mixing well after each addition. Add remaining ingredients; mix well. Spread into greased 8-inch square pan. Chill several hours; cut into squares.
1¾ pounds.

Variations: Omit vanilla and nuts; add few drops peppermint extract and ¼ cup crushed peppermint candy. Sprinkle with additional ¼ cup crushed peppermint candy before chilling.

Omit nuts; add 1 cup shredded coconut. Garnish with additional coconut.

Omit nuts; add ½ cup chopped maraschino cherries, drained. Garnish with whole cherries.

Double-Decker Fudge

    1 cup REESE'S Peanut Butter
        Chips
    1 cup HERSHEY'S Semi-Sweet
        Chocolate Chips
    2¼ cups sugar
    1¾ cups (7-ounce jar)
        marshmallow creme
    ¾ cup evaporated milk
    ¼ cup butter
    1 teaspoon vanilla

Measure peanut butter chips into one bowl and chocolate chips into another; set aside. Butter 8-inch square pan; set aside. Combine sugar, marshmallow creme, evaporated milk and butter in heavy 3-quart saucepan. Cook over medium heat, stirring constantly, until mixture boils; continue cooking and stirring for 5 minutes.

Remove from heat; stir in vanilla. Immediately stir half the hot mixture into peanut butter chips until completely melted. Quickly pour into prepared pan. Stir remaining hot mixture into chocolate chips until completely melted. Quickly spread over top of peanut butter layer; cool until set. Cut into 1-inch squares. Store in airtight container in cool, dry place.
About 4 dozen candies.

In glass dish: Double-Decker Fudge; on server: Chocolate-Almond Fudge; on counter: Nutty Rich Cocoa Fudge

Chocolate-Almond Fudge

    4 cups sugar
    1¾ cups (7-ounce jar)
        marshmallow creme
    1½ cups (12-ounce can)
        evaporated milk
    1 tablespoon butter or
        margarine
    2 cups (12-ounce package)
        HERSHEY'S MINI CHIPS
        Semi-Sweet Chocolate
    1 HERSHEY'S Milk Chocolate
        Bar with Almonds
        (8 ounces), chopped
    1 teaspoon vanilla
    ¾ cup chopped slivered almonds

Butter 9-inch square pan; set aside. Combine sugar, marshmallow creme, evaporated milk and butter in heavy 4-quart saucepan. Cook over medium heat, stirring constantly, until mixture comes to a full rolling boil; boil and stir 7 minutes. Remove from heat; *immediately* add MINI CHIPS Chocolate and chocolate bar pieces, stirring until completely melted. Blend in vanilla; stir in almonds. Pour into prepared pan; cool completely. Cut into 1-inch squares.
About 5 dozen candies.

Chocolate Truffles

    ½ cup unsalted butter, softened
    2½ cups confectioners' sugar
    ½ cup HERSHEY'S Cocoa
    ¼ cup heavy or whipping cream
    1½ teaspoons vanilla
        Centers: Pecan or walnut
        halves, whole almonds,
        candied cherries, after-
        dinner mints
        Coatings: Confectioners'
        sugar, flaked coconut,
        chopped nuts

Cream butter in large mixer bowl. Combine 2½ cups confectioners' sugar and the cocoa; add alternately with cream and vanilla to butter. Blend well. Chill until firm. Shape small amount of mixture around desired center; roll into 1-inch balls. Drop into desired coating and turn until well covered. Chill until firm.
About 3 dozen truffles.

Variation: Chocolate Rum Truffles: Decrease vanilla to 1 teaspoon and add ½ teaspoon rum extract.

Foolproof Dark Chocolate Fudge

3 (6-ounce) packages semi-sweet chocolate chips
1 (14-ounce) can EAGLE® Brand Sweetened Condensed Milk (NOT evaporated milk)
Dash salt
½ to 1 cup chopped nuts
1½ teaspoons vanilla extract

In heavy saucepan, over low heat, melt chips with sweetened condensed milk and salt. Remove from heat; stir in nuts and vanilla. Spread evenly into wax paper-lined 8- or 9-inch square pan. Chill 2 hours or until firm. Turn fudge onto cutting board; peel off paper and cut into squares. Store loosely covered at room temperature.
Makes about 2 pounds.

Microwave: In 1-quart glass measure, combine chips with sweetened condensed milk. Microwave on full power (high) 3 minutes. Stir until chips melt and mixture is smooth. Stir in remaining ingredients. Proceed as above.

Creamy Dark Chocolate Fudge: Melt 2 cups CAMPFIRE® Miniature Marshmallows with chips and sweetened condensed milk. Proceed as above.

Milk Chocolate Fudge: Omit 1 (6-ounce) package semi-sweet chocolate chips. Add 1 cup milk chocolate chips. Proceed as above.

Creamy Milk Chocolate Fudge: Omit 1 (6-ounce) package semi-sweet chocolate chips. Add 1 cup milk chocolate chips and 2 cups CAMPFIRE® Miniature Marshmallows. Proceed as above.

Mexican Chocolate Fudge: Reduce vanilla to 1 teaspoon. Add 1 tablespoon instant coffee and 1 teaspoon ground cinnamon to sweetened condensed milk. Proceed as above.

Butterscotch Fudge: Omit chocolate chips and vanilla. In heavy saucepan, melt 2 (12-ounce) packages butterscotch flavored chips with sweetened condensed milk. Remove from heat; stir in 2 tablespoons white vinegar, ⅛ teaspoon salt, ½ teaspoon maple flavoring and 1 cup chopped nuts. Proceed as above.

Foolproof Dark Chocolate Fudge

Easy Rocky Road

2 cups (12-ounce package) HERSHEY'S Semi-Sweet Chocolate Chips
¼ cup butter or margarine
2 tablespoons shortening
3 cups miniature marshmallows
¾ cup coarsely chopped nuts

Microwave: Butter 8-inch square pan; set aside. Place chocolate chips, butter and shortening in large micro-proof bowl. Microwave at MEDIUM (50%) for 5 to 7 minutes or until chips are softened and mixture is melted and smooth when stirred. Add marshmallows and nuts; blend well. Spread evenly in prepared pan. Cover; chill until firm. Cut into 2-inch squares.
16 squares.

Coconut Granola Snack

1⅓ cups (about) BAKER'S ANGEL FLAKE® Coconut
½ cup quick cooking rolled oats
2 tablespoons firmly packed brown sugar
¼ cup chopped pitted dried prunes
¼ cup chopped dried apricots
2 tablespoons sesame seed
2 tablespoons oil
2 tablespoons honey
¼ cup seedless raisins

Mix coconut with cereal, brown sugar, prunes, apricots and sesame seed in large bowl. Combine oil and honey in saucepan and bring to a boil over medium heat. Pour over cereal mixture and mix to coat well. Spread evenly in 13×9-inch pan. Bake at 325° for 20 minutes, stirring several times to toast evenly. Sprinkle with raisins and spread out on a tray to cool. Break into small pieces and store in airtight container.
Makes 3½ cups.

Chocolate Creams

1 package (8 squares) BAKER'S Semi-Sweet Chocolate
½ cup butter or margarine
1¾ cups sifted confectioners sugar
2 tablespoons light cream or half and half
1 teaspoon vanilla
1 cup finely chopped nuts or grated BAKER'S Semi-Sweet Chocolate

Melt chocolate with butter in saucepan over very low heat, stirring constantly until smooth. Blend in sugar, cream and vanilla. Chill about 30 minutes. Shape into ½-inch balls and roll in nuts. Store in refrigerator.
Makes about 4½ dozen.

Coconut Date Slices

    1 cup chopped or cut dates
 ³/₄ cup sugar
    2 eggs, well beaten
    1 cup chopped walnuts
    1 teaspoon vanilla
    2 cups POST Toasties Corn
        Flakes or POST 40% Bran
        Flakes
 ²/₃ cup (about) BAKER'S® ANGEL
        FLAKE® Coconut

Combine dates, sugar and eggs in 10-inch skillet. Cook over medium heat, stirring constantly, until mixture pulls away from sides of pan, about 5 minutes. Remove from heat. Stir in nuts and vanilla, then carefully stir in cereal and cool slightly. Moisten hands in cold water and shape mixture into two 6-inch logs, about 1½ inches in diameter. Roll in coconut, wrap in waxed paper and chill at least 1 hour. Cut into thin (about ³/₈-inch) slices.
Makes 3 dozen.

Fudgy Chocolate Truffles

 ½ cup margarine or butter
 ³/₄ cup unsweetened cocoa
    1 (14-ounce) can EAGLE® Brand
        Sweetened Condensed Milk
        (NOT evaporated milk)
    1 teaspoon vanilla extract *or*
        rum flavoring
        Additional unsweetened cocoa

In heavy saucepan, over low heat, melt margarine. Add *³/₄ cup* cocoa then sweetened condensed milk; mix until smooth and well blended. Over medium heat, cook and stir until thickened and smooth, about 5 minutes. Remove from heat; stir in vanilla. Chill 3 hours or until firm. Shape into 1¼-inch balls. Roll in additional cocoa. Chill until firm. Store covered in refrigerator.
Makes about 4 dozen.
Microwave: In 1-quart glass measure, melt margarine on 100% power (high) 1 minute. Add ³/₄ cup cocoa then sweetened condensed milk; mix until smooth and well blended. Cook on 100% power (high) 2 to 3 minutes or until thickened, stirring after each minute until smooth. Proceed as above.

Coconut Rum Balls

    4 cups vanilla wafer crumbs
 1¼ cups (about) BAKER'S®
        ANGEL FLAKE® Coconut
    1 cup finely chopped nuts
    1 can (14 ounces) sweetened
        condensed milk
 ½ cup rum*
        Confectioners sugar

Combine crumbs, coconut and nuts in bowl. Stir in condensed milk and rum, mixing well. Shape into 1-inch balls and roll in confectioners sugar to coat. Cover and store in refrigerator. Roll again in sugar just before serving.
Makes 6 dozen.
   *Or use ½ cup water and 1 teaspoon rum extract.
   Note: For best flavor store 24 hours; candies may be stored for several weeks. Recipe may be halved using ²/₃ cup sweetened condensed milk.

Bonbon Cups

    1 package (8 squares) BAKER'S®
        Semi-Sweet Chocolate
    1 cup sifted confectioners sugar
    1 tablespoon milk
    1 tablespoon light corn syrup
 ½ cup chopped mixed candied
        fruits
    1 teaspoon rum extract
        (optional)
    2 tablespoons butter or
        margarine

Melt 4 squares of the chocolate in saucepan over very low heat, stirring constantly until smooth. Remove from heat. Add sugar, milk and corn syrup. Stir in fruits and extract. Spoon into 3 dozen paper or aluminum foil bonbon cups; chill.
   Melt remaining 4 squares chocolate with the butter in saucepan over very low heat, stirring constantly until smooth. Cool slightly; spoon onto fruit filling in cups, mounding the chocolate. Chill until firm. Store in refrigerator.
Makes 3 dozen.

Chocolatey Peanut Treats

    1 8-ounce container Soft
        PHILADELPHIA BRAND
        Cream Cheese
 ½ cup peanut butter
    1 6-ounce package semi-sweet
        chocolate pieces, melted
 2¼ cups graham cracker crumbs
 ²/₃ cup finely chopped peanuts

Combine cream cheese and peanut butter, mixing until well blended. Blend in chocolate. Stir in graham cracker crumbs; mix well. Shape into 1-inch balls. Roll in peanuts; chill.
4 dozen.
   Variation: Omit peanuts. Prepare, shape and chill dough as directed. Roll in powdered sugar just before serving.

Coconut Date Slices (left), Coconut Rum Balls (right)

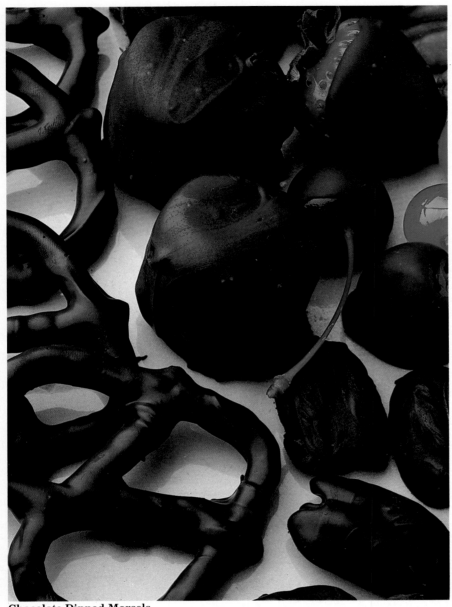

Chocolate-Dipped Morsels

Buckeyes

**2 (3-ounce) packages cream
cheese, softened
1 (14-ounce) can EAGLE® Brand
Sweetened Condensed Milk
(NOT evaporated milk)
2 (12-ounce) packages peanut
butter flavored chips
1 cup finely chopped peanuts
½ pound chocolate
confectioners' coating***

In large mixer bowl, beat cheese until fluffy. Gradually beat in sweetened condensed milk until smooth. In heavy saucepan, over low heat, melt peanut butter chips; stir into cheese mixture. Add nuts. Chill 2 to 3 hours; shape into 1-inch balls. In small heavy saucepan, over low heat, melt confectioners' coating. With wooden pick, dip each peanut ball into melted coating, not covering completely. Place on wax paper-lined baking sheets until firm. Store covered at room temperature or in refrigerator. *Makes about 7 dozen.*

*Chocolate confectioners' coating can be purchased in candy specialty stores.

Chocolate Pecan Critters

**1 (11½-ounce) package milk
chocolate chips
1 (6-ounce) package semi-sweet
chocolate chips
¼ cup margarine or butter
1 (14-ounce) can EAGLE® Brand
Sweetened Condensed Milk
(NOT evaporated milk)
⅛ teaspoon salt
2 cups coarsely chopped pecans
2 teaspoons vanilla extract
Pecan halves**

In heavy saucepan, over medium heat, melt chips and margarine with sweetened condensed milk and salt. Remove from heat; stir in chopped nuts and vanilla. Drop by teaspoonfuls onto wax paper-lined baking sheets. Top with pecan halves. Chill. Store tightly covered. *Makes about 5 dozen.*

Microwave: In 2-quart glass measure, microwave chips, margarine, sweetened condensed milk and salt on full power (high) 3 minutes, stirring after 1½ minutes. Stir to melt chips; stir in chopped nuts and vanilla. Proceed as above.

Chocolate-Dipped Morsels

**4 squares BAKER'S® Semi-
Sweet Chocolate
Assorted morsel centers***

Melt chocolate in saucepan over very low heat, stirring constantly until smooth. Insert wooden picks or skewers into fruit and marshmallow centers. Dip quickly, one at a time, into chocolate. (To dip pretzels or nuts, stir into chocolate; then remove with fork.) Let stand or chill on rack or waxed paper until chocolate is firm. For best eating quality, chill dipped fresh or canned fruits and serve the same day.
Makes 1 to 1½ dozen.

Suggested Morsel Centers.
Fruits: Firm strawberries, ½-inch banana slices, fresh pineapple wedges or drained canned pineapple chunks, peeled orange slices, orange wedges, well-drained stemmed maraschino cherries, dried figs, dried dates or dried apricots.

Unsalted Pretzels and Large Marshmallows.

Nuts: Walnuts or pecan halves or whole almonds or Brazil nuts.

Clockwise from top left: Chocolate Pecan Critters, Fruit Bon Bons, Milk Chocolate Bourbon Balls, Buckeyes, Foolproof Dark Chocolate Fudge (page 292), Peanut Butter Logs and Layered Mint Chocolate Candy

Peanut Butter Logs

- 1 (12-ounce) package peanut butter flavored chips
- 1 (14-ounce) can EAGLE® Brand Sweetened Condensed Milk (NOT evaporated milk)
- 1 cup CAMPFIRE® Miniature Marshmallows
- 1 cup chopped peanuts

In heavy saucepan, over low heat, melt chips with sweetened condensed milk. Add marshmallows; stir until melted. Remove from heat; cool 20 minutes. Divide in half; place each portion on a 20-inch piece of wax paper. Shape each into 12-inch log. Roll in nuts. Wrap tightly; chill 2 hours or until firm. Remove paper; cut into 1/4-inch slices.
Makes two 12-inch logs.

Microwave: In 2-quart glass measure, microwave chips, sweetened condensed milk and marshmallows on full power (high) 4 minutes or until melted, stirring after 2 minutes. Let stand at room temperature 1 hour. Proceed as above.

Peanut Butter Fudge: Stir peanuts into mixture. Spread into wax paper-lined 8- or 9-inch square pan. Chill 2 hours or until firm. Turn fudge onto cutting board; peel off paper and cut into squares.

Layered Mint Chocolate Candy

- 1 (12-ounce) package semi-sweet chocolate chips
- 1 (14-ounce) can EAGLE® Brand Sweetened Condensed Milk (NOT evaporated milk)
- 2 teaspoons vanilla extract
- 6 ounces white confectioners' coating*
- 1 tablespoon peppermint extract Few drops green or red food coloring, optional

In heavy saucepan, over low heat, melt chips with 1 cup sweetened condensed milk. Stir in vanilla. Spread half the mixture into wax paper-lined 8- or 9-inch square pan; chill 10 minutes or until firm. Hold remaining chocolate mixture at room temperature. In heavy saucepan, over low heat, melt coating with remaining sweetened condensed milk. Stir in peppermint extract and food coloring if desired. Spread on chilled chocolate layer; chill 10 minutes longer or until firm. Spread reserved chocolate mixture on mint layer. Chill 2 hours or until firm. Turn onto cutting board; peel off paper and cut into squares. Store loosely covered at room temperature.
Makes about 1 3/4 pounds.

*White confectioners' coating can be purchased in candy specialty stores.

Milk Chocolate Bourbon Balls

- 1 (12-ounce) package vanilla wafer cookies, finely crushed (about 3 cups crumbs)
- 5 tablespoons bourbon or brandy
- 1 (11 1/2-ounce) package milk chocolate chips
- 1 (14-ounce) can EAGLE® Brand Sweetened Condensed Milk (NOT evaporated milk) Finely chopped nuts

In medium mixing bowl, combine crumbs and bourbon. In heavy saucepan, over low heat, melt chips. Remove from heat; add sweetened condensed milk. Gradually add crumb mixture; mix well. Let stand at room temperature 30 minutes or chill. Shape into 1-inch balls; roll in nuts. Store tightly covered.
Makes about 5 1/2 dozen.

Tip: Flavor of these candies improves after 24 hours. They can be made ahead and stored in freezer. Thaw before serving.

Fruit Bon Bons

- 1 (14-ounce) can EAGLE® Brand Sweetened Condensed Milk (NOT evaporated milk)
- 2 (7-ounce) packages flaked coconut (5 1/3 cups)
- 1 (6-ounce) package fruit flavor gelatin, any flavor
- 1 cup ground blanched almonds
- 1 teaspoon almond extract Food coloring, optional

In large mixing bowl, combine sweetened condensed milk, coconut, 1/3 cup gelatin, almonds, extract and enough food coloring to tint mixture desired shade. Chill 1 hour or until firm enough to handle. Using about 1/2 tablespoon mixture for each, shape into 1-inch balls. Sprinkle remaining gelatin onto wax paper; roll each ball in gelatin to coat. Place on wax paper-lined baking sheets; chill. Store covered at room temperature or in refrigerator.
Makes about 5 dozen.

Crunchy Clusters

1 (12-ounce) package semi-sweet chocolate chips *or* 3 (6-ounce) packages butterscotch flavored chips
1 (14-ounce) can EAGLE® Brand Sweetened Condensed Milk (NOT evaporated milk)
1 (3-ounce) can chow mein noodles *or* 2 cups pretzel sticks, broken into ½-inch pieces
1 cup dry roasted peanuts *or* whole roasted almonds

In heavy saucepan, over low heat, melt chips with sweetened condensed milk. Remove from heat. In large mixing bowl, combine noodles and nuts; stir in chocolate mixture. Drop by tablespoonfuls onto wax paper-lined baking sheets; chill 2 hours or until firm. Store loosely covered in cool dry place.
Makes about 3 dozen.

Microwave: In 2-quart glass measure, combine chips and sweetened condensed milk. Microwave on full power (high) 3 minutes, stirring after 1½ minutes. Stir until smooth. Proceed as above.

Caramel Peanut Balls

3 cups *finely* chopped dry roasted peanuts
1 (14-ounce) can EAGLE® Brand Sweetened Condensed Milk (NOT evaporated milk)
1 teaspoon vanilla extract
½ pound chocolate confectioners' coating*

In heavy saucepan, combine nuts, sweetened condensed milk and vanilla. Over medium heat, cook and stir 8 to 10 minutes or until mixture forms ball around spoon and pulls away from side of pan. Cool 10 minutes. Chill if desired. Shape into 1-inch balls. In small heavy saucepan, over low heat, melt confectioners' coating. With wooden pick, dip each ball into melted coating, covering half of ball. Place on wax paper-lined baking sheets until firm. Store covered at room temperature or in refrigerator.
Makes about 4½ dozen.

*Chocolate confectioners' coating can be purchased in candy specialty stores.

Top to bottom: **Apricot Almond Chewies, Chipper Peanut Candy, Caramel Peanut Balls, Crunchy Clusters (Butterscotch and Chocolate)**

Chipper Peanut Candy

1 (6-ounce) package butterscotch flavored chips
1 (14-ounce) can EAGLE® Brand Sweetened Condensed Milk (NOT evaporated milk)
1 cup peanut butter
2 cups crushed WISE® Potato Chips
1 cup coarsely chopped peanuts

In heavy saucepan, melt butterscotch chips with sweetened condensed milk and peanut butter. Over medium heat, cook and stir until well blended. Remove from heat. Add potato chips and nuts; mix well. Press into aluminum foil-lined 8- or 9-inch square pan. Chill. Turn candy onto cutting board; peel off foil and cut into squares. Store loosely covered at room temperature.
Makes about 2 pounds.

Microwave: In 2-quart glass measure, combine sweetened condensed milk, butterscotch chips and peanut butter. Microwave on full power (high) 4 minutes, stirring after 2 minutes. Proceed as above.

Apricot Almond Chewies

- **4 cups finely chopped dried apricots (about 1 pound)**
- **4 cups flaked coconut or coconut macaroon crumbs (about 21 macaroons)**
- **2 cups slivered almonds, toasted and finely chopped**
- **1 (14-ounce) can EAGLE® Brand Sweetened Condensed Milk (NOT evaporated milk)**
- **Whole almonds, optional**

In large mixing bowl, combine all ingredients except whole almonds. Chill 2 hours. Shape into 1-inch balls. Top each with whole almond if desired. Store tightly covered in refrigerator. *Makes about 6¹/₂ dozen.*

Almond Toffee

- **1 cup butter or margarine**
- **1 cup sugar**
- **3 tablespoons water**
- **1 tablespoon light corn syrup**
- **¹/₃ cup chopped toasted blanched almonds**
- **1 package (8 squares) BAKER'S® Semi-Sweet Chocolate**
- **²/₃ cup chopped toasted blanched almonds**

Melt butter in heavy 2-quart saucepan over very low heat. Add sugar and stir until mixture starts to boil. Combine water and corn syrup; blend into sugar mixture. Cook and stir over medium heat until mixture comes to a boil. Reduce heat; cover and cook 3 minutes. Uncover and cook gently, stirring frequently to prevent burning, until a small amount of mixture forms a hard and brittle thread in cold water (or to a temperature of 300°). Remove from heat. Stir in ¹/₃ cup almonds. Spread evenly in well-buttered 15×10-inch jelly roll pan. Let stand until almost cool to the touch.

Melt 4 squares of the chocolate in saucepan over very low heat, stirring constantly until smooth. Spread over toffee; then sprinkle with ¹/₃ cup of the remaining almonds. Let stand until chocolate is firm. Turn toffee out onto waxed paper. (Toffee may break.) Melt remaining 4 squares chocolate and spread over toffee. Sprinkle with remaining ¹/₃ cup almonds. Let stand until chocolate is firm. Break into pieces. *Makes about 1¹/₂ pounds.*

Creamy Cocoa Taffy

- **1¹/₄ cups sugar**
- **³/₄ cup light corn syrup**
- **¹/₃ cup HERSHEY'S Cocoa**
- **¹/₈ teaspoon salt**
- **2 teaspoons white vinegar**
- **¹/₄ cup evaporated milk**
- **1 tablespoon butter**

Butter 9-inch square pan; set aside. Combine sugar, corn syrup, cocoa, salt and vinegar in heavy 2-quart saucepan. Cook over medium heat, stirring constantly, until mixture boils; add evaporated milk and butter. Continue to cook, stirring occasionally, to firm-ball stage, 248°F on a candy thermometer (or until syrup, when dropped into very cold water, forms a firm ball that does not flatten when removed from water). Bulb of candy thermometer should not rest on bottom of saucepan.

Pour mixture into prepared pan. Let stand until taffy is cool enough to handle. Butter hands; stretch taffy, folding and pulling until light in color and hard to pull. Place taffy on table; pull into ¹/₂-inch-wide strips (twist two strips together, if desired). Cut into 1-inch pieces with buttered scissors. Wrap individually in plastic wrap.
About 1¹/₄ pounds candy.

Gelatin Jiggles

Gelatin Jiggles

- **4 packages (4-serving size) or 2 packages (8-serving size) JELL-O® Brand Gelatin, any flavor**
- **2¹/₂ cups boiling water or fruit juice**

Completely dissolve gelatin in boiling water. Pour into 9-inch square pan. Chill until firm, about 4 hours. Cut with small cookie cutters that have been dipped in warm water, or cut into 1-inch squares. Carefully transfer cutouts to serving plates, using broad spatula that has been dipped in warm water. Flake remaining gelatin with fork; reserve for another use. *Makes about 1¹/₂ dozen cutouts.*

Note: To cut letters or shapes, place paper or cardboard pattern on firm gelatin; cut with sharp knife that has been dipped in warm water.

Fresh 'n Fruity Pops

- **1 envelope KNOX® Unflavored Gelatine**
- **¹/₂ cup cold water**
- **1 cup fruit juice, heated to boiling**
- **Suggested Fresh Fruits***
- **¹/₄ cup sugar or 6 packets aspartame sweetener**
- **1 tablespoon lemon juice**

In medium bowl, sprinkle unflavored gelatine over cold water; let stand 1 minute. Add hot juice and stir until gelatine is completely dissolved, about 5 minutes. Stir in remaining ingredients. Pour into 6 (5-ounce) Popsicle molds or paper cups; freeze until partially frozen, about 30 minutes. Insert wooden ice cream sticks; freeze until firm, about 4 hours. To serve, let stand at room temperature 5 minutes; remove from mold.
Makes 6 pops.

*Suggested Fresh Fruits: Use any of the following, pureed, to equal 1 cup—bananas, blueberries, pitted cherries, cantaloupe, nectarines, plums, peaches or strawberries.

DESSERTS

For the perfect finale to a great meal, turn to these delectable desserts. You'll find smooth Bavarian creams and mousses, fruity parfaits, elegant chocolate souffles, rich puddings, and a mouth-watering selection of cheesecakes. Provide a light touch with a refreshing fruit mold or tangy sorbet.

Mt. Gretna Chocolate Fondue

4 squares (4 ounces) HERSHEY'S Unsweetened Baking Chocolate
1 cup light cream
1 cup sugar
¼ cup creamy peanut butter
1½ teaspoons vanilla
Fondue Dippers

Combine chocolate and cream in medium saucepan. Cook over low heat, stirring constantly, until chocolate is melted and mixture is smooth. Add sugar and peanut butter; continue cooking until slightly thickened. Remove from heat; stir in vanilla. Pour into fondue pot or chafing dish; serve warm with Fondue Dippers.
About 2 cups fondue.

Fondue Dippers: In advance, prepare a selection of the following: marshmallows; angel food, sponge or pound cake pieces; strawberries; grapes; pineapple chunks; mandarin orange segments; cherries; fresh fruit slices. (Drain fruit well. Brush fresh fruit with lemon juice to prevent fruit from turning brown.)

Acapulco Flan

20 KRAFT Caramels
2 tablespoons water
1 8-ounce package PHILADELPHIA BRAND Cream Cheese, softened
½ cup sugar
6 eggs, beaten
1 teaspoon vanilla
2 cups milk

Melt caramels with water over low heat, stirring until smooth. Pour into greased 9-inch layer pan. Combine cream cheese and sugar, mixing until well blended. Blend in eggs and vanilla. Gradually add milk, mixing until well blended. Set layer pan in baking pan on oven rack; slowly pour milk mixture over caramel sauce.

Pour boiling water into baking pan to ½-inch depth. Bake at 350°, 45 minutes or until knife inserted 2 inches from edge of pan comes out clean. Remove from water immediately; cool 5 minutes. Invert onto serving dish with rim. Serve warm or chilled.
6 to 8 servings.

Butterscotch Apple Squares

¼ cup margarine or butter
1½ cups graham cracker crumbs
2 small all-purpose apples, pared and chopped (about 1¼ cups)
1 (6-ounce) package butterscotch flavored chips
1 (14-ounce) can EAGLE® Brand Sweetened Condensed Milk (NOT evaporated milk)
1 (3½-ounce) can flaked coconut (1⅓ cups)
1 cup chopped nuts

Preheat oven to 350° (325° for glass dish). In 3-quart shallow baking pan (13×9-inch), melt margarine in oven. Sprinkle crumbs evenly over margarine; top with apples. In heavy saucepan, over medium heat, melt chips with sweetened condensed milk. Pour butterscotch mixture evenly over apples. Top with coconut and nuts; press down firmly. Bake 25 to 30 minutes or until lightly browned. Cool. Chill thoroughly. Garnish as desired. Refrigerate leftovers.
Makes 12 servings.

Microwave: In 2½-quart shallow baking dish (12×7-inch), microwave margarine on full power (high) 1 minute or until melted. Sprinkle crumbs evenly over margarine; top with apples. In 1-quart glass measure, microwave chips with sweetened condensed milk on ⅔ power (medium-high) 2 to 3 minutes. Mix well. Pour butterscotch mixture evenly over apples. Top with coconut and nuts. Press down firmly. Microwave on full power (high) 8 to 9 minutes. Proceed as above.

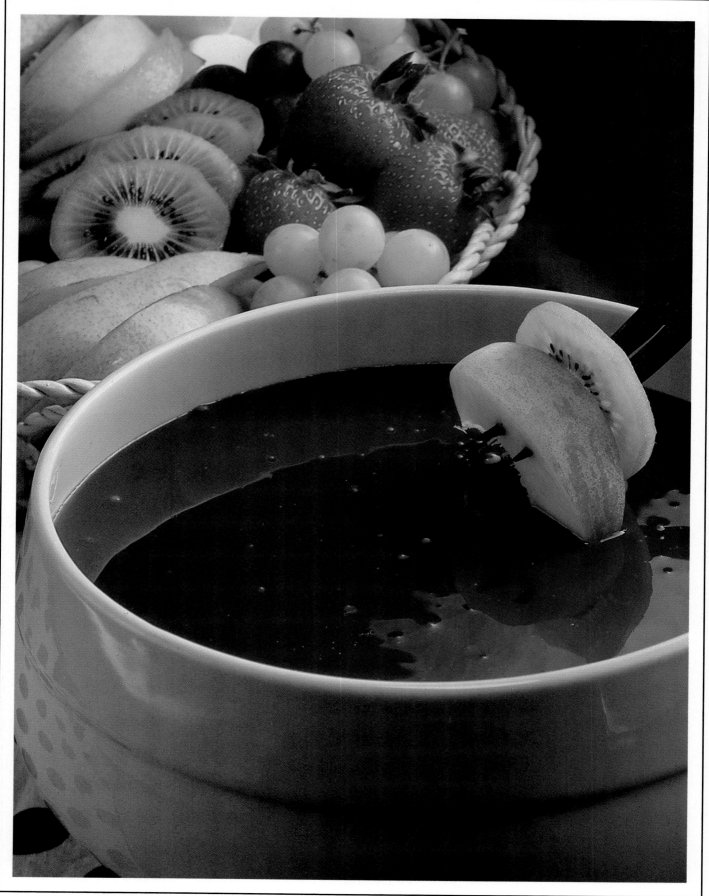

Mt. Gretna Chocolate Fondue

Mexicana Bread Pudding

- **1 cup SUN-MAID® Raisins**
- **1 cup orange juice**
- **³/₄ cup packed brown sugar**
- **¹/₂ teaspoon *each* ground cinnamon and grated orange peel**
- **¹/₄ teaspoon ground nutmeg**
- **5 cups lightly packed 1-inch French bread cubes (about 6 ounces)**
- **2¹/₂ cups shredded Monterey Jack cheese**
- **¹/₂ cup chopped DIAMOND® Walnuts**
- **Cream, lightly sweetened whipped cream or ice cream (optional)**

In small saucepan, combine raisins, juice, sugar, cinnamon, peel and nutmeg. Bring to boil over medium heat, stirring occasionally. In large bowl, toss bread with raisin mixture. Add 2 cups of the cheese and the walnuts; toss. Turn into buttered 1¹/₂-quart baking dish; sprinkle remaining ¹/₂ cup cheese on top. Bake in preheated 375°F oven 15 to 20 minutes or until cheese is melted. Serve warm, topped with cream, if desired.
Makes 6 servings.

Banana Mocha Layered Dessert

- **1 cup whipping cream**
- **2 tablespoons sugar**
- **1 teaspoon instant coffee powder**
- **¹/₂ teaspoon vanilla extract**
- **3 firm, medium DOLE™ Bananas**
- **1 package (8¹/₂ ounces) chocolate wafer cookies**

In large mixer bowl, beat cream, sugar, coffee powder and vanilla until stiff peaks form. Slice bananas. Crumble half the wafers into bottom of 8-inch square pan. Top with half the banana slices. Spread with half the mocha cream. Repeat layers. Refrigerate until ready to serve. Garnish with additional banana slices, if desired.
Makes 8 servings.

Mexicana Bread Pudding

Tropical Crisp

- **1 DOLE™ Fresh Pineapple**
- **4 DOLE™ Bananas**
- **1 cup brown sugar, packed**
- **1 cup flour**
- **³/₄ cup rolled oats**
- **¹/₂ cup flaked coconut**
- **¹/₂ teaspoon ground nutmeg**
- **¹/₂ cup butter or margarine, softened**

Preheat oven to 350°F. Twist crown from pineapple. Cut pineapple lengthwise into quarters. Remove fruit from shells with curved knife. Trim off core and cut fruit into chunks. Cut bananas into chunks. In 9-inch baking dish, toss bananas and pineapple with ¹/₄ cup brown sugar. In medium bowl, combine remaining ³/₄ cup brown sugar, flour, oats, coconut and nutmeg. Cut in butter until crumbly. Sprinkle over fruit mixture. Bake in preheated oven 45 to 50 minutes or until topping is crisp and juices have begun to bubble around edges.
Makes 8 servings.

Delightful Dessert Pancake

- **1 8-ounce package *Light* PHILADELPHIA BRAND Neufchâtel Cheese, softened**
- **3 tablespoons honey**
- **1 teaspoon grated lemon peel**
- **1 teaspoon lemon juice**

* * *

- **¹/₂ cup milk**
- **¹/₂ cup flour**
- **¹/₄ teaspoon salt**
- **2 eggs, beaten**
- **1 tablespoon PARKAY Margarine**
- **2 cups assorted fruit**
- **¹/₄ cup toasted flake coconut**

Combine neufchâtel cheese, honey, peel and juice, mixing until well blended. Chill.

Gradually add milk to combined flour and salt; beat until smooth. Beat in eggs. Heat heavy 10-inch ovenproof skillet in 450° oven until very hot. Add margarine to coat skillet; pour in batter immediately. Bake on lowest oven rack at 450°, 10 minutes. Reduce oven temperature to 350°; continue baking 10 minutes or until golden brown. Fill with fruit; sprinkle with coconut. Serve immediately with neufchâtel cheese mixture.
6 to 8 servings.

Thanksgiving Cranberry Cobbler

- **1 package DUNCAN HINES®
   Deluxe Yellow Cake Mix**
- **½ teaspoon ground cinnamon**
- **¼ teaspoon ground nutmeg**
- **1 cup (2 sticks) butter or
   margarine, softened**
- **½ cup chopped nuts**
- **1 can (21 ounces) peach pie
   filling**
- **1 can (16 ounces) whole
   cranberry sauce**
- **Vanilla ice cream or sweetened
   whipped cream**

1. Preheat oven to 350°F.
2. Combine dry cake mix, cinnamon and nutmeg in bowl. Cut in butter with pastry blender or two knives until crumbly. Stir in nuts; set aside.
3. Combine peach pie filling and cranberry sauce in ungreased 13×9×2-inch pan; mix well. Sprinkle crumb mixture over fruit.
4. Bake at 350°F for 45 to 50 minutes or until golden brown. Serve warm with ice cream or whipped cream.
16 servings.

Thanksgiving Cranberry Cobbler

Peanut Butter Snacking Cups

- **¾ cup graham cracker crumbs**
- **3 tablespoons butter or
   margarine, melted**
- **3½ cups (8 ounces) COOL WHIP®
   Non-Dairy Whipped Topping,
   thawed**
- **1 cup milk**
- **½ cup chunky peanut butter**
- **1 package (4-serving size)
   JELL-O® Vanilla Flavor
   Instant Pudding and Pie
   Filling**
- **¼ cup strawberry preserves**

Line 12-cup muffin pan with paper baking cups. Combine crumbs and butter; mix well. Press about 1 tablespoon of the crumb mixture into each cup. Top each with about 1 tablespoon of the whipped topping. Gradually blend milk into peanut butter in bowl. Add pudding mix. With electric mixer at low speed, beat until blended, 1 to 2 minutes. Fold in remaining whipped topping. Spoon into crumb-lined cups. Top each cup with 1 teaspoon of the preserves. Freeze about 4 hours; peel off papers.
Makes 12 servings.

Fruit Crumble

- **4 cups thinly sliced peeled
   apples**
- **¼ cup packed brown sugar**
- **1 teaspoon lemon juice**
- **¼ teaspoon ground cinnamon**
- **2 tablespoons butter or
   margarine**
- **1 cup coarsely crushed
   PEPPERIDGE FARM® Irish
   Oatmeal, Hazelnut or Lemon
   Nut Crunch Cookies**
- **½ cup chopped walnuts
   (optional)**

To Microwave:
1. In large bowl, toss together apples, brown sugar, lemon juice and cinnamon. Spoon mixture into 9-inch microwave-safe pie plate; set aside.
2. Place butter in medium microwave-safe bowl. Cover; microwave on HIGH 30 seconds or until melted. Stir in cookies and walnuts. Sprinkle over apple mixture.
3. Microwave, uncovered, on HIGH 7 minutes or until apples are tender, rotating dish twice during cooking. Let stand, uncovered, 5 minutes.
Makes 6 servings.

   Note: Substitute a 21-ounce can of apple or cherry pie filling for fresh apples. Omit brown sugar. Microwave as directed above.

Swedish Apple Cake

- **1 cup packed brown sugar**
- **2 tablespoons all-purpose flour**
- **¼ teaspoon ground nutmeg**
- **⅛ teaspoon salt**
- **1 cup water**
- **2 tablespoons butter or
   margarine**
- **1 can (20 ounces) apple pie
   filling**
- **1 package DUNCAN HINES®
   Deluxe Lemon Supreme
   Cake Mix**
- **3 large eggs**
- **⅓ cup CRISCO® Oil or PURITAN®
   Oil**
- **1¼ cups water**

1. For sauce, combine brown sugar, flour, nutmeg and salt in small baking dish. Gradually stir in 1 cup water. Add butter; set aside.
2. Spread apple pie filling in 13×9×2-inch pan.
3. Combine dry cake mix, eggs, oil and 1¼ cups water in large mixer bowl. Mix as directed on package. Spread batter evenly over apples.
4. Preheat oven to 350°F. Bake cake and sauce for 43 to 48 minutes or until toothpick inserted in center comes out clean.
5. To serve, spoon warm cake and apples in serving bowls and top with sauce.
16 to 20 servings.

Pots de Crème au Chocolat

**2 squares (2 ounces)
    HERSHEY'S Unsweetened
    Baking Chocolate, broken
    into pieces
1 cup light cream
2/3 cup sugar
2 egg yolks, slightly beaten
2 tablespoons butter or
    margarine, softened
1 teaspoon vanilla
    Sweetened whipped cream
    Candied violets (optional)**

Combine baking chocolate pieces and cream in medium saucepan. Cook over medium heat, stirring constantly with wire whisk, until chocolate flecks disappear and mixture is hot. Add sugar and continue cooking and stirring until mixture begins to boil. Remove from heat; gradually add to beaten egg yolks, stirring constantly. Stir in butter and vanilla. Pour into six crème pots or demitasse cups; press plastic wrap directly onto surface. Chill several hours or until set. Garnish with sweetened whipped cream and candied violets.
6 servings.

Tortoni Squares

**1 envelope unflavored gelatin
1/2 cup cold water
2 8-ounce containers Soft
    PHILADELPHIA BRAND
    Cream Cheese
2 tablespoons sugar
1 17-ounce can apricot halves,
    drained, chopped
2 tablespoons chopped
    almonds, toasted
1/4 teaspoon rum flavoring
2 cups thawed frozen whipped
    topping
2 cups macaroon cookies,
    crumbled**

Soften gelatin in water; stir over low heat until dissolved. Cool. Combine cream cheese and sugar, mixing until well blended. Gradually add gelatin, mixing until blended. Stir in apricots, almonds and flavoring. Fold in whipped topping. Place macaroons on bottom of 9-inch square baking pan; top with cream cheese mixture. Chill until set; cut into squares.
9 servings.

Cherry-Topped Icebox Cake

Cherry-Topped Icebox Cake

**20 whole graham crackers
2 cups cold milk
1 package (6-serving size)
    JELL-O® Vanilla or Chocolate
    Flavor Instant Pudding and
    Pie Filling
1 3/4 cups thawed COOL WHIP®
    Non-Dairy Whipped Topping
2 cans (21 ounces each) cherry
    pie filling**

Line 13×9-inch pan with some of the graham crackers, breaking crackers, if necessary. Pour cold milk into bowl. Add pudding mix. With electric mixer at low speed, beat until well blended, 1 to 2 minutes. Let stand 5 minutes; then blend in whipped topping. Spread half of the pudding mixture over crackers. Add another layer of crackers. Top with remaining pudding mixture and remaining crackers. Spread cherry pie filling over crackers. Chill about 3 hours.
Makes 12 servings.

Chocolate-Frosted Icebox Cake: Prepare Cherry-Topped Icebox Cake as directed, substituting 3/4 cup ready-to-spread chocolate fudge frosting for the cherry pie filling. Carefully spread frosting over top layer of graham crackers.

Peach Cream Cake

**1 (7-inch) prepared loaf angel
    food cake, frozen
1 (14-ounce) can EAGLE® Brand
    Sweetened Condensed Milk
    (NOT evaporated milk)
1 cup cold water
1 (3½-ounce) package instant
    vanilla pudding and pie
    filling mix
1 teaspoon almond extract
2 cups (1 pint) whipping cream,
    whipped
4 cups sliced, pared fresh
    peaches or 1 (20-ounce)
    package frozen sliced
    peaches, thawed**

Cut cake into 1/4-inch slices; arrange half the slices on bottom of 13×9-inch baking dish. In large mixer bowl, combine sweetened condensed milk and water; mix well. Add pudding mix; beat until well blended. Chill 5 minutes. Stir in extract; fold in whipped cream. Pour half the cream mixture over cake slices; arrange half the peach slices on top. Repeat layering, ending with peach slices. Chill 4 hours or until set. Cut into squares to serve. Refrigerate leftovers.
Makes 10 to 12 servings.

Creamy Lemon Sherbet

- **1 cup sugar**
- **2 cups (1 pint) BORDEN® or MEADOW GOLD® Whipping Cream, unwhipped**
- **½ cup REALEMON® Lemon Juice from Concentrate**
- **Few drops yellow food coloring**

In medium bowl, combine sugar and cream, stirring until sugar is dissolved. Stir in ReaLemon® brand and food coloring. Pour into 8-inch square pan or directly into sherbet dishes. Freeze 3 hours or until firm. Remove from freezer 5 minutes before serving. Return leftovers to freezer.
Makes about 3 cups.

Creamy Lime Sherbet: Substitute REALIME® Lime Juice from Concentrate for ReaLemon® brand and green food coloring for yellow.

Frozen Chocolate Graham Cups

- **1½ cups cold milk**
- **1 package (4-serving size) JELL-O® Chocolate Flavor Instant Pudding and Pie Filling**
- **1 cup thawed COOL WHIP® Non-Dairy Whipped Topping**
- **7 whole graham crackers, broken in pieces**
- **½ cup miniature marshmallows**
- **¼ cup chopped salted peanuts**

Pour cold milk into bowl. Add pudding mix. With electric mixer at low speed, beat until well blended, 1 to 2 minutes. Let stand 5 minutes. Fold in whipped topping, crackers, marshmallows and peanuts. Spoon into muffin pan lined with paper baking cups. Freeze until firm, about 3 hours. Garnish with additional whipped topping, if desired.
Makes about 8 servings.

Frozen Vanilla Graham Cups: Prepare Frozen Chocolate Graham Cups as directed, substituting vanilla flavor instant pudding and pie filling for the chocolate flavor pudding and ¼ cup chopped nuts or slivered almonds and ¼ cup diced maraschino cherries for the marshmallows and peanuts.
Makes 6 servings.

Sparkling Lemon-Lime Sorbet

- **1 envelope KNOX® Unflavored Gelatine**
- **½ cup sugar**
- **1 cup water**
- **1 cup Champagne, sauterne or ginger ale**
- **½ cup fresh lemon juice (about 3 lemons)**
- **⅓ cup fresh lime juice (about 3 limes)**

In medium saucepan, mix unflavored gelatine with sugar; blend in water. Let stand 1 minute. Stir over low heat until gelatine is completely dissolved, about 5 minutes. Let cool to room temperature; stir in remaining ingredients. Pour into 9-inch square baking pan; freeze 3 hours or until firm.

With electric mixer or food processor, beat mixture until smooth. Return to pan; freeze 2 hours or until firm. To serve, let stand at room temperature 15 minutes or until slightly softened. Spoon into dessert dishes or stemmed glassware. Garnish, if desired, with fresh mint.
Makes 6 servings; 110 calories per serving with Champagne or sauterne; 90 calories per serving with ginger ale.

Variation: For a Sparkling Citrus Mint Sorbet, increase water to 2 cups; omit Champagne. After gelatine is dissolved, add ¼ cup loosely packed mint leaves and simmer over low heat 5 minutes; strain. Let cool to room temperature, then proceed as above. *78 calories per serving.*

Very Berry Sorbet

- **1 envelope KNOX® Unflavored Gelatine**
- **½ cup sugar**
- **1½ cups water**
- **2 cups pureed strawberries or raspberries (about 1½ pints)***
- **½ cup creme de cassis (black currant) liqueur or cranberry juice cocktail**
- **2 tablespoons lemon juice**

In medium saucepan, mix unflavored gelatine with sugar; blend in water. Let stand 1 minute. Stir over low heat until gelatine is completely dissolved, about 5 minutes. Let cool to room temperature; stir in remaining ingredients. Pour into 9-inch square baking pan; freeze 3 hours or until firm.

With electric mixer or food processor, beat mixture until smooth. Return to pan; freeze 2 hours or until firm. To serve, let stand at room temperature 15 minutes or until slightly softened. Spoon into dessert dishes or stemmed glassware. Garnish, if desired, with fresh fruit.
Makes 8 servings; 119 calories per serving with creme de cassis; 78 calories per serving with cranberry juice cocktail.

*Substitution: Use 1 package (10 ounces) frozen strawberries or raspberries, partially thawed and pureed.

Creamy Lemon Sherbet

Frozen Passion

2 (14-ounce) cans EAGLE® Brand Sweetened Condensed Milk (NOT evaporated milk)
1 (2-liter) bottle or 5 (12-ounce) cans carbonated beverage, any flavor

In ice cream freezer container, combine ingredients; mix well. Freeze according to manufacturer's instructions. Store leftovers in freezer.
Makes 2 to 3 quarts.

Passion Shakes: In blender container, combine *one-half* can sweetened condensed milk, *1 (12-ounce) can* carbonated beverage and *3 cups* ice. Blend until smooth. Repeat for additional shakes. Store leftovers in freezer.
Makes 1 or 2 quarts.

Pudding Ice Cream

2 cups cold light cream or half and half
1 package (4-serving size) JELL-O® Vanilla or Chocolate Flavor Instant Pudding and Pie Filling
3½ cups (8 ounces) COOL WHIP® Non-Dairy Whipped Topping, thawed

Pour cold cream into bowl. Add pudding mix. With electric mixer at low speed, beat until well blended, 1 to 2 minutes. Let stand 5 minutes. Fold in whipped topping. Pour into 2-quart covered plastic container. Freeze until firm, about 6 hours.
Makes 6 cups or 12 servings.

Toffee Crunch Pudding Ice Cream: Prepare Pudding Ice Cream as directed, using vanilla flavor pudding mix and folding in ⅔ cup crushed chocolate-covered toffee bar with the whipped topping.

Rum Raisin Pudding Ice Cream: Prepare Pudding Ice Cream as directed, using vanilla flavor pudding mix. Soak ½ cup chopped raisins in 2 tablespoons light rum; fold in with the whipped topping.

Rocky Road Pudding Ice Cream: Prepare Pudding Ice Cream as directed, using chocolate flavor pudding mix and folding in 1 cup miniature marshmallows and ½ cup chopped walnuts with the whipped topping.

Cinnamon Walnut Pudding Ice Cream: Prepare Pudding Ice Cream as directed, using vanilla flavor pudding mix and adding 2 tablespoons light brown sugar and ½ teaspoon cinnamon to the pudding mix. Add ½ cup finely chopped walnuts with the whipped topping.

Fruit Pudding Ice Cream: Prepare Pudding Ice Cream as directed, folding in 1 cup pureed fruit (strawberries, peaches or raspberries) with the whipped topping.

Chocolate Chip Pudding Ice Cream: Prepare Pudding Ice Cream as directed, using chocolate flavor pudding mix and folding in ¾ cup BAKER'S® Real Semi-Sweet Chocolate Chips with the whipped topping.

Almond Creme

2 packages (4 ounces each) BAKER'S® GERMAN'S® Sweet Chocolate
¼ cup water
⅔ cup sweetened condensed milk
2 cups heavy cream
½ teaspoon vanilla
½ cup toasted slivered blanched almonds

Melt chocolate in water in saucepan over very low heat, stirring constantly until smooth. Cool. Combine chocolate, condensed milk, cream and vanilla in large bowl of electric mixer.

Chill; then whip until soft peaks form. Fold in almonds. Spoon into 9-inch square pan or 1½-quart freezer container. Freeze until firm, about 5 hours. Garnish with additional toasted almonds, if desired.
Makes 8 to 10 servings.

Melon Sorbet Cooler

1 envelope KNOX® Unflavored Gelatine
½ cup sugar
1 cup water
2½ cups pureed cantaloupe (about 1 large)*
⅓ cup rum (optional)
2 tablespoons lemon juice

In medium saucepan, mix unflavored gelatin with sugar; blend in water. Let stand 1 minute. Stir over low heat until gelatine is completely dissolved, about 5 minutes. Let cool to room temperature; stir in remaining ingredients. Pour into 9-inch square baking pan; freeze 3 hours or until firm.

With electric mixer or food processor, beat mixture until smooth. Return to pan; freeze 2 hours or until firm. To serve, let stand at room temperature 15 minutes or until slightly softened. Garnish, if desired, with fresh mint.
Makes about 8 servings.
***Variation:** Use 2½ cups pureed honeydew melon (about ½ medium).

Frozen Passion

Frozen Chocolate Banana Loaf

Banana Bonanza Ice Cream

2 cups milk
2 cups whipping cream
2 eggs, beaten
1¼ cups sugar
2 extra-ripe, medium DOLE™ Bananas
½ teaspoon vanilla extract
¼ teaspoon salt
⅛ teaspoon ground nutmeg

In large saucepan, combine milk, cream, eggs and sugar. Cook and stir over low heat until mixture thickens slightly and coats metal spoon. Cool to room temperature. Puree bananas in blender (1 cup). In large bowl, combine cooled custard, pureed bananas, vanilla, salt and nutmeg. Pour into ice cream freezer can. Freeze according to manufacturer's directions.
Makes 2 quarts.

Frozen Chocolate Banana Loaf

1½ cups chocolate wafer cookie crumbs (about 30 wafers)
¼ cup sugar
3 tablespoons margarine or butter, melted
1 (14-ounce) can EAGLE® Brand Sweetened Condensed Milk (NOT evaporated milk)
⅔ cup chocolate flavored syrup
2 small ripe bananas, mashed (¾ cup)
2 cups (1 pint) BORDEN® or MEADOW GOLD® Whipping Cream, whipped *(do not use non-dairy whipped topping)*

Line 9×5-inch loaf pan with aluminum foil, extending foil above sides of pan; butter foil. Combine crumbs, sugar and margarine; press firmly on bottom and halfway up sides of prepared pan. In large bowl, combine sweetened condensed milk, syrup and bananas; mix well. Fold in whipped cream. Pour into prepared pan; cover. Freeze 6 hours or until firm. To serve, remove from pan; peel off foil. Garnish as desired; slice. Return leftovers to freezer.
Makes 8 to 10 servings.

Raspberry Freeze

¼ cup honey
1 8-ounce package PHILADELPHIA BRAND Cream Cheese, softened
1 10-ounce package frozen raspberries, partially thawed, undrained
1 cup banana slices
2 cups KRAFT Miniature Marshmallows
1 cup whipping cream, whipped

Gradually add honey to cream cheese, mixing until well blended. Stir in fruit; fold in marshmallows and whipped cream. Pour into lightly oiled 9-inch square pan; freeze. Place in refrigerator 30 minutes before serving. Cut into squares.
9 servings.

Variations: Prepare mixture as directed. Spoon raspberry mixture into ten 5-ounce paper drinking cups; insert wooden sticks in center. Freeze.

Prepare mixture as directed. Pour raspberry mixture into lightly oiled 9-inch springform pan with ring insert; freeze. Place in refrigerator 1 hour before serving. Loosen dessert from rim of pan; remove rim of pan.

Chocolate Caramel Pecan Cheesecake

2 cups vanilla wafer crumbs
6 tablespoons PARKAY
     Margarine, melted

* * *

1 14-ounce bag KRAFT Caramels
1 5-ounce can evaporated milk
1 cup chopped pecans, toasted
2 8-ounce packages
     PHILADELPHIA BRAND
     Cream Cheese, softened
½ cup sugar
1 teaspoon vanilla
2 eggs
½ cup semi-sweet chocolate
     pieces, melted

Combine crumbs and margarine; press onto bottom and sides of 9-inch springform pan. Bake at 350°, 10 minutes.

In 1½-quart heavy saucepan, melt caramels with milk over low heat, stirring frequently, until smooth. Pour over crust. Top with pecans. Combine cream cheese, sugar and vanilla, mixing at medium speed on electric mixer until well blended. Add eggs, one at a time, mixing well after each addition. Blend in chocolate; pour over pecans. Bake at 350°, 40 minutes. Loosen cake from rim of pan; cool before removing rim of pan. Chill. Garnish with whipped cream, additional chopped nuts and maraschino cherries, if desired.
10 to 12 servings.

Miniature Cheesecakes

⅓ cup graham cracker crumbs
1 tablespoon sugar
1 tablespoon PARKAY
     Margarine, melted

* * *

1 8-ounce package
     PHILADELPHIA BRAND
     Cream Cheese, softened
¼ cup sugar
1½ teaspoons lemon juice
½ teaspoon grated lemon peel
¼ teaspoon vanilla
1 egg
     KRAFT Strawberry or Apricot
     Preserves

Combine crumbs, sugar and margarine. Press rounded measuring tablespoonful of crumb mixture onto bottom of each of six paper-lined muffin cups. Bake at 325°, 5 minutes.

Combine cream cheese, sugar, juice, peel and vanilla, mixing at medium speed on electric mixer until well blended. Blend in egg; pour over crust, filling each cup ¾ full. Bake at 325°, 25 minutes. Cool before removing from pan. Chill. Top with preserves just before serving.
6 servings.

Variation: Substitute fresh fruit for KRAFT Preserves.

Make Ahead: Wrap chilled cheesecakes individually in plastic wrap; freeze. Let stand at room temperature 40 minutes before serving.

Northwest Cheesecake Supreme

1 cup graham cracker crumbs
3 tablespoons sugar
3 tablespoons PARKAY
     Margarine, melted

* * *

4 8-ounce packages
     PHILADELPHIA BRAND
     Cream Cheese, softened
1 cup sugar
3 tablespoons flour
4 eggs
1 cup sour cream
1 tablespoon vanilla
1 21-ounce can cherry pie filling

Miniature Cheesecakes

Combine crumbs, sugar and margarine; press onto bottom of 9-inch springform pan. Bake at 325°, 10 minutes.

Combine cream cheese, sugar and flour, mixing at medium speed on electric mixer until well blended. Add eggs, one at a time, mixing well after each addition. Blend in sour cream and vanilla; pour over crust. Bake at 450°, 10 minutes. Reduce oven temperature to 250°; continue baking 1 hour. Loosen cake from rim of pan; cool before removing rim of pan. Chill. Top with cherry pie filling just before serving.
10 to 12 servings.

Variation: Substitute 1½ cups finely chopped nuts and 2 tablespoons sugar for graham cracker crumbs and sugar in crust.

Piña Colada Cheesecake

1½ cups vanilla wafer or graham
     cracker crumbs
½ cup flaked coconut, optional
3 tablespoons butter or
     margarine, melted
1 can (8 ounces) DOLE®
     Crushed Pineapple
3 packages (8 ounces each)
     cream cheese, softened
3 eggs
1 cup sugar
1 cup dairy sour cream
3 tablespoons dark rum
2 teaspoons coconut extract
     Pineapple Topping (recipe
     follows)

Preheat oven to 350°. In medium bowl, combine cookie crumbs, coconut and butter. Press onto bottom and sides of 9-inch springform pan. Bake 10 minutes. Cool.

Drain pineapple. In large bowl, beat cream cheese, eggs and sugar. Stir pineapple, sour cream, rum and coconut extract into cream cheese mixture. Pour into prepared crust. Bake in preheated oven 50 to 55 minutes or until set. Cool to room temperature; refrigerate until chilled. Spread Pineapple Topping over cheesecake just before serving.
Makes 16 servings.

PINEAPPLE TOPPING: In saucepan, combine 20 ounces (1 can) undrained Dole® Crushed Pineapple, ½ cup sugar, 1 tablespoon dark rum and 1 tablespoon cornstarch. Cook, stirring constantly, until thickened and clear. Cool.

Butterscotch Cheesecake

Butterscotch Cheesecake

- ⅓ **cup margarine or butter, melted**
- 1½ **cups graham cracker crumbs**
- ⅓ **cup firmly packed brown sugar**
- 1 **(14-ounce) can EAGLE® Brand Sweetened Condensed Milk (NOT evaporated milk)**
- ¾ **cup cold water**
- 1 **(3⅝-ounce) package butterscotch pudding and pie filling mix**
- 3 **(8-ounce) packages cream cheese, softened**
- 3 **eggs**
- 1 **teaspoon vanilla extract Whipped cream Crushed hard butterscotch candy**

Preheat oven to 375°. Combine margarine, crumbs and sugar; press firmly on bottom of 9-inch springform pan. In medium saucepan, combine sweetened condensed milk and water; mix well. Stir in pudding mix. Over medium heat, cook and stir until thickened and bubbly. In large mixer bowl, beat cheese until fluffy. Beat in eggs and vanilla then pudding mixture. Pour into prepared pan. Bake 50 minutes or until golden brown around edge (center will be soft). Cool to room temperature. Chill thoroughly. Garnish with whipped cream and crushed candy. Refrigerate leftovers.
Makes one 9-inch cheesecake.

Frozen Mocha Cheesecake

- 1¼ **cups chocolate wafer cookie crumbs (about 24 wafers)**
- ¼ **cup margarine or butter, melted**
- ¼ **cup sugar**
- 1 **(8-ounce) package cream cheese, softened**
- 1 **(14-ounce) can EAGLE® Brand Sweetened Condensed Milk (NOT evaporated milk)**
- ⅔ **cup chocolate flavored syrup**
- 1 **to 2 tablespoons instant coffee**
- 1 **teaspoon hot water**
- 1 **cup (½ pint) BORDEN® or MEADOW GOLD® Whipping Cream, whipped Additional chocolate crumbs, optional**

Combine crumbs, margarine and sugar; press firmly on bottom and up side of 8- or 9-inch springform pan or 13×9-inch baking pan. In large mixer bowl, beat cheese until fluffy. Gradually beat in sweetened condensed milk and chocolate syrup until smooth. In small bowl, dissolve coffee in water; add to cheese mixture. Mix well. Fold in whipped cream. Pour into prepared pan; cover. Freeze 6 hours or overnight. Garnish with additional chocolate crumbs if desired. Return leftovers to freezer.
Makes one 8- or 9-inch cheesecake.

Peaches in Port

- 6 **to 8 large fresh peaches, peeled and cut into sixths**
- 2 **teaspoons lemon juice**
- ¼ **cup tawny port wine**
- 2 **tablespoons butter or margarine**

Arrange peaches on 24×18-inch piece of heavy-duty foil. Sprinkle with lemon juice and port; dot with butter. Fold foil loosely around fruit and seal edges tightly. Grill packet, on covered grill, over medium-hot **KINGS-FORD® Charcoal Briquets** about 15 minutes or until fruit is hot, turning packet once.
Makes 4 to 6 servings.

"Philly" Fruit Clouds

1 8-ounce package
   PHILADELPHIA BRAND
   Cream Cheese, softened
½ cup sugar
1 tablespoon lemon juice
2 teaspoons grated lemon peel
1 cup whipping cream, whipped
   Assorted fruit

Combine cream cheese, sugar, juice and peel, mixing until well blended. Fold in whipped cream. With back of spoon, shape on wax paper–lined cookie sheet to form ten shells; freeze. Fill each shell with fruit. Garnish with fresh mint, if desired.
10 servings.

Variations: Prepare cream cheese mixture as directed. Spread into 8-inch square pan; freeze. Cut into squares; top with fruit.

Substitute *Light* PHILADELPHIA BRAND Neufchâtel Cheese for Cream Cheese.

Fresh Pineapple Melba

2 packages (10 ounces each)
   frozen raspberries, thawed
   Sugar
2 tablespoons cornstarch
3 tablespoons raspberry-
   flavored brandy
1 DOLE™ Fresh Pineapple
3 cups (1½ pints) vanilla ice
   cream
   Fresh raspberries for garnish,
   optional

In 2-quart saucepan, combine raspberries and their juice, sugar to taste and cornstarch. Stir until cornstarch is dissolved. Cook over medium heat, stirring constantly, until sauce turns clear and is slightly thickened. Remove from heat. Stir in brandy. Place plastic wrap directly on surface of sauce to cover. Refrigerate.

Twist crown from pineapple. Cut pineapple lengthwise into quarters. Remove fruit from shells with curved knife. Trim off core and cut fruit into chunks. Refrigerate, covered, until serving time.

To serve, spoon pineapple into 6 dessert dishes. Top each with scoop of ice cream. Drizzle with raspberry sauce; garnish with fresh raspberries, if desired.
Makes 6 servings.

"Philly" Fruit Clouds

Almond-Crumb Peaches

8 PEPPERIDGE FARM® Almond
   Supreme Cookies, finely
   crushed
2 tablespoons almond-flavored
   liqueur
4 ripe peaches, halved and
   pitted
   Whipped cream for garnish

To Microwave:
1. In small bowl, stir together cookies and liqueur.
2. Arrange peaches, cut-side up, in circular pattern on 10-inch microwave-safe plate. Spoon some of the cookie mixture into center of each peach. Microwave, uncovered, on HIGH 4 minutes or until peaches are tender, rotating dish once during cooking. Garnish with whipped cream.
Makes 4 servings.

Note: You can substitute 8 canned peach halves, drained, for fresh peaches. Reduce cooking time to 2 minutes or until peaches are heated through.

Fruit Kabobs with Whiskey Baste

2 tablespoons honey
2 tablespoons whiskey
1 tablespoon lemon juice
1 can (8 ounces) pineapple
   chunks, drained
1 large banana, diagonally sliced
   into 1-inch pieces
1 orange, peeled and sectioned
8 maraschino cherries

In large bowl, combine honey, whiskey and lemon juice; add pineapple chunks, banana pieces, orange sections and cherries. Gently toss to coat fruit well. Cover and refrigerate up to 2 hours or until ready to grill.

Remove fruit with slotted spoon, reserving whiskey baste. Alternately thread fruit on skewers. Grill fruit kabobs, on covered grill, over medium-low **KINGSFORD® Charcoal Briquets** 5 to 10 minutes or until fruit is warmed through, basting frequently with whiskey baste.
Makes 4 servings.

Cheddar Cheese Pears

3 fresh pears, peeled, cored and cut into halves *or* 1 can (29 ounces) pear halves, drained
2 teaspoons grated lemon peel
2 tablespoons fresh lemon juice
½ cup shredded Cheddar cheese (about 2 ounces)

Arrange pears on large square of heavy-duty foil. Sprinkle lemon peel and juice over pears. Fill pear halves with cheese. Fold up foil around pears; seal edges tightly. Grill packet over medium-hot **KINGSFORD® Charcoal Briquets** 15 minutes or until pears are hot and cheese is soft.
Makes 6 servings.

Hot Fruit Compote

1 (20-ounce) can pineapple chunks, drained
1 (17-ounce) can pitted dark sweet cherries, drained
1 (16-ounce) can sliced peaches, drained
1 (16-ounce) can pear halves, drained
1 (11-ounce) can mandarin orange segments, drained
¼ cup margarine or butter
½ cup firmly packed light brown sugar
½ cup orange juice
¼ cup REALEMON® Lemon Juice from Concentrate
½ teaspoon ground cinnamon
Sour cream and brown sugar

Preheat oven to 350°. In 13×9-inch baking dish, combine fruits. In small saucepan, melt margarine; add sugar, orange juice, ReaLemon® brand and cinnamon. Pour mixture over fruits. Bake 20 minutes or until hot. Serve warm with sour cream and brown sugar.
Makes 8 to 10 servings.

Bananas Foster

4 firm, small DOLE™ Bananas
½ cup brown sugar, packed
¼ cup butter or margarine
Dash cinnamon
⅓ cup light rum
Coffee or vanilla ice cream

Cut bananas into halves lengthwise, then crosswise. In 10-inch skillet, heat brown sugar and butter until sugar is melted. Cook and stir 2 minutes or until slightly thickened. Add bananas; cook slowly 1 to 2 minutes or until bananas are heated and glazed. Sprinkle lightly with cinnamon. Add rum. Carefully ignite rum with long match. Spoon liquid over bananas until flames die out, about 1 minute. Serve warm over ice cream.
Makes 4 servings.

Spiced Lemon Pears

1½ cups water
1 cup firmly packed light brown sugar
¼ cup REALEMON® Lemon Juice from Concentrate
2 cinnamon sticks
6 whole cloves
4 fresh pears, halved, pared and core removed

In large saucepan, combine all ingredients except pears. Bring to a boil; cook and stir until sugar dissolves. Add pears; cover and simmer 10 minutes or until pears are tender. Serve warm or chilled as a dessert, meat accompaniment or salad.
Makes 4 servings.
 Microwave: In 2-quart round baking dish, combine all ingredients except pears. Cover with plastic wrap; microwave on full power (high) 6 minutes or until mixture boils. Stir; add pears. Cover; microwave 6 minutes or until tender. Proceed as above.

Snow Topped Apples

2 medium baking apples
2 teaspoons raisins
2 teaspoons chopped nuts
Dash of cinnamon
2 teaspoons PARKAY Margarine
2 tablespoons *Light* PHILADELPHIA BRAND Neufchâtel Cheese

Core apples; remove peel around top of apples. Place each in 10-ounce custard cup. Fill center of apples with combined raisins, nuts and cinnamon; dot with margarine. Bake at 375°, 25 to 30 minutes or until soft. Top warm apples with neufchâtel cheese. Sprinkle with additional chopped nuts, if desired.
2 servings.
 Variation: Substitute Soft PHILADELPHIA BRAND Cream Cheese for Neufchâtel Cheese.
 Microwave: Prepare apples as directed. Cover custard cups with plastic wrap vented at one edge. Microwave on High 2½ to 3 minutes or until apples are soft. Serve as directed.

Bananas Foster

Pears au Chocolat

4 fresh pears
½ cup sugar
1 cup water
1 teaspoon vanilla
6 tablespoons finely chopped nuts
2 tablespoons confectioners' sugar
1 teaspoon milk
Chocolate Sauce

Core pears from bottom, leaving stems intact. Peel pears. Slice piece off bottom to make a flat base. Combine sugar and water in medium saucepan; add pears. Cover; simmer over low heat 10 to 20 minutes (depending on ripeness) or just until pears are soft. Remove from heat; add vanilla. Cool pears in syrup; chill. Combine nuts, confectioners' sugar and milk in small bowl. To serve, drain pears; spoon nut mixture into cavities. Place pears on dessert plates. Prepare Chocolate Sauce; pour or spoon sauce onto each pear. Serve with remaining sauce.
4 servings.

Chocolate Sauce

6 tablespoons water
6 tablespoons sugar
¼ cup butter or margarine
1⅓ cups HERSHEY'S MINI CHIPS Semi-Sweet Chocolate

Combine water, sugar and butter in small saucepan; bring to full boil. Remove from heat; stir in MINI CHIPS Chocolate. Stir until chocolate has completely melted; beat or whisk until smooth. Cool.

Flaming Pineapple

1 fresh pineapple
½ cup packed light brown sugar
½ teaspoon ground cinnamon
⅛ teaspoon freshly ground nutmeg
¼ cup butter or margarine
½ cup light rum
Ice cream, whipped cream or chilled soft custard (optional)

Cut pineapple in half lengthwise, leaving on green top. Cut each half lengthwise into four sections. Carefully cut pineapple away from peel. Remove core, then cut pineapple into 1-inch chunks; rearrange pineapple chunks on peel. Place in large baking pan or foil pan. Sprinkle with brown sugar, cinnamon and nutmeg; dot with butter. Place pan on edge of grill. Heat pineapple, on covered grill, over medium-hot **KINGSFORD**® **Charcoal Briquets** 10 minutes; remove pan from grill.

In small saucepan, heat rum on range-top over low heat just until hot. Carefully ignite with match; pour flaming rum over pineapple, stirring sauce and spooning over pineapple. Serve with ice cream.
Makes 8 servings.

Applesauce Yogurt Dessert

1 package (4-serving size) JELL-O® **Brand Sugar Free Gelatin, any red flavor**
1 cup boiling water
¾ cup chilled unsweetened applesauce
¼ teaspoon cinnamon
½ cup vanilla yogurt

Dissolve gelatin in boiling water. Measure ¾ cup of the gelatin; add applesauce and cinnamon. Pour into individual dessert glasses or serving bowl. Chill until set but not firm.

Chill remaining gelatin until slightly thickened. Blend in yogurt. Spoon over gelatin in glasses. Chill until set, about 2 hours. Garnish with additional yogurt and mint leaves, if desired.
Makes 2 cups or 4 servings.

Fruited Tilt

1 package (4-serving size) JELL-O® **Brand Gelatin, any flavor**
¾ cup boiling water
½ cup cold water
Ice cubes
1 cup sliced or diced fresh fruit*
1 cup thawed COOL WHIP® **Non-Dairy Whipped Topping**

Dissolve gelatin in boiling water. Combine cold water and ice cubes to make 1¼ cups. Add to gelatin, stirring until slightly thickened. Remove any unmelted ice. Fold in fruit. Spoon half of the fruited gelatin into individual parfait glasses. Tilt glasses in refrigerator by catching bases between bars of rack and leaning tops against wall; chill until set. Spoon whipped topping into glasses; top with remaining fruited gelatin. Stand glasses upright. Chill about 30 minutes.
Makes 6 to 8 servings.

*Do not use fresh pineapple, kiwifruit, mango, papaya or figs.

Pears au Chocolat

Fruit Whip

³/₄ cup boiling water
1 package (4-serving size)
**   JELL-O® Brand Gelatin, any**
**   flavor**
½ cup cold water or fruit juice
**   Ice cubes**
1 cup fresh or canned fruit
**   (optional)**

Pour boiling water into blender. Add gelatin. Cover and blend at low speed until gelatin is completely dissolved, about 30 seconds. Combine cold water and ice cubes to make 1¼ cups. Add to gelatin and stir until ice is partially melted; then blend at high speed for 30 seconds. Pour into dessert glasses or serving bowl. Spoon in fruit. Chill until firm, 20 to 30 minutes. Dessert layers as it chills. Garnish with additional fruit and mint, if desired.
Makes 4½ cups or 6 servings.
  *See note, page 310 (Fruited Tilt).

Molded Strawberries Romanoff

1 pint strawberries, hulled
2 tablespoons sugar
2 packages (4-serving size) or
**   1 package (8-serving size)**
**   JELL-O® Brand Strawberry**
**   Flavor Gelatin**
2 cups boiling water
2 tablespoons brandy*
1 tablespoon orange liqueur*
1³/₄ cups thawed COOL WHIP®
**   Non-Dairy Whipped Topping**

Slice strawberries, reserving a few whole berries for garnish, if desired. Sprinkle sliced berries with sugar; let stand 15 minutes. Drain, reserving liquid. Add enough cold water to liquid to make 1 cup. Dissolve gelatin in boiling water. Measure ³/₄ cup of the gelatin and add brandy, orange liqueur and ½ cup of the measured liquid. Chill until slightly thickened. Fold in whipped topping. Pour into 6-cup mold. Chill until set but not firm.
  Add remaining measured liquid to remaining gelatin. Chill until thickened; fold in sliced berries. Spoon over creamy layer in mold. Chill until firm, about 4 hours. Unmold. Garnish with reserved berries.
Makes 6 cups or 12 servings.
  ***Substitution:** Use ½ teaspoon brandy extract and 3 tablespoons orange juice for the brandy and orange liqueur.

Fruit Whip

Lime Chiffon Squares

¼ cup margarine or butter,
**   melted**
1 cup graham cracker crumbs
1 (3-ounce) package lime flavor
**   gelatin**
1 cup boiling water
1 (14-ounce) can EAGLE® Brand
**   Sweetened Condensed Milk**
**   (NOT evaporated milk)**
1 (8-ounce) can crushed
**   pineapple, undrained**
2 tablespoons REALIME® Lime
**   Juice from Concentrate**
4 cups CAMPFIRE® Miniature
**   Marshmallows**
1 cup (½ pint) BORDEN® or
**   MEADOW GOLD® Whipping**
**   Cream, whipped**

Combine margarine and crumbs; press firmly on bottom of 9-inch square *or* 12×7-inch baking dish. In large mixing bowl, dissolve gelatin in water; stir in sweetened condensed milk, pineapple and ReaLime® brand.

Fold in marshmallows and whipped cream. Pour into prepared dish. Chill 2 hours or until set. Garnish as desired. Refrigerate leftovers.
Makes 10 to 12 servings.

Fruit Juice Gelatine Cooler

1 envelope KNOX® Unflavored
**   Gelatine**
2 to 4 tablespoons sugar
2 cups fruit juice, heated to
**   boiling***

In medium bowl, mix unflavored gelatine with sugar; add hot juice and stir until gelatine is completely dissolved, about 5 minutes. Pour into 2-cup bowl, mold or dessert dishes; chill until firm, about 3 hours. To serve, unmold onto serving platter.
Makes about 4 servings.
  *Do not use fresh or frozen pineapple juice.

Piña Colada Ring

Ice Cream and Orange Dessert

**³/₄ cup boiling water
1 package (4-serving size) JELL-O® Brand Orange, Peach or Lemon Flavor Gelatin
1 cup (½ pint) vanilla ice cream
½ cup crushed ice
1 medium orange, peeled and cut into bite-size pieces**

Pour boiling water into blender. Add gelatin. Cover and blend at low speed until gelatin is completely dissolved, about 30 seconds. Add ice cream and crushed ice. Blend at high speed until ice is melted, about 30 seconds. Pour into bowl. Stir in orange. Chill until firm, about 1 hour. When ready to serve, spoon into flat-bottom ice cream cups or dessert dishes.
Makes about 3 cups or 6 servings.

Fruited Fruit Juice Gelatin

**2 packages (4-serving size) or 1 package (8-serving size) JELL-O® Brand Orange Flavor Sugar Free Gelatin*
1½ cups boiling water
1 cup cold apple juice*
Ice cubes
1½ cups diced apples***

Completely dissolve gelatin in boiling water. Combine cold fruit juice and ice cubes to make 2½ cups. Add to gelatin, stirring until slightly thickened. Remove any unmelted ice. Stir in apples. Pour into bowl or individual dessert glasses. Chill until set, about 4 hours. Garnish with celery leaves and additional fruit, if desired.
Makes 5 cups or 10 servings.

*Additional Flavor Combinations:
Use strawberry flavor gelatin with canned pineapple juice, 1½ cups diced apples and ¼ cup chopped nuts.

Use raspberry flavor gelatin with cranberry juice cocktail, 1½ cups diced oranges, 2 tablespoons chopped nuts and ¼ cup chopped celery.

Use strawberry-banana flavor gelatin with orange juice and 1½ cups sliced bananas.

Use strawberry flavor gelatin with grape juice and 1½ cups seedless green grapes.

Piña Colada Ring

**2 envelopes unflavored gelatin
2¼ cups (18 ounces) pineapple juice, unsweetened
1 package (8 ounces) Neufchatel cheese
⅓ cup sugar
1 teaspoon grated orange rind
1 teaspoon grated lemon rind
1½ teaspoons rum extract
½ cup dry CARNATION® Nonfat Dry Milk
½ cup ice water
2 tablespoons lemon juice
½ cup toasted flake coconut Fresh fruit**

Soften gelatin in pineapple juice; heat to dissolve. Pour into blender container. Add Neufchatel cheese, sugar, rinds, and rum extract. Cover; blend until smooth. Pour into large bowl. Chill until mixture mounds from a spoon. Place nonfat dry milk, ice water, and lemon juice in small mixer bowl. Beat on high speed until stiff peaks form, 4 to 6 minutes. Fold into gelatin mixture. Spoon into 6-cup ring mold. Chill until firm. Unmold onto serving platter. Sprinkle with toasted coconut. Garnish outer edge and center of mold with fresh fruit.
Makes 6 cups.

Self-Layering Dessert

**³/₄ cup boiling water
1 package (4-serving size) JELL-O® Brand Gelatin, any flavor
½ cup cold water
Ice cubes
½ cup thawed COOL WHIP® Non-Dairy Whipped Topping**

Pour boiling water into blender. Add gelatin. Cover and blend at low speed until gelatin is completely dissolved, about 30 seconds. Combine cold water and ice cubes to make 1¼ cups. Add to gelatin and stir until ice is partially melted. Then add whipped topping; blend at high speed for 30 seconds. Pour into dessert glasses. Chill about 30 minutes. Dessert layers as it chills. Garnish as desired.
Makes 3 cups or 6 servings.

Chocolate-Berry Parfaits

Chocolate Cream Pudding (see Index)
1 package (10 ounces) frozen sliced strawberries, thawed, or 1 cup sweetened sliced fresh strawberries
1 cup heavy or whipping cream*
¼ cup confectioners' sugar*
Fresh strawberries (optional)

Prepare Chocolate Cream Pudding; cool completely. Drain strawberries; puree in blender or sieve to equal ½ to ¾ cup. Beat cream and confectioners' sugar until stiff; fold in strawberry puree. Alternately layer chocolate pudding and strawberry cream in parfait glasses. Chill until set. Garnish with strawberries.
8 to 10 servings.

*You may substitute 2 cups frozen non-dairy whipped topping, thawed, for the cream and confectioners' sugar.

Fresh Fruit Parfaits

1 envelope KNOX® Unflavored Gelatine
1¾ cups cold water
9 packets aspartame sweetener or 3 tablespoons sugar
⅓ cup fresh lemon juice (about 2 lemons)
1 medium peach or nectarine, sliced
1 medium banana, sliced
1½ cups seedless green grapes, halved
1½ cups sliced strawberries

In medium saucepan, sprinkle unflavored gelatine over ½ cup cold water; let stand 1 minute. Stir over low heat until gelatine is completely dissolved, about 3 minutes. Stir in sweetener until dissolved, then add lemon juice and remaining 1¼ cups water.

In large bowl, combine fruit. Into 6 (8 ounce) parfait or dessert glasses, evenly divide fruit. Evenly pour gelatine mixture over fruit to cover; chill until firm, about 3 hours.
Makes 6 servings; 80 calories per serving with aspartame sweetener; 98 calories per serving with sugar.

Elegant Chocolate Mousse

3 squares BAKER'S® Unsweetened Chocolate
¾ cup water
¾ cup sugar
⅛ teaspoon salt
3 egg yolks, slightly beaten
1½ teaspoons vanilla
1¾ cups heavy cream*
3 tablespoons sugar*
¾ teaspoon vanilla*

Melt chocolate in water in saucepan over very low heat, stirring constantly until smooth. Stir in ¾ cup sugar and the salt. Bring to a boil over medium heat, stirring constantly. Reduce heat and simmer 5 minutes, stirring constantly.

Blend a small amount of the hot mixture into egg yolks; stir into remaining hot mixture. Cook and stir 1 minute longer. Cool to room temperature; then add 1½ teaspoons vanilla. Whip the cream with 3 tablespoons sugar and ¾ teaspoon vanilla until soft peaks form. Gradually blend in chocolate mixture. Spoon into 9-inch square pan or 1½-quart freezer container. Freeze until firm, at least 6 hours.
Makes 8 servings.

*Or use 3½ cups thawed COOL WHIP® Non-Dairy Whipped Topping.

Chocolate-Berry Parfaits

Microwave Hershey Bar Mousse

1 HERSHEY'S Milk Chocolate Bar (8 ounces), broken into pieces
¼ cup water
2 eggs, beaten
1 cup heavy or whipping cream

Microwave: Combine chocolate bar pieces and water in medium microproof bowl. Microwave at HIGH (100%) for 1½ to 2 minutes or until chocolate is softened and mixture is melted and smooth when stirred. Stir in eggs. Microwave at MEDIUM (50%) for 1½ to 2½ minutes or until mixture is hot; *do not boil.* Cool slightly. Whip cream until stiff; fold into cooled chocolate mixture. Pour into 8-inch square pan. Cover; freeze until firm. Cut into squares.
4 servings.

Cookies and Cream Parfaits

1 envelope KNOX® Unflavored Gelatine
¼ cup cold water
2 cups (1 pint) vanilla or chocolate ice cream, softened
1 cup (½ pint) whipping or heavy cream
22 chocolate sandwich cookies
1 teaspoon vanilla extract

In small saucepan, sprinkle unflavored gelatine over cold water; let stand 1 minute. Stir over low heat until gelatine is completely dissolved, about 3 minutes. Remove from heat and let stand until lukewarm, about 1 minute.

In blender or food processor, process ice cream, whipping cream, 10 cookies and vanilla until blended. While processing, through feed cap, gradually add lukewarm gelatine mixture and process until blended. Let stand until mixture is slightly thickened, about 5 minutes.

Meanwhile, coarsely crush remaining 12 cookies. In parfait glasses or dessert dishes, alternately layer gelatine mixture with crushed cookies; chill until set, about 2 hours. Garnish, if desired, with whipped cream and additional cookies.
Makes about 6 servings.

Fruit Glazed Baked Custards

3 eggs
1 (14-ounce) can EAGLE® Brand Sweetened Condensed Milk (NOT evaporated milk)
1 cup water
1 teaspoon vanilla extract
½ cup red currant jelly
2 tablespoons orange-flavored liqueur *or* orange juice
1 tablespoon cornstarch
Few drops red food coloring, optional
Fresh strawberries or other fruit

Preheat oven to 350°. In medium mixing bowl, beat eggs; stir in sweetened condensed milk, water and vanilla. Pour equal portions of mixture into six 6-ounce custard cups. Set cups in shallow pan; fill pan with 1 inch hot water. Bake 45 to 50 minutes or until knife inserted in center comes out clean. Cool. In small saucepan, combine jelly, liqueur and cornstarch. Cook and stir until jelly melts and mixture comes to a boil. Stir in food coloring if desired. Cool to room temperature. Invert custards onto serving plates. Top with sauce and strawberries. Refrigerate leftovers.
Makes 6 servings.

Quick Chocolate Mousse

1 (14-ounce) can EAGLE® Brand Sweetened Condensed Milk (NOT evaporated milk)
1 (4-serving size) package *instant* chocolate flavor pudding and pie filling mix
1 cup cold water
1 cup (½ pint) BORDEN® or MEADOW GOLD® Whipping Cream, whipped

In large mixer bowl, beat sweetened condensed milk, pudding mix and water; chill 5 minutes. Fold in whipped cream. Spoon into serving dishes; chill. Garnish as desired.
Makes 8 to 10 servings.

Quick Chocolate Mousse

Strawberry-Chocolate Bavarian Cream

1 package (10 ounces) frozen sliced strawberries, thawed
2 envelopes unflavored gelatine
½ cup sugar
1 cup HERSHEY'S Semi-Sweet Chocolate Chips
2¼ cups milk
1 teaspoon vanilla
2 cups heavy or whipping cream
1 teaspoon vanilla
2 or 3 drops red food color

Drain strawberries; reserve syrup. Add water to syrup to equal ³/₄ cup. Stir gelatine into liquid; set aside. Puree or mash berries to equal ½ cup; reserve.

Combine sugar, chocolate chips and ½ cup of the milk in medium saucepan. Cook over low heat, stirring constantly, until mixture is smooth and very hot. Add gelatine mixture, stirring until gelatine is dissolved. Remove from heat; add remaining 1³/₄ cups milk and 1 teaspoon vanilla. Pour into bowl; chill, stirring occasionally, until mixture mounds when dropped from a spoon.

Whip 1 cup of the cream until stiff; fold into chocolate mixture. Pour into oiled 5- or 6-cup mold; chill until firm.

Whip remaining 1 cup cream and 1 teaspoon vanilla in small mixer bowl until stiff. Fold in reserved puree and food color. Unmold Bavarian; garnish with strawberry mixture.
8 to 10 servings.

Creamy Low-Calorie Rice Pudding

1 package (4-serving size) JELL-O® Sugar Free Vanilla Pudding and Pie Filling
3 cups skim or low-fat milk
½ cup MINUTE® Rice
¼ cup raisins
⅛ teaspoon ground cinnamon

Combine all ingredients in medium saucepan. Bring to a boil over medium heat, stirring constantly. Pour into 1-quart casserole or individual dessert dishes. Place plastic wrap directly on surface of hot pudding. Chill 30 minutes; remove plastic wrap. Sprinkle with additional cinnamon, if desired.
Makes 8 servings.

Peanut Butter Shells with Chocolate-Almond Cream

2 cups (12-ounce package) REESE'S Peanut Butter Chips
2 tablespoons shortening*
Chocolate-Almond Cream Filling

Melt peanut butter chips and shortening in top of double boiler over hot, not boiling, water; stir until smooth. Remove from heat; cool slightly. Place 15 paper baking cups (2³/₄ inches in diameter) in muffin pans. Using a narrow, soft-bristled pastry brush, thickly and evenly coat the inside pleated surface and bottom of each cup with peanut butter mixture. (Reserve any remaining peanut butter mixture for touch-up.) Chill 10 minutes; coat any thin spots. (If peanut butter mixture thickens, stir over hot water until mixture becomes fluid again.) Cover; chill at least 1 hour or until firm.

Remove only a few peanut butter shells from refrigerator at a time; carefully peel paper from each cup. (Unfilled cups will keep for weeks in an airtight container in the refrigerator.) Fill each cup with Chocolate-Almond Cream Filling; chill several hours or overnight.
15 desserts.

*Do not substitute butter, margarine or oil.

Chocolate-Almond Cream Filling

1 HERSHEY'S Milk Chocolate Bar with Almonds (8 ounces)
1¹/₂ cups miniature or 15 large marshmallows
¹/₃ cup milk
1 cup heavy or whipping cream

Cut chocolate bar in pieces, chopping almonds into small pieces. Place in top of double boiler and melt with marshmallows and milk over hot, not boiling, water. Stir until chocolate and marshmallows are melted and mixture is smooth. Remove from heat; cool. Whip cream until stiff and fold into chocolate mixture. Cover; chill until ready to use.

Tip: You may prepare the shells weeks in advance of use, but for best results make the filling no earlier than a day ahead of serving time.

Creamy Banana Pudding

1 (14-ounce) can EAGLE® Brand Sweetened Condensed Milk (NOT evaporated milk)
1¹/₂ cups cold water
1 (3¹/₂-ounce) package instant vanilla pudding and pie filling mix
2 cups (1 pint) BORDEN® or MEADOW GOLD® Whipping Cream, whipped
36 vanilla wafers
3 medium bananas, sliced and dipped in lemon juice

In large mixing bowl, combine sweetened condensed milk and water. Add pudding mix; beat until well blended. Chill 5 minutes. Fold in whipped cream. Spoon *1 cup* pudding mixture into 2¹/₂-quart round glass serving bowl. Top with one-third each of the vanilla wafers, bananas and pudding. Repeat layering twice, ending with pudding mixture. Chill thoroughly. Garnish as desired. Refrigerate leftovers.
Makes 8 to 10 servings.

Tip: Mixture can be layered in individual serving dishes.

Old-Fashioned Rice Pudding

4 cups cold milk
1 cup MINUTE® Rice
1 package (4-serving size) JELL-O® Vanilla or Coconut Cream Flavor Pudding and Pie Filling
¹/₄ cup raisins (optional)
1 egg, well beaten
¹/₄ teaspoon ground cinnamon
¹/₈ teaspoon ground nutmeg

Combine milk, rice, pudding mix, raisins and egg in medium saucepan. Bring to a full boil over medium heat, stirring constantly. Remove from heat. Cool 5 minutes, stirring twice. Pour into individual dessert dishes or serving bowl. Sprinkle with cinnamon and nutmeg; serve warm. (For chilled pudding, place plastic wrap directly on hot pudding. Cool slightly; then chill about 1 hour. Stir before serving; sprinkle with cinnamon and nutmeg.)
Makes 10 servings.

Old-Fashioned Fruited Rice Pudding: Add 1 can (17¹/₂ oz.) drained fruit cocktail to pudding after cooling 5 minutes. Garnish as desired.

Creamy Banana Pudding

Clockwise from top: Pudding Tart-in-a-Dish, Quick Coffee Fluff, Pudding in a Cloud

Pudding Tart-in-a-Dish

1 package (4-serving size) JELL-O® Pudding and Pie Filling, any flavor except Lemon
2 cups milk
½ cup graham cracker crumbs or cookie crumbs
2 to 3 teaspoons butter or margarine, melted

Combine pudding mix and milk in medium saucepan; blend well. Cook and stir over medium heat until mixture comes to a full boil. Cool 5 minutes, stirring twice.

Combine crumbs and butter; mix well. Press mixture on bottom and sides of individual dessert glasses. Spoon pudding into crumb-lined glasses. Chill. Garnish with prepared whipped topping and additional crumbs, if desired.
Makes about 2½ cups or 4 servings.

Pudding in a Cloud

1 package (4-serving size) JELL-O® Pudding and Pie Filling, any flavor except Lemon
2 cups milk
2 cups thawed COOL WHIP® Non-Dairy Whipped Topping

Combine pudding mix and milk in medium saucepan; blend well. Cook and stir over medium heat until mixture comes to a full boil. Pour into bowl; cover surface of pudding with plastic wrap. Chill.

Spoon ⅓ cup of the whipped topping into each of 6 dessert glasses. Using the back of a spoon, make a depression in the center and spread topping up the sides of each glass. Spoon pudding mixture into glasses. Chill.
Makes about 3½ cups or 6 servings.

Quick Coffee Fluff

1 tablespoon MAXWELL HOUSE® or YUBAN® Instant Coffee
2¼ cups cold milk
1 envelope DREAM WHIP® Whipped Topping Mix
1 package (6-serving size) JELL-O® Vanilla Flavor Instant Pudding and Pie Filling
½ teaspoon cinnamon (optional)
½ cup chopped nuts (optional)

Dissolve coffee in milk in bowl. Add whipped topping mix, pudding mix and cinnamon. With electric mixer at low speed, beat until well blended, about 1 minute. Gradually increase beating speed and beat until mixture forms soft peaks, 3 to 6 minutes. Fold in nuts. Spoon into individual dessert glasses. Chill. Garnish with additional whipped topping and pecan halves.
Makes 8 or 9 servings.

"Philly" Banana Pudding

12 vanilla wafers
1 8-ounce container Soft PHILADELPHIA BRAND Cream Cheese
2 tablespoons milk
2 tablespoons sugar
1 teaspoon vanilla
2 cups thawed frozen whipped topping
2 medium bananas, sliced

Line bottom and sides of 1-quart serving bowl with wafers. Combine cream cheese, milk, sugar and vanilla, mixing until well blended. Fold in remaining ingredients. Spoon into bowl; chill.
6 servings.

Fruit and Juice Pudding

1 can (17 ounces) fruit cocktail
1 package (4-serving size) JELL-O® Vanilla Flavor Pudding and Pie Filling
1²/₃ cups milk

Microwave: * Drain fruit cocktail, reserving ¹/₃ cup syrup; set aside. Combine pudding mix and milk in 1½-quart microwave-safe bowl; blend well. Add reserved syrup. Cook at HIGH 3 minutes. Stir well and cook 2 minutes longer; then stir again and cook 1 minute or until mixture comes to a boil. Cover surface of pudding with plastic wrap. Chill. Fold in fruit. Spoon into individual dessert dishes.
Makes 3 cups or 6 servings.
*Ovens vary. Cooking time is approximate.

Pudding Tortoni

1¼ cups cold milk
1 package (4-serving size) JELL-O® Pistachio or Vanilla Flavor Instant Pudding and Pie Filling
1³/₄ cups thawed COOL WHIP® Non-Dairy Whipped Topping
³/₄ cup BAKER'S® ANGEL FLAKE® Coconut, toasted *
¼ cup chopped drained maraschino cherries
½ teaspoon almond extract

Pour cold milk into bowl. Add pudding mix. With electric mixer at low speed, beat until well blended, 1 to 2 minutes. Blend in whipped topping. Fold in coconut, cherries and almond extract. Spoon into muffin pan lined with paper baking cups. Freeze until firm, about 3 hours.
Makes 3½ cups or 6 servings.
To toast coconut: Spread coconut in a thin layer in shallow pan. Toast in preheated 350° oven for 7 to 12 minutes or until lightly browned, stirring frequently.

Baked Almond Pudding

¼ cup firmly packed brown sugar
³/₄ cup slivered almonds, toasted
1 (14-ounce) can EAGLE® Brand Sweetened Condensed Milk (NOT evaporated milk)
5 eggs
1 cup (½ pint) BORDEN® or MEADOW GOLD® Whipping Cream
½ teaspoon almond extract
Additional toasted almonds, optional

Preheat oven to 325°. In 8-inch round layer cake pan, sprinkle sugar; set aside. In blender or food processor container, grind nuts; add sweetened condensed milk, eggs, *½ cup* cream and extract. Blend thoroughly. Pour into prepared pan; set in larger pan. Fill larger pan with 1 inch hot water. Bake 40 to 45 minutes or until knife inserted near center comes out clean. Cool. Chill thoroughly; invert onto serving plate. Beat remaining cream for garnish; top with additional almonds if desired. Refrigerate leftovers.
Makes 8 to 10 servings.

Hot Fudge Sauce (top), Coconut Pecan Sauce (bottom)

Hot Fudge Sauce

1 (6-ounce) package semi-sweet chocolate chips *or*
4 (1-ounce) squares semi-sweet chocolate
2 tablespoons margarine or butter
1 (14-ounce) can EAGLE® Brand Sweetened Condensed Milk (NOT evaporated milk)
2 tablespoons water
1 teaspoon vanilla extract

In heavy saucepan, over medium heat, melt chips and margarine with sweetened condensed milk, water and vanilla. Cook and stir constantly until thickened, about 5 minutes. Serve warm over ice cream. Refrigerate leftovers.
Makes about 2 cups.
Mocha: Add 1 teaspoon instant coffee. Proceed as above.
Microwave: In 1-quart glass measure, combine ingredients. Cook on 100% power (high) 3 to 3½ minutes, stirring after each minute.
To Reheat: In small heavy saucepan, combine desired amount of sauce with small amount of water. Over low heat, stir constantly until heated through.

Coconut Pecan Sauce

1 (14-ounce) can EAGLE® Brand Sweetened Condensed Milk (NOT evaporated milk)
2 egg yolks, beaten
¼ cup margarine or butter
½ cup flaked coconut
½ cup chopped pecans
1 teaspoon vanilla extract

In heavy saucepan, combine sweetened condensed milk, egg yolks and margarine. Over medium heat, cook and stir until thickened and bubbly, about 8 minutes. Stir in remaining ingredients. Serve warm over ice cream or cake.
Makes about 2 cups.
Microwave: In 1-quart glass measure, combine sweetened condensed milk, egg yolks and margarine. Cook on 70% power (medium-high) 4 to 5 minutes, stirring after 3 minutes. Proceed as above.
To Reheat: In small heavy saucepan, combine desired amount of sauce with small amount of water. Over low heat, stir constantly until heated through.

Bananas Coco Lopez (left), Coconut Fudge Sauce (right)

Pineapple Orange Dessert Sauce

1 can (20 ounces) DOLE®
   Pineapple Chunks,
   undrained
1/2 cup orange juice
1 tablespoon cornstarch
1 tablespoon sugar
1 teaspoon ground ginger
1 teaspoon grated orange peel
   Vanilla ice cream
   DOLE™ Blanched Slivered
   Almonds, toasted

In saucepan, combine pineapple chunks, orange juice, cornstarch, sugar, ginger and orange peel. Cook and stir until sauce boils and thickens. Cool to room temperature. Spoon sauce over ice cream. Sprinkle with almonds.
Makes 2 cups sauce.

Chocolate Custard Sauce

1 egg, slightly beaten
1/4 cup sugar
1/4 teaspoon salt
1 1/2 cups milk
1 square BAKER'S®
   Unsweetened Chocolate,
   melted
1/2 teaspoon vanilla

Combine egg, sugar, salt and milk in saucepan. Cook and stir over medium heat until mixture begins to thicken slightly and coats a metal spoon, about 5 minutes. Remove from heat. Stir in chocolate and vanilla. Beat with hand or electric mixer until blended. Cover surface with plastic wrap. Chill. Serve over fruit, desserts or cake. Store any leftover sauce in refrigerator.
Makes 1 1/2 cups.

Chocolate Cream Pudding

1 cup sugar
1/4 cup HERSHEY'S Cocoa
1/3 cup cornstarch
1/4 teaspoon salt
3 cups milk
3 egg yolks, slightly beaten
2 tablespoons butter or
   margarine
1 1/2 teaspoons vanilla

Combine sugar, cocoa, cornstarch and salt in heavy saucepan; add milk and egg yolks. Cook over medium heat, stirring constantly, until mixture boils; boil and stir 1 minute. Remove from heat; blend in butter and vanilla. Pour into bowl or individual dessert dishes; press plastic wrap directly onto surface of pudding. Cool; chill until set.
6 to 8 servings.

Microwave Classic Chocolate Sauce

2 squares (2 ounces)
   HERSHEY'S Unsweetened
   Baking Chocolate
2 tablespoons butter or
   margarine
1 cup sugar
1/4 teaspoon salt
3/4 cup evaporated milk
1/2 teaspoon vanilla

Microwave: Place baking chocolate and butter in small micro-proof bowl. Microwave at HIGH (100%) for 1 minute or until chocolate is softened and mixture is melted and smooth when stirred. Add sugar, salt and evaporated milk; blend well. Microwave an additional 2 to 3 minutes, stirring with wire whisk after each minute, or until mixture is smooth and hot. Stir in vanilla. Serve warm.
About 1 1/2 cups sauce.

Bananas Coco Lopez

4 firm medium bananas, peeled
   and sliced
   REALEMON® Lemon Juice
   from Concentrate
1 cup COCO LOPEZ® Cream of
   Coconut
1/4 teaspoon ground cinnamon
1/2 teaspoon vanilla extract

Dip sliced bananas in ReaLemon® brand. In large skillet or chafing dish, combine cream of coconut and cinnamon; bring to a boil. Add bananas and vanilla. Over medium heat, cook and stir 2 to 3 minutes. Serve warm over ice cream or cake.
Makes 4 to 6 servings.
Microwave: Dip sliced bananas in ReaLemon® brand. In 2-quart glass measure, combine cream of coconut and cinnamon. Microwave on full power (high) 2 minutes or until mixture boils. Add bananas and vanilla. Microwave on full power (high) 1 1/2 to 2 minutes or until bananas are heated through *(do not overheat).*

Coconut Fudge Sauce

- 1 (6-ounce) package semi-sweet chocolate chips *or*
  4 (1-ounce) squares semi-sweet chocolate
- 1 (14-ounce) can EAGLE® Brand Sweetened Condensed Milk (NOT evaporated milk)
- 1 (15-ounce) can COCO LOPEZ® Cream of Coconut

In heavy saucepan, over medium heat, melt chips with sweetened condensed milk. Cook, stirring constantly, until sauce is slightly thickened, about 5 minutes. Gradually stir in cream of coconut; heat through. Serve warm over ice cream or with fresh fruit. Refrigerate leftovers.
Makes about 3½ cups.

Microwave: In 1-quart glass measure, combine chips and sweetened condensed milk. Microwave on full power (high) 3 to 3½ minutes, stirring after each minute. Gradually stir in cream of coconut; microwave on full power (high) 2 minutes, stirring after each minute.

Ginger Mandarin Sauce over Vanilla Ice Cream

- 1 can (20 ounces) lychee fruit
- 1 can (11 ounces) DOLE® Mandarin Orange Segments
- 1 tablespoon cornstarch
- ½ cup orange juice
- ¼ cup sugar
- 2 tablespoons butter or margarine
- 2 tablespoons finely chopped crystallized ginger
- 1 teaspoon grated orange peel
  Vanilla ice cream

Drain lychees and orange segments; reserve syrup. In saucepan, dissolve cornstarch in orange juice; add reserved syrup and sugar. Cook, stirring, until sauce boils and thickens. Stir in butter, ginger, orange peel and fruit. Heat through. Serve sauce warm or at room temperature over ice cream. Store leftover sauce in covered container in refrigerator up to 1 week.
Makes 4 cups sauce.

Black Russian Mini Soufflés

- 3 squares (1 ounce each) semi-sweet chocolate
- 1 envelope KNOX® Unflavored Gelatine
- ½ cup sugar
- 2 eggs, separated
- 1 cup milk
- 3 tablespoons coffee liqueur
- 2 tablespoons vodka
- 1 cup (½ pint) whipping or heavy cream, whipped

With vegetable peeler, make chocolate curls and shavings from 1 square chocolate; reserve for garnish.

In medium saucepan, mix unflavored gelatine with ¼ cup sugar; blend in egg yolks beaten with milk. Let stand 1 minute. Stir over low heat until gelatine is completely dissolved, about 5 minutes. Add remaining 2 squares chocolate and continue cooking, stirring constantly, until chocolate is melted. With wire whisk or rotary beater, beat mixture until chocolate is blended. Stir in liqueur and vodka. Pour into large bowl and chill, stirring occasionally, until mixture mounds slightly when dropped from spoon, about 40 minutes.

In large bowl, beat egg whites until soft peaks form; gradually add remaining ¼ cup sugar and beat until stiff. Fold into gelatine mixture.

Fold 1 cup whipped cream into gelatine mixture. Spoon into 6 (5-ounce) wine or Champagne glasses, each with 1½-inch collar; chill until set,

about 2 hours. Remove collars, then gently pat reserved chocolate shavings onto sides. Top with remaining whipped cream and reserved chocolate curls.
Makes 6 servings.

To Make Soufflé Collars: Cut 6 (3×6-inch) strips of wax paper or aluminum foil. Fold each in half lengthwise so that each strip measures 1½×6 inches. Wrap 1 strip around each of 6 wine or Champagne glasses forming a 1-inch collar; secure with tape.

Toasted Almond Souffle

- 1 8-ounce package PHILADELPHIA BRAND Cream Cheese, softened
- ⅓ cup sugar
- ½ teaspoon almond extract
- ¼ teaspoon salt
- 4 eggs, separated
- ½ cup half and half
- 2 tablespoons sliced almonds

Combine cream cheese, sugar, extract and salt, mixing until well blended. Lightly beat egg yolks; blend into cream cheese mixture. Gradually add half and half. Beat egg whites until stiff peaks form. Fold into cream cheese mixture; pour into 1½-quart souffle dish. With tip of spoon, make slight indentation or "track" around top of souffle 1 inch from edge to form top hat. Top with almonds. Bake at 325°, 50 minutes or until light golden brown.
6 to 8 servings.

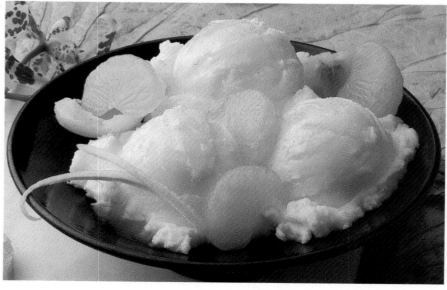

Ginger Mandarin Sauce over Vanilla Ice Cream

Hot Chocolate Soufflé

Chilly Strawberry Souffles

1 10-ounce package frozen
   strawberries, thawed
2 envelopes unflavored gelatin
2¼ cups cold water
1 8-ounce package *Light*
   PHILADELPHIA BRAND
   Neufchâtel Cheese, softened
¼ cup sugar
1 tablespoon lemon juice
   Few drops red food coloring
   (optional)
2 cups thawed frozen whipped
   topping

Drain strawberries, reserving liquid. Chop strawberries. Soften gelatin in ½ cup water; stir over low heat until dissolved. Add remaining water. Combine neufchâtel cheese and sugar, mixing until well blended. Gradually add gelatin mixture to neufchâtel cheese mixture, mixing until well blended. Stir in reserved liquid, juice and food coloring. Chill, stirring occasionally, until thickened but not set. Beat with electric mixer or wire whisk until smooth. Fold in strawberries and whipped topping. Wrap 3-inch collar of foil around individual dessert dishes; secure with tape. Pour mixture into dishes; chill until firm. Remove collar before serving.
8 to 10 servings.
   Variations: Substitute PHILA-DELPHIA BRAND Cream Cheese for Neufchâtel Cheese. Increase sugar to ⅔ cup. Substitute 1 cup whipping cream, whipped, for whipped topping.
   Substitute 1-quart souffle dish for individual dessert dishes.

Hot Chocolate Soufflé

1 tablespoon plus 1 cup sugar,
   divided
¾ cup HERSHEY'S Cocoa
½ cup unsifted all-purpose flour
¼ teaspoon salt
2 cups milk
6 egg yolks, well beaten
2 tablespoons butter
1 teaspoon vanilla
8 egg whites, at room
   temperature
¼ teaspoon cream of tartar
   Sweetened whipped cream
   (optional)

Lightly butter 2½-quart soufflé dish; sprinkle with 1 tablespoon sugar, tilting to coat. Measure length of heavy-duty aluminum foil to fit around soufflé dish; fold in thirds lengthwise. Lightly oil one side of collar; tape securely to outside of dish (oiled side in), allowing collar to extend at least 2 to 3 inches above rim. Set aside.
   Combine cocoa, ¾ cup sugar, the flour and salt in medium saucepan; gradually blend in milk. Cook over medium heat, stirring constantly with wire whisk, until mixture boils; remove from heat. Gradually stir small amount of chocolate mixture into beaten egg yolks; blend well. Return egg mixture to chocolate mixture in pan. Add butter and vanilla, stirring until combined. Set aside; cool to lukewarm.
   Beat egg whites with cream of tartar in large mixer bowl until soft peaks form. Add remaining ¼ cup sugar, 2 tablespoons at a time, beating until stiff peaks form. Gently fold one-third of the chocolate mixture into beaten egg whites. Fold in remaining chocolate mixture, half at a time, just until combined.
   Gently pour mixture, without stirring, into prepared dish; smooth top with spatula. Place dish in larger pan; place in oven on bottom rack. Pour hot water into pan to depth of 1 inch (be sure bottom of foil collar does not touch water bath). Bake at 350° for 1 hour and 10 minutes or until cake tester inserted halfway between edge and center comes out clean. Carefully remove foil. Serve immediately with sweetened whipped cream.
8 to 10 servings.

Individual Fudge Soufflés

½ cup butter or margarine,
   softened
1¼ cups sugar
1 teaspoon vanilla
4 eggs
⅔ cup milk
½ teaspoon instant coffee
   granules
⅔ cup unsifted all-purpose flour
⅔ cup HERSHEY'S Cocoa
1½ teaspoons baking powder
1 cup heavy or whipping cream
2 tablespoons confectioners'
   sugar

Grease and sugar eight 5- or 6-ounce custard cups or ramekins; set aside. Cream butter, sugar and vanilla in large mixer bowl until light and fluffy. Add eggs, one at a time, beating well after each addition. Scald milk; remove from heat and add coffee granules, stirring until dissolved. Combine flour, cocoa and baking powder; add alternately with milk-coffee mixture to creamed mixture. Beat 1 minute on medium speed.

Divide batter evenly among prepared custard cups. Place in two 8-inch square pans; place pans in oven. Pour hot water into pans to depth of 1/8 inch. Bake at 325° for 40 to 45 minutes for custard cups (50 to 55 minutes for ramekins), adding more water if necessary, until cake tester inserted halfway between edge and center comes out clean. Remove pans from oven and allow custard cups to stand in water 5 minutes. Remove custard cups from water; cool slightly. Serve in custard cups or invert onto dessert dishes. Beat cream with confectioners' sugar until stiff; spoon onto warm soufflés.
8 servings.

Fruited Chocolate Trifle

  2/3 cup sugar
  2 tablespoons cornstarch
  1/8 teaspoon salt
  2 eggs, slightly beaten
  3 cups milk, scalded
  3 squares BAKER'S®
    Unsweetened Chocolate
  3 tablespoons almond liqueur*
 12 ladyfingers, split
  1 pint fresh strawberries, hulled
    and halved
  1 can (16 ounces) apricot halves,
    drained

Combine sugar, cornstarch and salt in bowl. Add eggs and mix well. Gradually pour in hot milk, stirring constantly. Return to saucepan. Cook and stir over very low heat until mixture is smooth and thickened. Remove from heat. Add chocolate and liqueur; stir until chocolate is melted. Cool slightly.

Arrange half of the ladyfingers, fruits and chocolate custard in layers in a serving dish; repeat layers with remaining ingredients. Chill at least 2 hours. Before serving, garnish with sweetened whipped cream and additional strawberries, if desired.
Makes 8 to 10 servings.
*Or use 1/2 teaspoon almond extract.

Hawaiian Trifle

  2 packages (3 1/8 ounces each)
    vanilla flavor pudding and
    pie filling mix (not instant)
  2 cups milk
  1 1/2 cups DOLE® Chilled Pineapple
    Juice
  2 cups whipping cream
  1 package (16 ounces) frozen
    pound cake, thawed
  1/2 cup cream sherry
  1 cup raspberry jam, melted
  1 can (20 ounces) DOLE®
    Crushed Pineapple
    Maraschino cherries, optional

Prepare pudding mix according to package directions, using milk and pineapple juice as liquid. Place saucepan in bowl of ice water to cool pudding; stir often. In medium bowl, beat 1 cup cream until soft peaks form; fold into cooled pudding. Cut pound cake in half lengthwise. Drizzle sherry over cake; cut cake into chunks.

Spoon 1 cup pudding into 2 1/2- to 3-quart glass serving bowl. Top with half the cake and half the jam. Reserve 1/2 cup undrained pineapple for garnish. Spoon half the remaining pineapple on top of jam in serving bowl. Spoon half the remaining pudding on top. Repeat layering with remaining ingredients, ending with pudding. Refrigerate, covered, overnight.

In medium bowl, beat remaining 1 cup cream until soft peaks form; spread over top of trifle. Drain reserved 1/2 cup pineapple. Garnish trifle with pineapple and maraschino cherries, if desired.
Makes 8 servings.

Peach Melba Trifle

Peach Melba Trifle

  1 (14-ounce) can EAGLE® Brand
    Sweetened Condensed Milk
    (NOT evaporated milk)
  1 1/2 cups cold water
  1 (4-serving size) package
    instant vanilla flavor pudding
    and pie filling mix
  2 cups (1 pint) BORDEN® or
    MEADOW GOLD® Whipping
    Cream, whipped
  1/4 cup plus 1 tablespoon dry
    sherry *or* orange juice
  6 cups angel food cake cubes
    (about 10 ounces)
  1 1/2 pounds fresh peaches, pared
    and sliced *or* 1 (29-ounce)
    can sliced peaches, drained
  1/2 cup red raspberry preserves
    Toasted almonds and
    additional preserves,
    optional

In large bowl, combine sweetened condensed milk and water. Add pudding mix; beat well. Chill 5 minutes. Fold in whipped cream and *1 tablespoon* sherry. Place *3 cups* cake cubes in 3- to 4-quart glass serving bowl. Sprinkle with *2 tablespoons* sherry. Top with half the peach slices, *1/2 cup* preserves and half the pudding mixture. Repeat layering with remaining cake, sherry, peach slices and pudding. Garnish with almonds and preserves if desired. Chill thoroughly. Refrigerate leftovers.
Makes 10 to 12 servings.

PIES & PASTRIES

Though Americans did not invent the pie, it must be America's most popular dessert. All your favorites are here—aromatic fruit pies, smooth custard pies topped with meringue, chocolate pies, and rich nut pies. When time is short, concoct a superb pie from pantry-shelf ingredients.

ReaLemon Meringue Pie

    1 (9-inch) baked pastry shell
1²/₃ cups sugar
    6 tablespoons cornstarch
  ½ cup REALEMON® Lemon Juice from Concentrate
    4 eggs, separated*
1½ cups boiling water
    2 tablespoons margarine or butter
  ¼ teaspoon cream of tartar
       Mint leaves, optional

Preheat oven to 350°. In heavy saucepan, combine *1¹/₃ cups* sugar and cornstarch; add ReaLemon® brand. In small bowl, beat egg yolks; add to lemon mixture. Gradually add water, stirring constantly. Over medium heat, cook and stir until mixture boils and thickens, about 8 to 10 minutes. Remove from heat. Add margarine; stir until melted. Pour into prepared pastry shell. In small mixer bowl, beat egg whites with cream of tartar until soft peaks form; gradually add remaining *¹/₃ cup* sugar, beating until stiff but not dry. Spread on top of pie, sealing carefully to edge of shell. Bake 12 to 15 minutes or until golden brown. Cool. Chill before serving. Garnish with mint if desired. Refrigerate leftovers.
Makes one 9-inch pie.
  *Use only Grade A clean, uncracked eggs.

Easy Chocolate Mousse Pie

       Graham Cracker Crust
    1 package (8 ounces) cream cheese, softened
  ½ cup HERSHEY'S Cocoa
    1 cup confectioners' sugar
1½ teaspoons vanilla
    2 cups heavy or whipping cream

Prepare Graham Cracker Crust; set aside. Beat cream cheese and cocoa in large mixer bowl until fluffy and well blended. Gradually add confectioners' sugar; blend well. Stir in vanilla. Whip cream until stiff; fold into cheese mixture. Pour into cooled crust; chill until firm. Garnish as desired.
8 servings.

Graham Cracker Crust

1½ cups graham cracker crumbs
  ⅓ cup butter or margarine, melted
    3 tablespoons sugar

Combine graham cracker crumbs, melted butter and sugar in small bowl. Press mixture firmly onto bottom and up side of 9-inch pie pan. Bake at 350° for 10 minutes; cool.

Eggnog Pie

    1 cup cold dairy or canned eggnog
    1 package (6-serving size) JELL-O® Vanilla Flavor Instant Pudding and Pie Filling
    1 tablespoon rum or
  ¼ teaspoon rum extract
  ¼ teaspoon nutmeg
3½ cups (8 ounces) COOL WHIP® Non-Dairy Whipped Topping, thawed
    1 prepared 8- or 9-inch graham cracker crumb crust, cooled

Pour cold eggnog into bowl. Add pie filling mix, rum and nutmeg. With electric mixer at low speed, beat until blended, about 1 minute. Let stand 5 minutes. Fold in 2 cups of the whipped topping. Spoon into pie crust. Chill until firm, about 2 hours. Garnish with remaining whipped topping. Sprinkle with additional nutmeg, if desired.
Makes one 8- or 9-inch pie.

ReaLemon Meringue Pie

Create-a-Crust Apple Pie

- 2 medium all-purpose apples, pared and sliced (about 2 cups)
- 1 tablespoon REALEMON® Lemon Juice from Concentrate
- ½ cup plus 2 tablespoons biscuit baking mix
- 1 (14-ounce) can EAGLE® Brand Sweetened Condensed Milk (NOT evaporated milk)
- 1½ cups water
- 3 eggs
- ¼ cup margarine or butter, softened
- 1½ teaspoons vanilla extract
- ½ teaspoon ground cinnamon
- ½ teaspoon ground nutmeg

Preheat oven to 350°. In medium bowl, toss apples with ReaLemon® brand, then *2 tablespoons* biscuit mix. Arrange on bottom of buttered 10-inch pie plate. In blender container, combine remaining ingredients. Blend on low speed 3 minutes. Let stand 5 minutes. Pour evenly over apples. Bake 35 to 40 minutes or until golden brown around edge. Cool slightly; serve warm or chilled with vanilla ice cream. Refrigerate leftovers.
Makes one 10-inch pie.

Dutch Apple Raisin Pie

- 1½ cups SUN-MAID® Raisins
- 1 cup water
- ½ cup sugar
- 1 tablespoon all-purpose flour
- ½ teaspoon ground cinnamon
- ¼ teaspoon salt
- 1 tablespoon lemon juice
- 4 cups pared and sliced apples (4 to 6 apples)
- Pastry for double-crust 9-inch pie
- 1 egg, beaten, for glaze
- Sugar, for glaze

In large saucepan over low heat, simmer raisins in water until liquid is almost absorbed, 5 to 7 minutes. Meanwhile, in small bowl, mix sugar, flour, cinnamon and salt. Stir into raisin mixture along with lemon juice and apples. Turn into pastry-lined 9-inch pie plate. Cover with top crust, seal and flute edges. Cut slits for steam to escape. Brush with beaten egg and sprinkle with sugar. Bake in preheated 425°F oven 10 minutes; reduce heat to 350°F and bake 45 to 55 minutes longer or until crust is golden brown. Cool on wire rack. Serve warm or at room temperature.
Makes one 9-inch pie.
Note: If desired, sprinkle filling with grated Cheddar cheese just before covering with top crust.

Brandied Fruit Pie

- 1 KEEBLER® Ready-Crust® Graham Cracker Pie Crust
- 2 packages (8 ounces each) mixed, pitted dried fruit
- ¾ cup plus 1 tablespoon water
- ¼ cup plus 1 tablespoon brandy or cognac
- 5 thin slices lemon
- ¾ cup packed brown sugar
- 1 teaspoon ground cinnamon
- ¼ teaspoon ground nutmeg
- ¼ teaspoon ground cloves
- ¼ teaspoon salt
- ½ cup graham cracker crumbs
- ¼ cup butter or margarine, melted
- Hard sauce or whipped cream (optional)
- Lemon slices for garnish

In medium saucepan, combine dried fruit, ¾ cup of the water, ¼ cup of the brandy and the 5 lemon slices. Simmer over low heat 10 minutes or until liquid is absorbed. Remove and discard lemon slices. Stir in sugar, spices, salt, remaining 1 tablespoon water and remaining 1 tablespoon brandy; pour into pie crust. Sprinkle graham cracker crumbs evenly over top of pie. Drizzle melted butter over crumbs. Bake in preheated 350° oven 30 minutes. Cool on wire rack. Serve warm or at room temperature. If desired, serve with hard sauce or whipped cream; garnish with lemon slices.
Makes 8 servings.

Brandied Fruit Pie

Apple Chess Pie

- 1 (9-inch) unbaked pastry shell
- 4 eggs
- 1 (14-ounce) can EAGLE® Brand Sweetened Condensed Milk (NOT evaporated milk)
- 1 cup applesauce
- ½ cup margarine or butter, melted
- ¼ cup REALEMON® Lemon Juice from Concentrate
- 2 tablespoons cornmeal

Preheat oven to 425°. Bake pastry shell 8 minutes; remove from oven. Reduce oven temperature to 350°. In large mixer bowl, beat eggs. Add remaining ingredients except pastry shell; mix well. Pour into prepared

Cherry Cheese Pie

(continued)

pastry shell. Bake 40 to 45 minutes or until knife inserted near center comes out clean. Cool. Serve warm or chilled. Refrigerate leftovers.
Makes one 9-inch pie.

Almond Ginger Ice Cream Pie

    Almond Crust (recipe follows)
 1 can (20 ounces) DOLE®
      Crushed Pineapple
 1 quart vanilla ice cream,
      softened
 ½ cup DOLE™ Blanched Slivered
      Almonds, toasted
 ¼ cup crystallized ginger,
      chopped
 3 tablespoons almond-flavored
      liqueur
 1 tablespoon grated orange peel

Prepare Almond Crust. Drain pineapple; reserve all but ½ cup juice. In large bowl, combine pineapple, reserved juice and remaining ingredients. Spoon into prepared crust; freeze overnight or until firm. Let soften slightly before slicing. Garnish as desired.
Makes 8 to 10 servings.   (continued)

ALMOND CRUST: In bowl, combine 1½ cups vanilla wafer crumbs, ⅔ cup toasted ground Dole™ Almonds and ¼ cup melted butter or margarine. Press onto bottom and sides of 9-inch pie plate. Freeze until ready to use.

Cherry Cheese Pie

 1 (9-inch) graham cracker crumb
      crust
 1 (8-ounce) package cream
      cheese, softened
 1 (14-ounce) can EAGLE® Brand
      Sweetened Condensed Milk
      (NOT evaporated milk)
 ⅓ cup REALEMON® Lemon Juice
      from Concentrate
 1 teaspoon vanilla extract
      Canned cherry pie filling,
      chilled

In large bowl, beat cheese until fluffy. Gradually add sweetened condensed milk; beat until smooth. Stir in ReaLemon® brand and vanilla. Pour into prepared crust. Chill 3 hours or until set. Top with desired amount of pie filling before serving. Refrigerate leftovers.
Makes one 9-inch pie.   (continued)

Topping Variations:
Ambrosia: In small saucepan, combine ½ cup BAMA® Peach or Apricot preserves, ¼ cup flaked coconut, 2 tablespoons orange-flavored liqueur and 2 teaspoons cornstarch; cook and stir until thickened. Remove from heat. Chill thoroughly. Arrange fresh orange sections (1 or 2 oranges) on top of pie; drizzle with sauce.
Makes about ½ cup.

Glazed Strawberry: In saucepan, combine 3 tablespoons BAMA® Apple Jelly and 1 tablespoon ReaLemon® brand. Cook and stir until jelly melts. Combine ½ teaspoon cornstarch and 1 tablespoon water; add to jelly mixture. Cook and stir until thickened and clear. Cool 10 minutes. Arrange sliced strawberries over top of pie; spoon glaze over strawberries.

Cranberry Nut: In small bowl, combine 1 cup chilled cranberry-orange relish, ½ cup chopped walnuts and 1 teaspoon grated orange rind. Spread over pie. Garnish with orange twists if desired.
Makes about 1 cup.

Caribbean Fudge Pie

 ¼ cup butter or margarine,
      softened
 ¾ cup packed brown sugar
 3 eggs
 1 package (12 ounces) real
      semisweet chocolate pieces
 2 teaspoons instant coffee
      powder
 1 teaspoon rum flavoring
 ¼ cup all-purpose flour
 1 cup coarsely broken
      DIAMOND® Walnuts
 1 (9-inch) unbaked pie shell
 ½ cup DIAMOND® Walnut halves

In large bowl, cream butter and brown sugar. Add eggs, one at a time, beating well after each addition. In top of double boiler, melt chocolate over hot, not boiling, water and add to creamed mixture with coffee and rum flavoring. Stir in flour and the 1 cup walnuts. Pour into unbaked pie shell and decorate top with the ½ cup walnut halves. Bake, below oven center, in preheated 375°F oven 25 minutes or until knife inserted near center comes out clean. Cool on wire rack. Store in refrigerator, covered. Serve topped with whipped cream or ice cream, if desired.
Makes 8 servings.

Sweet Potato Pecan Pie

1 (9-inch) unbaked pastry shell
1 pound (2 medium) yams or
    sweet potatoes, cooked and
    peeled
¼ cup margarine or butter
1 (14-ounce) can EAGLE® Brand
    Sweetened Condensed Milk
    (NOT evaporated milk)
1 teaspoon grated orange rind
1 teaspoon vanilla extract
1 teaspoon ground cinnamon
½ teaspoon ground nutmeg
¼ teaspoon salt
2 eggs
    Pecan Topping

Preheat oven to 350°. In large mixer bowl, beat hot yams with margarine until smooth. Add remaining ingredients except pastry shell and Pecan Topping; mix well. Pour into pastry shell. Bake 30 minutes. Remove from oven; spoon Pecan Topping evenly over top. Return to oven; bake 20 to 25 minutes or until golden brown. Cool. Serve warm or chilled. Refrigerate leftovers.
Makes one 9-inch pie.
PECAN TOPPING: In small mixer bowl, combine 1 egg, 3 tablespoons dark corn syrup, 3 tablespoons firmly packed light brown sugar, 1 tablespoon margarine, melted, and ½ teaspoon maple flavoring; mix well. Stir in 1 cup chopped pecans.

Banana Mocha Ice Cream Pie

1 pint chocolate ice cream,
    softened
1 pint coffee ice cream,
    softened
¼ cup coffee-flavored liqueur
1 firm, medium DOLE™ Banana,
    peeled, diced
    Chocolate Cookie Crust
    (recipe follows)

Combine softened ice creams with liqueur. Fold in diced banana. Pour into prepared Chocolate Cookie Crust. Freeze until firm. Garnish with sliced bananas and mocha-flavored candies.
Makes one 8- or 9-inch pie.
CHOCOLATE COOKIE CRUST: Combine 2 cups chocolate wafer crumbs and ½ cup melted butter. Blend well. Pour into buttered 8- or 9-inch pie pan. Press evenly over bottom and sides of pan. Chill.

Banana Layered Pie

Classic Banana Cream Pie

2 eggs
½ cup plus 2 tablespoons sugar
¼ cup flour
2 cups milk, scalded
½ cup unsalted butter or
    margarine
1 tablespoon vanilla extract
5 firm, medium DOLE™ Bananas
1 baked 9-inch pastry shell
1 cup whipping cream

In heavy saucepan, beat eggs, ½ cup sugar and flour until pale lemon color. Gradually beat hot milk into egg mixture. Cook, stirring constantly, over medium heat until sauce thickens, about 5 minutes. Remove from heat. Stir in butter and vanilla until blended. Place plastic wrap directly on surface of filling to cover. Cool.

To assemble pie, slice bananas; reserve a few slices for garnish, if desired. Fold remaining bananas into filling; spoon into baked pastry shell. Beat cream with remaining 2 tablespoons sugar until soft peaks form. Spread on top of pie.
Makes 8 servings.

Banana Layered Pie

2¼ cups cold milk
1 package (6-serving size)
    JELL-O® Vanilla Flavor
    Instant Pudding and Pie
    Filling
1 baked 9-inch pie shell or
    prepared graham cracker
    crumb crust, cooled
2 medium bananas
½ cup thawed COOL WHIP® Non-
    Dairy Whipped Topping
    Lemon juice

Pour cold milk into bowl. Add pie filling mix. With electric mixer at low speed, beat until blended, about 1 minute. Pour ½ cup of the pie filling into pie shell.

Slice 1 banana; arrange slices on filling in shell. Top with ¾ cup of the pie filling.

Blend whipped topping into remaining pie filling. Spread over filling in pie shell. Chill about 3 hours. Slice remaining banana; brush with lemon juice. Arrange banana slices on pie. Garnish with additional whipped topping, if desired.
Makes one 9-inch pie.

Chocolate Turtle Pie

**¼ cup caramel- or butterscotch-
    flavored dessert topping
1 baked 8- or 9-inch pie shell,
    cooled
¾ cup pecan halves
1 package (4-serving size)
    JELL-O® Chocolate Flavor
    Pudding and Pie Filling
1¾ cups milk
1¾ cups thawed COOL WHIP®
    Non-Dairy Whipped Topping**

Place caramel topping in small saucepan. Heat over medium heat until topping comes to a boil, stirring constantly. Pour into pie shell. Arrange pecans on topping and chill.

Combine pie filling mix and milk in medium saucepan; blend well. Cook and stir over medium heat until mixture comes to a full boil. Cool 5 minutes, stirring twice. Pour over nuts in pie shell. Cover surface with plastic wrap. Chill about 3 hours. Remove plastic wrap. Pipe whipped topping around edge of pie. Drizzle with additional topping and garnish with additional pecans, if desired.
Makes one 8- or 9-inch pie.

Impossible Pie

**1 (14-ounce) can EAGLE® Brand
    Sweetened Condensed Milk
    (NOT evaporated milk)
1½ cups water
½ cup biscuit baking mix
3 eggs
¼ cup margarine or butter,
    softened
1½ teaspoons vanilla extract
1 cup flaked coconut**

Preheat oven to 350°. In blender container, combine all ingredients except coconut. Blend on low speed 3 minutes. Pour mixture into buttered 10-inch pie plate; let stand 5 minutes. Sprinkle coconut over top. Carefully place in oven; bake 35 to 40 minutes or until knife inserted near edge comes out clean. Cool slightly; serve warm or cool. Refrigerate leftovers.
Makes one 10-inch pie.

Tip: Pie can be baked in buttered 9-inch pie plate but it will be extremely full.

Impossible Lemon Pie: Add 3 tablespoons REALEMON® Lemon Juice from Concentrate and 1 tablespoon grated lemon rind to ingredients in blender.

Fluffy Grasshopper Pie

**2 cups finely crushed creme-
    filled chocolate sandwich
    cookies (about 20 cookies)
¼ cup margarine or butter,
    melted
1 (8-ounce) package cream
    cheese, softened
1 (14-ounce) can EAGLE® Brand
    Sweetened Condensed Milk
    (NOT evaporated milk)
3 tablespoons REALEMON®
    Lemon Juice from
    Concentrate
¼ cup green creme de menthe
¼ cup white creme de cacao
1 (4-ounce) container frozen
    non-dairy whipped topping,
    thawed *or* 1 cup (½ pint)
    BORDEN® or MEADOW
    GOLD® Whipping Cream,
    stiffly whipped**

Combine crumbs and margarine; press firmly on bottom and up side of buttered 9-inch pie plate. Chill. Meanwhile, in large mixer bowl, beat cheese until fluffy; gradually beat in sweetened condensed milk until smooth. Stir in ReaLemon® brand and liqueurs. Fold in whipped topping. Chill 20 minutes; pile into crust. Chill or freeze 4 hours or until set. Garnish as desired. Refrigerate or freeze leftovers.
Makes one 9-inch pie.

Peach Surprise Pie

**2 8-ounce packages *Light*
    PHILADELPHIA BRAND
    Neufchâtel Cheese, softened
¼ cup sugar
½ teaspoon vanilla
    Pastry for 1-crust 9-inch pie,
    baked
1 16-ounce can peach slices,
    drained
¼ cup KRAFT Red Raspberry
    Preserves
1 teaspoon lemon juice**

Combine neufchâtel cheese, sugar and vanilla, mixing until well blended. Spread onto bottom of crust; chill several hours or overnight. Top with peaches just before serving. Combine preserves and juice, mixing until well blended. Spoon over peaches. Garnish with fresh mint, if desired.
6 to 8 servings.

Peach Surprise Pie

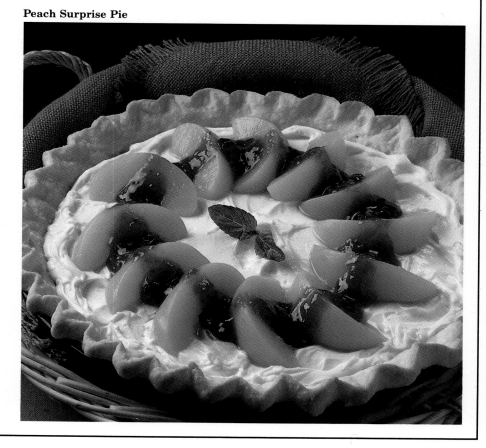

Frozen Peanut Butter Pie

**3½ cups (8 ounces) COOL WHIP®
    Non-Dairy Whipped Topping,
    thawed
1 prepared 9-inch graham
    cracker crumb crust, cooled
⅓ cup strawberry jam
1 cup cold milk
½ cup chunky peanut butter
1 package (4-serving size)
    JELL-O® Vanilla Flavor
    Instant Pudding and Pie
    Filling**

Spread 1 cup of the whipped topping
in bottom of pie crust; freeze for about
10 minutes. Carefully spoon jam over
whipped topping.

Gradually add milk to peanut butter in bowl, blending until smooth.
Add pie filling mix. With electric
mixer at low speed, beat until well
blended, 1 to 2 minutes. Fold in remaining whipped topping. Spoon over
jam in pie crust. Freeze until firm,
about 4 hours. Garnish with additional whipped topping and chopped
nuts, if desired.
Makes one 9-inch pie.

Margarita Pie

**½ cup margarine or butter
1¼ cups finely crushed pretzels
¼ cup sugar
1 (14-ounce) can EAGLE® Brand
    Sweetened Condensed Milk
    (NOT evaporated milk)
⅓ cup REALIME® Lime Juice
    from Concentrate
2 to 4 tablespoons tequila
2 tablespoons triple sec or other
    orange-flavored liqueur
1 cup (½ pint) BORDEN® or
    MEADOW GOLD® Whipping
    Cream, whipped
Additional whipped cream,
    orange twists and mint
    leaves or pretzels for
    garnish, optional**

In small saucepan, melt margarine;
stir in pretzel crumbs and sugar. Mix
well. Press crumbs on bottom and up
side of buttered 9-inch pie plate; chill.
In large bowl, combine sweetened condensed milk, ReaLime® brand, tequila and triple sec; mix well. Fold in
whipped cream. Pour into prepared

crust. Freeze or chill until firm, 4
hours in freezer or 2 hours in refrigerator. Garnish as desired. Refrigerate
or freeze leftovers.
Makes one 9-inch pie.

Orange 'n Vanilla Mousse Pie

**1 envelope KNOX® Unflavored
    Gelatine
¼ cup cold water
1 cup (½ pint) whipping or
    heavy cream, heated to
    boiling
1 package (8 ounces) cream
    cheese, softened
1 can (6 ounces) frozen orange
    juice concentrate, partially
    thawed and undiluted
¾ cup confectioners sugar
1½ teaspoons vanilla extract
1 (9-inch) graham cracker crust**

In blender, sprinkle unflavored gelatine over cold water; let stand 1 minute. Add hot cream and process at low
speed until gelatine is completely dissolved, about 2 minutes. Add cream
cheese, orange juice concentrate,
sugar and vanilla; process until
blended. Chill blender container until
mixture is slightly thickened, about
15 minutes. Pour into prepared crust;
chill until firm, about 3 hours. Garnish, if desired, with whipped cream
and orange slices.
Makes about 8 servings.

Cranberry Crumb Pie

**1 (9-inch) unbaked pastry shell
1 (8-ounce) package cream
    cheese, softened
1 (14-ounce) can EAGLE® Brand
    Sweetened Condensed Milk
    (NOT evaporated milk)
¼ cup REALEMON® Lemon Juice
    from Concentrate
3 tablespoons light brown sugar
2 tablespoons cornstarch
1 (16-ounce) can whole berry
    cranberry sauce
¼ cup cold margarine or butter
⅓ cup unsifted flour
¾ cup chopped walnuts**

Preheat oven to 425°. Bake pastry
shell 8 minutes; remove from oven.
Reduce oven temperature to 375°. In
large mixer bowl, beat cheese until
fluffy. Gradually beat in sweetened
condensed milk until smooth. Stir in
ReaLemon® brand. Pour into prepared
pastry shell. In small bowl, combine *1
tablespoon* sugar and cornstarch; mix
well. Stir in cranberry sauce. Spoon
evenly over cheese mixture. In medium mixing bowl, cut margarine into
flour and remaining *2 tablespoons*
sugar until crumbly. Stir in nuts.
Sprinkle evenly over cranberry mixture. Bake 45 to 50 minutes or until
bubbly and golden. Cool. Serve at
room temperature or chill thoroughly.
Refrigerate leftovers.
Makes one 9-inch pie.

Margarita Pie

Traditional Pumpkin Pie with Sour Cream Topping (left) and Streusel Topping (right)

Traditional Pumpkin Pie

1 (9-inch) unbaked pastry shell
1 (16-ounce) can pumpkin (about 2 cups)
1 (14-ounce) can EAGLE® Brand Sweetened Condensed Milk (NOT evaporated milk)
2 eggs
1 teaspoon ground cinnamon
½ teaspoon ground ginger
½ teaspoon ground nutmeg
½ teaspoon salt

Preheat oven to 425°. In large mixer bowl, combine all ingredients except pastry shell; mix well. Pour into prepared pastry shell. Bake 15 minutes. Reduce oven temperature to 350°; continue baking 35 to 40 minutes or until knife inserted 1 inch from edge comes out clean. Cool. Garnish as desired. Refrigerate leftovers.
Makes one 9-inch pie.

Topping Variations:

Sour Cream Topping: In medium mixing bowl, combine 1½ cups BORDEN® or MEADOW GOLD® Sour Cream, 2 tablespoons sugar and 1 teaspoon vanilla extract. After 30 minutes of baking, spread evenly over top of pie; bake 10 minutes longer. Garnish as desired.

Streusel Topping: In medium mixing bowl, combine ½ cup firmly packed light brown sugar and ½ cup unsifted flour; cut in ¼ cup cold margarine or butter until crumbly. Stir in ¼ cup chopped nuts. After 30 minutes of baking, sprinkle on top of pie; bake 10 minutes longer.

No-Bake Pumpkin Pie

1 egg
1 (14-ounce) can EAGLE® Brand Sweetened Condensed Milk (NOT evaporated milk)
1 teaspoon ground cinnamon
½ teaspoon *each* ground ginger, nutmeg and salt
1 envelope KNOX® Unflavored Gelatine
2 tablespoons water
1 (16-ounce) can pumpkin (about 2 cups)
1 KEEBLER® Ready-Crust® Graham Cracker Pie Crust

In medium bowl, beat egg; beat in sweetened condensed milk and spices. In medium saucepan, sprinkle gelatine over water; let stand 1 minute. Over *low* heat, stir until gelatine dissolves. Add sweetened condensed milk mixture; over *low* heat, cook and stir constantly until mixture thickens slightly, 5 to 10 minutes. Remove from heat. Add pumpkin. Pour into crust. Chill 4 hours or until set. Garnish as desired. Refrigerate leftovers.
Makes one pie.

Paradise Pumpkin Pie

Pastry for 1-crust 9-inch pie
1 8-ounce package PHILADELPHIA BRAND Cream Cheese, softened
¼ cup sugar
½ teaspoon vanilla
1 egg

* * *

1¼ cups canned pumpkin
1 cup evaporated milk
½ cup sugar
2 eggs, beaten
1 teaspoon cinnamon
¼ teaspoon ground ginger
¼ teaspoon ground nutmeg
Dash of salt
Maple syrup
Pecan halves

On lightly floured surface, roll pastry to 12-inch circle. Place in 9-inch pie plate. Turn under edge; flute. Combine cream cheese, sugar and vanilla, mixing at medium speed on electric mixer until well blended. Blend in egg. Spread onto bottom of pastry shell.

Combine all remaining ingredients except syrup and pecans; mix well. Carefully pour over cream cheese mixture. Bake at 350°, 65 minutes. Cool. Brush with syrup; top with pecan halves.
8 servings.

Berry-Bottomed Walnut Pie

Cranberry Filling (recipe follows)
2 eggs
³/₄ cup dark corn syrup
¹/₃ cup packed brown sugar
3 tablespoons butter or margarine, melted
1 teaspoon grated orange peel
2 cups DIAMOND® Walnuts
1 (9-inch) unbaked pie shell
Sweetened whipped cream, for garnish

Prepare Cranberry Filling; cool. In medium bowl, beat eggs, corn syrup, sugar, butter and orange peel. Mix in walnuts. Spread Cranberry Filling evenly in pie shell. Top with walnut mixture. Bake in preheated 350°F oven about 45 minutes or until filling is set and crust is browned. Cool on wire rack. Serve at room temperature. Top with sweetened whipped cream, if desired.
Makes one 9-inch pie.

CRANBERRY FILLING: In medium saucepan, combine 1¹/₂ cups fresh cranberries, 6 tablespoons orange juice and 3 tablespoons granulated sugar. Bring to boil over high heat. Reduce heat to medium; cook 3 minutes. In small dish, mix 2 teaspoons cornstarch with 1 tablespoon water. Stir into cranberry mixture. Cook and stir until mixture is the consistency of thick jam.

Simply Superb Pecan Pie

3 eggs, beaten
1 cup sugar
¹/₂ cup dark corn syrup
1 teaspoon vanilla
6 tablespoons butter or margarine, melted, cooled
1 cup pecan pieces or halves
1 (9-inch) unbaked pie shell

In large bowl, beat eggs, sugar, corn syrup, vanilla and butter. Stir in pecans. Pour into unbaked pie shell. Bake in preheated 350° oven 45 to 60 minutes or until knife inserted halfway between outside and center comes out clean. Cool on wire rack.
Makes one 9-inch pie.

*Favorite recipe from **National Pecan Marketing Council, Inc.***

Fluffy Orange Pie

Chess Pie

¹/₂ cup butter or margarine, softened
¹/₂ cup packed brown sugar
¹/₂ cup granulated sugar
4 eggs
¹/₂ teaspoon salt
1 teaspoon grated lemon peel
1 teaspoon lemon juice
1 teaspoon vanilla
1 cup finely chopped DIAMOND® Walnuts
1 cup finely chopped SUN-MAID® Raisins
1 (9-inch) unbaked pie shell
Walnut Cream Topping:
1 cup whipping cream
2 tablespoons powdered sugar
¹/₂ cup finely chopped or ground DIAMOND® Walnuts

In medium bowl, cream butter and brown and granulated sugars until fluffy. Beat in eggs, one at a time, until well blended. Stir in salt, lemon peel and juice, vanilla, walnuts and raisins. (Mixture will appear slightly curdled.) Pour into unbaked pie shell. Bake, below oven center, in preheated 350°F oven 40 to 45 minutes or until just barely set in center. Top will be a deep brown. Cool on wire rack. Serve with Walnut Cream Topping.
Makes 8 servings.

To prepare Walnut Cream Topping: In medium bowl, beat cream until soft peaks form. Fold in powdered sugar and walnuts.

Fluffy Orange Pie

2 cups vanilla wafer crumbs (about 50 wafers)
¹/₃ cup margarine or butter, melted
1 (8-ounce) package cream cheese, softened
1 (14-ounce) can EAGLE® Brand Sweetened Condensed Milk (NOT evaporated milk)
1 (6-ounce) can frozen orange juice concentrate, thawed
1 cup (¹/₂ pint) BORDEN® or MEADOW GOLD® Whipping Cream, whipped

Combine crumbs and margarine; press firmly on bottom and up side of 9-inch pie plate. Chill. Meanwhile, in large mixer bowl, beat cheese until fluffy; gradually beat in sweetened condensed milk then juice concentrate until smooth. Fold in whipped cream. Pile into crust. Chill 2 hours or until set. Garnish as desired. Refrigerate leftovers.
Makes one 9-inch pie.

Classic Meringue Pie

⅔ cup sugar
⅓ cup flour
½ teaspoon salt
2¾ cups milk
    2 squares BAKER'S®
    Unsweetened Chocolate
    3 eggs, separated
    2 teaspoons butter or margarine
    2 teaspoons vanilla
    1 baked 9-inch Pie Shell, cooled
    (recipe follows)
    6 tablespoons sugar

Mix ⅔ cup sugar, the flour and salt in saucepan. Gradually stir in milk; add chocolate. Cook and stir over medium heat until mixture is smooth and thickened; then cook and stir 5 minutes longer. Remove from heat. Beat egg yolks slightly. Stir a small amount of the hot mixture into egg yolks, mixing well. Return to remaining hot mixture in saucepan. Cook 2 minutes longer. Blend in butter and vanilla. Cover surface with plastic wrap and cool 30 minutes without stirring. Pour into pie shell.

Beat egg whites until foamy throughout. Gradually add 6 tablespoons sugar and continue beating until meringue forms stiff peaks. Pile lightly on filling; then spread to edge of pie shell to seal well. Bake at 425° for 8 minutes, or until meringue is lightly browned. Cool to room temperature before serving.
Makes one 9-inch pie.

Pie Shell

1¼ cups flour
½ teaspoon salt
½ cup shortening
3 tablespoons (about) cold water

Mix flour and salt in bowl. Lightly cut in shortening with a pastry blender until mixture resembles coarse meal. Sprinkle in water, a small amount at a time, mixing lightly with pastry blender or fork until all particles are moistened and cling together when pastry is pressed into a ball. Cover with a damp cloth and let stand a few minutes. Roll pastry thin (less than ⅛ inch) on lightly floured board. Line a 7-, 8- or 9-inch pie pan with pastry. Trim 1 inch larger than pan; fold under to form standing rim; flute edge.

For a baked pie shell, prick pastry thoroughly with fork. Bake at 425° for 12 to 15 minutes or until lightly browned. Cool.

Fresh Pineapple Pie

    Nut Crust (recipe follows)
    1 large DOLE™ Fresh Pineapple
½ cup sugar
    2 tablespoons cornstarch
    1 teaspoon grated lemon peel
⅛ teaspoon ground nutmeg
1½ cups water
    3 drops yellow food coloring,
    optional

Prepare Nut Crust. Twist crown from pineapple. Cut pineapple lengthwise into quarters. Remove fruit from shells with curved knife. Trim off core and cut fruit into bite-size chunks. In large saucepan, combine sugar, cornstarch, lemon peel and nutmeg. Stir in water and food coloring. Cook, stirring constantly, until sauce is clear and thickened. Remove from heat. Add pineapple. Cool. Spoon pineapple mixture into prepared crust. Refrigerate, covered, overnight.
Makes 6 to 8 servings.
NUT CRUST: Preheat oven to 400°F. In large bowl, combine 1¾ cups vanilla wafer crumbs, ⅔ cup ground toasted walnuts, 5 tablespoons melted butter or margarine and 1 tablespoon sugar. Press onto bottom and sides of 9-inch pie plate. Bake in preheated oven 8 minutes. Cool.

Frozen Peach Cream Pies

    1 (8-ounce) package cream
    cheese, softened
    1 (14-ounce) can EAGLE® Brand
    Sweetened Condensed Milk
    (NOT evaporated milk)
    2 cups chopped pared fresh,
    canned or frozen peaches,
    pureed (about 1½ cups)
    1 tablespoon REALEMON®
    Lemon Juice from
    Concentrate
¼ teaspoon almond extract
    Few drops yellow and red food
    coloring, optional
    1 (8-ounce) container frozen
    non-dairy whipped topping,
    thawed
    2 (6-ounce) packaged graham
    cracker crumb crusts
    Additional peach slices

In large mixer bowl, beat cheese until fluffy. Gradually beat in sweetened condensed milk, then pureed peaches, ReaLemon® brand, extract and food coloring if desired. Fold in whipped topping. Pour equal portions into crusts. Freeze 4 hours or until firm. Remove from freezer 5 minutes before serving. Garnish with additional peaches. Return ungarnished leftovers to freezer.
Makes 2 pies.

Frozen Peach Cream Pies

Microwave Hershey Bar Pie

Chocolate Crumb Crust or
Graham Cracker Crust (see
Index)
1 HERSHEY'S Milk Chocolate
Bar (8 ounces), broken into
pieces
1/3 cup milk
1 1/2 cups miniature marshmallows
1 cup heavy or whipping cream
Sweetened whipped cream
Chilled cherry pie filling

Bake crumb crust; set aside. Combine chocolate bar pieces, milk and miniature marshmallows in medium microproof bowl. Microwave at HIGH (100%) for 1 1/2 to 2 1/2 minutes or until chocolate is softened and mixture is melted and smooth when stirred. Cool completely.

Whip cream until stiff; fold into chocolate mixture. Spoon into crust. Cover; chill several hours or until firm. Garnish with sweetened whipped cream; serve with chilled cherry pie filling.
8 servings.

Chocolate Crumb Crust

1/2 cup butter or margarine
1 1/2 cups graham cracker crumbs
6 tablespoons HERSHEY'S
Cocoa
1/3 cup confectioners' sugar

Grease micro-proof 9-inch pie plate. In small micro-proof bowl, microwave butter at HIGH (100%) for 1 minute or until melted. Stir in graham cracker crumbs, cocoa and confectioners' sugar until well blended. Press on bottom and up side of prepared pie plate. Microwave an additional 1 to 1 1/2 minutes until bubbly. (Do not overcook.) Cool crust completely before filling.

Fresh Strawberry Pie

1 (9-inch) baked pastry shell
1 1/4 cups sugar
1 tablespoon cornstarch
1 1/2 cups water
3 tablespoons REALEMON®
Lemon Juice from
Concentrate
1 (4-serving size) package
strawberry flavor gelatin
1 quart fresh strawberries,
cleaned and hulled

In medium saucepan, combine sugar and cornstarch; add the water and ReaLemon® brand. Over high heat, bring to a boil. Reduce heat; cook and stir until slightly thickened and clear, 4 to 5 minutes. Add gelatin; stir until dissolved. Cool to room temperature. Stir in strawberries; turn into prepared pastry shell. Chill 4 to 6 hours or until set. Refrigerate leftovers.
Makes one 9-inch pie.

Fresh Strawberry Pie

Praline Ice Cream Pudding Pie

2 tablespoons light brown sugar
2 tablespoons butter or
margarine
1/3 cup chopped nuts
1 lightly baked 9-inch pie shell*
1 1/2 cups cold milk
1 cup (1/2 pint) vanilla ice cream,
softened
1 package (6-serving size)
JELL-O® Butter Pecan Flavor
Instant Pudding and Pie
Filling

Combine brown sugar, butter and nuts in small saucepan. Heat over medium heat until butter is melted. Pour into pie shell. Bake in preheated 450° oven for 5 minutes or until bubbly. Cool on wire rack.

Combine milk and ice cream in medium bowl until thoroughly blended. Add pie filling mix. With electric mixer at low speed, beat until blended, about 1 minute. Pour immediately over nut mixture in pie shell. Chill until set, about 3 hours. Garnish with whipped topping and pecan halves or chopped nuts, if desired.
Makes one 9-inch pie.

*Decrease recommended baking time by 5 minutes.

Harvest Cherry Pie

Pastry for 2-crust pie
1 1/3 cups (one-half jar) NONE
SUCH® Ready-to-Use
Mincemeat (Regular or
Brandy & Rum)
3/4 cup chopped nuts
1 (21-ounce) can cherry pie
filling
1 egg yolk plus 2 tablespoons
water, optional

Place rack in lower half of oven; preheat oven to 425°. In small bowl, stir together mincemeat and nuts; turn into pastry-lined 9-inch pie plate. Spoon cherry pie filling over mincemeat. Cover with top crust; cut slits near center. Seal and flute. For a more golden crust, mix egg yolk and water; brush over entire surface of pie. Bake 25 to 30 minutes or until golden brown. Serve warm or cool. Garnish as desired.
Makes one 9-inch pie.

Peachy Mince Pie with Cheddar Crust (left), Harvest Cherry Pie (right)

Peachy Mince Pie with Cheddar Crust

> **1 (9-ounce) package pie crust mix**
> **1 cup (4 ounces) shredded sharp Cheddar cheese**
> **1 jar NONE SUCH® Ready-to-Use Mincemeat (Regular *or* Brandy & Rum)**
> **1 (16-ounce) can sliced peaches, drained**
> **1 egg yolk plus 2 tablespoons water, optional**

Place rack in lower half of oven; preheat oven to 425°. Prepare pie crust mix as package directs for 2-crust pie, adding cheese. Turn mincemeat into pastry-lined 9-inch pie plate. Top with peach slices. Cover with top crust; cut slits near center. Seal and flute. For a more golden crust, mix egg yolk and water; brush over entire surface of pie. Bake 20 minutes or until golden. Serve warm or cool. Garnish as desired.
Makes one 9-inch pie.

Single Pie Crust

> **1¹/₃ cups unsifted all-purpose flour**
> **¹/₂ teaspoon salt**
> **6 tablespoons CRISCO® Oil**
> **3 tablespoons milk**

Preheat oven to 375°F. Combine flour and salt in medium mixing bowl. Blend Crisco® Oil and milk. Add to flour mixture. Stir with fork until mixture forms a ball. Shape into ball; flatten slightly. Place between sheets of waxed paper. Roll to a cricle 2 inches larger than inverted 9-inch pie plate. Remove top sheet of waxed paper. Carefully slide your hand under bottom sheet of waxed paper. Turn over into pie plate so waxed paper is on top, easing pastry to fit pie plate. Remove waxed paper. Trim and flute edges. Prick thoroughly with fork. Bake at 375°F, 12 to 15 minutes, or until light golden brown. Cool.
One 9-inch pie crust.

Lemon Pastry

> **1 cup unsifted flour**
> **¹/₂ teaspoon salt**
> **¹/₃ cup shortening**
> **1 egg, beaten**
> **1 tablespoon REALEMON® Lemon Juice from Concentrate**

Preheat oven to 400°. In medium bowl, combine flour and salt; cut in shortening until crumbly. In small bowl, beat egg and ReaLemon® brand. Sprinkle over flour mixture; stir until dough forms a ball. On floured surface, roll out to about ¹/₈-inch thickness. Line 9-inch pie plate; flute edges. Prick with fork. Bake 12 to 15 minutes or until golden.
Makes one 9-inch pastry shell.

Pastry for Two-Crust Pie

> **2²/₃ cups unsifted all-purpose flour**
> **1 teaspoon salt**
> **³/₄ cup CRISCO® Oil**
> **6 tablespoons milk**

Combine flour and salt in medium mixing bowl. Blend Crisco® Oil and milk. Add to flour mixture. Stir with fork until mixture forms a ball. Divide dough in half; set one half aside. Shape remaining half into a ball; flatten slightly. Place between sheets of waxed paper. Roll to a circle at least 2 inches larger than inverted 9-inch pie plate. Remove top sheet of waxed paper. Carefully slide your hand under bottom sheet of waxed paper. Turn over into pie plate so waxed paper is on top, easing pastry to fit pie plate. Remove waxed paper. Add filling. Roll out remaining dough. Place over filling. Trim and flute edges. Cut slits in top so steam can escape. Bake according to pie recipe.
One 9-inch double pie crust.

Mini Fruit Cheese Tarts

Coconut Custard Pie

**1 (9-inch) unbaked pastry shell
1 cup flaked coconut
3 eggs
1 (14-ounce) can EAGLE® Brand
   Sweetened Condensed Milk
   (NOT evaporated milk)
1¼ cups hot water
1 teaspoon vanilla extract
¼ teaspoon salt
⅛ teaspoon ground nutmeg**

Preheat oven to 425°. Toast ½ *cup* coconut; set aside. Bake pastry shell 8 minutes; cool slightly. Meanwhile, in medium mixing bowl, beat eggs. Add sweetened condensed milk, water, vanilla, salt and nutmeg; mix well. Stir in remaining ½ *cup* coconut. Pour into prepared pastry shell. Sprinkle with toasted coconut. Bake 10 minutes. Reduce oven temperature to 350°; continue baking 25 to 30 minutes or until knife inserted near center comes out clean. Cool. Chill if desired. Refrigerate leftovers.
Makes one 9-inch pie.

Raisin Sour Cream Pie

**¾ cup sugar
2 tablespoons cornstarch
¼ teaspoon salt
2 eggs, beaten
2 cups dairy sour cream
1 cup SUN-MAID® Raisins
2 tablespoons lemon juice
1 (9-inch) pie shell, baked, or
   crumb crust**

In top of double boiler, blend together sugar, cornstarch and salt. In small bowl, combine beaten eggs, 1½ cups of the sour cream, the raisins and lemon juice. Stir into sugar mixture. Set over hot, not boiling, water and cook until thick, stirring frequently. Pour into baked pie shell. When cool, top with remaining ½ cup sour cream. Chill several hours.
Makes one 9-inch pie.

Plum Pudding Pie

**⅓ cup plus 2 tablespoons
   KAHLÚA®
½ cup golden raisins
½ cup chopped pitted dates
⅓ cup chopped candied cherries
½ cup chopped walnuts
⅓ cup dark corn syrup
½ teaspoon pumpkin pie spice
¼ cup butter or margarine,
   softened
¼ cup packed brown sugar
2 tablespoons all-purpose flour
¼ teaspoon salt
2 eggs, slightly beaten
1 (9-inch) unbaked pie shell
1 cup whipping cream
   Maraschino cherries (optional)**

In medium bowl, combine ⅓ cup of the Kahlúa®, the raisins, dates and cherries; mix well. Cover; let stand 1 to 4 hours. Stir in walnuts, corn syrup and spice. In large bowl, cream butter, sugar, flour and salt. Stir in eggs. Add fruit mixture; blend well. Pour into unbaked pie shell. Bake in preheated 350° oven 35 minutes or until filling is firm and crust is golden. Cool completely on wire rack. When ready to serve, in small bowl, beat whipping cream with remaining 2 tablespoons Kahlúa® just until soft peaks form. Spoon cream into pastry bag fitted with large star tip and pipe decoratively on top. If desired, garnish with maraschino cherries.
Makes 8 servings.

Strawberry Tart Glace

**Pastry for 1-crust 9-inch pie
2 8-ounce packages Light
   PHILADELPHIA BRAND
   Neufchâtel Cheese, softened
½ cup sugar
1 tablespoon milk
¼ teaspoon vanilla
1 quart strawberries, hulled
1 tablespoon cornstarch
¼ cup water
   Few drops red food coloring
   (optional)**

On lightly floured surface, roll pastry to 12-inch circle. Place in 10-inch quiche dish. Prick bottom and sides of pastry with fork. Bake at 450°, 9 to 11 minutes or until golden brown.

Combine neufchâtel cheese, ¼ cup sugar, milk and vanilla, mixing at medium speed on electric mixer until well blended. Spread onto bottom of crust. Puree 1 cup strawberries. Top neufchâtel cheese mixture with remaining strawberries. Combine remaining sugar and cornstarch in saucepan; gradually add pureed strawberries and water. Cook, stirring constantly, over medium heat until mixture is clear and thickened. Stir in food coloring. Pour over strawberries; chill.
8 servings.

Variations: Substitute PHILADELPHIA BRAND Cream Cheese for Neufchâtel Cheese.

Substitute 9-inch pie plate for 10-inch quiche dish.

Substitute almond extract for vanilla.

Mini Fruit Cheese Tarts

**24 (2- or 3-inch) prepared tart-
   size crusts
1 (8-ounce) package cream
   cheese, softened
1 (14-ounce) can EAGLE® Brand
   Sweetened Condensed Milk
   (NOT evaporated milk)
⅓ cup REALEMON® Lemon Juice
   from Concentrate
1 teaspoon vanilla extract
   Assorted fruit (strawberries,
   blueberries, bananas,
   raspberries, orange
   segments, cherries,
   kiwifruit, grapes, pineapple,
   etc.)
¼ cup BAMA® Apple Jelly,
   melted**

Cinnamon Fruit Tart with Sour Cream Filling

In large mixer bowl, beat cheese until fluffy. Gradually beat in sweetened condensed milk until smooth. Stir in ReaLemon® brand and vanilla. Spoon equal portions into crusts. Top with fruit; brush with jelly. Chill 2 hours or until set. Refrigerate leftovers.
Makes 24 tarts.

Cinnamon Fruit Tart with Sour Cream Filling

- **1 envelope KNOX® Unflavored Gelatine**
- **¼ cup cold water**
- **1 cup (8 ounces) creamed cottage cheese**
- **¾ cup canned pineapple juice**
- **½ cup sour cream**
- **½ cup milk**
- **¼ cup sugar**
- **1 teaspoon lemon juice**
  Cinnamon Graham Cracker Crust (recipe follows)
  Suggested Fresh Fruit*
- **2 tablespoons orange or apricot marmalade, melted**

In small saucepan, sprinkle unflavored gelatine over cold water; let stand 1 minute. Stir over low heat until gelatine is completely dissolved, about 3 minutes.

In blender or food processor, process cottage cheese, pineapple juice, sour cream, milk, sugar and lemon juice until blended. While processing, through feed cap, gradually add gelatine mixture and process until blended. Pour into Cinnamon Graham Cracker Crust; chill until firm, about 3 hours. To serve, top with Suggested Fresh Fruit, then brush with marmalade.
Makes 12 servings, 223 calories per serving.

*Suggested Fresh Fruit: Use any combination of the following to equal 2 cups—sliced strawberries, kiwi or oranges; blueberries or raspberries.
CINNAMON GRAHAM CRACKER CRUST: In small bowl, combine 2 cups graham cracker crumbs, 1 tablespoon sugar, ½ teaspoon ground cinnamon and ¼ cup melted butter. Press into 10-inch tart pan. Bake at 375°, 8 minutes; cool.

Strawberry and Cream Napoleons

- **1 package (17¼ ounces) frozen puff pastry sheets, thawed according to package directions**
- **1 envelope KNOX® Unflavored Gelatine**
- **¼ cup cold water**
- **2 cups (1 pint) whipping or heavy cream**
- **¼ cup raspberry liqueur**
- **½ cup confectioners sugar**
- **½ cup strawberry preserves, heated**
- **4 cups sliced strawberries (about 2 pints)**
  Strawberry Glaze (recipe follows)

Preheat oven to 425°.

On lightly floured surface, unfold pastry sheets, then separate, using perforated lines, into 3 rectangles. Cut each rectangle in half crosswise.* Place on ungreased baking sheets and bake 20 minutes or until puffed and golden. On wire rack, cool completely.

Chill large mixing bowl at least 15 minutes. Meanwhile, in small saucepan, sprinkle unflavored gelatine over cold water; let stand 1 minute. Stir over low heat until gelatine is completely dissolved, about 3 minutes. In chilled bowl, while beating cream on low speed, gradually add gelatine mixture and liqueur, then beat on medium speed until thickened, about 5 minutes. Add sugar, then beat on high speed until soft peaks form, about 2 minutes.

To serve, with long, serrated knife, cut each pastry rectangle in half horizontally. Reserve the 8 best rectangles for tops. Evenly brush 8 rectangles with ½ preserves, then top with ½ strawberries and ½ cream mixture. Repeat layers, ending with reserved pastry tops. Decoratively drizzle tops with Strawberry Glaze.
Makes 8 large napoleons.
*Hint: For smaller napoleons, cut each pastry rectangle in thirds crosswise and proceed as above.
STRAWBERRY GLAZE: In small bowl, thoroughly blend ½ cup sifted confectioners sugar, 2 teaspoons water and 1 teaspoon strawberry preserves, heated.

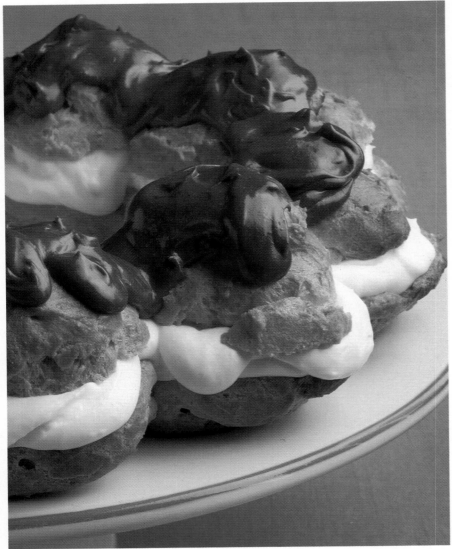

"Philly" Cream Puff Ring

Chocolate-Almond Tarts

Chocolate Tart Shells
3/4 cup sugar
1/4 cup HERSHEY'S Cocoa
2 tablespoons cornstarch
2 tablespoons flour
1/4 teaspoon salt
2 cups milk
2 egg yolks, slightly beaten
2 tablespoons butter or
  margarine
1/4 teaspoon almond extract
Sliced almonds

Prepare Chocolate Tart Shells; set aside. Combine sugar, cocoa, cornstarch, flour and salt in medium saucepan; blend in milk and egg yolks. Cook over medium heat, stirring constantly, until mixture boils; boil and stir 1 minute. Remove from heat; blend in butter and almond extract.

Pour into cooled shells; press plastic wrap directly onto surface. Chill. Garnish tops with sliced almonds.
6 tarts.

Chocolate Tart Shells

1 1/2 cups vanilla wafer crumbs
  (about 45 wafers)
1/3 cup confectioners' sugar
1/4 cup HERSHEY'S Cocoa
6 tablespoons butter or
  margarine, melted

Combine crumbs, confectioners' sugar, cocoa and melted butter in medium bowl; stir until completely blended. Divide mixture among six 4-ounce tart pans; press mixture firmly onto bottoms and up sides of pans. Bake at 350° for 5 minutes. Cool.

Napoleons

2 sheets (17 1/4-ounce package)
  frozen puff pastry
Chocolate Cream Filling
Vanilla Frosting
Chocolate Glaze

Thaw folded pastry sheets as directed; gently unfold. Roll each on floured surface to 15×12-inch rectangle. Place on ungreased cookie sheets; prick each sheet thoroughly with fork. Bake at 350° for 18 to 22 minutes or until puffed and lightly browned. Cool completely on cookie sheets. Prepare Chocolate Cream Filling.

"Philly" Cream Puff Ring

1 cup water
1/2 cup PARKAY Margarine
1 cup flour
1/4 teaspoon salt
4 eggs
2 8-ounce packages
  PHILADELPHIA BRAND
  Cream Cheese, softened
1 1/2 cups powdered sugar
1 teaspoon vanilla
1 cup whipping cream, whipped
2 bananas, sliced
1 1-ounce square unsweetened
  chocolate, melted
1 tablespoon milk

Bring water and margarine to boil. Add flour and salt; stir vigorously over low heat until mixture forms ball. Remove from heat. Add eggs, one at a time, beating well after each addition. Drop ten 1/2 cupfuls of dough on lightly greased cookie sheet to form 9-inch ring. Bake at 400°, 50 to 55 minutes or until golden brown. Remove from cookie sheet immediately; cool.

Combine cream cheese, 1 cup sugar and vanilla, mixing until well blended. Reserve 1/2 cup cream cheese mixture; fold whipped cream and bananas into remaining mixture. Chill. Carefully cut top from ring; fill with whipped cream mixture. Replace top. Add remaining sugar, chocolate and milk to reserved cream cheese mixture; mix well. Spread over ring.
10 servings.

Cut one rectangle lengthwise into three equal pieces. Place one piece on serving plate; spread with one-fourth of the Chocolate Cream Filling. Top with second piece of pastry; spread with one-fourth of the filling. Place remaining piece on top; set aside. Repeat procedure with remaining pastry and filling.

Prepare Vanilla Frosting; spread half the frosting on each rectangle. Prepare Chocolate Glaze; drizzle half of the glaze in decorative design over frosting on each rectangle. Cover; chill at least 1 hour or until filling is firm. Cut each rectangle into six pieces.

12 servings.

Chocolate Cream Filling

½ cup sugar
3 tablespoons cornstarch
1½ cups milk
3 egg yolks, slightly beaten
¾ cup HERSHEY'S MINI CHIPS Semi-Sweet Chocolate
½ teaspoon vanilla

Combine sugar, cornstarch and milk in medium saucepan. Cook over medium heat, stirring constantly, until mixture just begins to boil. Remove from heat. Gradually stir small amount of mixture into egg yolks; blend well. Return egg mixture to mixture in pan. Cook over medium heat, stirring constantly, 1 minute. Remove from heat; add MINI CHIPS Chocolate and vanilla, stirring until chips are melted and mixture is smooth. Press plastic wrap directly onto surface. Cool; chill thoroughly.

Vanilla Frosting

1½ cups confectioners' sugar
1 tablespoon light corn syrup
¼ teaspoon vanilla
1 to 2 tablespoons hot water

Combine confectioners' sugar, corn syrup, vanilla and hot water in small mixer bowl; beat to spreading consistency.

Chocolate Glaze

¼ cup butter or margarine
⅓ cup HERSHEY'S Cocoa

Melt butter in small saucepan. Remove from heat; stir in cocoa until smooth. Cool slightly.

Chocolate-Filled Cream Puffs

1 cup water
½ cup butter or margarine
¼ teaspoon salt
1 cup unsifted all-purpose flour
4 eggs
Chocolate Cream Filling
Confectioners' sugar

Heat water, butter and salt to rolling boil in medium saucepan. Add flour all at once; stir vigorously over low heat about 1 minute or until mixture leaves side of pan and forms a ball. Remove from heat; add eggs, one at a time, beating well after each addition until smooth and velvety.

Drop by scant ¼ cupfuls onto ungreased cookie sheet. Bake at 400° for 35 to 40 minutes or until puffed and golden brown. While puff is warm, horizontally slice off small portion of top; reserve tops. Remove any soft filaments of dough; cool puffs. Prepare Chocolate Cream Filling; fill puffs. Replace tops; dust with confectioners' sugar. Chill.

About 12 cream puffs.   *(continued)*

Chocolate Cream Filling

1¼ cups sugar
⅓ cup HERSHEY'S Cocoa
⅓ cup cornstarch
¼ teaspoon salt
3 cups milk
3 egg yolks, slightly beaten
2 tablespoons butter or margarine
1½ teaspoons vanilla

Combine sugar, cocoa, cornstarch and salt in medium saucepan; stir in milk. Cook over medium heat, stirring constantly, until mixture boils; boil and stir 1 minute. Remove from heat. Gradually stir small amount of chocolate mixture into egg yolks; blend well. Return egg mixture to chocolate mixture in pan; stir and heat just until boiling. Remove from heat; blend in butter and vanilla. Pour into bowl; press plastic wrap directly onto surface. Cool.

Variation—Miniature Cream Puffs: Drop dough by level teaspoonfuls onto ungreased cookie sheet. Bake at 400° for about 15 minutes. Fill as directed above.

About 8 dozen miniature cream puffs.

Chocolate-Filled Cream Puffs (top), Chocolate-Almond Tarts (middle), Napoleons (bottom)

CAKES

Every celebration is a good reason to show off your baking skills with a tender cake, high and moist. A specially filled angel cake will draw raves at a party. Delight the children with whimsical shapes and decorations. And for the birthday honoree, present the traditional chocolate layer cake.

Chocolatetown Special Cake

- **½ cup HERSHEY'S Cocoa**
- **½ cup boiling water**
- **⅔ cup shortening**
- **1¾ cups sugar**
- **1 teaspoon vanilla**
- **2 eggs**
- **2¼ cups unsifted all-purpose flour**
- **1½ teaspoons baking soda**
- **½ teaspoon salt**
- **1⅓ cups buttermilk or sour milk***

Stir together cocoa and boiling water in small bowl until smooth; set aside. Cream shortening, sugar and vanilla in large mixer bowl until light and fluffy. Add eggs; beat well. Combine flour, baking soda and salt; add alternately with buttermilk to creamed mixture. Blend in cocoa mixture.

Pour into three greased and floured 8-inch or two 9-inch layer pans. Bake at 350° for 25 to 30 minutes for 8-inch pans or 35 to 40 minutes for 9-inch pans, or until cake tester comes out clean. Cool 10 minutes; remove from pans. Cool completely; frost as desired.

8 to 10 servings.

*To sour milk: Use 4 teaspoons vinegar plus milk to equal 1⅓ cups.

Pound Cake

- **1 package (2-layer size) yellow cake mix or pudding-included cake mix**
- **1 package (4-serving size) JELL-O® Vanilla, Butterscotch, Butter Pecan or Lemon Flavor Pudding and Pie Filling**
- **1 cup (½ pint) sour cream or plain yogurt**
- **⅓ cup vegetable oil**
- **4 eggs**
- **⅛ to ¼ teaspoon mace (optional)**

Combine all ingredients in large bowl. With electric mixer at low speed, blend just to moisten, scraping sides of bowl often. Then beat at medium speed for 4 minutes. Pour batter into 2 greased and floured 9×5-inch loaf pans. Bake in preheated 350° oven for 40 to 45 minutes or until cake tester inserted in center of cake comes out clean and cakes begin to pull away from sides of pans. Cool in pans on wire rack 15 minutes. Remove from pans and finish cooling on wire racks. Sprinkle with confectioners sugar, if desired.

Makes two 9×5-inch loaves.

Tomato Soup Spice Cake

- **1 tablespoon sugar**
- **1 box (about 18 ounces) spice cake mix**
- **1 can (10¾ ounces) CAMPBELL'S® Condensed Tomato Soup**
- **2 eggs**
- **2 tablespoons water**
- **1 cup sour cream**
- **¼ cup packed brown sugar**
- **1 teaspoon vanilla extract**

To Microwave:
1. Generously grease 14-cup microwave-safe Bundt® pan. Sprinkle pan with sugar.
2. In large bowl, combine cake mix, soup, eggs and water. With mixer, beat 2 minutes or until well mixed, constantly scraping side and bottom of bowl.
3. Pour into prepared pan. Microwave, uncovered, at 50% power 9 minutes, rotating pan once during cooking.
4. Increase power to HIGH. Microwave, uncovered, 5 minutes or until toothpick inserted into cake comes out clean. Let stand directly on countertop 15 minutes. Invert onto serving plate; cool completely.
5. In small bowl, stir together sour cream, brown sugar and vanilla until sugar dissolves. Spoon evenly over cooled cake.

Makes 12 servings.

Chocolatetown Special Cake

Cinnamon Ripple Cake

    1 package DUNCAN HINES®
       Deluxe Angel Food Cake Mix
1⅓ cups water
3½ teaspoons ground cinnamon
    ¾ cup whipping cream
    ½ cup cold milk
    ⅓ cup confectioners' sugar
    1 teaspoon vanilla extract

1. Preheat oven to 375°F.
2. Prepare cake with water as directed on package. Spoon one-fourth of batter into ungreased 10-inch tube pan and spread evenly. With small fine sieve, sprinkle one teaspoon cinnamon over batter. Repeat layering two more times, ending with batter.
3. Bake at 375°F for 30 to 40 minutes or until top crust is golden brown, firm and looks very dry. Do not underbake.
4. To cool cake, hang pan upside down on bottle or funnel. When completely cooled, remove from pan.
5. To serve, beat whipping cream and milk in chilled bowl with chilled beaters until thick. Blend in confectioners' sugar, vanilla extract and remaining ½ teaspoon cinnamon. Cut cake into slices and top with cinnamon cream.
12 to 16 servings.

Cinnamon Ripple Cake

French Apple Cake

    3 cooking apples, pared, cored
       and sliced (about 3 cups)
    ⅔ cup sugar
    1 tablespoon all-purpose flour
    ½ teaspoon ground cinnamon
    2 tablespoons butter or
       margarine, melted
    2 tablespoons lemon juice
    1 package DUNCAN HINES®
       Deluxe White Cake Mix
    3 large eggs
    ⅓ cup CRISCO® Oil or PURITAN®
       Oil
1¼ cups water

1. Preheat oven to 350°F. Grease 13×9×2-inch pan.
2. Arrange apples in pan. Mix sugar, flour and cinnamon; sprinkle over apples. Combine melted butter and lemon juice; drizzle over apples.
3. Place dry cake mix, eggs, oil and water in large mixer bowl. Mix cake as directed on package. Turn batter into pan over apples and spread evenly.
4. Bake at 350°F for 40 to 50 minutes or until toothpick inserted in center comes out clean. Cool 1 to 2 minutes in pan. Invert on large platter or tray; remove pan after 1 to 2 minutes. Serve warm.
12 to 16 servings.

Marble Chiffon Cake

    ⅓ cup HERSHEY'S Cocoa
    2 tablespoons sugar
    ¼ cup water
    2 tablespoons vegetable oil
    2 cups unsifted all-purpose flour
1½ cups sugar
    3 teaspoons baking powder
    1 teaspoon salt
    ½ cup vegetable oil
    7 egg yolks, at room
       temperature
    ¾ cup cold water
    2 teaspoons vanilla
    7 egg whites, at room
       temperature
    ½ teaspoon cream of tartar
       Cocoa Glaze

Combine cocoa, 2 tablespoons sugar, ¼ cup water and 2 tablespoons oil in small bowl until smooth; set aside. Combine flour, 1½ cups sugar, the baking powder and salt in large mixer bowl; add ½ cup oil, the egg yolks, ¾ cup cold water and the vanilla. Beat on low speed until combined. Beat 5 minutes on high speed. With clean beaters, beat egg whites and cream of tartar in another large mixer bowl until stiff peaks form.

Pour batter in thin stream over entire surface of egg whites; fold in lightly, using rubber spatula. Remove one-third of the batter to another bowl; gently fold in chocolate mixture. Pour half the vanilla batter into ungreased 10-inch tube pan; spread half the chocolate batter over vanilla. Repeat layers; gently swirl with spatula or knife for marbled effect. Bake at 325° for 65 to 70 minutes or until cake springs back when touched lightly. Invert cake over heat-proof funnel or bottle until completely cool. Loosen cake from pan; invert onto serving plate. Spread top with Cocoa Glaze.
12 to 16 servings.

Cocoa Glaze

    2 tablespoons butter or
       margarine
    ¼ cup HERSHEY'S Cocoa
    3 tablespoons water
    ½ teaspoon vanilla
1¼ cups confectioners' sugar

Melt butter in small saucepan over low heat. Stir in cocoa and water. Cook, stirring constantly, until mixture thickens; *do not boil.* Remove from heat. Stir in vanilla. Gradually add confectioners' sugar; beat with wire whisk until smooth.

Carrot Cake (left), Chocolate Yogurt Cake (right)

Carrot Cake

2¼ cups unsifted all-purpose flour
1½ cups sugar
2 teaspoons baking soda
1½ teaspoons ground cinnamon
½ teaspoon ground nutmeg
½ teaspoon salt
1 cup CRISCO® Oil
3 eggs
½ cup milk
2 cups shredded carrot
1½ cups flaked coconut
¾ cup chopped nuts
½ cup currants or raisins
Frosting:
    1 package (3 ounces) cream
      cheese, softened
    2 tablespoons butter or
      margarine, softened
    2 tablespoons milk
    ¼ teaspoon vanilla
    Dash salt
    2 to 2¼ cups confectioners
      sugar

Preheat oven to 325°F. Oil and flour 13×9-inch baking pan. Set aside.

Mix flour, sugar, baking soda, cinnamon, nutmeg and salt in large mixing bowl. Add Crisco® Oil, eggs, milk and carrot. Beat with electric mixer at low speed until ingredients are moistened, scraping bowl constantly. Beat at medium speed 2 minutes, scraping bowl occasionally. Stir in coconut, nuts and currants. Pour into prepared pan. Bake at 325°F, 55 to 60 minutes, or until wooden pick inserted in center comes out clean. Cool completely on wire rack.

For frosting, blend cream cheese and butter in small mixing bowl. Add milk, vanilla and salt. Mix well. Stir in enough confectioners sugar until thick enough to spread. Spread on cooled cake.
One 13×9-inch cake.

Chocolate Yogurt Cake

2 cups unsifted all-purpose flour
1½ cups sugar
½ cup unsweetened cocoa
2 teaspoons baking soda
1 teaspoon salt
1 cup plain yogurt
3 eggs
⅔ cup CRISCO® Oil
1½ teaspoons vanilla
Frosting:
    1 package (6 ounces) semisweet
      chocolate chips
    ¼ cup butter or margarine
    ⅔ cup plain yogurt
    ½ teaspoon vanilla
    ⅛ teaspoon salt
    2½ to 3 cups confectioners sugar

Preheat oven to 350°F. Grease and flour two 9-inch round layer pans. Set aside.

Mix flour, sugar, cocoa, baking soda and salt in large mixing bowl. Add yogurt, eggs, Crisco® Oil and vanilla. Beat with electric mixer at low speed until ingredients are moistened, scraping bowl constantly. Beat at medium speed 2 minutes, scraping bowl occasionally. Pour into prepared pans. Bake at 350°F, 30 to 35 minutes, or until wooden pick inserted in center comes out clean. Cool 10 minutes. Remove from pans. Cool completely on wire rack.

For frosting, combine chocolate chips and butter in small saucepan. Cook over low heat, stirring constantly, until melted. Transfer mixture to medium mixing bowl. Cool slightly. Blend in yogurt, vanilla and salt. Stir in enough confectioners sugar until frosting is thick enough to spread. Fill and frost cooled cake.
One 2-layer cake.

Easy German Chocolate Cake

**1 package DUNCAN HINES®
    Deluxe Swiss Chocolate
    Cake Mix**
3 large eggs
**½ cup CRISCO® Oil or PURITAN®
    Oil**
1¼ cups water
1 cup chopped nuts
**⅓ cup butter or regular
    margarine, melted**
1 cup packed light brown sugar
**1 can (3½ ounces) flaked
    coconut**
¼ cup milk

1. Preheat oven to 350°F. Grease and flour 13×9×2-inch pan.
2. Combine dry cake mix, eggs, oil and water in large mixer bowl. Mix cake as directed on package. Stir in ½ cup nuts. Turn batter into pan and spread evenly.
3. Bake at 350°F for 35 to 40 minutes or until toothpick inserted in center comes out clean. Cool in pan on rack.
4. For topping, combine butter, brown sugar, coconut, milk and remaining ½ cup nuts. Spread evenly over cooled cake. Place under broiler and broil 2 to 3 minutes or until bubbly.
12 to 16 servings.

Petits Fours

Cocoa-Spice Snackin' Cake

**¼ cup butter or margarine,
    melted**
¼ cup HERSHEY'S Cocoa
¾ cup applesauce
1¼ cups unsifted all-purpose flour
1 cup sugar
¾ teaspoon baking soda
½ teaspoon cinnamon
¼ teaspoon nutmeg
¼ teaspoon salt
1 egg, beaten
½ cup chopped nuts

Combine melted butter and cocoa; blend in applesauce. Combine flour, sugar, baking soda, cinnamon, nutmeg and salt in large bowl. Blend in cocoa mixture and egg until dry ingredients are moistened. Stir in nuts.
    Spread in greased 9-inch square pan. Bake at 350° for 30 to 35 minutes or until cake tester comes out clean. Cool in pan.
8 to 10 servings.

Petits Fours

**1 package DUNCAN HINES®
    Deluxe White or Yellow Cake
    Mix**
3 large eggs
**⅓ cup CRISCO® Oil or PURITAN®
    Oil**
1¼ cups water
3 cups granulated sugar
¼ teaspoon cream of tartar
1½ cups hot water
1 teaspoon vanilla extract
**2¼ cups confectioners' sugar
    Food coloring, if desired
    Frosted roses or candy
    decorations, if desired**

1. Line 15½×10½×1-inch jelly roll pan with waxed paper. Preheat oven to 350°F.
2. Combine dry cake mix, eggs, oil and 1¼ cups water in large mixer bowl. Mix cake as directed on package. Turn batter into pan and spread evenly.
3. Bake at 350°F for 25 to 30 minutes or until toothpick inserted in center comes out clean. Immediately turn cake out onto towel and peel off paper. Cool.
4. Cut cooled cake into seventy 1½-inch shapes. Place on racks with waxed paper under racks.
5. For frosting, combine granulated sugar, cream of tartar, and 1½ cups hot water in heavy saucepan. Cook over medium heat until syrup reaches 226°F on candy thermometer. Cool until lukewarm (110°F). Stir in vanilla extract. Gradually beat in confectioners' sugar until frosting is of good pouring consistency. Tint frosting with food coloring, if desired.
6. Pour frosting over cakes on racks. After frosting one rack, remove frosting from waxed paper and return to bowl of frosting. If frosting becomes too thick, heat over hot water or add a few drops of hot water. Repeat until all cakes are frosted. Decorate with frosted roses or candy decorations.
70 cakes.

Kahlúa® Sweetheart Cake

¾ **cup unsweetened cocoa**
1 **teaspoon instant coffee crystals**
1 **cup boiling water**
½ **cup plus 2 tablespoons KAHLÚA®**
½ **cup butter or margarine, softened**
¼ **cup shortening**
1¾ **cups sugar**
3 **eggs**
1 **teaspoon vanilla**
2 **cups sifted all-purpose flour**
1½ **teaspoons baking soda**
¾ **teaspoon salt**
¼ **teaspoon baking powder**
  KAHLÚA® Fudge Frosting (recipe follows)

In small heatproof bowl, blend cocoa, coffee and water. Stir in ½ cup Kahlúa®; cool. In large bowl, beat butter, shortening, sugar, eggs and vanilla until light and fluffy. In small bowl, combine flour, baking soda, salt and baking powder. Add flour mixture to butter mixture alternately with cocoa mixture, beating well after each addition. Line bottoms of two 9-inch round pans with parchment paper; lightly grease sides of pans. Divide batter evenly between prepared pans. Bake in preheated 350° oven 25 to 30 minutes or just until toothpick inserted into center comes out clean. Do not overbake. Let cool in pans on wire racks 5 minutes. Loosen edges; remove from pans. Peel off parchment paper; cool completely on wire racks. Prepare Kahlúa® Fudge Frosting. Brush bottom of each layer with 1 tablespoon of remaining Kahlúa®. Fill and frost layers with frosting. Decorate as desired. Let stand until frosting is set.
Makes 10 to 12 servings.
KAHLÚA® FUDGE FROSTING: In medium saucepan, combine 1 package (6 ounces) semisweet chocolate chips, ¼ cup *each* Kahlúa® and half-and-half and 1 cup butter or margarine. Stir over medium heat until chocolate melts. Remove from heat; blend in 2½ cups powdered sugar. Beat until frosting is cool and holds its shape. (Pan may be placed over ice water to hasten cooling.)

Cool and Minty Party Cake

1 **(14-ounce) can EAGLE® Brand Sweetened Condensed Milk (NOT evaporated milk)**
2 **teaspoons peppermint extract**
8 **drops green food coloring**
2 **cups (1 pint) BORDEN® or MEADOW GOLD® Whipping Cream, whipped (do not use non-dairy whipped topping)**
1 **(18¼- or 18½-ounce) package white cake mix**
  Green creme de menthe
1 **(8-ounce) container frozen non-dairy whipped topping, thawed**

In large mixing bowl, combine sweetened condensed milk, extract and food coloring. Fold in whipped cream. Pour into aluminum foil-lined 9-inch round layer cake pan; cover. Freeze at least 6 hours or overnight. Meanwhile, prepare and bake cake mix as package directs for two 9-inch round layers. Remove from pans; cool thoroughly. With table fork, poke holes in layers 1 inch apart halfway through each layer. Spoon small amounts of creme de menthe in holes. Place 1 cake layer on serving plate; top with ice cream layer then second cake layer. Trim ice cream layer to fit cake layers. Frost quickly with topping. Return to freezer until ready to serve. Garnish as desired.
Makes one 9-inch cake.
  Tip: Cake can be made 1 week ahead and stored in freezer.

Lickety-Split Cocoa Cake

1½ **cups unsifted all-purpose flour**
1 **cup sugar**
¼ **cup HERSHEY'S Cocoa**
1 **teaspoon baking soda**
½ **teaspoon salt**
1 **cup water**
¼ **cup plus 2 tablespoons vegetable oil**
1 **tablespoon vinegar**
1 **teaspoon vanilla**

Combine flour, sugar, cocoa, baking soda and salt in large bowl. Add water, oil, vinegar and vanilla; stir with spoon or wire whisk just until batter is smooth and ingredients are well blended.

Pour into greased and floured 9-inch layer pan or 8-inch square pan. Bake at 350° for 35 to 40 minutes or until cake tester comes out clean. Cool in pan; frost as desired.
6 to 8 servings.

Cool and Minty Party Cake

Strawberry Tunnel Cream Cake

- 1 (10-inch) prepared round angel food cake
- 2 (3-ounce) packages cream cheese, softened
- 1 (14-ounce) can EAGLE® Brand Sweetened Condensed Milk (NOT evaporated milk)
- ⅓ cup REALEMON® Lemon Juice from Concentrate
- 1 teaspoon almond extract
- 2 to 4 drops red food coloring, optional
- 1 cup chopped fresh strawberries
- 1 (12-ounce) container frozen non-dairy whipped topping, thawed (5¼ cups)
- Additional fresh strawberries, optional

Invert cake onto serving plate. Cut 1-inch slice crosswise from top of cake; set aside. With sharp knife, cut around cake 1 inch from center hole and 1 inch from outer edge, leaving cake walls 1 inch thick. Remove cake from center, leaving 1-inch-thick base on bottom of cake. Reserve cake pieces. In large mixer bowl, beat cheese until fluffy. Gradually beat in sweetened condensed milk until smooth. Stir in ReaLemon® brand, extract and food coloring if desired. Stir in reserved torn cake pieces and chopped strawberries. Fold in *1 cup* whipped topping. Fill cavity of cake with strawberry mixture; replace top slice of cake. Chill 3 hours or until set. Frost with remaining whipped topping; garnish with strawberries if desired. Store in refrigerator.
Makes one 10-inch cake.

German Chocolate Cake

- 1 package (4 ounces) BAKER'S® GERMAN'S® Sweet Chocolate
- ½ cup boiling water
- 2 cups flour
- 1 teaspoon baking soda
- ½ teaspoon salt
- 1 cup butter or margarine
- 2 cups sugar
- 4 egg yolks
- 1 teaspoon vanilla
- 1 cup buttermilk
- 4 egg whites
- Coconut-Pecan Filling and Frosting

Melt chocolate in boiling water. Cool. Mix flour, soda and salt. Cream butter and sugar until light and fluffy. Add egg yolks, one at a time, beating thoroughly after each. Blend in vanilla and chocolate. Alternately add flour mixture and buttermilk, beating after each addition until smooth. Beat egg whites until stiff peaks form. Fold into batter.

Pour into three 9-inch layer pans, lined on bottoms with waxed paper. Bake at 350° for 30 to 35 minutes, or until a cake tester inserted in centers comes out clean. Immediately run spatula around pans between cakes and sides. Cool in pans 15 minutes. Remove from pans; remove paper and finish cooling on racks. Spread filling and frosting between layers and over top of cake.
Makes one 9-inch layer cake.

COCONUT-PECAN FILLING AND FROSTING: Combine 1 cup evaporated milk or heavy cream, 1 cup sugar, 3 slightly beaten egg yolks, ½ cup butter or margarine and 1 teaspoon vanilla in saucepan. Cook and stir over medium heat until mixture thickens, about 12 minutes. Remove from heat and stir in 1⅓ cups (about) BAKER'S® ANGEL FLAKE® Coconut and 1 cup chopped pecans. Cool until of spreading consistency, beating occasionally.
Makes 2½ cups.

Chocolate Sheet Cake

- 1¼ cups margarine or butter
- ½ cup unsweetened cocoa
- 1 cup water
- 2 cups unsifted flour
- 1½ cups firmly packed brown sugar
- 1 teaspoon baking soda
- 1 teaspoon ground cinnamon
- ½ teaspoon salt
- 1 (14-ounce) can EAGLE® Brand Sweetened Condensed Milk (NOT evaporated milk)
- 2 eggs
- 1 teaspoon vanilla extract
- 1 cup confectioners' sugar
- 1 cup nuts

Preheat oven to 350°. In small saucepan, melt *1 cup* margarine; stir in *¼ cup* cocoa, then water. Bring to a boil; remove from heat. In large mixer bowl, combine flour, brown sugar, baking soda, cinnamon and salt. Add cocoa mixture; beat well. Stir in *⅓ cup* sweetened condensed milk, eggs and vanilla. Pour into greased 15×10-inch jellyroll pan. Bake 15 minutes or until cake springs back when lightly touched. In small saucepan, melt remaining *¼ cup* margarine; add remaining *¼ cup* cocoa and remaining sweetened condensed milk. Stir in confectioners' sugar and nuts. Spread on *warm* cake.
Makes one 15×10-inch cake.

Strawberry Tunnel Cream Cake

Drum Layer Cake

- 1 package DUNCAN HINES®
Deluxe Cake Mix (any flavor)
- 3 large eggs
CRISCO® Oil or PURITAN® Oil
Water
- 5 cups confectioners' sugar
- ¾ cup CRISCO® Shortening
- ⅓ cup non-dairy creamer
- 2 teaspoons vanilla extract
- ½ cup water
- ½ teaspoon salt
Licorice twists and strings
- 2 lollipops

1. Preheat oven to 350°F. Grease and flour two 8×1½-inch round layer pans.
2. Combine dry cake mix, eggs and the amount of oil and water listed on package in large mixer bowl. Mix, bake and cool cake as directed on package.
3. For decorator frosting, beat confectioners' sugar, shortening, non-dairy creamer, vanilla extract, ½ cup water and salt in large mixer bowl. Beat 3 minutes at medium speed, then 5 minutes at high speed. Add more confectioners' sugar to thicken or water to thin frosting as needed.
4. Spread frosting between cooled layers and on sides and top of cake. Cut lengths of licorice twists and make pattern around sides of cake. For top and bottom borders, braid three licorice strings together and place on cake. Place lollipops on top for drumsticks.
12 to 16 servings.

Choco-Coconut Cake Roll

- 4 egg whites, at room
temperature
- ½ cup sugar
- 4 egg yolks, at room
temperature
- ⅓ cup sugar
- 1 teaspoon vanilla
- ½ cup unsifted all-purpose flour
- ⅓ cup HERSHEY'S Cocoa
- ½ teaspoon baking powder
- ¼ teaspoon baking soda
- ⅛ teaspoon salt
- ⅓ cup water
Cherry-Coconut Filling
Confectioners' sugar

Line 15½×10½×1-inch jelly roll pan with aluminum foil; generously grease foil. Set aside. Beat egg whites in large mixer bowl until foamy; grad-

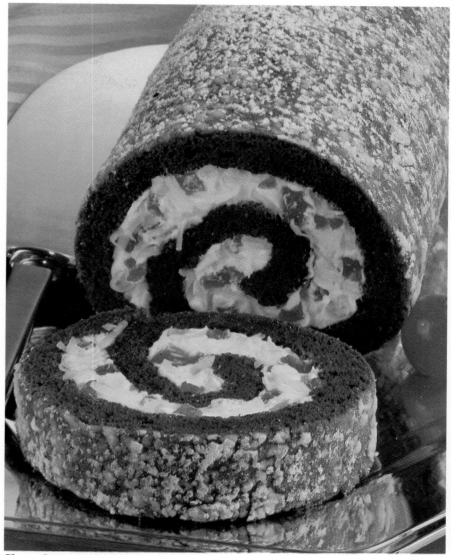

Choco-Coconut Cake Roll

ually add ½ cup sugar and beat until stiff peaks form. Set aside.

Beat egg yolks in small mixer bowl 3 minutes on high speed. Gradually add ⅓ cup sugar and the vanilla; continue beating 2 additional minutes. Combine flour, cocoa, baking powder, baking soda and salt; add alternately with water to egg yolk mixture, beating on low speed just until batter is smooth. Gradually fold chocolate mixture into beaten egg whites until mixture is well blended.

Spread batter evenly in prepared pan. Bake at 375° for 12 to 15 minutes or until cake springs back when touched lightly. Invert onto towel sprinkled with confectioners' sugar; carefully peel off foil. Immediately roll cake and towel together starting from narrow end; place on wire rack to cool completely.

Prepare Cherry-Coconut Filling. Carefully unroll cake; remove towel. Spread cake with filling; reroll and chill. Sprinkle with confectioners' sugar just before serving.
8 to 10 servings.

Cherry-Coconut Filling

- 1 cup heavy or whipping cream
- 3 tablespoons confectioners'
sugar
Few drops red food color
(optional)
- ⅓ cup chopped maraschino
cherries, well drained
- ½ cup flaked coconut

Beat cream until slightly thickened. Add confectioners' sugar and food color; beat until stiff. Fold in cherries and coconut.

Golden Crunch Cake

Golden Crunch Cake

    2 cups fine vanilla wafer crumbs
    1 cup finely chopped pecans
    1/2 cup sugar
    1/4 cup (1/2 stick) butter or
        margarine
    1 package DUNCAN HINES®
        Butter Recipe Golden Cake
        Mix
    3 large eggs
    1/2 cup (1 stick) butter or
        margarine, softened
    2/3 cup water

1. Preheat oven to 375°F. Grease two 9×5×3-inch pans.
2. Combine wafer crumbs, pecans and sugar in bowl. Add 1/4 cup butter and cut in with pastry blender until crumbs are fine. Divide evenly in pans; press on bottom and sides.
3. Combine dry cake mix, eggs, 1/2 cup butter and water in large mixer bowl. Mix cake as directed on package. Divide batter evenly in pans.
4. Bake at 375°F for 50 to 60 minutes or until toothpick inserted in center comes out clean. Cool in pans on racks 5 minutes. Carefully loosen cake from pans and turn upside down on racks; cool completely.
20 servings.

Cranberry Pudding Cake with Sauce

    1 package (2-layer size) yellow
        cake mix*
    1 package (4-serving size)
        JELL-O® Lemon Flavor
        Instant Pudding and Pie
        Filling
    4 eggs
    1 cup (1/2 pint) sour cream*
    1/4 cup vegetable oil
    1/2 cup chopped nuts
    1 can (16 ounces) whole berry
        cranberry sauce or jellied
        cranberry sauce cut in small
        cubes
    1 package (4-serving size)
        JELL-O® Lemon Flavor
        Pudding and Pie Filling
    1/2 cup sugar
    1/4 teaspoon salt
    1 tablespoon butter or
        margarine

Combine cake mix, instant pudding mix, eggs, sour cream, oil and nuts in large bowl. With electric mixer at low speed, blend just to moisten, scraping sides of bowl often. Then beat at medium speed for 4 minutes. Fold in half of the cranberry sauce. Pour batter into 2 greased and floured 9×5-inch loaf pans. Bake in preheated 350° oven for 50 to 55 minutes or until cake tester inserted in center of cake comes out clean and cake begins to pull away from sides of pan. Do not underbake. Cool in pans on wire rack 15 minutes. Remove from pans and finish cooling on wire rack.

Add water to remaining cranberry sauce to make 2 1/2 cups. Combine pudding mix, sugar, salt and measured liquid in medium saucepan. Cook and stir over medium heat until mixture comes to a full boil and is thickened. Remove from heat. Stir in butter. Serve warm over cake.
Makes two 9×5-inch loaves.
 Substitution: Use pudding-included cake mix, decreasing sour cream to 3/4 cup.

Banana Mocha Cake

    2 extra-ripe, medium DOLE™
        Bananas
    1 teaspoon instant coffee
        powder
    1 1/4 cups flour
    2/3 cup sugar
    1/4 cup cornstarch
    3 tablespoons cocoa
    1 teaspoon baking soda
    1/2 teaspoon salt
    1/3 cup vegetable oil
    1 egg, lightly beaten
    1 tablespoon vinegar
    1 teaspoon vanilla extract
        Silky Mocha Frosting (recipe
        follows)

Preheat oven to 350°F. Puree bananas in blender (1 cup). Stir coffee powder into pureed bananas. In 9-inch square baking pan, combine flour, sugar, cornstarch, cocoa, baking soda and salt. Blend well. Make a well in center of dry ingredients. Add banana mixture, oil, egg, vinegar and vanilla.

Stir in dry mixture with fork until well blended. Bake in preheated oven 30 minutes. Cool completely on wire rack. Spread cake with Silky Mocha Frosting.

Makes 12 servings.

SILKY MOCHA FROSTING: In large mixer bowl, combine 3 tablespoons butter or margarine, 1½ cups sifted powdered sugar, 2 tablespoons cocoa and 1 teaspoon instant coffee powder. Add 2 tablespoons milk and ½ teaspoon vanilla extract. Beat until smooth.

Pineapple Upside-Down Cake

        1 can (20 ounces) DOLE®
            Pineapple Slices
    ²/₃ cup butter or margarine
    ²/₃ cup brown sugar, packed
      10 maraschino cherries
    ³/₄ cup granulated sugar
        2 eggs, separated
        1 teaspoon grated lemon peel
        1 teaspoon lemon juice
        1 teaspoon vanilla extract
    1½ cups flour
    1³/₄ teaspoons baking powder
    ¼ teaspoon salt
    ½ cup dairy sour cream

Preheat oven to 350°F. Drain pineapple; reserve 2 tablespoons liquid. In 9- or 10-inch cast iron skillet, melt ⅓ cup butter. Remove from heat. Add brown sugar and stir until blended. Arrange pineapple slices in skillet. Place 1 cherry in center of each slice.

In large bowl, beat remaining ⅓ cup butter with ½ cup granulated sugar until fluffy. Beat in egg yolks, lemon peel and juice, and vanilla. In medium bowl, combine flour, baking powder and salt. Blend dry ingredients into creamed mixture alternately with sour cream and reserved pineapple liquid. In large bowl, beat egg whites until soft peaks form. Gradually beat in remaining ¼ cup granulated sugar until stiff peaks form. Fold into batter. Spread evenly over pineapple in skillet.

Bake in preheated oven about 35 minutes or until cake springs back when touched. Let stand in skillet on wire rack 10 minutes. Invert onto serving plate. Serve warm or cold.

Makes 8 to 10 servings.

Fudgey Pecan Cake

    ³/₄ cup butter or margarine,
        melted
    1½ cups sugar
    1½ teaspoons vanilla
        3 egg yolks
    ½ cup plus 1 tablespoon
        HERSHEY'S Cocoa
    ½ cup unsifted all-purpose flour
        3 tablespoons vegetable oil
        3 tablespoons water
    ³/₄ cup finely chopped pecans
        3 egg whites, at room
            temperature
    ⅛ teaspoon cream of tartar
    ⅛ teaspoon salt
        Royal Glaze (see Index)
        Pecan halves (optional)

Line bottom of 9-inch springform pan with aluminum foil; butter foil and side of pan. Set aside. Combine ³/₄ cup melted butter, the sugar and vanilla in large mixer bowl; beat well. Add egg yolks, one at a time, beating well after each addition. Blend in cocoa, flour, oil and water; beat well. Stir in chopped pecans. Beat egg whites, cream of tartar and salt in small mixer bowl until stiff peaks form. Carefully fold into chocolate mixture. Pour into prepared pan. Bake at 350° for 45 minutes or until top begins to crack slightly. (Cake will not test done in center.) Cool 1 hour. Cover; chill until firm. Remove side of pan.

Prepare Royal Glaze. Pour over cake, allowing glaze to run down side. With

narrow metal spatula, spread glaze evenly on top and side. Allow to harden. Garnish with pecan halves. *10 to 12 servings.*

Mocha Fudge Pudding Cake

    ³/₄ cup sugar
        1 cup unsifted all-purpose flour
        2 teaspoons baking powder
    ¼ teaspoon salt
    ½ cup butter or margarine
        1 square (1 ounce) HERSHEY'S
            Unsweetened Baking
            Chocolate
    ½ cup milk
        1 teaspoon vanilla
    ½ cup sugar
    ½ cup packed light brown sugar
    ¼ cup HERSHEY'S Cocoa
        1 cup hot strong coffee
            Ice cream

Combine ³/₄ cup sugar, the flour, baking powder and salt in medium bowl. Melt butter with baking chocolate in small saucepan over low heat; add to dry ingredients with milk and vanilla. Beat until smooth. Pour into 8- or 9-inch square pan.

Combine ½ cup sugar, the brown sugar and cocoa in small bowl; sprinkle evenly over batter. Pour coffee over top; *do not stir.* Bake at 350° for 40 minutes or until center is almost set. Serve warm with ice cream.

8 to 10 servings.

Pineapple Upside-Down Cake

Easy Pina Colada Cake

1 (18¼- to 18½-ounce) package
    yellow cake mix*
1 (4-serving size) package
    instant vanilla flavor pudding
    and pie filling mix
1 (15-ounce) can COCO LOPEZ®
    Cream of Coconut
½ cup plus 2 tablespoons rum
⅓ cup vegetable oil
4 eggs
1 (8-ounce) can crushed
    pineapple, *well drained*
    Whipped cream, pineapple
    chunks, maraschino
    cherries, toasted coconut
    for garnish

Preheat oven to 350°. In large mixer bowl, combine cake mix, pudding mix, *½ cup* cream of coconut, *½ cup* rum, oil and eggs. Beat on medium speed 2 minutes. Stir in pineapple. Pour into well-greased and floured 10-inch bundt or tube pan. Bake 50 to 55 minutes. Cool 10 minutes. Remove from pan. With a table knife or skewer, poke holes about 1 inch apart in cake almost to bottom. Combine remaining cream of coconut and remaining *2 tablespoons* rum; slowly spoon over cake. Chill thoroughly. Garnish as desired. Store in refrigerator.
Makes one 10-inch cake.

   *If cake mix with "pudding in" is used, omit pudding mix.

Easy Pina Colada Cake

Rum-Nut Pudding Cake

1 cup chopped pecans or
    walnuts
1 package (2-layer size) yellow
    cake mix*
1 package (4-serving size)
    JELL-O® Vanilla or Butter
    Pecan Flavor Instant
    Pudding and Pie Filling
4 eggs
¾ cup water*
¼ cup vegetable oil
⅔ cup dark rum
1 cup sugar
½ cup butter or margarine

Sprinkle nuts evenly in bottom of greased and floured 10-inch tube or fluted tube pan. Combine cake mix, pudding mix, eggs, ½ cup of the water, the oil and ⅓ cup of the rum in large bowl. With electric mixer at low speed, blend just to moisten, scraping sides of bowl often. Then beat at medium speed for 4 minutes. Pour batter into pan. Bake in preheated 325° oven for about 1 hour or until cake tester inserted in center comes out clean and cake begins to pull away from sides of pan. Do not underbake. Cool in pan on wire rack 15 minutes.

   Meanwhile, combine sugar, butter and remaining ¼ cup water in small saucepan. Cook and stir over medium-high heat until mixture comes to a boil; boil 5 minutes, stirring constantly. Stir in remaining rum and bring just to a boil.

   Invert cake onto serving plate and prick with cake tester or wooden pick. Carefully spoon warm syrup over warm cake. Garnish with whipped topping and pecans, if desired.
Makes one 10-inch cake.

   Substitution: Use pudding-included cake mix, reducing water in batter to ¼ cup.

Kentucky Jam Cake

1½ cups flour
1 teaspoon baking soda
½ teaspoon salt
1 teaspoon allspice
¼ teaspoon cinnamon
¾ cup buttermilk
2 tablespoons whiskey, bourbon
    or fruit juice
⅓ cup shortening
½ cup granulated sugar
½ cup firmly packed brown sugar
3 eggs, separated
½ cup seedless raspberry or
    blackberry jam
2 squares BAKER'S®
    Unsweetened Chocolate,
    melted and cooled
1 cup raisins
½ cup chopped nuts*

Mix flour, soda, salt and spices. Combine buttermilk and whiskey. Cream shortening. Gradually beat in sugars and continue beating until light and fluffy. Add egg yolks and beat thoroughly. Alternately add flour and buttermilk mixtures, beating after each addition until smooth. Blend in jam and chocolate. Fold in raisins and nuts. Beat egg whites until stiff peaks form; fold into batter.

   Pour into well-greased 9-inch tube pan. Bake at 350° for 50 to 55 minutes, or until cake tester inserted in center of cake comes out clean. Cool in pan 15 minutes. Remove sides of pan and finish cooling upright on rack. Loosen from tube and bottom; invert onto rack. Wrap in aluminum foil or plastic wrap. Store in refrigerator at least 2 days to mellow flavors. Serve at room temperature. Sprinkle with confectioners sugar and garnish with raspberries, if desired.
Makes one 9-inch cake.

   *Or use 8 squares Baker's® Semi-Sweet Chocolate, cut into large (⅜-inch) chunks.

Surprise Carrot Cake

1 8-ounce package
   PHILADELPHIA BRAND
   Cream Cheese, softened
¼ cup sugar
1 egg, beaten

*   *   *

2 cups flour
1¾ cups sugar
2 teaspoons baking soda
2 teaspoons cinnamon
1 teaspoon salt
1 cup oil
3 eggs, beaten
3 cups shredded carrot
½ cup chopped nuts

Combine cream cheese, sugar and egg, mixing until well blended. Set aside.

Combine dry ingredients. Add combined oil and eggs, mixing just until moistened. Fold in carrots and nuts. Reserve 2 cups batter; pour remaining batter into greased and floured 9-inch bundt pan. Pour cream cheese mixture over batter; carefully spoon reserved batter over cream cheese mixture, spreading to cover. Bake at 350°, 55 minutes or until wooden pick inserted in center comes out clean. Cool 10 minutes; remove from pan. Cool thoroughly. Sprinkle with powdered sugar, if desired.
12 servings.

Variation: Substitute *Light* PHILADELPHIA BRAND Neufchâtel Cheese for Cream Cheese.

Surprise Carrot Cake

Pudding Poke Cake

1 package (2-layer size) yellow
   cake mix or pudding-
   included cake mix*
   Ingredients for cake mix
2 packages (4-serving size)
   JELL-O® Chocolate Flavor
   Instant Pudding and Pie
   Filling*
1 cup confectioners sugar
4 cups cold milk

Prepare and bake cake as directed on package for 13×9-inch cake. Remove from oven. Poke holes at once down through cake to pan with round handle of wooden spoon. (Or poke holes with plastic drinking straw, using turning motion to make large holes.) Holes should be at 1-inch intervals.

Only after the holes are made, combine pudding mix with sugar in large bowl. Gradually stir in milk. Beat with electric mixer at low speed for not more than 1 minute. Do not overbeat. Quickly, before pudding thickens, pour about half of the thin pudding evenly over warm cake and into holes. (This will make stripes in cake.) Allow remaining pudding to thicken slightly; then spoon over the top, swirling it to "frost" the cake. Chill at least 1 hour. Store cake in refrigerator.
Makes one 13×9-inch cake.

Peanut Butter Poke Cake: Prepare Pudding Poke Cake as directed, using chocolate flavor instant pudding and pie filling. Add ½ cup peanut butter to pudding mix and confectioners sugar with ½ cup of the milk; blend well before adding remaining milk and beating.

*Additional Flavor Combinations:
Use yellow cake mix with butterscotch or pistachio flavor pudding mix.

Use chocolate cake mix with chocolate, vanilla, coconut cream, banana cream· or pistachio flavor pudding mix.

Use lemon cake mix with lemon flavor pudding mix.

Use white cake mix with butterscotch, chocolate, pistachio or vanilla pudding mix.

Old-Fashioned Lemon Pudding Cake

3 eggs, separated
1 cup sugar
¼ cup unsifted flour
¼ teaspoon salt
1 cup BORDEN® or
   MEADOW GOLD® Milk
¼ cup REALEMON® Lemon Juice
   from Concentrate

Preheat oven to 325°. In small mixer bowl, beat egg whites until stiff but not dry; set aside. In medium bowl, combine sugar, flour and salt. In small bowl, beat egg yolks; stir in milk and ReaLemon® brand. Add to flour mixture; mix well. Fold in egg whites; pour into 1-quart baking dish. Place in larger pan; fill with 1 inch hot water. Bake 50 to 55 minutes or until top is well browned. Cool about 30 minutes before serving. Spoon pudding over cake in serving dishes. Refrigerate leftovers.
Makes 6 to 8 servings.

Individual Servings: Pour mixture into 8 (6-ounce) custard cups; place in shallow pan. Fill with 1 inch hot water. Bake 35 to 40 minutes.

Strawberries Romanoff on Angel Slices

New Orleans Crumb Cake

**1 package DUNCAN HINES®
    Deluxe Devil's Food Cake
    Mix
3 large eggs
½ cup CRISCO® Oil or PURITAN®
    Oil
1⅓ cups water
1 cup graham cracker crumbs
3 tablespoons CRISCO®
    Shortening, melted
1 package (6 ounces) semisweet
    chocolate pieces (1 cup)
½ cup chopped nuts
    Sweetened whipped cream, if
    desired**

1. Preheat oven to 350°F. Grease and flour 13×9×2-inch pan.
2. Combine dry cake mix, eggs, oil and water in large mixer bowl. Mix cake as directed on package. Turn batter into pan and spread evenly.
3. Combine graham cracker crumbs and melted shortening; mix well. Stir in chocolate pieces and nuts. Sprinkle evenly over batter.
4. Bake at 350°F for 40 to 50 minutes or until toothpick inserted in center comes out clean. Cool in pan on rack. Serve with whipped cream.
16 servings.

Birthday Cakelets

**2 packages DUNCAN HINES®
    Deluxe Devil's Food Cake
    Mix
6 large eggs
1 cup CRISCO® Oil or PURITAN®
    Oil
2⅔ cups water
2 cups light corn syrup
4 large egg whites
⅛ teaspoon salt
    Red food coloring
½ teaspoon peppermint extract**

1. Preheat oven to 350°F. Grease and flour two 13×9×2-inch pans.
2. Combine dry cake mix, whole eggs, oil and water in large mixer bowl. Mix, bake and cool cakes as directed on package. Freeze cooled cakes at least 2 hours.
3. For frosting, heat syrup to boiling. Beat egg whites in large mixer bowl at medium speed until frothy. Add salt and continue beating until soft peaks form. Turn mixer to high speed and gradually add hot corn syrup,

Strawberries Romanoff on Angel Slices

**1 package DUNCAN HINES®
    Deluxe Angel Food Cake Mix
1⅓ cups water
1½ pints fresh strawberries,
    hulled and halved
    lengthwise
⅓ cup orange juice
3 tablespoons orange-flavored
    liqueur
2 tablespoons sugar
1 cup whipping cream
½ teaspoon vanilla extract**

1. Preheat oven to 375°F.
2. Prepare cake with water as directed on package. Pour batter into ungreased 10-inch tube pan. Cut through batter with knife or spatula to remove large air bubbles.
3. Bake at 375°F for 30 to 40 minutes or until top crust is golden brown, firm and dry. Do not underbake. To cool, hang pan upside down on funnel or bottle at least 1½ hours.
4. Place strawberries in bowl. Combine orange juice, 2 tablespoons of the liqueur and sugar; pour over strawberries. Cover with plastic wrap. Refrigerate, occasionally spooning liquid over strawberries.
5. Beat whipping cream until soft peaks form. Beat in remaining 1 tablespoon liqueur and vanilla extract. Beat until thick. Refrigerate until ready to use.
6. To serve, cut cake into slices. Spoon some strawberrries and liquid over cake slices; top with whipped cream.
12 to 16 servings.

beating until soft peaks form. Fold in food coloring to tint delicate pink. Fold in peppermint extract.

4. Draw heart on 3-inch square of cardboard; cut out. Set heart pattern on lower left corner of one cake. Cut around pattern through cake. Cut out 11 more hearts before removing cake pieces. Repeat with remaining cake.

5. Frost sides and tops of each cake heart. Insert pink birthday candle in center of each heart.

24 servings.

Continental Flair Frosting

1 cup sugar
1 cup heavy cream or evaporated milk
4 squares BAKER'S® Unsweetened Chocolate
½ cup butter or margarine, at room temperature
1 teaspoon rum extract or vanilla

Combine sugar and cream in saucepan. Bring to a boil over medium heat, stirring constantly. Reduce heat and simmer gently for 6 minutes. Remove from heat. Add chocolate and stir until chocolate is melted. Blend in butter and rum extract. Chill until mixture begins to thicken; then beat until thick, creamy and of spreading consistency.

Makes about 2½ cups, or enough to cover tops and sides of two 8- or 9-inch cake layers, the top and sides of one 9-inch square or 13×9-inch cake, or the tops of 24 cupcakes.

Note: Recipe may be halved.

Royal Glaze

8 squares (8 ounces) HERSHEY'S Semi-Sweet Baking Chocolate, broken into pieces*
½ cup heavy or whipping cream

Combine chocolate pieces and cream in small saucepan. Cook over very low heat, stirring constantly, until chocolate is melted and mixture is smooth; *do not boil.* Remove from heat; cool, stirring occasionally, until mixture begins to thicken, about 10 to 15 minutes.

About 1 cup.

*You may substitute 1⅓ cups HERSHEY'S Semi-Sweet Chocolate Chips for the baking chocolate.

Lemon Icing

2 tablespoons margarine or butter
3 to 4 teaspoons REALEMON® Lemon Juice from Concentrate
1 cup confectioners' sugar

In small saucepan, melt margarine with ReaLemon® brand; remove from heat. Stir in sugar; mix well. Drizzle warm icing over 10-inch bundt or tube cake, coffee cake or sweet rolls.

Makes about ½ cup.

Classic Fudge Frosting

4 squares BAKER'S® Unsweetened Chocolate
2 tablespoons butter or margarine
1 pound (4 cups) confectioners sugar
Dash of salt
½ cup milk
1 teaspoon vanilla

Melt chocolate with butter over very low heat, stirring constantly until smooth. Remove from heat. Combine sugar, salt, milk and vanilla. Add chocolate, blending well. If necessary, let stand until of spreading consistency, stirring occasionally. Spread quickly, adding a small amount of additional milk if frosting thickens.

Makes about 2½ cups, or enough to cover tops and sides of two 8- or 9-inch layers, the top and sides of one 9-inch square or 13×9-inch cake, or the tops of 24 cupcakes.

Chocolate Cream Cheese Frosting

3 packages (3 ounces each) cream cheese, softened
⅓ cup butter or margarine, softened
5 cups confectioners' sugar
1 cup HERSHEY'S Cocoa
5 to 7 tablespoons light cream

Blend cream cheese and butter in large mixer bowl. Combine confectioners' sugar and cocoa; add alternately with cream to cream cheese mixture. Beat to spreading consistency.

About 3 cups frosting.

Birthday Cakelets

Chocolate-Coconut Frosting

⅓ cup sugar
1 tablespoon cornstarch
¾ cup evaporated milk
1 HERSHEY'S Milk Chocolate Bar (4 ounces), broken into pieces
1 tablespoon butter or margarine
1 cup flaked coconut
½ cup chopped nuts

Combine sugar and cornstarch in small saucepan; blend in evaporated milk. Cook over medium heat, stirring constantly, until mixture boils; remove from heat. Add chocolate bar pieces and butter; stir until chocolate is melted and mixture is smooth. Stir in coconut and nuts. Immediately spread on cake.
About 2 cups frosting.

Bittersweet Glaze

2 squares BAKER'S® Unsweetened Chocolate
2 tablespoons butter or margarine
Dash of salt
1¾ cups confectioners sugar
3 tablespoons (about) hot water

1. Melt chocolate with butter in saucepan over very low heat, stirring constantly until smooth. Remove from heat and add salt. Alternately add sugar with water until of spreading consistency.
Makes 1 cup, or enough for a 9- or 10-inch tube cake, 9-inch square cake, 10-inch cake roll or about 3½ dozen cookies.

Chocolate Glaze

3 squares BAKER'S® Semi-Sweet Chocolate*
3 tablespoons water
1 tablespoon butter or margarine
1 cup sifted confectioners sugar
Dash of salt
½ teaspoon vanilla

Place chocolate, water and butter in saucepan. Stir constantly over very low heat until mixture is smooth. Re-move from heat. Combine sugar and salt in bowl. Gradually blend in chocolate mixture and vanilla. For thinner glaze, add a small amount of hot water. For thicker glaze, cool until of desired consistency.
Makes about ¾ cup, or enough for a 9- or 10-inch tube cake, 8- or 9-inch layer cake, 13×9-inch cake or a 10-inch cake roll.

*Or, use 1 package (4 ounces) BAKER'S® GERMAN'S® Sweet Chocolate.

Chocolate Butter Frosting

6 tablespoons butter or margarine
Dash of salt
1 pound (4 cups) confectioners sugar
2 squares BAKER'S® Unsweetened Chocolate, melted and cooled
4 tablespoons (about) milk
1½ teaspoons vanilla

Cream butter with salt. Gradually beat in part of the sugar. Blend in chocolate. Alternately add remaining sugar with milk until of spreading consistency, beating after each addition until smooth. Blend in vanilla.
Makes 3 cups, or enough to cover tops and sides of two 8- or 9-inch layers or the top and sides of one 13×9-inch cake.

Quick Chocolate Frosting

4 squares (4 ounces) HERSHEY'S Unsweetened Baking Chocolate
¼ cup butter or margarine
3 cups confectioners' sugar
1 teaspoon vanilla
⅛ teaspoon salt
⅓ cup milk

Melt baking chocolate and butter in small saucepan over very low heat, stirring constantly, until chocolate is melted and mixture is smooth. Pour into small mixer bowl; add confectioners' sugar, vanilla and salt. Blend in milk; beat to spreading consistency. (If frosting is too thick, add additional milk, 1 teaspoonful at a time, until frosting is desired consistency.)
About 2 cups frosting.

Chocolate Satin Glaze

2 tablespoons sugar
2 tablespoons water
½ cup HERSHEY'S MINI CHIPS Semi-Sweet Chocolate

Combine sugar and water in small saucepan; cook over medium heat, stirring constantly, until mixture boils and sugar is dissolved. Remove from heat; immediately add MINI CHIPS Chocolate, stirring until melted. Continue stirring until glaze is desired consistency.
About ½ cup glaze.

Chocolate Zucchini Cupcakes

1½ cups unsifted all-purpose flour
¾ cup sugar
¼ cup unsweetened cocoa
1½ teaspoons baking soda
½ teaspoon salt
1 cup shredded, peeled zucchini
⅓ cup CRISCO® Oil
⅓ cup buttermilk
1 egg
1 teaspoon vanilla
Frosting:
1½ cups confectioners sugar
2 tablespoons butter or margarine, softened
2 to 3 tablespoons milk, divided
¼ teaspoon vanilla

Preheat oven to 350°F. Place paper liners in 12 muffin cups. Set aside.

Mix flour, sugar, cocoa, baking soda and salt in medium mixing bowl. Add remaining cake ingredients. Beat with electric mixer at low speed until ingredients are moistened, scraping bowl constantly. Beat at high speed 1 minute, scraping bowl occasionally. Pour into lined muffin cups, filling each about ⅔ full. Bake at 350°F, 20 to 25 minutes, or until wooden pick inserted in center comes out clean. Remove from pan. Cool completely on wire rack.

For frosting, combine confectioners sugar, butter, 1 tablespoon milk and vanilla in small mixing bowl at low speed until smooth, scraping bowl frequently. Beat in additional milk until thick enough to spread. Spread on cooled cupcakes.
1 dozen cupcakes.

Fudge 'n' Banana Cupcakes

Fudge 'n' Banana Cupcakes

- **1 package DUNCAN HINES®**
  Deluxe Devil's Food Cake
  Mix
- **3 large eggs**
- **½ cup CRISCO® Oil or PURITAN®**
  Oil
- **1⅓ cups water**
- **½ cup (1 stick) butter or**
  margarine
- **2 ounces (2 squares)**
  unsweetened chocolate
- **1 pound confectioners' sugar**
- **½ cup half-and-half**
- **1 teaspoon vanilla extract**
- **4 medium bananas**
- **2 tablespoons lemon juice**

1. Preheat oven to 350°F. Line 24 muffin cups with paper baking cups.
2. Combine dry cake mix, eggs, oil and water in large mixer bowl. Mix, bake and cool cupcakes as directed on package.
3. For frosting*, melt butter and chocolate in heavy saucepan over low heat. Remove from heat. Add confectioners' sugar alternately with half-and-half, mixing until smooth after each addition. Beat in vanilla extract. Add more confectioners' sugar to thicken or milk to thin as needed.

4. Using small paring knife, remove cone-shaped piece from top center of each cupcake. Dot top of each cone with frosting. Frost top of each cupcake spreading frosting down into cone-shaped hole. Slice bananas and dip in lemon juice. Stand three banana slices in each hole. Set cone-shaped pieces, pointed-side-up, on banana slices.
24 cupcakes.
   *Or use 1 can Duncan Hines® Dark Dutch Fudge or Chocolate Frosting.

Creme-Filled Cupcakes

- **¾ cup shortening**
- **1¼ cups sugar**
- **2 eggs**
- **1 teaspoon vanilla**
- **1¾ cups unsifted all-purpose flour**
- **½ cup HERSHEY'S Cocoa**
- **1 teaspoon baking soda**
- **½ teaspoon salt**
- **1 cup milk**
  Vanilla Creme

Cream shortening and sugar in large mixer bowl. Add eggs and vanilla; blend well. Combine flour, cocoa, baking soda and salt; add alternately with milk to creamed mixture. Fill paper-lined muffin cups (2½ inches in diameter) two-thirds full with batter.

Bake at 375° for 20 to 25 minutes or until cake tester comes out clean. Cool completely.
   Prepare Vanilla Creme; spoon into pastry bag with open star tip. Insert tip into center of top of cupcake; gently squeeze until cupcake begins to peak. Cover top with swirl of filling. (Or cut a 1½-inch cone from top of cupcake. Fill; replace cone. Swirl filling over top.)
About 2 dozen cupcakes.

Vanilla Creme

- **¼ cup unsifted all-purpose flour**
- **½ cup milk**
- **¼ cup butter or margarine,**
  softened
- **¼ cup shortening**
- **2 teaspoons vanilla**
- **¼ teaspoon salt**
- **4 cups confectioners' sugar**

Combine flour and milk in small saucepan; cook over low heat, stirring constantly with wire whisk, until mixture thickens and just begins to boil. Remove from heat; chill. Cream butter and shortening in large mixer bowl; blend in vanilla, salt and the chilled flour mixture. Gradually add confectioners' sugar; beat to spreading consistency.

Chocolate Butterscotch Chip Cupcakes

½ **cup cake flour**
1 **package (6 ounces) butterscotch-flavored pieces (1 cup), divided**
1 **package (6 ounces) semisweet chocolate pieces (1 cup), divided**
1 **package DUNCAN HINES® Deluxe White Cake Mix**
3 **egg whites or 3 whole eggs**
⅓ **cup CRISCO® Oil or PURITAN® Oil**
1¼ **cups water**

1. Preheat oven to 350°F. Line 24 muffin cups with paper baking cups.
2. Combine cake flour, ½ cup butterscotch pieces and ½ cup chocolate pieces in small bowl.
3. Combine dry cake mix, egg whites or whole eggs, oil and water in large mixer bowl. Mix cake as directed on package. Stir in chocolate-butterscotch mixture. Spoon batter into muffin cups, filling about two-thirds full.
4. Bake at 350°F for 18 to 23 minutes or until toothpick inserted in centers comes out clean. Cool in pans on racks 10 minutes. Remove from pans; cool completely on racks.
5. For chocolate-butterscotch frosting, melt remaining ½ cup butterscotch and ½ cup chocolate pieces in small saucepan over low heat; stir until smooth. Spread over cooled cupcakes.
24 cupcakes.

Chocolatetown Cupcakes

½ **cup butter or margarine, softened**
1 **cup sugar**
1 **teaspoon vanilla**
4 **eggs**
1¼ **cups unsifted all-purpose flour**
¾ **teaspoon baking soda**
1½ **cups (16-ounce can) HERSHEY'S Syrup**

Cream butter, sugar and vanilla in large mixer bowl until light and fluffy. Add eggs; beat well. Combine flour and baking soda; add alternately with syrup to creamed mixture. Fill paper-lined muffin cups (2½ inches in diameter) half full with bat-

Black Bottom Cupcakes

ter. Bake at 375° for 15 to 20 minutes or until cake tester comes out clean. Cool; frost as desired.
About 2½ dozen cupcakes.

Black Bottom Cupcakes

2 **packages (3 ounces each) cream cheese, softened**
1⅓ **cups sugar**
1 **egg**
1 **package (6 ounces) chocolate chips**
1½ **cups flour**
¼ **cup unsweetened cocoa**
1 **teaspoon baking soda**
½ **teaspoon salt**
2 **extra-ripe, medium DOLE™ Bananas**
⅓ **cup vegetable oil**
1 **teaspoon vanilla extract**
1 **firm, large DOLE™ Banana**

Preheat oven to 350°F. Line 18 muffin cups with paper liners. In small bowl, beat cream cheese and ⅓ cup sugar until light and fluffy. Add egg; beat until well blended. Stir in chocolate chips. Set aside.

In large bowl, combine remaining 1 cup sugar, flour, cocoa, baking soda and salt; mix well. Puree extra-ripe bananas in blender (1 cup). Combine pureed bananas with oil and vanilla. Stir banana mixture into dry ingredients until smooth.

Divide batter evenly among prepared muffin cups. Thinly slice firm banana; place 2 slices in center of batter in each muffin cup. Divide cream cheese mixture evenly over bananas in muffin cups. Bake in preheated oven 30 minutes or until wooden pick inserted in center comes out clean. Cool in pan on wire rack.
Makes 18 cupcakes.

Spicy Walnut Fruitcake

1 **cup DIAMOND® Walnuts, coarsely chopped**
1 **cup SUN-MAID® Raisins**
1 **cup pitted dates, coarsely chopped**
⅔ **cup SUN-MAID® Zante Currants**
½ **cup sliced dried apricots**
½ **cup halved candied cherries**
¼ **cup chopped candied orange peel**
¼ **cup chopped candied lemon peel**
⅓ **cup butter or margarine, softened**
½ **cup sugar**
½ **teaspoon salt**
1 **teaspoon ground cinnamon**
½ **teaspoon *each* ground allspice, nutmeg and mace**
¼ **teaspoon ground ginger**
2 **eggs, beaten**
⅛ **teaspoon baking soda**
¼ **cup molasses**
1 **cup all-purpose flour**
Powdered Sugar Glaze (recipe follows)
DIAMOND® Walnut halves and candied fruit, for garnish

In large bowl, combine chopped walnuts, fruits and peels; mix well. In another large bowl, cream butter, sugar, salt and spices until fluffy. Beat in eggs. Add soda, molasses and flour; mix to moderately stiff batter. Stir in walnut-fruit mixture. Pack batter into well-greased and floured 6-cup mold or pan. Bake in preheated 275°F oven about 2½ hours or until center springs back when lightly touched. Cool completely, then loosen edges and remove from pan. Wrap in foil and store at least 48 hours in a cool, dry place. Before serving, glaze with Powdered Sugar Glaze and decorate with walnut halves and candied fruits.
Makes one cake.
POWDERED SUGAR GLAZE: In small bowl, combine 1 cup sifted powdered sugar, ½ teaspoon vanilla and enough milk (1 to 2 tablespoons) to make of drizzling consistency.

Ever-So-Easy Fruitcake

2½ cups unsifted flour
1 teaspoon baking soda
2 eggs, slightly beaten
1 jar NONE SUCH® Ready-to-Use Mincemeat (Regular *or* Brandy & Rum)
1 (14-ounce) can EAGLE® Brand Sweetened Condensed Milk (NOT evaporated milk)
2 cups (1 pound) mixed candied fruit
1 cup coarsely chopped nuts

Preheat oven to 300°. Grease and flour 10-inch bundt pan. Combine flour and baking soda; set aside. In large bowl, combine remaining ingredients; blend in dry ingredients. Pour batter into prepared pan. Bake 1 hour and 45 to 50 minutes or until wooden pick comes out clean. Cool 15 minutes. Turn out of pan. Garnish as desired.
Makes one 10-inch cake.

Tip: To substitute condensed mincemeat for ready-to-use mincemeat, crumble 2 (9-ounce) packages None Such® Condensed Mincemeat into small saucepan; add 1½ cups water. Boil briskly 1 minute. Cool. Proceed as above.

Chocolate Fruitcake: Prepare fruitcake batter as above, adding 3 (1-ounce) squares unsweetened chocolate, melted. For glaze, melt 3 (1-ounce) squares semi-sweet chocolate with 2 tablespoons margarine or butter. Spoon over fruitcake.

Fruitcake-in-a-Can: Grease three 1-pound coffee cans; fill each can with about 2⅔ cups batter. Bake 1 hour and 20 to 25 minutes. *Or,* grease eight 10¾-ounce soup cans; fill each with 1 cup batter. Bake 50 to 55 minutes.

Fruitcake Bars: Grease 15×10-inch jellyroll pan; spread batter evenly in pan. Bake 40 to 45 minutes. Cool. Glaze if desired. Makes about 4 dozen bars.

Fruitcake Loaves: Grease two 9×5-inch loaf pans. Pour half the batter into each pan. Bake 1 hour and 20 to 25 minutes.

Fruitcake Cookies: Drop by rounded tablespoonfuls, 2 inches apart, onto greased baking sheets. Bake 15 to 18 minutes. Makes about 5½ dozen cookies.

Fruitcake Mini Loaves: Grease twelve 4½×2½-inch loaf pans. Fill each pan ⅔ full. Bake 35 to 40 minutes.

Sherried Fruit-Spice Cake

½ cup cream sherry
½ cup SUN-MAID® Raisins
½ cup finely chopped dried figs
½ cup chopped pitted prunes
½ cup finely chopped dried apricots
1½ cups milk
5 cups all-purpose flour
⅔ cup granulated sugar
1 package active dry yeast
½ teaspoon salt
¾ cup butter or margarine, softened
½ cup packed brown sugar
2 eggs
1 teaspoon ground cinnamon
½ teaspoon ground nutmeg
⅛ teaspoon ground cloves
1 cup chopped DIAMOND® Walnuts
Sherry Icing (recipe follows)
DIAMOND® Walnut halves, for garnish
Dried figs, prunes or apricots, for garnish

In small saucepan over low heat, warm sherry; add the ½ cup each raisins, figs, prunes and apricots. Remove from heat. Let stand, covered, several hours or overnight. In small saucepan over low heat, scald milk; cool to lukewarm (110° to 115°F). In large bowl, combine 1½ cups of the flour, ⅓ cup of the granulated sugar, the yeast and salt. Add milk, stirring until combined. Cover; let rise in warm place (85°F) until doubled, 45 to 60 minutes.

Stir yeast mixture down. In large bowl, beat butter, brown sugar and remaining ⅓ cup granulated sugar until fluffy. Add eggs, one at a time, beating 1 minute after each addition. Stir in fruit-sherry and yeast mixtures. In medium bowl, combine remaining 3½ cups flour, the cinnamon, nutmeg and cloves. Stir into dough along with the 1 cup walnuts. Place dough into greased and lightly floured 10-inch fluted tube pan. Cover; let rise in warm place until nearly doubled, about 1½ hours. Bake in preheated 350°F oven about 1 hour or until cake pulls away from edge of pan. Cover with foil the last 15 minutes, if necessary, to prevent over-browning. Loosen edges and invert onto wire rack; cool completely. Glaze cake with Sherry Icing. Top with walnut halves. Garnish with figs, prunes and apricots, if desired.
Makes one 10-inch cake.
SHERRY ICING: In medium bowl, combine 1 cup sifted powdered sugar, ½ teaspoon vanilla and enough cream sherry (1 to 2 tablespoons) to make of drizzling consistency.

Sherried Fruit-Spice Cake

Viennese Cherry Cheese Torte

Spread remaining cream cheese filling over top layer and top with remaining cherry filling. Refrigerate until ready to serve.
12 to 16 servings.

Viennese Chocolate Torte

- **1 cup flour**
- **½ teaspoon salt**
- **½ cup ground walnuts**
- **¾ cup unsalted butter**
- **1¼ cups confectioners sugar**
- **8 egg yolks**
- **1 package (8 squares) BAKER'S® Semi-Sweet Chocolate, melted and cooled**
- **1 teaspoon vanilla**
- **8 egg whites**
- **1 cup (10-ounce jar) apricot jam Continental Flair Frosting, half recipe (see Index)**
- **Sweetened whipped cream or thawed COOL WHIP® Whipped Topping**

Mix flour, salt and walnuts. Cream butter. Gradually beat in sugar and continue beating until light and fluffy. Add egg yolks, a few at a time, beating thoroughly after each addition. Gradually stir in chocolate. Add flour mixture and vanilla, stirring just to blend. Beat egg whites until soft peaks form. Blend about ¼ cup of the beaten egg whites into the chocolate mixture; gently fold in remaining egg whites.

Pour into 2 greased and floured 9-inch layer pans. Bake at 350° for 40 to 45 minutes, or until cake tester inserted in centers comes out clean. Cool in pans 10 minutes. Remove from pans and finish cooling on racks.

Split layers horizontally, making 4 layers. Stir jam in saucepan over low heat until melted. Spread about ⅓ cup over tops of three layers. Stack on a rack placed on a tray; top with fourth layer. Prepare frosting as directed, cooling only slightly. Pour quickly over cake, covering top and sides. Place cake on serving plate. If desired, spoon frosting drippings into plastic-lined decorating bag fitted with writing tip; pipe a name or greeting on cake. Store in refrigerator at least one day to mellow flavors. Serve at room temperature with sweetened whipped cream.
Makes one 9-inch torte.

Festive Cranberry Torte

- **1 8-ounce package PHILADELPHIA BRAND Cream Cheese, softened**
- **¼ cup sugar**
- **½ cup whipping cream, whipped**
- **1 10¾-ounce frozen pound cake, thawed**
- **1 14-ounce jar cranberry orange sauce**

Combine cream cheese and sugar, mixing until well blended. Fold in whipped cream. Split cake horizontally into four layers. Spread bottom layer with ½ cup cranberry orange sauce; top with second layer. Spread second layer with ⅔ cup cream cheese mixture; top with third layer. Spread third layer with ½ cup cranberry orange sauce. Cover with top cake layer. Frost top and sides of torte with remaining cream cheese mixture. Chill several hours or overnight. Top with remaining cranberry orange sauce just before serving. Garnish with whole cranberries and fresh mint, if desired.
10 to 12 servings.

Variation: Substitute *Light* PHILADELPHIA BRAND Neufchâtel Cheese for Cream Cheese.

Viennese Cherry Cheese Torte

- **1 package DUNCAN HINES® Butter Recipe Golden Cake Mix**
- **3 large eggs**
- **½ cup (1 stick) butter or margarine, softened**
- **⅔ cup water**
- **1 package (8 ounces) plus 1 package (3 ounces) cream cheese, softened**
- **⅔ cup sugar**
- **¼ teaspoon ground nutmeg**
- **2 tablespoons milk**
- **1 can (21 ounces) cherry pie filling**

1. Preheat oven to 375°F. Grease and flour two 8×1½- or 9×1½-inch round layer pans.
2. Combine dry cake mix, eggs, butter and water in large mixer bowl. Mix, bake and cool as directed on package. Refrigerate layers to make splitting easier. Split each cake into 2 thin layers.
3. For filling, beat cream cheese, sugar, nutmeg and milk until smooth.
4. Place one layer on cake plate. Spread with ½ cup cream cheese filling; top with ½ cup cherry filling. Repeat layers, ending with cake layer.

Open House Ribbon Torte

- 1 package DUNCAN HINES®
  Deluxe Fudge Marble Cake
  Mix
- 3 large eggs
- ⅓ cup CRISCO® Oil or PURITAN®
  Oil
- 1¼ cups water
- 1 cup whipping cream
- 1 cup milk
- 1 package (4-serving-size)
  chocolate instant pudding
  and pie filling mix

1. Preheat oven to 350°F. Grease and flour two 8×1½- or 9×1½-inch round layer pans.
2. Combine dry cake mix, eggs, oil and water in large mixer bowl. Mix as directed on package but do not add contents of small packet. Turn half of batter (about 2½ cups) into one pan. Blend contents of small packet into remaining batter and turn into remaining pan.
3. Bake and cool layers as directed on package. Chill cooled layers to make splitting easier. Split each layer into two thin layers.
4. Whip cream until stiff. Blend in milk and pudding mix. Let set for 1 minute.
5. Place one chocolate layer on plate. Spread one-fourth pudding mixture over layer. Top with remaining layers, alternating light and dark layers and spreading pudding mixture between layers. Frost top layer with pudding mixture. Refrigerate until ready to serve.
12 to 16 servings.

Chocolate Almond "Philly" Torte

- 1 8-ounce package
  PHILADELPHIA BRAND
  Cream Cheese, softened
- ¼ cup PARKAY Margarine
- 1 cup sugar
- 2 eggs
- ½ teaspoon vanilla
- 1½ cups flour
- 1 teaspoon baking soda
- ½ teaspoon baking powder
- ½ cup milk
- 2 1-ounce squares unsweetened
  chocolate, melted
- Almond and Chocolate
  "Philly" Cream Frostings

Combine cream cheese, margarine and sugar, mixing until well blended. Blend in eggs and vanilla. Add combined dry ingredients alternately with milk, mixing well after each addition. Blend in chocolate. Spread batter into wax paper-lined 15×10×1-inch jelly roll pan. Bake at 350°, 12 to 15 minutes or until wooden pick inserted in center comes out clean. Cool thoroughly. Cut crosswise into four equal sections; remove from pan. Spread three sections with almond frosting; chill until frosting is firm. Stack. Top with remaining layer; frost top and sides with chocolate frosting. *12 servings.*

Almond and Chocolate "Philly" Cream Frostings

- 1 8-ounce package
  PHILADELPHIA BRAND
  Cream Cheese, softened
- 6½ cups sifted powdered sugar
- ½ cup whipping cream
- ½ cup chopped almonds, toasted
- 2 1-ounce squares unsweetened
  chocolate, melted

Beat cream cheese at medium speed on electric mixer. Gradually add 5 cups sugar, mixing well after each addition. Add whipping cream, beating at high speed until creamy. Divide mixture in half. Add remaining sugar and almonds to one half, mixing until well blended. Stir chocolate into remaining half. Chill chocolate frosting until thickened for spreading consistency.

Black Forest Torte

- 1 (18¼- or 18½-ounce) package
  chocolate cake mix
- 1 (21-ounce) can cherry pie
  filling, drained and chilled,
  reserving ½ cup sauce
- 1 (6-ounce) package semi-sweet
  chocolate chips
- 1 (14-ounce) can EAGLE® Brand
  Sweetened Condensed Milk
  (NOT evaporated milk)
- ½ teaspoon almond extract

Preheat oven to 350°. Prepare and bake cake mix as package directs for two 9-inch round layers. Remove from pans; cool thoroughly. In heavy saucepan, over medium heat, melt chips with sweetened condensed milk. Cook and stir until mixture thickens, about 10 minutes. Cool 20 minutes. Meanwhile, combine cherries, reserved sauce and extract. Place 1 cake layer on serving plate, top side up. With sharp knife, remove crust from top of cake layer to within ½ inch of edge; top with half the chocolate mixture then the cherries. Top with second cake layer and remaining chocolate mixture. Garnish as desired. *Makes one 9-inch cake.*

Open House Ribbon Torte

Lemon Cream Almond Torte

- ½ cup sifted cake flour
- ½ teaspoon baking powder
- ⅛ teaspoon salt
- ½ cup butter or margarine, softened
- ¾ cup granulated sugar
- 1 cup BLUE DIAMOND® Blanched Almond Paste
- 3 eggs
- 1 tablespoon brandy
- 1 teaspoon vanilla
- ⅛ teaspoon almond extract
  Lemon Cream (recipe follows)
  Powdered sugar (optional)
  Lemon slices (optional)

In small bowl, combine flour, baking powder and salt. In large bowl, cream butter and granulated sugar. Add almond paste; beat until smooth. Add eggs, 1 at a time, beating well after each addition. Mix in brandy, vanilla and almond extract. Stir in flour mixture. Pour into greased and floured 8×2-inch round pan. Bake in preheated 325° oven 45 minutes or until toothpick inserted into center comes out clean. Let cool in pan on wire rack 15 minutes. Loosen edge; remove from pan. Cool completely on wire rack. Meanwhile, prepare Lemon Cream. Slice cake horizontally in half. Spread Lemon Cream over cut side of bottom layer; top with second layer, cut side down. Refrigerate until serving time. To serve, if desired, place lace doily over top of torte. Sift powdered sugar evenly over top; carefully remove doily. Garnish with lemon slices.
Makes 8 to 10 servings.

Lemon Cream

- 3 egg yolks
- ⅓ cup granulated sugar
- 2 tablespoons all-purpose flour
- 1 cup milk, scalded
- 2 teaspoons grated lemon peel
- 2 tablespoons lemon juice
- ½ teaspoon vanilla

In medium saucepan, beat egg yolks and sugar until thick and pale yellow. Stir in flour. Gradually pour in hot milk, stirring constantly. Stir in lemon peel. Bring mixture to a boil over medium heat, stirring constantly. Stir and boil 1 minute. Remove from heat; add lemon juice and vanilla. Cool completely, stirring occasionally.

Mexican Cocoa Torte

- 1 cup sugar
- ½ cup HERSHEY'S Cocoa
- ¼ teaspoon cinnamon
- ⅓ cup shortening
- ½ cup strong coffee
- 1 package (11 ounces) pie crust mix
- 2 cups heavy or whipping cream
  HERSHEY'S MINI CHIPS Semi-Sweet Chocolate (optional)

Combine sugar, cocoa, cinnamon, shortening and coffee in small saucepan. Cook over very low heat, stirring constantly, until smooth and creamy. Cool to room temperature. Place pie crust mix in medium mixing bowl; stir in ¾ cup of the cocoa mixture, blending thoroughly. Shape into smooth ball; chill 1 hour.

Divide dough into 4 pieces. Line two cookie sheets with aluminum foil; mark two 8-inch circles on each. Place balls of dough on foil; press with fingers into marked circles. Bake at 375° for 10 to 12 minutes or until almost set; cool on cookie sheets.

Add remaining cocoa mixture to cream in small mixer bowl; beat until stiff. Place one pastry round on serving plate; spread with one-fourth of the whipped cream mixture. Repeat layering with remaining three rounds and whipped cream mixture, ending with whipped cream. Chill several hours. Garnish with MINI CHIPS Chocolate.
8 to 10 servings.

Elegant Angel Torte

- 1 package DUNCAN HINES® Deluxe Angel Food Cake Mix
- 1⅓ cups water
- 2 cups whipping cream
- ¼ cup chocolate syrup
- 1 tablespoon sugar
- ⅓ cup orange marmalade
- 6 red maraschino cherries with stems, if desired
- 6 pecan halves, if desired
- ¼ cup chocolate curls, if desired

1. Preheat oven to 375°F.
2. Prepare cake with water as directed on package. Pour batter into ungreased 10-inch tube pan. Cut through batter with knife or spatula to remove large air bubbles.
3. Bake at 375°F for 30 to 40 minutes or until top crust is golden brown, firm and dry. Do not underbake. To cool, hang pan upside down on funnel or bottle at least 1½ hours.
4. Slice cooled cake crosswise into four 1-inch layers.
5. Whip cream until stiff. Beat in chocolate syrup and sugar. Place bottom cake slice on serving plate; spread with ⅓ cup whipped cream. Top with next layer; spread with orange marmalade. Top with next layer; spread with ⅓ cup whipped cream. Add final layer. Frost sides and top with remaining whipped cream. Decorate with cherries, pecans and chocolate curls.
12 to 16 servings.

Elegant Angel Torte

Crème de Cacao Torte

- **2/3 cup butter or margarine, softened**
- **1 2/3 cups sugar**
- **3 eggs**
- **1/2 teaspoon vanilla**
- **2 cups unsifted all-purpose flour**
- **2/3 cup HERSHEY'S Cocoa**
- **1 1/4 teaspoons baking soda**
- **1/4 teaspoon baking powder**
- **1 1/3 cups milk**
- **2 tablespoons creme de cacao**
- **Crème de Cacao Filling**
- **Chocolate Ganache Glaze**

Cream butter, sugar, eggs and vanilla in large mixing bowl until light and fluffy. Combine flour, cocoa, baking soda and baking powder; add alternately with milk to creamed mixture, blending just until combined.

Pour into two greased and floured 9-inch layer pans. Bake at 350° for 30 to 35 minutes or until cake tester comes out clean. Cool 10 minutes; remove from pans. Sprinkle each layer with 1 tablespoon crème de cacao; cool completely.

Meanwhile, prepare Crème de Cacao Filling. Split each cake layer horizontally into 2 layers. Place one layer on serving plate; spread with one-third of the filling. Repeat layering with remaining cake and filling, ending with cake layer. Cover tightly; chill at least 8 hours. Prepare Chocolate Ganache Glaze; spoon on top of chilled cake, allowing glaze to drizzle down side. Chill. Garnish as desired. *10 to 12 servings.*

Crème de Cacao Filling

- **1 cup heavy or whipping cream**
- **2 tablespoons crème de cacao**
- **1 tablespoon HERSHEY'S Cocoa**

Beat cream, crème de cacao and cocoa until stiff. Cover; chill.

Chocolate Ganache Glaze

- **1 HERSHEY'S SPECIAL DARK Sweet Chocolate Bar (8 ounces), broken into pieces**
- **1/4 cup heavy or whipping cream**
- **1 tablespoon butter or margarine**
- **1 1/2 teaspoons crème de cacao**

Combine chocolate bar pieces, cream and butter in medium saucepan. Cook over low heat, stirring constantly, until mixture is melted and smooth. Stir in crème de cacao. Cool to lukewarm (glaze will be slightly thickened).

Crème de Cacao Torte

Chocolate Coconut Pecan Torte

- **1 (18 1/4- or 18 1/2-ounce) package chocolate cake mix**
- **1 (14-ounce) can EAGLE® Brand Sweetened Condensed Milk (NOT evaporated milk)**
- **3 egg yolks, beaten**
- **1/2 cup margarine or butter**
- **1 (3 1/2-ounce) can flaked coconut (1 1/3 cups)**
- **1 cup chopped pecans**
- **1 teaspoon vanilla extract**
- **2 cups frozen non-dairy whipped topping, thawed, *or* 1 cup (1/2 pint) BORDEN® or MEADOW GOLD® Whipping Cream, whipped**
- **Pecan halves, optional**

Preheat oven to 350°. Prepare cake mix as package directs. Pour batter into three well-greased and floured 8- or 9-inch round layer cake pans. Bake 20 minutes or until wooden pick inserted near center comes out clean. Remove from pans; cool thoroughly. Meanwhile, in heavy saucepan, combine sweetened condensed milk, egg yolks and margarine. Over medium heat, cook and stir until thickened or bubbly, about 10 minutes. Stir in coconut, pecans and vanilla. Cool 10 minutes. With sharp knife, remove crust from top of each cake layer to within 1/2 inch of edge. Spread equal portions of coconut pecan mixture between layers and on top to within 1/2 inch of edge. Frost side and 1/2-inch rim on top of cake with whipped topping. Garnish with pecan halves if desired. Store cake in refrigerator. *Makes one 8- or 9-inch cake.*

ACKNOWLEDGMENTS

The publishers would like to thank the companies and organizations
listed below for the use of their recipes in this book.

American Dairy Association
Armour Food Company
Bel Paese Sales Company, Inc.
Best Foods, a Division of CPC International Inc.
Blue Diamond Growers
Borden Kitchens, Borden, Inc.
Campbell Soup Company
Carnation Co.
The Creamette Company
Diamond Walnut Growers, Inc.
The Dole Food Company
Durkee-French Foods, Division of Reckitt &
    Colman Inc.
Filippo Berio Brand, Imported Italian Olive Oil
General Foods USA
Hershey Foods Corporation
The HVR Company
Keebler Company
Kellogg Company
Kikkoman International Inc.
The Kingsford Products Company
Kraft, Inc.

Land O'Lakes, Inc.
Lawry's Foods, Inc.
Maidstone Wine & Spirits, Inc.
McIlhenny Company
Mrs. Paul's Kitchens, Inc.
Nabisco Brands, Inc.
National Live Stock and Meat Board
National Pecan Marketing Council
National Pork Producers Council
Norseland Foods, Inc.
Pepperidge Farm Incorporated
Pet Incorporated
Procter & Gamble
The Quaker Oats Company
Rice Council of America
Roman Meal Company
StarKist Seafood Co.
Sun-Maid Growers of California
Swift-Eckrich, Inc.
Thomas J. Lipton, Inc.
Vlasic Foods, Inc.
Washington Apple Commission

PHOTO CREDITS

The publishers would like to thank the companies and organizations
listed below for the use of their photographs in this book.

American Dairy Association
Armour Food Company
Bel Paese Sales Co., Inc.
Borden Kitchens, Borden, Inc.
Campbell Soup Company
Carnation Co.
The Dole Food Company
Durkee-French Foods, Division of Reckitt &
    Colman Inc.
General Foods USA
Hershey Foods Corporation
Keebler Company
Kikkoman International Inc.

Kraft, Inc.
McIlhenny Company
Nabisco Brands, Inc.
National Live Stock and Meat Board
National Pork Producers Council
Norseland Foods, Inc.
Procter & Gamble
Rice Council of America
Sun-Maid Growers of California and Diamond
    Walnut Growers, Inc.
Swift-Eckrich, Inc.
Thomas J. Lipton, Inc.

INDEX

A

Acapulco Flan, 298
Aegean Lamb Stew, 135
Albóndingas Soup, 59
All-American Meat Loaf, 113
All-in-One Tuna Casserole, 202
Almond Creme, 304
Almond-Crumb Peaches, 308
Almond Crust, 325
Almond Frosting, 279
Almond Ginger Ice Cream Pie, 325
Almondine Butter Sauce, 234
Almondine Fish, 174
Almond Melting Moments, 275
Almond "Philly" Cream Frosting, 357
Almond Shortbread Cookies, 279
Almond Toffee, 297
Ambrosia, 75
Ambrosia Topping, 325
American-Style Cassoulet, 193
Any-Way-You-Like'm Cookies, 273
Appetizer Ham Logs, 21
Appetizers, 6–31 (*see also* **Canapes;
    Dips and spreads; Paté**)
  Appetizer Ham Logs, 21
  Baked Artichoke Squares, 20
  Baked Stuffed Clams, 20
  Baked Stuffed Shrimp, 20
  Beef Kushisashi, 19
  Beer Batter Fried Veggies 'n Things,
    19
  Beer-Batter Shrimp, 28
  Buffalo-Style Chicken Wings, 22
  Cajun-Style Chicken Nuggets, 26
  Cantonese Meatballs, 25
  Cheese & Nut Stuffed Bread Slices,
    18
  Cheese Stuffed Tomatoes, 18
  Cheesy Potato Skins, 19
  Chicken Wings with Honey &
    Orange Sauce, 23
  Chicken with Oriental Dipping
    Sauce, 10
  Chinese-Style Spareribs, 125
  Crispy Fried Mushrooms, 24
  Crispy Wontons, 27
  Curried Chicken Puffs, 26
  Deviled Stuffed Eggs, 24
  Empress Chicken Wings, 26
  Filled New Potatoes, 23
  Flaky Crab Puffs, 26
  Flaky Ham Puffs, 27
  Golden Mini Quiches, 24
  Grilled Cheese, 24
  Grilled Oysters, 25
  Ham-Wrapped Oysters, 21
  Herb Appetizer Cheesecake, 19
  Herbed Mussels in Wine, 28

Appetizers (*continued*)
  Italian Pepperoni Puffs, 260
  Marinated Antipasto, 22
  Marinated Mushrooms, 22
  Mexican Shrimp Cocktail, 18
  Miniature Teriyaki Pork Kabobs, 23
  Mini Cocktail Meatballs, 26
  Mini Monte Cristo Sandwiches, 17
  Party Quiche Squares, 29
  "Philly" Stuffed Mushrooms, 25
  Rumaki, 22
  Sausage Antipasto Platter, 29
  Seafood Cocktails with Watercress
    Sauce, 28
  Spring Rolls, 25
  Steamed Mussels in White Wine, 182
  Thai Chicken Strips, 23
Apple & Herb Stuffing, 161
Apple & Tarragon Salad with
    Watercress, 83
Apple and Veal Scallop, 135
Applecakes, 222
Apple-Cheese Soup, 54
Apple Chess Pie, 324
Apple Crumb Squares, 286
Apple Raisin Snack Bars, 284
Apple-Raisin Stuffed Chicken Breasts,
    149
Apples
  Apple & Tarragon Salad with
    Watercress, 83
  Applecakes, 222
  Apple Chess Pie, 324
  Applesauce Yogurt Dessert, 310
  Butterscotch Apple Squares, 298
  Cherry Waldorf Gelatin, 70
  Create-a-Crust Apple Pie, 324
  Dutch Apple Raisin Pie, 324
  Fruit Crumble, 301
  Golden Apple Boston Brown Bread,
    265
  Old-Fashioned Apple Loaf, 265
  Red Cabbage 'n' Apples, 217
  Snow Topped Apples, 309
  Swedish Apple Cake, 301
Applesauce Yogurt Dessert, 310
Apricot Almond Chewies, 297
Apricot Crumble Cake, 263
Apricots
  Tortoni Squares, 302
Apricot-Stuffed Lamb Chops, 133
Arizona's 7-Layer Taco Sandwich, 241
Artichokes
  Baked Artichoke Squares, 20
  Frittata Romano, 255
  Hot Artichoke Dip, 13
  Risotto with Vegetables, 229
Asparagus
  Asparagus-Ham Roll-Ups, 128
  Asparagus in Anchovy Sauce, 216

Asparagus (*continued*)
  Fish Rolls with Asparagus, 177
  Fresh Asparagus Soufflé, 253
  Sausage-Asparagus Souffle
    Sandwiches, 253
Asparagus-Ham Roll-Ups, 128
Asparagus in Anchovy Sauce, 216
Autumn Pear 'n Apple Salad, 74
Avocado & Bacon Pitas, 244
Avocados
  Avocado & Bacon Pitas, 244
  Avocado Sauce, 243
  Guacamole, 11
Avocado Sauce, 243

B

Bacon
  Avocado & Bacon Pitas, 244
  Bacon & Chicken Sandwiches, 240
  Bacon & Egg Potato Salad, 77
  Bacon-Horseradish Dip, 6
  B.L.T.E. Breakfast Pockets, 249
  Cheese & Bacon Potato Bake, 228
  Citrus, Avocado & Bacon Salad, 66
  Creamy Spinach Fettucini, 210
  Loaf Sandwiches with Bacon & Ham,
    244
  Santa Monica Sandwich, 243
  Spinach Salad with Raspberry
    Dressing, 66
Bacon & Chicken Sandwiches, 240
Bacon & Egg Potato Salad, 77
Bacon and Green Pepper Stuffing, 163
Bacon-Horseradish Dip, 6
Bacon-Wrapped Shrimp, 188
Bacon-Wrapped Tuna, 170
Bagels
  Crispy Bagel Chips, 30
Bake & Glaze Teri Ribs, 125
Baked Almond Pudding, 317
Baked Apricot Chicken, 140
Baked Artichoke Squares, 20
Baked Celery and Almonds, 221
Baked Chicken Breasts with Rice &
    Vegetable Stuffing, 155
Baked Cream Cheese Appetizer, 8
Baked Ham with Glazed Vegetables,
    129
Baked Ham with Wine & Onion Glaze,
    129
Baked Stuffed Clams, 20
Baked Stuffed Shrimp, 20
Banana Bonanza Ice Cream, 305
Banana Chutney Dressing, 91
Banana Layered Pie, 326
Banana Mocha Cake, 346
Banana Mocha Ice Cream Pie, 326

Banana Mocha Layered Dessert, 300
Banana-Orange Shake, 32
Bananas
  Banana Bonanza Ice Cream, 305
  Banana Layered Pie, 326
  Banana Mocha Cake, 346
  Banana Mocha Ice Cream Pie, 326
  Banana Mocha Layered Dessert, 300
  Bananas Coco Lopez, 318
  Bananas Foster, 309
  Banana Shake, 32
  Chocolate Chip Banana Bread, 265
  Classic Banana Cream Pie, 326
  Creamy Banana Pudding, 315
  Favorite Banana Bread, 266
  Frozen Chocolate Banana Loaf, 305
  Gingery Banana Waffles, 250
  "Philly" Banana Pudding, 316
Bananas Coco Lopez, 318
Bananas Foster, 309
Banana Shake, 32
Barbecue: see **Outdoor grilling**
Barbecued Garlic, 221
Barbecued Pork Leg, 117
Barbecued Sausage Kabobs, 130
Barbecued Shrimp on a Skewer, 186
Barbecued Spareribs, 125
Barbecued Turkey with Herbs, 164
Barbecue Ham Sandwiches, 245
Bar cookies, 281–289
  Apple Crumb Squares, 286
  Apple Raisin Snack Bars, 284
  Best Brownies, 289
  Cheesecake Bars, 288
  Cherry Scotchies, 287
  Chocolate 'n' Oat Bars, 282
  Chocolate Pecan Bars, 286
  Chocolate Streusel Bars, 284
  Coconut Dream Bars, 282
  Coconut Lemon Bars, 281
  Crunch Bars, 283
  Double-Deck Brownies, 288
  Festive Cookie Bars, 282
  Frosted Toffee Bars, 282
  Fruit & Nut Snack Bars, 285
  Fruitcake Bars, 355
  Granola Bars, 279
  Jungle Bars, 285
  Lebkuchen Jewels, 285
  Lemon Iced Ambrosia Bars, 288
  Lemon Pecan Bars, 281
  Lemony Raisin-Coconut Squares, 289
  Macaroon Almond Crumb Bars, 281
  Magic Cookie Bars, 284
  Marble Squares, 287
  Minty Chocolate Squares, 287
  Peanut Butter Paisley Brownies, 288
  Peanutty Chocolate Snack Squares, 287
  Pecan Pie Bars, 283
  Pineapple Dream Bars, 286
  Pumpkin Cheesecake Bars, 286
  Raspberry Oatmeal Bars, 285
  Rich Lemon Bars, 281
  Scrumptious Chocolate Layer Bars, 288
  Seven Layer Magic Cookie Bars, 284
  Toffee Bars, 281
  Triple Layer Cookie Bars, 283

Barley
  Barley with Corn and Red Pepper, 217
  Beefy Vegetable Soup, 59
  Chunky Beef Barley Soup, 61
  Turkey-Barley Soup, 54
Barley with Corn and Red Pepper, 217
Basque Lamb, 135
Bavarian Pea Soup, 51
Bean and Kraut Franks, 130
Beans
  Bean and Kraut Franks, 130
  Black Bean Soup with Rice and Sherry, 50
  Brazilian Beans and Rice, 113
  Buffet Bean Bake, 214
  Chili in Tortilla Cups, 111
  Cincinnati Chili, 110
  Country Bean Barbecue, 214
  Country French Cassoulet, 192
  Country-Style Baked Beans, 216
  Dilly Bean Salad, 65
  Grandpa Snub's Chili, 130
  Individual Taco Salads, 86
  Louisiana Beans and Rice, 227
  Peppy Bean Dip, 16
  Sopa de Sonora, 58
  Spicy Bean Toss, 224
  Tex-Mex Rice and Beans, 229
  Three Bean Rice Salad, 79
  Turkey Cassoulet, 198
  Two-Bean Chili, 110
  Two-Bean Franks, 130
  Two-Bean Soup, 49
  Warm Bean Salad, 68
Beans, green
  Buffet Bean Bake, 214
  Cajun-Style Green Beans, 223
  Creamy Green Beans Almondine, 223
  Green Beans Napoli, 223
  Original Green Bean Casserole, 223
  Spicy Bean Toss, 224
  Sprout-Green Bean Salad, 67
  Three Bean Rice Salad, 79
Bean Sprout & Spinach Salad, 65
Bearnaise Sauce, 165
Béchamel Sauce, 213
Beef, 94–114 (see also **Beef, corned; Beef, ground; Beef ribs; Liver**)
  Beef and Bean Sprout Stir-Fry, 109
  Beef Burgundy, 105
  Beef Fajitas, 240
  Beef Goulash, 103
  Beef Kushisashi, 19
  Beef Ragoût, 106
  Beef Stew, 103
  Beef Stew with Dumplings, 106
  Beef Stroganoff, 102
  Beef Tenderloin Dijon, 94
  Beef with Leafy Greens, 108
  Beefy Vegetable Soup, 59
  Beer Marinated Steak, 100
  Broccoli & Beef Stir-Fry, 107
  Burgundy Beef Stroganoff, 102
  Cheese-Stuffed Beef Rolls, 194
  Chinese-Style Beef & Vegetables, 107
  Chuckwagon Roast and Vegetables, 97
  Chunky Beef Barley Soup, 61
  Classic Chinese Pepper Steak, 106

Beef (continued)
  Confetti Beef Salad, 85
  Country French Beef Stew, 104
  Eight Flavors Pot Roast, 96
  Fiery Beef Stir-Fry, 108
  Flank Steak Bearnaise, 100
  French-Style Pot Roast, 96
  German Beef Roulade, 96
  German-Style Pot Roast, 96
  Ginger Beef, 108
  Grilled Flank Steak Sangrita, 99
  Grilled Steak with Mushroom-Wine Sauce, 100
  Grilled Tenderloin with Cognac, 98
  Islander's Beef Barbecue, 96
  Italian-Style Pot Roast, 96
  Layered Picnic Club Sandwich, 239
  Lime Kabobs Polynesian, 108
  Marinated Beef Salad, 85
  Marinated Flank Steak, 102
  Marinated Oriental Beef Salad, 87
  Mexican Beef Stew, 104
  Mongolian Beef, 98
  Old-Fashioned Pot Roast, 96
  Orange-Flavored Grilled Beef, 106
  Oriental Steak Kabobs, 107
  Oven-Baked Bourguignonne, 104
  Pepper-Stuffed Flank Steak, 99
  Peppery Rib Steaks, 99
  Rouladen, 94
  Sauerbraten, 103
  Savory Steak, 100
  Simmered Beef and Vegetables, 105
  Souper Pot Roast, 97
  Standing Rib Roast with Madeira Sauce, 97
  Steak Salad in Red-Wine Dressing, 86
  Steak with Hearty Mustard Marinade, 99
  Stir-Fried Beef and Vegetables, 101
  Stroganoff Superb, 105
  Stuffed Flank Steak, 98
  Szechuan Beef & Snow Peas, 109
  Texas-Style Chili, 110
  Texas-Style Steak on Hot Bread, 245
  Vegetable-Stuffed Flank Steak, 101
  Wine-Simmered Beef and Vegetables, 105
Beef, corned
  Corned Beef & Cabbage Chowder, 58
  Hash-and-Egg Brunch, 253
Beef, ground
  Albóndingas Soup, 59
  All-American Meat Loaf, 113
  Beef and Bean Chimichangas, 240
  Beef and Wild Rice Casserole, 194
  Brazilian Beans and Rice, 113
  Cantonese Meatballs, 25
  Cheeseburger Pie, 195
  Chili Beef and Corn Casserole, 193
  Chili Burritos, 243
  Chili in Tortilla Cups, 111
  Cincinnati Chili, 110
  Country Paté, 17
  Easy Cheesy Meat Loaf, 112
  Individual Taco Salads, 86
  Italian-Style Salisbury Steaks, 111
  Lasagna Deliciousa, 213
  Lasagna with White and Red Sauces, 213

Beef, ground (*continued*)
Lipton Onion Burgers, 241
Meatball Stew, 114
Meat Loaf Italiano, 110
Meat Loaf Supreme, 112
Meat 'n' Tater Pie, 190
Meatza Pizzas, 113
Mexican Meatloaf Roll, 112
Mini Cocktail Meatballs, 26
Mini Meat Loaves, 112
Nutty Burgers, 243
Picadillo-Stuffed Peppers, 113
Quick 'n Easy Tacos, 245
Sloppy Joes, 244
Souper Quick "Lasagna," 212
Split Pea and Meatball Soup, 57
Stuffed Cheese Burgers, 244
Tortilla Lasagna, 192
Two-Bean Chili, 110
Zesty Meat Loaf, 111
Beef and Bean Chimichangas, 240
Beef and Bean Sprout Stir-Fry, 109
Beef and Wild Rice Casserole, 194
Beef Burgundy, 105
Beef Fajitas, 240
Beef Goulash, 103
Beef Kushisashi, 19
Beef Ragoût, 106
Beef ribs
Honey-Mustard Beef Ribs, 108
Red-Cooked Short Ribs, 107
Beef Stew, 103
Beef Stew with Dumplings, 106
Beef Stroganoff, 102
Beef Tenderloin Dijon, 94
Beef with Leafy Greens, 108
Beefy Mary, 32
Beefy Vegetable Soup, 59
Beer Batter Fried Veggies 'n Things, 19
Beer-Batter Shrimp, 28, 185
Beer Cheese Bread, 266
Beer Marinated Steak, 100
Beets
Borscht, 47
Berry-Bottomed Walnut Pie, 330
Berry Mint Ice Ring, 40
Best Brownies, 289
Beverages, alcoholic, 38–41 (*see also* **Punches**)
Bloody Mary, 39
Bourbon Slush, 38
Death Mix, The, 39
Devilish Daiquiri, 39
Frozen Margaritas, 39
Hot Maple Toddy, 41
Lemon Toddy, 41
Lemony Light Cooler, 40
Melon Citrus Cooler, 39
Mulled Cider, 41
Party Mai Tais, 38
Piña Colada, 38
Pineapple Margarita, 38
Seaside Mary, 39
Simmered Sherry Bouillon, 41
Spirited Coffee Lopez, 41
Spirited Egg Nog, 41
Syllabub, 41
White Sangria, 40

Beverages, nonalcoholic, 32–38 (*see also* **Cocoa; Lemonade; Milk shakes; Punches; Tea; Tea, iced**)
Beefy Mary, 32
Bullshot, 37
Checkmate, 34
City Slicker, 35
Hot Buttered Pineapple Smoothie, 38
Hot Cranberry Cider, 38
Hot Mulled Pineapple Juice, 37
Hot Tomato Sipper, 32
Island Fruit Cooler, 34
Passion Shakes, 304
Pineapple Mint Tulip, 34
Pineapple Orange Slush, 36
Pineapple Passion, 34
Sparkling V8, 35
Spicy Warmer, 37
Tonic Thyme, 35
Toro, 32
Zesty V8, 35
Birthday Cakelets, 350
Bittersweet Glaze, 352
Black Bean Soup with Rice and Sherry, 50
Black Bottom Cupcakes, 354
Black-Eyed Susans, 273
Black Forest Torte, 357
Black Russian Mini Soufflés, 319
Bloody Mary, 39
B.L.T.E. Breakfast Pockets, 249
BLT Soup, 60
Blueberries 'n Cheese Coffeecake, 262
Blueberry Muffins, 258
Blue Cheese Dressing, 93
Blue Cheese Walnut Spread, 8
Blushing Onions, 225
Blushing Onion Soup, 45
Bohemian Rye Bread, 269
Bonbon Cups, 293
Borscht, 47
Bourbon Slush, 38
Braised Chinese Duckling, 158
Bran
Treasure Bran Muffins, 259
Brandied Fruit Pie, 324
Brazilian Beans and Rice, 113
Breads, 256–269: *see* **Breads, quick; Breads, yeast; Coffee cakes; Doughnuts; Rolls; Sweet rolls**
Breads, quick, 264–267
Beer Cheese Bread, 266
Chocolate Chip Banana Bread, 265
Favorite Banana Bread, 266
Gingerbread, 264
Golden Apple Boston Brown Bread, 265
Golden Fruit Loaves, 264
Golden Raisin Spice Bread, 264
Lemon Bread, 265
Mandarin Orange French Toast, 250
Mexican Corn Bread, 266
Old-Fashioned Apple Loaf, 265
Orange Corn Bread, 162
Pumpkin Nut Bread, 266
Raisin Scones, 258
Soda Bread, 264
Southern Hush Puppies, 260

Breads, yeast, 267–269
Bohemian Rye Bread, 269
Cheese Casserole Bread, 268
Cinnamon-Raisin Swirl Loaf, 267
Double-Braided Saffron Bread, 268
Italian Pepperoni Puffs, 260
Savory Bubble Cheese Bread, 268
V8 Cheese Bread, 267
Breakfast Pizza, 249
Broccoli
Broccoli and Celery Oriental, 219
Broccoli and Pasta, 218
Broccoli and Rice with Walnuts, 216
Broccoli Cheese Soup, 46
Broccoli-Mushroom Omelet, 255
Cheddar Broccoli Corn Bake, 216
Curried Smoked Turkey Salad, 85
Party Quiche Squares, 29
Sesame Broccoli, 217
Broccoli & Beef Stir-Fry, 107
Broccoli and Celery Oriental, 219
Broccoli and Pasta, 218
Broccoli and Rice with Walnuts, 216
Broccoli Cheese Soup, 46
Broccoli-Mushroom Omelet, 255
Browned Garlic-Butter Sauce, 114
Brownies
Best Brownies, 289
Double-Deck Brownies, 288
Peanut Butter Paisley Brownies, 288
Brunswick Stew, 145
Brussels Sprouts Amandine, 216
Buckeyes, 294
Buffalo-Style Chicken Wings, 22
Buffet Bean Bake, 214
Buffet Slaw, 72
Bulgur
Stir-Fried Vegetables with Bulgur, 235
Tabbouleh, 80
Bullshot, 37
Burgundy Beef Stroganoff, 102
Butterscotch Apple Squares, 298
Butterscotch Cheesecake, 307
Butterscotch Fudge, 292

C

Cabbage
Mustard Glazed Sausage with Sauteed Cabbage, 131
Red Cabbage 'n' Apples, 217
Spiced Red Cabbage, 218
Stuffed Cabbage Leaves, 126
Sweet 'n Sour Cabbage, 218
Cajun Dirty Rice, 227
Cajun Fish, 183
Cajun-Style Chicken Nuggets, 26
Cajun-Style Green Beans, 223
Cake rolls
Choco-Coconut Cake Roll, 345
Cakes, 338–359 (*see also* **Cake rolls; Cakes, layer; Cakes from mixes; Fruitcakes; Tortes**)
Banana Mocha Cake, 346
Carrot Cake, 341
Chocolate Sheet Cake, 344
Cocoa-Spice Snackin' Cake, 342
Fudgey Pecan Cake, 347

Cakes (*continued*)
Kentucky Jam Cake, 348
Lickety-Split Cocoa Cake, 343
Marble Chiffon Cake, 340
Mocha Fudge Pudding Cake, 347
Old-Fashioned Lemon Pudding Cake, 349
Pineapple Upside-Down Cake, 347
Surprise Carrot Cake, 349
Tomato Soup Spice Cake, 338
Cakes, layer
Chocolatetown Special Cake, 338
Chocolate Yogurt Cake, 341
German Chocolate Cake, 344
Kahlúa® Sweetheart Cake, 343
Cakes from mixes
Birthday Cakelets, 350
Cinnamon Ripple Cake, 340
Cool and Minty Party Cake, 343
Cranberry Pudding Cake with Sauce, 346
Drum Layer Cake, 345
Easy German Chocolate Cake, 342
Easy Pina Colada Cake, 348
Elegant Angel Torte, 358
French Apple Cake, 340
Golden Crunch Cake, 346
New Orleans Crumb Cake, 350
Open House Ribbon Torte, 357
Peanut Butter Poke Cake, 349
Petits Fours, 342
Pound Cake, 338
Pudding Poke Cake, 349
Rum-Nut Pudding Cake, 348
Strawberries Romanoff on Angel Slices, 350
Strawberry Tunnel Cream Cake, 344
California Bisque, 44
California Classic, The, 245
California-Style Chicken, 196
Calypso Shrimp Salad, 91
Canapes
Herbed Cheese Pinwheel Canapes, 18
Salmon Canapes, 27
Candies, 290–297
Almond Toffee, 297
Apricot Almond Chewies, 297
Bonbon Cups, 293
Buckeyes, 294
Butterscotch Fudge, 292
Caramel Peanut Balls, 296
Cherry Fudge, 290
Chipper Peanut Candy, 296
Chocolate-Almond Fudge, 291
Chocolate Creams, 292
Chocolate-Dipped Morsels, 294
Chocolate Pecan Critters, 294
Chocolate "Philly" Fudge, 291
Chocolate Rum Truffles, 291
Chocolate Truffles, 291
Chocolatey Peanut Treats, 293
Coconut Date Slices, 293
Coconut Rum Balls, 293
Confetti Fudge, 290
Creamy Cocoa Taffy, 297
Creamy Dark Chocolate Fudge, 292
Creamy Milk Chocolate Fudge, 292
Creamy White Fudge, 290
Crunchy Clusters, 296
Dorchester Fudge, 290

Candies (*continued*)
Double-Decker Fudge, 291
Easy Rocky Road, 292
Foolproof Dark Chocolate Fudge, 292
Fruit Bon Bons, 295
Fudgy Chocolate Truffles, 293
Layered Mint Chocolate Candy, 295
Marshmallow-Nut Cocoa Fudge, 290
Mexican Chocolate Fudge, 292
Milk Chocolate Bourbon Balls, 295
Milk Chocolate Fudge, 292
Mocha Almond Fudge, 290
Nutty Rich Cocoa Fudge, 291
Peanut Butter Fudge, 290, 295
Peanut Butter Logs, 295
Praline Fudge, 290
Raspberry Fudge Balls, 290
Rich Cocoa Fudge, 290
Rum Raisin Fudge, 290
Cantonese Chicken Salad, 81
Cantonese Meatballs, 25
Capon
Grilled Capon, 146
Caramel Peanut Balls, 296
Caribbean Fudge Pie, 325
Caribbean Pork Chops, 114
Carrot Cake, 341
Carrot Nut Pudding, 220
Carrot Pineapple Salad, 75
Carrots
Carrot Cake, 341
Carrot Nut Pudding, 220
Carrot Saute, 218
Chilled Carrot Soup, 45
Dilled Carrots and Parsnips, 219
Golden Salad, 71
Hot & Spicy Glazed Carrots, 220
Layered Carrot-Pineapple Salad, 73
Lemon Orange Carrots, 219
Neapolitan Vegetable Mold, 71
Onion-Glazed Carrots, 219
Surprise Carrot Cake, 349
Watercress-Carrot Salad, 67
Carrot Saute, 218
Cashew Chicken, 152
Cashew Pork Stir-Fry, 122
Cashew-Shrimp Salad, 90
Catfish
Tangy Catfish, 179
Cauliflower
Cauliflower au Gratin, 220
Golden Cauliflower Soup, 49
Italian-Style Cauliflower Salad, 67
Cauliflower au Gratin, 220
Celery Seed Dressing, 92
Champagne Sherbet Punch, 40
Checkmate, 34
Cheddar Broccoli Corn Bake, 216
Cheddar Cheese Pears, 309
Cheese
Arizona's 7-Layer Taco Sandwich, 241
Baked Cream Cheese Appetizer, 8
Beer Cheese Bread, 266
Blue Cheese Walnut Spread, 8
Breakfast Pizza, 249
Broccoli Cheese Soup, 46
Broccoli-Mushroom Omelet, 255
California Classic, The, 245
Cheddar Broccoli Corn Bake, 216
Cheddar Cheese Pears, 309

Cheese (*continued*)
Cheese & Bacon Potato Bake, 228
Cheese & Nut Stuffed Bread Slices, 18
Cheese Casserole Bread, 268
Cheese-Mushroom Strata, 203
Cheese Strata, 251
Chili con Queso, 9
Chili Soup Jarlsberg, 61
Colorful Ham Omelet, 252
Cracked Black Pepper and Herb Spread, 6
Cream Cheese Kugel, 254
Creamy Fettucini Alfredo, 207
Easy "Hollandaise" Sauce, 234
Eggplant Parmesan, 202
Fettucine Alfredo, 206
Galbani® Fontina Potato Surprise, 228
Garden Vegetable Spread, 12
Golden Mini Quiches, 24
Golden Squash Bake, 230
Greek-Style Puffy Pancake, 251
Grilled Cheese, 24
Ham and Cheese Strata, 190
Hearty Herbed Cheese Spread, 12
Herb Appetizer Cheesecake, 19
Herbed Cheese Pinwheel Canapes, 18
Hot Chili con Queso, 9
Lasagna Deliciousa, 213
Lasagna with White and Red Sauces, 213
Leeks with Bel Paese®, 219
Loaf Sandwiches with Bacon & Ham, 244
Molded Cheese, 11
Neapolitan Pizza, 238
Nutty Blue Cheese Vegetable Dip, 14
Party Cheese Ball, 14
Party Pizza, 238
Party Quiche Squares, 29
"Philly" Brunch Quiche, 246
Phyllo Spinach Pie, 254
Piña Pepper Spread, 15
Pineapple-Almond Cheese Spread, 15
Pineapple Brunch Casserole, 252
Pine Nut Cheese Spread, 14
Potato and Cheese Casserole, 227
Quiche Florentine, 248
Quick Mexican Spread, 15
Santa Fe Pasta, 207
Savory Bubble Cheese Bread, 268
Savory Cheddar Spread, 15
Savory Onion Cheese Tart, 248
Savory Sunday Eggs, 255
Smoked Sausage Stuffed Pasta Shells, 206
Smoky Macaroni and Cheese, 203
Souper Easy Quiche, 249
Souper Quick "Lasagna," 212
Southwestern Egg Puff, 249
Sunny Fries, 228
Swiss Chicken Quiche, 248
Tagliatelle with Creamy Sauce, 212
Tangy Blue Cheese Vegetables, 233
Tempting Cheese Crepes, 246
Thick 'n Cheesy Vegetable Pizza, 238
Toasted Sesame Cheese Spread, 9
Tortellini in Cream Sauce, 204
Turkey and Caper Quiche, 248

Cheese (*continued*)
Warm Herb Cheese Spread, 12
Wisconsin Cheese 'n Beer Soup, 48
Cheese & Bacon Potato Bake, 228
Cheese & Nut Stuffed Bread Slices, 18
Cheese and Red Bean Salad, 62
Cheeseburger Pie, 195
Cheesecake Bars, 288
Cheesecakes, 306–307
Butterscotch Cheesecake, 307
Chocolate Caramel Pecan
Cheesecake, 306
Frozen Mocha Cheesecake, 307
Miniature Cheesecakes, 306
Northwest Cheesecake Supreme, 306
Piña Colada Cheesecake, 306
Cheese Casserole Bread, 268
Cheese-Mushroom Strata, 203
Cheese Strata, 251
Cheese-Stuffed Beef Rolls, 194
Cheese Stuffed Tomatoes, 18
Cheesy Chicken Tetrazzini, 198
Cheesy Pork Chops 'n Potatoes, 192
Cheesy Potato Skins, 19
Chef's Salad, 88
Cherries
Cherry Cheese Pie, 325
Harvest Cherry Pie, 332
Viennese Cherry Cheese Torte, 356
Cherry Cheese Pie, 325
Cherry-Coconut Filling, 345
Cherry Fudge, 290
Cherry Scotchies, 287
Cherry-Topped Icebox Cake, 302
Cherry Waldorf Gelatin, 70
Chess Pie, 330
Chicken, 138–157 (*see also* **Capon;**
Chicken breasts, boneless;
Chicken livers)
Apple & Tarragon Salad with
Watercress, 83
Bacon & Chicken Sandwiches, 240
Baked Apricot Chicken, 140
Brunswick Stew, 145
Buffalo-Style Chicken Wings, 22
Cajun-Style Chicken Nuggets, 26
California-Style Chicken, 196
Cantonese Chicken Salad, 81
Chicken Adobo, 145
Chicken and Ham Supreme, 197
Chicken and Pasta Soup, 53
Chicken & Rice Gumbo, 52
Chicken Breasts in Wine Sauce, 144
Chicken Cacciatore, 141
Chicken-Corn Soup Santa Fe, 52
Chicken Enchiladas, 195
Chicken Kyoto, 145
Chicken Marinated with Orange &
Tarragon, 143
Chicken Noodle Chowder, 52
Chicken Noodle Soup, 53
Chicken Paprika, 138
Chicken Puff Bravo, 197
Chicken Roma, 143
Chicken Salad Supreme, 81
Chicken-Vegetable Soup, 52
Chicken Wings with Honey &
Orange Sauce, 23
Chicken with Oriental Dipping
Sauce, 10

Chicken (*continued*)
Chicken with Potatoes & Peppers,
144
Corn-Stuffed Chicken, 148
Country Captain, 142
Country Chicken and Peppers, 140
Country Paté, 17
Country-Style Chicken Dinner, 195
Creamy Chicken Tarragon, 140
Creole Chicken Jambalaya, 200
Curried Chicken Puffs, 26
Curried Pineapple Pasta Salad, 84
Dan D's Chicken BBQ, 141
Deluxe Chicken Walnut Salad, 82
Elegant Chicken Piccata, 142
Empress Chicken Wings, 26
Festive Chicken Salad, 82
French Quarter Rice Salad, 85
Fried Chicken, 143
Garden Chicken Salad, 84
Garden-Fresh Pitas, 241
Golden Glazed Stuffed Chicken, 147
Grilled Curried Chicken, 141
Herb-Roasted Chicken, 148
Hot Chicken Salad, 81
Italian Chicken, 145
Layered Chicken Salad, 83
Lemon Herbed Chicken, 142
Lemony Chicken Mold, 83
Lettuce and Chicken Soup, 52
Mexican Chicken with Spicy Bacon,
147
Old-Fashioned Chicken Pot Pie, 196
Orange-Honey Chicken, 143
Oven-Baked Buttermilk Chicken,
138
Oven Barbecued Chicken, 144
Roasted Dill Chicken, 147
Sausage-Chicken Creole, 199
Spicy Orange Chicken, 141
Sweet and Spicy Chicken Barbecue,
146
Swiss Chicken Quiche, 248
Tequila-Orange Chicken, 146
Thai Chicken Strips, 23
Versatile Chicken, 138
Waldorf Chicken Salad, 82
Chicken Adobo, 145
Chicken and Broccoli, 156
Chicken and Ham Supreme, 197
Chicken and Pasta Soup, 53
Chicken & Rice Gumbo, 52
Chicken breasts, boneless, 148–157
Apple-Raisin Stuffed Chicken
Breasts, 149
Baked Chicken Breasts with Rice &
Vegetable Stuffing, 155
Cashew Chicken, 152
Cheesy Chicken Tetrazzini, 198
Chicken and Broccoli, 156
Chicken Breasts Florentine, 151
Chicken Breasts with Artichoke-
Cheese Stuffing, 156
Chicken Cordon Bleu with Golden
Cream Sauce, 156
Chicken 'n Vegetable Stir Fry, 157
Chicken Parisian, 156
Chicken-Vegetable Kabobs, 151
Chicken Walnut Stir-Fry, 153
Colorful Dragon Stir-Fry, 155

Chicken breasts, boneless (*continued*)
Crunchy Almond Chicken Cutlets,
155
Golden Chicken Stir-Fry, 154
Jade & Ruby Stir-Fry, 153
Lemon Chicken, 155
Mongolian Pot, 152
Moo Goo Gai Pan, 153
Mushroom-Stuffed Chicken Breasts,
154
Orange-Cashew Chicken, 157
Quick Chicken Curry, 150
Rolled Chicken Breasts Florentine,
150
Shanghai Chicken, 189
Shantung Chicken, 149
Special Lemony Chicken, 148
Spinach & Pesto Stuffed Chicken
Breasts, 148
Sweet-and-Sour Chicken, 152
Tandoori-Style Chicken Kabobs, 151
Chicken Breasts Florentine, 151
Chicken Breasts in Wine Sauce, 144
Chicken Breasts with Artichoke-Cheese
Stuffing, 156
Chicken Cacciatore, 141
Chicken Cordon Bleu with Golden
Cream Sauce, 156
Chicken-Corn Soup Santa Fe, 52
Chicken Enchiladas, 195
Chicken Kyoto, 145
Chicken Liver Pâté, 10
Chicken livers
Cajun Dirty Rice, 227
Chicken Liver Pâté, 10
Chicken Livers in Wine Sauce, 141
Rumaki, 22
Sauteed Chicken Livers, 144
Chicken Livers in Wine Sauce, 141
Chicken Marinated with Orange &
Tarragon, 143
Chicken Noodle Chowder, 52
Chicken Noodle Soup, 53
Chicken 'n Vegetable Stir Fry, 157
Chicken Paprika, 138
Chicken Parisian, 156
Chicken Puff Bravo, 197
Chicken Roma, 143
Chicken Salad Supreme, 81
Chicken-Vegetable Kabobs, 151
Chicken-Vegetable Soup, 52
Chicken Walnut Stir-Fry, 153
Chicken Wings with Honey & Orange
Sauce, 23
Chicken with Oriental Dipping Sauce,
10
Chicken with Potatoes & Peppers, 144
Chile Dressing, 69
Chili
Chili in Tortilla Cups, 111
Cincinnati Chili, 110
Fire and Ice Chili, 127
Grandpa Snub's Chili, 130
Texas-Style Chili, 110
Two-Bean Chili, 110
Chili Beef and Corn Casserole, 193
Chili Burritos, 243
Chili con Queso, 9
Chili Dogs, 242
Chili in Tortilla Cups, 111

Chili Soup Jarlsberg, 61
Chilled Carrot Soup, 45
Chilled Rigatoni Salad, 79
Chilly Strawberry Souffles, 320
Chinese Noodle Cakes, 187
Chinese Spinach, 231
Chinese-Style Beef & Vegetables, 107
Chinese-Style Spareribs, 125
Chinese Trout, 172
Chip Macaroons, 275
Chipper Peanut Candy, 296
Choco-Coconut Cake Roll, 345
Chocolate
  Best Brownies, 289
  Black Bottom Cupcakes, 354
  Black Forest Torte, 357
  Black Russian Mini Soufflés, 319
  Bonbon Cups, 293
  Caribbean Fudge Pie, 325
  Cherry Fudge, 290
  Chip Macaroons, 275
  Choco-Coconut Cake Roll, 345
  Chocolate-Almond Fudge, 291
  Chocolate Almond "Philly" Torte, 357
  Chocolate-Almond Tarts, 336
  Chocolate-Berry Parfaits, 313
  Chocolate Caramel Pecan Cheesecake, 306
  Chocolate Chip Banana Bread, 265
  Chocolate Chip Whole Wheat Cookies, 272
  Chocolate Coconut Pecan Torte, 359
  Chocolate Cookie Sandwiches, 272
  Chocolate Crackles, 280
  Chocolate Cream Pudding, 318
  Chocolate Creams, 292
  Chocolate Custard Sauce, 318
  Chocolate-Filled Cream Puffs, 337
  Chocolate Fruitcake, 355
  Chocolate Kahlúa® Bears, 274
  Chocolate 'n' Oat Bars, 282
  Chocolate Pecan Bars, 286
  Chocolate Pecan Critters, 294
  Chocolate "Philly" Fudge, 291
  Chocolate Rum Truffles, 291
  Chocolate Sauce, 310
  Chocolate Sheet Cake, 344
  Chocolate Streusel Bars, 284
  Chocolatetown Cupcakes, 354
  Chocolatetown Special Cake, 338
  Chocolate Truffles, 291
  Chocolate Turtle Pie, 327
  Chocolate Waffles, 250
  Chocolate Yogurt Cake, 341
  Chocolatey Peanut Treats, 293
  Classic Meringue Pie, 331
  Cocoa-Spice Snackin' Cake, 342
  Coconut Fudge Sauce, 319
  Confetti Fudge, 290
  Creamy Brownie Frosting, 289
  Creamy Cocoa Taffy, 297
  Creamy Dark Chocolate Fudge, 292
  Creamy Hot Chocolate, 37
  Creamy Milk Chocolate Fudge, 292
  Creamy White Fudge, 290
  Crème de Cacao Torte, 359
  Dorchester Fudge, 290
  Double-Decker Fudge, 291

Chocolate (continued)
  Double-Dip Chocolate Chunk Cookies, 274
  Easy Chocolate Mousse Pie, 322
  Easy German Chocolate Cake, 342
  Easy Rocky Road, 292
  Elegant Chocolate Mousse, 313
  Foolproof Dark Chocolate Fudge, 292
  Frosty Chocolate Shake, 36
  Frozen Chocolate Banana Loaf, 305
  Frozen Mocha Cheesecake, 307
  Fudgey Pecan Cake, 347
  Fudgy Chocolate Truffles, 293
  German Chocolate Cake, 344
  Hershey's™ Great American Chocolate Chip Cookies, 273
  Hot Chocolate Soufflé, 320
  Hot Cocoa Mix, 37
  Hot Fudge Sauce, 317
  Individual Fudge Soufflés, 320
  Lacy Chocolate Crisps, 278
  Layered Mint Chocolate Candy, 295
  Lickety-Split Cocoa Cake, 343
  Marble Squares, 287
  Marshmallow-Nut Cocoa Fudge, 290
  Mexican Chocolate Fudge, 292
  Mexican Cocoa Torte, 358
  Microwave Classic Chocolate Sauce, 318
  Microwave Hershey Bar Mousse, 313
  Microwave Hershey Bar Pie, 332
  Microwave Hot Cocoa, 37
  Milk Chocolate Bourbon Balls, 295
  Milk Chocolate Chip Cookies, 273
  Milk Chocolate Fudge, 292
  Minty Chocolate Squares, 287
  Mocha Almond Fudge, 290
  Mocha Fudge Pudding Cake, 347
  Mt. Gretna Chocolate Fondue, 298
  New Orleans Crumb Cake, 350
  Nutty Rich Cocoa Fudge, 291
  Peanut Butter Fudge, 290
  Peanut Butter Shells with Chocolate-Almond Cream, 315
  Peanutty Chocolate Snack Squares, 287
  Pears au Chocolat, 310
  Pinwheels and Checkerboards, 276
  Pots de Crème au Chocolat, 302
  Praline Fudge, 290
  Quick Chocolate Mousse, 314
  Quick Pudding Chip Cookies, 274
  Raspberry Fudge Balls, 290
  Reese's Chewy Chocolate Cookies, 272
  Reese's Cookies, 281
  Rich Cocoa Fudge, 290
  Rum Raisin Fudge, 290
  Scrumptious Chocolate Layer Bars, 288
  Strawberry-Chocolate Bavarian Cream, 314
  Super Chocolate Chunk Cookies, 274
  Super Coconut Chocolate Chunk Cookies, 274
  Super Peanut Butter Chocolate Chunk Cookies, 274
  Thumbprint Cookies, 270
  Viennese Chocolate Torte, 356
Chocolate-Almond Cream Filling, 315

Chocolate-Almond Fudge, 291
Chocolate Almond "Philly" Torte, 357
Chocolate-Almond Tarts, 336
Chocolate-Berry Parfaits, 313
Chocolate Butter Frosting, 352
Chocolate Butterscotch Chip Cupcakes, 354
Chocolate Caramel Pecan Cheesecake, 306
Chocolate Chip Banana Bread, 265
Chocolate Chip Whole Wheat Cookies, 272
Chocolate-Coconut Frosting, 352
Chocolate Coconut Pecan Torte, 359
Chocolate Cookie Crust, 326
Chocolate Cookie Sandwiches, 272
Chocolate Crackles, 280
Chocolate Cream Cheese Frosting, 351
Chocolate Cream Filling, 337
Chocolate Cream Pudding, 318
Chocolate Creams, 292
Chocolate Crumb Crust, 332
Chocolate Custard Sauce, 318
Chocolate-Dipped Morsels, 294
Chocolate-Filled Cream Puffs, 337
Chocolate Fruitcake, 355
Chocolate Ganache Glaze, 359
Chocolate Glaze, 337, 352
Chocolate Icing, 274
Chocolate Kahlúa® Bears, 274
Chocolate 'n' Oat Bars, 282
Chocolate Pecan Bars, 286
Chocolate Pecan Critters, 294
Chocolate "Philly" Cream Frosting, 357
Chocolate "Philly" Fudge, 291
Chocolate Rum Truffles, 291
Chocolate Satin Glaze, 352
Chocolate Sauce, 310
Chocolate Sheet Cake, 344
Chocolate Streusel Bars, 284
Chocolate Tart Shells, 336
Chocolatetown Cupcakes, 354
Chocolatetown Special Cake, 338
Chocolate Truffles, 291
Chocolate Turtle Pie, 327
Chocolate Waffles, 250
Chocolate Yogurt Cake, 341
Chocolatey Peanut Treats, 293
Chocolate Zucchini Cupcakes, 352
Chowders
  Chicken Noodle Chowder, 52
  Corned Beef & Cabbage Chowder, 58
  Creamed Corn Chowder, 44
  New England Style Turkey Chowder, 53
  Sausage Corn Chowder, 57
Christmas Carol Punch, 36
Chuckwagon Roast and Vegetables, 97
Chunky Beef Barley Soup, 61
Cider-Glazed Pork Roast, 118
Cincinnati Chili, 110
Cinnamon Fruit Tart with Sour Cream Filling, 335
Cinnamon Graham Cracker Crust, 335
Cinnamon-Nut Topping, 263
Cinnamon-Raisin Swirl Loaf, 267
Cinnamon Ripple Cake, 340
Cinnamon Walnut Pudding Ice Cream, 304

Citrus, Avocado & Bacon Salad, 66
Citrus Candied Sweet Potatoes, 235
City Slicker, 35
Clam & Tomato Molded Salad, 72
Clam Noodle Florentine, 201
Clams
 Baked Stuffed Clams, 20
 Clam & Tomato Molded Salad, 72
 Clam Noodle Florentine, 201
 Creamy Clam Bisque, 57
 Deep-Fried Clams, 185
 Manhattan Clam Dip, 9
 Pasta with Clam Sauce, 212
 Seafood Cacciatore, 184
Classic Banana Cream Pie, 326
Classic Chinese Pepper Steak, 106
Classic Fudge Frosting, 351
Classic Meringue Pie, 331
Classic Pizza, 236
Classic Spanish Rice, 228
Classic Spinach Salad, 62
Classic Tomato Aspic, 70
Clear Japanese Soup, 45
Clear Lemon Glaze, 265
Clear Vegetable Soup, 49
Clove Glazed Turkey, 164
Cobb Salad, 81
Cocoa
 Creamy Hot Chocolate, 37
 Hot Cocoa Mix, 37
 Microwave Hot Cocoa, 37
Cocoa Glaze, 340
Cocoa-Spice Snackin' Cake, 342
Coconut
 Almond Melting Moments, 275
 Chip Macaroons, 275
 Coconut Custard Pie, 334
 Coconut Date Slices, 293
 Coconut Dream Bars, 282
 Coconut Lemon Bars, 281
 Coconut Macaroons, 275
 Coconut Pecan Sauce, 317
 Coconut Rum Balls, 293
 Coconut Thumbprints, 270
 Coconut Washboards, 275
 Florentines, 278
 Fruit Bon Bons, 295
 Fruited Macaroons, 275
 Hawaiian Coconut Spread, 15
 Impossible Pie, 327
 Lacy Chocolate Crisps, 278
 Melting Moments, 275
 Nut Macaroons, 275
 Raisin Macaroons, 275
 Super Coconut Chocolate Chunk
  Cookies, 274
 Super Peanut Butter Chocolate
  Chunk Cookies, 274
 toasting directions, 317
 Tropical Fruit Dip, 9
Coconut Cream Dressing, 73
Coconut Custard Pie, 334
Coconut Date Slices, 293
Coconut Dream Bars, 282
Coconut Fudge Sauce, 319
Coconut Granola Snack, 292
Coconut Lemon Bars, 281
Coconut Macaroons, 275
Coconut-Pecan Filling and Frosting,
 344

Coconut Pecan Sauce, 317
Coconut Rum Balls, 293
Coconut Thumbprints, 270
Coconut Washboards, 275
Coffee cakes, 262–263
 Apricot Crumble Cake, 263
 Blueberries 'n Cheese Coffeecake,
  262
 Cream Cheese Swirl Coffee Cake, 263
 Easy Apple Kuchen, 262
 Fruity Swirl Coffeecake, 262
 Orange Wake-Up Cake, 263
Coleslaw
 Country Pineapple Coleslaw, 68
 Sunflower Seed Cole Slaw, 65
 Tangy Coleslaw, 69
Colorful Carrot Dip, 6
Colorful Dragon Stir-Fry, 155
Colorful Ham Omelet, 252
Colorful Stir-Fried Pork, 121
Confetti Beef Salad, 85
Confetti Cones, 277
Confetti Fried Rice, 226
Confetti Fudge, 290
Continental Flair Frosting, 351
Cookies, 270–289: see Bar cookies;
 Cookies, drop; Cookies,
 refrigerator; Cookies, rolled;
 Cookies, shaped
 Cookies and Cream Parfaits, 313
Cookies, drop
 Chip Macaroons, 275
 Chocolate Chip Whole Wheat
  Cookies, 272
 Chocolate Cookie Sandwiches, 272
 Coconut Macaroons, 275
 Double-Dip Chocolate Chunk
  Cookies, 274
 Florentines, 278
 Fruitcake Cookies, 355
 Fruited Macaroons, 275
 Granola Cookies, 279
 Hershey's™ Great American
  Chocolate Chip Cookies, 273
 Milk Chocolate Chip Cookies, 273
 Nut Macaroons, 275
 Quick Pudding Chip Cookies, 274
 Quick Pudding Cookies, 274
 Raisin Macaroons, 275
 Reese's Chewy Chocolate Cookies,
  272
 Reese's Cookies, 281
 Super Chocolate Chunk Cookies, 274
 Super Coconut Chocolate Chunk
  Cookies, 274
 Super Peanut Butter Chocolate
  Chunk Cookies, 274
 Wheat Germ Cookies, 270
Cookies, refrigerator
 Slice 'n' Bake Lemon Cookies, 279
Cookies, rolled
 Black-Eyed Susans, 273
 Chocolate Kahlúa™ Bears, 274
 Coconut Washboards, 275
 Favorite Butter Cookies, 277
 Gingerbread People, 276
 Kris Kringle Cookies, 277
 Old-Fashioned Butter Cookies, 277
 Pinwheels and Checkerboards, 276
 Swiss Cinnamon Cookies, 278

Cookies, shaped
 Almond Melting Moments, 275
 Almond Shortbread Cookies, 279
 Any-Way-You-Like'm Cookies, 273
 Chocolate Crackles, 280
 Coconut Thumbprints, 270
 Confetti Cones, 277
 Cream Cheese and Jelly
  Thumbprints, 270
 Easy Peanut Butter Cookies, 273
 Jam Thumbprints, 270
 Jelly Jewels, 279
 Lacy Chocolate Crisps, 278
 Lemon Blossom Cookies, 274
 Lemon Sugar Cookies, 270
 Lollipop Cookies, 276
 Melting Moments, 275
 Peanut Blossoms, 273
 Peanut Butter & Jelly Gems, 273
 Pecan Tassies, 280
 "Philly" Apricot Cookies, 280
 Raisin Oatmeal Crispies, 280
 Thumbprint Cookies, 270
 Walnutty Ribbons, 280
Cookies and Cream Parfaits, 313
Cool and Creamy Cucumber Spread, 11
Cool and Minty Party Cake, 343
Cordon Bleu Rice, 165
Cordon Bleu Sauce, 165
Corn
 Barley with Corn and Red Pepper,
  217
 Cheddar Broccoli Corn Bake, 216
 Corncakes, 222
 Corn Fritters, 220
 Corn-Pepper-Sausage Skillet, 131
 Corn Relish Salad, 65
 Country Corn Bake, 222
 Creamed Corn Chowder, 44
 Fresh Corn Maque Choux, 222
 Sausage Corn Chowder, 57
 Southwestern Egg Puff, 249
Corncakes, 222
Corned Beef & Cabbage Chowder, 58
Corn Fritters, 220
Cornish hens
 Cornish Hens with Chestnut-Sausage
  Stuffing, 160
 Cornish Hens with Oyster Stuffing,
  161
 Glazed Stuffed Cornish Hens, 158
 Grilled Cornish Game Hens, 160
 Grilled Game Hens Texas-Style, 157
 Lemon Herb Cornish Hens, 159
 Oriental Game Hens, 158
 Raisin-Stuffed Cornish Game Hens
  with Apples, 160
 Thai Hens, 159
Cornish Hens with Chestnut-Sausage
 Stuffing, 160
Cornish Hens with Oyster Stuffing,
 161
Cornmeal
 Louisiana Corn Muffins, 256
 Mexican Corn Bread, 266
 Polenta, 131
Corn-Pepper-Sausage Skillet, 131
Corn Relish Salad, 65
Corn-Stuffed Chicken, 148
Cottage Herb Rolls, 269

Country Bean Barbecue, 214
Country Captain, 142
Country Chicken and Peppers, 140
Country Corn Bake, 222
Country French Beef Stew, 104
Country French Cassoulet, 192
Country Paté, 17
Country Pineapple Coleslaw, 68
Country-Style Baked Beans, 216
Country-Style Chicken Dinner, 195
Country-Style Veal, 136
Couscous
Vegetable Couscous, 220
Crab and Rice Primavera, 187
Crabmeat
Crab and Rice Primavera, 187
Crab-Stuffed Trout, 173
Dilled Crab Salad Mold, 89
Flaky Crab Puffs, 26
Hasty Shore Dinner, 202
Hot Crabmeat Appetizer, 12
Layered Crab Spread, 14
Seafood Salad Sandwiches, 242
Crab-Stuffed Trout, 173
Cracked Black Pepper and Herb
Spread, 6
Crackers
Sesame Cheese Crackers, 30
Cranberries
Berry-Bottomed Walnut Pie, 330
Cranberry Crumb Pie, 328
Cranberry Pudding Cake with Sauce,
346
Festive Cranberry Torte, 356
Cranberry Crumb Pie, 328
Cranberry Filling, 330
Cranberry Glazed Pork Roast, 119
Cranberry Muffins and Creamy Orange
Spread, 258
Cranberry Nut Topping, 325
Cranberry Pudding Cake with Sauce,
346
Cranberry-Sausage Stuffing, 163
Cream Cheese and Jelly Thumbprints,
270
Cream Cheese Kugel, 254
Cream Cheese Swirl Coffee Cake, 263
Creamed Corn Chowder, 44
Creamed Turkey Stack-Ups, 169
Creamy Baked Mashed Potatoes, 230
Creamy Baked Onions, 225
Creamy Banana Pudding, 315
Creamy Brownie Frosting, 289
Creamy Chicken Tarragon, 140
Creamy Chili Dip, 9
Creamy Clam Bisque, 57
Creamy Cocoa Taffy, 297
Creamy Dark Chocolate Fudge, 292
Creamy Fettucini Alfredo, 207
Creamy Garden Salad, 74
Creamy Green Beans Almondine, 223
Creamy Hot Chocolate, 37
Creamy Lemon Sherbet, 303
Creamy Lime Sherbet, 303
Creamy Low-Calorie Rice Pudding,
314
Creamy Milk Chocolate Fudge, 292
Creamy Nectarine Mold with
Strawberry Sauce, 70
Creamy Red Potato Salad, 77

Creamy Shrimp 'n Yogurt Salad with
Dill, 91
Creamy Spinach Fettucini, 210
Creamy Tomato Bisque, 48
Creamy Topped Fruit Salad, 75
Creamy Tortellini Primavera, 208
Creamy Turkey & Broccoli, 198
Creamy V8 Dressing, 92
Creamy White Fudge, 290
Create-a-Crust Apple Pie, 324
Crème de Cacao Filling, 359
Crème de Cacao Torte, 359
Creme-Filled Cupcakes, 353
Creme Filling, 272
Creole Chicken Jambalaya, 200
Creole Tartar Sauce, 28
Crepes
Kensington Crepes, 166
Tempting Cheese Crepes, 246
Crisp Onion-Roasted Potatoes, 231
Crispy Bagel Chips, 30
Crispy Fried Mushrooms, 24
Crispy Fried Pork and Apples, 120
Crispy Wontons, 27
Croutons
Kavli Croutons, 46
Crown Roast of Pork with Cognac
Glaze, 121
Crullers, 262
Crunch Bars, 283
Crunchy Almond Chicken Cutlets, 155
Crunchy Clusters, 296
Crunchy Scalloped Celery, 221
Crusts
Almond Crust, 325
Chocolate Cookie Crust, 326
Chocolate Crumb Crust, 332
Chocolate Tart Shells, 336
Cinnamon Graham Cracker Crust,
335
Graham Cracker Crust, 322
Lemon Pastry, 333
Nut Crust, 331
Pastry for Two-Crust Pie, 333
Piecrust, 249
Pie Shell, 331
Single Pie Crust, 333
Cucumbers
Cool and Creamy Cucumber Spread,
11
Cucumber Salad, 69
Refreshing Cucumber Dip, 15
White Gazpacho, 50
Cucumber Salad, 69
Cucumber Sauce, 239
Cupcakes
Black Bottom Cupcakes, 354
Chocolate Butterscotch Chip
Cupcakes, 354
Chocolatetown Cupcakes, 354
Chocolate Zucchini Cupcakes, 352
Creme-Filled Cupcakes, 353
Fudge 'n' Banana Cupcakes, 353
Curried Chicken Puffs, 26
Curried Peanut Dip, 6
Curried Pineapple Pasta Salad, 84
Curried Popcorn Mix, 30
Curried Pork, 123
Curried Smoked Turkey Salad, 85
Curried Zucchini Soup, 50

Curry dishes
Curried Pork, 123
Lamb Curry, 133, 135
Quick Chicken Curry, 150
Turkey Curry, 165

D

Dan D's Chicken BBQ, 141
Death Mix, The, 39
Deep Dish Turkey Pie, 197
Deep-Fried Clams, 185
Delightful Dessert Pancake, 300
Deluxe Chicken Walnut Salad, 82
Desserts, 298–321 (*see also individual
types*)
Acapulco Flan, 298
Almond Creme, 304
Almond-Crumb Peaches, 308
Banana Mocha Layered Dessert, 300
Bananas Foster, 309
Butterscotch Apple Squares, 298
Cheddar Cheese Pears, 309
Cherry-Topped Icebox Cake, 302
Chocolate-Berry Parfaits, 313
Delightful Dessert Pancake, 300
Flaming Pineapple, 309
Fresh Pineapple Melba, 308
Frozen Chocolate Banana Loaf, 305
Frozen Chocolate Graham Cups, 303
Frozen Vanilla Graham Cups, 303
Fruit Crumble, 301
Fruited Chocolate Trifle, 321
Fruit Glazed Baked Custards, 314
Fruit Kabobs with Whiskey Baste,
308
Hawaiian Trifle, 321
Hot Fruit Compote, 309
Mexicana Bread Pudding, 300
Mt. Gretna Chocolate Fondue, 298
Peach Cream Cake, 302
Peaches in Port, 307
Peach Melba Trifle, 321
Peanut Butter Shells with Chocolate-
Almond Cream, 315
Peanut Butter Snacking Cups, 301
Pears au Chocolat, 310
"Philly" Fruit Clouds, 308
Pots de Crème au Chocolat, 302
Raspberry Freeze, 305
Snow Topped Apples, 309
Spiced Lemon Pears, 309
Strawberry-Chocolate Bavarian
Cream, 314
Swedish Apple Cake, 301
Thanksgiving Cranberry Cobbler, 301
Tortoni Squares, 302
Tropical Crisp, 300
Desserts, gelatin, 310–313
Applesauce Yogurt Dessert, 310
Cookies and Cream Parfaits, 313
Fresh Fruit Parfaits, 313
Fruited Fruit Juice Gelatin, 312
Fruited Tilt, 310
Fruit Juice Gelatine Cooler, 311
Fruit Whip, 311
Ice Cream and Orange Dessert, 312
Lime Chiffon Squares, 311

Desserts, gelatin (*continued*)
Molded Strawberries Romanoff, 311
Piña Colada Ring, 312
Self-Layering Dessert, 312
Dessert toppings, 317–318
Ambrosia Topping, 325
Bananas Coco Lopez, 318
Chocolate Custard Sauce, 318
Chocolate Sauce, 310
Coconut Fudge Sauce, 319
Coconut Pecan Sauce, 317
Cranberry Nut Topping, 325
Ginger Mandarin Sauce over Vanilla
Ice Cream, 319
Glazed Strawberry Topping, 325
Hot Fudge Sauce, 317
Microwave Classic Chocolate Sauce,
318
Pecan Topping, 326
Pineapple Orange Dessert Sauce, 318
Sour Cream Topping, 329
Strawberry-Banana Topping, 246
Streusel Topping, 329
Walnut Cream Topping, 330
Deviled Stuffed Eggs, 24
Devilish Daiquiri, 39
Dijon Breaded Pork Chops, 116
Dill Dressing, 65
Dilled Carrots and Parsnips, 219
Dilled Crab Salad Mold, 89
Dilled Salmon Loaf, 180
Dilly Bean Salad, 65
Dips and spreads, 6–17
Bacon-Horseradish Dip, 6
Baked Cream Cheese Appetizer, 8
Blue Cheese Walnut Spread, 8
Chili con Queso, 9
Colorful Carrot Dip, 6
Cool and Creamy Cucumber Spread,
11
Cracked Black Pepper and Herb
Spread, 6
Creamy Chili Dip, 9
Curried Peanut Dip, 6
Eggplant Caviar, 8
Eggplant Spread, 10
Florentine Dip, 12
Garden Vegetable Spread, 12
Garlic Spread, 8
Guacamole, 11
Hawaiian Coconut Spread, 15
Hearty Herbed Cheese Spread, 12
Hot Artichoke Dip, 13
Hot Beef Dip, 13
Hot Chili con Queso, 9
Hot Crabmeat Appetizer, 12
Layered Crab Spread, 14
Lipton Onion Butter, 30
Manhattan Clam Dip, 9
Mexican-Style Appetizer, 13
Molded Cheese, 11
Nutty Blue Cheese Vegetable Dip, 14
Party Cheese Ball, 14
Peppy Bean Dip, 16
Pesto Spread, 29
Piña Pepper Spread, 15
Pineapple-Almond Cheese Spread, 15
Pine Nut Cheese Spread, 14
Quick Mexican Spread, 15
Refreshing Cucumber Dip, 15

Dips and spreads (*continued*)
Roasted Red Pepper Mousse Spread,
16
Salmon Mousse, 16
Savory Cheddar Spread, 15
Shrimp Spread, 16
Spicy Appetizer Dip, 17
Toasted Sesame Cheese Spread, 9
Tropical Fruit Dip, 9
Vegetable Dip Verde, 9
Warm Herb Cheese Spread, 12
Zucchini Chive Dip, 15
Dole's Summer Vegetable Salad, 65
Dorchester Fudge, 290
Double-Braided Saffron Bread, 268
Double-Deck Brownies, 288
Double-Decker Fudge, 291
Double-Dip Chocolate Chunk Cookies,
274
Double Onion Soup Gratinee, 45
Doughnuts
Crullers, 262
French Breakfast Puffs, 261
Glazed Raised Doughnuts, 261
Raised Doughnuts, 261
Drum Layer Cake, 345
Duck
Braised Chinese Duckling, 158
Roasted Duckling with Orange &
Plum Sauce, 159
Spicy Smoked Duck, 157
Dutch Apple Raisin Pie, 324

E

Easy Apple Kuchen, 262
Easy Cheesy Meat Loaf, 112
Easy Chocolate Mousse Pie, 322
Easy German Chocolate Cake, 342
Easy "Hollandaise" Sauce, 234
Easy Peanut Butter Cookies, 273
Easy Pina Colada Cake, 348
Easy Rocky Road, 292
Egg Drop Soup, 51
Eggnog Pie, 322
Eggplant
Eggplant Caviar, 8
Eggplant Parmesan, 202
Eggplant Salad, 67
Eggplant Spread, 10
Fried Eggplant, 222
Eggplant Caviar, 8
Eggplant Parmesan, 202
Eggplant Salad, 67
Eggplant Spread, 10
Eggs
B.L.T.E. Breakfast Pockets, 249
Broccoli-Mushroom Omelet, 255
Cheese-Mushroom Strata, 203
Cheese Strata, 251
Colorful Ham Omelet, 252
Deviled Stuffed Eggs, 24
Egg Salad Magnifique, 239
Eggs Arnold, 252
Fresh Asparagus Soufflé, 253
Frittata Romano, 255
Golden Mini Quiches, 24
Hash-and-Egg Brunch, 253

Eggs (*continued*)
Huevos Rancheros, 253
Party Quiche Squares, 29
"Philly" Brunch Quiche, 246
Phyllo Spinach Pie, 254
Pineapple Brunch Casserole, 252
Quiche Florentine, 248
Sausage-Asparagus Souffle
Sandwiches, 253
Sausage 'n Egg Brunch Special, 254
Sausage Omelet, 254
Savory Sunday Eggs, 255
Souper Easy Quiche, 249
Southwestern Egg Puff, 249
Swiss Chicken Quiche, 248
Turkey and Caper Quiche, 248
Egg Salad Magnifique, 239
Eggs Arnold, 252
Eight Flavors Pot Roast, 96
Elegant Angel Torte, 358
Elegant Chicken Piccata, 142
Elegant Chocolate Mousse, 313
Emperor's Sweet & Sour Fish, 181
Empress Chicken Wings, 26
Enchiladas
Chicken Enchiladas, 195
Ever-So-Easy Fruitcake, 355
Extra-Good Mushroom Cream Soup, 44

F

Fabulous Fish Terrine, 179
Fajitas
Beef Fajitas, 240
Favorite Banana Bread, 266
Favorite Butter Cookies, 277
Festival Shrimp, 185
Festive Chicken Salad, 82
Festive Cookie Bars, 282
Festive Cranberry Torte, 356
Fettucine Alfredo, 206
Fettucine with Roasted Red Pepper
Sauce, 206
Fiery Beef Stir-Fry, 108
Filled New Potatoes, 23
Fire and Ice Chili, 127
Firecracker Salad, 62
Fish, 170–183 (*see also individual
types*)
Almondine Fish, 174
Emperor's Sweet & Sour Fish, 181
Fabulous Fish Terrine, 179
Fisherman's Bouillabaisse, 56
Fisherman's Light Fillets, 178
Ginger Fish Fillets, 179
Grilled Fish Steaks with Vegetable
Butter, 178
Grilled Fish with Salsa, 172
Grilled Oriental Fish Steaks, 176
Halibut Provençale, 180
Herb-Baked Fish & Rice, 201
Lemon Broiled Fish, 181
Lemony Fish Fillets, 172
Oriental Steamed Fish, 175
Pineapple-Tomato Salsa and Fish,
175
Saucy Fish Fillets, 172
Savory Seafood Stew, 189

Fish (*continued*)
Skillet Fish Italiano, 180
So-Easy Fish Divan, 201
Fisherman's Bouillabaisse, 56
Fisherman's Favorite Cioppino Salad, 91
Fisherman's Light Fillets, 178
Fish Rolls with Asparagus, 177
Fish Soup Florentine, 55
Flaky Crab Puffs, 26
Flaky Ham Puffs, 27
Flaming Pineapple, 310
Flank Steak Bearnaise, 100
Florentine Dip, 12
Florentines, 278
Flounder
Fish Rolls with Asparagus, 177
Fish Soup Florentine, 55
Lemony Stuffed Flounder, 181
Tomato-Shrimp Soup, 56
Fluffy Grasshopper Pie, 327
Fluffy Orange Pie, 330
Fondue
Mt. Gretna Chocolate Fondue, 298
Foolproof Dark Chocolate Fudge, 292
Frank and Vegetable Soup, 58
Frankfurters
Bean and Kraut Franks, 130
Chili Dogs, 242
Frank and Vegetable Soup, 58
Two-Bean Franks, 130
French Apple Cake, 340
French Breakfast Puffs, 261
French Dressing, 93
French Green Peas, 225
French Quarter Rice Salad, 85
French-Style Pot Roast, 96
French toast
Mandarin Orange French Toast, 250
Fresh and Creamy Potato Salad, 77
Fresh Asparagus Soufflé, 253
Fresh Corn Maque Choux, 222
Fresh Fruit Parfaits, 313
Fresh 'n Fruity Pops, 297
Fresh Pineapple Melba, 308
Fresh Pineapple Pie, 331
Fresh Spinach Soup, 42
Fresh Strawberry Pie, 332
Fresh Vegetable Ring, 233
Fresh Vegetable Salad, 64
Fried Chicken, 143
Fried Eggplant, 222
Fried Potato Wedges, 229
Frittata Romano, 255
Frosted Toffee Bars, 282
Frostings and icings, 351–352 (*see also* **Glazes**)
Almond Frosting, 279
Almond "Philly" Cream Frosting, 357
Bittersweet Glaze, 352
Chocolate Butter Frosting, 352
Chocolate-Coconut Frosting, 352
Chocolate Cream Cheese Frosting, 351
Chocolate Glaze, 352
Chocolate Icing, 274
Chocolate "Philly" Cream Frosting, 357
Classic Fudge Frosting, 351

Frostings and icings (*continued*)
Coconut-Pecan Filling and Frosting, 344
Continental Flair Frosting, 351
Creamy Brownie Frosting, 289
Kahlúa® Fudge Frosting, 343
Lemon Icing, 288, 351
Powdered Sugar Icing, 267
Quick Chocolate Frosting, 352
Sherry Icing, 355
Silky Mocha Frosting, 347
Vanilla Frosting, 337
Frosty Chocolate Shake, 36
Frozen Chocolate Banana Loaf, 305
Frozen Chocolate Graham Cups, 303
Frozen Margaritas, 39
Frozen Mocha Cheesecake, 307
Frozen Passion, 304
Frozen Peach Cream Pies, 331
Frozen Peanut Butter Pie, 328
Frozen Vanilla Graham Cups, 303
Fruit and Juice Pudding, 317
Fruit & Nut Snack Bars, 285
Fruit Bon Bons, 295
Fruitcake Bars, 355
Fruitcake Cookies, 355
Fruitcake-in-a-Can, 355
Fruitcake Loaves, 355
Fruitcake Mini Loaves, 355
Fruitcakes, 354–355
Chocolate Fruitcake, 355
Ever-So-Easy Fruitcake, 355
Fruitcake-in-a-Can, 355
Fruitcake Loaves, 355
Fruitcake Mini Loaves, 355
Sherried Fruit-Spice Cake, 355
Spicy Walnut Fruitcake, 354
Fruit Crumble, 301
Fruited Chocolate Trifle, 321
Fruited Fruit Juice Gelatin, 312
Fruited Macaroons, 275
Fruited Tilt, 310
Fruit Glazed Baked Custards, 314
Fruit Juice Gelatine Cooler, 311
Fruit Kabobs with Whiskey Baste, 308
Fruit Punch, 36
Fruits (*see also individual types*)
Ambrosia, 75
Autumn Pear 'n Apple Salad, 74
Brandied Fruit Pie, 324
Calypso Shrimp Salad, 91
Cinnamon Fruit Tart with Sour Cream Filling, 335
Creamy Nectarine Mold with Strawberry Sauce, 70
Creamy Topped Fruit Salad, 75
Fresh Fruit Parfaits, 313
Fresh 'n Fruity Pops, 297
Fruit and Juice Pudding, 317
Fruited Chocolate Trifle, 321
Fruited Fruit Juice Gelatin, 312
Fruited Tilt, 310
Fruit Kabobs with Whiskey Baste, 308
Fruit Salad with Orange Almond Dressing, 76
Fruit Salad with Poppy Seed Dressing, 76
Fruit Whip, 311
Hawaiian Trifle, 321

Fruits (*continued*)
Holiday Fruit Salad, 71
Hot Fruit Compote, 309
Indian Fruit Salad, 76
Jungle Bars, 285
Luau Fruit Salad, 76
Mai Tai Compote, 76
Minted Fruit Salad, 75
Old-Fashioned Fruited Rice Pudding, 315
Peach Melba Trifle, 321
"Philly" Fruit Clouds, 308
Piña Colada Ring, 312
Rainbow Fruit Salad, 75
Sparkling Berry Salad, 72
Thanksgiving Cranberry Cobbler, 301
Tropical Crisp, 300
Winter Fruit Bowl, 70
Fruit Salad with Orange Almond Dressing, 76
Fruit Salad with Poppy Seed Dressing, 76
Fruit Whip, 311
Fruity Swirl Coffeecake, 262
Fruity Wine Sauce, 99
Fudge
Butterscotch Fudge, 292
Cherry Fudge, 290
Chocolate-Almond Fudge, 291
Chocolate "Philly" Fudge, 291
Confetti Fudge, 290
Creamy Dark Chocolate Fudge, 292
Creamy Milk Chocolate Fudge, 292
Creamy White Fudge, 290
Dorchester Fudge, 290
Double-Decker Fudge, 291
Easy Rocky Road, 292
Foolproof Dark Chocolate Fudge, 292
Marshmallow-Nut Cocoa Fudge, 290
Mexican Chocolate Fudge, 292
Milk Chocolate Fudge, 292
Mocha Almond Fudge, 290
Nutty Rich Cocoa Fudge, 291
Peanut Butter Fudge, 290, 295
Praline Fudge, 290
Rich Cocoa Fudge, 290
Rum Raisin Fudge, 290
Fudge 'n' Banana Cupcakes, 353
Fudgey Pecan Cake, 347
Fudgy Chocolate Truffles, 293

G

Galbani® Fontina Potato Surprise, 228
Garden Chicken Salad, 84
Garden-Fresh Pitas, 241
Garden Macaroni Salad, 79
Garden Medley Rice, 227
Garden Patch Salad, 88
Garden Vegetable Spread, 12
Garlic Dressing, 93
Garlic Mushrooms, 98
Garlic Spread, 8
Garnishes
green onion brushes, 32
Green Onion Firecracker, 39
Onion & Olive Pick, 39
Gazpacho, 48
Gazpacho Dressing, 69

Gelatin Jiggles, 297
German Beef Roulade, 96
German Chocolate Cake, 344
German-Style Potato Salad, 78
German-Style Pot Roast, 96
Ginger Beef, 108
Gingerbread, 264
Gingerbread People, 276
Ginger Fish Fillets, 179
Ginger Mandarin Sauce over Vanilla
    Ice Cream, 319
Ginger Pineapple Mold, 73
Ginger-Soy Dressing, 92
Gingery Banana Waffles, 250
Glazed Ham Steak, 129
Glazed Pork Roast, 118
Glazed Pork Tenderloin, 124
Glazed Raised Doughnuts, 261
Glazed Strawberry Topping, 325
Glazed Stuffed Cornish Hens, 158
Glazed Turkey Kabobs, 167
Glazes (*see also* **Frostings and
    icings**)
    Bittersweet Glaze, 352
    Chocolate Ganache Glaze, 359
    Chocolate Glaze, 337, 352
    Chocolate Satin Glaze, 352
    Clear Lemon Glaze, 265
    Cocoa Glaze, 340
    Lemon Glaze, 285
    Powdered Sugar Glaze, 354
    Royal Glaze, 351
    Strawberry Glaze, 335
Golden Apple Boston Brown Bread, 265
Golden Cauliflower Soup, 49
Golden Chicken Stir-Fry, 154
Golden Crunch Cake, 346
Golden Fruit Dressing, 92
Golden Fruit Loaves, 264
Golden Gate Grill, 243
Golden Glazed Ham Loaf, 127
Golden Glazed Stuffed Chicken, 147
Golden Mini Quiches, 24
Golden Oatmeal Muffins, 256
Golden Raisin Spice Bread, 264
Golden Salad, 71
Golden Squash Bake, 230
Graham Cracker Crust, 322
Grandpa Snub's Chili, 130
Granola Bars, 279
Granola Cookies, 279
Greek Lemon Soup, 51
Greek-Style Puffy Pancake, 251
Greek-Style Shrimp, 183
Green Beans Napoli, 223
Grill-Baked Sweet Potatoes, 235
Grilled Capon, 146
Grilled Cheese, 24
Grilled Cornish Game Hens, 160
Grilled Curried Chicken, 141
Grilled Fish Steaks with Vegetable
    Butter, 178
Grilled Fish with Salsa, 172
Grilled Flank Steak Sangrita, 99
Grilled Game Hens Texas-Style, 157
Grilled Lobster with Spicy Sauce, 184
Grilled Oriental Fish Steaks, 176
Grilled Oysters, 25
Grilled Salmon Steaks with Watercress
    Sauce, 176

Grilled Sausage with Apples & Onions,
    131
Grilled Smoked Sausage, 133
Grilled Smoked Turkey 'n Muenster
    Sandwiches, 240
Grilled Steak with Mushroom-Wine
    Sauce, 100
Grilled Tenderloin with Cognac, 98
Grilled Tomatoes, 232
Grilled Trout with Two Sauces, 174
Guacamole, 11
Gumbo
    Chicken & Rice Gumbo, 52

H

Haddock
    Vegetable-Stuffed Fish Rolls, 174
Halibut Provençale, 180
Ham, 127–129
    Appetizer Ham Logs, 21
    Asparagus-Ham Roll-Ups, 128
    Baked Ham with Glazed Vegetables,
        129
    Baked Ham with Wine & Onion
        Glaze, 129
    Barbecue Ham Sandwiches, 245
    Chef's Salad, 88
    Chicken and Ham Supreme, 197
    Colorful Ham Omelet, 252
    Confetti Fried Rice, 226
    Country Paté, 17
    Creamy Spinach Fettucini, 210
    Creole Chicken Jambalaya, 200
    Flaky Ham Puffs, 27
    Glazed Ham Steak, 129
    Golden Glazed Ham Loaf, 127
    Ham and Cheese Strata, 190
    Ham and Pea Noodle Soup, 60
    Ham Pasta Primavera, 204
    Ham-Pasta Salad Vinaigrette, 86
    Ham-Sauced Sweet Potatoes, 128
    Ham-Stuffed Peppers, 129
    Ham-Wrapped Oysters, 21
    Holiday Baked Ham, 128
    Jambalaya, 200
    Layered Salad Extraordinaire, 87
    Loaf Sandwiches with Bacon & Ham,
        244
    Mini Monte Cristo Sandwiches, 17
    Pineapple and Ham Pasta Salad, 85
    Pineapple Brunch Casserole, 252
    Pineapple-Glazed Ham and Sweets,
        127
    Pineapple-Orange Glazed Ham, 128
    Rice Pilaf Salad, 80
    Sausage Antipasto Platter, 29
    Shaved Ham Salad, 85
    Souper Easy Quiche, 249
Ham and Cheese Strata, 190
Ham and Pea Noodle Soup, 60
Ham Pasta Primavera, 204
Ham-Pasta Salad Vinaigrette, 86
Ham-Sauced Sweet Potatoes, 128
Ham-Stuffed Peppers, 129
Ham-Wrapped Oysters, 21
Harvest Cherry Pie, 332
Harvest Pork Chops, 115

Harvest Sausage Stuffing, 163
Harvest Vegetable Scallop, 225
Hash-and-Egg Brunch, 253
Hasty Shore Dinner, 202
Hawaiian Coconut Spread, 15
Hawaiian Pork Stew, 126
Hawaiian Roast Pork, 121
Hawaiian Trifle, 321
Hearty Herbed Cheese Spread, 12
Hearty Vegetable Soup, 57
Hell-Fire Crispy Balls, 31
Herb Appetizer Cheesecake, 19
Herb-Baked Fish & Rice, 201
Herbed Buttermilk Dressing, 93
Herbed Cheese Pinwheel Canapes, 18
Herbed Mussels in Wine, 28
Herbed Pork Sauté, 126
Herb-Marinated Pork Roast, 118
Herb-Roasted Chicken, 148
Hershey's™ Great American Chocolate
    Chip Cookies, 273
Holiday Baked Ham, 128
Holiday Fruit Salad, 71
Homespun Scalloped Potatoes, 226
Homestyle Zucchini & Tomatoes, 214
Honey-Apple Dressing, 93
Honey Dressing for Fruit, 93
Honey-Lemon Muffins, 256
Honey-Lime Vinaigrette, 75
Honey-Mustard Beef Ribs, 108
Horseradish Cream, 74
Hot & Sour Soup, 51
Hot and Sour Soup, 58
Hot & Spicy Glazed Carrots, 220
Hot Artichoke Dip, 13
Hot Beef Dip, 13
Hot Buttered Pineapple Smoothie, 38
Hot Chicken Salad, 81
Hot Chili con Queso, 9
Hot Chocolate Soufflé, 320
Hot Cocoa Mix, 37
Hot Crabmeat Appetizer, 12
Hot Cranberry Cider, 38
Hot Fruit Compote, 309
Hot Fudge Sauce, 317
Hot Maple Toddy, 41
Hot Mulled Pineapple Juice, 37
Hot Potato Salad, 77
Hot Spiced Lemonade, 38
Hot Tomato Sipper, 32
Huevos Rancheros, 253
Hunan Pork Stir-Fry, 120
Hunan Stir-Fry with Tofu, 132

I

Ice Cream and Orange Dessert, 312
Ice creams
    Banana Bonanza Ice Cream, 305
    Cinnamon Walnut Pudding Ice
        Cream, 304
    Creamy Lemon Sherbet, 303
    Creamy Lime Sherbet, 303
    Frozen Passion, 304
    Melon Sorbet Cooler, 304
    Pudding Ice Cream, 304
    Rocky Road Pudding Ice Cream, 304
    Rum Raisin Pudding Ice Cream, 304

Ice creams (*continued*)
    Sparkling Lemon-Lime Sorbet, 303
    Toffee Crunch Pudding Ice Cream, 304
    Very Berry Sorbet, 303
Ice Ring, 40
Impossible Lemon Pie, 327
Impossible Pie, 327
Indian Fruit Salad, 76
Individual Fudge Soufflés, 320
Individual Taco Salads, 86
Islander's Beef Barbecue, 96
Island Fruit Cooler, 34
Italian Chicken, 145
Italian Pasta Salad, 79
Italian Pepperoni Puffs, 260
Italian-Style Cauliflower Salad, 67
Italian-Style Pot Roast, 96
Italian-Style Roasted Peppers, 226
Italian-Style Salisbury Steaks, 111
Italian Vegetable Sauté, 235
Italian Vegetable Soup, 46

J

Jade & Ruby Stir-Fry, 153
Jamaican Sweet Buns, 261
Jambalaya, 200
Jam Thumbprints, 270
Jelly Jewels, 279
Jungle Bars, 285

K

Kabobs
    Barbecued Sausage Kabobs, 130
    Chicken-Vegetable Kabobs, 151
    Fruit Kabobs with Whiskey Baste, 308
    Glazed Turkey Kabobs, 167
    Grilled Sausage with Apples & Onions, 131
    Lime Kabobs Polynesian, 108
    Marinated Kabobs, 134
    Miniature Teriyaki Pork Kabobs, 23
    Oriental Steak Kabobs, 107
    Seafood Kabobs, 185
    Skewered Vegetables, 232
    Tandoori-Style Chicken Kabobs, 151
Kahlúa® Fudge Frosting, 343
Kahlúa® Sweetheart Cake, 343
Kamaaina Spareribs, 125
Kavli Croutons, 46
Kensington Crepes, 166
Kentucky Jam Cake, 348
Kris Kringle Cookies, 277

L

Lacy Chocolate Crisps, 278
Lamb, 132–135
    Aegean Lamb Stew, 135
    American-Style Cassoulet, 193
    Apricot-Stuffed Lamb Chops, 133
    Basque Lamb, 135

Lamb (*continued*)
    Lamb Chops with Lemony Apple Glaze, 134
    Lamb Curry, 133, 135
    Lamb Pilaf, 134
    Lamb Stew, 132
    Lemon and Garlic Lamb Chops, 134
    Marinated Kabobs, 134
    Roasted Leg of Lamb with Lemon-Rosemary Glaze, 132
    Western Lamb Riblets, 132
Lamb Chops with Lemony Apple Glaze, 134
Lamb Curry, 133, 135
Lamb Pilaf, 134
Lamb Stew, 132
Lasagna
    Lasagna Deliciousa, 213
    Lasagna with White and Red Sauces, 213
    Souper Quick "Lasagna," 212
    Tortilla Lasagna, 192
Lasagna Deliciousa, 213
Lasagna with White and Red Sauces, 213
Layered Carrot-Pineapple Salad, 73
Layered Chicken Salad, 83
Layered Crab Spread, 14
Layered Mint Chocolate Candy, 295
Layered Peach Salad, 73
Layered Picnic Club Sandwich, 239
Layered Salad Extraordinaire, 87
Layered Seafood Quiche, 200
Lebkuchen Jewels, 285
Leeks with Bel Paese®, 219
Lemon
    Impossible Lemon Pie, 327
    Old-Fashioned Lemon Pudding Cake, 349
    ReaLemon Meringue Pie, 322
Lemonade
    Hot Spiced Lemonade, 38
    Lemonade Syrup Base, 35
    Low Calorie Lemonade, 35
Lemonade Syrup Base, 35
Lemon and Garlic Lamb Chops, 134
Lemon Blossom Cookies, 274
Lemon Bread, 265
Lemon Broiled Fish, 181
Lemon Chicken, 155
Lemon Cream, 358
Lemon Cream Almond Torte, 358
Lemon-Dill Lobster Tails, 187
Lemon Glaze, 285
Lemon Herb Cornish Hens, 159
Lemon Herbed Chicken, 142
Lemon Iced Ambrosia Bars, 288
Lemon Icing, 288, 351
Lemon-Mustard Dressing, 89
Lemon Orange Carrots, 219
Lemon Pastry, 333
Lemon Pecan Bars, 281
Lemon Sugar Cookies, 270
Lemon Swordfish, 182
Lemon Tea Muffins, 259
Lemon Tea Sparkler, 34
Lemon Toddy, 41
Lemony Chicken Mold, 83
Lemony Fish Fillets, 172
Lemony Light Cooler, 40

Lemony Low Cal Dressing, 93
Lemony Raisin-Coconut Squares, 289
Lemony Stuffed Flounder, 181
Lentil and Brown Rice Soup, 42
Lentil-Pasta Soup, 47
Lentils
    Lentil and Brown Rice Soup, 42
    Sausage and Lentil Soup, 61
Lettuce and Chicken Soup, 52
Lickety-Split Cocoa Cake, 343
Light and Lively Turkey Soup, 54
Lime Chiffon Squares, 311
Lime Kabobs Polynesian, 108
Linguine Tuna Salad, 91
Linguine with Red Seafood Sauce, 206
Lipton Onion Burgers, 241
Lipton Onion Butter, 30
Liver (*see also* **Chicken livers**)
    Liver and Onions, 101
    Smothered Liver and Onions, 101
Liver and Onions, 101
Loaf Sandwiches with Bacon & Ham, 244
Lobster
    Grilled Lobster with Spicy Sauce, 184
    Lemon-Dill Lobster Tails, 187
Lollipop Cookies, 276
Louisiana Beans and Rice, 227
Louisiana Corn Muffins, 256
Low-Calorie Dressing, 82
Low Calorie Lemonade, 35
Luau Fruit Salad, 76
Lynn's Salad, 64

M

Macaroon Almond Crumb Bars, 281
Magic Cookie Bars, 284
Mai Tai Compote, 76
Mandarin Orange French Toast, 250
Mandarin Pork Chops, 116
Manhattan Clam Dip, 9
Marble Chiffon Cake, 340
Marble Squares, 287
Margarita Pie, 328
Marinated Antipasto, 22
Marinated Beef Salad, 85
Marinated Flank Steak, 102
Marinated Kabobs, 134
Marinated Mushrooms, 22
Marinated Oriental Beef Salad, 87
Marinated Potato and Mushroom Salad, 77
Marinated Shrimp & Vegetables, 90
Marinated Tomatoes & Cucumbers, 64
Marinated Vegetables, 69
Marshmallow-Nut Cocoa Fudge, 290
Meatballs
    Cantonese Meatballs, 25
    Mini Cocktail Meatballs, 26
    Split Pea and Meatball Soup, 57
Meatball Stew, 114
Meat loaf
    All-American Meat Loaf, 113
    Easy Cheesy Meat Loaf, 112
    Golden Glazed Ham Loaf, 127
    Meat Loaf Italiano, 110
    Meat Loaf Supreme, 112

Meat loaf (*continued*)
Mexican Meatloaf Roll, 112
Mini Meat Loaves, 112
Zesty Meat Loaf, 111
Meat Loaf Italiano, 110
Meat Loaf Supreme, 112
Meat 'n' Tater Pie, 190
Meatza Pizzas, 113
Mediterranean Orange and Red Onion Salad, 72
Mediterranean Pasta, 211
Melon
Melon Sorbet Cooler, 304
Melon Wedges, 71
Minted Melon Mold, 73
Melon Citrus Cooler, 39
Melon Sorbet Cooler, 304
Melon Wedges, 71
Melting Moments, 275
Mexicana Bread Pudding, 300
Mexican Beef Stew, 104
Mexican Chicken with Spicy Bacon, 147
Mexican Chocolate Fudge, 292
Mexican Cocoa Torte, 358
Mexican Corn Bread, 266
Mexican Fried Rice, 188
Mexican Meatloaf Roll, 112
Mexican Sauce, 175
Mexican Shrimp Cocktail, 18
Mexican-Style Appetizer, 13
Mexican Style Tuna Loaf, 175
Mexican Tossed Salad, 68
Microwave Classic Chocolate Sauce, 318
Microwave cooking times, 5
Microwave Hershey Bar Mousse, 313
Microwave Hershey Bar Pie, 332
Microwave Hot Cocoa, 37
Microwave recipes
Albóndingas Soup, 59
Almond-Crumb Peaches, 308
Apple-Cheese Soup, 54
Apple-Raisin Stuffed Chicken Breasts, 149
Asparagus-Ham Roll-Ups, 128
Baked Stuffed Clams, 20
Baked Stuffed Shrimp, 20
Bananas Coco Lopez, 318
Barbecued Spareribs, 125
Barbecue Ham Sandwiches, 245
Bavarian Pea Soup, 51
Bean and Kraut Franks, 130
Beef Ragoût, 106
Beef Stroganoff, 102
Blushing Onions, 225
Blushing Onion Soup, 45
Broccoli and Celery Oriental, 219
Brunswick Stew, 145
Bullshot, 37
Butterscotch Fudge, 292
Cajun-Style Chicken Nuggets, 26
California Bisque, 44
Cheese-Stuffed Beef Rolls, 194
Cheesy Pork Chops 'n Potatoes, 192
Cherry Fudge, 290
Chicken Adobo, 145
Chicken and Ham Supreme, 197
Chicken Breasts Florentine, 151
Chicken-Corn Soup Santa Fe, 52

Microwave recipes (*continued*)
Chicken Enchiladas, 195
Chicken Liver Pâté, 10
Chicken Marinated with Orange & Tarragon, 143
Chicken 'n Vegetable Stir Fry, 157
Chicken Roma, 143
Chicken Wings with Honey & Orange Sauce, 23
Chicken with Oriental Dipping Sauce, 10
Chili Beef and Corn Casserole, 193
Chili Burritos, 243
Chili Dogs, 242
Chipper Peanut Candy, 296
Chocolate Crackles, 280
Chocolate Crumb Crust, 332
Citrus Candied Sweet Potatoes, 235
Coconut Fudge Sauce, 319
Coconut Pecan Sauce, 317
Colorful Ham Omelet, 252
Confetti Fudge, 290
cooking times, 5
Corned Beef & Cabbage Chowder, 58
Country Captain, 142
Country Paté, 17
Country-Style Baked Beans, 216
Cream Cheese Kugel, 254
Creamy Baked Mashed Potatoes, 230
Creamy Chicken Tarragon, 140
Creamy Dark Chocolate Fudge, 292
Creamy Hot Chocolate, 37
Creamy Milk Chocolate Fudge, 292
Creamy Tortellini Primavera, 208
Creamy Turkey & Broccoli, 198
Creamy White Fudge, 290
Crunchy Clusters, 296
Curried Zucchini Soup, 50
Dilled Carrots and Parsnips, 219
Dilled Salmon Loaf, 180
Double Onion Soup Gratinee, 45
Easy "Hollandaise" Sauce, 234
Easy Rocky Road, 292
Egg Drop Soup, 51
Eggplant Parmesan, 202
Emperor's Sweet & Sour Fish, 181
Extra-Good Mushroom Cream Soup, 44
Fabulous Fish Terrine, 179
Foolproof Dark Chocolate Fudge, 292
French-Style Pot Roast, 96
Fresh Spinach Soup, 42
Fresh Vegetable Ring, 233
Fruit and Juice Pudding, 317
Fruit Crumble, 301
Fudgy Chocolate Truffles, 293
Garden Chicken Salad, 84
Garden Medley Rice, 227
German-Style Pot Roast, 96
Ginger Beef, 108
Glazed Pork Roast, 118
Glazed Stuffed Cornish Hens, 158
Golden Glazed Ham Loaf, 127
Golden Glazed Stuffed Chicken, 147
Greek Lemon Soup, 51
Grilled Fish Steaks with Vegetable Butter, 178
Ham-Sauced Sweet Potatoes, 128
Harvest Vegetable Scallop, 225
Hash-and-Egg Brunch, 253

Microwave recipes (*continued*)
Hasty Shore Dinner, 202
Herb-Baked Fish & Rice, 201
Homestyle Zucchini & Tomatoes, 214
Hot Artichoke Dip, 13
Hot Chicken Salad, 81
Hot Fudge Sauce, 317
Hot Maple Toddy, 41
Hot Spiced Lemonade, 38
Hot Tomato Sipper, 32
Italian Chicken, 145
Italian-Style Pot Roast, 96
Lamb Curry, 133, 135
Lamb Stew, 132
Lemon Toddy, 41
Lemony Stuffed Flounder, 181
Lentil and Brown Rice Soup, 42
Lentil-Pasta Soup, 47
Lettuce and Chicken Soup, 52
Linguine with Red Seafood Sauce, 206
Lipton Onion Burgers, 241
Louisiana Beans and Rice, 227
Louisiana Corn Muffins, 256
Meatza Pizzas, 113
Mexican Chocolate Fudge, 292
Mexican Sauce, 175
Mexican Style Tuna Loaf, 175
Microwave Classic Chocolate Sauce, 318
Microwave Hershey Bar Mousse, 313
Microwave Hershey Bar Pie, 332
Microwave Hot Cocoa, 37
Milk Chocolate Fudge, 292
Mulled Cider, 41
Mushroom-Stuffed Chicken Breasts, 154
Nouvelle Fettucini, 209
Okra-Bacon Casserole, 224
Old-Fashioned Pot Roast, 96
Oriental Game Hens, 158
Oriental Pork, 122
Oriental Vegetable Soup, 44
Original Green Bean Casserole, 223
Oven-Baked Bourguignonne, 104
Paella Olé, 188
Party Scramble, 31
Pasta with Clam Sauce, 212
Pasta with Vegetables, 204
Peach Melba Pancakes, 251
Peanut Butter Fudge, 295
Peanut Butter Logs, 295
Peanutty Chocolate Snack Squares, 287
Pecan-Stuffed Squash, 230
Pennsylvania Dutch Chow Chow, 64
Picadillo-Stuffed Peppers, 113
Pineapple-Glazed Ham and Sweets, 127
Poached Sole with Dill Sauce, 178
Pork Chops and Sauerkraut, 116
Potato and Cheese Casserole, 227
Praline Fudge, 290
Quick Chicken Curry, 150
Quick 'n Easy Tacos, 245
Raisin-Stuffed Cornish Game Hens with Apples, 160
Red Cabbage 'n' Apples, 217
Rolled Chicken Breasts Florentine, 150

Microwave recipes (*continued*)
Rum Raisin Fudge, 290
Salmon Steaks in Dill Sauce, 170
Santa Fe Pasta, 207
Saucy Fish Fillets, 172
Saucy Garden Patch Vegetables, 231
Savory Cheddar Spread, 15
Seafood Cacciatore, 184
Seafood Creole, 176
Simmered Sherry Bouillon, 41
Skillet Fish Italiano, 180
Sloppy Joes, 244
Smothered Liver and Onions, 101
Snow Topped Apples, 309
Souper Pot Roast, 97
Souper Quick "Lasagna," 212
Southern Tomato-Bean Soup, 46
Spiced Lemon Pears, 309
Spicy Warmer, 37
Spinach and Noodles Parmesan, 209
Sunny Fries, 228
Superb Fillet of Sole & Vegetables, 202
Swiss Vegetable Medley, 233
Tangy Blue Cheese Vegetables, 233
Tex-Mex Rice and Beans, 229
Tomato Soup Spice Cake, 338
Tortellini in Cream Sauce, 204
Traditional Gravy, 162
Tuna-Pasta Casserole, 201
Turkey Cottage Pie, 196
Turkey Divan, 195
Two-Bean Franks, 130
Veal Stew, 137
Vegetables in Cheese Sauce, 218
Vegetable-Stuffed Fish Rolls, 174
Vegetable-Stuffed Flank Steak, 101
Vegetable Sunburst, 232
Warm Bean Salad, 68
Warm Herb Cheese Spread, 12
Zesty Barbecued Ribs, 124
Zesty Meat Loaf, 111
Middle East Pita Pockets, 242
Milk Chocolate Bourbon Balls, 295
Milk Chocolate Chip Cookies, 273
Milk Chocolate Fudge, 292
Milk shakes
Banana-Orange Shake, 32
Banana Shake, 32
Frosty Chocolate Shake, 36
Passion Shakes, 304
Quick Banana Malt, 35
Quick Wink Breakfast Drink, 35
Strawberry-Banana Shake, 32
Minestrone, 47
Miniature Cheesecakes, 306
Miniature Cream Puffs, 337
Miniature Teriyaki Pork Kabobs, 23
Mini Cocktail Meatballs, 26
Mini Fruit Cheese Tarts, 334
Mini Meat Loaves, 112
Mini Monte Cristo Sandwiches, 17
Minted Fruit Salad, 75
Minted Melon Mold, 73
Minty Chocolate Squares, 287
Mocha Almond Fudge, 290
Mocha Fudge Pudding Cake, 347
Moist Orange Mince Muffins, 259
Molasses Muffins, 259
Molded Cheese, 11

Molded Strawberries Romanoff, 311
Mongolian Almonds, 31
Mongolian Beef, 98
Mongolian Pot, 152
Moo Goo Gai Pan, 153
Mousses
Elegant Chocolate Mousse, 313
Microwave Hershey Bar Mousse, 313
Quick Chocolate Mousse, 314
Mt. Gretna Chocolate Fondue, 298
Muffin Pan Snacks, 71
Muffins, 256–259
Blueberry Muffins, 258
Cranberry Muffins and Creamy
Orange Spread, 258
Golden Oatmeal Muffins, 256
Honey-Lemon Muffins, 256
Lemon Tea Muffins, 259
Louisiana Corn Muffins, 256
Moist Orange Mince Muffins, 259
Molasses Muffins, 259
Orange Raisin Muffins, 259
Treasure Bran Muffins, 259
Walnut Streusel Muffins, 258
Mulled Cider, 41
Mushroom & Pepper Stuffed Chops, 117
Mushrooms
Crispy Fried Mushrooms, 24
Extra-Good Mushroom Cream Soup, 44
Garlic Mushrooms, 98
Marinated Mushrooms, 22
"Philly" Stuffed Mushrooms, 25
Mushroom-Stuffed Chicken Breasts, 154
Mussel Rice Soup, 56
Mussels
Herbed Mussels in Wine, 28
Mussel Rice Soup, 56
safe to eat, 28
Seafood over Angel Hair Pasta, 208
Steamed Mussels in White Wine, 182
Mustard Glazed Sausage with Sauteed
Cabbage, 131
Mustard Sauce, 16

N

Napoleons, 336
Neapolitan Pizza, 238
Neapolitan Sauce, 212
Neapolitan Vegetable Mold, 71
New England Style Turkey Chowder, 53
New Orleans Crumb Cake, 350
New Year Fried Rice, 227
No-Bake Pumpkin Pie, 329
Northwest Cheesecake Supreme, 306
Norwegian Pea Soup, 46
Nouvelle Fettucini, 209
Nut Crust, 331
Nut Macaroons, 275
Nutritional analysis information, 5
Nuts
Almondine Butter Sauce, 234
Baked Almond Pudding, 317
Berry-Bottomed Walnut Pie, 330
Caramel Peanut Balls, 296
Caribbean Fudge Pie, 325
Carrot Nut Pudding, 220

Nuts (*continued*)
Chess Pie, 330
Chocolate Coconut Pecan Torte, 359
Chocolate Fruitcake, 355
Chocolate Pecan Critters, 294
Confetti Cones, 277
Curried Popcorn Mix, 30
Ever-So-Easy Fruitcake, 355
Fruitcake Bars, 355
Fruitcake Cookies, 355
Fruitcake-in-a-Can, 355
Fruitcake Loaves, 355
Fruitcake Mini Loaves, 355
Fudgey Pecan Cake, 347
Mongolian Almonds, 31
Nut Macaroons, 275
Pecan Tassies, 280
Peppered Pecans, 31
Sherried Fruit-Spice Cake, 355
Simply Superb Pecan Pie, 330
Spiced Apple Party Mix, 30
Spicy Walnut Fruitcake, 354
Sweet Potato Pecan Pie, 326
Swiss Cinnamon Cookies, 278
Walnut Streusel Muffins, 258
Walnutty Ribbons, 280
Nutty Blue Cheese Vegetable Dip, 14
Nutty Burgers, 243
Nutty Rich Cocoa Fudge, 291

O

Oatmeal Dinner Rolls, 269
Oatmeal Griddlecakes, 250
Oats
Apple Crumb Squares, 286
Apple Raisin Snack Bars, 284
Chocolate 'n' Oat Bars, 282
Frosted Toffee Bars, 282
Golden Oatmeal Muffins, 256
Granola Bars, 279
Granola Cookies, 279
Oatmeal Dinner Rolls, 269
Oatmeal Griddlecakes, 250
Raisin Oatmeal Crispies, 280
Raspberry Oatmeal Bars, 285
Octoberfest Sausage Soup, 60
Okra
Okra-Bacon Casserole, 224
Southern-Style Squash and Okra, 230
Okra-Bacon Casserole, 224
Old-Fashioned Apple Loaf, 265
Old-Fashioned Bread Stuffing, 163
Old-Fashioned Butter Cookies, 277
Old-Fashioned Chicken Pot Pie, 196
Old-Fashioned Fruited Rice Pudding, 315
Old-Fashioned Lemon Pudding Cake, 349
Old-Fashioned Pot Roast, 96
Old-Fashioned Rice Pudding, 315
Omelets
Broccoli-Mushroom Omelet, 255
Colorful Ham Omelet, 252
Frittata Romano, 255
Sausage Omelet, 254
Onion-Buttered Popcorn, 31
Onion-Glazed Carrots, 219

Onion Green Goddess Dressing, 93
Onion Party Puffs, 30
Onion Rings, 224
Onions
  Blushing Onions, 225
  Blushing Onion Soup, 45
  Creamy Baked Onions, 225
  Double Onion Soup Gratinee, 45
  Onion Rings, 224
Open House Ribbon Torte, 357
Orange Almond Dressing, 76
Orange-Cashew Chicken, 157
Orange Corn Bread, 162
Orange-Flavored Grilled Beef, 106
Orange-Honey Chicken, 143
Orange 'n Vanilla Mousse Pie, 328
Orange Raisin Muffins, 259
Oranges
  Fluffy Orange Pie, 330
  Ginger Mandarin Sauce over Vanilla
    Ice Cream, 319
  Mediterranean Orange and Red
    Onion Salad, 72
  Orange 'n Vanilla Mousse Pie, 328
Orange Tea Punch, 36
Orange Wake-Up Cake, 263
Oriental Game Hens, 158
Oriental Pork, 122
Oriental Pork Chops, 117
Oriental Steak Kabobs, 107
Oriental Steamed Fish, 175
Oriental Turkey Terrine, 168
Oriental Vegetable Soup, 44
Original Green Bean Casserole, 223
Orloff Rice, 166
Orloff Sauce, 166
Outdoor grilling
  Bacon-Wrapped Shrimp, 188
  Bacon-Wrapped Tuna, 170
  Barbecued Garlic, 221
  Barbecued Pork Leg, 117
  Barbecued Sausage Kabobs, 130
  Barbecued Shrimp on a Skewer, 186
  Barbecued Turkey with Herbs, 164
  Basque Lamb, 135
  Beef Fajitas, 240
  Beer Marinated Steak, 100
  Cajun Fish, 183
  Cheddar Cheese Pears, 309
  Chicken Kyoto, 145
  Chicken-Vegetable Kabobs, 151
  Cider-Glazed Pork Roast, 118
  Corn-Pepper-Sausage Skillet, 131
  Corn-Stuffed Chicken, 148
  Crab-Stuffed Trout, 173
  Dan D's Chicken BBQ, 141
  Flaming Pineapple, 310
  Garlic Mushrooms, 98
  Grill-Baked Sweet Potatoes, 235
  Grilled Capon, 146
  Grilled Cheese, 24
  Grilled Cornish Game Hens, 160
  Grilled Curried Chicken, 141
  Grilled Fish with Salsa, 172
  Grilled Flank Steak Sangrita, 99
  Grilled Game Hens Texas-Style, 157
  Grilled Lobster with Spicy Sauce, 184
  Grilled Oysters, 25
  Grilled Sausage with Apples &
    Onions, 131

Outdoor grilling (*continued*)
  Grilled Smoked Sausage, 133
  Grilled Steak with Mushroom-Wine
    Sauce, 100
  Grilled Tenderloin with Cognac, 98
  Grilled Tomatoes, 232
  Grilled Trout with Two Sauces, 174
  Honey-Mustard Beef Ribs, 108
  Islander's Beef Barbecue, 96
  Lemon-Dill Lobster Tails, 187
  Lemon Herb Cornish Hens, 159
  Lemon Herbed Chicken, 142
  Lemon Swordfish, 182
  Lipton Onion Burgers, 241
  Mexican Chicken with Spicy Bacon,
    147
  Nutty Burgers, 243
  Orange-Flavored Grilled Beef, 106
  Oriental Game Hens, 158
  Oriental Pork Chops, 117
  Oriental Steak Kabobs, 107
  Pacific Coast Barbecued Salmon, 177
  Parmesan Seasoned Turkey, 164
  Peaches in Port, 307
  Pepper-Stuffed Flank Steak, 99
  Peppery Rib Steaks, 99
  Satay Pork, 122
  Savory Steak, 100
  Seafood Kabobs, 185
  Skewered Vegetables, 232
  Southern-Style Squash and Okra, 230
  Spicy Country Ribs, 124
  Spicy Orange Chicken, 141
  Steak with Hearty Mustard
    Marinade, 99
  Stuffed Cheese Burgers, 244
  Sweet & Sour Pork Loin, 122
  Sweet and Spicy Chicken Barbecue,
    146
  Sweet Jalapeno Ribs, 125
  Tandoori-Style Chicken Kabobs, 151
  Tequila-Orange Chicken, 146
  Texas-Style Steak on Hot Bread, 245
  Turkey Fillets in Spicy Cilantro
    Marinade, 168
  Western Lamb Riblets, 132
Oven-Baked Bourguignonne, 104
Oven-Baked Buttermilk Chicken, 138
Oven Barbecued Chicken, 144
Oysters
  Grilled Oysters, 25
  Ham-Wrapped Oysters, 21
Oyster Stuffing, 164

P

Pacific Coast Barbecued Salmon, 177
Pacific Salad, 91
Paella Olé, 188
Pancakes
  Creamed Turkey Stack-Ups, 169
  Delightful Dessert Pancake, 300
  Greek-Style Puffy Pancake, 251
  Oatmeal Griddlecakes, 250
  Peach Melba Pancakes, 251
  Potato Pancakes, 226
  Puffy Pancake, 251
Paradise Pasta, 209

Paradise Pumpkin Pie, 329
Parmesan Dressing, 93
Parmesan Seasoned Turkey, 164
Parsnips
  Dilled Carrots and Parsnips, 219
Party Cheese Ball, 14
Party Mai Tais, 38
Party Pizza, 238
Party Quiche Squares, 29
Party Scramble, 31
Passion Shakes, 304
Pasta, 204–213 (*see also* **Lasagna**)
  Broccoli and Pasta, 218
  Chilled Rigatoni Salad, 79
  Chinese Noodle Cakes, 187
  Creamy Fettucini Alfredo, 207
  Creamy Spinach Fettucini, 210
  Creamy Tortellini Primavera, 208
  Curried Pineapple Pasta Salad, 84
  Fettucine Alfredo, 206
  Fettucine with Roasted Red Pepper
    Sauce, 206
  Garden Macaroni Salad, 79
  Ham Pasta Primavera, 204
  Ham-Pasta Salad Vinaigrette, 86
  Italian Pasta Salad, 79
  Linguine with Red Seafood Sauce,
    206
  Mediterranean Pasta, 211
  Nouvelle Fettucini, 209
  Paradise Pasta, 209
  Pasta Primavera, 211
  Pasta Vegetable Medley, 78
  Pasta with Clam Sauce, 212
  Pasta with Vegetables, 204
  Peanut Noodles, 211
  Potluck Pasta Salad, 78
  Salad Taverna, 88
  Santa Fe Pasta, 207
  Seafood over Angel Hair Pasta,
    208
  Sea Salad, 89
  Shrimp Milano, 208
  Smoked Sausage Stuffed Pasta
    Shells, 206
  Smoky Macaroni and Cheese, 203
  Spaghetti Mediterranean, 210
  Spaghetti with Cream Sauce, 210
  Spinach and Noodles Parmesan,
    209
  Summer Spaghetti, 210
  Tagliatelle with Creamy Sauce, 212
  Tortellini in Cream Sauce, 204
  Tortellini Soup, 48
Pasta Primavera, 211
Pasta sauces
  Neapolitan Sauce, 212
  Pesto, 207
Pasta Vegetable Medley, 78
Pasta with Clam Sauce, 212
Pasta with Vegetables, 204
Pastries
  Chocolate-Filled Cream Puffs, 337
  Curried Chicken Puffs, 26
  Miniature Cream Puffs, 337
  Napoleons, 336
  "Philly" Cream Puff Ring, 336
  Strawberry and Cream Napoleons,
    335
Pastry for Two-Crust Pie, 333

Paté
Chicken Liver Pâté, 10
Country Paté, 17
Quick Paté Mold, 10
Paul Bunyan Sticky Buns, 260
Peach Cream Cake, 302
Peaches
Almond-Crumb Peaches, 308
Frozen Peach Cream Pies, 331
Layered Peach Salad, 73
Peach Cream Cake, 302
Peaches in Port, 307
Peach Surprise Pie, 327
Peachy Mince Pie with Cheddar Crust, 333
Peaches in Port, 307
Peach Melba Pancakes, 251
Peach Melba Trifle, 321
Peach Surprise Pie, 327
Peachy Mince Pie with Cheddar Crust, 333
Peanut Blossoms, 273
Peanut butter
Any-Way-You-Like'm Cookies, 273
Buckeyes, 294
Chipper Peanut Candy, 296
Curried Peanut Dip, 6
Double-Decker Fudge, 291
Easy Peanut Butter Cookies, 273
Frozen Peanut Butter Pie, 328
Peanut Blossoms, 273
Peanut Butter & Jelly Gems, 273
Peanut Butter Fudge, 290, 295
Peanut Butter Logs, 295
Peanut Butter Paisley Brownies, 288
Peanut Butter Poke Cake, 349
Peanut Butter Shells with Chocolate-Almond Cream, 315
Peanut Butter Snacking Cups, 301
Peanut Noodles, 211
Peanutty Chocolate Snack Squares, 287
Reese's Chewy Chocolate Cookies, 272
Reese's Cookies, 281
Peanut Butter & Jelly Gems, 273
Peanut Butter Fudge, 290, 295
Peanut Butter Logs, 295
Peanut Butter Paisley Brownies, 288
Peanut Butter Poke Cake, 349
Peanut Butter Shells with Chocolate-Almond Cream, 315
Peanut Butter Snacking Cups, 301
Peanut Noodles, 211
Peanutty Chocolate Snack Squares, 287
Pears
Cheddar Cheese Pears, 309
Pears au Chocolat, 310
Spiced Lemon Pears, 309
Pears au Chocolat, 310
Peas
American-Style Cassoulet, 193
French Green Peas, 225
Norwegian Pea Soup, 46
Split Pea and Meatball Soup, 57
Pecan Pie Bars, 283
Pecan-Stuffed Squash, 230
Pecan Tassies, 280
Pecan Topping, 326
Pennsylvania Dutch Chow Chow, 64
Peppered Pecans, 31

Peppers
Barley with Corn and Red Pepper, 217
Fettucine with Roasted Red Pepper Sauce, 206
Fresh Corn Maque Choux, 222
Ham-Stuffed Peppers, 129
Italian-Style Roasted Peppers, 226
Pork Steaks with Peppers, 133
Roasted Red Pepper Mousse Spread, 16
roasting, 229
Sausage and Peppers, 131
Spanish Stuffed Bell Peppers, 180
Pepper-Stuffed Flank Steak, 99
Peppery Rib Steaks, 99
Peppy Bean Dip, 16
Pesto, 207
Pesto Spread, 29
Petits Fours, 342
"Philly" Apricot Cookies, 280
"Philly" Banana Pudding, 316
"Philly" Brunch Quiche, 246
"Philly" Cream Puff Ring, 336
"Philly" Fruit Clouds, 308
"Philly" Stuffed Mushrooms, 25
Phyllo Spinach Pie, 254
Picadillo-Stuffed Peppers, 113
Piecrust, 249
Pies, 322–334 (*see also* **Crusts; Pastries; Tarts**)
Almond Ginger Ice Cream Pie, 325
Apple Chess Pie, 324
Banana Layered Pie, 326
Banana Mocha Ice Cream Pie, 326
Berry-Bottomed Walnut Pie, 330
Brandied Fruit Pie, 324
Caribbean Fudge Pie, 325
Cherry Cheese Pie, 325
Chess Pie, 330
Chocolate Turtle Pie, 327
Classic Banana Cream Pie, 326
Classic Meringue Pie, 331
Coconut Custard Pie, 334
Cranberry Crumb Pie, 328
Create-a-Crust Apple Pie, 324
Dutch Apple Raisin Pie, 324
Easy Chocolate Mousse Pie, 322
Eggnog Pie, 322
Fluffy Grasshopper Pie, 327
Fluffy Orange Pie, 330
Fresh Pineapple Pie, 331
Fresh Strawberry Pie, 332
Frozen Peach Cream Pies, 331
Frozen Peanut Butter Pie, 328
Harvest Cherry Pie, 332
Impossible Lemon Pie, 327
Impossible Pie, 327
Margarita Pie, 328
Microwave Hershey Bar Pie, 332
No-Bake Pumpkin Pie, 329
Orange 'n Vanilla Mousse Pie, 328
Paradise Pumpkin Pie, 329
Peach Surprise Pie, 327
Peachy Mince Pie with Cheddar Crust, 333
Plum Pudding Pie, 334
Praline Ice Cream Pudding Pie, 332
Raisin Sour Cream Pie, 334
ReaLemon Meringue Pie, 322

Pies (*continued*)
Simply Superb Pecan Pie, 330
Sweet Potato Pecan Pie, 326
Traditional Pumpkin Pie, 329
Pie Shell, 331
Piña Colada, 38
Piña Colada Cheesecake, 306
Pina Colada Punch, 40
Piña Colada Ring, 312
Piña Pepper Spread, 15
Piñata Salad, 69
Pineapple
Almond Ginger Ice Cream Pie, 325
Carrot Pineapple Salad, 75
Curried Pineapple Pasta Salad, 84
Flaming Pineapple, 310
Fresh Pineapple Melba, 308
Fresh Pineapple Pie, 331
Ginger Pineapple Mold, 73
Layered Carrot-Pineapple Salad, 73
Mai Tai Compote, 76
Piña Colada Cheesecake, 306
Piña Pepper Spread, 15
Pineapple-Almond Cheese Spread, 15
Pineapple and Ham Pasta Salad, 85
Pineapple Brunch Casserole, 252
Pineapple Juice Cubes, 34
Pineapple Orange Dessert Sauce, 318
pineapple shells, to make, 82
Pineapple Upside-Down Cake, 347
Spicy Appetizer Dip, 17
Turkey Pineapple Salad, 82
Pineapple-Almond Cheese Spread, 15
Pineapple and Ham Pasta Salad, 85
Pineapple Brunch Casserole, 252
Pineapple Citrus Glazed Pork Roast, 120
Pineapple Dream Bars, 286
Pineapple-Glazed Ham and Sweets, 127
Pineapple Juice Cubes, 34
Pineapple Lime Dressing, 75
Pineapple Margarita, 38
Pineapple Mint Tulip, 34
Pineapple Orange Dessert Sauce, 318
Pineapple-Orange Glazed Ham, 128
Pineapple Orange Slush, 36
Pineapple Passion, 34
Pineapple Pizza, 239
Pineapple-Tomato Salsa and Fish, 175
Pineapple Upside-Down Cake, 347
Pine Nut Cheese Spread, 14
Pinwheels and Checkerboards, 276
Pizza, 236–238
Breakfast Pizza, 249
Classic Pizza, 236
Neapolitan Pizza, 238
Party Pizza, 238
Pineapple Pizza, 239
Pizza Bread Pronto, 236
Thick 'n Cheesy Vegetable Pizza, 238
Pizza Bread Pronto, 236
Planter's Punch, 40
Plum Pudding Pie, 334
Poached Red Snapper, 176
Poached Sole with Dill Sauce, 178
Polenta, 131
Popcorn
Curried Popcorn Mix, 30
Onion-Buttered Popcorn, 31

Pork, 114–126 (see also **Ham; Pork chops; Sausage; Spareribs**)
American-Style Cassoulet, 193
Barbecued Pork Leg, 117
Cashew Pork Stir-Fry, 122
Cider-Glazed Pork Roast, 118
Colorful Stir-Fried Pork, 121
Country French Cassoulet, 192
Cranberry Glazed Pork Roast, 119
Crispy Wontons, 27
Crown Roast of Pork with Cognac Glaze, 121
Curried Pork, 123
Fire and Ice Chili, 127
Glazed Pork Roast, 118
Glazed Pork Tenderloin, 124
Golden Glazed Ham Loaf, 127
Grandpa Snub's Chili, 130
Hawaiian Pork Stew, 126
Hawaiian Roast Pork, 121
Herbed Pork Sauté, 126
Herb-Marinated Pork Roast, 118
Hot and Sour Soup, 58
Hunan Pork Stir-Fry, 120
Hunan Stir-Fry with Tofu, 132
Miniature Teriyaki Pork Kabobs, 23
Oriental Pork, 122
Pineapple Citrus Glazed Pork Roast, 120
Pork and Peanut Stir-Fry, 123
pork loin roast, to butterfly, 119
Pork Roast with Corn Bread & Oyster Stuffing, 118
Pork Roast with Sausage & Spinach Stuffing, 119
Pork Steaks with Peppers, 133
Roast Loin of Pork Oriental-Style, 123
Satay Pork, 122
Sopa de Sonora, 58
Spring Rolls, 25
Stuffed Cabbage Leaves, 126
Sweet-and-Sour Pork, 123
Sweet & Sour Pork Loin, 122
Tasty Pork Ragout, 119
Tofu & Vegetable Stir-Fry, 120
Pork and Peanut Stir-Fry, 123
Pork chops, 114–117
Caribbean Pork Chops, 114
Cheesy Pork Chops 'n Potatoes, 192
Crispy Fried Pork and Apples, 120
Dijon Breaded Pork Chops, 116
Harvest Pork Chops, 115
Mandarin Pork Chops, 116
Mushroom & Pepper Stuffed Chops, 117
Oriental Pork Chops, 117
Pork Chops and Sauerkraut, 116
Pork Chops Roma, 115
Pork Chops with Browned Garlic-Butter Sauce, 114
Pork Chops with Sweet Red Peppers, 116
Sweet and Sour Pork Chops, 115
Pork Chops and Sauerkraut, 116
Pork Chops Roma, 115
Pork Chops with Browned Garlic-Butter Sauce, 114
Pork Chops with Sweet Red Peppers, 116

Pork Roast with Corn Bread & Oyster Stuffing, 118
Pork Roast with Sausage & Spinach Stuffing, 119
Pork Steaks with Peppers, 133
Potato and Cheese Casserole, 227
Potatoes
Bacon & Egg Potato Salad, 77
Cheese & Bacon Potato Bake, 228
Cheesy Potato Skins, 19
Creamy Baked Mashed Potatoes, 230
Creamy Red Potato Salad, 77
Crisp Onion-Roasted Potatoes, 231
Filled New Potatoes, 23
Fresh and Creamy Potato Salad, 77
Fried Potato Wedges, 229
Galbani® Fontina Potato Surprise, 228
German-Style Potato Salad, 78
Hash-and-Egg Brunch, 253
Homespun Scalloped Potatoes, 226
Hot Potato Salad, 77
Marinated Potato and Mushroom Salad, 77
Potato and Cheese Casserole, 227
Potato Pancakes, 226
Potato-Tuna Salad, 89
Sausage 'n Egg Brunch Special, 254
Skillet Potatoes, 229
Spinach-Potato Soup, 50
Sunny Fries, 228
Zesty Potato Salad, 78
Potato Pancakes, 226
Potato-Tuna Salad, 89
Potluck Pasta Salad, 78
Pot roast
Chuckwagon Roast and Vegetables, 97
Eight Flavors Pot Roast, 96
French-Style Pot Roast, 96
German-Style Pot Roast, 96
Italian-Style Pot Roast, 96
Old-Fashioned Pot Roast, 96
Sauerbraten, 103
Souper Pot Roast, 97
Pots de Crème au Chocolat, 302
Poultry: see individual types
Pound Cake, 338
Powdered Sugar Glaze, 354
Powdered Sugar Icing, 267
Praline Fudge, 290
Praline Ice Cream Pudding Pie, 332
Pronto Zucchini, 234
Pudding Ice Cream, 304
Pudding in a Cloud, 316
Pudding Poke Cake, 349
Puddings
Baked Almond Pudding, 317
Chocolate Cream Pudding, 318
Creamy Banana Pudding, 315
Creamy Low-Calorie Rice Pudding, 314
Fruit and Juice Pudding, 317
Old-Fashioned Fruited Rice Pudding, 315
Old-Fashioned Rice Pudding, 315
"Philly" Banana Pudding, 316
Pudding in a Cloud, 316
Pudding Tart-in-a-Dish, 316

Puddings (continued)
Pudding Tortoni, 317
Quick Coffee Fluff, 316
Pudding Tart-in-a-Dish, 316
Pudding Tortoni, 317
Puffy Pancake, 251
Pumpkin
No-Bake Pumpkin Pie, 329
Paradise Pumpkin Pie, 329
Pumpkin Cheesecake Bars, 286
Pumpkin Nut Bread, 266
Traditional Pumpkin Pie, 329
Pumpkin Cheesecake Bars, 286
Pumpkin Nut Bread, 266
Punches
Champagne Sherbet Punch, 40
Christmas Carol Punch, 36
Fruit Punch, 36
Orange Tea Punch, 36
Pina Colada Punch, 40
Planter's Punch, 40
Rosé Wine Cooler, 40
Sparkling Harvest Cider, 36
Tropical Cream Punch, 37
Volcano Punch, 36

Q

Quiche Florentine, 248
Quiches
Golden Mini Quiches, 24
Layered Seafood Quiche, 200
Party Quiche Squares, 29
"Philly" Brunch Quiche, 246
Quiche Florentine, 248
Savory Onion Cheese Tart, 248
Souper Easy Quiche, 249
Swiss Chicken Quiche, 248
Turkey and Caper Quiche, 248
Quick and Easy Tuna Rice with Peas, 175
Quick Banana Malt, 35
Quick Chicken Curry, 150
Quick Chocolate Frosting, 352
Quick Chocolate Mousse, 314
Quick Coffee Fluff, 316
Quick Deli Turkey Soup, 53
Quick Mexican Spread, 15
Quick 'n Easy Tacos, 245
Quick Paté Mold, 10
Quick Pudding Chip Cookies, 274
Quick Pudding Cookies, 274
Quick Wink Breakfast Drink, 35

R

Rainbow Fruit Salad, 75
Raised Doughnuts, 261
Raisin Macaroons, 275
Raisin Oatmeal Crispies, 280
Raisins
Black-Eyed Susans, 273
Chess Pie, 330
Cinnamon-Raisin Swirl Loaf, 267
Dutch Apple Raisin Pie, 324
Golden Raisin Spice Bread, 264

Raisins (*continued*)
Kris Kringle Cookies, 277
Mexicana Bread Pudding, 300
Raisin Macaroons, 275
Raisin Oatmeal Crispies, 280
Raisin Scones, 258
Raisin Sour Cream Pie, 334
Raisin Scones, 258
Raisin Sour Cream Pie, 334
Raisin-Stuffed Cornish Game Hens
with Apples, 160
Raspberries
Fresh Pineapple Melba, 308
Raspberry Freeze, 305
Scandinavian Raspberry Soup, 54
Raspberry Freeze, 305
Raspberry Fudge Balls, 290
Raspberry Oatmeal Bars, 285
ReaLemon Meringue Pie, 322
Red Cabbage 'n' Apples, 217
Red-Cooked Short Ribs, 107
Reese's Chewy Chocolate Cookies, 272
Reese's Cookies, 281
Refreshing Cucumber Dip, 15
Relishes
Corn Relish Salad, 65
Warm Dried Fruit Compote, 121
Rice
Beef and Wild Rice Casserole, 194
Brazilian Beans and Rice, 113
Broccoli and Rice with Walnuts, 216
Cajun Dirty Rice, 227
Classic Spanish Rice, 228
Confetti Fried Rice, 226
Cordon Bleu Rice, 165
Crab and Rice Primavera, 187
Creamy Low-Calorie Rice Pudding,
314
French Quarter Rice Salad, 85
Garden Medley Rice, 227
Lamb Pilaf, 134
Louisiana Beans and Rice, 227
Mexican Fried Rice, 188
New Year Fried Rice, 227
Old-Fashioned Fruited Rice Pudding,
315
Old-Fashioned Rice Pudding, 315
Orloff Rice, 166
Paella Olé, 188
Quick and Easy Tuna Rice with Peas,
175
Rice Pilaf Salad, 80
Risotto with Vegetables, 229
South-of-the-Border Salad, 80
Stuffed Tomatoes, 232
Tandoori Rice, 151
Tex-Mex Rice and Beans, 229
Three Bean Rice Salad, 79
Wild Rice and Seafood Salad, 89
Wild Rice Salad, 80
Rice Pilaf Salad, 80
Rich Cocoa Fudge, 290
Rich Lemon Bars, 281
Risotto with Vegetables, 229
Roasted Dill Chicken, 147
Roasted Duckling with Orange & Plum
Sauce, 159
Roasted Leg of Lamb with Lemon-
Rosemary Glaze, 132
Roasted Red Pepper Mousse Spread, 16

Roast Loin of Pork Oriental-Style, 123
Rocky Road Pudding Ice Cream, 304
Rolled Chicken Breasts Florentine,
150
Rolls
Cottage Herb Rolls, 269
Oatmeal Dinner Rolls, 269
Rosé Wine Cooler, 40
Rosy Blue Cheese Dressing, 92
Rouladen, 94
Royal Glaze, 351
Rumaki, 22
Rum-Nut Pudding Cake, 348
Rum Raisin Fudge, 290
Rum Raisin Pudding Ice Cream, 304

S

Salada di Antipasto, 88
Salad dressings, 92–93
Banana Chutney Dressing, 91
Blue Cheese Dressing, 93
Celery Seed Dressing, 92
Chile Dressing, 69
Coconut Cream Dressing, 73
Creamy V8 Dressing, 92
Dill Dressing, 65
French Dressing, 93
Garlic Dressing, 93
Gazpacho Dressing, 69
Ginger-Soy Dressing, 92
Golden Fruit Dressing, 92
Herbed Buttermilk Dressing, 93
Honey-Apple Dressing, 93
Honey Dressing for Fruit, 93
Honey-Lime Vinaigrette, 75
Horseradish Cream, 74
Lemon-Mustard Dressing, 89
Lemony Low Cal Dressing, 93
Low-Calorie Dressing, 82
Onion Green Goddess Dressing, 93
Orange Almond Dressing, 76
Parmesan Dressing, 93
Pineapple Lime Dressing, 75
Rosy Blue Cheese Dressing, 92
Vinaigrette Dressing, 93
Yogurt Dressing, 90
Zesty Dressing, 68
Salads, 62–93 (*see also* **Coleslaw;**
Salads, fruit; Salads, gelatin;
Salads, main-dish; Salads, pasta;
Salads, potato; Salads, rice;
Salads, vegetable)
Cheese and Red Bean Salad, 62
Tabbouleh, 80
Salads, fruit, 75–76
Ambrosia, 75
Carrot Pineapple Salad, 75
Creamy Topped Fruit Salad, 75
Fruit Salad with Orange Almond
Dressing, 76
Fruit Salad with Poppy Seed
Dressing, 76
Indian Fruit Salad, 76
Luau Fruit Salad, 76
Mai Tai Compote, 76
Minted Fruit Salad, 75
Rainbow Fruit Salad, 75

Salads, gelatin, 70–74
Apple & Tarragon Salad with
Watercress, 83
Autumn Pear 'n Apple Salad, 74
Buffet Slaw, 72
Cherry Waldorf Gelatin, 70
Clam & Tomato Molded Salad, 72
Classic Tomato Aspic, 70
Creamy Garden Salad, 74
Creamy Nectarine Mold with
Strawberry Sauce, 70
Creamy Shrimp 'n Yogurt Salad with
Dill, 91
Dilled Crab Salad Mold, 89
Ginger Pineapple Mold, 73
Golden Salad, 71
Holiday Fruit Salad, 71
Layered Carrot-Pineapple Salad, 73
Layered Peach Salad, 73
Lemony Chicken Mold, 83
Mediterranean Orange and Red
Onion Salad, 72
Melon Wedges, 71
Minted Melon Mold, 73
Muffin Pan Snacks, 71
Neapolitan Vegetable Mold, 71
Snack Cups, 70
Sparkling Berry Salad, 72
Tomato-Garden Aspic with
Horseradish Cream, 74
Winter Fruit Bowl, 70
Salads, main-dish, 81–91
Apple & Tarragon Salad with
Watercress, 83
Calypso Shrimp Salad, 91
Cantonese Chicken Salad, 81
Cashew-Shrimp Salad, 90
Chef's Salad, 88
Chicken Salad Supreme, 81
Cobb Salad, 81
Confetti Beef Salad, 85
Creamy Shrimp 'n Yogurt Salad with
Dill, 91
Curried Pineapple Pasta Salad, 84
Curried Smoked Turkey Salad, 85
Deluxe Chicken Walnut Salad, 82
Dilled Crab Salad Mold, 89
Egg Salad Magnifique, 239
Festive Chicken Salad, 82
Fisherman's Favorite Cioppino Salad,
91
French Quarter Rice Salad, 85
Garden Chicken Salad, 84
Garden Patch Salad, 88
Ham-Pasta Salad Vinaigrette, 86
Hot Chicken Salad, 81
Individual Taco Salads, 86
Layered Chicken Salad, 83
Layered Salad Extraordinaire, 87
Lemony Chicken Mold, 83
Linguine Tuna Salad, 91
Marinated Beef Salad, 85
Marinated Oriental Beef Salad, 87
Marinated Shrimp & Vegetables, 90
Pacific Salad, 91
Pineapple and Ham Pasta Salad, 85
Potato-Tuna Salad, 89
Salada di Antipasto, 88
Salad Taverna, 88
Seafood Salad Sandwiches, 242

Salads, main-dish (*continued*)
Sea Salad, 89
Shaved Ham Salad, 85
Stay Slim Salad, 82
Steak Salad in Red-Wine Dressing, 86
Summer Kielbasa Salad, 87
Tuna & Cracked Wheat Salad, 90
Turkey Pineapple Salad, 82
Turkey Salad with Pita Bread, 84
Waldorf Chicken Salad, 82
Wild Rice and Seafood Salad, 89
Salads, pasta, 78–79
Chilled Rigatoni Salad, 79
Curried Pineapple Pasta Salad, 84
Garden Macaroni Salad, 79
Ham-Pasta Salad Vinaigrette, 86
Italian Pasta Salad, 79
Pasta Vegetable Medley, 78
Potluck Pasta Salad, 78
Salad Taverna, 88
Sea Salad, 89
Salads, potato, 77–78
Bacon & Egg Potato Salad, 77
Creamy Red Potato Salad, 77
Fresh and Creamy Potato Salad, 77
German-Style Potato Salad, 78
Hot Potato Salad, 77
Marinated Potato and Mushroom Salad, 77
Potato-Tuna Salad, 89
Zesty Potato Salad, 78
Salads, rice, 79–80
French Quarter Rice Salad, 85
Rice Pilaf Salad, 80
South-of-the-Border Salad, 80
Three Bean Rice Salad, 79
Wild Rice and Seafood Salad, 89
Wild Rice Salad, 80
Salads, vegetable, 62–69 (*see also* **Coleslaw**)
Bean Sprout & Spinach Salad, 65
Citrus, Avocado & Bacon Salad, 66
Classic Spinach Salad, 62
Corn Relish Salad, 65
Cucumber Salad, 69
Dilly Bean Salad, 65
Dole's Summer Vegetable Salad, 65
Eggplant Salad, 67
Firecracker Salad, 62
Fresh Vegetable Salad, 64
Italian-Style Cauliflower Salad, 67
Lynn's Salad, 64
Marinated Tomatoes & Cucumbers, 64
Marinated Vegetables, 69
Mexican Tossed Salad, 68
Pennsylvania Dutch Chow Chow, 64
Piñata Salad, 69
Salada di Antipasto, 88
Simple Salad Élégante, 65
Spinach Salad, 68
Spinach Salad with Raspberry Dressing, 66
Sprout-Green Bean Salad, 67
Tomato and Onion Salad, 62
Warm Bean Salad, 68
Watercress-Carrot Salad, 67
Zesty Mushroom Salad, 67
Salad Taverna, 88

Salmon
Dilled Salmon Loaf, 180
Grilled Salmon Steaks with Watercress Sauce, 176
Pacific Coast Barbecued Salmon, 177
Salmon Canapes, 27
Salmon Cheese Puff Pies, 182
Salmon Mousse, 16
Salmon Steaks in Dill Sauce, 170
Salmon Steaks with Cucumber Sauce, 177
Salmon Canapes, 27
Salmon Cheese Puff Pies, 182
Salmon Mousse, 16
Salmon Steaks in Dill Sauce, 170
Salmon Steaks with Cucumber Sauce, 177
Sam's Mop Sauce, 117
Sandwiches, 239–245
Arizona's 7-Layer Taco Sandwich, 241
Avocado & Bacon Pitas, 244
Barbecue Ham Sandwiches, 245
Bacon & Chicken Sandwiches, 240
Beef and Bean Chimichangas, 240
Beef Fajitas, 240
B.L.T.E. Breakfast Pockets, 249
California Classic, The, 245
Chili Burritos, 243
Chili Dogs, 242
Egg Salad Magnifique, 239
Garden-Fresh Pitas, 241
Golden Gate Grill, 243
Grilled Smoked Turkey 'n Muenster Sandwiches, 240
Layered Picnic Club Sandwich, 239
Lipton Onion Burgers, 241
Loaf Sandwiches with Bacon & Ham, 244
Middle East Pita Pockets, 242
Mini Monte Cristo Sandwiches, 17
Nutty Burgers, 243
Quick 'n Easy Tacos, 245
Santa Monica Sandwich, 243
Seafood Salad Sandwiches, 242
Sloppy Joes, 244
Stuffed Cheese Burgers, 244
Texas-Style Steak on Hot Bread, 245
Turkey Cranberry Croissant, 241
Turkey-Topped Biscuits, 242
Vegetarian Sandwiches, 239
Santa Fe Pasta, 207
Santa Monica Sandwich, 243
Satay Pork, 122
Sauces (*see also* **Dessert toppings**)
Almondine Butter Sauce, 234
Avocado Sauce, 243
Bearnaise Sauce, 165
Béchamel Sauce, 213
Browned Garlic-Butter Sauce, 114
Cordon Bleu Sauce, 165
Creole Tartar Sauce, 28
Cucumber Sauce, 239
Easy "Hollandaise" Sauce, 234
Fruity Wine Sauce, 99
Mexican Sauce, 175
Mustard Sauce, 16
Orloff Sauce, 166
Sam's Mop Sauce, 117
Sesame Vegetable Topping, 234
Spiced Currant Sauce, 164

Sauces (*continued*)
Tangy Cocktail Sauce, 186
Tarragon Cream Sauce, 174
Traditional Gravy, 162
Walnut Butter Sauce, 174
Saucy Fish Fillets, 172
Saucy Garden Patch Vegetables, 231
Saucy Shrimp over Chinese Noodle Cakes, 187
Sauerbraten, 103
Sauerkraut
Bean and Kraut Franks, 130
Pork Chops and Sauerkraut, 116
Sausage
Barbecued Sausage Kabobs, 130
Brazilian Beans and Rice, 113
Breakfast Pizza, 249
Corn-Pepper-Sausage Skillet, 131
Country Chicken and Peppers, 140
Country French Cassoulet, 192
Creole Chicken Jambalaya, 200
Garden Patch Salad, 88
German-Style Potato Salad, 78
Grilled Sausage with Apples & Onions, 131
Grilled Smoked Sausage, 133
Lasagna Deliciousa, 213
Mediterranean Pasta, 211
Mini Meat Loaves, 112
Mustard Glazed Sausage with Sauteed Cabbage, 131
Octoberfest Sausage Soup, 60
Party Pizza, 238
Pineapple Pizza, 239
Pizza Bread Pronto, 236
Sausage and Lentil Soup, 61
Sausage and Peppers, 131
Sausage Antipasto Platter, 29
Sausage-Asparagus Souffle Sandwiches, 253
Sausage-Chicken Creole, 199
Sausage Corn Chowder, 57
Sausage 'n Egg Brunch Special, 254
Sausage Omelet, 254
Savory Sunday Eggs, 255
Smoked Sausage Noodle Bake, 190
Smoked Sausage Stuffed Pasta Shells, 206
Summer Kielbasa Salad, 87
Turkey Cassoulet, 198
Two-Bean Chili, 110
Vermont Vegetable Stew, 60
Sausage and Lentil Soup, 61
Sausage and Peppers, 131
Sausage Antipasto Platter, 29
Sausage-Asparagus Souffle Sandwiches, 253
Sausage-Chicken Creole, 199
Sausage Corn Chowder, 57
Sausage 'n Egg Brunch Special, 254
Sausage Omelet, 254
Sauteed Chicken Livers, 144
Savory Bubble Cheese Bread, 268
Savory Cheddar Spread, 15
Savory Corn Bread Stuffing, 163
Savory Onion Cheese Tart, 248
Savory Seafood Stew, 189
Savory Steak, 100
Savory Sunday Eggs, 255
Scalloped Turkey, 196

Scallops
Linguine with Red Seafood Sauce, 206
Scallops with Golden Cream Sauce, 186
Seafood Kabobs, 185
Seafood over Angel Hair Pasta, 208
Stir-Fried Scallops & Vegetables, 188
Scallops with Golden Cream Sauce, 186
Scandinavian Raspberry Soup, 54
Scones
Raisin Scones, 258
Scrumptious Chocolate Layer Bars, 288
Seafood: *see* **Fish; Shellfish;**
individual types
Seafood Bisque, 56
Seafood Cacciatore, 184
Seafood Cocktails with Watercress Sauce, 28
Seafood Creole, 176
Seafood Kabobs, 185
Seafood over Angel Hair Pasta, 208
Seafood Salad Sandwiches, 242
Sea Salad, 89
Seaside Mary, 39
Self-Layering Dessert, 312
Sesame Broccoli, 217
Sesame Cheese Crackers, 30
Sesame Vegetable Topping, 234
Seven Layer Magic Cookie Bars, 284
Shanghai Chicken, 189
Shanghai Shrimp, 189
Shanghai Turkey Stir-Fry, 167
Shantung Chicken, 149
Shaved Ham Salad, 85
Shellfish (*see also individual types*)
Fisherman's Bouillabaisse, 56
Fisherman's Favorite Cioppino Salad, 91
Savory Seafood Stew, 189
Seafood Bisque, 56
Seafood Cocktails with Watercress Sauce, 28
Sherried Fruit-Spice Cake, 355
Sherry Icing, 355
Shrimp
Bacon-Wrapped Shrimp, 188
Baked Stuffed Shrimp, 20
Barbecued Shrimp on a Skewer, 186
Beer-Batter Shrimp, 28, 185
Calypso Shrimp Salad, 91
Cashew-Shrimp Salad, 90
Creamy Shrimp 'n Yogurt Salad with Dill, 91
Festival Shrimp, 185
Greek-Style Shrimp, 183
Hasty Shore Dinner, 202
Jambalaya, 200
Linguine with Red Seafood Sauce, 206
Marinated Antipasto, 22
Marinated Shrimp & Vegetables, 90
Mexican Shrimp Cocktail, 18
Pacific Salad, 91
Paella Olé, 188
Saucy Shrimp over Chinese Noodle Cakes, 187
Seafood Cacciatore, 184
Seafood Kabobs, 185
Seafood over Angel Hair Pasta, 208
Sea Salad, 89

Shrimp (*continued*)
Shanghai Shrimp, 189
Shrimp & Mushroom Stuffed Sole, 170
Shrimp & Vegetable Stir-Fry, 189
Shrimp Bisque Orleans, 55
Shrimp Creole, 186
Shrimp Creole Soup, 55
Shrimp Etouffée, 187
Shrimp Milano, 208
Shrimp Oriental, 184
Shrimp Scampi Italiano, 188
Shrimp Spread, 16
Skillet Seafood Bisque, 55
Tomato-Shrimp Soup, 56
Wild Rice and Seafood Salad, 89
Shrimp & Mushroom Stuffed Sole, 170
Shrimp & Vegetable Stir-Fry, 189
Shrimp Bisque Orleans, 55
Shrimp Creole, 186
Shrimp Creole Soup, 55
Shrimp Etouffée, 187
Shrimp Milano, 208
Shrimp Oriental, 184
Shrimp Scampi Italiano, 188
Shrimp Spread, 16
Silky Mocha Frosting, 347
Simmered Beef and Vegetables, 105
Simmered Sherry Bouillon, 41
Simple Salad Élégante, 65
Simply Superb Pecan Pie, 330
Single Pie Crust, 333
Skewered Vegetables, 232
Skillet Fish Italiano, 180
Skillet Potatoes, 229
Skillet Seafood Bisque, 55
Slice 'n' Bake Lemon Cookies, 279
Sloppy Joes, 244
Smoked Sausage Noodle Bake, 190
Smoked Sausage Stuffed Pasta Shells, 206
Smoky Macaroni and Cheese, 203
Smothered Liver and Onions, 101
Snack Cups, 70
Snacks
Coconut Granola Snack, 292
Crispy Bagel Chips, 30
Curried Popcorn Mix, 30
Fresh 'n Fruity Pops, 297
Gelatin Jiggles, 297
Hell-Fire Crispy Balls, 31
Mongolian Almonds, 31
Onion-Buttered Popcorn, 31
Onion Party Puffs, 30
Party Scramble, 31
Peppered Pecans, 31
Sesame Cheese Crackers, 30
Spiced Apple Party Mix, 30
Toasty Onion Sticks, 30
Snapper
Cajun Fish, 183
Poached Red Snapper, 176
Seafood Creole, 176
Snow Topped Apples, 309
Soda Bread, 264
So-Easy Fish Divan, 201
Sole
Poached Sole with Dill Sauce, 178
Shrimp & Mushroom Stuffed Sole, 170

Sole (*continued*)
Superb Fillet of Sole & Vegetables, 202
Teriyaki Fish Fillets, 173
Sopa de Sonora, 58
Souffles
Black Russian Mini Soufflés, 319
Chilly Strawberry Souffles, 320
collars for, making, 319
Fresh Asparagus Soufflé, 253
Hot Chocolate Soufflé, 320
Individual Fudge Souffles, 320
Toasted Almond Souffle, 319
Souper Easy Quiche, 249
Souper Pot Roast, 97
Souper Quick "Lasagna," 212
Soups, 42–61 (*see also* **Chowders; Gumbo; Soups, cold**)
Albóndigas Soup, 59
Apple-Cheese Soup, 54
Bavarian Pea Soup, 51
Beefy Vegetable Soup, 59
Black Bean Soup with Rice and Sherry, 50
BLT Soup, 60
Blushing Onion Soup, 45
Borscht, 47
Broccoli Cheese Soup, 46
California Bisque, 44
Chicken and Pasta Soup, 53
Chicken-Corn Soup Santa Fe, 52
Chicken Noodle Soup, 53
Chicken-Vegetable Soup, 52
Chili Soup Jarlsberg, 61
Chunky Beef Barley Soup, 61
Clear Japanese Soup, 45
Clear Vegetable Soup, 49
Creamy Clam Bisque, 57
Creamy Tomato Soup, 48
Double Onion Soup Gratinee, 45
Egg Drop Soup, 51
Extra-Good Mushroom Cream Soup, 44
Fisherman's Bouillabaisse, 56
Fish Soup Florentine, 55
Frank and Vegetable Soup, 58
Fresh Spinach Soup, 42
Golden Cauliflower Soup, 49
Greek Lemon Soup, 51
Ham and Pea Noodle Soup, 60
Hearty Vegetable Soup, 57
Hot & Sour Soup, 51
Hot and Sour Soup, 58
Italian Vegetable Soup, 46
Lentil and Brown Rice Soup, 42
Lentil-Pasta Soup, 47
Lettuce and Chicken Soup, 52
Light and Lively Turkey Soup, 54
Minestrone, 47
Mussel Rice Soup, 56
Norwegian Pea Soup, 46
Octoberfest Sausage Soup, 60
Oriental Vegetable Soup, 44
Quick Deli Turkey Soup, 53
Sausage and Lentil Soup, 61
Seafood Bisque, 56
Shrimp Bisque Orleans, 55
Shrimp Creole Soup, 55
Skillet Seafood Bisque, 55
Sopa de Sonora, 58

Soups (*continued*)
Southern Tomato-Bean Soup, 46
Spinach-Potato Soup, 50
Spinach-Rice Soup, 42
Split Pea and Meatball Soup, 57
Tomato-Shrimp Soup, 56
Tortellini Soup, 48
Tortilla Soup, 49
Turkey-Barley Soup, 54
Turkey Vegetable Soup, 53
Two-Bean Soup, 49
Vermont Vegetable Stew, 60
Wisconsin Cheese 'n Beer Soup, 48
Soups, cold
Chilled Carrot Soup, 45
Curried Zucchini Soup, 50
Gazpacho, 48
Scandinavian Raspberry Soup, 54
White Gazpacho, 50
Sour Cream Topping, 329
Southern Hush Puppies, 260
Southern-Style Squash and Okra, 230
Southern Tomato-Bean Soup, 46
South-of-the-Border Salad, 80
Southwestern Egg Puff, 249
Spaghetti Mediterranean, 210
Spaghetti with Cream Sauce, 210
Spanish Stuffed Bell Peppers, 180
Spareribs
Bake & Glaze Teri Ribs, 125
Barbecued Spareribs, 125
Chinese-Style Spareribs, 125
Kamaaina Spareribs, 125
Spicy Country Ribs, 124
Sweet Jalapeno Ribs, 125
Zesty Barbecued Ribs, 124
Sparkling Berry Salad, 72
Sparkling Harvest Cider, 36
Sparkling Lemon-Lime Sorbet, 303
Sparkling V8, 35
Special Lemony Chicken, 148
Spiced Apple Party Mix, 30
Spiced Currant Sauce, 164
Spiced Lemon Pears, 309
Spiced Red Cabbage, 218
Spiced Tea, 38
Spicy Appetizer Dip, 17
Spicy Bean Toss, 224
Spicy Country Ribs, 124
Spicy Orange Chicken, 141
Spicy Smoked Duck, 157
Spicy Vegetable Stir-Fry, 235
Spicy Walnut Fruitcake, 354
Spicy Warmer, 37
Spinach
Bean Sprout & Spinach Salad, 65
Chinese Spinach, 231
Classic Spinach Salad, 62
Florentine Dip, 12
Fresh Spinach Soup, 42
Neapolitan Vegetable Mold, 71
Phyllo Spinach Pie, 254
Quiche Florentine, 248
Spinach Almond Casserole, 231
Spinach and Noodles Parmesan, 209
Spinach-Potato Soup, 50
Spinach-Rice Soup, 42

Spinach (*continued*)
Spinach Salad, 68
Spinach Salad with Raspberry Dressing, 66
Spinach Almond Casserole, 231
Spinach and Noodles Parmesan, 209
Spinach & Pesto Stuffed Chicken Breasts, 148
Spinach-Potato Soup, 50
Spinach-Rice Soup, 42
Spinach Salad, 68
Spinach Salad with Raspberry Dressing, 66
Spirited Coffee Lopez, 41
Spirited Egg Nog, 41
Split Pea and Meatball Soup, 57
Spring Rolls, 25
Sprout-Green Bean Salad, 67
Squash
Golden Squash Bake, 230
Pecan-Stuffed Squash, 230
Southern-Style Squash and Okra, 230
Standing Rib Roast with Madeira Sauce, 97
Stay Slim Salad, 82
Steak Salad in Red-Wine Dressing, 86
Steak with Hearty Mustard Marinade, 99
Steamed Mussels in White Wine, 182
Steamed Trout with Orange & Ginger, 182
Stews
Aegean Lamb Stew, 135
Beef Burgundy, 105
Beef Goulash, 103
Beef Ragoût, 106
Beef Stew, 103
Beef Stew with Dumplings, 106
Brunswick Stew, 145
Country French Beef Stew, 104
Hawaiian Pork Stew, 126
Lamb Stew, 132
Meatball Stew, 114
Mexican Beef Stew, 104
Tasty Pork Ragout, 119
Veal Marengo, 137
Veal Stew, 137
Stir-Fried Beef and Vegetables, 101
Stir-Fried Scallops & Vegetables, 188
Stir-Fried Vegetables with Bulgur, 235
Stir-fry dishes
Beef and Bean Sprout Stir-Fry, 109
Beef with Leafy Greens, 108
Broccoli & Beef Stir-Fry, 107
Cashew Chicken, 152
Cashew Pork Stir-Fry, 122
Chicken and Broccoli, 156
Chicken 'n Vegetable Stir Fry, 157
Chicken Walnut Stir-Fry, 153
Chinese Spinach, 231
Chinese-Style Beef & Vegetables, 107
Classic Chinese Pepper Steak, 106
Colorful Dragon Stir-Fry, 155
Colorful Stir-Fried Pork, 121
Fiery Beef Stir-Fry, 108
Golden Chicken Stir-Fry, 154
Hot & Spicy Glazed Carrots, 220
Hunan Pork Stir-Fry, 120
Hunan Stir-Fry with Tofu, 132
Jade & Ruby Stir-Fry, 153

Stir-fry dishes (*continued*)
Mongolian Beef, 98
Moo Goo Gai Pan, 153
Orange-Cashew Chicken, 157
Pork and Peanut Stir-Fry, 123
Saucy Shrimp over Chinese Noodle Cakes, 187
Shanghai Chicken, 189
Shanghai Shrimp, 189
Shanghai Turkey Stir-Fry, 167
Shantung Chicken, 149
Shrimp & Vegetable Stir-Fry, 189
Spicy Vegetable Stir-Fry, 235
Stir-Fried Beef and Vegetables, 101
Stir-Fried Scallops & Vegetables, 188
Sweet-and-Sour Chicken, 152
Sweet-and-Sour Pork, 123
Sweet 'n Sour Stir Fry, 234
Szechuan Beef & Snow Peas, 109
Tofu & Vegetable Stir-Fry, 120
Vegetable Stir-Fry, 217
Strawberries
Chilly Strawberry Souffles, 320
Chocolate-Berry Parfaits, 313
Fresh Strawberry Pie, 332
Molded Strawberries Romanoff, 311
Strawberries Romanoff on Angel Slices, 350
Strawberry and Cream Napoleons, 335
Strawberry-Chocolate Bavarian Cream, 314
Strawberry Tart Glace, 334
Strawberry Tunnel Cream Cake, 344
Very Berry Sorbet, 303
Strawberries Romanoff on Angel Slices, 350
Strawberry and Cream Napoleons, 335
Strawberry-Banana Shake, 32
Strawberry-Banana Topping, 246
Strawberry-Chocolate Bavarian Cream, 314
Strawberry Glaze, 335
Strawberry Tart Glace, 334
Strawberry Tunnel Cream Cake, 344
Streusel Topping, 329
Stroganoff Superb, 105
Stuffed Cabbage Leaves, 126
Stuffed Cheese Burgers, 244
Stuffed Flank Steak, 98
Stuffed Tomatoes, 232
Stuffed Veal Cutlets, 136
Stuffings
Apple & Herb Stuffing, 161
Bacon and Green Pepper Stuffing, 163
Cornish Hens with Chestnut-Sausage Stuffing, 160
Cornish Hens with Oyster Stuffing, 161
Cranberry-Sausage Stuffing, 163
Harvest Sausage Stuffing, 163
Old-Fashioned Bread Stuffing, 163
Oyster Stuffing, 164
Savory Corn Bread Stuffing, 163
Turkey with American Stuffing, 163
Turkey with Garlic and Chili Pepper Stuffing, 160
Turkey with Sausage and Orange Corn Bread Stuffing, 162

Summer Kielbasa Salad, 87
Summer Spaghetti, 210
Sunflower Seed Cole Slaw, 65
Sunny Fries, 228
Superb Fillet of Sole & Vegetables, 202
Super Chocolate Chunk Cookies, 274
Super Coconut Chocolate Chunk Cookies, 274
Super Peanut Butter Chocolate Chunk Cookies, 274
Surprise Carrot Cake, 349
Swedish Apple Cake, 301
Sweet-and-Sour Chicken, 152
Sweet-and-Sour Pork, 123
Sweet and Sour Pork Chops, 115
Sweet & Sour Pork Loin, 122
Sweet and Spicy Chicken Barbecue, 146
Sweet Jalapeno Ribs, 125
Sweet 'n Sour Cabbage, 218
Sweet 'n Sour Stir Fry, 234
Sweet potatoes
    Baked Ham with Glazed Vegetables, 129
    Citrus Candied Sweet Potatoes, 235
    Grill-Baked Sweet Potatoes, 235
    Ham-Sauced Sweet Potatoes, 128
    Pineapple-Glazed Ham and Sweets, 127
    Sweet Potato Pecan Pie, 326
Sweet Potato Pecan Pie, 326
Sweet rolls
    Jamaican Sweet Buns, 261
    Paul Bunyan Sticky Buns, 260
Swiss Chicken Quiche, 248
Swiss Cinnamon Cookies, 278
Swiss Vegetable Medley, 233
Swordfish
    Lemon Swordfish, 182
    Swordfish Steaks with Dill-Mustard Sauce, 173
Swordfish Steaks with Dill-Mustard Sauce, 173
Syllabub, 41
Szechuan Beef & Snow Peas, 109

T

Tabbouleh, 80
Tacos
    Quick 'n Easy Tacos, 245
Tagliatelle with Creamy Sauce, 212
Tandoori Rice, 151
Tandoori-Style Chicken Kabobs, 151
Tangy Blue Cheese Vegetables, 233
Tangy Catfish, 179
Tangy Cocktail Sauce, 186
Tangy Coleslaw, 69
Tarragon Cream Sauce, 174
Tarts
    Chocolate-Almond Tarts, 336
    Cinnamon Fruit Tart with Sour Cream Filling, 335
    Mini Fruit Cheese Tarts, 334
    Strawberry Tart Glace, 334
Tasty Pork Ragout, 119

Tea
    Orange Tea Punch, 36
    Spiced Tea, 38
Tea, iced
    Lemon Tea Sparkler, 34
Tempting Cheese Crepes, 246
Tequila-Orange Chicken, 146
Teriyaki Fish Fillets, 173
Texas-Style Chili, 110
Texas-Style Steak on Hot Bread, 245
Tex-Mex Rice and Beans, 229
Thai Chicken Strips, 23
Thai Hens, 159
Thanksgiving Cranberry Cobbler, 301
Thick 'n Cheesy Vegetable Pizza, 238
Three Bean Rice Salad, 79
Thumbprint Cookies, 270
Toasted Almond Souffle, 319
Toasted Sesame Cheese Spread, 9
Toasty Onion Sticks, 30
Toffee Bars, 281
Toffee Crunch Pudding Ice Cream, 304
Tofu
    Hunan Stir-Fry with Tofu, 132
    Tofu & Vegetable Stir-Fry, 120
Tofu & Vegetable Stir-Fry, 120
Tomato and Onion Salad, 62
Tomatoes
    BLT Soup, 60
    Cheese Stuffed Tomatoes, 18
    Clam & Tomato Molded Salad, 72
    Classic Tomato Aspic, 70
    Creamy Tomato Bisque, 48
    Grilled Tomatoes, 232
    Homestyle Zucchini & Tomatoes, 214
    Italian Vegetable Sauté, 235
    Marinated Tomatoes & Cucumbers, 64
    Paradise Pasta, 209
    Southern Tomato-Bean Soup, 46
    Spaghetti Mediterranean, 210
    Stuffed Tomatoes, 232
    Summer Spaghetti, 210
    Tomato and Onion Salad, 62
    Tomato-Garden Aspic with Horseradish Cream, 74
    Tomato-Shrimp Soup, 56
    Tomato Soup Spice Cake, 338
Tomato-Garden Aspic with Horseradish Cream, 74
Tomato-Shrimp Soup, 56
Tomato Soup Spice Cake, 338
Tonic Thyme, 35
Toppings (see also **Dessert toppings**)
    Cinnamon-Nut Topping, 263
    Sesame Vegetable Topping, 234
    Sour Cream Topping, 329
    Streusel Topping, 329
Toro, 32
Tortellini in Cream Sauce, 204
Tortellini Soup, 48
Tortes
    Black Forest Torte, 357
    Chocolate Almond "Philly" Torte, 357
    Chocolate Coconut Pecan Torte, 359
    Crème de Cacao Torte, 359
    Elegant Angel Tarts, 358
    Festive Cranberry Torte, 356
    Lemon Cream Almond Torte, 358

Tortes (continued)
    Mexican Cocoa Torte, 358
    Open House Ribbon Torte, 357
    Viennese Cherry Cheese Torte, 356
    Viennese Chocolate Torte, 356
Tortilla Cups, 111
Tortilla Lasagna, 192
Tortilla Soup, 49
Tortoni Squares, 302
Traditional Gravy, 162
Traditional Pumpkin Pie, 329
Treasure Bran Muffins, 259
Trifles
    Fruited Chocolate Trifle, 321
    Hawaiian Trifle, 321
    Peach Melba Trifle, 321
Triple Layer Cookie Bars, 283
Tropical Cream Punch, 37
Tropical Crisp, 300
Tropical Fruit Dip, 9
Trout
    Chinese Trout, 172
    Crab-Stuffed Trout, 173
    Grilled Trout with Two Sauces, 174
    Steamed Trout with Orange & Ginger, 182
Tuna
    All-in-One Tuna Casserole, 202
    Bacon-Wrapped Tuna, 170
    Layered Seafood Quiche, 200
    Linguine Tuna Salad, 91
    Mexican Style Tuna Loaf, 175
    Potato-Tuna Salad, 89
    Quick and Easy Tuna Rice with Peas, 175
    Spanish Stuffed Bell Peppers, 180
    Tuna & Cracked Wheat Salad, 90
    Tuna Loaf, 183
    Tuna-Pasta Casserole, 201
Tuna & Cracked Wheat Salad, 90
Tuna Loaf, 183
Tuna-Pasta Casserole, 201
Turkey, 164–169
    Arizona's 7-Layer Taco Sandwich, 241
    Barbecued Turkey with Herbs, 164
    California Classic, The, 245
    Chef's Salad, 88
    Clove Glazed Turkey, 164
    Creamed Turkey Stack-Ups, 169
    Creamy Turkey & Broccoli, 198
    Curried Smoked Turkey Salad, 85
    Deep Dish Turkey Pie, 197
    Glazed Turkey Kabobs, 167
    Golden Gate Grill, 243
    Grilled Smoked Turkey 'n Muenster Sandwiches, 240
    Kensington Crepes, 166
    Layered Picnic Club Sandwich, 239
    Light and Lively Turkey Soup, 54
    New England Style Turkey Chowder, 53
    Oriental Turkey Terrine, 168
    Parmesan Seasoned Turkey, 164
    Quick Deli Turkey Soup, 53
    Santa Monica Sandwich, 243
    Scalloped Turkey, 196
    Shanghai Turkey Stir-Fry, 167
    Turkey à la Cordon Bleu, 165
    Turkey and Caper Quiche, 248
    Turkey-Barley Soup, 54

Turkey (*continued*)
Turkey Cassoulet, 198
Turkey Cottage Pie, 196
Turkey Cranberry Croissant, 241
Turkey Curry, 165
Turkey Cutlets with Ginger & Lime Sauce, 169
Turkey Divan, 195
Turkey Fillets in Spicy Cilantro Marinade, 168
Turkey Florentine, 166
Turkey Hash, 166
Turkey Marengo, 169
Turkey Orloff, 166
Turkey Oscar, 165
Turkey Paprikash, 168
Turkey Parmesan, 169
Turkey Parmigiana, 167
Turkey Pineapple Salad, 82
Turkey Salad with Pita Bread, 84
Turkey Schnitzel, 167
Turkey Tetrazzini, 199
Turkey-Topped Biscuits, 242
Turkey Vegetable Soup, 53
Turkey with American Stuffing, 163
Turkey with Garlic and Chili Pepper Stuffing, 160
Turkey with Sausage and Orange Corn Bread Stuffing, 162
Turkey with Wine-Glazed Vegetables, 168
Turkey à la Cordon Bleu, 165
Turkey and Caper Quiche, 248
Turkey-Barley Soup, 54
Turkey Cassoulet, 198
Turkey Cottage Pie, 196
Turkey Cranberry Croissant, 241
Turkey Curry, 165
Turkey Cutlets with Ginger & Lime Sauce, 169
Turkey Divan, 195
Turkey Fillets in Spicy Cilantro Marinade, 168
Turkey Florentine, 166
Turkey Hash, 166
Turkey Marengo, 169
Turkey Orloff, 166
Turkey Oscar, 165
Turkey Paprikash, 168
Turkey Parmesan, 169
Turkey Parmigiana, 167
Turkey Pineapple Salad, 82
Turkey Salad with Pita Bread, 84
Turkey Schnitzel, 167
Turkey Tetrazzini, 199
Turkey-Topped Biscuits, 242
Turkey Vegetable Soup, 53
Turkey with American Stuffing, 163
Turkey with Garlic and Chili Pepper Stuffing, 160
Turkey with Sausage and Orange Corn Bread Stuffing, 162
Turkey with Wine-Glazed Vegetables, 168

Two-Bean Chili, 110
Two-Bean Franks, 130
Two-Bean Soup, 49

V

V8 Cheese Bread, 267
Vanilla Creme, 353
Vanilla Frosting, 337
Veal, 135–137
Apple and Veal Scallop, 135
Country-Style Veal, 136
Stuffed Veal Cutlets, 136
Veal Chops Stuffed with Fontina, 137
Veal Marengo, 137
Veal Parmesan, 137
Veal Scallopini with Brandy Cream Sauce, 136
Veal Stew, 137
Veal Chops Stuffed with Fontina, 137
Veal Marengo, 137
Veal Parmesan, 137
Veal Scallopini with Brandy Cream Sauce, 136
Veal Stew, 137
Vegetable Couscous, 220
Vegetable Dip Verde, 9
Vegetables (*see also individual types*)
Baked Celery and Almonds, 221
Barbecued Garlic, 221
Beer Batter Fried Veggies 'n Things, 19
Chilled Rigatoni Salad, 79
Crunchy Scalloped Celery, 221
Fresh Vegetable Ring, 233
Garden Chicken Salad, 84
Garden Medley Rice, 227
Harvest Vegetable Scallop, 225
Italian Pasta Salad, 79
Leeks with Bel Paese®, 219
Middle East Pita Pockets, 242
Nouvelle Fettucini, 209
Pasta Primavera, 211
Pasta Vegetable Medley, 78
Potluck Pasta Salad, 78
Rice Pilaf Salad, 80
Saucy Garden Patch Vegetables, 231
Skewered Vegetables, 232
Skillet Potatoes, 229
Spicy Vegetable Stir-Fry, 235
Stir-Fried Vegetables with Bulgur, 235
Sweet 'n Sour Stir Fry, 234
Swiss Vegetable Medley, 233
Tangy Blue Cheese Vegetables, 233
Vegetables in Cheese Sauce, 218
Vegetable Stir-Fry, 217
Vegetable Sunburst, 232
Vegetables in Cheese Sauce, 218
Vegetable Stir-Fry, 217
Vegetable-Stuffed Fish Rolls, 174

Vegetable-Stuffed Flank Steak, 101
Vegetable Sunburst, 232
Vegetarian Sandwiches, 239
Vermont Vegetable Stew, 60
Versatile Chicken, 138
Very Berry Sorbet, 303
Viennese Cherry Cheese Torte, 356
Viennese Chocolate Torte, 356
Vinaigrette Dressing, 93
Volcano Punch, 36

W

Waffles
Chocolate Waffles, 250
Gingery Banana Waffles, 250
Waldorf Chicken Salad, 82
Walnut Butter Sauce, 174
Walnut Cream Topping, 330
Walnut Streusel Muffins, 258
Walnutty Ribbons, 280
Warm Bean Salad, 68
Warm Dried Fruit Compote, 121
Warm Herb Cheese Spread, 12
Watercress-Carrot Salad, 67
Western Lamb Riblets, 132
Wheat Germ Cookies, 270
White Gazpacho, 50
White Sangria, 40
Wild Rice and Seafood Salad, 89
Wild Rice Salad, 80
Wine-Simmered Beef and Vegetables, 105
Winter Fruit Bowl, 70
Wisconsin Cheese 'n Beer Soup, 48

Y

Yogurt Dressing, 90

Z

Zesty Barbecued Ribs, 124
Zesty Dressing, 68
Zesty Meat Loaf, 111
Zesty Mushroom Salad, 67
Zesty Potato Salad, 78
Zesty V8, 35
Zucchini
Curried Zucchini Soup, 50
Homestyle Zucchini & Tomatoes, 214
Italian Vegetable Sauté, 235
Pasta with Vegetables, 204
Pronto Zucchini, 234
Spaghetti with Cream Sauce, 210
Vegetable Couscous, 220
Zucchini Chive Dip, 15